A Reference Grammar of
Modern French

A Reference Grammar of Modern French

Anne Judge
Lecturer in French and Linguistics, University of Surrey

F.G. Healey
Professor of French, University of Surrey

Edward Arnold

© Anne Judge and F.G. Healey 1983

First published 1983 by
Edward Arnold (Publishers) Ltd
41 Bedford Square, London WC1B 3DQ

Edward Arnold (Australia) Pty Ltd
80 Waverley Road
Caulfield East 3145
PO Box 234
Melbourne

First published in United States of America 1983 by
Edward Arnold
300 North Charles Street
Baltimore
Maryland 21201

British Library Cataloguing in Publication Data

Judge, Anne
  A reference grammar of modern French.
  1. French language—Grammar
  I. Title   II. Healey, F.G.
  448.2′421   PC2112

  ISBN 0-7131-6285-6

Text set in 9/10pt Times Compugraphic by Colset Private Limited, Singapore.
Printed and bound in Great Britain by Richard Clay (The Chaucer Press) Ltd, Bungay, Suffolk

Contents

Part III   The modifiers: adjectives and adverbs   261

Chapter 11   The adjective   263

Acknowledgements

The authors wish to give special thanks to Solange Lamothe, Professor in Grammar and Stylistics in the department of French at Lyon III University, who has been a virtual third author of this book. She has been closely involved in the project over the years checking and revising all our drafts and providing much useful guidance. In particular, she has contributed many interesting historical insights together with authoritative information and specific examples of current usage. Without her invaluable help our task would have been much heavier and the book would have been less complete than the authors hoped it to be. Many of the good points are hers; any errors are our responsibility.

Thanks are also due to our publishers, Edward Arnold, who were not only responsible for initiating and commissioning this work, but who have also guided our efforts during its long period of gestation. They have given constant support at all stages and have contributed many useful and enlightening criticisms of content and treatment at the editorial stage.

Finally our thanks are due to the University of Surrey for its material assistance, and to our colleagues in the Department of Linguistic and International Studies for their encouragement and support over the years. A special mention should be made of our colleague, Janine Cole, for having always been ready to discuss linguistic problems as they arose.

A.J.
F.G.H.

Introduction

Writing a Reference Grammar is a difficult task at any time but it is even more so in the last quarter of a century which has seen most of the major developments in linguistics. There are nowadays so many different 'schools' of linguistics, each of which has developed its own approach to grammar, that some kind of decision has to be made at the outset as to what sort of theoretical basis is to be used. The specific aims of a given grammar will also clearly influence the working hypotheses of its authors. It is the purpose of this Introduction to make explicit the theoretical basis of this book and to explain its aims.

The main choices facing the authors when beginning this work were as follows.

A synchronic or a diachronic grammar?

By *synchronic* is meant the study of the language at one particular stage of its development (usually the stage it has reached at the moment of writing), whereas *diachronic* indicates the study of the development of the language, i.e., its passage from one state to another. The main aim of this Reference Grammar is to be synchronic – to deal with the present state of the French language. Some attention has been given to diachronic aspects, however, since in certain instances a knowledge of previous states of the language is essential for a full understanding of the system as it is today. Some knowledge of previous states of the language is also necessary in order to understand completely the language of the great writers of the past, and although this book does not claim to be in any sense a historical grammar nor yet a history of the language, it does nevertheless include a certain amount of explanatory historical material where this is felt to be necessary or desirable. In a similar way examples have been taken from a very wide span of language use including, where appropriate, some from the sixteenth and seventeenth centuries as well as later periods.

Prescriptive or descriptive grammar?

A prescriptive grammar is a work which describes what *should* be said or written; it is a grammar of *le bon usage*, whereas a descriptive grammar describes what is *really* said or written.

Traditionally grammars have been prescriptive, based on certain norms of 'good' or 'accepted' usage, and as such they have been incomplete since they do not describe the language as spoken or written by many of those who use it. It is, however, the 'mistakes' people make in using a language at any given moment which may provide the most likely indications of the way the language is going to develop. A descriptive grammar, on the other hand, passes no judgments as to what is 'good' or 'bad' French. All forms likely to be met with are listed, thus making for a very complete form of grammar.

This particular grammar is descriptive in the sense that it does not limit itself to *le bon usage*; but it is also prescriptive, in that it makes clear which forms of the language are considered to belong to *le bon usage* and which are not. Constructions which are felt to be quite unacceptable in prescriptive terms may be given, but they are preceded by an asterisk (*) to indicate their status, or lack of it, in the language. More doubtful cases, i.e. constructions which are acceptable to some but not to others, are preceded by a question mark. The authors feel that it is important that students should not be confronted on arrival in France with forms of the language not encountered in their grammar books, since they will not know whether these are acceptable but simply omitted from their books, or unacceptable in prescriptive terms.

The choice of examples

This problem is related to the previous one and has been resolved in the following manner: where the rule described is a straightforward one which is still productive, an example has been invented, on the principle that hundreds of other examples of a similar kind could also be invented. Where the rule described is archaic or has stylistic overtones (this applies particularly to the written language), examples have been borrowed from literature. Where the example illustrates something which is *said* but which is not accepted in prescriptive terms as 'correct', the examples quoted have all been heard in use in France.

The place of linguistic theories in the book

It was decided that the approach in *A Reference Grammar of Modern French* should be purely pragmatic, making no effort to follow closely the theories of any particular school of linguistics, nor indeed to exclude *per se* theories or ideas taken from any of them. Adherence to any particular school of linguistic theory generally appears to make a given grammar both partial in the range of phenomena it can deal with and also usually impenetrable to those not trained in that particular school of linguistics. Since this book is aimed above all at undergraduate learners of French and not at graduates in, or even students of, linguistics, we have thought it proper to choose whatever angle of approach to a problem will be most enlightening and accessible to the language learner and to the general reader, irrespective of its theoretical provenance. As a result this book is a compromise in that, although it contains many concepts foreign to traditional grammars, it retains those aspects and concepts of traditional grammar, including much of its terminology, which still work efficiently, or which would cause unacceptable confusion to students if replaced by other and more acceptable terminology from the point of view of modern linguistics.

This grammar is not transformationalist, although it has recourse to the concept of 'deep structure' and, for example, explains the idea of the passive as being the result of the 'passivization' of the active voice, i.e., a transformation. It may be said to be 'structuralist' in the sense that language is seen as '*un tout dans lequel tout se tient*', but it is recognized that the principle that elements, when they appear in a language, displace others, while elements which disappear are replaced by yet others, does not work perfectly (for example, the compound past tense has been unable to fill completely the void left in the General system by the disappearance of the past historic, which now belongs only to the Narrative system (see Ch. 4)). Similarly the plan of this grammar may be said to be 'functionalist' − at least in the French sense − since the main headings refer to the functions the elements may fulfil: 'Noun phrase', 'Verb phrase', 'Modifiers', 'Link words' are all 'functional' labels. While the keen seeker after such things will no doubt be able to identify yet further linguistic influences in this grammar, it is hoped that enough has been said here on this point to make it plain that our aim has been to make use of whatever theories or insights could assist in better describing the phenomena of French grammar.

A major consequence of the approach outlined above has been the necessity of making theoretical choices when dealing with any specific problem. It is these choices which are in fact explained in the various sections headed 'General considerations' or 'Theoretical considerations', and it is to these that the reader should refer in order to find out why a particular chapter is organized in the way it is. If such linguistic niceties are not the immediate concern of the reader, who may merely wish to check a grammatical point such as agreement for compound nouns, for example, then these sections (which are numbered 0) may be ignored. The grammar may thus be used at two levels: as a straightforward reference work for checking points of grammar or as a basic textbook on French linguistics.

A second reason for the sections entitled 'General' or 'Theoretical considerations' is that many students may not have studied English grammar at school, or at least not in any depth, and may therefore find terms such as 'adverb', 'syntactical links' or 'modifiers' difficult to understand. It is precisely for this reason that the sections referred to are used to analyse the meaning of the words used within the body of the particular chapter. The chapters themselves tend to correspond to the traditional parts of speech.

Within the chapters the usual order followed has been: morphological considerations; syntactical considerations; semantic considerations; stylistic considerations; and contrastive problems (all of the last three as and when necessary). In other words, the sections on morphological and syntactical considerations are common to all chapters and correspond, in terms of content, to what is found in traditional grammars such as those of Grevisse, Wagner and Pinchon, Baylon and Fabre and others. The remaining sections are more unorthodox.

Overall plan of the grammar

The book is divided into five parts: the noun phrase; the verb phrase; modifiers; link words; and the clause, the sentence and textual organization. Each of these parts contains an introduction explaining what it is about and this is followed by the chapters, each of which starts with the section referred to above, numbered '0', detailing the main problems. These are the sections which may be omitted if the reader is merely using the work in its purely reference function. It may also be useful to indicate here that the final two chapters of the whole book, those on the textual organization of the written and of the spoken language, are largely unique to this Grammar.

In conclusion, it may be useful to say a word about the genesis of this grammar and the manner in which it is envisaged that it may be used. It owes its origins partly to the fact that no really comprehensive grammar of French expressly designed for advanced anglophone students of that language has appeared in the recent past, and partly also to the fact that the authors, and the first author in particular, have been developing fresh approaches to the teaching of French language over a number of years at the University of Surrey. In the course of the development of such new courses it also became apparent that no French grammar (published in Britain at least) took account either of the many recent developments in linguistics nor of the large quantity of research carried out in recent years, especially in France, on the grammar of French. The role of spoken French, which has been gradually gaining in importance in higher education courses in Britain during the last three decades, is almost totally neglected by traditional grammars, as is the fact that the French language is in a constant state of flux. All of these factors combined to convince the authors of the need for a new French grammar, comprehensive in its scope, developmental in its attitude to language, and aimed at meeting the kinds of difficulty peculiar to anglophone learners of French. It was also hoped that it might be possible to produce a book which might serve as a means of making grammar less of a prescriptive and more of a reasoned study by attempting to provide, as far as could be done, a *rationale* of French grammar. While it is clear that much in grammar must remain purely arbitrary and inaccessible to reasoned explanation, there is nevertheless much also which can now be satisfactorily accounted for with reasonable scientific accuracy at levels which do not demand a prior detailed study either of linguistics or of logic. Although no grammar book can hope to become popular material for light reading, it is hoped that some at least of the chapters in this book will be found instructive and maybe even interesting reading rather than mere reference tables.

In producing *A Reference Grammar of Modern French* it was the authors' intention to meet the needs of students of French at the tertiary education level and primarily those of undergraduate students reading for degrees in which French played a substantial role. At the same time it was felt that it might be of use to all those studying the language beyond A-level GCE, whether in universities, polytechnics, institutes of higher education, technical and commercial colleges etc. While it is clearly not intended for general use in schools it may well be found suitable for advanced sixth-form classes as well as a reference work for teachers. In particular, although as its name implies this grammar is intended to provide an up-to-date reference work both for students and teachers of French, it is also hoped that it may provide a useful and badly needed textbook for a number of those classes which are to be found today in French Departments in universities and polytechnics under the rubrics 'advanced grammar', 'advanced French language study', 'French grammar and style' etc.

Note

?   before a word or construction: form considered 'incorrect' by some native speakers; usually typical of informal speech; may act as a sociolinguistic marker if used in an appropriate register.
*   before a word or construction: form unacceptable to nearly all native speakers; if used, functions as a sociolinguistic marker.

Part I The nominal phrase

Nouns have traditionally been defined as words denoting persons, things or concepts; but this type of definition leads to difficulties, since words such as *red* may be considered either as nouns or as adjectives:

Give me the *red* dress (adjective)
The *red* of that dress suits you (noun)

Also, nouns such as *fire* or *race* (in the sense of contest of speed) refer to actions rather than to 'persons, things or concepts'.

Modern grammarians prefer, therefore, to define nouns by their possible forms and functions, i.e. they prefer to define them *formally* and *syntactically* rather than semantically. English nouns, for example, normally have two forms, a plural and a singular (*dog/dogs*). In French, on the other hand, they usually have two forms in the written language only (*chien/chiens*) since the -*s* of the plural is silent. In the spoken language – with a few exceptions (*cheval/chevaux*) – they only have one form, the distinction between singular and plural being indicated by the determiner (*le chien/les chiens*). On the other hand, French nouns have gender, also indicated by the determiner (*le chien/la table*) although in some cases the noun itself may carry gender (*le chien/la chienne*).

Thus it may be seen that nouns are defined in English as words which inflect for number in both the written and the spoken language; in French they rarely inflect for number in the spoken language, but are preceded by determiners which carry both the concepts of number and gender to be attributed to the noun. French nouns are defined in Chapter 1.

Nouns may function as the subject or object of a clause, or may be part of a prepositional phrase. A noun phrase is a word or group of words with a noun as its head, and functioning as the subject, object or adverbial complement of a clause. The minimal noun phrase is made up of a proper noun; if a common noun is used, the minimal phrase is made up of a determiner + noun. When no determiner is used, a common noun is seen as an abstract concept, i.e. as a dictionary entry. It is the determiner which 'actualizes' it, i.e. brings it into concrete existence: *a dog/the dog/this dog/my dog/all dogs/these dogs* are in opposition to the abstract concept *dog*. Determiners differ in French and English, in that in French they express the concepts of number and gender as well as those of specificity, whereas in English they merely specify. Determiners include articles, demonstrative adjectives, possessive adjectives, numerals and indefinite adjectives. These are examined in Chapter 2.

Pronouns are defined in traditional grammar as a part of speech used instead of a noun. Thus *he* may replace *that boy* in *that boy helped me to do it*. Pronouns include personal pronouns, demonstrative pronouns, possessive pronouns, indefinite pronouns, relative pronouns and interrogative pronouns. Although one may quibble with the traditional definition of pronouns, it works well enough for French not to make it worth using a more complex one. Chapter 3 deals with pronouns; but some of the pronouns mentioned above, namely relative pronouns and interrogative pronouns, will not be included and instead appear respectively under Subordinators in Chapter 14 and under Interrogative Sentences in Chapter 19.

The noun phrase may include modifiers. The determiner + noun unit may be modified by one or several adjectives (e.g. *the old grey stone houses*). It may also be modified by a complement (e.g. *the top of the hill*) or by a relative clause (e.g. *the man who came this morning* . . .). Modification of the determiner + noun by adjectives is examined in Chapter 11 and modification by a relative clause in Chapter 14.

Chapter 1

The noun

0   General considerations

0.1   Gender and number

(i) The noun may be defined morphologically, in that it is a word or lexical unit which is marked for gender and number, although these categories are often covert (i.e. hidden). The noun itself may be seen in terms of three types of semantic categories: animate/inanimate; count nouns/mass nouns; or common nouns/proper nouns. These semantic distinctions may affect either gender or number or both (see *ii, iii* and *iv*).

(ii) There are two genders, masculine and feminine; gender in French is, however, *grammatical* rather than *natural*, in the sense that there is no natural reason why *chaise* should be feminine and *fauteuil* masculine.[1] This is particularly true where inanimates are concerned, since these would have to be in a neutral gender for there to be a connection between grammatical gender and natural gender; since there is no neutral gender in French, gender for inanimates has to be *unmotivated* at least as far as nature is concerned (although some genders are sometimes motivated grammatically – see 1.1.1.2). There is however sometimes a link between animates and natural gender (*un chat/une chatte*).

(iii) Nouns may be singular or plural, but this only applies to count nouns (*la table/les tables*), for mass nouns only appear in the singular (*du sable, de l'eau*), whilst some may change meaning depending on whether they are treated as count nouns or as mass nouns, e.g. *donne-moi les poires* (countable) v. *la poire est chère cette année*, in which *poire* used in the singular as a mass noun takes on a generic meaning.

There are also some nouns which may only be used in one or other number: adjectives used as nouns, such as *le vrai*, are only used in the singular, whereas some nouns such as *les mœurs* may only appear in the plural.

(iv) It is also necessary to distinguish between common nouns and proper nouns, since proper nouns have their own set of rules both where number is concerned and where the use of determiners is concerned (see Ch. 2).

0.2   Difficulties associated with the use of nouns

(i) Gender is difficult only in so far as, being usually unmotivated, the genders are difficult to remember. The only problems presented by number are those of agreement (1.2.2), particularly where compound nouns are concerned.

(ii) The noun presents few problems from a functional point of view, since it may fulfil the same functions, and in roughly the same manner, as the English noun.

(iii) There are some translating problems associated with nominalization through syntax, English being far more flexible than French in this respect (see 4.1). There are also problems due to the fact that English may nominalize through derivation more easily than French (see 4.2). But the most difficult of all is the translation of English compound nominal phrases: English being a largely *synthetic* language and French a

largely *analytical* one, there is no equivalent in French to the limitless ability in English to create nominal phrases of the *do-it-yourself shop* type, and a translation into French often ends up being an explanation rather than a direct equivalent structure (see 4.3.2).

1   Morphological considerations

1.1   Gender

1.1.1   *Generalities*

1.1.1.1 *Fixed and variable gender; marked and unmarked gender*
(i) Nouns have a fixed gender: it is *'le* soleil' and *'la* lune'. But some nouns may belong to both genders. This may arise for two reasons: a difference in gender may entail a difference in meaning (*un manoeuvre* (the person) and *une manoeuvre* (the action); *un aide* (the person) and *une aide* (the action); *un trompette* (the person) and *une trompette* (the instrument); − but *une clarinette* corresponds to both instrument and player); or two originally different words may have become homonyms in Modern French (*une moule* from the Latin *musculum* and *un moule* from the Latin *modulum*).
(ii) There are also a certain number of words which may change gender by the addition of a suffix; in this case the change in gender often corresponds to male/female distinction: *un chat* (masculine)/*une chatte* (feminine), i.e. a tom-cat and a she-cat; *un pécheur* (a male sinner)/*une pécheresse* (a female sinner).
(iii) Generally speaking the masculine gender is unmarked, i.e. it does not automatically refer to a natural gender distinction. *Le chat de ma voisine* could indicate a male or a female cat, the implication being that its sex is unknown to the speaker; but in *la chatte de ma voisine*, the feminine gender corresponds to natural gender. Similarly the masculine gender may refer to something unspecific, whereas the feminine gender refers to something specific: *un truc, un machin, un chose* (as against *une chose*[2] which is specific). The feminine gender is sometimes indicated morphologically by the addition of an *-e* or of a suffix of a more elaborate nature (*chat/chatte*; *pécheur/pécheresse*), but it may also be indicated by the use of the appropriate article and agreement of the modifying adjective if there is one (*un petit enfant/une petite enfant*).

1.1.1.2 *Motivated and unmotivated gender*   Gender, in French, is usually conventional; one thus distinguishes between *natural* gender and *grammatical* gender. There are however a few cases in which gender is motivated.
There are four different types of motivation, only one of which corresponds to identity between grammatical gender and natural gender:
(i) The masculine/feminine distinction may correspond to a male/female distinction (see 1.1.1.1 *iii*).
(ii) The gender may be motivated by morphological analogy: *une après-midi* for *un après-midi* by analogy with *une matinée*; *une ombrelle* − which was masculine in the eighteenth century − became feminine because most words ending in *-elle* are feminine (*jouvencelle, nouvelle*).
(iii) The gender may be motivated by semantic analogy: *une jeep* because of *une voiture*, *une redingote* because of *une veste*.
(iv) In cases of the metonymic[3] use of nouns, they take the gender of the noun they are related to: *un hollande* (= *du fromage de Hollande*), *un Picasso* (= *un tableau de Picasso*).
New words tend to be masculine if there is nothing to indicate otherwise: *un laisser-*

passer, un radar, un laser. . . . But if the new word is one which exists in another sense and is used figuratively, it keeps its gender: a silicon chip is *une puce à protubérance*.

1.1.1.3 *Historical notes on the origins of gender* There is no natural link between gender and reality where inanimates are concerned: there is no particular reason why *chaise* should be feminine whilst *fauteuil* is masculine (see 0.1). Gender in these cases is the result of the historical development of each word from Latin to modern French, changes of gender having sometimes taken place on the way.

Where animates are concerned, matters are more complex, since in this case natural gender exists. Originally, in Indo-European, one distinguished between inanimates and animates: inanimates were neutral, and animates were divided into masculine and feminine. Many 'inanimates', however, were classified as animates since they were often associated with ideas of force and energy; in other words, inanimates were normally considered as nondynamic, and if they were dynamic for cultural reasons they became animate. Hence *water, sun, earth* and other nouns were personalized by being given a gender; conversely, to make an animate neutral was to depersonalize it.

As far as the masculine/feminine distinction is concerned, the feminine used to be derived in certain cases from the masculine by changing or adding a suffix, as is the case today in French (*auditeur/auditrice*); but even then the masculine was the most normal unmarked gender. Although Latin kept the three genders, the opposition inanimate/animate was no longer marked morphologically. The natural masculine and feminine genders were not linked to the declensions, although gender was still marked syntactically in the adjective, which has three forms – masculine, feminine and neuter. What is more, gender in Latin was not a very stable category, and in many cases neuter nouns became masculine in Latin before ending up as masculine in French. On the other hand, nouns such as *brasse, cervelle, feuille, joie* which are all feminine today come from the plural nominative and accusative forms of certain neuter nouns, these forms ending in -*a*: since the -*a* ending was associated with the feminine gender, they became feminine by analogy. (See Monteil, *Eléments de phonétique et de morphologie du Latin*, 133-7.)

It is therefore not surprising that even where animates are concerned gender is usually conventional rather than natural. Thus although – as in Indo-European – one may still make a masculine into a feminine by derivation (*chat/chatte*) or by use of different lexical items (*un bélier/une brebis*), there are many cases in which there is a clash between grammatical and natural gender; there are, for example, many words referring to army life which are feminine where one could expect a masculine: *recrue, sentinelle, ordonnance*, for example. Gender therefore has to be learnt for each word. Masculine words ending in -*e* are particularly problematic, for students tend to think of words such as *système, problème, vote, manque*, as being feminine by analogy with the feminine forms of adjectives (*petit/petite, joli/jolie* . . .) whereas they are, in fact masculine.

As a general rule, one can say that:
(i) Nouns which are feminine in French come either from feminine words in Latin or from the plural form of neuter nouns in Latin.
(ii) Nouns which are masculine in French come from masculine nouns in Latin, but in some cases they come from neuter nouns. Thus, *bràcchium* (singular and neuter) gave *bras*, which is masculine, whereas *bràcchia* (plural and neuter) gave *brasse,* which is feminine. This can be explained in terms of what the French call *l'usure phonétique* ('phonetic erosion') which affected unstressed syllables following the stressed ones. Of the unstressed syllables in this case, only the -*a* survived, first of all as an -*e*, but in most cases then becoming 'mute', although it is usually retained in spelling (cf. *brasse*).

1.1.2   *Changes of gender obtained through suffixation*

1.1.2.1   *The addition of '-e' to the masculine form to obtain the feminine form*   There are several possibilities:

(i) Adding the *-e* does not change the pronunciation of the word, e.g. *un ami/une amie*; *un ours/une ourse*.

(ii) Adding the *-e* entails the pronunciation of a consonant which is mute in the masculine form, e.g. *un marchand/une marchande*; *un bourgeois/une bourgeoise*.

(iii) The addition of the *-e* entails both pronunciation and spelling changes. In some cases the final consonant is doubled, e.g. *-el* becomes *-elle* (*colonel/colonelle*); *-eau* becomes *-elle (chameau/chamelle)*; *-en* and *-on* become *-enne* and *-onne (gardien/gardienne*; *breton/bretonne*). But endings in *-an* do not normally become *-anne*, e.g. *courtisan/courtisane*, *mahométan/mahométane*, *persan/persane*. (Exceptions are *paysan/paysanne* and sometimes *lapon/laponne* or *lapone* — both orthographies are to be found).

The ending *-et* becomes *-ette* (*cadet/cadette*; exception *prefet/prefète*). But words in *-at* and *-ot* do not double their final consonant (*avocat/avocate*; *dévot/dévote*) except for *chat/chatte*; *boulot/boulotte*; *linot/linotte*; *sot/sotte*.

(*Note:* Favori becomes *favorite* because it comes from the Italian *favorita*. Métis becomes *métisse*. Andalou, which used to be spelt 'andalous', becomes *andalouse*.)

(iv) The addition of *-e* entails a change in the quality either of the final vowel or of the final consonant. Words ending in *-er* (closed *e*) become *-ère* with an open *e* indicated by a grave accent: (*berger/bergère*; *écolier/écolière*). *-f* becomes *-v* (*juif/juive*; *veuf/veuve*). *-c* becomes *-que* (in order to maintain the 'c' sound, since *ce* is pronounced 'se' (*turc/turque*; *Frédéric/Frédérique*; but *Grec/Grecque*).

(*Note:* An ending in *-e* does not automatically indicate a feminine gender when it is not a suffix, e.g. *le problème*, *le système*, *le vote*, *le manque*.)

1.1.2.2   *Nouns in '-eur'*

(i) Some change the *-eur* into *-euse* (*menteur/menteuse*; *danseur/danseuse*; *pêcheur/pêcheuse* (fisherman, fisherwoman)). These are nouns which derive from verbs.

Exceptions include *enchanteur/enchanteresse*; *pécheur/pécheresse* (sinner); *vengeur/vengeresse*; *exécuteur/exécutrice*; *inspecteur/inspectrice*; *inventeur/inventrice*; *persécuteur/persécutrice*.

(ii) Some nouns ending in *-eur* (rather than *-teur*) also have their feminine form in *-drice*, *-trice*, e.g. *ambassadeur/ambassadrice; empereur/impératrice*. (*Chanteur* follows the rule in *i* and gives *chanteuse*, but there also exists *cantatrice*, which is borrowed from Italian.)

(iii) Some change *-eur* to *-eresse*. These usually refer to legal or biblical matters, or are poetic terms: *demandeur* and *vendeur* give *demandeuse* and *vendeuse* in nontechnical contexts, but in law these become *demanderesse* and *venderesse*.

1.1.2.3   *Feminine forms in '-esse'*   The *-esse* derives from the Latin *-itia*, e.g. Latin *pigritia* gave *paresse* (*perece* in Old French). As such, *-esse* is used in such pairs as *chanoine/chanoinesse*; *prince/princesse*.

1.1.2.4   *Cases of odd derivations*   Many feminine forms are unpredictable in that their masculine and feminine forms may derive from different Latin words. For example, *roi* comes from *regem* and *reine* from *reginam*. Sometimes the feminine form corresponds to an older masculine form which has been replaced by another: *mule*, which is feminine, is used for *mul*, which was masculine but which disappeared and was replaced by *mulet*. In some cases the feminine form may come from a different root, e.g. *bélier/brebis*; *taureau/vache*; *oncle/tante*; *gendre/bru*.

1.1.2.5 *Areas of hesitation* The opening up to women of professions previously exclusively reserved for men is causing linguistic problems, in the sense that a new feminine form has to be found to refer to these professions when practised by women. Sometimes a feminine form already exists, but referring to the wife of the man practising that profession. *Ambassadrice*, for example, used to refer to the wife of an ambassador. This has meant calling lady ambassadors *Madame l'Ambassadeur* to distinguish between these two statuses; in the press, however, one reads about *les ambassadrices de la mode/de la haute couture* . . ., in which case *ambassadrice* is seen to be the feminine of *ambassadeur* and not as designating the wife of an ambassador. The same problem occurs with *mairesse*, which used to refer exclusively to the wife of a mayor; a lady mayor becomes *Madame le Maire* in order to distinguish between the two.

Another way of forming the feminine is by either anteposing or postposing the word *femme: une femme peintre, une femme professeur* or *un peintre femme, un professeur femme*. This kind of distinction is spreading to the extent that one talks of *une femme facteur* even though the word *factrice* exists.[4] Schoolchildren often simplify the problem and use the expression *la professeur* or *la prof.*, in the same way as one can say *une enfant, une gosse, une archiviste, une bibliothécaire*. One may indeed read in newspapers sentences such as, *une otage américaine a été libérée en raison de sa maladie*. This is the simplest solution to the problem, but one that is far from generally accepted.

As for the university grade of *maître assistant*, no solution seems to have been worked out. One may find *maître-assistante, maîtresse-assistant* or *maître-assistant*. The second alternative is the least acceptable because *maîtresse* is mainly used in the context of primary school teaching. There seems to be a movement towards the third solution, in which there is no agreement – as is the case for *professeur* and *docteur*. Indeed, this is sometimes true even where the feminine form exists – *doctoresse* exists, but is rejected by the medical profession. One writes *Madame le Docteur X*, or *Docteur* + first name + surname (*Docteur Nicole Lefèvre*).

Note: In one particular case, a woman gynaecologist wanted to make her sex known on her nameplate; she could not use the solution mentioned above, for her first name, Dominique, may be either masculine or feminine. She got round the problem by writing, *Docteur Dominique X, Gynécologue diplomée de la Faculté*.

The following example, taken from a 1980 issue of the Lyons daily newspaper *Le Progrès*, illustrates these problems:

Une seconde femme recteur 'sort' de l'Université Lyon III

Un professeur de l'université Lyon III (Jean-Moulin), Mme Rolande Gadille vient d'être *nommée* recteur de l'académie de Reims: c'est la seconde *femme recteur*, la première – *nommée* il y a quelques mois recteur de l'académie de Dijon – était également *professeur* à Lyon III: Mme Lambert-Faivre (qui était *directrice* de l'Institut d'assurances de la faculté de droit de Lyon III).

Mme Rolande Gadille est *une géographe réputée*. Professeur *agrégée* en 1951, *maître-assistant* à la faculté des lettres de Dijon en 1964, *maître de conférences* en 1968, elle arriva à Lyon en 1970. Elle était *doyen* de la faculté des lettres depuis 1977, fonction où elle sut faire apprécier une compétence et un dévouement sans faille (. . . .)

Avec *elle, c'est le* 4e recteur que l'université Lyon III 'donne' au ministère. . . .

For other areas of hesitation, see 1.1.3.6 and 1.1.3.7.

1.1.3 *General guidelines for the determination of gender*

It has been pointed out that, except in those cases in which a noun may appear either in the masculine form or in the feminine form to indicate the difference between male and female, it is not possible to determine in most cases the gender of the noun from its form alone. Thus *sentinelle* refers (normally) to a man but is grammatically feminine; *plage, page, cage, rage, image* are feminine but *courage, gage* and *adage* are masculine. There are even some cases in which a noun tends to be masculine in the singular and feminine in the plural: *un amour*, but *de folles amours*; *gens* is normally masculine, but in certain cases may be preceded by an adjective in the feminine form. (See Ch. 11, 2.1.2 *vi* and also sections 1.1.3.6 and 1.1.3.7 below.)

There are a few rules which may help, however.

1.1.3.1 *Masculine categories*
(i) All names of trees, with the exception of *aubépine* (and *épine*), *ronce, vigne, virone* and *yeuse*.
(ii) All words ending with the following suffixes: *-ier, -age, -as, -ement, -ament, -et, -in, -is, -illon* and *-oir*. (This does not include *rage, cage, plage, image, gage* and *nage*, in which *-age* is not a suffix and which are feminine.)
(iii) The names of metals and chemicals, and the names of animals and plants which are still in their Latin form, e.g. *fer, soufre, felis rubiginosa, viola canina*.

1.1.3.2 *Feminine categories*
(i) Nouns referring to sciences, e.g. *chimie, géologie*
(ii) Nouns ending with the following suffixes: *-ade, -aie, -aille, -aine, -aison, -ison, -ande, -ée* (except those which come from Greek *-eum*, such as *le lycée, le musée*), *-ence, -esse, -ie, -ille, -ise, -te, -tion* (except for *le bastion*), *-ure* and abstract nouns ending in *-eur* such as *peur* (with the exception of *honneur, labeur, bonheur* and *malheur*, which are masculine).

1.1.3.3 *The gender of compound nouns*
(i) If the compound noun is made up of a noun and an adjective, the gender is that of the noun, e.g. *un bateau-mouche, une chauve-souris*; but there are exceptions to this: *un rouge-gorge* (by analogy with *un oiseau*).
(ii) If the compound noun is made up of a verb and its complement, it is usually masculine, e.g. *un abat-jour, un pare-brise*. There are some exceptions, however: *une garde-robe, une perce-neige* (although nowadays *un perce-neige* is becoming the norm).
(iii) If the compound noun is made up of a preposition and a noun, it is usually masculine, e.g. *un sous-main*.

1.1.3.4 *Letters of the alphabet*   According to prescriptive grammarians, the letters of the alphabet are masculine, except for: *une f, une h, une m, une n, une r*, and *une s*. Nowadays, however, the tendency is to use the masculine in all cases.

1.1.3.5 *Names of towns*   It is not possible to predict the gender of names of towns, e.g. *Vaison-la-Romaine, la Venise du Nord*, but *Le Havre, Le Caire*. When in doubt it is easiest to say *la ville de*. . . .

1.1.3.6 *Nouns which may take two genders*
(i) Amour was traditionally masculine in the singular and feminine in the plural, except when referring to Cupid, when it is written with a capital 'A', e.g. *un amour fou*; *de folles amours*; *sculpter de petits Amours*. Nowadays, however, *amour* tends to be masculine in both singular and plural.
(ii) Chose, used in expressions such as *autre chose, grand-chose, peu de chose* and *quelque chose*, is masculine instead of feminine:

j'ai quelque chose à vous dire et ce quelque chose est important

but

c'est une chose importante que celle que vous venez de me dire

(See also Ch. 1, note 2.)

(iii) Foudre, which is normally feminine, is masculine in the fossilized expressions *foudre de guerre* and *foudre d'éloquence:*

Je suis donc un foudre de guerre (La Fontaine)

(iv) Gens is normally treated as masculine plural, but it may in certain cases be considered feminine when preceded by an adjective (see Ch. 11, 2.1.2*vi*): *des gens méchants* but *de méchantes gens*.

(v) Merci is feminine when used in the sense of 'mercy' and masculine when used as a form of politeness: *je suis à sa merci* but *dites-lui un bien grand merci de ma part*.

(vi) Œuvre is always feminine in the plural but masculine in the singular when referring to architecture: *faire de bonnes œuvres*; *le gros œuvre est fini* (i.e. the main building works). This used also to apply to the works of an artist: *l'œuvre entier de Picasso*, but this usage is now archaic, the feminine being the norm: *l'œuvre entière de Picasso*.

(vii) Orgue is traditionally masculine in both its singular and plural forms: *l'orgue de cette église est très beau*; *les orgues de ces deux églises sont très beaux*. But used in the feminine plural it refers to one instrument only: *les orgues de cette église sont très belles*.

Nowadays, however, one can also hear *les orgues de ces deux églises sont très belles*.

(viii) Pâque used in the feminine singular with an article refers to the Jewish feast, whereas used in the feminine plural with an article it refers to the Christian feast: *la Pâque juive* but *passez de bonnes Pâques*. It may also be used in the masculine singular, but without an article, as in *je vous verrai à Pâques prochain*.

(ix) Personne is feminine when preceded by a determiner, but masculine when not preceded by a determiner; in this last case it will also be singular: *je connais beaucoup de personnes intéressantes* but *personne n'est content de cette décision*.

1.1.3.7 *Nouns with problematic genders*

(i) Grevisse (*Le Bon usage*) quotes some 200 masculine nouns and some 150 feminine nouns on which the French themselves may hesitate concerning gender; a native speaker may hesitate between *un pétale* and *une pétale*, for example (it is in fact masculine).

(ii) Grevisse also lists words such as *alvéole, après-midi, avant-guerre, après-guerre, chromo, disparate, effluve, entrecôte, interview, ordonnance, palabre, pample-mousse, perce-neige, phalène* and *steppe* as words which are either given different genders by different dictionaries or which are given one gender in dictionaries and another in everyday usage. *Entrecôte* is an example: it is masculine according to the Littré dictionary, and the Robert dictionary mentions that it was masculine until the beginning of the twentieth century; but in everyday usage it is always feminine.

1.2 Number

1.2.1 *Generalities*

(i) Nouns may be subdivided into countable and noncountable (or mass) nouns. For example, *office* is a count noun, since one can speak of *one office, two offices* etc., but *office space* is not a count noun, since one cannot count *office space;* similarly one

may count *tables* but not *sand*. Where count nouns are concerned, one may distinguish between singular and plural. In Indo-European there used to exist two forms of the plural: one corresponded to a plurality which could be counted and was therefore analytical, and the other corresponded to a plural which was not countable and was therefore synthetic. The latter survives lexically – but not morphologically – in both English and French: *people* are countable, whereas *a crowd* is not. Similarly it is possible to refer to *trois personnes* but not *trois gens*: *gens* is not a count noun.

(ii) Number in French is usually marked by the addition of *-s* at the end of the noun. This does not usually entail a change in the pronunciation of the word: *(une) table* sounds the same as *(des) tables*. In most cases, therefore, plurality is expressed by the determiner (*une/des* in this case). Sometimes plurality is expressed by agreement with the verb: *la table est à vendre*; *les tables sont à vendre*; but this is far from always being the case. With *(la) chanteuse chante* and *(les) chanteuses chantent*, agreement is purely visual and not aural. It is therefore the determiner which is the most important carrier of number in the spoken language, but in the written language the plural is indicated morphologically.

(iii) Although the plural is normally expressed by the addition of an *-s*, this is not always the case: there are a number of exceptions. The following cases will be examined: nouns ending in *-al*, *-ou*; in *-au*, *-eau*, *-eu*; and in *-ail*; nouns which may take two plurals; proper nouns; compound nouns; and the plurals of foreign words.

1.2.2   *Formation of the plural*

1.2.2.1   *The addition of '-s'*   In most cases this does not entail a change in the pronunciation of the noun: *un chat/des chats* (pronounced [ʃa] in both cases).

There are a few exceptions, e.g. *un œuf* [œnœf]/*des œufs* [dɛzø]; *un bœuf* [œbœf]/ *des bœufs* [debø].

1.2.2.2   *Plural forms identical to the singular*   Such identicality occurs when the noun ends *-s*, *-x* or *-z*, e.g. *un pois/des pois*; *une croix/des croix*; *un nez/des nez*.

1.2.2.3   *Nouns ending in '-al'*   These make their plural in *-aux*, e.g. *journal/journaux*.

Exceptions: *bal*, *cal*, *carnaval*, *chacal*, *festival*, *régal* (to which one may add a certain number of other words which are now archaic) take an *-s*. *Val* and *idéal* have two plurals, *vals/vaux*, *idéals/idéaux* (but not *étals/étaux*, since *étals* is the plural of *étal*, whereas *étaux* is the plural of *étau*, a quite different word from *étal*).

1.2.2.4   *Nouns ending in '-ou'*   These make their plural in *-ous*: *clou/clous*.

Exceptions: (*des*) *bijoux*, *cailloux*, *choux*, *genoux*, *hiboux*, *joujoux*, *poux*, which take an *-x* (and which are learnt by rote in French primary schools).

1.2.2.5   *Nouns ending in '-au'/'-eau' and '-eu'*   These make their plural in *-x*: *manteau/manteaux*.

Exceptions: *landau*, *sarrau*, *bleu*, *pneu*, *émeu*, *lieu* (the fish, not the word for 'place') all take *-s*.

1.2.2.6   *Nouns ending in '-ail'*   These take an *-s* in the plural: *détail/détails*.

Exceptions: *aspirail*, *bail*, *corail*, *émail*, *soupirail*, *travail*, *vantail*, *ventail* and *vitrail* make their plural in *-aux* (e.g. *vitraux*). *Ail* ('garlic') has its plural in *aulx*, to distinguish it from *aux* (= *à les*).

1.2.2.7   *Nouns with two plural forms*   These include *aieul*: *aieuls/aieux* (*aieuls* = grandfather(s) and grandmother(s) – archaic; *aieux* = ancestors – literary); *ciel*:

ciels/cieux (*ciels* is used mainly to refer to 'skies' in painting); *œil/yeux*, but *œils* in *œils-de-boeuf, œils-de-perdrix* (a kind of corn).

1.2.2.8   *The plural of proper nouns*
(i) They do not take the plural when referring to the members of one family: *les Martin, les Dupont*.
(ii) They do take the plural if they refer to the members of famous families: *les Bourbons, les Condés*, or to the artistic works produced by one person, e.g. *des Picassos* (although *des Picasso* is also acceptable).

Note: There has been a lack of uniformity in the past as to whether certain proper nouns should take the mark of the plural or not; subtle distinctions have been made as to whether the noun was considered as symbolic of a new concept represented by that person, or whether one was referring to the family as a whole, e.g. *On dirait des petits Napoléon(s)*. Grevisse quotes two examples in this respect (*Le Bon Usage,*):

Mais l'aigle des Habsbourgs a des aiglons sans nombre (Rostand)
Le prognathisme des Habsbourg (Cocteau)

Some writers prefer *des Picasso* rather than *des Picassos*, since one could argue that the underlying structure is *des tableaux de Picasso*; but according to the *Arrêté* of 26 February 1901, both usages are acceptable.

1.2.2.9   *Foreign words*   The norm is to apply the same rules as to French words, if the foreign word has really entered the language, e.g. *des agendas, des impromptus, des quatuors, des mémorandums*.

Exceptions are those words still felt to be foreign to the language (see the *Arrêté* of 26 February 1901).
(i) Latin words such as *Magnificat, Te Deum, Kyrie, amen, verbo/interim* remain invariable. But certain words such as *maximum* and *minimum* make their plural both in -*a* and, more usually, in -*s*: *des maximums/des maxima*; if one is using them adjectivally, one has the choice between *un tarif minimal/minimum* and *des tarifs minimums/minima/minimaux*!
(ii) Some Italian words keep their plural in -i: *des confetti, des graffiti*; but one tends to use the same form in the singular, i.e. *un confetti*.
(iii) English words either keep their English form in the plural, as in *des barmen*, or they may take an -*s*, as in *des barmans*; if the word is of a recent borrowing its plural will be in -*s*: *un perchman/des perchmans*.[5]
(iv) Similarly, German words may keep their German plural form, or one may add an -*s* to the singular (*des lieder* or *des lieds*).

1.2.2.10   *Compound nouns*
(i) If these are written in one word, they are treated the same as simple nouns, e.g. *un passeport/des passeports; un portemanteau/des portemanteaux*.

Exceptions: *madame/mesdames; monsieur/messieurs; bonhomme/bonshommes*, because the two concepts which make up the word are still felt to be present, whereas in other cases such as *passeports* and *portemanteaux* the compound noun corresponds to one concept only.

(*Note: Monsieur, madame* and *mademoiselle* are sometimes used with a 'regular' plural), as in *des monsieurs, des mademoiselles*, in which case one is referring to rank rather than to an individual. Such plurals belong to children's speech only, and when used by adults express either irony or familiarity.)
(ii) The compound noun which is clearly made up of several words — which may or may not be joined by a dash (*chef-d'œuvre* is, but *pomme de terre* is not) — may present problems: should both terms take the plural, or only the one which functions as the head word? To come to a decision, it is necessary to work out what the internal

syntactic structure of the compound noun is. There are six possibilities, but the rule in all six is predictable.

(a) The noun is modified by an adjective: both words take the plural, e.g. *un coffre-fort/des coffres-forts*; *une basse-cour/des basses-cours*.
Exception: the case of *grand*. One may write either *des grand-mères* or *des grands-mères* (for further details see Ch. 11, 1.1.6 *iii*). Non-agreement used to be the rule, but the Arrêté of 28 December 1976 allows for agreement to take place, which is more logical. What is less logical is that no mention is made of *grand-route*, probably an oversight because this term is rarely used. Thus the old rule still stands: *une grand-route/des grand-routes*.
(See also Ch. 11 on the Adjective for the apparent non-agreement of gender (1.1.6.)
(b) The two nouns are coordinated, and both take the plural, e.g. *un sourd-muet/des sourds-muets* (= *des sourds et muets*).
(c) If the compound noun is made up of a noun and an invariable word (preposition or adverb), the latter remains invariable, e.g. *une arrière-boutique/des arrière-boutiques*; *un nouveau-né/des nouveau-nés* (= *nouvellement né − nouveau* is used adverbially.)
(d) Where the compound noun is made up of a noun modified by a prepositional phrase, the agreement of the noun included in the latter will depend on logic, e.g. *des arcs-en-ciel* (there is but one sky); *des timbres-poste* (= de la poste).
(e) Where the compound noun is made up of a noun and a verb, the noun being the complement or direct object of the verb, agreement will depend on logic, e.g. *un abat-jour/des abat-jour* (= *objet qui abat le jour*);[6] *un cache-pot/des cache-pot* (= *objet qui cache le pot)*; but *un accroche-cœur/des accroche-cœurs* (= *pour accrocher un cœur/des cœurs*); *un tire-bouchon/des tire-bouchons* (= *pour tirer un bouchon/des bouchons*).
In some cases the direct object is always in the plural, e.g. *un chasse-mouches* (= *pour chasser les mouches*); *un porte-cigarettes* (= *pour porter les cigarettes*).
(f) Compound nouns derived from verbs and verbal phrases remain invariable, e.g. *un laisser-passer/des laisser-passer*; *un pare-chocs/des pare-chocs*

1.2.2.11   *Historical note on '-s' as mark of the plural*   In Old French one had a two-case system which clearly distinguished between plural and singular:

	Singular	Plural
Subject case	*murs* (Lat. nominative *murus*)	*mur* (Lat. nom. *muri*)
Oblique[7] case	*mur* (Lat. accusative *murum*)	*murs* (Lat. acc. *muros*)

It is because the subject case disappeared that the -*s* became, after the fourteenth century, the mark of the plural. The -*s* was pronounced in those days. It often used to replace the consonant it followed, hence some difficulties of orthography which still exist in present-day French: *clef/clés* (but *clé* is acceptable); *nerf/ners* (written *nerfs* nowadays); *œuf/œus* (written *œufs* nowadays).
    Words ending in -*l* had a clearly different sound in the plural, since the -*l* became vocalized, e.g. *cheval/chevaus* (now *chevaux*), which was pronounced to rhyme with 'Strauss'.
    But from the sixteenth century onwards two important factors emerged:
(i) The -*s* gradually disappeared from pronunciation: *Paris* became *Pari*, and the -*s* at the end of *dames* was no longer pronounced; and from then on French no longer had, generally speaking, an aural form for number, but only a written form.
(ii) Double forms became simplified: *clef* is pronounced *clé* today, and one may still hear *un œuf/des œuf(s)*; the same applies to *des bœuf(s)*. The pronunciation of the *f* is seen in both cases to indicate a lack of education. Where the masculine form was most

frequently heard, it became the accepted form for both singular and plural, e.g. *un rossignol/des rossignols* (instead of *rossignous*). Where the plural form was the most commonly used, it sometimes changed the form of the singular, e.g. *des genous* became *un genou* and the original singular *genouil* disappeared. Even today this tendency is still at work: the singular of *matériaux* is *matériau* for architects (as against *matériel*, which has a different meaning) because *matérial* has disappeared.

Where singular and plural were equally frequent, both survived, e.g. *un œil/des yeux.*

Some nouns and adjectives have found themselves at certain points in time without either a singular or a plural form, in the case in which one of these was rarely used. Thus in the seventeenth century the plural of *naval* was still *navaux*; by the nineteenth century there is hesitation between *navaux* and *navals,* which is why *combats sur mer* was more frequently used until the twentieth century, when *navals* became the norm. Thus many words of the 'irregular plural' type have changed through time: *madrigaux* has at times been *madrigals*; *cristaux* has been *cristals, bocaux* was once *bocals.* . . .

2   Syntactic considerations

2.1   Generalities: the replacement of case by word-order

French, having come from Latin, has developed from a language which had cases, case being a grammatical category of a noun or similarly inflected word such as a pronoun or an adjective indicating its relationship to other words in the sentence. Whereas Indo-European had eight cases, Latin had only six, and these became two in Old French: the Subject case and the Oblique case. An example of a Latin declension follows:

	Singular	Plural
Nominative	*murus*	*muri*
Vocative	*(mure)*	*(muri)* (semantically unlikely)
Accusative	*murum*	*muros*
Genitive	*muri*	*murorum*
Dative	*muro*	*muris*
Ablative	*muro*	*muris*

Given that already in Latin the same endings may correspond to several cases, it is not surprising that in Old French the whole system should have been reduced to two cases:

	Singular	Plural
Nominative = subject	*murs*	*mur*
Oblique	*mur*	*murs*

The subject case corresponds to the nominative and vocative in Latin, the oblique case to all the others.

This reduction in the number of cases was due to many factors, most of them phonetic. The development of the use of prepositions in Vulgar Latin also contributed to the downfall of the case system by making some of the cases redundant. In Old French the tendency to use the word order subject/verb/object finally made the distinction between subject and object case redundant. Thus, although in Old French one could still write either *Rolanz fiert Charlon* or *Charlon fiert Rolanz* (= *Roland frappe Charles*), the former became more and more frequent.

Since the most frequently used case was the oblique case,[8] it is the one which survived most frequently both in the singular and the plural. Hence the *-s* − originally the mark of the nominative singular case − became in modern French the most usual form of the plural. The case system was, however, preserved where confusion could have occurred, namely in the case of pronouns (*je/me/moi, tu/te/toi*. . .) — *je* being the subject case and *me* and *moi* the unstressed and stressed forms which developed from the Latin accusative *me*.

2.2 The functions of the noun

When following Latin through to Modern French, one goes from a language in which the noun is autonomous — in the sense that it may occur in many places in the sentence, its case inflection making its function clear — to a language in which the function of the noun is bound to its position in the sentence.

2.2.1 *The noun as subject*

The general rule is that its place in the sentence will depend on the type of sentence. In the most common case, i.e. in declarative sentences, the subject normally precedes the verb: *Paul bat Pierre* (Paul does the beating), *Pierre bat Paul* (Pierre does the beating).

2.2.2 *The noun as complement*

This may be either of another noun, of an adjective, or of a verb.

2.2.2.1 *The noun as complement of another noun*   In this case the underlying structures (also called 'deep structures') may vary, even though they may appear the same on the surface (also called 'surface structures'), which makes these sentences ambiguous when considered out of context.

(i) The relationship may be that of subject to verb or of verb to object:

> *La peur du roi* = *la peur que le roi éprouve* = *le roi a peur* (subject)
> = *la peur que le roi inspire* = *on a peur du roi* (object)

Similarly,
> *L'amour des parents*   = *les parents aiment* (subject)
> = *les parents sont aimés* (object)

(*Note:* In Old French there was no such confusion: *la paour le roi* = *la peur que le roi éprouve*; *la paour du (del) roi* = *la peur que le roi inspire.*)

(ii) The relationship may be that of noun to adverbial: *une promenade à la campagne* = place adverbial.

(iii) The relationship may be epithetic (see Ch. 11): *un homme à la retraite* = *un retraité*; *un vol de nuit* = *un vol nocturne*.

2.2.2.2 *The noun as complement of an adjective*   These are fairly rare if one excludes those cases in which the noun functions as an adjectival adverb as in *vert bouteille (= du vert d'une bouteille); gris souris (= du gris d'une souris)*. Examples do exist, however, both using and not using the article (see Ch. 2): *il est plein d'amertume; c'est bien naturel aux bêtes intempérantes que nous sommes* (Duhamel).

2.2.2.3 *The noun as complement of a verb*
(i) It may be the direct object of the verb, e.g. *il mange du pain*.
(ii) It may be indirect, e.g. *annoncer une nouvelle* (direct) *à une personne* (indirect), in which case it is introduced by a preposition (see Ch. 13).
(iii) It may refer to the agent of the process or action, e.g. *cette résolution a été approuvée par tout le monde*.
(iv) It may be an adverbial (or circumstantial complement), e.g. *il est dans la voiture*.

2.2.3 *The noun as attribute*

(i) In this case it expresses a quality of the subject, and normally appears after an intensive verb:[9] this is an attribute of the subject, e.g. *L'homme est un roseau, le plus faible de la nature* (Pascal).
(ii) It may be an attribute of the object (or 'complement of the object'), e.g. *les membres du comité ont élu M. X président* (*président* is the attribute of *M. X*).

An attribute may refer indirectly to the object, i.e. through the intermediary of a preposition, or of an adverb functioning as such, e.g. *je l'ai eu longtemps comme collègue.*

2.2.4 *The noun in apposition*

It may modify a preceding noun in a nonrestrictive construction,[10] e.g. *Paris, la capitale de la France,. . . .*

2.2.5 *The noun in 'apostrophe'*

In this case the noun is either a proper noun or one referring to rank, e.g. *Cécile, viens voir ce qui se passe!*

3 The creation of new nouns[11]

3.1 The possibilities

A living language needs to be constantly creating new words, in order that the language should match the changing cultural and technological environment in which it functions. The main ways of creating new nouns in French are the following, listed roughly in order of importance.

3.1.1 *Use of the name of the inventor*

Examples: *un bic, un frigidaire, un calepin, une poubelle, un watt, un ohm.*

3.1.2 *Use of initials or abbreviations*

Some phrases may be abbreviated to acronyms, which then function as nouns, e.g. *les PTT, la SNCF, la CGT.* (Some of them are now sometimes written with only the first letter as a capital, e.g. *la Cgt, l'Otan,* but this is true mainly of unions and political bodies, and only in journalism. It is felt to be unacceptable by many French people.) In some cases they become fully integrated as 'ordinary' nouns: *un cégétiste* (a member of the *CGT*); *un capésien* (one who has a grant to study for the *CAPES – Certificat d'Aptitude à l'Enseignement Secondaire*).

3.1.3 *Borrowings from other languages*
Some of these are so integrated into French (*naturalisés)* that they are now no longer recognizable as foreign words: *café* and *zéro* come from Arabic, *piano* and *balcon* from Italian, *redingote* and *bouledogue* from English. Others are in the process of being integrated, which means that there may be some hesitation in terms of their spelling, and in terms of agreement (e.g. the question of whether words such as *building* should end in *-ing* or *-ingue).*

3.1.4   *Derivation*

This is a grammatical process and will therefore be examined in more detail in 3.2.

Nouns which are created through derivation are words which function as one 'noun-unit' although they are made up of at least two elements, one of these being the root and a lexical unit in its own right, the other (or others) being an affix which is a lexical unit which cannot exist in its own right. In other words, the root is the 'free form', whereas the affix is a 'bound form':

un *pré*salaire = un salaire payé *avant* le vrai salaire
lav*age* = *action* de laver
chambre/chambr*ette* = une *petite* chambre

Prefixes, in French, do not change the grammatical category of the noun. Suffixes may do so (*laver/lavage*: a verb has become a noun); but a suffix may also simply modify the meaning of another noun (*chambre/chambrette*). If the suffix changes the category of word it is *exocentric*; if it changes the meaning but not the category, it is *endocentric* (see 3.2 for the practical application of these distinctions).

3.1.5   *Compound nouns ('mots composés')*

These are lexical units made up of several free forms, as is the case, for example, with *remonte-pente* or *pomme de terre*. In some cases they may be written as one word, although made up of several, e.g. *vinaigre* (= *vin aigre*). (There are problems, however, in defining free forms and affixes – see 3.3.1.)

This process is very productive where technical terms are concerned: for example, a medicine called 'Adiazine' has the technical name 'paraminophenylsulfamido 2 pyrimidine' (example from Bonnard, *Grammaire française des lycées et collèges*, 228).

3.1.6   *Syntactic nominalization*

It is sometimes possible to create a noun from a word which already exists in a different class by placing it in a nominal context: any adjective may become a noun if preceded by a determiner, e.g. *le nucléaire* (see Ch. 11, 3.5); the past participle *rentré* may become the noun *la rentrée*; some infinitives may be nominalized (although far less easily than in Old French), e.g. *le boire et le manger*; even prepositions may become nouns, as in the expression *le pour et le contre*. It is far less easy, however, to nominalize in this way in French than in English (with the exception of adjectives), and this entails a number of translation problems (see 4.1 and 4.2).

3.2   The creation of new nouns through derivation

3.2.1   *Prefixes*

These change the meaning and not the class of the word; their origin is usually Greek or Latin. Some of these are no longer productive (i.e. no longer used to create new nouns), whilst others are used increasingly frequently. Examples of productive prefixes are:

anti = *contre* , e.g. *antiraciste*
auto = *qui agit de soi-(même)*, e.g. *autosuggestion, autorail*
hyper = *qui surpasse*, e.g. *hypermarché, hypersensibilité*
super = *qui dépasse*, e.g. *supermarché, superproduction*
micro = *très petit*, e.g. *microphone, microsillon*
mini = *diminutive*, e.g. *minijupe, minibus*

poly = plusieurs, e.g. *polyclinique, polyculture*
télé = au loin, e.g. *télévision, téléguidage, télésiège*

3.2.2 *Suffixes*

3.2.2.1 *Exocentric suffixes* These change the grammatical category of the word by the process of nominalization through derivation.

(i) Nouns may be derived from verbs using the following suffixes: *-age* (*arracher/arrachage*); *-ade* (*noyer/noyade*); *-erie* (*tromper/tromperie*); *-is* (*abattre/abattis*); *-isme* (*déterminer/déterminisme*; also endocentric, e.g. *abstention/abstentionisme*); *-oir* (*abattre/abattoir*); *-ation, -isation, -ification* (*motoriser/motorisation, confisquer/confiscation*); *-ure* (*fêler/fêlure*).
(ii) Nouns derived from adjectives: *-* (*anonyme/anonymat*); *-ce* (*violent/violence*); *-erie* (*gauche/gaucherie*); *-esse* (*riche/richesse*); *-ie* (*jaloux/jalousie*); *-isme* (cf. *(i)*) (*colonial/colonialisme*); *-ise* (*franc/franchise*); *-té* (*habile/habileté*).

3.2.2.2 *Endocentric suffixes* These change the meaning of a word and not its grammatical category: *serf/servage* (= *état du serf*); *consul/consulat* (= *fonction de consul*); *duc/duché* (= *territoire administré par le duc*); *Bouddha/bouddhisme* (= *croyance en Bouddha*); *Bouddha/bouddhiste* (= *partisan de Bouddha*); *colonne/ colonnade* (= *ensemble de colonnes*); *vin/vinasse* (pejorative = *mauvais vin*); *rue/ ruelle* (diminutive = *petite rue*); *lion/lionceau* (= *petit lion*; there are many diminutives); *France/français* (= *originaire de la France*); *cuillère/cuillerée* (= *contenu d'une cuillère*); *rose/rosacée* (= *plantes de la famille des roses*).

3.3 Compound nouns[12]

3.3.1 *Problems of definition*

(i) There are two factors which make compound nouns difficult to define. The first, and the most important, is that it is often difficult to distinguish between an affix – which is a bound form – and a free form: *kilo-*, for example, is a 'learned' prefix meaning a thousand; it appears as such in words such as *kilogramme, kilomètre*. But it also appears as a word in its own right, in the spoken language at least: *un kilo de pommes*. Has it therefore become a free form, and is *kilogramme* a compound noun and not a noun obtained through derivation?

The second problem is due to the fact that there are many compound nouns which are 'learned' compound nouns, i.e. made up of Greek or Latin terms (mainly Greek). These are no longer felt to be compound in the same way as those based on French words. Compare, for example:

un anti-monte-lait (= *appareil qui empêche le lait de monter* (*et par conséquent de déborder*))
un anthropophage (= *mangeur d'hommes*, from *anthropo* (*homme*) and *phage* (*manger*))

Whereas the meaning of *anti-monte-lait* is obvious to a French person, all the words being French, the meaning of *anthropophage* has to be learnt, and it is not obvious to all which part means *homme* and which *manger*.
(ii) But even though there may be difficult borderline cases between compound nouns and nouns formed from derivation, there are still essential differences between these two processes of word formation. One way of defining compound nouns is to say that derivation is the association of one or more bound forms – or affixes – to a free form or root, whereas compound nouns are the association of two or more potentially

free forms ('potentially' covers the fact that in learned compound nouns the original 'free form' may no longer be felt to be so). Compound nouns may also be defined in semantic terms: a compound noun is a noun which is made up of several other words, none of which is autonomous within the new formation. In *pomme de terre*, for example, each noun needs the other to express the concept 'potato', since *pomme* on its own means apple and *terre* on its own means earth. *Pomme de terre* to a French person is the same as *potato* to an English person (except from a cultural point of view: the French eat far less of them) and there is no idea of it being 'the apple of the earth'.

(*Note*: a convenient way of checking whether a group of words forms a compound noun or not is to try to modify the individual nouns which make it up: if one or the other may be modified, the group of words considered does not form a compound noun; if none of the nouns may be modified, it is a compound noun. Taking *bain de soleil* as an example, one cannot say **des bain prolongés de soleil* nor **des bains de soleil pâle*; one can, however, modify the group of words taken as a whole: *de bons bains de soleil*. Therefore *bain de soleil* is a compound noun (see 3.3.2v).)

3.3.2   *Characteristics of compound nouns*

Compound nouns display the following characteristics, although none of these is strictly compulsory:

(*i*) The compound noun may be made up of several words (*une grande surface*), of words joined by a dash (*chef-d'œuvre*), or it may be written in one word (*vinaigre*). Joining up the words or writing in a dash emphasizes the compound nature of the noun.

Note: One may sometimes wonder whether a dash is required or not: is it *timbre poste* or *timbre-poste*; *chou fleur* or *chou-fleur*? According to the *Arrêté* of 26 February 1901 it does not matter: 'Il est inutile de fatiguer les enfants à apprendre des contradictions que rien ne justifie. L'absence d'un trait d'union dans *pomme de terre* n'empêche pas cette expression de former un véritable mot composé aussi bien que *chef-d'œuvre* par exemple. Ces mots pourront toujours s'écrire sans trait d'union.' Many people, and teachers in particular, feel this to be a blatant example of 'linguistic permissiveness'. Nobody however disputes the need to retain the dash (*trait d'union*) in the very rare cases in which intelligibility would be affected, e.g. *petite fille* ('little girl') but *petite-fille* 'granddaughter'.

(*ii*) In a compound noun one gender will dominate, that of the head noun, e.g. *un* (masculine) *chou* (masculine) *-fleur* (feminine).

(*iii*) It is often difficult to add a prefix or a suffix to a compound noun.

(*iv*) Whereas a prefix can never become a suffix and vice versa, the elements of a compound noun may appear in both positions, e.g. *anthropophage* (= *mangeur d'hommes*), *philanthrope* (= *ami de l'homme*).

What normally happens is that the modifier comes first and the modified element comes second, thus:

> *pithécanthrope* = *un homme qui est un singe*
> *anthropopithèque* = *un singe qui est un homme*
anthropos meaning 'man' and *pithekos* meaning 'monkey'.

This is an extremely important characteristic for determining the difference between nouns formed by derivation and compound nouns (see 3.3.1*i*).

(*v*) Compound nouns have an inner or 'deep' syntactical structure; the latter may be simple, e.g. *vinaigre* = *vin* (noun) + *aigre* (adjective); it may include preposition, e.g. *machine à coudre*; *canne à sucre*, where the same preposition may take on a different meaning in each case; or it may be elliptical, e.g. *chirurgien-dentiste* (= *un dentiste qui est chirurgien des dents.*) (See 3.3.3.)

(*vi*) A compound noun made up of several individual words functions as a whole where modification is concerned; it is not possible to modify separately the nouns which may make it up (see 3.3.1 *ii Note*).

(vii) In some cases the meaning of each element remains unchanged. In this case the meaning of the underlying structures will be of the type 'x *is* something', e.g. *un château fort* (= *un château qui est fort*), 'x *has* something', e.g. *un polygame* (= *quelqu'un qui a plusieurs femmes*), or 'somebody or something is *both* x *and* y', e.g. *un sourd-muet* (= *quelqu'un qui est à la fois sourd et muet*).

In other cases, however, the meaning of the compound noun may be different from the sum of the meanings of the individual constituents: *un grand brûlé* is somebody who has been grievously burned, and not somebody burned who is also tall; *un chirurgien cardiaque* is a specialist in heart surgery and not a surgeon who has had a heart attack; *le demi-jour* is not half a day, but light which lacks intensity, as it would at dawn or dusk (i.e. 'half a day's light'). This area of study belongs more to semantics than to grammar.

3.3.3 *Summary of the types of formation of compound nouns*

Some are based on verbs, some on nouns, and some on whole sentences.

(i) Different kinds of compound nouns may use the verb as a base:

Combination	Functions involved	Examples
Verb + Noun	(1) The noun is the direct object	*un pousse-café*
		un casse-croûte
		un abat-jour
	(2) The noun is an adverbial (this may involve the use of a preposition)	*un réveille-matin*
		un appel de fonds
		une mise en ordre
Verb + Verb	The second verb is the complement of the first one (Note repetition of the same verb, e.g. *un pousse-pousse*)	*le savoir-faire*
		un laisser-passer
Preposition + Verb	The preposition introduces the verb	*un pourboire*
Adverb + Verb	The adverb modifies the verb	*le bien-être*
Adjective + Past Participle	The adjective modifies the participle, which functions as a noun	*un nouveau-né*

Note: If the verb used is a 'learned verb', there is usually an *-o-* inserted if the word is of Greek origin, and an *-i-* if it is of Latin origin. In these cases, the verb is not felt to be a verb by the average native speaker, who accepts the word as a whole:

anthrop*o*phage (*-phage* being the verbal element)
hipp*o*drome (*-drome* meaning 'course')
plomb*i*fère (*-fère*, from the Latin meaning 'which carries').

(ii) Compound nouns may be based on nouns:

Combination	Functions involved	Examples
Noun + Noun	(1) Something is both *x* and *y* (apposition or coordination)	*un chirurgien-dentiste*
		un chou-fleur
		des cumulo-nimbus
	(2) The second noun is complement of the first, despite the absence of a preposition	*un timbre-poste*
		un thé-citron
	(3) A preposition links the two nouns	*une pomme de terre*
		un moulin à vent
Noun + Adjective	The adjective modifies the noun	*du vinaigre*
		un pot-pourri

| Adverb + Noun | The adverb is complement of the noun | *une avant-garde* |
| Preposition + Noun | The preposition introduces the noun | *un(e) après-midi* |

(iii) Some sentences (complete or not) may be nominalized through the presence of a determiner, e.g. *le qu'en-dira-t-on*; *un va-et-vient*; *un sauve-qui-peut*; *un je-ne-sais-quoi*. The use of dashes emphasizes that the sentences are functioning as nouns. In some cases one may even add a suffix: *le j'm'en-fout-isme* (vulgar).

(iv) Abbreviation of compound nouns is common mainly in the spoken language. Abbreviation (the French call it *amputation*) may take place either at the beginning of the word (*amputation par la gauche*) as in *bus* for *autobus*, the head word being *bus*, or, more frequently, at the end of the word (*amputation par la droite*), in which case the first element is the head element: *radio, ciné, télé, auto, para, métro* (for *métropolitain*), *congélo* (for *congélateur*).

These may sometimes take the pejorative and rather vulgar suffix *-oche*, e.g.

cinéma—ciné—cinoche (vulgar)
télévision—télé—téloche (vulgar)

4   Translation problems

4.1   Nominalization through syntax

(i) Generally speaking, English has far more flexibility in terms of syntactical nominalization than French, since in English almost any word, given the right syntactical context, may function as nearly any part of speech:

(1) 'Is it *right* to say no *right* may wrong no man?'
(2) 'It will *right* itself in the end.'

In French this is not possible in either case:

(1a) *Peut-on vraiment dire que ce qui est juste ne peut faire de tort à personne?*
(2a) *Tout s'arrangera en fin de compte.*

In each case, the word 'right' has to be translated quite differently in French.

(ii) There is one exception to this, however: it is possible to nominalize any French adjective, e.g. *le beau, le bon, le vrai, le petit, le bleu*.

4.2   Nominalization through derivation

Although French has a large number of suffixes with which it may nominalize various classes of words, it is less flexible in this respect than English. In English, for example, many verbs of action may be nominalized by the addition of the otherwise verbal suffix '-ing' ('ride/riding', 'hunt/hunting', 'kill/killing', as in 'riding is fun', 'hunting tigers is illegal', and 'the killing of the deer'). The same does not apply to French; thus, 'ride' = *monter à cheval*; 'riding' = *faire de l'équitation*; and 'riding is fun' = *c'est amusant de faire de l'équitation*. 'Hunting tigers is illegal' = *la chasse aux tigers est illégale* or *chasser le tigre est illégal* (but *la chasse* and *chasser* are both less dynamic than 'hunting'); 'the killing of the deer' = *la mise à mort du cerf, le fait de tuer un cerf*. In all these cases '-ing' may correspond to *le fait de* + *action* – *le fait de faire du cheval, le fait de chasser les tigres, le fait de tuer le cerf*.

4.3 Formation of compound nouns (see 4.3.1) and compound nominal phrases (see 4.3.2)

4.3.1 *The different potential in English and French for creating compound nouns*

Although French can be seen to create compound nouns quite easily, there are a number of cases when a compound noun in English cannot be translated by a compound noun in French, but has to be translated by the 'basic sentence' underlying the compound noun:

the cupboard door = *la porte de l'armoire*
a war story = *une histoire de guerre/une histoire sur la guerre/une histoire écrite pendant la guerre*

The English compound noun may be seen to be sometimes ambiguous, since it is a reduced sentence; in the French version, which is complete, the ambiguity is removed. The problem is that sometimes it is difficult to decide which meaning the English is supposed to carry. It also sometimes happens that the ambiguity of the compound noun is important: it is a way of expressing several things at once, yet one cannot write several alternatives into the French version.

4.3.2 *Compound nominal phrases*

Compound nominal phrases differ, in that they are accidental or temporary, created to fulfil the need of a moment. Some of these may, it is true, become compound nouns, as is the case with *a do-it-yourself shop*; but 'compound nominal phrases' is a term used to cover these 'temporary' compound nouns, as they are created. English has a quite extraordinary propensity to create compound nominal phrases, a propensity which French does not have, and which therefore entails major translation problems. Sinclair writes the following on the subject (d = determiner, n = noun, h = head noun):[13]

Nouns can modify nouns. If you knock a small hole in a wall you can call it a *vent* (dh);[14] if you fit a *control* on it for opening and shutting it you can call that a *vent control* (dnh); If the control has a *knob* so that it can be operated, that can be the *vent control knob* (dnnh). If it is a knob which unscrews with a special *key* that can be your *vent control knob key* (dnnnh) – and, to become slightly absurd, you could require a special *lubricant* for the key, supplied in a *can* (a *vent control knob key lubricant can* (dnnnnnh)) and then the can could have a control with knob, key, etc. There is no limit to the power of compounding nouns in Modern English.[15]

The problem is that the English language enables one to produce any number of synthetic constructions such as the one in Sinclair's example. These are particularly common in journalese:

Who, after all, gives a moment's thought these days to the sight of some rent-a-crowd parading through the streets, whether it's for full employment, student grants, abortion, or peace? (P. Toynbee, *The Guardian,* 23 June 1980)

. . . a whipped-up, top-spin backhand (BBC sports commentary)

French, on the other hand, cannot create such compound nominal phrases with anywhere near the same flexibility as English. In this respect French remains far more analytical than English.
    There are two consequences of this:
(i) It is often impossible to translate exactly the conceptual and semantic connotations of 'words' such as *do-it-yourself* or *rent-a-crowd*; since a synthetic construction is semantically different from an analytical one.

Where a new reality is created in French, a word will be created, but not in the same way as in English. Thus one has in France *des magasins de bricolage* in place of the English *do-it-yourself shop*. To translate the journalistic example above, however, one has really to explain in French what the English *rent-a-crowd* means. Here is a possible translation:

> *Qui accorde désormais la moindre attention à ces foules qui, rassemblées à la demande, défilent aussi bien en faveur du plein emploi, des bourses d'études, de l'avortement ou de la paix?*

(ii) The English synthetic construction may be ambiguous, and this ambiguity has to be removed when going from a synthetic construction to an analytical one. For example, *a coal merchants' foundation* could mean either 'a foundation *for* coal merchants' or 'a foundation created *by* coal merchants' or 'a foundation *for* and *by* coal merchants'. In this case accurate translation is possible only if the context makes clear which one it is. The following are some possible translations for *a coal merchants' foundation*:

> a foundation for coal merchants = *une société de bienfaisance pour charbonniers*
> a foundation by coal merchants = *une société de bienfaisance créée par les charbonniers*

But it is possible to combine the translation of *for* and *by* with the French *de*:

> a foundation for and by coal merchants = *une société bénévole de charbonniers.*

Notes

1 There are morphological reasons, however − see 1.1.1.2 on the origins of French genders.

2 *'une chose* = terme le plus général par lequel on désigne tout ce qui existe et qui est concevable comme un objet unique (concret; abstrait; réel; mental). *Un chose* = (familier) ce qu'on ne peut ou ne veut pas nommer. Voir *machin, truc' (Dictionnaire du français primordial* (Micro-Robert), Paris, Garnier Flammarion, 1973.)

3 Metonymy is the substitution of the name of an attribute or adjunct for that of the thing meant (e.g. 'crown' for 'king', 'the turf' for 'horse-racing' − see *Concise Oxford Dictionary.*)

4 It is true that *factrice* is not really the feminine of *facteur* in the sense of 'postman': it corresponds instead to the verb *faire*, in the sense of 'making' as in *un facteur/ une factrice d'orgues* = *un fabricant d'orgues/une femme qui fabrique des orgues.*

5 A skiing term used to refer to the men who hand over the poles of the ski-lifts to the skiers.

6 Some grammarians think that *abat* and *cache* are imperatives.

7 There are terminological problems related to the term 'oblique case'. In English, one uses the term 'oblique case' for all but the nominative and vocative cases (see B. Hall Kennedy's *Revised Latin primer* (London, Longman, 1959). Ménard uses the term *cas régime* to refer to the same concept (*Manuel d'Ancien Français, Syntaxe*). But other French grammarians keep the term *oblique* to refer to those cases which correspond, very often, to the use of a preposition in French, namely the genitive, dative and ablative.

8 Thus *comte*, in the oblique case, won over *cuens* in the nominative case; but sometimes both forms survived, each having a slightly different meaning, as in the case of *on/homme* (*homo/hominem*).

9 An intensive verb is one which introduces a complement or attribute of the subject.

10 A nonrestrictive structure in a sentence is one which gives additional information

about some element in the sentence but is not essential to the general meaning of the sentence. This term is used mainly in relation to relative clauses (see Ch. 14, 0.1*i*).

11 Only certain aspects of noun creation are, strictly speaking, grammatical, namely derivation and compound nouns. The subject as a whole belongs to lexicology, but since grammar and lexicology are bound to overlap, brief mention is made here of these matters.

12 The most recent and complete work on the subject was done by S. Lamothe as a Thèse d'Etat, *Les Mots composés formés de 2 éléments lexicaux* (1978). The present summary takes this work into consideration.

13 J.M. Sinclair, *A course in spoken English: Grammar* (London, Oxford University Press, 1972).

14 *d* stands for determiner, *n* for noun and *h* for head.

15 'Compound nouns' is the term usually used both for what have been called 'compound nouns' in this chapter and for what have been called 'compound nominal phrases'. The distinction seems important since, although French has plenty of compound nouns, it cannot easily create compound nominal phrases.

Chapter 2

The determiners

0 General considerations

0.1 Definition

(i) Determiners are those parts of speech which transform a noun from the abstract concept it represents as a dictionary entry to an actual concept which is realized in a given context. (The French say that 'le déterminant *actualise* le nom'.)

(ii) Determiners may indicate specificity (*le chien que je vois*), deixis or spatiotemporal reference (*ce chien qui est là-bas*), or possession (*mon chien*). Certain indefinite adjectives may also function as indefinite determiners (*certains chiens*). Those determiners which indicate specificity are called 'articles' (see 1); those which indicate deixis are called 'demonstrative adjectives'[1] (see 2); those which indicate possession are called 'possessive adjectives' (see 3); and those which function as indefinite determiners are 'indefinite adjectives functioning as determiners' (see 4). Numerals are discussed in section 5.

(iii) All determiners have the characteristic of being mutually exclusive: one may say *le chien* or *mon chien*, but not **le mon chien*.

(iv) In French, as in English, determiners precede the noun, although they may be separated from them by adjectives: *le chien* and *le petit chien*.

(v) There are cases in which the noun is not preceded by a determiner: the absence of a determiner indicates indefiniteness. This is sometimes called 'the zero article' (see 1.4). The latter was far more frequent in Old French than in modern French. It is often represented by the sign Ø.

0.2 Numerals

There are two types of numerals: cardinal numerals, e.g. *un*, *deux*, *trois*, *vingt*; and ordinal numerals, e.g. *premier*, *deuxième*, *troisième*, *vingtième*.

Ordinal numerals function exactly as do ordinary adjectives: *mon petit livre* (ordinary adjective); *mon premier livre* (ordinal adjective). Since the ordinal numerals are adjectives they should, logically, be classified as adjectives. They are, however, morphologically dependent upon the cardinal numerals, which may function either as indefinite articles (*un livre/deux livres/vingt livres*) or as modifiers of the noun (*les trois livres/les vingt livres*). It is because the ordinal numerals are morphologically dependent on the cardinal numerals – which themselves *may* function as determiners – that the former are dealt with in this particular chapter.

0.3 Interrogative and exclamative adjectives

The interrogative and exclamative adjective *quel* is often classified as a determiner, since *quel* and the other determiners are mutually exclusive: *un homme/quel homme?/quel homme!* but never **le quel homme*. There is, nonetheless, an essential difference between *quel* and determiners: determiners transform a noun from the abstract concept it represents to an actual concept which is realized in a given context; but *quel* does not 'determine' the noun in any way. *Quel* serves to 'transform' a declarative clause or sentence either into an interrogative or an exclamative sentence:

un homme est venu réparer la chaudière
quel homme est venu réparer la chaudière?
quel homme est venu réparer la chaudière!

(See Ch. 19.)

0.4 The modern system of determiners[2]

A distinction is made between the specific and the generic (the latter meaning either 'general', i.e. not specific, or characteristic of a class or large group (see 0.4.2)).

0.4.1 *Expression of the specific*[3]

Increasing degrees of specificity

Identity of the determined is unclear	Identity of the determined is known	Reference is made to a possessor	Localization in terms of space
J'aperçois UN chien et DES chats	*Tiens! LE chien poursuit LES chats*	*Mais c'est MON chien! Mais ce sont VOS chats!*	*CE chien est bien méchant; et CES chats aussi*
This often corresponds to a transient state of affairs	Refers to shared knowledge (and by extension to what is well known)		A gesture may be used at the same time

0.4.2 *Expression of the generic*

(i) in the sense of general, not specific, e.g. *un homme averti en vaut deux* (i.e. 'any man'); *un cadeau qui vous tombe du ciel, cela fait toujours plaisir* (or *des cadeaux. . . !*).
(ii) in the sense of characteristic of a whole class or large group, e.g. *le chien est un animal affectueux*; *j'aime les mathématiques*.

A brief summary is given in 0.5 of the development of the French system of determiners. This is a very confusing area for English speakers, since it is the system used in Old French which resembles that used in modern English. A summary of the reasons why the system had to change is included in order to make it more understandable.

See also, in this respect, section 6 on translation problems.

0.5 Historical development

0.5.1 *The system used in Old French*

The system of determiners used in Old French closely resembled that of modern English, except that the determiners were marked for both case and gender.
(i) Complete indefiniteness was indicated by the zero article, e.g. *chat/chats* ('cat/cats'). The final *-s* was pronounced, as it is in English.
(ii) Partial definiteness was expressed by the indefinite article, e.g. *un chat/(des) chats*[4] ('a cat/(some) cats'). In this case *un* meant *un quelconque*. Its use was the exception and not the rule.

(iii) Definiteness was expressed then, as now, by the definite article, the possessive adjective and the demonstrative adjective: *le chat/les chats*; *mon chat/mes chats*; *ce chat/ces chats*, but the use of the definite article was more emphatic then than now.

0.5.2   *The collapse of the old system and the beginnings of the new*

The collapse of the old system was mainly due to the fact that the *-s* of the plural ceased to be pronounced (the loss of the cases also weakened the system). The result of this was that it became impossible to distinguish orally between the singular and plural, when there was no article expressed. To compensate for this, when count nouns were used, they became preceded by *des*, a new plural indefinite article, which developed from *de*: the *des* in *des chats* became essential to the expression of number. But when mass nouns were used, number was irrelevant: *boire vin* continued to be used, although *boire de vin* also existed. When referring to a certain quantity of something taken from a determined whole, however, *de* + the definite article was used, e.g. *il boit du (de le) vin de son père*. Little by little the use of *de* + definite article to refer to a certain quantity of something taken from a determined whole, became used whether or not the whole was determined, hence: *il boit du vin de son père/il boit du vin* (see 1.3.3).

The 'zero article' was thus replaced either by the indefinite or partitive articles, or by the definite article when used in a generic sense.

1   The article

There are four kinds of articles: the definite article (1.1), the indefinite article (1.2), the 'partitive article' (1.3) and the 'zero article' or absence of article (1.4).

1.1   The definite article: 'le/la/les'

1.1.1.   *General characteristics*

The definite article serves to indicate the difference between a noun in its abstract dictionary sense and a noun used either as a definite specific referent (*l'homme que j'ai vu ce matin*) or as representing all the referents of a category (*l'homme est le plus destructeur de tous les animaux*). In this last case it has a 'generalizing' role.
(ii) A noteworthy property of the definite article is its ability to nominalize nearly any other part of speech: *le bien*, *le manger*, *le garde-à-vous*. The indefinite article may be used in the same way, but this is done far less frequently (e.g. *un beau vert*.)
(iii) In Old French there were three degrees of specificity:[5] complete indefiniteness, indicated by the zero article; partial indefiniteness indicated by the indefinite article; and definiteness indicated by the definite article.

The near disappearance of the zero article means that the whole system has shifted, and the definite article is no longer as 'definite' as it used to be. This creates serious translation problems for anglophones (see 6.1), since English has retained its zero article:

'books'	'some books'	'the books'
—	*des livres*	*les livres*

'books represent the progress of mankind'
les livres représentent les progrès de l'humanité
'the books are on the table'
les livres sont sur la table

In this case the English zero article is translated in French by a definite article which represents the whole category of possible referents (this is also called generic reference). These problems are examined in section 6.1.

1.1.2. *Morphology*

(i)

Singular		Plural
Masculine	Feminine	Masculine and Feminine
le, l'	*la, l'*	*les*

(ii) The definite article undergoes elision of its final vowel in the singular (both masculine and feminine) before a noun beginning with a vowel, and before an aspirate *h-*, e.g. *l'aspirateur, l'homme.*

(iii) The masculine singular form *le* combines with the prepositions *à* and *de* to produce *au* and *du*:

*j'irai à le retour de ma promenade gives *j'irai au retour de ma promenade*
*le problème de le retour en Angleterre gives *le problème du retour en Angleterre*

The plural form *les* combines with *à* and *de* to give *aux* and *des* (which must not be confused with its homonym *des*, the plural of *un*):

*aller à les courses gives *aller aux courses*
*revenir de les magasins gives *revenir des magasins*

Note: The 'aspirated *h*' is often called in French either the 'so-called aspirated *h*' or the 'disjunctive *h*'. It is called the 'so-called aspirated *h*' because it is no longer aspirated – at least in standard French; it is called the 'disjunctive *h*' because where a word starts with such an *h*, neither liaison nor elision takes place. Around 65 words in modern standard French start with a 'disjunctive *h*'. These are: *la hache, la haie, la haine, le hâle, le hall, les halles, le halo, le hamac, le hameau, la hanche, les handicapés, le hangar, hanter, happer, harasser, harceler, hardi, le harem, le hareng, le haricot, la harpe, le harpon, le hasard, la hâte, la hausse, le haut, le hautbois, la hauteur, Le Havre, hérisser, la hernie, le héros, la herse, le hêtre, heurter, le hibou, le hideux, la hiérarchie, hocher, les Hollandais, le homard, la Hongrie, la honte, honteux, le hors-jeu, la hotte, la houille, la housse, le hublot, la huée, le huguenot, le huit* (but for *dix-huit, vingt-huit* etc. the liaison is made), *hurler, le hussard.*

One may contrast these with words starting with a mute *h*, in which case the *h* exists only in the written form, and elision and liaison take place normally, e.g. *l'haleine, l'hameçon, l'helléniste, l'hémistiche, l'héroïne, l'héroïque, l'huissier. L'hippisme* (horse-racing) is thus distinguished from *le hippysme* (the 'hippy' movement) by the absence of a disjunctive h.

Historically speaking, the disjunctive *h* appears in words which are germanic in origin (e.g. *haga< haie*); these were originally aspirated. This was still the case in the sixteenth century, but aspiration was by then much weaker. There were many cases of hesitation between the two kinds of *h*, and some Latin words became pronounced with a disjunctive *h*, *le héros* being an example (although the *h* in *héroïne* is not disjunctive, hence *l'héroïne*); proper names starting with an *h* also tended to become disjunctive (*de Hector* rather than **d'Hector, de Hugo* and not **d'Hugo*).

This is still an area of uncertainty in modern French.

1.1.3   *Use*

1.1.3.1   *Particularization of the noun*   The definite article indicates the fact that a specific realization of the noun is being referred to. Further information about that referent cannot be conveyed by the definite article, but must be conveyed by the context, e.g.

> *j'ai vu le chien*
> *j'ai vu le chien enragé*
> *j'ai vu le chien enragé que le gendarme a tué*

All three sentences may refer either to the same dog, or to two or three different dogs; all the article tells us is that in each sentence it is a definite dog which is being referred to, and not dogs in general.

1.1.3.2   *Indication of uniqueness*   The definite article is also used to indicate a single referent: *la France, la lune, le surréalisme*.

1.1.3.3   *Exophoric reference*   In this case what is being referred to is well known or visible for the interlocutor, e.g.

> donne-moi *la* pioche; ferme *la* porte

1.1.3.4   *Generic reference*   In this case the term 'definite article' takes on a general meaning so wide that the term 'definite' seems hardly appropriate: it refers to all the members of that category:

> *l'homme est un animal belliqueux* (= *tous les hommes sont belliqueux* or *les hommes sont, dans l'ensemble, belliqueux*)

1.1.3.5   *Historical and explanatory note*   There were no articles in Classical Latin; their development has therefore taken place concurrently with the development of French itself. Like the personal pronouns *il* and *elle*, the definite articles have developed from the Latin demonstrative *ille*, which slowly lost its purely deictic signification (deictic = which makes spatio-temporal references). The indefinite article developed from the numeral *unus*.

The articles, both definite and indefinite, were originally used to express something concrete; but through time they have taken on various abstract meanings as well, abstract ideas having become 'concretized' through their use. This increase in the use of the article was due to the disappearance from the spoken language of the *-s* of the plural (which English has retained): the article was needed to express number. Thus the article became used both in those contexts in which it was used before, and in other contexts from which it used to be absent (see 0.5): the article invaded the 'zero article' area, thus acquiring two values; one for specific reference and one for abstract reference.

1.1.3.6   *Use with proper nouns*   French uses the definite article far more often than English does (see 6.1):
(i) with the names of families, dynasties, or any kind of team: *les Durand, les Bourbons, les verts* (the football team from St-Etienne). The article may also be used to refer to a group of people in expressions such as *Hé! les gars!* or *Les parisiens sont arrivés!*
(ii) with the names of countries, except when these are used with the preposition *en*: *traverser la Belgique* but *aller en Belgique* (see Ch. 13).
(iii) with names used pejoratively (such as those of the unpopular mistresses of the Bourbon kings: *la Montespan, la Pompadour*).

(iv) with a name followed by a nickname: *Pépin le Bref, Jojo la Terreur*.

(v) with a title followed by a function: *Monsieur le Président*.

(*Note 1*: This does not always apply with army ranks. In this case the rule is as follows:

If one is oneself in the army, one uses the expression *mon commandant, mon lieutenant* etc. when addressing one's superior; if addressing inferior ranks, one simply says *lieutenant* (one never says *mon sergent*, but simply *sergent*).

If one is not in the army, one says *Bonjour, commandant*; *Bonjour, général*. Below the rank of commandant one uses *Monsieur*.

When speaking *of* somebody in the army one uses the definite article, as is the case for other professions entailing the use of a title, e.g. *le général de Gaulle, le caporal Martin*, in the same way as one would say *le professeur Dubois* or *le docteur Durand*.)

(*Note 2*: In law, one uses the title *Maître* without an article: *Maître Legrand a été chargé de la défense de l'accusé*.)

(vi) with certain names of Italian or Spanish origin, e.g. *le Cid, le Tintoret, la Callas*; this is neologistic, however, since it imitates Spanish and Italian.

1.1.3.7 *Use in expression of time, date and season*

(i) The definite article is used to refer to a specific date: *le 30 juin, la semaine prochaine*; and to refer to the days of the week in a frequentative way: *le dimanche* (= 'on Sundays'). For vague indications of time other than midday or midnight one uses the plural definite article: *vers les huit heures*.[6]

(Note: One says *au printemps*, but *en été, en automne* and *en hiver*. This is because *printemps* starts with a consonant, whereas the other three nouns start with a vowel or a mute *h-*.)

(ii) There is a distinction between the use of the numeral *un* and the definite article: *dans une semaine, dans un mois* (i.e. at the end of the period stated) but *dans la semaine, dans le mois* (i.e. during the period stated).

1.1.3.8 *Use in fixed verbal expressions*   The definite article is used in a number of fixed expressions of the *avoir l'air de* or *avoir l'habitude de* type, in which the noun is normally followed by a complement, as in *avoir l'air de comprendre*.

1.1.3.9 *Use in the expression of quantity*

(i) The definite article is used in various commercial distributive situations relating to weights and measures, e.g. *beurre à 12 francs le kilo; œufs 6 francs la douzaine; artichauts 3 francs la pièce* (although this is often shortened to *3 francs pièce*).

The preposition *à* entails, in such cases, the use of the definite article (*vendre les pommes au kilo, acheter un tissu au mètre*), whereas the preposition *en* precludes the use of the article (*vente en gros*).

(ii) It is also used with fractions: *prenez la moitié du melon; prenez le tiers du melon*; but the indefinite article is just as likely: *prenez une moitié du melon; prenez un tiers du melon*.

When referring to more than one unit of a fraction, the article *les* is possible but not obligatory: *prenez (les) trois quarts du gâteau*.

(*Note*: One may refer to *un trois-quarts*, i.e. to a member of a rugby football team, and to *un quatre-quarts*, which is a cake; but in these cases *trois-quarts* and *quatre-quarts* are compound nouns and not fractions.)

1.1.3.10 *Use of the definite article for parts of the body*

(i) where the noun forms part of a complement indicating manner, e.g. *elle marchait le dos courbé contre la pluie; il est sorti le fusil à la main*.

(ii) where there is an object followed by an attribute, e.g. *il avait les mains sales*.

(iii) where there is no ambiguity as to the possessor, and when the noun is not the

subject of the clause: *j'ai mal à la tête* (obviously 'my head'); *on risque de se casser le cou* ('one's own neck'); *va te laver les mains* ('your hands'). One may also hear *ne marche pas sur mes pieds*, in which case the use of *mes* is emphatic (*ne me marche pas sur les pieds* would also be possible).

(iv) But when the noun is the subject, the possessive adjective must be used:

> *leurs mains sont sales*; *qu'ils aillent se les laver!*
> *Leurs pieds roses éperonnés coupaient l'air bleu* (Jammes).

(v) The possessive adjective is also obligatory where the noun is modified by an adjective:

> *On le vit manœuvrer des léviers, se pencher en avant, comprimer son gros ventre. Le moteur ronfla. Siméon Bramberger, debout, une mèche de cheveux gris dansant comme une flamme, au sommet de sa tête, regarda s'éloigner la voiture.* (van der Meersch)

*Comprimer le gros ventre would be totally unacceptable; but *au sommet de la tête* is possible, since no ambiguity would arise. *Sa tête* is chosen here rather than *la tête* because the expression is metaphorical: *sa* emphasizes the fact that this is not a straightforward description of a normal state of affairs.

Further examples of the obligatory use of the possessive adjective for parts of the body are:

> *Sur ses genoux est son petit métier de brodeuse*
> *Ses ongles brillent dans le treillis des fils* (Mauclair)

In this example we find *ses genoux* because *les genoux* would be ambiguous; and *ses ongles* because *ongles* is the subject of the verb.

(vi) In poetry the possessive adjective is sometimes used instead of the article because of its being more suggestive, given that it also refers to the possessor:

> *Tu la trouveras baignant ses pieds sous les rouches*[7]

>   (la Tour du Pin)

1.1.4.   *Further determination of the 'definite article + noun' group*

The definite article + noun may be made more precise in two ways, either through the use of the adjective *tout/toute/tous/toutes*, or through the use of cardinal numerals.

1.1.4.1   *Determination by 'tout'*

> *Tous les livres que je voulais ont été vendus*
> *Toutes les filles sont arrivées en retard*

(*Note 1*: There are some cases in which *tout* may be used as a determiner on its own, e.g. *à tout seigneur, tout honneur*; *toute vérité n'est pas bonne à dire.* (See 4.))

(*Note 2*: When *tout* is used to modify the definite article, it precedes the definite article. When it follows the determiner, it usually functions as part of a compound noun, as in *le tout-Paris*; *la toute-puissance du Seigneur*. In these cases a dash links the adjective *tout* to the noun.)

1.1.4.2   *Determination by cardinal numerals*

> *Les deux livres qui sont sur la table sont à moi*

In this case *deux* introduces extra precision to *les livres*. Whereas *tout* is placed before the article + noun group, the cardinal numeral always immediately follows the article. (If an adjective is included in the nominal group the same applies: *Les deux petits livres.*)

1.2 The indefinite article: 'un/une/des'

1.2.1 *General characteristics*

(i) Like the definite article, the indefinite article serves to indicate the difference between a noun used in its abstract dictionary sense and a noun pointing to a specific referent, although the identity of the referent is not made explicit: in *un homme est venu ce matin, un homme* is specific but one does not know exactly who it is. We may therefore distinguish between articles which are specific and definite (1.1) and articles which are specific and indefinite (1.2).

In other words, the indefinite article refers to one or several referents in a whole category – *un chat* (= *un quelconque chat*)/*des chats* – without their identity being made explicit.

(ii) The indefinite article may be used to nominalize an adjective: *c'est un beau vert.*

(iii) *Un* is a homonym of the numeral *un*; in other words *un* may mean 'a' or 'one', e.g. *un livre* = 'a book' and 'one book'. The plural indefinite article *des* is a homonym of the plural partitive *des*, e.g. *des livres* can mean 'some books' or 'of the books' as in *la vente des livres* (= 'the sale of the books').

(*Note*: The indefinite article *un/une* derives from the Latin numeral *unus*; historically speaking, the indefinite article is therefore a numeral. But in French *je me suis acheté un vase* does not mean 'I have bought one vase' (as against two or three) but simply 'I have bought a vase'. It is, in fact, important not to confuse the indefinite article *un* with its homonym, the numeral *un*:

je voudrais manger un gâteau (*un* = any cake)
j'en voudrais un morceau seulement (*un* = and not two, three . . .)

1.2.2 *Morphology*

(i)

Singular		Plural
Masculine	Feminine	Masculine and Feminine
un	*une*	*des*

(ii) In the context adjective + noun, *de* is used instead of *des*: *de belles fleurs* rather than *des belles fleurs.*

(*Note*: This does not apply if adjective + noun form a compound noun: *des jeunes filles, des fines champagnes.*)

1.2.3 *Use of the indefinite article*

1.2.3.1 *With one or several unspecified referents*

je cherche un homme qui puisse m'aider (*un homme* is not distinguished from other men)

It is normally used in this sense to refer to somebody or something for the first time at the beginning of a story: *il était une fois une petite fille qui s'appelait Cendrillon.*

(ii) It is also used to refer to somebody one does not know much about: *un Monsieur Dupont a cherché à vous joindre ce matin au téléphone.*

(iii) It is used to refer to a non-identified member of an otherwise identified family: *il a épousé une demoiselle Dupont.*

1.2.3.2   *Reference to one or several members of a group*   It is in this sense that the indefinite article is used with *c'est* to indicate membership of a group. Compare:

> *il est médecin* (*médecin* is an attribute of *il* and functions as an adjective)
> *c'est un médecin* (he is a member of the group of people called *médecins*)
> *c'est un communiste* (he is a member of the group of people called *communistes*)

(See also *c'est* v. *il est*, Ch. 3,2.4.2.4.)

1.2.3.3   *Indication of uniqueness*   In this case, the indefinite article is applied to something or someone unique, to render that uniqueness exemplary:

> *Après un Jean-Sébastien Bach, on pense: telle est la musique; survient un Mozart, un Beethoven. . . .* (Gide)
> *je voudrais avoir l'âme d'un Lamartine pour exprimer la grandeur de ce paysage*

1.2.3.4   *Generalization*   In this case the indefinite article is used to make an unspecified referent stand for the whole category of such referents: *un repas sans fromage n'est pas un vrai repas* (*un* = any/all).

1.2.3.5   *Emphasis*
(i) *Des* may be used to stress number or quantity, e.g. *j'attends depuis des heures!* or *il a gagné des millions!*
(ii) *D'un/d'une* may be used in the spoken language to express emphasis:

> *le ciel est d'un bleu!* (= *d'un bleu très intense, ou spécial*)
> *tu parles d'un fou!* (= *il est complètement fou*)

1.2.4   *Numerals functioning as indefinite articles*

(i) Cardinal numerals may function as indefinite articles: in *donnez-moi un livre* or *donnez-moi trois livres*, reference is specific but indefinite, in that one does not know which particular books are required.
(ii) The indefinite article *un* is historically the same as the cardinal numeral *un* (they both derive from the Latin numeral *unus*), although their meaning is different nowadays: *je suis resté un mois à la campagne* (*un* = 1); but *une couleur que je n'aime pas pour les intérieurs est le vert* (*une* = a colour amongst other colours).
   There are cases of ambiguity, however, e.g. *je prends un pain*. In this case we do not know if *un* is a cardinal numeral, in opposition with other cardinal numerals, as in *je prends deux pains, trois pains . . .* , or whether *un* is an indefinite article in opposition with *le* or *ce*, as in *je prends le pain que vous avez mis de côté pour moi*.
   (*Note*: In the spoken language, the ambiguity could be removed in the case of *un* = 1 by stressing the *un*:

> *je prends un pain* (*et non pas deux, trois, . . .*))

1.3   The 'partitive articles': 'du', 'de la' and 'des'

The partitive article serves to refer to an indefinite quantity of something, i.e. one which has not been measured or counted.

1.3.1   *The two meanings (or dual role) of the partitive article*

(i) Not all grammarians accept that there is a separate entity called 'the partitive article', since the partitive element in *je veux de la soupe* is expressed by the preposition *de*. Also, *de* does not combine only with the definite article to express the

partitive: *je veux de ta soupe* (*de* + possessive adjective) and *je veux de cette soupe* (*de* + demonstrative adjective) both express the same kind of idea (see 1.3.4).

(ii) There can be a difference, however, between *je veux de la soupe* and *je veux de ta soupe/je veux de cette soupe*: when *de* combines with the demonstrative or the possessive adjective, it refers to some quantity of a determined whole; when *de* is used with the definite article to express the partitive, the speaker may be referring either to part of a determined whole, or to part of an indeterminate whole. It is in this second case that the partitive article differs from the other constructions which may express the partitive. Hence *je veux de la soupe* is ambiguous when out of context: it could mean either a portion of a specific soup, or simply 'some soup', i.e. any soup. Similarly, *je veux du gâteau* could mean either that I want a slice of a particular cake, or that I would like some cake, 'cake' being used in a general sense. This is illustrated by the fact that these sentences could have two possible translations in English, depending on the meaning attributed to them:

je veux de la soupe = 'I want some soup' (indeterminate)
　　　　　　　　　　　 'I want some of the soup' (a part of a specific whole)
je veux du gâteau = 'I want some cake'
　　　　　　　　　　 'I want some of the cake'

1.3.2　*Morphology*

(i) The partitive article is made up of the preposition *de* + the definite article. This gives the following forms:

Singular		Plural
Masculine	Feminine	Masculine and Feminine
du	*de la/de l'*	*(des)*

(ii) Des is in brackets since not all grammarians accept that there is such a thing as a 'plural partitive', given that the partitive refers by definition to what is not countable. But there are cases in which nouns are used only in the plural, e.g. *rillettes*, hence the use of *des* instead of *du* in *prenez des rillettes*. In other cases a singular form exists but it is meaningless: one would not say *prenez une lentille* (meaning 'lentils') but *prenez des lentilles*. Similarly, in English 'some' may apply to singular or plural nouns ('some cheese', 'some grapes'). *Des* is therefore a morphologically plural partitive used for nouns which, although morphologically plural, are not really 'count nouns'.

1.3.3　*Historical development (see also 0.5)*

(i) In Old French an article was used only when the noun was employed in a clearly specific manner. When the noun employed was not specific an article was not used. Compare:

il boit vin (nowadays *il boit du vin*)
il mange pain (nowadays *il mange du pain*)

but

il boit le vin de son père (as in Modern French)

(ii) To refer to a certain quantity of something taken from an unspecified whole, the preposition *de* was used, from the Latin *de* referring to an origin:

boire de vin (in Modern French *boire du vin*)
manger de pain (in Modern French *manger du pain*)

This still survives in negative constructions; e.g.

il ne boit pas de vin; *il ne mange pas de pain*

(iii) When referring to a certain quantity of something taken from a determined whole, it was the preposition *de* with the definite article which was formerly used: *il mange de la soupe de sa mère*; *il boit del* (= *de* + *le*) *vin de son père* (*del* later changed to *du*).

(iv) Little by little the use of *de* with the definite article became used to mean 'a certain quantity of something', whether or not that whole was determined: *il mange du pain* and *il boit du vin* no longer refer to a part taken from a specific whole. This means that nowadays the 'partitive articles' *du*, *de la* and *des* may take on two meanings. They may refer to a certain quantity of something taken from a whole, as in *je mange de la soupe que tu as faite ce matin* (= a part of); and they may also refer to an indeterminate quantity not taken from a specified whole, as in *je mange de la soupe* (= 'some soup', i.e. an indeterminate amount of soup).

1.3.4   *Partitive articles v. partitive determiners*

In the same way as *du/de la/des* may function as partitive articles, 'partitive determiners' based on determiners other than the definite article may also be used:
(i) partitive determiner based on the possessive adjective − *de mon/de ton*:

donne-moi de ton eau (= *une quantité indéterminée de ton eau*)

(ii) partitive determiner based on the demonstrative adjective − *de ce/de cette/de ces*:

donne-moi de cette eau

(iii) partitive determiner based on an indefinite adjective functioning as a determiner:

donne-moi de tous les plats
donne-moi de chaque plat

1.3.5   *Other ways of expressing the partitive: the indefinite quantifiers*

The quantifying adverbs may also function as determiners: they refer to quantities which are not exactly quantifiable (see Ch. 12, 2.1.1). The most commonly used are *peu de*, *assez de*, *pas mal de*, *beaucoup de*, *trop de*, *moins de*, *plus de*. They are all used in association with *de*. Compare *peu de gens sont venus* (adverb + *de* functioning as a determiner) with *des gens sont venus* (indefinite article) and *quelques personnes sont venus* (indefinite adjective functioning as a determiner).

For indefinite adjectives functioning as determiners, see section 4.

1.4   The absence of article or 'zero article'

1.4.1   *Historical note*

In Old French the difference between a noun used to refer to a specific referent − definite or indefinite − and a noun used in the abstract sense was dependent on the presence or absence of a determiner. The determiner, and in particular the article, turned the noun from a 'virtual' or abstract concept into one seen as realized (or *actualisé*). It was therefore quite normal for a noun to appear on its own, without being preceded by an article or any other form of determiner, e.g.

cuers ne puet mentir (= *le cœur ne peut mentir*)
courtoisie passe beaulté (= *la courtoisie a plus de valeur que la beauté*)

(examples borrowed from P. Ménard, *Manuel d'Ancien Français*, vol. 3, 17).

In modern French this is rarely the case: the article – both definite and indefinite – has, little by little, filled what was a meaningful void in Old French. There are still, however, a number of cases in which no article is used (or in which the 'zero article' is used).

1.4.2 *Cases in which no article is used (the 'zero article')*

1.4.2.1 *Cases in which 'de' is not followed by an article*

(i) when the preposition + noun functions as an adjective as in *un instrument de musique* (a musical instrument); in this case the second noun remains an abstract non specific entity. This may occur with collective nouns (*une boîte d'allumettes, un plat de lentilles*, in which *allumettes* and *lentilles* are not determined in terms of specificity), with mass nouns (*une tasse à thé*), with abstract nouns (*des produits de beauté, un instrument de travail*), and with count nouns (*le nombre de chômeurs*).
Note: One may contrast *le nombre de chômeurs* and *le nombre des chômeurs*: in the second case, *les chômeurs* is specific; *un accident de travail* (any kind of accident at work) and *un accident du travail* (an industrial injury, i.e. a specific type of accident); *un poisson de rivière* (a fresh water fish) and *un poisson de la rivière* (a fish taken from a specific river). See also (vi) below.
(ii) in most compound nouns made up of several free forms, e.g. *pomme de terre, anti-monte-lait, chien de race* (see Ch. 1, 3.3).
(iii) in negative statements before a noun complement, e.g. *tu n'as plus de voiture? je n'ai pas d'amis.*
(iv) when certain quantifying adverbs + *de* form the equivalent of a determiner (see 4.1iii), e.g. *j'ai beaucoup d'amis; j'ai assez de place.*
(v) in certain set adverbial phrases, such as *à vive allure, de manière imprévue, foncer tête baissée.*
(vi) in certain set verbal phrases, such as *accuser de vol, avoir raison, avoir peur, faire fortune, donner congé.* One may contrast some of these set expressions with similar expressions containing an article: *accuser de vol* ('to accuse of theft') and *accuser d'un vol* ('to accuse of a particular theft')

1.4.2.2 *The case of the other prepositions*

(i) En is used in most cases without an article: *en France, en hiver* (but *en l'air*).
(ii) A and *par* are used without an article in adverbial expressions: *à genoux, à tâtons, à reculons, voyager par mer, une fois par an, par monts et par vaux.*
(iii) Avec and *sans* are frequently used without the article when these refer to an abstract concept: *avec courage, avec plaisir, sans peur, sans doute.* Many of these represent fossilized expressions which have come down to us from Old French without any changes in this respect. The same applies to *après, avant, contre, hors, pour, selon, sauf, sous* and *sur*. (See Ch. 13.)

1.4.2.3 *Absence of the article from certain syntactic contexts*

(i) from *ni . . . ni . . .* constructions: *je n'ai pu acheter ni pain ni sucre.*
(ii) in so-called telegraphic style: *bateau à vendre, service compris, solde.*
(iii) in certain superlative constructions with negative implications:

jamais homme ne fut plus rusé (= *il n'y eut jamais d'homme plus rusé*)
Connaissez-vous femme plus élégante? (Mauger) (= *il n'y a pas de femme plus élégante*)

(iv) Before nouns in apposition it is usual but not essential to drop the article: *ma tante Amélie, (une) cuisinière parfaite*; *Paris, (la) capitale de la France.*

(v) In enumerations, irrespective of syntactic function and whether or not preceded by a preposition:

> *Brouettes à une roue avec des têtes de bébé qui pendaient entre deux bols, pousse-pousse, petits chevaux poilus, voitures à bras, camions chargés de soixante personnes, matelas monstrueux peuplés de tout un mobilier, hérissés de pieds de table, géants protégeant leurs bras tendus. . . .* (Malraux)

This is not an immutable rule, although it represents the norm; but in the following example a stylistic effect is created by keeping the articles:

> *Le long du mur de première ligne, sur une sorte de remblai, de corniche, de piédestal, se tenaient, de place en place, les guetteurs. Ce mur se composait de tout, comme le reste de la ville. Outre les sacs, on le sentait fait avec des armoires à glace, des commodes, des fauteuils, des dessus de piano, de l'ennui, de la tristesse, du silence.* (Cocteau)

Fait avec des could have been replaced by *fait d'armoires, de tristesse.* . . . The use of the article serves to stress the elements being determined.)

(vi) In vocatives and expletives: *Ô rage, ô désespoir* (Corneille); *Horreur! Nom d'une pipe!* (the very vulgar *Putain!* is one of the most frequently used).

1.4.2.4   *Absence of the article before names and titles*

(i) The article is absent before names referring to specific individuals, e.g. *Jean est arrivé.* But in rural areas first names are sometimes preceded either by an article, e.g. *le Jean m'a dit*, or by a possessive adjective, e.g. *mon Jean est arrivé*, the latter expressing strong affection.

(ii) Before the nouns used in some book titles, the use of the article gives the title an air of fame: *Le Guide Michelin, La Cuisine du marché* (written by the famous Paul Bocuse). Titles such as *Vol de nuit* (Saint-Exupéry) do not make such claims to fame.

(iii) In proverbs and popular sayings; e.g. *chat échaudé craint l'eau froide*, which were created at a time when the zero article was normally used in such cases.

2 The demonstrative adjectives: 'ce/cette/ces'

2.1 Definition and historical development

2.1.1 *Definition*

(i) The demonstrative adjectives are determiners which indicate both specificity and deixis (spatio-temporal reference). The demonstrative adjective is therefore more 'definite' than the definite article.

(ii) It has been noted (see 1.1.3.5-9 and specifically 6.1) that the French definite article is often used to translate the English zero article. This is because it is frequently used to express the generic rather than the specific. The definite article being no longer associated solely with the specific, it is somewhat less definite in its connotations than its English equivalent. The consequence of this is the frequent use of the demonstrative adjective – which is always specific – to translate the English definite article, particularly in legal and administrative texts (cf. 6.3).

2.1.2 *Historical note*

(i) The French demonstrative adjectives come from the Latin demonstrative

adjectives; but whereas Latin had three demonstrative adjectives, these give only one in French: *ce/cet* and its variants for gender and number, *cette* and *ces*.

The Latin demonstrative adjectives were:
hic (= 'this', indicating something associated with the speaker)
iste (= 'that', indicating something associated with the listener)
ille (= 'that', indicating something associated with neither, and by extension 'over there')

Old French had a two-tier system made up of *cist* ('this') and *cil* ('that'). What happened in fact was that *hic* disappeared, its role being taken on by *iste* (which gives *esta* in Spanish, as in *esta casa*). The role of *iste* was in turn taken over by *ille*: thus it was the third distinction of 'that over there' which was lost in this shift from one term to the other. The Old French forms *icist* or *cist* and *icil* or *cil* are based on *iste* and *ille* preceded by the adverb *ecce* ('behold').[8]

(ii) In Modern French there is also a two-tier system, but it is a 'French' creation: one may contrast *ce livre*, *ce livre-ci* and *ce livre-là*. Thus the adverbs *ici* (which becomes *-ci* in this context) and *là* came to be used in association with *ce* to express nearness or distance: *ce livre*, *ce livre-ci* (expresses nearness to the speaker) and *ce livre-là* (expresses distance from the speaker).

2.2 Morphology

The forms of the demonstrative adjectives are as follows:
(i)

Simple forms			Compound forms	
	Sing.	Plur.	Sing.	Plur.
Masc.	*ce* *cet*	*ces*	*ce. . .ci* *cet. . .ci* *ce. . .là* *cet. . .là*	*ces. . .ci*
Fem.	*cette*	*ces*	*cette. . .ci* *cette. . .là*	*ces. . .ci* *ces. . .là*

(ii) Masculine forms ending in *-t* are used before nouns beginning with a vowel or a mute *h-*: *ce livre*, but *cet homme*, *cet angle*. (See 1.1.2 for note on mute *h*.)
(iii) The second part of the compound forms follows the noun determined and is joined to the latter by a hyphen: *cet homme-ci*, *cet homme-là*.

2.3 Uses of the simple forms

(i) To introduce a noun relating to a referent (or referents) the existence of which is made specific by some kind of gesture: *cet homme vous le dira*; *donnez-moi ce journal*; *cette robe vous plaît?*
(ii) To introduce a noun which will be made specific − temporally or spatially − by a following relative clause or a participial clause:

Un lion parbleu!
Non! un âne, un de ces tout petits ânes qui sont si communs en Algérie. (Daudet)

(iii) To refer back to a noun which has already been used, determined simply by an indefinite article. This is very common at the beginning of stories: one starts with an indefinite article in the first sentence, and this becomes *ce/cette/ces* in the second:

Il y avait une fois une petit fille qui vivait dans les bois. Cette petite fille. . . .

(The same applies to English, of course.)

(iv) The simple forms of the demonstrative adjective may indicate disdain or disgust: *ces gens qui vous embêtent avec leurs histoires* (informal speech, *négligé*).

2.3.2   *Use of the complex forms*

(i) The difference between the simple French demonstrative adjective and the simple English ones is that the English ones indicate spatial and temporal reference in terms of 'closeness' and 'distance' ('this/that'). French does not make closeness or distance explicit since it has only one demonstrative adjective. This means that in terms of translation *ce* has to be translated either by 'this' or by 'that', depending on the context.

(ii) If one wants to make the distinction of closeness and distance explicit, one uses the compound forms *ce . . . ci/ce . . . là*, *ci* standing for *ici* and *là* for *là-bas*, e.g. *passez-moi ce livre-là* (*ce . . . là* = 'that'); *prenez ce livre-ci* (*ce . . . ci* = 'this').

These forms may be used equally well for spatial or temporal reference:

> *ce mois-là, il n'avait pas eu de quoi payer son loyer, cette année-ci, nous allons passer nos vacances en Bretagne*

(iii) In the spoken language the compound demonstrative adjectives may be used to express a choice: *préférez-vous ce gâteau-ci ou cette brioche-là?* (or simply *préférez-vous ce gâteau-ci ou cette brioche?*, in which case the second demonstrative is the simple demonstrative).

(iv) The demonstrative ending in *-là* is sometimes used in spoken French to express disdain: *moi, je n'aime pas ces histoires-là!*

3   Possessive adjectives

3.1   General characteristics

(i) Possessive adjectives are so called because they ascribe ownership or relationship to a person or thing in terms of the three grammatical personal pronouns.

(ii) They behave as true adjectives in that they always qualify a noun; but matters are complicated by the presence of both what is possessed and one or more possessors (see 3.3*ii*).

3.2   Morphology

3.2.1   *Different forms of the possessive adjective*

There are two forms, one unstressed, the other stressed; but only the unstressed form is in common use in Modern French. The stressed version belongs to earlier stages of the language, and is normally only used today for archaic effect in literature or for special emphasis by rather pedantic speakers.

3.2.2 *Unstressed forms*

The singular is used where the *thing possessed* is singular:

Possessors	Thing possessed	
	Masc. sing. (and fem. sing. with initial vowel	Fem. sing. (except with initial vowel)
1st pers. sing.	*mon (livre)*	*ma (table)*
2nd pers. sing.	*ton (auto − fem.)*	*ta*
3rd pers. sing.	*son*	*sa*
		Masc. and fem. sing.
1st pers. plur.		*notre (lit/table)*
2nd pers. plur.		*votre*
3rd pers. plur.		*leur*

The plural is used where the *things possessed* are plural:

Possessors	Things possessed
	Masc. and fem. plur.
1st pers. sing.	*mes (lits/tables)*
2nd pers. sing.	*tes*
3rd pers. sing.	*ses*
1st pers. plur.	*nos*
2nd pers. plur.	*vos*
3rd pers. plur.	*leurs*

Note: There is denasalization when *mon, ton* or *son* are followed either by a noun starting with a mute *h* or by a noun starting with a vowel, e.g.

       mon livre is pronounced /mɔ̃ livrə

but   mon habit is pronounced /mɔ nabi/

       mon auto is pronounced /mɔ noto/

(See 1.1.2 for note on mute *h*)

3.2.3   *Stressed forms (now rather archaic in adjectival form[9])*

Singular (thing possessed):

Possessor(s)	Thing possessed	
	Masc. sing.	Fem. sing.
1st pers. sing.	*mien*	*mienne*
2nd pers. sing.	*tien*	*tienne*
3rd pers. sing.	*sien*	*sienne*
	Masc. and fem. sing.	
1st pers. plur.	*nôtre*	
2nd pers. plur.	*vôtre* (e.g. *cette maison est vôtre*)	
3rd pers. plur.	*leur*	

Plural (things possessed):

Possessor(s)	Things possessed	
	Masc. plur.	Fem. plur.
1st pers. sing.	*miens*	*miennes*
2nd pers. sing.	*tiens*	*tiennes*
3rd pers. sing.	*siens*	*siennes*
	Masc. and fem. plur.	
1st pers. plur.	*nôtres* (e.g. *ces fermes ont été nôtres depuis des siècles*)	
2nd pers. plur.	*vôtres*	
3rd pers. plur.	*leurs*	

3.3   Agreement

(i) Agreement is with the noun determined and not, as in English, with the possessor:

elle a perdu son livre (= 'she has lost her book')
elle a perdu sa clé (= 'she has lost her key')

(ii) If the possessor is singular, the possessive adjective will agree for both gender and number with the noun determined: *mon fauteuil, ma chaise, mes papiers*. Before a feminine noun beginning with a vowel the masculine forms *mon/ton/son* are used, e.g. *mon amie*. (There is however a difference in pronunciation: see 3.2.2 *Note*.) If the possessor is plural, no distinction of gender is made: *mes fauteuils, mes chaises*.
(iii) Where the possessor is plural, agreement is only for number: *notre maison/notre jardin*; *nos maisons/nos jardins*.

3.4   Uses of the possessive adjective

(i) Generally the possessive adjective in French, as in English, is used to underline

actual possession of something, e.g. *c'est mon livre*; *voilà ton chien*; but it may also indicate non-physical attributes 'belonging' to someone or something, e.g. *cela a duré pendant toute ma jeunesse*; *son attitude envers moi n'est pas toujours bonne.*

(ii) With parts of the body, where English uses the possessive adjective French often uses the definite article (see 1.1.3.10).

(iii) Stylistically, considerable emotive use is made of the possessive adjective in French. It is often used to indicate scorn, as in the following from Molière's *Tartuffe*:

> *Mais quoi! si votre père est un bourru fieffé*
> *Qui s'est de son Tartuffe entièrement coiffé, . . .*

Such a use of the possessive adjective is common in the spoken language: *tu m'ennuies avec tes histoires.*

(*Note*: The stressed form was used in the past for stylistic effect, but its use is now archaic (e.g. *un mien ami*, *un sien ami*):

> *Le patron jura qu'un vieux sien matelot était cuisinier remarquable.* (Mérimée, quoted by Wagner and Pinchon, *Grammaire du français classique et moderne*)

(iv) Where the possessor to whom the possessive adjective refers is not actually mentioned, or is otherwise indeterminate, the possessive adjective is used in the third person singular:

> *on ne peut pas toujours manger à sa faim*
> *chacun doit suivre son propre destin*
> *il faut être sur ses gardes*

(*Note*: This use of the third person pronoun corresponds, in English, to the use of 'one's'.)

4 Indefinite adjectives functioning as determiners

4.1 General remarks

(i) The indefinite adjectives constitute an ill-defined category which has close similarities of form and meaning with the indefinite pronouns (see Ch. 3, 4). They may also be thought of as a loosely delineated subclass of the numeral adjectives, since many of them refer to number.

(ii) It is important to note that, from a semantic point of view, there may be differences of meaning between indefinite adjectives used as adjectives and indefinite adjectives used as determiners. For example, in *certaines personnes pensent que . . .* , *certaines* corresponds to 'some', whereas in *il est certain qu'il viendra*, *certain* − which functions as an adjective − means 'certain'. Only their meaning when functioning as determiners is examined in this section.

(iii) When used as determiners, they may differ according to whether they are used in the plural or in the singular; thus *quelques* used in the plural functions as a quantifier meaning 'a few' (see 4.3.2*i*), whereas *quelque* used in the singular functions as an identifier meaning 'a' in the sense of 'any' (see section 4.4.1*i*).

(iv) Finally, some indefinite adjectives such as *tout* and *quelque* may also function as adverbs, in which case their meaning will again be different. One may thus contrast *tout homme qui pense que . . .* ('any man who thinks that . . .') with *il est tout petit* ('he is very small').

The use of the indefinite adjectives therefore presents a number of semantic problems for anglophones.

4.2   Morphology

4.2.1   *Absence of morphological unity*

There is no morphological unity among the indefinite adjectives. They consist of a number of terms of different historical origins, related only by syntactic and semantic functions. They are probably best considered as forming a quantitative (but non-numerical) scale from nothing (*nul, aucun*) to totality (*tous, toutes*), but with a secondary group which refers to 'identity' or 'lack of identity' ('identity' in the sense of being a specified person or thing). For indefinite adjectives referring to quantities, see section 4.3; for those referring to identity see section 4.4.

4.2.2.   *The main indefinite adjectives functioning as determiners*

(i) Quantifiers:

nul, aucun (refer to a zero quantity)
quelques, plusieurs, certains, maints, divers, différents (refer to plurality)
chaque, tous, toutes (refer to totality in the sense of 'each' and 'every')

(ii) Identifiers:

quelque, chaque, tel, tout (refer to the vagueness of identity of the referent)
certain(s), autre(s), même(s) (give a definite indication of identity but without actually naming names)

It will be noted that whereas *quelque* and *certain* appear in the singular when functioning as indicators of identity, they appear in the plural when functioning as quantifiers; their meanings in each case are different.

4.2.3   *Agreement of indefinite adjectives*

(i) Indefinite adjectives agree in gender with the noun which they determine, e.g. *certain/certaine, aucun/aucune* (unless they themselves already end in *-e* in the singular). *Plusieurs*, however, remains invariable.
(ii) Those adjectives which are capable of indicating plurality also agree in number with the noun, e.g. *certains livres/certaines œuvres*.

4.3   The main indefinite adjectives functioning as 'quantifiers'

4.3.1   *The negative quantifiers 'nul(le)' and 'aucun(e)'*

(i) *Nul(le)* and *aucun(e)* normally require the negative particle *ne* before the verb:

nulle femme ne l'aime ('no woman loves him')
aucun train n'est encore arrivé ('no train has yet arrived')

(ii) If *aucun* is not used with a negative particle, it takes on the positive sense[10] of 'any':

croyez-vous qu'aucun auditeur aurait osé le contredire? (Collins-Robert Dictionary)

(iii) When used with *sans*, *aucun* may follow the noun it refers to, although in spoken French this tends to create a rather pretentious effect, e.g. *sans exception aucune* instead of the normal *sans aucune exception*.
(iv) *Aucun(e)* and *nul(le)* are normally used only in the singular, although in literary texts they may occasionally be found in the plural in fairly recent writing. In the seven-

teenth century the plural of *aucun* was still in use, in literature at least. Today it is found only when it refers to a noun which has only a plural form, or which has a different meaning in the singular, e.g. *aucunes funérailles, aucuns pourparlers, aucuns frais.*

4.3.2 *The quantifiers expressing plurality: 'quelques', 'certains', 'plusieurs', 'maints', 'divers', 'différents'*

(i) Quelques refers to a small but indefinite number of items; it very often corresponds to 'a few', e.g. *je suis sorti avec quelques amis.*

(ii) Plusieurs also refers to a small number of items, generally more than two; but whereas *quelques* does not stress the idea of plurality, *plusieurs* does; *plusieurs* therefore often corresponds to 'several' as against 'one', e.g. *je suis sorti avec plusieurs amis* (*et non pas avec un seul*).

(iii) Certains in its plural form refers to a certain number of items taken from within a larger group:

> *j'ai certains amis qui pensent que la peine de mort est nécessaire*

Certains, referring to a subsection within a group, tends to imply opposition to the other members of the group; thus the sentence above implies that my other friends — and maybe most of my friends — believe the opposite. *Certains* thus implies the idea *mais d'autres ne sont pas du même avis.* Because of this implication, *certains* may easily be used to convey pejorative overtones. Whereas *quelques* refers to an indefinite number, and *plusieurs* stresses plurality, *certains* is more definite in that it refers to a subsection within a group. (Note, however, that anglophones tend to use *certains* instead of the neutral *quelques.*)

(iv) Maint(s), meaning 'many', is used both in the singular and in the plural, e.g. *à mainte reprise* and *à maintes reprises.* There is no agreement amongst grammarians as to which is the preferable form. *Maint(s)* is, in any case, confined to literary language, except in the set expression above.

(v) Divers and <u>*différent(s)*</u> both refer to a number of items, usually a small number; but whereas *divers* emphasizes the idea of variety (it corresponds usually to 'various'), *différent(s)* emphasizes the dissimilarity of the items (it usually corresponds to 'different'); often they may be interchanged, but this entails a shift in emphasis as described above:

> *nous avons acheté différents journaux mais tous publiaient la même photo*
> *nous avons acheté divers journaux . . .* (more emphatic)

4.3.3 *Quantifiers referring to totality:* 'chaque', 'tous/toutes' *and* 'tout' *before proper names*

(i) Chaque is always singular and has the meaning of 'each': *remettez chaque chose à sa place.*

(ii) Tous and *toutes* may function as determiners, but such a use is rare and archaic: *la voiture roulait, tous feux éteints.*

But such constructions are common in set expressions such as *tout compte fait, toutes proportions gardées, toutes sortes de* (as in *je lui ai raconté toutes sortes de sornettes*).

(iii) Tous and *toutes* are however frequently used as 'predeterminers', i.e. as a determiner of a 'determiner + noun' group:

> *nous y allons tous les soirs* (*tous les* = 'every')

and this is their normal use in modern French.

(iv) Tout may be used in the singular with the same meaning as *tous* and *toutes* when it functions as a determiner to a proper noun indicating some kind of collectivity such as the inhabitants of a town, or the works of an artist:

> *j'aime tout Mozart*
> *tout Paris a suivi le cortège de J.-P. Sartre*

(The expression *le Tout-Paris* does not come under this heading, since *Tout-Paris* may be considered to be a compound noun.)

(v) One must not confuse *tout* used in this sense with *tout* used as an identifier (see 4.4.1*(iv)*), nor with the adverb *tout* meaning 'very', as in *il est tout petit* (i.e. *très petit*) or *tout mécontent qu'il soit* (i.e. *aussi mécontent qu'il soit*).

4.4.   The main indefinite adjectives functioning as 'identifiers'

4.4.1   *Identifiers stressing the vagueness of identity of the referents: 'quelque', 'chaque', 'tel(le)', 'tout(e)'*

(i) Quelque is used in the singular to refer to somebody or something of unknown identity, e.g. *quelque homme avait déjà habité cette île. Quelque* in the singular resembles *quelques* in the plural in that they both express the idea of the indefinite; but in the singular it is simply the identity which is indefinite, whereas in the plural it is both identity and the exact number which are indefinite.

Quelque is not to be confused with *quelque* the adverb which means 'however much', as in *quelque mécontent qu'il soit* ('however displeased he may be'). It may also mean 'around', as in *quelque vingt personnes* ('around twenty people').

It is also important not to confuse *quelque* with *quel(le) que*, written as two words and meaning 'whichever', as in *quelle que soit la route que vous preniez, cela reviendra au même.*

(ii) Chaque refers to the idea of totality (see 4.3.3*i*), but it also stresses the vagueness of identity of each referent, and corresponds both to 'each' and to 'every': *remets chaque chose à sa place.*

(iii) Tel(le) may be used to refer to an item at first picked at random but later specified, usually by a relative clause, e.g. *tel enfant qui se croit menacé devient agressif* (example from Collins-Robert Dictionary). *Tel* could in such cases be replaced by *tout*, e.g. *tout enfant qui se croit menacé devient agressif.*

Tel is more literary and more archaic than *tout*, and corresponds roughly to the English eighteenth-century construction 'such children as . . .'. It is also used to emphasize the lack of importance of precise identity when used in the construction *tel ou tel*, e.g. *que m'importe que tel ou tel candidat soit élu* (example from *Micro-Robert Dictionnaire du français primordial*).

(iv) Tout(e) is the most commonly used indefinite adjective functioning as a determiner to refer to any item picked at random (it corresponds semantically to *n'importe quel*, i.e. to both 'any' and 'all'):

> *Tout homme né dans l'esclavage naît pour l'esclavage* (Rousseau)

4.4.2   *Identifiers indicating a more definite identity: 'certain', 'autre(s)', 'même(s)'*

(i) Certain used in the singular may fulfil this role, but such a construction is now slightly archaic, as in:

> *Certain renard gascon, d'autres disent normand. . . .* (La Fontaine)

although one may still sometimes hear sentences such as:

> *l'autre jour j'ai rencontré certain collègue que je croyais*
> *pourtant bien loin!*

This use of *certain* implies suspicion.

In modern French however *certain* tends to function more often as an adjective than as a determiner: *un certain renard gascon.* . . .

(ii) Autre(s) only functions as a determiner in set expressions which are no more than a vestige of what was fairly common usage in earlier periods of the language. It is used in the plural in the expression *autres temps, autres mœurs* and in the singular in the commonly used expressions *autre chose* (e.g. *passons maintenant à autre chose*) and *autre part* (*allons autre part*).

(iii) Même(s) indicates either complete identity or similarity of kind, according to the context:

> *j'ai le même stylo que toi* (similarity)
> *j'ai le même stylo depuis deux ans* (identity)

5 The numerals (cardinal and ordinal)

5.1 General considerations

Both cardinal and ordinal numerals are listed here, although they do not necessarily function as determiners: ordinal numerals (*premier, deuxième, troisième*) are always adjectives but they are obtained − with the exception of *premier* and *second* − from the corresponding cardinal numerals which function either as indefinite articles (see 1.2.4) or as further determiners of the noun.

Given the morphological links between these two types of numerals, it is more convenient to deal with both under the same heading, rather than keep cardinal numerals under determiners and ordinal numbers under adjectives.

5.2 Morphology

5.2.1 *Defining cardinal and ordinal numerals*

(i) Cardinal numerals are the written and spoken forms which correspond to the arithmetical series of numbers having a unit progression from 0 to infinity (see table in 5.4).

(ii) Ordinal numerals correspond in a similar way to numbers denoting rank order in a series (1st, 2nd, 3rd etc.). The same terms may also correspond to fractions (a third, a fourth, a fifth etc.). There are however exceptions, such as 'a half', *un demi or une moitié* 'a third' which is not **un troisième* but *un tiers*; similarly 'a fourth' is not **un quatrième* but *un quart.*

5.2.2 *Number and gender of the cardinal and ordinal numerals*

(i) They are not marked for gender, except for *un/une, premier/première* and *second/seconde.*

(ii) Ordinal numerals are marked for number, e.g. *les premières gelées sont arrivées.* Ordinals in fractions are also marked for number, e.g. *les trois huitièmes du gâteau.*

(iii) Cardinal numerals are not marked for number except for multiples of *vingt* and *cent: quatre-vingts* but *quatre-vingt-un;*[11] *deux cents* but *deux cent un.* (*Note: mille* is always invariable − but see Appendix, section IV for the new 'lenient' attitudes now to be adopted in cases of 'mistakes' in this area.)

5.2.3 *Formation of the cardinal and ordinal numerals*

5.2.3.1 *The cardinal numerals*
(i) The simple forms run from 0 to 16, then for each multiple of 10 up to 60, then 100, 1,000, 1,000,000 etc. The compound forms include all other numbers (see table in 5.4).
(ii) Certain numerals have alternative forms.

According to prescriptive grammar, *mille*[12] is used for numbers, whereas *mil* is used in preference to *mille* for dates: 1789 is written *mil sept cent quatre-vingt-neuf* (but see Appendix on '*Les tolérances grammaticales*' for tolerance of *mille* in all cases nowadays). There are in fact two ways of expressing dates: 1789 can be written either as *mil* (or *mille*) *sept cent quatre-vingt-neuf*, or as *dix-sept cent quatre vingt neuf* (this latter way of writing dates is not used for dates BC).

In Belgium, Canada and Switzerland, as well as in parts of eastern and northern France, 70 is *septante* (instead of *soixante-dix*), 80 is *octante* (instead of *quatre-vingts*) and 90 is *nonante* (instead of *quatre-vingt-dix*). *Huitante* for *quatre-vingts* also exists.
(iv) A perplexing problem for anglophones and francophones alike is the non-correspondence between the two languages of the ways of indicating decimals and multiples through the use of commas and full stops. In English one writes '2.3' (two point three') and '1,300' ('thirteen hundred'). In French, however, the decimal point becomes a comma, and the comma for multiples becomes a point: '2.3' becomes 2,3 (pronounced *deux virgule trois*), and '1,300' becomes 1.300. Thus 1.000.000 in French would be written 1,000,000 in English.

5.2.3.2 *The ordinal numerals* Except for *premier* and *second*, the ordinals are formed by the addition of the suffix *-ième* to the cardinal form: *deux/deuxième*, *trois/troisième*. Where the cardinal ends in -x (*deux*, *six*, *dix*) this is pronounced 'z' in the corresponding ordinal numeral (*deuxième*, *sixième*, *dixième*). (*Note*: *neuf* becomes *neuvième* (i.e. the 'f' becomes voiced.)

5.3 Syntactic considerations

(i) The cardinal numbers may function either as indefinite articles or as further determiners of the 'definite article + noun' group (see 1.2.4 and 1.1.4.2).
(ii) The ordinal numerals always function as adjectives modifying the noun: *c'est la deuxième buse que j'aie vue ce matin*.
(iii) The cardinal numerals may also function as other parts of speech. They may function as nouns, e.g. *trois fois six font dix-huit*; in this case they function as if they were proper nouns, and are not preceded by an article. But they may also function as common nouns, e.g. *le trois est mal fait*, in which case they are preceded by a masculine article.

The ordinal numerals may, like other adjectives, be nominalized: *donnez-moi le troisième*.
(iv) If the cardinal numeral functions as an indefinite article, it occupies the first position in the phrase: *dix petits canards*. If it determines the 'definite article + noun' group it immediately follows the definite article: *les dix canards*, *les dix petits canards*.

Ordinal numbers also immediately follow the article, whatever else follows: *un premier canard arriva*, *un premier petit canard arriva*.

5.4 Summary table and notes

No.	Cardinal numeral Masc.	Fem.	Ordinal numeral Sing.	Plur.
1	*un*	*une*	*premier/* *première*	*premiers/* *premières*
2	*deux*		*deuxième* *second/* *seconde*	*deuxièmes* *seconds/secondes[1]*
3	*trois*		*troisième[2]*	*troisièmes*
4	*quatre*		*quatrième[2]*	*quatrièmes*
5	*cinq*		*cinquième*	*cinquièmes* (etc.)
6	*six*		*sixième*	
7	*sept*		*septième*	
8	*huit*		*huitième*	
9	*neuf*		*neuvième*	
10	*dix*		*dixième*	
11	*onze[3]*		*onzième*	
12	*douze*		*douzième*	
13	*treize*		*treizième*	
14	*quatorze*		*quatorzième*	
15	*quinze*		*quinzième*	
16	*seize*		*seizième*	
17	*dix-sept*		*dix-septième*	
18	*dix-huit*		*dix-huitième*	
19	*dix-neuf*		*dix-neuvième*	
20	*vingt*		*vingtième*	
21	*vingt et un*		*vingt et unième*	
22	*vingt-deux*		*vingt-deuxième*	
30	*trente*		*trentième*	
31	*trente et un*		*trente et unième*	
60	*soixante*		*soixantième*	
70	*soixante-dix/* *septante[4]*		*soixante dixième/* *septantième*	
71	*soixante et onze*		*soixante et onzième*	
72	*soixante douze*		*soixante douzième*	
80	*quatre-vingts/* *octante[4]*		*quatre-vingtième/* *octantième*	
81	*quatre-vingt-un[5]*		*quatre-vingt-unième*	
90	*quatre-vingt* *dix/nonante[4]*		*quatre-vingt-dixième/* *nonantième*	
100	*cent*		*centième*	
101	*cent un*		*cent unième*	
200	*deux cents[6]*		*deux centième*	
201	*deux cent un*		*deux cent unième*	
1.000[7]	*mille[8]* (but *mil* for dates)		*millième*	
2.000	*deux mille*		*deux millième*	
1.000.000	(see section 5.5)		*millionième*	

Notes:
1 The form *second* is normally used when the count does not go beyond 2.
2 In forming ordinals from cardinals ending in *-e*, the final *-e* always drops.
3 When *onze* is used with an article, as in dates, in Modern French there is no elision of the *-e* of the article: *le onze*.

4 *Septante, octante* and *nonante* are alternatives to *soixante-dix, quatre-vingts* and *quatre-vingt-dix* used in various francophone countries other than France and in some regions of France.
5 One writes *quatre-vingts* but *quatre-vingt-un*.
6 One writes *deux cents* but *deux cent un*.
7 In French 'a thousand' is written in numerals with a 'multiple point' (and not a 'multiple comma', as in English).
8 *Mille* is always invariable.

5.5   The case of numbers above 'mille'

Compare the following:

'a hundred workers' = *cent travailleurs*
'two hundred workers' = *deux cents travailleurs*

but /

'two million workers' = *deux millions de travailleurs* (also *deux milliards de francs,* etc.)

This is because *million* and *milliard* are nouns. The nouns corresponding to *cent* and *mille* are *centaine* and *millier*, e.g. *une centaine de travailleurs, un millier de travailleurs.*
Whereas French presents no problems for these very large numbers, British and American English differ in the names given to them:

No.	French	British English	American English
1 000 000	*un million*	a million	a million
1 000 000 000	*un milliard* (synonym: *un billion*)	a thousand millions (synonym: a milliard)	a billion
1 000 000 000 000	*un trillion* (also *mille billions* and *un million de millions*)	a billion	a trillion

The French system resembles the American rather than the British system.

6   Translation problems

6.1   Translation problems involving the use of the definite article in French but not in English

6.1.1   *Reasons for the differences*

It was pointed out in 1.1.3.6 that French uses the definite article far more often than English does; indeed, French uses the article with certain proper nouns where English does not. French also uses the definite article for the expression of time, date and season, in cases in which English does not: *je viens la semaine prochaine* (see 1.1.3.7).
French and English differ yet again in the expression of quantities (see 1.1.3.9), and

the use of determiners with words for the parts of the body is always a problem for anglophones (see 1.1.3.10).

This is not surprising when one realizes that the articles fulfil quite different roles in French and in English. In French the article expresses number and gender, whereas in English the article expresses neither gender nor number; but both English and French articles may express the specific, definite and indefinite, and the generic. This is therefore their area of overlap.

They overlap in the following manner († indicates that the two languages diverge in their use of articles):

Specific			Specific	
Definite			Indefinite	
Count nouns	Mass nouns		Count nouns	Mass nouns
'the tiger' = *le tigre/ la tigresse* 'the tigers' = *les tigres*	'the ink' = *l'encre*		'a tiger' = *un tigre/ une tigresse* Ø '(some)' tigers' = † *des tigres*	'ink' = † *de l'encre* (the 'partitive article')

Generic	
Count nouns	Mass nouns/Abstract nouns
'the tiger' = *le tigre* 'a tiger' = † *le tigre/ un tigre* = very rare Ø 'tigers' = † *les tigres*	'ink' = † *l'encre* 'English' = † *l'anglais*

(These tables are adapted from Quirk *et al.*, *A university grammar of English*.)
It can be seen from these tables that:
(i) Articles are used in much the same way where the definite article is concerned.
(ii) Indefiniteness may be expressed by an absence of article in English (or by the zero article), but this is no longer possible in French. This means that, whereas Ø is the English plural of 'a', in French *des* is the plural of *un*; and the zero article used with mass nouns is translated in French by the partitive article.
(iii) All the English articles (including the zero article) may be used to express the generic, but this is not the case in French. Only the definite article is really productive in French, hence the numerous cases in which an indefinite article or a zero article in English will correspond to a definite article in French.

6.1.2 *Examples of the differences*

(i) with the English indefinite articles:

the zero article (Ø) is used for plural count nouns: 'there are Ø brambles at the bottom of my garden' = *il y a des ronces au fond de mon jardin*
with mass nouns: 'I want Ø water' = *je veux de l'eau*

(ii) with the English generic articles:

with the generic indefinite article: 'a dog is an affectionate animal' = *le chien est un animal affectueux* (the second 'a' is translated as *un* because it is used as an indefinite article and not as a generic one).
(There are cases in which French uses its indefinite article generically, although this is quite rare: *Un Anglais, comme homme libre, va au Ciel par le chemin qui lui plaît* (Voltaire).)
with the generic plural Ø article: 'English people go abroad mainly for the sun' = *les Anglais vont à l'étranger surtout pour le soleil*
with the generic Ø article used for mass nouns: 'Ø rain is good for Ø grass' = *la pluie est bonne pour l'herbe*
with the Ø article used before abstract nouns: 'I am studying Ø English literature, Ø mathematics and Ø French' = *j'étudie la littérature anglaise, les mathématiques et le français*
See also examples in 6.3.

6.2   Translation problems involving the use of cardinal numerals

These are relatively simple:

6.2.1   *Confusion arising from differing uses of ordinals and cardinals*

In the titles of monarchs French and English follow similar written conventions: *Georges V, Louis XIII, Edouard VII*; but these correspond to different spoken conventions: 'George the fifth' = *Georges cinq*; 'Louis the thirteenth' = *Louis treize*; 'Edward the seventh' = *Edouard sept*. (Note, however, that there is a growing tendency in American English to say 'Louis fourteen' or 'Charles ten' where *French* kings are concerned.)

6.2.2   *Use of cardinal numerals in French to indicate uncertain quantities*

(i) Various cardinal numerals may be used in this way, particularly with *fois: merci mille fois* means 'many thanks' or 'thanks a lot' (rather than 'a thousand thanks').
(ii) Similarly, *vingt fois* and *cent fois* are rarely to be taken literally but simply mean 'very frequently' or some equivalent: *je te l'ai répété cent fois* = 'I have told you so over and over again'.
(iii) Dix and *une dizaine* may often be used in French where English, being the language of a nation which has only recently adopted the decimal system, tends to talk of 'a dozen' or 'dozens'.

6.3   Translation of the English definite article by the French demonstrative adjective

There is a 'cline' in the amount of 'determination' expressed in English by the zero article, the indefinite article, the definite article and of the demonstrative adjective which is not exactly matched in French, the latter not having a zero article any more. As a result *le* tends to be less definite in French than in English; the consequence is a tendency to use the demonstrative adjective where in English one may use a definite article (see in extract below 'the breakthrough' translated as *cette percée*).
Text illustrating the different use made of articles and demonstrative adjectives in English and French (taken from ILO information vol 17, no. 2):

Of robots and jobs

'Mechatronics' – *the* combination of mechanical and electronic sciences – has at last realised man's dream of creating machines to replace him at work. But *the* breakthrough – made possible by the microchip computer – has coincided with recession and in some countries almost unprecedented levels of unemployment. Vistas of *a* new industrial civilisation have opened but at the same time fears of redundancy have been kindled. While many countries hesitate and some find themselves forced to invest in old technology, Japan has embarked on a policy of almost explosive growth in such high technology. Kyril Tidmarsh, Chief of the ILO Bureau of Public Information, talked with Japanese government, employer and worker partners in this venture. His report follows on page 3.

Robot, mon ami

La «mécatronique» – combinaison de *la* mécanique et de *l'*électronique – a enfin réalisé *le* rêve de *l'*homme: créer des machines capables de travailler à sa place. Mais *cette percée* – rendue possible par le micro-ordinateur – a coïncidé avec *la* récession et, dans certains pays, avec des taux de chômage sans précédent ou presque.

*L'*ouverture *de nouvelles perspectives* de civilisation industrielle a suscité la crainte de voir apparaître un excédent de main-d'œuvre. Si de nombreux pays hésitent à investir dans *l'*ancienne technologie et si certains autres s'y trouvent contraints, *le* Japon s'est lancé dans une politique de croissance quasiment explosive dans cette technologie de pointe. Kyril Tidmarsh, chef du Bureau de l'information publique du BIT, s'est entretenu de ces questions avec *les* représentants du gouvernement, *des* employeurs et *des* travailleurs japonais. Il livre en page 3 l'essentiel de *ces* entretiens.

Notes

1 The term 'adjective' is a misnomer in both cases; it would be more accurate to use the terms 'demonstrative determiners' and 'possessive determiners'.
2 Numerals and indefinite adjectives are excluded from this table, since they are not basic to the system.
3 This table is adapted from Baylon and Fabre's *Grammaire systématique de la langue française*.
4 *Des*, as such was not used then, but its equivalent, the plural form of *un*, was, since the latter inflected for case, gender and number.
5 Old French is similar to English in this respect; see section 0.5
6 Some people do say *vers les midi* and *vers les minuit*, even though such expressions are hardly logical.
7 *Rouches* is a dialectal form meaning 'rushes'.
8 In relation to this section see G. Price, *The French language: present and past*, 120 – 7.
9 The corresponding pronouns *le mien, le tien* etc. are however still in constant use (see Ch. 3, 3).
10 Historically *aucun* was normally positive, having the same meaning as the modern *un*, and was used in the plural to indicate 'some' or 'several'.
11 According to prescriptive grammar, there should be a hyphen only between the words referring to units and tens, hence the hyphen in *dix-huit*; but this is considered unnecessary elsewhere, except in *quatre-vingts, quatre-vingt-un* etc. Thus one writes *deux cents* and *deux cent un* without hyphens.
12 This rule, although taught in English schools, is felt to be quite archaic in France, where *mille* is nearly universally written in dates in the same way as for numbers.

Chapter 3

The basic pronouns

0 General remarks

0.1 Definition: pro-nouns or pro-forms?

In traditional grammar pronouns have been defined somewhat loosely as words which 'stand for nouns'. The modern term 'pro-form' could be thought to be more accurate since pronouns may stand for either nouns (1), adjectives (2), adverbials (3), or even clauses (4):

(1) *Pierre est venu me voir; il m'a dit que . . .(il = Pierre)*
(2) *Pierre est triste; je le suis aussi (le = triste)*
(3) *Pierre va a Paris; moi, j'en reviens* (en = *de Paris*)
(4) *Tu savais qu'il fallait y aller dimanche? oui, je le savais (le = qu'il fallait y aller dimanche)*

It is true, however, that pronouns reflect the categories of nouns in the sense that they tend to inflect for number and gender. In French, in some instances, they inflect for case, which French nouns no longer do; and there are some pronouns which represent a gender which does not exist in French, the neuter. But these are all nonetheless categories typical of nouns, and they explain the general use of the term 'pronoun'. The term is retained, because even when these items do not stand for nouns they *function* as nouns.

0.2 Problems

English and French have similar categories of pronouns, in that both languages have personal pronouns, demonstrative pronouns, possessive pronouns, relative and interrogative pronouns, and a set of words loosely described as indefinite pronouns. But they sometimes reflect differently the categories of gender and case: thus, whereas in French the possessive pronoun agrees for gender with the noun it stands for (*mon livre = le mien*; *ma table = la mienne*), in English it agrees only with the possessor ('my book' = 'mine'), since English does not have gender as a category of the noun. Other problems belong rather more to sociolinguistics than to grammar, for example, when should one use *tu* and when *vous*, since English does not make this distinction. Finally, the pronouns happen to be an area of considerable syntactic uncertainty in both languages. In English, for example, should one say 'it is I' or 'it is me' in answer to 'who is it?'? When should one use which of the following relative constructions: 'the girl whom I saw'/'the girl who I saw'/'the girl that I saw'/'the girl I saw'?

0.3 The role of pronouns

Pronouns may be used either for abbreviating a construction or for avoiding repetition. Pronouns are particularly important when used across sentences to ensure cohesion: the use of a pronoun in one clause or sentence will normally link it with an item which has appeared in a previous clause or sentence. This is called *anaphora*. In some cases the pronoun may precede what it refers to; in this case one is dealing with *cataphora*. In the spoken language the pronoun may refer to an object or person present in the situational context but not otherwise referred to: this is *exophora*.

anaphora:	J'ai demandé à Jean de venir. Malheureusement *il* n'est pas libre ce soir.
cataphora:	*Il* ne pourra pas venir ce soir, Jean.
exophora:	Laisse tout *ça* tranquille

Pronouns do not always function as cohesive devices, however: the 1st and 2nd person personal pronouns refer to the speaker(s) and the addressee(s) and not to an element in a previous or future stretch of language. As such they are not cohesive.

0.4 The different kinds of pronouns

There are three different kinds of pronouns:

Group A includes personal pronouns, demonstrative pronouns and possessive pronouns. These are the basic pronouns, in the sense that they simply act as substitutes for a variety of elements; these elements are usually nouns, but where this is not the case they become nominalized the moment a pronoun takes their place, since a pronoun must fulfil a nominal function. Group A includes:

(i) personal pronouns, involving the substitution of a nominal phrase by a pronoun which stands for it: *Jean est fatigué: il a trop travaillé (il = Jean)*; (see section 1).

(ii) demonstrative pronouns, usually involving a rather different type of relation: not one of simple substitution, but of pointing out a particular item within a group: *ces dessins sont beaux*; *j'aimerais bien celui-ci*; (see section 2).

(iii) possessive pronouns, similar to personal pronouns except that they have two co-referents (or antecedents): the object or person referred to and its possessor; (see section 3).

Group B is made up of the so-called 'indefinite pronouns'; this is a somewhat mythical category in the sense that there are no paradigms of indefinite pronouns as such. The words which may function in this role form a very heterogeneous class; they may be nouns which are not actualized by a determiner, or are actualized by specific indefinite determiners (e.g. *personne* and *quelqu'un*;) or they may be elliptical constructions, the noun in the noun phrase being the missing element (as in *certains* or *les uns, les autres*). (See section 4.)

Group C includes relative and interrogative pronouns. The difference between relative pronouns and other pronouns is that the relative pronoun also functions as a syntactic link, as does the subordinating conjunction; but unlike the subordinating conjunction it also has a specific function in the clause it introduces, e.g. *c'est Pierre qui me l'a dit (qui = Pierre*, and is the subject of *a dit*). This group is examined in Chapter 14 under 'Syntactic links'.

Interrogative pronouns are basically relative pronouns without an antecedent: it is the antecedent which is being asked for, e.g. *qui est là?* (direct question); *je me demande qui est là* (indirect question). In the second example the interrogative pronoun also functions as a syntactic link. Interrogative pronouns are examined along with interrogative adjectives and interrogative adverbs in Chapter 19; they are also mentioned in Chapter 15, since they may function as syntactical links in indirect questions.

Note: Contrast the following uses of *qui:*

(1) *je sais que c'est Pierre qui l'a fait (qui = Pierre)*
(2) *j'aime qui m'aime (qui* is a relative pronoun without an antecedent)

(3)   *Qui veut noyer son chien l'accuse de la rage* (Molière, *Les Femmes Savantes*)
      (qui is the equivalent of the indefinite pronoun *quiconque)*

In (1) the use of *qui* is typical of relative pronouns: it has an antecedent and is the
subject of the verb in the clause it introduces. In (2) the same applies, except that it has
no antecedent. It is in this case similar to *quiconque* but also acts as a syntactical link as
in (1). In (3) the use of *qui* is similar to that of an indefinite pronoun; it does not even
function as a syntactical link in this case.

1   Personal pronouns

1.1   General considerations

(i) Despite the term 'personal', personal pronouns may refer either to animates or
inanimates. They may refer:

to the speaker *(je)* or to the speaker and addressee(s) *(nous)*
to the addressee *(tu* or *vous)* or to the addressees *(vous)*
to a third person or to an inanimate *(il(s)/elle(s)*, depending on gender and number.

Thus *le docteur* may be *il* and in the same way *le livre* may be *il.*
     (It is however true to say that in the spoken language the *il* of inanimates is often
replaced by the demonstrative pronoun *ça*: see 1.4.1.5, 1.7.2.2, 2.1.*ii* and 2.5.3*iii.*)
(ii) The 3rd person personal pronoun usually replaces a nominal phrase which may
have occurred in the previous clause or sentence:

*Le jardin est beau en ce moment: il est plein de rhododendrons en fleurs (il = le
jardin)*

As such the 3rd person personal pronoun functions as a cohesive tie, in that the second
sentence or clause is only interpretable if one refers back to the first.
     Although this is usually the case, there are exceptions:

the 3rd person may be a 'dummy subject', i.e. it may not stand for anything, e.g. *il
pleut*
it may be used cataphorically, usually in disjunctive constructions in the spoken
language, as in *il vient, Jean?*
it may be used to refer to the nonverbal context, as in *ne le casse pas* (i.e. *le vase que
tu tiens)*

(iii) The main difference between personal pronouns and demonstrative pronouns is
that there is identity between the personal pronoun and its coreferent,[1] whereas this is
not necessarily the case for the demonstrative pronoun:

*J'ai acheté une nouvelle table. Elle ira très bien dans le salon (elle = une nouvelle
table)*

but

*Ces bouquets de fleurs sont très jolis. Donnez-moi celui-là (celui-là = le bouquet de
fleurs qui est là* and not *ces bouquets)*

It can be seen from this that the relationship of substitution between these two types of
pronouns and the nouns to which they refer is quite different.
     Both the demonstrative pronoun and the possessive adjective may in fact refer to the
concept represented by the antecedent rather than to the one specified in the context:

Le chien est carnivore, mais le mien [celui-ci] s'est bien habitué aux légumes
(Bonnard)

They differ in this from both the personal pronoun and the relative pronoun.

(iv) The personal pronouns overlap with the demonstrative pronouns (see 2.1*ii*):

> *Elle m'a prêté le dernier Prix Goncourt. Il/Celui-ci m'a beaucoup plu.*

There are both grammatical and stylistic considerations which have to be taken into account in this respect (see 1.6.1). The *c'est* and *il est* constructions also imply problems for both native and non-native speakers (see 2.4.2.4).

(v) The morphology itself is very complicated: there are many more functions than there are forms, and yet some of these functions may be filled by two different forms, an unstressed and a stressed. This means that the same forms – namely the 1st and 2nd persons plural – tend to reappear in many 'function boxes' in tables, with the 3rd person being the only one to change consistently.

The problem of correspondence of form and function is analysed from a functional point of view under the heading Morphology (see 1.2). But in 1.3, dealing with the position of the pronoun complements, the same problem is seen from the opposite point of view: given the forms – which are quite limited in number – how can they combine? Both approaches are needed to give a full picture of this complex area of grammar.

1.2 Morphology of the personal pronouns according to function

1.2.1 *Stressed and unstressed forms*

For the 1st, 2nd and 3rd persons singular and for the 3rd plural masculine, different forms of the personal pronoun exist according to whether or not they carry a tonic stress. *Nous* and *vous*, although not changing their forms, may carry a stress according to syntactic function and position in the sentence. Historically both forms of the French pronoun object were derived from Latin accusative case pronouns, with the exception of the 3rd person forms *lui, elle* (stressed), derived from Latin datives, and *leur* from a Latin genitive. It was the existence or development of tonic stress which brought about the separate formation of the so-called stressed pronouns. See 1.2.10 for further historical notes.

1.2.2 *Forms of the pronoun as subject (see 1.2.10)*

Person	Singular		Plural	
	Unstressed	Stressed*	Unstressed	Stressed*
1st	*je*	*moi*	*nous*	*nous*
2nd	*tu*	*toi*	*vous*	*vous*
3rd	*il, elle*[2]	*lui, elle*	*ils, elles*	*eux, elles*

*The stressed forms of pronouns are not used on their own as pronoun subject; but they do occur quite commonly in speech, in apposition with unstressed forms, as subjects: *toi, tu n'es pas sérieux; eux, ils ne le feront jamais.*

1.2.3 *Forms of the pronoun as direct object (see 1.2.10)*

Person	Singular	Plural
1st	*me*	*nous*
2nd	*te*	*vous*
3rd	*le, la*	*les*

Only the unstressed form can really be said to exist in this function, although cases will be found of the stressed form added at the end of the sentence to lend stress to the direct object pronoun, e.g. *nous les avons vus, eux.* This kind of stress is more generally achieved in speech, however, by expressions such as *nous les avons vus, ces gens-là.*

1.2.4   *Forms of the pronoun as indirect object (see 1.2.10)*

	Singular		Plural	
Person	Unstressed	Stressed	Unstressed	Stressed
1st	*me*	*moi*	*nous*	*nous*
2nd	*te*	*toi*	*vous*	*vous*
3rd	*lui*	*lui, elle*[3]	*leur*	*eux, elles*

Constructions with pronoun indirect objects are to be found in French either with or without a preceding preposition. These constructions are by no means optional or freely interchangeable (see 1.4.3.2 below). Where such a preposition occurs, the pronoun used will be in the stressed form.

1.2.5   *Summary of uses of pronoun forms*

Position		Form				
Subject placed next to the verb		*je*	*tu*	*il*		*elle*
		nous	*vous*	*ils*		*elles*
Complement placed before the verb	transitive direct	*me*	*te*	*le*		*la*
		nous	*vous*		*les*	
	transitive indirect	*me*	*te*		*lui*	
		nous	*vous*		*leur*	
All other positions, whatever the function		*moi*	*toi*	*lui*		*elle*
		nous	*vous*	*eux*		*elles*

A complete table including all the personal pronouns is included under 1.2.11.

The following table shows examples of the use of the stressed and unstressed forms. Stressed forms are indicated in small capitals, unstressed in italics. (Note that the stressed form of the pronoun is mobile, e.g. *MOI, je parle* and *je parle, MOI.*)

Person	Singular	Plural
1st person:		
Subject	MOI, *je* parle	NOUS, *nous* parlons
Direct Object	il *me* voit, MOI	il *nous* voit, NOUS
Indirect Object	il *me* parle, à MOI	il *nous* parle, à NOUS
2nd person:		
Subject	TOI, *tu* parles	VOUS, *vous* parlez

Person	Singular	Plural
1st person:		
Direct Object	il *te* voit, TOI	il *vous* voit, VOUS
Indirect Object	il *te* parle, à TOI	il *vous* parle, à VOUS
3rd person:		
Subject:		
masc.	LUI, *il* parle	EUX, *ils* parlent
fem.	ELLE, *elle* parle	ELLES, *elles* parlent
Direct Object:		
masc.	je *le* vois, LUI	je *les* vois, EUX
fem.	je *la* vois, ELLE	je *les* vois, ELLES
Reflexive:		
masc.	il *se* plaint, LUI	ils *se* plaignent, EUX
fem.	elle *se* plaint, ELLE	elles *se* plaignent, ELLES
Indirect Object:		
masc.	je *lui* parle, à LUI	je *leur* parle, à EUX
fem.	je *lui* parle, à ELLE	je *leur* parle, à ELLES
Reflexive:		
masc.	il *se* nuit, à LUI (-même)	ils *se* nuisent, à EUX (-mêmes)
fem.	elle *se* nuit, à ELLE (-même)	elles *se* nuisent, à ELLES (-mêmes)

(This table is adapted from Brunot and Bruneau, *Précis de grammaire historique de la langue française*, 277.)

1.2.6 The case of 'on'

On derives from the Latin nominative *homo* (whereas *homme* comes from the Latin accusative *hominem*). It is normally regarded as the nonspecific form of the 3rd person singular pronoun subject.

Although historically it was regarded as masculine, *on* may refer to persons of either sex and may be followed by a feminine adjective, e.g. *à soixante ans on est moins belle qu' à vingt ans.*

On may also stand for persons other than the 3rd person singular, namely the 1st person plural and the 2nd person singular. These uses belong to familiar speech and not to the written language (see 1.5.4).

1.2.7 The case of 'soi'

The stressed Latin pronouns gave:

mé	moi
té	toi
sé	soi

whereas the unstressed pronouns gave:

mè	me
tē	te
sē	se

But *soi* no longer corresponds to *moi* and *toi* as far as its possibilities in terms of use are concerned. Nowadays it may only be used to refer to nonspecified persons in association with *on: on a souvent besoin d'un plus petit que soi.*

In Old French and in Middle French its use was much more general, e.g. *il travaille pour soi.* This is no longer acceptable: nowadays one would have to say, *il travaille pour lui-même*, because *il* refers to a specific person.

1.2.8   *The reflexive form of the personal pronoun*

This occurs only with so-called 'reflexive' or pronominal verbs (*verbes pronominaux*), e.g. *se moquer de*, *se louer*, or with verbs which have been made reflexive although not normally so (in contexts where English normally uses a passive construction): *en Angleterre les œufs se vendent à la douzaine* ('in England eggs are sold by the dozen').

Person	Singular	Plural
1st	*me*	*nous*
2nd	*te*	*vous*
3rd	*se*	*se*

Only the 3rd person forms differ from the pronoun objects. See 1.5.5 for special uses in the spoken language.

1.2.9   *The case of 'y' and 'en'*

These are personal pronouns in that they may function in the same way as nouns:
(i) when these are indirect objects, e.g.

je parle souvent de nos vacances = j'en parle souvent (*en = de nos vacances*)
je réfléchis au problème = j'y réfléchis (*y = au problème*)

(ii) when these function as adverbials:

je vais à Paris = j'y vais
je reviens de Paris = j'en reviens

It is true, however, that both *y* and *en* were originally adverbial, *y* deriving from Latin *ibi* and *en* from Latin *inde*. The pronoun *en* is a chance homonym of the preposition *en,* since the latter derives from the Latin *in*.

1.2.10   *Development of the personal pronouns from Latin into French*

The French personal pronouns came into existence because of the changes which took place in the Latin system in terms of vowel length and stress. In the following table an asterisk indicates a reconstructed form.

Pronoun form	Derivation
je	*ĕgo* > **ĕo* (*jo* by the twelfth century)[1]
tu	*tū*
il	**ĭlli* (in Classical Latin *ĭlle*)[2]
elle	*ĭlla* and in Old French *ele*[2]
nous	*nōs*
vous	*vōs*
ils	*ĭllos*
elles	*ĭllas* and then *eles* in Old French
leur	(*ĭl*) *lōrum* and then *lor* in Old French
eux	*ĭllos* and then *eus* in Old French

Pronoun form	Derivation
me	*me* (unstressed)
te	*te*
se	*se*
moi	*me* (stressed)
toi	*te*
soi	*se*
lui	*(il)lui* (in Classical Latin *illi*)

1 The evolution from *ĕgo* to **eo* in the Vulgar Latin gave two sets of possibilities:
*eo gave in Old French *ieu, ié, jé, gié*
*eó gave in Old French *io, jo, jou* and then *je*
2 According to other grammarians, *il* and *elle* come from **illum* and *illam*.

1.2.11 *General table of personal pronouns*

	Unstressed forms			Stressed forms
Person	Subject	Direct object	Indirect object	One form only
1st sing.	*je*	*me*	*me*	*moi*
2nd sing.	*tu*	*te*	*te*	*toi*
3rd sing.	*il/elle*	*le/la*	*lui*	*lui/elle*
1st plur.	*nous*	*nous*	*nous*	*nous*
2nd plur.	*vous*	*vous*	*vous*	*vous*
3rd plur.	*ils/elles*	*les*	*leur*	*eux/elles*
3rd pers. reflexive		*se*	*se*	*lui/elle* soi
Indefinite 3rd pers.	*on**			
'adverbial' or 'inanimate pronouns			*y* (= *à* + noun phrase) *en* (= *de* + noun phrase)	

1.2.12 *The use of the hyphen between verb and personal pronoun*

Hyphens are used in the following cases:
(i) between a verb and a personal pronoun functioning as a subject and placed after the verb, e.g. *dit-il, dis-je.*
(ii) between an imperative and the personal pronoun functioning as a complement, on condition that they form one intonation or rhythmic group (for rhythmic or intonation group, see Ch. 17, section 5). One thus writes *dites-le* or *crois-moi*, since there is no pause possible between the two words. On the other hand one would write *veuillez me suivre* without hyphens, since pauses are possible in this case, *me* being the complement of *suivre* and not of *veuillez*.
(iii) between the imperative and two personal pronouns functioning as complements; in this case two hyphens may be used, as in *donne-le-moi* or *allez-vous-en*. But if the verb and pronouns may be separated by pauses there may be no hyphen, as in *viens me*

voir dimanche, or just one hyphen, as in *laissez-moi vous aider,* since in this case just two of the items are inseparable from a phonetic point of view.

Note: According to the *Arrêté* of 1976 (see Appendix, Section X), it is now permissible not to use hyphens in those cases in which liaison does not take place.

1.3 Position of the pronoun complements in the clause or sentence

(For an account of the position of subject pronouns, see 1.4.1)

1.3.1 *General considerations*

An elaborate description of the position of the complement pronouns according to their specific functions makes the whole matter appear very complex. If, on the other hand, instead of starting from the functions that they may fill (i.e. direct object versus indirect object, stressed versus unstressed), one starts from a table of their forms, each form being entered only once, the picture becomes clear, for all pronoun complements follow a strict order of precedence which is the same for all voices and moods. The only point to remember is that this order of precedence occurs *before* the verb in all cases except where the affirmative imperative is concerned, in which case the order of precedence remains the same but occurs *after* the verb.

1.3.2 *Word-order of pronoun complements*

This invariable order of precedence, which applies to pronoun complements with verbs in all voices and moods, including the imperative and infinitive, can be represented by a rank order table as follows. The figures in the top row represent the order of precedence of the pronouns in the vertical columns: those in column 1 will always precede those in all the other columns, and so on down to *en*, which never precedes any other pronoun.

1	2	3	4	5
me		*moi**		
te	*le*	*toi**		
se	*la*	*lui*		
			y	
				en
nous	*les*	*nous**		
vous		*vous**		
		leur		

with imperatives only

Examples: *je le lui ai demandé, je l'y ai conduit*; *ne me le demandez pas*; *ne l'y conduisez pas*; but *demandez-le-moi*; *conduisez-l'y* (the pronouns follow the verb in the affirmative imperative).

1.3.3 *Word-order in a construction including a modal verb + infinitive*

This obligatory order will precede the verb in a simple tense, or the auxiliary verb if the latter is *être* or *avoir*,[4] or the factitive *faire*:[5] *je le lui demanderai; je le lui ai demandé; je te le ferai envoyer.* But in constructions in which there is a modal verb followed by an infinitive, this obligatory order will precede the infinitive: *je dois le lui demander; j'ai dû le lui demander; il ne pouvait pas lui répondre.*

1.3.4 *Word-order when infinitival clauses are included*

Where the verb is followed by an infinitive functioning as an infinitival clause, the order of the complement pronouns follows the normal rules:

> *j'envoie Pierre chercher du lait/des pommes (= pour qu'il cherche)*
> *je l'envoie en/les chercher*

In this case *Pierre = l'*, and precedes the verb of which it is the object, i.e. *envoie*; *lait* or *pommes* are the objects of *chercher* and therefore precede *chercher*. A similar example is:

> *j'ai vu Pierre construire sa maison (= qui construisait)*
> *je l'ai vu la construire*

In this case another construction is possible: *je la lui ai vue construire*; but the 'deep structure' of the sentence is different ('I saw it being built by him').

1.3.5 *Emphatic constructions including three pronoun complements*

Only two pronoun complements may occur in French in the same clause. There are examples of a third being added in order to emphasize the indirect object pronoun, but in this case there are still only two nouns which are being referred to: *il faut que tu me le donnes à moi* (*à moi* used to emphasize *me*)

1.3.6 *The case of pronominal verbs*

Pronoun complements in the same rank of precedence never normally occur together in the same phrase. The only situation in which this is apparently likely is with a reflexive pronoun, but in such cases the indirect object is expressed by *à* + the disjunctive pronoun, e.g. *je me fie à vous*; *il s'intéresse à elle*.

1.3.7 *Attributive v. indirect complement*

It is interesting to note the difference between:

> *je parle à François/je lui parle*
> *je pense à François/je pense à lui*

For many French grammarians the difference in these two forms of pronominalization reflects the difference between 'attributive complements' and 'indirect object complements'. Thus if *à* + noun may be replaced by *lui*, it will show that *à* + noun is an attributive complement; if, on the contrary, *à* + noun has to be replaced by *à lui* this is an indirect object complement (see Ch. 9, 1.1*iii*).

1.4 Functions of the personal pronouns

1.4.1 *The pronoun as subject*

1.4.1.1 *The unstressed subject pronouns* These are the pronouns which normally function as subjects.
(i) Their full forms are *je, tu, il, elle, nous, vous, ils, elles*. Also included is *on*, which functions in the same manner as *il*. *Je* normally elides to *j'* before an auxiliary or a verb starting with a vowel: *j'achète; j'ai vu*. *Tu* may be elided to *t'* in the same conditions but only in the spoken language and then only in informal usage; for some this would be a sociolinguistic marker indicating lack of education, e.g. *t'as vu les soldes rue du Pont Neuf?*[6]

(ii) In declarative sentences the subject pronoun will always precede the verb unless there is also a pronoun complement, interposed between the subject and verb,[7] e.g. *il donne la rose à sa mère* but *il la lui donne*.

(iii) Inversion of the subject and verb takes place after certain prepositions such as *aussi: il est arrivé en retard au théâtre aussi a-t-il manqué le premier acte*.

(iv) In interrogative sentences there may be inversion of the subject and verb since this constitutes one of the methods used in French for producing interrogative sentences: *elle est jolie* but *est-elle jolie*?

NOTE: In this construction there is always a hyphen linking pronoun subject to verb. With the pronoun subjects *il, elle* and *on* there is a liaison introduced between the final consonant of the verb and the subject, e.g. *vient-il? sort-elle? vend-il? vendent-ils?* and this final consonant is always pronounced as *-t*. With verbs, such as those of the *-er* conjugations (e.g. *porter, aimer, marcher*), where there is no final *-t* or *-d*, the *-t* is introduced: *il porte/porte-t-il? elle aime/aime-t-elle?*

1.4.1.2   *The use of the impersonal 'il'*
(i) The impersonal pronoun *il* is used as the grammatical subject of impersonal verbs which can take no other, e.g. *il faut, il s'agit*.

(ii) It is used as the grammatical subject of verbs referring to the state of the weather: *il pleut, il neige*.

(iii) It is used to express the time: *il est six heures*.

(iv) It is used in the extremely common expression *il y a*, which corresponds both to 'there is' and to 'there are' in English.

1.4.1.3 *Syntactic restrictions on the use of 'il' as a subject*   *Il est* must be followed by an adjective, or by a noun used adjectivally, e.g. *il est médecin* (where *médecin* is used adjectivally as a quality since it is not preceded by a determiner). It cannot be followed by a noun: **il est un médecin* is not acceptable. One has to say instead *c'est un médecin*.

1.4.1.4 *The stressed subject pronouns*   These are *moi, toi, lui, elle, nous, vous, eux, elles*. Although they are not usually used on their own as pronoun subjects, they may appear in the following constructions:

(i) In apposition, to lend stress to an unstressed pronoun subject: *moi, je ne sais pas*; *je ne sais pas, moi*.

(ii) When followed immediately by a relative pronoun:

> *Lui qui avait toujours détourné les yeux parce qu'il avait l'impression qu'on le regardait avec ironie* (Simenon)

(iii) In apposition to a noun subject: *moi, chef d'équipe, je le veux; toi, vieil idiot, tais-toi*.

(iv) As the notional subject of a nonfinite part of a verb: *moi, faire cela, jamais!*; or of a past participle in a subordinate preposition: *lui parti, qu'est-ce qu'elle va faire?*

(v) In an elliptical expression where the verb is suppressed: *qui a fait cela? moi!*

(vi) Stressed pronouns are used in sentences in which the unstressed pronoun appears ambiguous:

> *nous le ferons = lui et moi, nous le ferons*
> *vous êtes coupables = vous et lui, vous êtes coupables*

(vii) In English there are two forms of the complement subject, e.g. 'it is I' and 'it is me'. There is no such choice in French: one uses the stressed form of the subject: *c'est moi, c'est lui*.

1.4.1.5   *The 3rd person personal pronouns and the neuter demonstrative pronouns* *(i)* The 3rd person pronoun functioning as subject is sometimes replaced by *ce, c', cela* or *ça* in informal spoken French. This happens when the 3rd person pronoun refers to inanimates which are seen as the sum of their parts rather than as simple objects. This may be illustrated as follows:

> *As-tu vu la lampe que j'ai achetée?*
> *Oui, elle est très jolie* (and not **c'est très joli* – see 1.4.1.2)

but

> *As-tu vu le nouvel arrangement* (or *la nouvelle disposition) de mon salon?*
> *Oui, c'est très joli* (i.e. 'the whole thing')

(ii) There is a tendency to extend the use of *ça* in the spoken language beyond the limits described in *(i)*:

> *Ça me fait mal aux pieds, ces chaussures* (shoes come in pairs: they are seen globally)
> *Fais attention en bougeant cette télé; c'est lourd ça* (in this case the television is seen as the sum of its many parts, which is why it is heavy)

These examples are typical of very informal spoken French; the use of *ça* tends to be emphatic.
(iii) When used to refer to animates, *ça* may be strongly pejorative, and such use is often considered a vulgarism, e.g. (of a child) *ça n'a pas encore dix ans et ça croit tout savoir*. (See 2.1.2, 2.4.2.4 and 2.5.3*ii* and *iii*.)

1.4.2 *The pronoun as direct object*

1.4.2.1 *The normal direct object pronouns*
(i) These are *me (m'), te (t'), le (l'), la (l'), nous, vous, les*. The elided forms are used before auxiliaries or verbs starting with a vowel or before the pronoun *y*, e.g. *elle la cherche* but *elle l'a trouvée, je l'y ai trouvé*.
(ii) Le may be used in a neutral sense, i.e. to refer back to a whole statement, e.g. *il est très fatigué, je le sais* (*le = il est très fatigué*).
(iii) Position: see 1.3.2 and 1.3.3.
Note: There is an area of syntactical uncertainty related to the normal direct object pronoun. In the Lyons and St Etienne area, it is quite common to replace the direct object pronoun – when it is neutral – by *y*, e.g. *je sais pas y faire* for *je ne sais pas le faire*; *je vais y porter sur la table* for *je vais le porter sur la table*. This is unacceptable in prescriptive terms and is a sociolinguistic marker.
The grammarian S. Lamothe recalls:

> *Je me bats avec mes petits enfants à ce sujet, et ils me répondent que le maître d'école dit comme cela! J'ai vérifié. . . . C'est hélas vrai!*

She adds,

> *Je crois que je reléguerais en notes ces remarques sur les fautes de pronoms. C'est leur donner trop d'importance que de les placer dans le corps de la grammaire. Elles ne se trouvent que dans le langage parlé, et si un étranger ne comprend pas, l'usager français rectifiera de lui-même pour être compris.*

This indicates an interesting awareness of the mistakes made.

1.4.2.2 *The case of reflexive pronouns* The role of *me, te, se, nous, vous* is either to indicate that the action of the verb turns back on the subject itself (*je me lave*) or that the action is something which the (plural) subjects do to each other (*ils se battent*). (See Ch. 9.) Their origin and development is a matter of some doubt (see Price, *The French language*, 152-3). For odd emphatic uses in the spoken language, see 1.5.5.

One must distinguish three contexts in which reflexive pronouns may be used:

(i) In declarative sentences one uses the unstressed reflexive forms quoted above: *je me lave, tu te laves, il se lave, nous nous lavons, vous vous lavez, ils se lavent.*

(ii) In an affirmative imperative sentence one uses the stressed subject pronouns: *lave-toi, lavons-nous, lavez-vous* (but the 1st and 2nd person plural are the same whether stressed or unstressed).

(iii) With a negated imperative one uses the direct object pronoun (as in *(i)*): *ne te lave pas*; *ne nous lavons pas*; *ne vous lavez pas.*

Note: This seems a somewhat unstable area of the language, since sentences such as **assieds-toi pas* (instead of *ne t'assieds pas*) or **plaignez-vous pas* (instead of *ne vous plaignez pas*) are extremely common. Such forms are unacceptable in prescriptive terms.

1.4.3   *The pronoun as indirect object*

1.4.3.1   *The unstressed indirect object pronouns*

(i) These are *me, te, lui, nous, vous* and *leur*. Only *lui* and *leur* differ from the direct object pronouns (*le, la, les*).

For discussion of the position of the indirect object pronouns, see 1.3.2 and 1.3.3. Basically, in declarative, interrogative and negative imperative clauses or sentences, the 1st and 2nd persons precede the direct object if the latter is *le, la* or *les*; but the 3rd persons *lui* and *leur* follow *le, la* or *les*, e.g. *je te le donne* but *je le lui donne*; *ne me le donne pas* but *ne le lui donne pas.*

(ii) If the sentence is an imperative affirmative, one uses the stressed indirect object pronouns; in this case the indirect object pronoun follows the direct object pronoun *le, la* or *les*, e.g. *ne me le donne pas* but *donne-le-moi.* (But see 1.4.3.3*ii* for exceptions in the spoken language.)

1.4.3.2   *The stressed indirect object pronouns*

(i) These are *moi, toi, lui, elle, nous, vous, eux, elles,* and are the same forms as for the stressed subject pronouns (for *soi*, see 1.2.7 and 1.4.6). The characteristic of these pronouns is that they occur after an introductory preposition and are usually placed at the end of the clause or sentence: *je pense à toi*; *ils se sont moqués de moi*; *je l'ai fait pour lui.*

(ii) The stressed indirect pronouns must be used instead of the unstressed pronouns in the following cases:

(a) In imperative affirmative constructions (see 1.4.3.1), e.g. *donne-le-moi.*

(b) With reflexive or pronominal verbs followed by a preposition, e.g. *nous nous sommes fiés à eux; ils se sont moqués de moi.*

(c) After verbs such as *penser à, venir à, être à, avoir affaire à, plaire à, renoncer à, rêver à,* e.g. *je penserai à toi; je suis à toi; tu auras affaire à moi.* But this is not true of all indirect transitive verbs, e.g. *cela m'appartient; il me semble* (and not **cela appartient à moi* or **il semble à moi*).

(d) With verbs taking both direct and indirect objects (i.e. ditransitive verbs), the indirect object pronoun will be stressed if the direct object is in the 1st or 2nd person, e.g. *je te recommande à eux* as against *je le leur recommande.*

(e) When the complement follows a preposition: *tu m'as trahi auprès d'eux.*

(f) After *ne . . . que* in constructions of the type *ce n'est que moi*, e.g. *il n'y avait que lui à la maison ce jour-là.*

(iii) These stressed pronouns may be used for emphasis in the following cases:

(a) When the unstressed pronoun is already present: in this case the construction will be disjunctive, i.e. the pronoun will be detached from the main construction by a

pause or a comma, e.g. *il vous l'a avoué, à vous!*

(b) When the unstressed pronoun is not present, the stressed pronoun will be used either with the *ne . . . que* construction (see *(ii)*) or with the modifier *seul*, e.g. *il l'a avoué à vous seul* or *il ne l'a avoué qu'à vous.*

1.4.3.3 *The 3rd person indirect object pronoun: an area of syntactic uncertainty*
(i) The pronoun *lui* tends to be replaced in popular speech by *y* in quite a systematic manner, particularly in the Paris region, e.g. *je lui ai dit que . . .* becomes **j'y ai dit que. . . .* The latter form is unacceptable in prescriptive terms and belongs to what some French teachers call *un langage populaire très négligé.*
(ii) It has been stated in 1.4.3.1*ii* that the affirmative imperative makes use of the stressed rather than the unstressed indirect object pronouns; in popular speech this is not always the case, hence **donne-me-le* instead of *donne-le-moi*; or **confie-me-le* instead of *confie-le-moi*. This is probably due to analogy with *ne me le donne pas* and *ne me le confie pas*, the affirmative imperative being the odd form out. This kind of 'mistake' (in prescriptive terms) seems to be common over the whole of France.

1.4.4 *The use of 'y'*

The pronoun *y* may function either as an indirect object (1.4.4.1) or as an adverbial (1.4.4.2).

1.4.4.1 *'Y' used as an indirect object*
(i) *Y* stands essentially for inanimates in an *à* + noun construction, when the former is the equivalent of *à cela* or *à quelque chose,* e.g.

> *j'ai laissé mes papiers en désordre sur la table; n'y touchez surtout pas!* (= *ne touchez surtout pas à cela*)

(ii) *Y* is used instead of *lui* to differentiate *quelque chose* from *quelqu'un,* e.g.

> *je renonce à quelqu'un = je renonce à lui*
> *je renonce à quelque chose = j'y renonce*

(iii) *Y* is used in opposition to *lui* to refer to a whole statement, e.g. *pensez à vos examens qui sont bientôt = pensez-y.* *Y* in this sense, functioning as an indirect object, resembles *le* standing for a whole statement, but as a direct object (see 1.4.2.1*ii*).
Note: One may contrast the following responses to the sentence *pense à moi!*

> (1) *oui, je pense à toi*
> (2) *oui, j'y pense*

In (1) *toi* stands for a person; in (2) *y* stands for a whole statement, i.e. *je pense à ce que tu m'as demandé de faire pour toi.*

1.4.4.2 *'Y' used as an adverbial* This is the so-called 'adverbial pronoun'.
(i) It may stand either for *à* + noun or for *dans* + noun:

> *je vais à Paris = j'y vais*
> *j'ai fait un trou dans le plâtre = j'y ai fait un trou*
> *je m'engage dans ce tunnel = je m'y engage*

(ii) *Y* may stand for the adverbs *ici* and *là:*

> *j'y suis, j'y reste* (= *je suis ici, je reste ici*)
> *nous y voilà* (= *nous sommes là*, i.e. 'we've got to the crux of the matter')

(iii) It is more or less an 'empty' pronoun in fixed expressions such as *il y a.*

Although there is a vague kind of spatial implication in its use, expressions such as these are felt to form a semantic whole.

In constructions such as *je n'y suis pour rien* it resembles the 'global it' of the possible English translation, 'I had nothing to do with it'or 'it is not my fault'. In this case its usage resembles that in *(ii)* above.

1.4.5 *The use of 'en'*

En comes from the Latin *unde* meaning *de cela*; as such it may function as a partitive complement (1.4.5.1). *Unde* also means *de là*: *en* may also function as an adverbial (1.4.5.2).

1.4.5.1 *'En' used as a partitive complement*
(i) En stands for 'indicator of quantity + noun'; this idea of quantity may be expressed either by an adverb of quantity, by a numeral or by a partitive. In these cases the deep structure corresponds to a *de cela* construction:

je veux du vin = j'en veux (= je veux de cela)
j'ai deux voitures = j'en ai deux (= j'ai deux de cela)

In the following case an animate is pronominalized in a similar fashion:

je vois des/trois/quelques hommes qui travaillent = j'en vois/trois/quelques uns qui travaillent

(ii) En may be used for an inanimate, in contrast with an animate expressed by *lui*. In this case *en* means *de quelque chose*:

je m'approche de la berge = je m'en approche (= je m'approche de quelque chose)

but

je m'approche de Jean = je m'approche de lui (de quelqu'un)

In this *en* is similar to *y* (see 1.4.4.1*ii).*

The same applies where possessive adjectives are concerned: *en* is in competition with *son*: *Paul habite Lyon; connaissez-vous son adresse? Ce restaurant est à Lyon; en connaissez-vous l'adresse?* (Dubois and Lagane, *La Nouvelle grammaire française).*
(iii) En may stand for a whole statement:

Elle veut absolument partir. Il n'y a rien que je puisse faire pour l'en empêcher
(= pour l'empêcher de faire cela)

(iv) In some cases *en* may stand for an animate. Despite the fact that grammarians have tried to make *en* refer only to inanimates, there is a certain amount of flexibility in this area of the language; and there are standard (i.e. prescriptively acceptable) cases in which *en* may stand for an animate:
(a) When pronominalizing a direct object determined by an indefinite determiner or a numeral (see 1.4.5.1*i*), e.g. *je vois trois enfants dans la cour = j'en vois trois.*
(b) When referring to the agent of a passive verb, e.g. *il aimait ses enfants et en était aimé (=de* or *par ses enfants).*
(c) En may stand for an animate with verbs such as *avoir des nouvelles de* and *recevoir des nouvelles de*:

Savez-vous où est Jean?
Oui, j'en ai eu des nouvelles récemment

(d) When it enables one to avoid repetition:

Ce que j'ai vu d'elles, ce qu'on m'en avait raconté (Proust)

But one could argue that *en* means *à leur sujet*, i.e. *ce qu'on m'avait raconté à leur sujet*: in this case the *en* (like the *y* of 1.4.4.1*iii)* refers back to a statement rather than only to an animate.

(e) En may be used cataphorically (i.e. to refer forwards), as in *en voilà un qui n'a pas froid aux yeux!*

(f) En may also be used to emphasize, in the spoken language, the direct object:

> *j'en ai vu, des gens ruinés par cette guerre!*
> *des difficultés, nous en prévoyons beaucoup*
> (Examples borrowed from Wartburg and Zumthor, *Précis de syntaxe du français contemporain*.)

In these cases the use of *en* is always linked with an idea of indeterminacy in terms of number.

(v) En can definitely not be used to replace a noun contained in a prepositional phrase acting as complement of another noun: *(cet incident est sérieux;) je songe aux conséquences de cet incident* cannot be rendered as **j'en songe aux conséquences*.

1.4.5.2 *'En' used as an adverbial* This is the so-called adverbial pronoun
(i) In this case it stands for *de* + noun, and may refer to place of origin, e.g. *je viens de Paris* = *j'en viens*.
(ii) By extension it may also refer to *avec* + noun, meaning an origin other than spatial, e.g. *j'ai acheté de la viande hachée et j'en ai fait des boulettes* (= *j'ai fait des boulettes avec/à partir de la viande*).
(iii) A large number of fixed expressions exist in current usage in which *en* appears to have become fossilized, although the meaning in *(ii)* seems to be present', e.g. *en vouloir à quelqu'un* ('to have it in for somebody'); *s'en aller* ('to go away'); *en avoir marre* (slang, 'to be fed up'); *n'en pouvoir plus* ('to be at the end of one's tether').

1.4.5.3 *'En' in imperative constructions* Taking as example the question *j'ai des pommes: en veux-tu?* the following constructions are all possible:

> *oui, donne-m'en!*
> *oui, donne-m'en une!*
> *oui, donnes-en moi une!* (the final *-s* added to the imperative is euphonic)

Note: The following forms, although unacceptable in prescriptive terms, are frequently heard in children's speech and in uneducated speech:

> **donnes-en-moi!*
> **donne-moi-z-en!*
> **donne-moi-z-en une!*

1.4.6 *The case of 'soi'*

(i) In the past *soi* was much more commonly used than it is today; but it has been generally displaced by *lui*, or by *lui-même* whenever it refers to a noun subject (see 1.2.7).
(ii) In modern usage it practically never functions as subject or attribute. It is normally found referring to an indefinite human subject *(on, nul, personne, quiconque, tel, celui qui* etc.),[8] e.g. *on ne travaille que pour soi; tel travaille pour soi, tel autre pour le bien de tous*.
 Soi is also used where a semantic subject is not actually mentioned, as with an infinitive and after impersonal verbs: *il faut le faire soi-même; rester soi; être soi et non un autre*.
 Like the stressed pronouns, with which it may be classed, it is often preceded by a

preposition when in an accentuated position: *penser à soi*; *l'amour de soi*.

(iii) Soi is also frequently seen in the fixed expression *soi-disant,* an invariable adjectival expression meaning 'so-called': *les soi-disant réformateurs*; *les soi-disant libéraux*. It may also apply to abtract qualities: *ce soi-disant mérite*. In this usage *soi-disant* always immediately precedes the noun it qualifies.

When referring to inanimates *soi-disant* is replaced by *prétendu*, e.g. *ce prétendu chef-d'œuvre ne m'a pas paru génial*.

Note: *Soi-disant* is also sometimes used in this context, but this is judged to be incorrect for semantic reasons: it is somewhat illogical for inanimate objects to 'say' things about themselves. *Ce soi-disant mérite* is a case of metonymy: it is the merit of the person.

Soi-disant is occasionally used adverbially, e.g. *ils sont partis, soi-disant pour aller le chercher* (Larousse).

1.5   The semantics of personal pronouns

The significance of some of the personal pronouns in French is not always parallel to that of their English counterparts. Embarrassing misunderstandings can arise from a faulty knowledge of these differences. Since these matters are really the province of sociolinguistics rather than grammar, only a bare outline is provided below.

1.5.1   *The 1st person pronouns*

Je rarely presents problems, although it is less used in formal written language than the English 'I'. The French classical tradition has encouraged the sentiment, first enunciated by Blaise Pascal, that *le moi est haïssable*, and that the 1st person pronouns should be replaced by the more modest-seeming *nous* or *on*, together with a corresponding change in the person of the verb (see 1.5.4.1 for *on*).

Nous is used by those in high authority in formal proclamations (cf. the royal 'we' in English). Not unnaturally, French grammarians tend to quote instances of administrative formulae such as *Nous, Préfet de la Seine Maritime, décrétons que*. . . .

Nous is also used in a somewhat similar way to the English editorial 'we' as a device of mock modesty by authors, editors etc. Its use is obligatory in all French academic theses: the following example comes from the printed thesis of Jacqueline Pinchon, *Les Pronoms adverbiaux 'en' et 'y'*:

C'est encore une étude particulière que nous présenterons ici. . . .

1.5.2   *The 2nd person pronouns*

The *tu/vous* pair is the most fertile source of problems, especially as the singular form 'thou' has disappeared from current English.

Tu is no longer the singular of *vous* and has not been for a long time. It is the familiar mode of address between friends and workmates, children, pupils at school and students, members of a family (except possibly in certain families in the highest reaches of French society), lovers, old classmates and similar categories. It cannot be taken for granted even between equals in certain areas such as management teams in industry or commerce, or in the civil service. Its use may well be increasing, however, on the social level, among the young and the young middle-aged. Outside the limits of school or student contacts or similar, it is wiser for the non-native speaker to leave the initiative in *tutoiement* to the native-speaker interlocutor.

Vous, apart from being the second person plural form, is also the polite mode of address used to all persons one does not know well enough to address as *tu*, or who may be one's superiors in a work or business situation.

Changes from *tu* to *vous* and vice versa can be both traumatic and dramatic, and have been much exploited in literature of all types. Corneille's *Le Cid* provides a number of examples of dramatic uses of *tu* and *vous*. In Act 3, for example, Rodrigue comes to Chimène to offer her vengeance for her father, whom he has killed:

Don Rodrigue:	*N'épargnez* point mon sang: goûtez sans résistance.
	La douceur de ma perte et de votre vengeance.
Chimène:	Hélas!
Don Rodrigue:	*Ecoute*-moi.

Racine provides numerous examples, such as the following from the crucial encounter of Hippolyte and Phèdre:

Hippolyte:	Dieux! qu'est-ce que j'entends? Madame, oubliez-vous
	Que Thésée est mon père, et qu'il est *votre* époux?
Phèdre:	Et sur quoi jugez-*vous* que j'en perds la mémoire,
	Prince? Aurais-je perdu tout le soin de ma gloire?
Hippolyte:	Madame, *pardonnez:* j'avoue, en rougissant
	Que j'accusais à tort un discours innocent.
	Ma honte ne peut plus soutenir *votre vue;*
	Et je vais . . .
Phèdre:	Ah, cruel! *tu* m'as trop entendue!

Equally dramatic is the change from *vous* to *tu* when the police arrest a suspect, according to Simenon (*Le Temps d'Anaïs*):

> – *C'est* vous *l'homme qui avez téléphoné?*
> *Alors cela se passa comme un tour de prestidigitation, à croire que la scène avait été patiemment répétée. Bauche sentit les mains d'un des gendarmes glisser le long de son corps, sans doute pour s'assurer qu'il ne portait pas d'arme. L'autre, campé en face de lui, désignait ses poignets.*
> – Tes *mains!*

Finally, it should be remembered that French Protestants use *tu* when speaking to God, as in this version of the Lord's Prayer from the 1805 Paris printing of the Bible:

> *Notre Père qui es aux cieux, que ton nom soit sanctifié, que ton règne vienne, que ta volonté soit faite sur la terre comme au ciel. . . .*

(This has recently also become true for Catholics.)

Over the centuries there have been several politically motivated attempts to enforce or encourage the use of *tu* as the normal singular 2nd person pronoun. Each revolution since 1789 has attempted this, as did the revolution of 1968, and it is probably true that *tutoiement* has become somewhat more common since that date, at least among intellectuals and middle-class people who were young [9] at the time. Today it is very rare to find man and wife addressing each other as *vous*, but in Zola's *Au Bonheur des dames* we find the following:

> *Vallagnosc était devant elle, ce mari d'un mois dont le tutoiement la gênait encore; et il la questionnait, en s'étonnant de sa stupeur.*[10]

The use of *tu* is also likely to change in future, probably broadly reflecting social attitudes, and it is also different in francophone countries outside France, e.g. Canada and also Belgium.

1.5.3 *The 3rd person pronouns*

Il may indicate not only 'he' but also the neutral 'it' in expresssions such as *il pleut* and *il est six heures.* Frequently, however, the neutral 'it' is rendered by *ce* (see 1.4.1.5*i*).

Il and *elle* are also used in certain somewhat exaggerated situations of politeness: *Et monsieur, qu'est-ce qu'il désire? Votre Altesse, que désire-t-elle?*

Ils, in addition to meaning 'they', referring to some person or things which have already been named or indicated, also has a similar meaning to the English 'they' meaning rather vaguely 'the government', 'the powers that be' etc.: *ils ont augmenté l'essence encore une fois; ils vont faire bâtir tout un nouveau faubourg par là.*

1.5.4   *The case of 'on'*

1.5.4.1   *The indefinite 'on'*
(i)   On may refer to people unknown, e.g. *on dit que.* . . . In this case it is grammatically singular but semantically plural.

(ii)   On may refer to a specific person whose identity is unknown to the speaker, e.g. *on m'a volé mon portefeuille.*

(iii)   On may refer to persons whose identity is known to the speaker, but felt to be irrelevant in a given context, e.g. *on est en train de nous refaire toute notre tuyauterie.*

(iv)   On may refer to everybody in general, e.g. *on ne porte plus de faux-col aujourd'hui.*

See 1.7.1 for translation problems.

1.5.4.2   *The definite 'on'*
(i) It may be used instead of *nous* in informal spoken French, e.g. *ma femme et moi, on va au cinéma tous les dimanches.* (This may have something to do with the fact that 3rd person verb endings are shorter and more frequently used than 1st person plural endings.)

(ii) It may be used to refer to *je* + an indefinite number of persons, e.g. *on en a marre!* (slang and vulgar).

(iii) It may be used for *tu* when speaking to children or animals: *alors on a bien dormi?* or *on a bien mangé sa soupe?* Or it may be used in adult speech to express condescension, in which case it may correspond to *vous,* as in *alors, Madame Martin, on prend le frais!* This kind of formula is fairly frequent in the theatre.

(iv) It may be used to refer to *je* + *tu* or to *je* + *vous,* e.g. *alors, on y va?* This form is used in questions when one does not know exactly what the reactions of the other person(s) are going to be.

1.5.4.3   *'On' and problems of style*
(i) If *on* is being used as a 'real' indefinite pronoun, i.e. if it cannot be replaced by a definite pronoun, its use is perfectly acceptable in the written language, since there is no alternative to it; if it is a 'false' indefinite pronoun, in that it may be replaced by another definite pronoun, its use is banned from formal written French (except when *(ii)* applies).

(ii)   On may be used instead of a definite pronouns such as *vous* to express slight contempt for the addressee or to express the powerful position of the speaker (see 1.5.4.2.*iii*)

In some rare cases *on* may be used instead of *je*, as in the following sentence from Marivaux:

On (= *je*) *vous épousera, toute fière que l'on* (= *vous*) *est*

In this case the first *on* is similar to a kind of royal 'we' − implying power − whereas the second one implies contempt due to the speaker's power. (This use of *on* = *je* was inherited from the *Précieuses*, who felt the use of *je* to be too direct.)

Note: On is sometimes used in modern French with the meaning of *je* to express insolence: *on lui dira*, referring to oneself, is a way of ignoring an order or piece of advice. The following incident illustrates this expression: a youth parks his moped next to the entrance of a small shop; the shopkeeper asks the youth to remove it; the youth answers, *C'est ça, mon petit père! On lui dira*! Fury of insulted shopkeeper.

1.5.5   *Use of the reflexive pronouns in the spoken language*

Reflexive pronouns are sometimes used in the spoken language to emphasize the fact that the person referred to has acted of his own free will:

   il se l'est bien épousée (= 'after all, he did marry her')

In this case the auxillary has to be changed from *avoir* to *être* (instead of *il l'a épousée*).

   puisque c'est comme ça, je me le garde (instead of *je le garde*) (= 'since things are as they are I shall definitely keep it')

Such constructions are in frequent use in the southern part of France; they tend to be considered vulgar.

1.6   Grammatical and stylistic 'mistakes' to be avoided in formal French

1.6.1   *'Il' v. 'celui-ci'*

When two clauses follow each other, *il(s)* or *elle(s)* at the beginning of the second clause always stands for the subject of the first clause if the latter is of the same gender and number, e.g.

   Pierre a battu Paul; il est vraiment trop agressif (*il* = *Pierre*)

But in the following example the use of *il* becomes illogical:

   *Pierre a battu Paul; il est malheureusement trop petit pour pouvoir se défendre

In this case *il* has *Pierre* as its grammatical co-referent, whereas logic demands that *il* should have *Paul* as its co-referent. To make this distinction one must replace *il* by *celui-ci*, since *celui-ci/celle-ci* always stands for the last noun of that gender and number. The example above should therefore be rendered as follows to become acceptable at least in formal written French, which is more prescriptive than the spoken language:

   Pierre a battu Paul; celui-ci est malheureusement trop petit pour pouvoir se défendre

This rule applies obligatorily if there is identity of gender and number between the pronoun used and the noun one does *not* want it to refer to, as in the last example above; if there is no confusion possible, one may use the personal pronoun to refer to a noun other than the subject:

   les enfants de la grande école ont battu Paul; il/celui-ci a porté plainte

In this case either pronoun is possible, since *il* can only refer to Paul. The use of *celui-ci* where there is a choice, as here, makes the text more formal. But in the spoken language *il* is the preferred form: the speaker relies on the intelligence of the listener not to misinterpret what is being said.

1.6.2   *Personal pronouns standing for a 'determiner + noun' construction*

A personal pronoun must always stand for a nominal phrase, i.e. either for a proper noun or for a noun which is preceded by a determiner (i.e. it must be preceded by either an article, a numeral, a possessive adjective, a demonstrative adjective or an indefinite adjective).

One is therefore told, in prescriptive grammar at least, not to write **j'ai demandé pardon; il m'a été accordé*, but *j'ai demandé mon pardon; il m'a été accordé*; not **vous m'enverrez copie du contrat; elle doit me parvenir avant jeudi*, but *vous m'enverrez une copie du contrat; elle doit. . . .*

It is possible however to use a pronoun to refer to the complement of a collective partitive:

> *j'ai acheté un grand nombre de livres d'occasion; ils vont vous être expédiés sous peu (de livres d'occasion* is the complement of the collective partitive *un grand nombre)*

1.6.3   *Repetition of subject by personal pronoun*

The pronouns *il* or *elle* should not be used in formal written French where another noun is already the subject, even if it no longer immediately precedes the verb:

> **Pierre, mon voisin de l'étage du dessous, il m'a dit que. . .*

Such constructions are however typical of spontaneous spoken French.

1.6.4   *Repetition of object by personal pronoun*

Similarly, repetition of the object is considered poor style, although such repetition is common in the spoken language and acceptable in that context, e.g. *tu le vois souvent, Pierre, ces temps-ci?* In this case *le* is cataphoric (i.e. refers forward).

1.6.5   *The use of 'on'*

It has been noted that only the 'real' indefinite *on* is considered good style in formal written French (see 1.5.4.3). The 'false' indefinite *on* belongs mainly to the spoken language.

1.6.6   *Areas of syntactic uncertainty*

The personal pronoun is an area of great syntactic uncertainty, in the sense that many of the uses of the object pronouns which one may hear will be considered unacceptable in the written language. The 3rd person singular is often replaced by a demonstrative pronoun in the spoken language where the item referred to is inanimate (see 1.4.1.5); 1.4.3.3 shows areas of uncertainty where the 3rd person indirect object is concerned; 1.4.4.2 refers to areas of instability where *y* is concerned; and 1.4.2.2 *Note* shows the use of reflexive pronouns to be uncertain in affirmative imperative constructions.

1.6.7   *Use of pronoun complements in coordinated verbal constructions*

Another area of uncertainty is where two verbs share the same pronoun complement. There are two possibilities:

(i) In cases where two coordinated verbs each have a pronoun – both pronouns functioning either as direct or as indirect object and both having the same coreferent – the subject of the second verb should not be repeated, nor the auxiliary if the verb is in a compound tense:

elle le lave et l'habille (no repetition of subject)
elle l'a lavé et habillé (no repetition of subject or of auxiliary)

and not:

*elle l'a lavé et l'a habillé

(ii) In cases where the two pronouns have the same coreferent but different functions, they should be repeated, even though they may appear to be morphologically the same:

elle m'a habillé avec goût et elle m'a appris à vivre

In this case the *me* is repeated because it is the direct object of *habiller* and the indirect object of *apprendre* (*habiller quelqu'un* but *apprendre quelque chose à quelqu'un*). This did not stop Françoise Sagan from writing in *Bonjour Tristesse, Elle m'a habillé avec goût et appris à vivre*, which is why Grevisse (*Le Bon usage*) states:

Cette règle n'est pas absolue: d'excellents auteurs se dispensent . . . de répéter . . . le pronom (et l'auxiliaire), faisant cumuler au pronom, exprimé une seule fois devant le premier verbe, deux fonctions différentes.[11]

(See also L.C. Harmer, *Uncertainties in French grammar*, 123 – 8.)

1.7 Contrastive problems

For the *il est/c'est* problem, see 2.4.2.4.

1.7.1 *The translation of 'on'*

(i) The indefinite *on* may be translated by 'one' or 'they':

on dit que . . . ('they say that . . .')
on aurait pu s'attendre à ce que . . . ('one could have expected that . . .')

(ii) The indefinite *on* may be translated by 'somebody':

on m'a volé mon portefeuille ('somebody has stolen my wallet')

(iii) The indefinite *on* is frequently translated by the passive, *(a)* when referring to everybody in general (*on ne porte plus le faux col* – 'detachable collars are no longer worn') or *(b)* when the identity of the person(s) is known but irrelevant in a given context:

on est en train de nous refaire notre tuyauterie ('we are having all the plumbing redone')

1.7.2 *Problems arising from the absence of 'it' in French*

1.7.2.1 *The possible ambiguity of 'il' and 'elle'* *Il* and *elle* may become ambiguous. When writing about a book written by a man, one may not know, given the context, whether *il* refers to the author or to the book, whereas in English the existence of a neuter pronoun 'it' removes all ambiguity. When translating from English into French, therefore, either the pronoun 'it' may have to be translated by a repetition of its coreferent by contextual synonym[12], or the syntax may have to be changed.

From a window in her office at the Shipyards, Penelope Wain Stood watching the evening draw over the water. It was invading the Stream like a visible and moving body. (H. MacLennan, *Barometer rising*)

The following suggested translation is borrowed from Vinay and Darbelnet, *Stylistique comparée du français et de l'anglais:*

> *Debout à une fenêtre de son bureau aux chantiers de construction navale, Penelope Wain regardait s'allonger sur l'eau les ombres du crépuscule. L'obscurité envahissait la baie comme une masse visible et mouvante.*

The following translation, suggested by the present authors, involves a change in the syntax:

> *Debout à une fenêtre de son bureau aux chantiers de construction navale, Penelope Wain regardait s'allonger sur l'eau les ombres du crépuscule, envahissant la baie comme une masse visible et mouvante.*

Elle does not appear in either translation since it would necessarily refer to *Penelope.*

1.7.2.2 *The use of 'il' and 'elle' for inanimates* There is a general tendency among native speakers to avoid the repeated use of *il/elle* for inanimates. In the spoken language, *il/elle* are taken up as *ça* whenever possible, in order to avoid this problem (see 1.4.1.5):

> *t'as vu le film?*
> *oui, ça m'a bien plu (*for *il m'a bien plu)*

Since such a solution is unacceptable in the written language, the tendency in the latter is to use contextual synonyms, preceded by a suitable demonstrative adjective or definite article. There follows an English text containing a problematic 'it', together with our suggested translation:

> No more precise indication may be given as to its origin and *it* is not known what bright spirit invented the idea of the game. *It* was then called 'chaturanga' and though the game differed in some respects from the modern version *it* was clearly chess. (H. Golombek, *The game of chess*)

> *Aucune indication plus précise ne peut être donnée quant à son origine et personne ne sait quel est l'homme de génie qui en eut le premier l'idée. Ce jeu s'appelait à l'origine le 'chaturanga' et bien que celui-ci ait différé à certains égards du jeu d'échecs tel que nous le connaissons aujourd'hui, il s'agit bien, néanmoins, du même jeu.*

This translation shows that, when the coreferent of 'it' is not clear and explicit, 'it' cannot be translated by *il* or *elle.*

Of course, once an English pronoun has been translated in French by a nominal phrase, the whole principle of the succession of nouns and their pronouns is interrupted – hence the non-correspondence of nouns and pronouns between the translation and the original English text.

This non-correspondence between the use of pronouns and contextual synonyms in French and English presents major problems to anglophones as soon as they begin to work on texts rather than on separate sentences.

1.7.2.3 *'Il' used with a nonspecific coreferent* 'It' in English may take on a kind of 'global' diffused meaning which no French equivalent pronoun may do; in this case, once again, the French translation will have to make the meaning of 'it' precise and explicit:

> *Dinah:* Darling, you haven't kissed me yet.
> *Brian:* I oughtn't to, but then one never ought to do nice things.
> *Dinah:* Why oughtn't you?

Brian: Well, we said we'd be good until we'd told your uncle and aunt all about it [their engagement]. . . .

Translation suggested in Vinay and Darbelnet, *Stylistique comparée. . .,* 227 – 8.

Dinah: Mon chéri, tu ne m'as pas encore embrassée!
Brian: Est-ce que ce n'est pas défendu? C'est toujours défendu de faire des choses agréables!
Dinah: Pourquoi serait-ce défendu de m'embrasser?
Brian: Tu sais bien que nous avons promis d'être sages jusqu'à ce que ton oncle et ta tante soient au courant de nos fiançailles.

Another solution to the problem, however, would be . . . *que ton oncle et ta tante soient au courant de tout.* The latter is, in fact, more likely than the rather stilted translation suggested. It does however illustrate the point of the non-translatability of the English 'it'.
Note: For the use *c'est défendu* instead of *il est défendu,* see 2.4.2.4.

1.7.3 *The lack of ellipsis relating to the French personal pronouns*

1.7.3.1 *The explicitness of French constructions* It is necessary in French that all the elements necessary to a construction from a syntactical point of view should be made explicit (but see 1.7.3.3 for classical French):

'but I told him! = *mais je le lui ai dit!*
'I won't have time' = *je n'en aurai pas le temps/je n'aurai pas le temps de le faire*

In other words, where a direct or indirect object or adverbial is understood in English ('but I told him (something); 'I won't have time (to do something)', or 'I won't have (enough) time (for it)'), it must be made syntactically explicit in French. Many students make the following type of mistake:* *je lui ai dit* for *je le lui ai dit.* Thus, 'he seems very pleased with himself, but I am not' (i.e. 'pleased with him') is translated by: *il a l'air trés content de lui, mais moi je ne le suis pas,* or in more informal language by *il a l'air très content de lui, mais moi pas.*

1.7.3.2 *Cases in which the pronoun object is omitted*
(i) There are some cases in which the pronoun object is not necessary. Compare *dis-le lui* with *prévenez-le,* and *je m'en vais* with *je pars.* In the dictionary one will find that *dire* must take both direct and indirect objects (*dire quelque chose à quelqu'un*); but that *prévenir* takes only a direct object (*prévenir quelqu'un*). The verb *aller* requires a complement (*aller quelque part,*) whereas *partir* does not. Careful attention should therefore be given to the kind of structure which is inherent to a specific vocabulary entry.
(But see 1.7.3.3 for exceptions both in classical French and in the spoken language.)
(ii) There is one case in which the English construction demands the pronoun 'it' whereas the French one does not. This is when the subordinate clause is the explicit object of the verb, and here the French construction avoids unnecessary repetition:

j'ai jugé nécessaire qu'il se couche tôt, vu son état de santé ('I thought it advisable that he should go to bed early given his state of health')
je trouve un peu difficile de lui donner raison ('I find it a little difficult to say that he is right')

1.7.3.3 *Syntactic uncertainties*
The rule described in 1.7.3.1 is a difficult one in that it has not always been strictly followed in formal language in the past (see *(i)* below), and it is often not followed in informal language in the present (see *(ii)* below).

(i) This rule was not followed to the same extent in Classical French; thus Racine wrote:

Le pape envoie le formulaire tel qu'on lui demandait

instead of

Le pape envoie le formulaire tel qu'on le lui demandait

(see Vinay and Darbelnet, *Stylistique comparée du français et de l'anglais.*
(ii) This rule is not followed completely in the informal spoken language:

tu veux des chocos? (*chocos* are a kind of chocolate biscuit eaten by French children
   for tea)
non, j'aime pas (instead of *non, je ne les aime pas*)

(*Ne/n'* is often dropped in informal speech: see Ch. 12, 7.1*v*.)

2   Demonstrative pronouns

2.1   Areas of overlap between personal and demonstrative pronouns

(i) Some of these have been examined in 1.4.1.5 and 1.6.1. The formal written language uses *celui-ci* to avoid grammatical (and sometimes semantic) ambiguity.
   Compare:

(1) *Marie s'est disputée avec sa sœur; elle est allée se plaindre auprès de sa mère*
(2) *Marie s'est disputée avec sa sœur; celle-ci est allée se plaindre auprès de sa mère*

The first sentence is ambiguous in that *elle* could refer either to *Marie* or to *sa sœur*; the second sentence is not ambiguous since *celle-ci* has to refer to the previous noun phrase.
   In the spoken language the personal pronoun is the preferred form, the speaker leaving it to the intelligence of the hearer (helped by the context) not to misinterpret what is being said.
(ii) In some cases it may be possible to see the same thing − a picture, for example − either as a single unit or as the sum of its parts. In this case one has a choice between using the personal pronoun − which refers to a unit − or the demonstrative pronoun, which refers to the whole:

Regardez ce tableau!
Oui, il est beau (*il = le tableau*)
Oui, c'est beau (*c'* = *cela* = the global effect)

(iii)   The personal and demonstrative pronouns overlap where the neuter forms are concerned: *c'est* and the impersonal *il est* often present problems for both native and non-native speakers (2.4.2.4).

2.2   Areas of no overlap

(i) The demonstrative pronoun differs from the 3rd person pronouns in that it includes in its meaning some form of spatial reference, e.g.

j'aime en général les tableaux modernes, mais celui-là ne me plaît pas du tout

In this case a picture is being pointed at (i.e. the reference is exophoric).
(ii) The demonstrative may serve to pick out one item within a group:

J'aime ces grandes tasses
Prends-les or *Prends en une*

J'aime ces grandes tasses
Prends celle-ci

Whereas the personal pronoun stands for the noun, the demonstrative pronoun points at one item in the group.

(iii) Location in space may be extended to a nonspatial context. For example, in a text *celui-ci* will refer to the nearest possible co-referent (or antecedent), whereas *celui-là* will refer to the furthest:

First noun	Second noun	*celui-ci*	*celui-là*

(See example in 2.5.2*ii*.) These terms are not however as flexible as 'the former' and 'the latter' − see 2.5.2*ii* − and are a source of error for most students.

By extension, however, *-là* may indicate psychological distance, i.e. it may take on pejorative connotations (see 2.5.2*iii*).

(iv) The demonstrative may stand for a whole statement. In this it is in complementary distribution[13] with the personal pronouns:

cela/c'/ça = subject pronoun
le = object pronoun
y and *en* = indirect object pronouns

Examples:

Tu sais que tu vas être en retard si tu ne te dépêches pas
(1) *Cela m'est bien égal* (subject)   (2) *Je le sais* (object)
Tu vas à Paris?   Oui, j'y vais (adverbial)
Tu as acheté du pain?   Oui, j'en ai acheté (partitive complement)

Note: It is because *cela* tends to be associated with the idea of a whole statement that it may also be used to refer to something in a global manner (see 2.1*ii*).

2.3 Morphology

2.3.1 *General characteristics*

(i) The French system of demonstrative pronouns is a two-tier set of forms, one of which is simple and the other compound, having an additional adverb (*-ci* or *-là*) joined to it, originally in order to indicate nearness or distance of the speaker.

(ii) The French system of demonstrative pronouns still includes three genders: in addition to the masculine and feminine forms in both singular and plural, there is also a set of neuter forms which can apply to either gender or to none.

The following table summarizes the system:

	Masculine	Feminine	Neuter
Simple forms	*celui* *ceux*	*celle* *celles*	*ce*
Compound forms	*celui-ci/là* *ceux-ci/là*	*celle-ci/là* *celles-ci/là*	*ceci-cela (ça)*

The simple forms cannot appear on their own: they have to be completed either by a prepositional phrase (*de* + noun) or by a relative clause:

le livre de mon frère = *celui de mon frère*
le livre qui est à mon frère = *celui qui est à mon frère*

but this is an area of syntactic uncertainty (see 2.4.2.1*ii*).

Ce may be either unstressed (which is the norm) or stressed:

c'est moi qui l'ai fait (unstressed)
sur ce, je m'en vais (stressed)

Note: In synchronic terms the demonstrative pronouns are the result of two sets of substitutions: the first at the level of the determiner, the second at the level of the noun:

First	*Le* +	noun *qui est ici/là*	⟶	*ce* + noun + *ci/là*
substitution:	(*le*	*livre qui est ici/là*	⟶	*ce* *livre-ci/là*)

Second	*Ce* +	noun + *ci/là*	⟶	*ce* + pronoun + *ci/là*
substitution:	(*ce*	*livre-ci/là˙*	⟶	*ce* *lui-ci/là*
			=	*celui-ci/là*)

The so-called 'simple forms' are in fact elliptical or incomplete.

2.4   Syntactic functions

2.4.1   *The compound or 'complete' forms*
These may function as subject, object (indirect or direct) or attribute, e.g.

celui-ci/celle-ci/ceci ⎫		
celui-là/celle-là/cela ⎬ *est à moi*	(= subject)
c'est ⎰ *celui-ci/celle-ci/ceci*	(= attribute)
⎱ *celui-là/celle-là/cela*	
je veux ⎰ *celui-ci/celle-ci/ceci*	(= object)
⎱ *celui-là/celle-là/cela*	
je m'adresse à ⎰ *celui-ci/celle-ci*	(= indirect object (animate))
⎱ *celui-là/celle-là*	
je m'intéresse à cela	(= indirect object (inanimate))

2.4.2   *The simple or 'incomplete' forms*
2.4.2.1   *'Celui'/'celle'/'ceux'/'celles'*
(i) These too may function as subject, object or attribute; but because these forms are incomplete, their use implies specific kinds of sentence structure which will serve to fill the gap left by the absence of *-ci* or *-là*. This gap may be filled by a relative clause or by a prepositional phrase, usually introduced by the preposition *de*, e.g. *celui qui l'a fait doit être très habile; j'ai emprunté celui de mon frère.*

This gap may in legal and administrative texts be completed by a participial clause, e.g. *tous ceux désirant se plaindre sont priés de s'adresser aux bureaux compétents.*
(ii) There is a tendency in contemporary French to multiply the number of cases in which *celui* is completed by a past participle, which is not really acceptable in prescriptive terms,[14] e.g.

*j'aime ce tableau, mais je n'aime pas celui exposé dans la grande salle

the 'correct' form being:

j'aime ce tableau, mais je n'aime pas celui qui est dans la grande salle

Since *de* indicating possession is often replaced by *à* (see Ch. 13), there is a tendency, particularly in rural areas, to say **celui à* instead of *celui de,* e.g. *mon tracteur est en panne; *j'ai pris celui à Paul,* instead of *j'ai pris celui de Paul.*

2.4.2.2 *The neuter pronoun 'ce' ('c'' before a vowel)*
(i) Just like the other incomplete or simple forms of the demonstrative pronouns, this may be completed by a relative clause:

> *ce qui fait le malheur des uns fait le bonheur des autres* (subject)
> *je n'aime pas ce que tu me dis* (object)
> *je vais me plaindre de ce que vous faites* (indirect object)

(ii) *Ce* may also appear in the construction *ce. . . que,* in which *que* is a subordinating conjunction: *que* may sometimes be replaced by *comme, quand* or *si*:

> *ce* + noun/pronoun + *que,* e.g.
> *c'est une nécessité pour les infirmes que le téléphone*
> (This construction is emphatic.)
>
> *ce* + infinitive + *que,* e.g.
> *c'est une vraie joie au printemps (que) de manger des fraises*
> *(Que* is often left out in present-day French.)
>
> *ce* + subordinate clause + *que/si,* e.g.
> *c'est vrai qu'il ne nous aime pas*
> *c'est écœurant comme il mange*
> *c'est dommage si vous manquez cette sortie*

These all belong to spoken French rather than to formal written French. In all of these cases one is dealing with emphatic constructions, emphasis being achieved by making the comment (*vrai, écœurant, dommage, nécessité*) into a main clause.
(iii) *Ce* may also appear in the construction *c'est. . . qui/c'est. . . que.* (This kind of construction is sometimes called *un gallicisme,* in the sense that it appeared during the development from Vulgar Latin into French but did not have an equivalent form in Latin.) This construction closely parallels the English expression 'it is . . . that' and 'it is . . . who':

> *c'est de lui que je parle* ('it is of him that I speak' – but today we are much more likely to say, 'I am talking about him', whereas the French phrase above remains quite normal)
> *c'est son attitude qui me plaît* ('it's his attitude that I like')
> *c'est qu'il ne me plaît pas du tout* ('I really don't like him at all')

This is an extremely frequently used form in both the written and spoken language. In these cases the *ce* or *c'* is used cataphorically (to refer forwards).
(iv) *Ce* or *c'* may be used on its own with the verb *être* (or *pouvoir être* or *devoir être*):

> *c'est un homme très habile* (i.e. *la personne dont nous parlons)*
> *c'est vrai, ça* (i.e. *ce que vous dites)*

In this case it is anaphoric (i.e. it refers backwards).
(v) *Ce* or *c'* may be used on its own when it is used exophorically (i.e. to refer to somebody or something outside the purely verbal situational context, e.g. *c'est moi; c'est Jean: c'est Monsieur Dupont.*

2.4.2.3 *Agreement in number when 'ce'/'c'' is the subject*
(i) In Old French *ce* was the attribute of the subject and not the subject, e.g.

ce suis-je	*ce sommes-nous*
ce es-tu	*ce estes-vous*
ce est il/ele	*ce sont-ils/eles*

(*Ele/eles* were the Old French orthographic forms of *elle/elles.* No hyphens were used in Old French in these constructions.)

Little by little, *ce* came to be seen as the subject; the pronoun subject became the pronoun complement, and the verb agreed with *ce/c'*, except in the 3rd person plural:

c'est moi	*c'est nous*
c'est toi	*c'est vous*
c'est lui/elle	*ce sont eux/elles*

The only exception to the change in verb agreement is the 3rd person plural.

(ii) In modern French this seems to be an area of uncertainty. Normal practice appears to indicate that, where there is a 3rd person plural direct object, the plural of the verb will be used, at least in the written language (i.e the rule described in *(i)* is followed), e.g. *ce sont les gens qui ont volé notre voiture*; but when there are two coordinated direct objects, matters are more complex:

in the case of two singular nouns, the singular form of the verb is acceptable, e.g. *c'était la fille et le fils de nos voisins*

in the case in which a singular noun is followed by a plural noun, the singular is possible, e.g. *c'est la fille de Mme Leblanc et ses deux enfants*

in the case in which a plural noun is followed by a singular noun, the plural is the norm, e.g. *ce sont les cousines de Mme Leblanc et sa fille Jeanne*

2.4.2.4   *'C'est' v. 'il est'*

(i) Where *il* is personal, one has the choice between *il est* + *adjective* or *c'est* + determiner + noun (see 1.4.1.3), e.g.

il est professeur[15]*/c'est un professeur*
il est gentil/c'est un gentil garçon

(ii) Where il is impersonal, the use of *il est* + adjective is cataphoric, i.e. refers forwards, e.g.

il est vrai qu'il est riche (presentation of new information)

whereas *c'est* + adjective is anaphoric, i.e. refers backwards, e.g.

c'est vrai qu'il est riche (repetition of information)

In very narrow prescriptive terms there is no choice in this case between *c'est* and *il est:* one or the other will be judged correct, depending on the context. But in everyday spoken French *c'est* has nearly entirely displaced the impersonal *il est,* and the same applies to most written French.

Note: Traditional grammars usually state the prescriptive rules governing the use of the impersonal *il est* in the following terms:

Il est is used instead of *c'est* when followed by:

an adjective indicating national or regional origin, e.g.
il est lillois; il est angevin; il est Anglais
an attribute indicating trade or profession used without an article, e.g.
il est médecin; elle est couturière

an adjective which refers to a following phrase (often an infinitive) introduced by *de* or *que*, e.g.
il est difficile de dire cela (but *c'est facile à dire*); *il est impossible que nous soyons de retour ce soir.*

Il est is also used in the following cases:

when talking of time, e.g.
quelle heure est-il? il est midi

when *il est* could be replaced by *il y a*, e.g.
il est peu de gens qui croient aux fées (This is particularly frequent in the past

tense, as in *il était une fois. . .* (a fossilized expression corresponding to 'once upon a time').

All of these rules are however summarized in *(i)* and *(ii)* above.

2.5 Semantics of the demonstrative pronouns

2.5.1 *The incomplete or simple forms*

It has been seen that these are syntactically — and therefore semantically — dependent on the elements which complete them.

2.5.2 *The complete or compound personal forms*

(i) The meaning of these forms is reasonably clear if the adverbial particles *-ci* and *-là* are indicators of place, e.g.

> *ne prenez pas celles-ci* (= *qui sont ici*) *mais plutôt celles-là* (*qui sont là, plus loin*)

NOTE: The adverbs *là* and *ici* have, however, lost some of their meaning as specific indicators of place; in particular, *là* seems to be used in a number of contexts in which one would expect *ici*, e.g. (an adult speaking to a child):

> *viens ici, à côté de moi!*
> *viens là, à côté de moi!*

This is probably due to the fact that *là* is far less precise than *ici*. This also explains why there is a greater sense of urgency associated with *ici*. One could thus contrast *viens ici que je te donne une paire de claques!* with *viens là que je te donne un bonbon!*

As a result, French speakers of English frequently use 'there' for 'here'.

(ii) The concept of place was extended in the past to include other types of relationships such as distance in terms of words written on a page:

> *Dans une ménagerie*
> *De volatiles remplie*
> *Vivaient le Cygne et l'Oison;*
> *Celui-là destiné pour les regards du maître;*
> *Celui-ci pour son goût*   (La Fontaine, *Fables*).

In this case *celui-là* corresponds to 'the former' (or furthest) and *celui-ci* to 'the latter' (or nearest). But these terms may only be used in this way in the context of a single sentence, and to refer to the first and second elements of a coordinated structure. One cannot use the term *celui-là* to refer back any further than that, whereas with the English 'the former' one can. This is the source of many mistakes where students are concerned. Even in the narrow context of the sentence, *celui-ci* and *celui-là* appear to be used but very infrequently.

The equivalents of 'the former' and 'the latter' are not, therefore, the demonstrative pronouns, but rather expressions such as *le dernier* and numerals:

> 'I prefer the former alternative to the latter' = *je préfère la première alternative à la dernière*
> 'the former's victory over the latter' = *la victoire du premier sur le dernier* (see *Harrap's Standard French-English Dictionary*)

(iii) This concept of place and distance was also extended to cover psychological distance, hence the pejorative connotation attached to *celui-* (*celle-*) *là* used disjunctively e.g. *oui, je le connais, celui-là, c'est un vaurien.*

2.5.3 *The complete or compound neuter demonstrative pronouns*

(i) Ceci and *cela*, although generally similar in significance to their cognates *celui-ci* and *celui-là*, tend to indicate generalities and things not already named or possibly difficult to name, or to refer to a proposition already stated or understood, as in *qu'à cela ne tienne* (= *si cela ne tient qu'à ça*); *une histoire de fantômes, cela te fait peur?; tout ceci n'est qu'un fatras pour nous en imposer; qu'est-ce que c'est que cela (ceci)?*

Ceci and *cela* never refer to persons.

(ii) Ça is a shortened form of *cela* which has, since the seventeenth century, gradually become ever more accepted as normal usage in the spoken language. There are still people, however, for whom *ça* remains a vulgarism.[16]

Although *ça* is more or less accepted in the spoken language, it remains stylistically unacceptable in the written language, except when reporting direct speech.

(iii) Ça usually simply replaces *cela*, as in *comment ça va?* or *est-ce que ça vous plaît?*

Ça may also be used instead of personal pronouns (see 1.4.1.5). It is often used in this case in disjunctive constructions to express emphasis:

> *les enfants, ça mange toujours*

In this case *ça* refers to children globally and condescendingly.

> *la voiture, ça coute beaucoup pour l'entretien*

In this case the use of *ça* is strongly pejorative (the car, in this case, is seen as the sum of its parts, all of which are presumably costly). Generally speaking, *ça* used for a noun in the singular may be either pejorative or affectionate, as in *ça va?*

3 Possessive pronouns

3.1 General considerations

(i) Possessive pronouns are pronouns which have two coreferents: the object or person or concept referred to (or for which the possessive pronoun 'stands') and the possessor of the said object, person or concept.

(ii) They resemble the personal pronouns in that they indicate person as the personal pronoun does; but the system is considerably simpler, since it merely has personal forms and no impersonal ones, nor do the possessive pronouns vary in form for case.

(iii) They are similar to the demonstrative pronouns (and different from personal pronouns) in that they stand for a noun and not a noun phrase. Compare:

> *Jean est arrivé. Il est à la cuisine* (*il = Jean*)
> *Je ne veux pas de cette tasse; elle est ébréchée. Prends celle-là à la place* (*cella-là* is a
>   different cup)

> *Ne prends pas cette tasse: elle est ébréchée. Prends la mienne à la place* (*la mienne* is a
>   different cup)

In the case of the demonstrative pronoun the distinction between the two items referred to is made spatially; in the case of the possessive pronoun this distinction is made by way of the possessor. Where the personal pronoun is concerned, there is identity between the pronoun and its coreferent.

3.2 Morphology

The forms of the possessive pronouns are precisely those of the stressed possessive adjective (see Ch. 2), with the addition of a preceding definite article which forms an integral part of the form:

	Possessive adjective (stressed form)	Possessive pronoun
Singular:		
1st person	*mien(ne)(s)*	*le mien, la mienne, les mien(ne)s*
2nd	*tien(ne)(s)*	*le tien, la tienne, les tien(ne)s*
3rd	*sien(ne)(s)*	*le sien, la sienne, les sien(ne)s*
Plural:		
1st	*nôtre(s)*	*le nôtre, la nôtre, les nôtres*
2nd	*vôtres(s)*	*le vôtre, la vôtre, les vôtres*
3rd	*leur(s)*	*le leur, la leur, les leurs*

(i) It will be seen from the table that the possessive pronoun is marked for number in all persons, both by changes in the definite article and by addition of final *-s*. Gender is marked in all persons, both singular and plural, by change of definite article; but it is only in the singular that gender is marked also by change in the ending of the possessive itself.

(ii) The possessive pronoun carries a heavy load of information, since it has two coreferents. As such it is less likely to be used than the other pronouns.

(iii) The possessive, like the demonstrative, is the result of two substitutions:

First substitution:	*le* + noun + *de* + noun ⟶ possessive adjective + noun
	(le livre de Pierre son livre)

Second substitution:	possessive adjective + noun ⟶ possessive pronoun
	(son livre ⟶ le sien)

3.3 Functions

Semantically the possessive pronoun attributes the possession of somebody or something — the existence of which has already been made obvious, verbally or otherwise — to somebody specific. Possessive pronouns do not normally attribute possession to inanimate objects.

Syntactically, possessive pronouns can fulfil any of the functions of the noun: subject (*le mien est plus beau que les autres; prenons ta voiture, la nôtre est en panne*); direct object (*ma voiture est en panne, prenons la vôtre; as-tu de l'argent? j'ai dépensé le mien*); indirect object (*ton cheval n'a plus faim, donne cette avoine au mien; on a volé mon portefeuille, prenez garde au vôtre*); and attribute (*c'est le mien*).

3.4 Lexicalization

In certain usages possessive pronouns have acquired status as nouns with specific meaning:

être des nôtres = 'to be one of us, on our side, to belong to our gang', etc.
les mien/les tiens/les siens = 'my/your/his/her near family'
*du mien/du tien/*etc., in certain contexts, e.g. *il y a mis du sien* = 'he has put a lot into it'

3.5 Contrastive problems

English students of French tend to find some difficulty in the early stages, due to the fact that English possessive pronouns are invariable for gender, except for the 3rd person singular ('his', 'hers'). This change, however, follows the gender of the possessor, whereas in French the pronoun agrees in gender and number with that which is possessed:

	Possessive pronoun		Possessive pronoun
his dog	his	*son chien*	*le sien*
her dog	hers	*son chien*	*le sien*
his mother	his	*sa mère*	*la sienne*
her mother	hers	*sa mère*	*la sienne*
his dogs	his	*ses chiens*	*les siens*
your aunts	yours	*tes* ⎡ *tantes*	*les tiennes*
		vos ⎣	*les vôtres*
your garden	yours	*ton* ⎡ *jardin*	*le tien*
		votre ⎣	*le vôtre*
my shirts	mine	*mes chemises*	*les miennes*
our dreams	ours	*nos rêves*	*les nôtres*
our friends	ours	*nos ami(e)s*	*les nôtres*

See 1.4.5.1*v* for the compulsory use of the possessive pronoun in place of *en*.

4   The 'indefinite pronouns'

4.1   General considerations

Grammarians have listed under this category some very different kinds of words and constructions, and their definitions of 'indefinite pronouns' have often been contradictory, in that they often classify under this heading pronominalized forms which are not indefinite in any way.

There are two types of construction which have been put under this heading:
(i) words used as nouns from a functional point of view which are not however preceded by a determiner, or which are preceded by an indefinite determiner:

> *je ne vois rien* (no determiner, although a determiner may be used in other contexts such as in *un rien l'amuse*, in which *rien* no longer functions as an indefinite pronoun but as an ordinary noun)

or

> *quelqu'un est venu me réparer la chaudière* (indefinite pronoun made up of *un*, used nominally, and *quelque*, which is an indefinite adjective functioning as a determiner − see 4.2.1)

This category also includes relative pronouns not preceded by an antecedent as in *qui dort dîne* (= *n'importe quelle personne* or *toute personne*).
(ii) words or constructions which function as indefinite pronouns, but which are in reality elliptical constructions from which a noun is missing. One may distinguish two cases, depending on whether or not the missing noun is retrievable from the verbal context.

Examples in which the missing noun is not retrievable from the verbal context are:

> *certains disent que . . .* (= *certaines personnes*)
> *beaucoup sont arrivés en retard* (= *beaucoup de personnes*)

See 4.2.2.1.

Examples in which the missing noun is retrievable from the verbal context are:

> − *Regarde mon lave-vaisselle; il est tout neuf!*
> − *Tiens! J'ai le même (= lave-vaisselle)*

– *Comme ces pêches sont belles!*
– *Oui, donne-m'en une (= de ces pêches)*

See 4.2.2.2.

4.2 Words classed as indefinite pronouns

4.2.1 *The indefinite nouns*

These are indefinite from a syntactical point of view, since they are either not preceded by a determiner *(i)* or are preceded by an indefinite determiner *(ii)*. Sometimes it is a whole clause which functions as an indefinite pronoun *(iv)*.
(i) The noun is not preceded by a determiner in the case of *rien* and *personne*.
   In the case of *rien* there is a shift in its basic meaning of 'zero quantity' to 'very small quantity', depending on whether the determiner is absent or present:

je ne fais rien ('I am not doing anything')
un rien la contrarie ('the slightest thing annoys her')

In the case of *personne* the shift is from 'nobody' to 'somebody':

personne n'est venu ('nobody came')
une personne est venue ('somebody came')

(ii) In cases where the noun is preceded by an indefinite determiner, the determiner employed is *quelque*: *quelqu'un/quelqu'une*; *quelques-uns/quelques-unes*. Of these four forms, all are in frequent use except *quelqu'une*, which is no longer used (*quelqu'une de mes amies* becomes *une de mes amies*).
(iii) Relative pronouns may function as indefinite pronouns.   This happens when the relative pronoun does not have an antecedent, as in *qui dort dîne*, in which case *qui* refers to 'anybody' or 'he who . . .'. There is also one indefinite relative pronoun in its own right – *quiconque*, as in *quiconque m'aime me suive*.
(iv) A whole clause may function as an indefinite pronoun in the case of 'fossilized' clauses such as *je ne sais qui, je ne sais quoi* and *n'importe qui, n'importe quoi*: *il dit n'importe quoi*; *c'est le je ne sais quoi de cette affaire qui m'intéresse*. *N'importe qui/quoi* is not preceded by a determiner, whereas *je ne sais qui/quoi* is.

4.2.2 *Items functioning as indefinite pronouns which are in reality elliptical constructions*

4.2.2.1 *Adjectival and adverbial determiners functioning as indefinite pronouns*   In this case the missing noun is not usually directly retrievable from the verbal context; the missing noun will be a noun such as *gens, personnes* or *hommes*, i.e. it will refer to people in general. The absence of these nouns leaves either adverbs of quantity, determiners + adjectives, or certain determiners on their own, functioning as the noun phrase (see 4.1*ii*):

peu/plusieurs/beaucoup sont venus (adverbs of quantity)
ce sont toujours les mêmes qui se dévouent (article + adjective)
certains/tous disent que . . . (determiners)

4.2.2.2 *Numerals, or expressions based on numerals, or nominalized adjectives, functioning as indefinite pronouns*   In this case the missing noun is usually directly retrievable from the verbal context:
(i) One may use the pronominalized forms of the cardinal numerals, e.g.

les deux étaient là (= *les deux frères*)
deux étaient là (= *deux des frères*)

If the cardinal numeral is preceded by a definite determiner, one is referring to the total number of items in that set; if no determiner is used, one is referring to only part of the set considered. In English the determiner used in the first case would be 'all', e.g. *ma chatte a eu cinq petits, mais les cinq sont morts* ('all five').

Ordinals may also be used in this manner, e.g. *le premier film est de Hitchcock, le deuxième d'un inconnu.*

(ii) There are also indefinite pronouns based on *un*: *un, l'un/l'autre, chacun* and *aucun*. In all of these cases the pronoun has in fact a coreferent which is indefinite in the case of *un* and *chacun* and definite in the case of *l'un/l'autre* and *aucun*.

Un is a numeral used as an indefinite pronoun, e.g.

Quelles belles pêches! Donne-m'en une (= *une pêche*)

Un may become *l'un* without the *l'* being an article: it is simply there to avoid having several vowels in a row in phrases such as *si l'un de vous.* . . .

L'un . . . *l'autre* and *les uns* . . . *les autres* may express opposition, reciprocity or indefinite reference:

l'un part, l'autre reste (opposition)
ils se sont tués l'un l'autre en duel (reciprocity)
*quelques personnes attendaient, assises sur un banc; l'une tricotait, l'autre lisait,
    tandis qu'une troisième dormait* (indefinite reference)

Chacun is used to express a general indefinite singular (*que chacun pense ce qu'il veut*) or to refer to a specific coreferent (*nos invités sont passés à table; donne à chacun une serviette*).

Aucun is the negative form of *chacun: j'attends des invités mais aucun n'est encore arrivé.*

Aucun also used to have the positive meaning of *quelque*:

Est-il aucun moment (= *quelque moment*)
Qui vous puisse assurer d'un second seulement (La Fontaine, *Fables*)

It still retains this meaning in its plural form, e.g. *d'aucuns préfèrent Corneille à Racine* (= *quelques personnes*). But *d'aucuns* is archaic nowadays.

(iv) Any determiner + adjective may be used on its own as a nominal phrase if the missing noun is retrievable within the verbal context, e.g. *donne-moi le grand* (*tableau, drap,* . . .); *choisis le plus beau; c'est le plus riche.*

4.3　Gender and number of certain indefinite nouns and pronouns

4.3.1　*Gender*

Quelque chose is a set expression, which is why, despite the feminine gender of *chose* as a noun, it is treated as masculine, e.g. *donne-moi un petit quelque chose.* (This has not always been the case: in Middle French one could still say *quelque chose bonne.*)

Personne, although originally a feminine noun, is also treated as masculine in its pronominal form: *personne ici n'est assez grand pour l'atteindre.*

Other indefinite pronouns, especially those ending in *-un*, e.g. *aucun, chacun, l'un*, but also *nul, tout, certain*, agree in gender with the nouns to which they refer, unless the pronoun has no coreferent, in which case it is used in its masculine form.

*parmi les dames du palais certaines haïssaient la duchesse
pas une ne l'avait vu entrer dans le sérail
aucune ne voulait devenir sa femme*

but:

> *nul n'est tenu à l'impossible*
> *chacun est responsable de ses propres fautes*

4.3.2 *Number*

The following are the only indefinite forms to be used as plurals:
(i) D'aucuns (archaic), *d'autres, certains, les uns . . . les autres, la plupart, plusieurs, quelques-uns, quelques autres, les mêmes, tels, tous.*
(ii) Plusieurs and *la plupart* are treated as plural in terms of agreement of adjectives and used with plural verbs, except for *la plupart* when used alone as subject, without any plural reference. In that case it may have either a singular or a plural verb:

> *plusieurs y sont allés avant nous*
> *voici l'équipe opposante, dont la plupart ont très mauvaise mine*
> *je pensais avoir trop de travail, mais finalement la plupart [du travail] a été fait par un collègue*

Agreement with *la plupart* is therefore with its complement. Where there is no complement, the plural is the norm (*la plupart s'en vont*) and the singular is literary in style (*la plupart s'en va*: see the Micro-Robert dictionary).

4.4 Syntactic peculiarities: the use of the indefinite pronouns and nouns in relation to the negative adverb 'ne'

(i) Aucun, nul, personne, rien all imply negation and are all accompanied by *ne*, whatever their function:

> *personne ne veut le faire*
> *nul ne le connaît*

(ii) Certain archaisms also come into this category.
Aucun had, in Old and Middle French, a positive meaning, being synonymous with *quelqu'un*. This positive meaning survives in its plural forms *aucuns* and *d'aucuns*, which are used without the *ne*, e.g. *d'aucuns* (= *certains*) *le croient immortel*.
Personne may sometimes be used positively, in which case it is used without the *ne*:

> *Y a-t-il personne d'assez hardi?* (quoted by Grevisse, *Le Bon usage)*

4.5 Stylistic choices available

One may want to make the following kind of choice:

> *on arrive* (indefinite personal pronoun, = *je* or *nous*; informal)
> *il arrive* ('somebody is coming (the person is known to me)')
> *quelqu'un arrive* (indefinite pronoun — 'somebody is coming (but I do not know who it is)')

> *il y en a qui disent que* . . . (very informal)
> *ils disent que* . . . (relatively informal)
> *certains disent que* . . . (formal)

> *on a trafiqué ce moteur* (indefinite personal pronoun = 'I do not know the culprit')
> *quelqu'un a trafiqué ce moteur* (more formal than *on*)
> *certains d'entre vous ont trafiqué ce moteur* (= 'I could name them if I chose')

4.6   Contrastive problems

(i) When an 'indefinite pronoun' is used before an adjective, the preposition *de* has to be added between the two: it is the equivalent, in this case, of the relative construction *qui est* or *qui soit*:

> *il n'y a rien de nouveau* (= *il n'y a rien qui soit nouveau*)
> *y a-t-il quelqu'un de blessé?* (= *y a-t-il quelqu'un qui soit blessé?*)

In English no such preposition is needed:

> 'there is nothing new' ('there is nothing which is new')
> 'is there anyone hurt?' ('is there anyone who is hurt?')

(ii) The 'indefinite pronouns' which are made up of fossilized clauses function in exactly the same way as English 'indefinite pronouns':

> *n'importe qui saurait le faire* ('anyone could do it')
> *il ferait n'importe quoi pour lui faire plaisir* ('he would do anything to please him/her')

Notes

1 A *referent* is an item which refers to another lexical item (the *coreferent*).
2 For *on*, see 1.2.6.
3 For *soi*, see 1.2.7.
4 In Classical French it was possible to place the pronoun object before the modal or auxilliary verb. Thus Corneille, in *Horace*, first wrote:

> *Je la dois/attaquer,/mais tu la dois/défendre* (3/3/4/3 syllables)

which he then changed to:

> *Je la dois/attaquer,/mais tu dois/la défendre* (3/3/3/4)

for reasons of rhythm. This stylistic convention was followed up to the mid-nineteenth century in certain literary works, e.g.

> *Je commençai par m'en aller excuser* (de Nerval)

Also in Classical French the unstressed pronoun functioning as direct object was often omitted, e.g. *il m'a donné le livre pour elle et je lui ai confié* (= *je le lui ai confié*).
5 For further comments on the use of pronoun complements with *faire*, see Harmer, *Uncertainties of French grammar*, 200 – 228.
6 According to S. Lamothe, *t'as vu* instead of *tu as vu* is comparable to 'dropping one's aitches' in English.
7 There is one case, however, in which the pronoun subject may be separated from the verb by something other than a pronoun object: this is the now ossified expression used only in legal and administrative texts, and in testimonials: *je, soussigné, atteste que. . . .* In this case *je* is stressed.
8 But *soi* may be used with *cela* (inanimate) in the fossilized expression *cela va de soi* (or *ça va de soi* in informal spoken French).
9 Age seems to be an all-important factor in this respect: many of the older generation in university teaching posts say *vous* to all their colleagues. Thus a colleague writes, 'Je ne tutoie aucun de mes collègues et en appelle fort peu par leur prénom' (1981). The same does not apply to the younger generation.
10 'Dans la "gentry" française, il est toujours "de bon ton" de se vouvoyer entre mari et femme. Certains parents, même de la bourgeoisie, demandent le "vous" à leurs enfants. Dans ma famille, c'est partagé: moitié-moitié' (S. Lamothe, 1981).

The present author, however, not belonging to 'the gentry', has encountered very few such cases. (*AJ*)

11 Some grammarians feel that Grevisse is not being prescriptive enough in accepting Sagan's sentence as 'correct'.

12 Contextual synonyms (or near-synonyms) are words which may be synonymous within one context but not necessarily within another; this applies in particular to superordinates such as 'flowers', for example, which could become, in a specific context, synonymous for a particular type of flower being spoken about (e.g. 'roses').

13 'Complementary distribution' is the term used to describe the situation where two variants are mutually exclusive in a particular environment. Members of a declension are therefore in complementary distribution.

14 S. Lamothe comments: 'Pour la tournure "celui + participe passé", je me bats avec mes étudiants qui l'emploient tout le temps' (1981).

15 *Professeur* is used to refer to a quality, since it is not preceded by an article; it is used adjectivally.

16 S. Lamothe writes: '*Ça* reste interdit en langage parlé d'un certain niveau. Dans un salon, ou entre professeurs, ce serait mal vu.' For others, the non-use of *ça* would appear synonymous with conservatism.

Part II

The verbal phrase: tense, aspect, mood and voice

0   Introduction

This is one of the most difficult areas of the French language, since both the concepts and the terminologies involved are confusing. The case of tense, which expresses both time and aspect, is examined in section 1, the case of mood in section 2, the case of voice in section 3, and the problem of how to label French tenses in section 4.

1   Tense

1.1   One form but two concepts: time and aspect

The word 'tense' has traditionally covered both what could be termed 'time' − which is a familiar concept − and what is now called 'aspect', which is less so.[1] In other words, tense may express both time and aspect.
Compare:

> *hier je marchais dans la rue, quand tout à coup. . . .*
> *hier j'ai marché toute la journée*

Both sentences refer to the same time, 'yesterday', but they differ in the way they describe the action: in the first case the action is seen as ongoing, whereas in the second case the action is seen as completed. These two past tenses differ in terms of aspect but not in terms of time. Aspect may therefore be said to refer not so much to the location of the action in time, but to the stage reached by the action or to its duration. In English there are two aspects which are expressed morphologically − the perfect (action completed):

> I have read that book (present)
> I had read that book (past)

and the progressive:

> I am reading that book (present)
> I was reading that book (past)

In French, time and tense are combined in the various tense forms, but in ways which are not always easy to analyse, given that time and aspect are fused, whereas in English they are clearly defined specific morphological forms.

1.2   Dating the action or process: the various possible time (or 'temporal') situations

(i) Time is a universal concept involving the past, the present and the future. But it is a nonlinguistic concept. What is meant by tense is the correspondence between specific linguistic forms and time as a universal concept. Although some languages are considered to be tenseless, in that they do not have specific verbal forms to translate the idea of time, no language is timeless: time will be expressed in other ways than through tenses. French however has a particularly rich tense system, since it has 7 tense

forms which may refer to the past. The difficulty is distinguishing between them. This has to be done on the grounds of aspect.

(ii) One can distinguish 'absolute time' and 'relative time'. Absolute time is defined in terms of the relationship existing between the process or action and the time of speaking or writing. Relative time is defined in terms of the time relationship existing between the action or process and another action or process. Absolute time includes therefore the basic concepts of present, past and future. Relative time means anteriority or posteriority. In other words, if the past and future are seen in relation to the present, they come under absolute time, but if they are seen to precede or follow some action situated at some point in time in the past or future, they come under relative time.

(iii) The following is a table of some of the correspondences existing between absolute and relative time and the French tenses (this table does not include all French tenses). In this table, AT stands for absolute time and RT for relative time. The names of the tenses used are in parenthesis. P is the point in time corresponding to the moment of speaking or writing.

	RT(1)	Acts or events anterior to Then: *quand il avait fini son repas* (pluperfect), *il allait se promener au jardin/dès qu'il eut fini son repas* (past anterior), *il alla se promener au jardin*
PAST	AT(2)	Then (e.g. *le 3 mars*) (not seen in relation to Now): *le 3 mars il est allé* (compound past)/*il alla* (past historic)/*il allait* (imperfect) *à Paris*
	RT(3)	Acts or events posterior to Then: *il lui dit qu'il la reverrait le lendemain* (conditional)
	RT(1)	Acts or events anterior to Now: *il était toujours gai* (imperfect), *mais maintenant il ne l'est plus/il a toujours été très gai . . .* (compound past)
PRESENT	AT(2)	Now: *je chante pour passer le temps* (present)
	RT(3)	Acts or events posterior to Now: *je finirai ce travail demain* (future)
	RT(1)	Acts or events anterior to Then: *j'aurai fini ce travail* (future anterior) *avant que tu ne reviennes*
FUTURE	AT(2)	Then (e.g. *lundi prochain*) (not seen in relation to Now): *je finirai ce travail lundi* (future)
	RT(3)	Acts or events posterior to Then: *après lundi je serai en vacances* (future)

We may note several points at this stage:

(1) Absolute time tends to be expressed by simple tenses and relative time tends to be expressed by compound tenses; there are however important exceptions to this general trend (i.e. the compound past and the conditional).

(2) Tenses referring to the past are far more numerous than those referring to the

future. Most problems will therefore be found in relation to the past.

(3)   There are sometimes several tenses per 'time slot', and the same tense may appear in several slots (i.e. compound past).

(4)   The time 'past' does not involve exactly the same tenses when it is seen in terms of absolute time and in terms of relative time (relative to Now): it does not include the past historic when it is seen to be a relative time.

1.3   Aspect

1.3.1   *The stage reached by the action*

(i) The action may be seen as beginning (inchoative aspect):

> *je commence à faire mes devoirs*
> *je me mets à faire mes devoirs*

This may be represented on the diagram by adding a kind of box in a dotted line which will represent the portion of the action under consideration:[2]

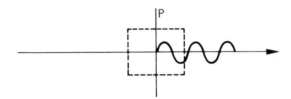

(ii) The action may be seen as finishing (the terminative aspect):

> *je finis de faire mes devoirs*

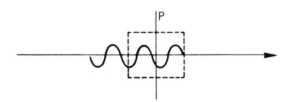

(iii) The action may be seen as midstream (in French *aspect sécant* resembles the imperfective):

> *je fais mes devoirs*

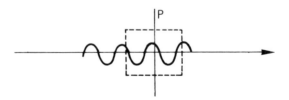

or

> *je faisais mes devoirs*

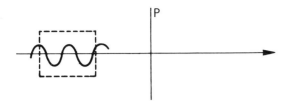

(iv) The action may be seen as progressing (the progressive) and the arrow in this diagram translates the idea of progression:

je suis en train de faire mes devoirs

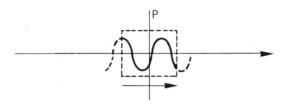

(v) The action may be seen as completed:

j'ai fait mes devoirs

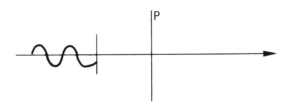

The vertical line indicates the insistence on the action being finished.
(vi) The action or process could also be seen in its totality, with no reference being made to its beginning, middle or end. The duration in this case does not matter since the action is seen as a whole, hence the diagram for:

je fis mes devoirs

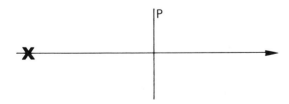

We see from this that aspect is expressed either by tense alone or by tenses backed up by 'auxiliaries' of aspect such as *commencer* or *finir*.

1.3.2   *Duration of the action*

The action may be seen as limited or not limited in time because of its meaning. Thus the length of time involved in *il ferme la porte* is by necessity extremely short. Other actions such as *il déjeune* may have a duration which may vary quite considerably, but without the action going on indefinitely. Other verbs, on the other hand, may express an action which may go on indefinitely as in *il lit sans arrêt* or in *la terre tourne*. These lexical aspects are called respectively the punctual, the noncontinuous and the continuous aspects.[3]

1.3.3   *The single action or repeated: the 'semelfactive' aspect and the iterative aspect*

A consequence of the point made in 1.3.1 is that if a verb with a noncontinuous meaning (the punctual being a special case of the noncontinuous) is used in a context in which a length of time is specified, the action will be seen not as one action but as an action which is repeated throughout that period:

   il mange tous les jours au restaurant

This is called the iterative aspect. But the following sentence is ambiguous, in that the context does not make clear whether the action described is an action repeated daily or one which takes place on one specific occasion:

   il mange au restaurant

In this case it is not clear whether one is dealing with the iterative aspect or what is called in French the 'semelfactive' aspect, by which one means that the action is seen to be one single action. This is a matter of context. Adverbials play a major role in this respect.

1.3.4   *The three ways of expressing aspect in French*

(i) Aspect may be expressed grammatically, i.e. by the tense forms. The action may be seen as midstream (*aspect sécant*), it may be seen as completed, it may be seen in its totality, and it may be omnitemporal; some tenses also imply speed of action.
(ii) Aspect may be expressed lexically: an action may be seen to be continuous, noncontinuous or punctual because of the intrinsic meaning of the verb which expresses it (*sortir* is punctual for example, whereas *rester* is continuous).
Auxiliaries of aspect are periphrastic constructions based on verbs which express aspect lexically (*commencer* and *finir* are auxiliaries of aspect).
(iii) Aspect may be expressed contextually: the iterative and the semelfactive are expressed by a combination of tense and context, i.e. the presence or absence of suitable adverbials.

2   Mood

2.1   The number of moods in French

Grammarians disagree on the number of moods which exist in French. Traditionally, they have stated that there were 4 personal moods, i.e. moods which inflect to some degree at least for person, and 3 impersonal moods, i.e. moods which do not inflect at all for person. The 4 personal moods would be the indicative, the subjunctive, the conditional and the imperative. The three impersonal moods would be the infinitive, the participle and the gerund.

   According to other grammarians there are only two personal moods: the indicative and the subjunctive, and two impersonal moods, the infinitive and the participle.

Seven moods are difficult to justify from a morphological point of view: the conditional is made up from indicative forms, the imperative is made up of a mixture of indicative and subjunctive forms, and the gerund is really a participle preceded by *en*. But 7 moods may be justified from a functional point of view: the conditional may function as a mood (this is the 'modal conditional' as against the 'temporal conditional'); the imperative differs syntactically from the moods it is based on; and the gerund differs in function from the participle to which it corresponds formally. It is the functional point of view which is adopted here, and 5 moods are identified: the indicative, the subjunctive, the imperative and the conditional, the 3 impersonal moods being regrouped under the heading 'nominal mood'.

2.2 The function of moods

Mood defines the attitude of the speaker or writer towards the action or state of affairs described.

2.2.1 *The personal moods*

All 4 personal moods are present in the following example:[4]

> *Apprenez-moi l'orthographe. . . . . Je suis*
> *amoureux d'une personne de qualité, et je souhaiterais*
> *que vous m'aidassiez à lui écrire quelque chose* (Molière, *Le Bourgeois Gentilhomme*)

(i) The indicative is the main mood, since one cannot do without it, whereas one could do without the others, at least up to a certain point. It is amodal, in that it does not express a particular attitude of the speaker or writer towards the action or state described. Being amodal, it is perfectly suited to the expression of time, which is its main role. Because of this it is said to be 'the mood of the action realized' (*l'action actualisée*) – which does not mean that the action takes place, merely that it is 'seen' or 'described' as if it were taking place.
(ii) The subjunctive, on the other hand, gives no clear idea of time; it is the mood of the amorphous, the action being seen merely as 'prospective' or 'retrospective'. It therefore shows the action as merely envisaged (either in the past or future) rather than as realized.
(iii) The conditional – when functioning as a mood and not as a tense – is the mood of the imaginary, an imaginary which may or may not turn out to be possible. It is often ambiguous in this respect.
(iv) The imperative is the mood for giving orders.

2.2.2 *The nominal mood: the infinitive, the participle and the gerund*

The term 'nominal mood' corresponds to the fact that these forms belong partly to the verbal system and partly to the nominal one. They are nominal in that, unlike verbs, they do not express person or time. The infinitive may function as a noun (e.g. *lire me fatigue les yeux*); the participle may function as an adjective (e.g. *un enfant souriant/une femme souriante, un enfant très aimé/une femme très aimée*); the gerund always expresses the progressive (e.g. *il travaille en chantant*); and the infinitive and participle may express either noncompletion or completion (e.g. *lire/avoir lu, chantant/ayant chanté*).

2.2.3 *The French modal system and the expression of time*

One finds in French the following gradation as far as time is concerned, from (1) the vague to (3) the most specific:[5]

(1) the nominal mood (not inflected for person or time; indicates aspect)
(2) the imperative, the subjunctive, the conditional (inflected for person, number and aspect, but only vaguely indicative of time)
(3) the indicative (clearly inflected for number and person; carrier of both time and aspect)

3   Voice

3.1   Definition

Voice is either a verb form or a particular syntactic construction indicating certain relationships between the subject, the object and the verb.

(i) Generally speaking, the active voice indicates that the subject carries out the action: the grammatical subject is the actor: *le chat attrape la souris.*

(ii) The passive voice indicates that the grammatical subject is the goal or sufferer: *la souris est attrapée par le chat.*

(iii) The pronominal voice indicates that an action is performed on the actor or for his own benefit: *le chat se lave* (which form is usually called the reflexive).

But in French it may take on other roles: it may be the equivalent of a passive construction: *le blé se vend bien cette année*; it may express reciprocity: *nous nous voyons souvent*; and it may refer to a situation in which there is no actor and no goal: *le Mont Blanc s'élève à 4.807 mètres.*

Some verbs only appear in a pronominal form (they are essentially i.e. lexically pronominal) in which case the constructions they appear in will be identical, except in form, to simple active constructions:

il se repent (= il regrette ses actions)

(The verb *se repentir* only exists in its pronominal form; there is no verb *repentir*.)

3.2   The expression of voice in French

Morphologically speaking there is only one voice in French: the active voice. The other two voices are obtained by adding *être* to the construction for the passive, and a reflexive pronoun in the case of the pronominal voice. It is therefore more accurate to speak in terms of passivization where the passive voice is concerned, and of pronominal forms where the pronominal voice is concerned.

4   The problem of labelling tenses

4.1   Defining the problem

There are two problems involved. Firstly, these labels sometimes differ in English and French: the 'perfect', for example, corresponds in French to *le passé composé*, the 'subjunctive past' corresponds to *l'imparfait du subjonctif*, whereas *le passé du subjonctif* corresponds in English to the 'perfect subjunctive'. The terminology is therefore very confusing when going from one language to the other. The second problem is of a different nature: the labels may be based either on form or on function. In most cases they are based on function, which is unfortunate, since each tense tends to have more than one function and these functions have sometimes changed through time, leaving the labels out of date. Ideally one would wish to change the whole system of labelling of tenses; a new system is, in fact, suggested in 4.4. But this new system has not been adopted in this book for pedagogical reasons, since it is felt it would be too confusing for readers used to the old terminology. One would hope, however, that such a terminology may be accepted one day.

4.2 Changing the labels

No attempt has been made to change those labels which − although not entirely satisfactory − are not misleading (see *(i)*). Where changes have been made, the new labels have been borrowed from French (see *(ii)*) where the French label has been felt to be reasonably accurate. An effort has been made to use the same labels for all the moods (see *(iii)*). Where no suitable label was available, a morphologically descriptive one has been coined (see *(iv)*).

(i) The following labels remain unchanged: the 'present' (e.g. *je parle*), the 'imperfect' (e.g. *je parlais*), the 'future' (e.g. *je parlerai*), the 'pluperfect' (e.g. *j'avais parlé*), and the 'past historic' (e.g. *je parlai*).

(ii) The following labels have been borrowed from French: the 'present perfect' has become the 'compound past'[6] (*le passe composé*), e.g. *j'ai parlé*; the 'past perfect' has become the 'past anterior' (*le passé antérieur*), e.g. *j'eus parlé* − this label being accurate in modern French, since it is nowadays only used in subordinate clauses. The 'future perfect' has become the 'future anterior' (*le futur antérieur*), e.g. *j'aurai parlé*, this label being an accurate one.

(iii) An effort has been made to keep the names of the tenses the same in the other moods, hence the term 'subjunctive compound past' (or *le passe composé du subjonctif* − which term is not normally used in French), e.g. *que j'aie parlé*; the 'subjunctive imperfect' (*l'imparfait du subjonctif* which term does exist in French), e.g. *que je parlasse*.

(iv) We shall use the terms 'double compound past' (*passé surcomposé*), e.g. *j'ai eu parlé*, 'compound pluperfect', e.g. *j'avais eu parlé*, double compound future, e.g. *j'aurai eu parlé*, 'double compound conditional' e.g. *j'aurais eu parlé* and 'double compound past subjunctive', e.g. *que j'aie eu parlé*. (Only the double compound past is used with any frequency.) See 4.3*i* Note.

Similarly we shall use the labels 'compound' and 'double compound' infinitive for *avoir parlé* and *avoir eu parlé*; and the labels 'compound participle' and 'double compound participle' for *ayant parlé* and *ayant eu parlé*.

4.3 Labels used in this grammar

(i) We shall use as example the verb *finir*, a verb belonging to the 2nd conjugation (*parler*, a verb of the 1st conjugation, having been used in 4.2)

present/compound past/double compound past, e.g.
   je finis/j'ai fini/j'ai eu fini
imperfect/pluperfect/compound pluperfect, e.g.
   je finissais/j'avais fini/j'avais eu fini
past historic/past anterior, e.g.
   je finis/j'eus fini
future/future anterior/double compound future, e.g.
   je finirai/j'aurai fini/j'aurai eu fini
present conditional/compound or 'past' conditional/double compound conditional, e.g.
   je finirais/j'aurais fini/j'aurais eu fini
present subjunctive/compound past subjunctive/double compound past subjunctive, e.g.
   que je finisse/que j'aie fini/que j'aie eu fini
imperfect subjunctive/pluperfect subjunctive, e.g.
   que je finisse/que j'eusse fini
simple infinitive/compound infinitive/double compound infinitive, e.g.
   finir/avoir fini/avoir eu fini

present participle/past participle/compound participle/double compound participle, e.g.

   finissant/fini/ayant fini/ayant eu fini
gerund, e.g.
   en finissant

Note: Some grammarians use the term 'double compound form' for all the double compound tenses: 'double compound past', but also 'double compound pluperfect' and 'double compound future anterior'. This seems tautologous. Grevisse (*Le Bon usage*) describes tenses as *simples, composés* and *surcomposés*, but does not give the compound pluperfect, the double compound future or the double compound conditional separate names: he simply places the compound and the double compound forms under the same heading (i.e. as different forms of the pluperfect, future anterior or compound conditional), which is logical from a functional point of view.

(ii) We shall use the term 'conditional' to refer to the conditional forms, 'modal conditional' to refer to its modal use (e.g. *si j'étais riche, j'achèterais un bateau*), and 'temporal conditional' to refer to its temporal use, i.e. to refer to the future seen from the past (e.g. *je savais qu'il viendrait.*) Some French grammarians use the expression *la forme en − rais* to refer to the 'temporal conditional'.

4.4   An ideal terminology

An ideal terminology, from a theoretical point of view, would be one which was entirely formal.

There would be four simple tenses: the present, the imperfect, the future, the past historic (these are unchanged)

There would be four compound forms: the compound present, the compound imperfect, the compound future, and the compound past historic.

There would be three double compound forms: the double compound present, the double compound imperfect, the double compound future.

This terminology would apply to both the indicative and the subjunctive.

In the conditional, there would be three labels: a simple conditional, a compound conditional and a double compound conditional. Such a terminology has not been adopted here for pedagogical reasons.

Notes

1 Aspect appears in most French grammars in current use today. One of the most famous of these, Bonnard's *Grammaire française des lycées et collèges*, explained the concept as early as 1950. But it was G. Guillaume who developed the concept for French early on in the century. Grevisse, however, in *Le Bon usage*, dismisses this concept as not being relevant to French (559). In this he constitutes an exception.
2 This convention is borrowed from Bonnard's *Grammaire française des lycées et collèges*. Bonnard writes, '*ces graphiques portent un rectangle en pointillé gras qui limite, sur la ligne du temps, la partie qu'embrasse la pensée*' (90).
3 French tends to use the terms 'conclusive', 'potentially conclusive' and 'nonconclusive'.
4 Example borrowed from Bonnard, *Grammaire française des lycées et collèges*, 94.
5 This system corresponds to Guillaume's *Temps et verbe: théorie des aspects, des modes et des temps*.
6 The term 'compound present' would be far more logical, but difficult to use, being too new. It also would have the inconvenience of being functionally misleading, since in many cases in modern French it simply refers to the past.

Chapter 4

The indicative mood

0 General considerations

(i) The indicative system of tenses is complicated for a number of reasons. In the first place, the indicative system in modern French differs considerably from those which existed in the earlier stages of the language; and in the second place, there is not one indicative system but two, one of which includes the past historic and the past anterior. Finally, tenses are sometimes used to express modality rather than time and aspect. Although the aim of this book is to deal with the language synchronically, some attention must be given to diachronic aspects. In many cases an understanding of previous systems is necessary to grasp the system functioning in modern French; furthermore, knowledge of the previous systems is essential if one is to have a full understanding of the great writers of the past. We shall therefore approach the problem through an analysis of the development of the verbal system as a whole.

(ii) The approach chosen here is a structuralist one in the sense that the tenses are considered to form a system, the role of each tense being determined by the presence of the others. This means that if a tense disappears from the language, the other tenses have to shift in order to fill the gap. This is exactly what has happened in French: the modern intense specialization of the past historic has excluded it from most registers:[1] hence two systems: the 'general' or 'usual' system, which does not include it (see section 2) and the 'narrative' system, which does (see section 3).

Similarly, it is the decline of certain forms in certain moods − namely the imperfect and pluperfect subjunctive − which has led to the development of the modal potential of certain tenses in the indicative, the imperfect being the most striking example (see section 4).

1 Changes within the tense system

1.1 Existing forms

The forms which exist in the system are the following:

il chante	il a chanté	il a eu chanté
il chantait	il avait chanté	il avait eu chanté
il chanta	il eut chanté	—
il chantera	il aura chanté	il aura eu chanté
il chanterait	il aurait chanté	il aurait eu chanté

It is the role played by each form in relation to the system as a whole which has changed.

1.2 The system in Old French[2]

The tense system changed greatly between the end of the ninth and the sixteenth century. But by the end of this period one finds in the language all the forms given in 1.1; their roles may be defined as follows:

Unmarked for aspect of completion	Completed action or anteriority	Completed action in relation to a previously completed action
il chante	*il a chanté**	*il a eu chanté*
*il chantait**	*il avait chanté*	*il avait eu chanté*
*il chanta**	*il eut chanté*	—
il chantera	*il aura chanté*	*il aura eu chanté*
il chanterait	*il aurait chanté*	*il aurait eu chanté*

(The spelling used is that of contemporary French.)

The forms with an asterisk are those which present major differences between their use towards the end of the Old French period and their use in modern French.

(i) The past historic was unmarked for aspect: one could say, for example, *il eut un long nez* where in modern French one has to say *il avait un long nez*.

(ii) The compound past was still only a perfect; thus *il l'a mort*, i.e. *il l'a tué*, literally meant 'the body of the dead person was before his eyes'.

(iii) All the double compound forms were possible but rare; they may, however, have been frequent in the spoken language. The following is an example of the use of a double compound form:

> *une femme qui a épousé un deuxième mari, en a eu épousé précédemment un premier*

(iv) The imperfect was used to describe an action or state of affairs which preceded another in the past, but continues after this other one has ceased:

> *une chapèle estoit sur la falaise; li chevaliers i fu o sun ami . . .*

Its use was, however, very rare, at least until the thirteenth century.

1.3 The system in Classical French

1.3.1 *The true Classical system*

(i) To avoid redundancy, specialization between the two past tenses takes place: the past historic is used to express actions seen in their totality, i.e. with no reference to their beginning or end, while the imperfect remains unmarked aspectually:

		Completed action or anteriority	Completed action in relation to a previously completed action
The action is seen from within (it is not completed)	*il chante* *il chantait* *il chantera* *il chanterait*	*il a chanté** *il avait chanté* *il aura chanté* *il aurait chanté*	*(il a eu chanté)* *(il avait eu chanté)* *(il aura eu chanté)* *(il aurait eu chanté)*
The action is seen from outside: it is completed	*il chanta*	*il eut chanté*	

(ii) The double compound forms are in parenthesis because they were eventually banned from written French as being clumsy. They continued to be used in the spoken language (particularly in the south), but from then on their life was underground.

(iii) The compound past is followed by an asterisk in the table above because it will be the cause of the breakdown in the system. The problem is that the line dividing a

'completed action' from 'an action situated in the past and seen from the outside' is an extremely fine one: when did a 'completed action' become a 'definite past action'?

It was to solve this problem that the grammarians and rule makers of the seventeenth century set up what was called 'the 24 hours rule'. This established that anything further than 24 hours in the past would be in the past historic and anything more recent would be in the compound past:

Je vis, hier, Madame de G. . . elle m'a chargé de vous faire mille amitiés.

(If one had written instead *elle me chargea*, the action would be seen as purely in the past. The use of the compound past *elle m'a chargé* brings the action into the present: seeing Madame de G. is indeed an action in the past, but *elle m'a chargé de vous faire mille amitiés* refers to the time when the author does so, i.e. the present.)

This rule was followed by most classical writers: Corneille, for example, is known to have corrected his tenses when critics pointed out that he had failed to follow the rule. This rule was however highly artificial, and towards the end of the seventeenth century both past historic and compound past were being used for the description of a past over 24 hours old. But although these tenses were no longer carriers of 'real' time distinctions (i.e. recent past versus distant past), they had become the carriers of distinctions in psychological time, and although the 24-hour rule was gradually to disappear, it was replaced by another which was to stay: the use of the compound past implies some psychological link uniting past and present, whereas the past historic implies a sense of detachment between the two. Once again, the two tenses would be in complementary distribution.

1.3.2 *Instability of the new Classical system*

In the new Classical system the compound past figures twice: both as a perfect and as a definite past. This in turn entails the shift of the double compound past to the middle column (see Table below): it no longer functions only as a double compound past, but it also functions as a compound past.

		Completed action or anteriority	Completed action in relation to a previously completed action
Unmarked for aspect of completion	*il chante* *il chantait* *il chantera* *il chanterait*	*il a chanté* *il avait chanté* *il aura chanté* *il aurait chanté*	*il a eu chanté* *il avait eu chanté* *il aura eu chanté* *il aurait eu chanté*
Marked for aspect of completion	*il chanta** *il a chanté**	*il eut chanté* *il a eu chanté**	

(As in the preceding Table, an asterisk denotes a 'shifting tense', i.e. one developing a new function.)

1.3.3 *The two modern French systems*

In Modern French the problem of the competition existing between the past historic and the compound past has been solved in the following manner.

1.3.3.1   *The General System,[3] excluding the past historic and past anterior.*   The 'general' system is the system used in the spoken language and in writing in most cases except that of story-telling (this term being used in its broadest sense). In this system the compound past has a dual role: that of expressing the perfect and the definite past. Only the syntactical context can give a precise meaning to these forms (see 2.3). (This is in fact in keeping with the development of French from a morphologically based language to a predominantly syntactically based language). The double compound past, taking the place of the compound past to express completion or anteriority, becomes much more necessary to the language, and therefore much more acceptable in prescriptive terms.

Tenses functioning as simple tenses		Completed action or anteriority	Completed action in relation to a previously completed action
il chante *il chantait* *il chantera* *il chanterait*	unmarked for aspect of completion	il a chanté il avait chanté il aura chanté il aurait chanté	il a eu chanté il avait eu chanté il aura eu chanté il aurait eu chanté
il a chanté	completed	il a eu chanté	

1.3.3.2   *The Narrative System,[3] including the past historic and past anterior*   This system is very simple when used on its own (but see 1.3.3.3).

Simple tenses: marked and unmarked for aspect	Completed action or anteriority
il chantait (unmarked for completion)	*il avait chanté*
il chanta (marked for completion and more)	*il eut chanté*
il chanterait (unmarked for completion)	*il aurait chanté*

The past historic is 'marked for completion and more' in the sense that it is very specialized: it does not simply refer to the end of an action, but describes the action seen as a whole, with no reference to its beginning, middle or end. This is what has been termed 'the aspect of totality' (see Introduction to Part II and, in this chapter, 3.1.1).

1.3.3.3   *The intertwining of the two systems*   The narrative system is ideally suited to story-telling, the story-teller being anonymous; but stories tend to be told by people who interrupt the narrative from time to time; thus interruptions will happen, using the general system. The general system may also be used to highlight certain events or opinions (this is similar to the effects obtained in the cinema when using close-ups and zooming):

> . . . . *elle l'entraînait avec elle vers des perspectives inconnues. Puis elle disparut. Il souhaita passionnément la revoir une troisième fois. Et elle reparut en effet, mais sans lui parler plus clairement, en lui causant une volupté plus profonde: il était comme un homme dans la vie de qui une passante qu'il a aperçue vient de faire entrer l'image d'une beauté nouvelle qui donne à sa propre sensibilité une valeur plus grande, sans qu'il sache seulement s'il pourra jamais revoir celle qu'il aime déjà et dont il ignore jusqu'au nom.* (Proust, *Du côté de chez Swann*)

2 The indicative tenses in the General System

These tenses are the present, the imperfect, the compound past, the future, the pluperfect, the future anterior and the double compound forms.

2.1 The present

The present poses problems for English speakers because a far greater use is made of the French present than of its English equivalent.

2.1.1 *Normal or basic meaning*

(i) It refers to an action taking place or a state of affairs existing at the moment of speaking or writing: *je travaille.* As such it tends to include a portion of the immediate past and the immediate future (hence its use for other times than the 'present' – see 2.1.3 and 2.1.4).
(ii) It may refer to an action which is:

punctual, e.g. *je vous félicite*
limited in time, e.g. *je mange*
eternal, e.g. *la terre tourne*
timeless, e.g. *l'eau bout à 100°*

In other words, it represents the action or state of affairs as seen from the subject's point of view, with no reference to the beginning or end of the action.
(iii) Where the action described is an ongoing action, the verb may combine with *être en train de* in order to emphasize the progressive aspect, e.g. *je suis en train de travailler.*

2.1.2 *The present expressing the habitual*

(i) The present may be used to express the habitual in conjunction with suitable adverbials:

tous les ans, je passe mes vacances de Pâques à Paris

whereas

je passe mes vacances de Pâques à Paris

is ambiguous (it could be this year or every year).
(ii) If the verb refers to a noncontinuous action, the action will be seen as referring either to the habitual or to a specific occasion, depending on the absence or presence of a direct object:

il boit un café (= specific occasion)
cet homme boit (= habitual: this man is an alcoholic)

2.1.3 *The present referring to the future*

(i) When used instead of the future, the present announces that the realization of the future is seen as very definite in the speaker's mind:

Tu peux venir demain? Non, demain je travaille (instead of *travaillerai*)
vous nous téléphonez dès que vous savez quelque chose (instead of *téléphonerez* and *saurez*)

This use of the present is extremely common in the spoken language.
(ii) One may use *être* + adjective in the present to refer to the future on condition that

the adjective is compatible with the idea of the prospective. One may thus write:

demain je suis libre

but not

*demain je suis prêt

(Adjectives may be modified, in some cases, to make them potentially prospective; thus the following sentence is acceptable: *demain je suis prêt à t'accompagner*.)

2.1.4   *The present referring to the past*

(i) One may use the present in statements on past events:

c'est en 1715 que Louis XIV est mort (instead of *mourut*)

(ii) When referring to a film or play − if the version referred to can still be seen − it is normal to use the present:

X est excellent dans ce film

(iii) The 'narrative present' or *présent historique* is a stylistic use of the present in a text otherwise in the past:

> *Hervine fut repêchée; mais elle déclara que François l'avait jetée bas. Les bonnes fondent sur moi; je leur échappe; je cours me barricader dans la cave de la maison: l'armée femelle me pourchasse. Mon père et ma mère étaient heureusement sortis.*
> (Chateaubriand, example borrowed from Baylon and Fabre, *Grammaire systématique de la langue française*)

(iv) It is important not to confuse the 'narrative present' with the use of the present made in *la nouvelle histoire*. In the latter, the historian does not seek to give an impression of objectivity. Instead he describes history as it unfolds before his eyes; his use of the present therefore corresponds to a 'normal' use of the present. For there to be *présent historique* there must be contrast with the past historic. For example, in the conclusion to a chapter written in the past historic, an author could write:

> *Louis XIV meurt en 1715. Il laisse la France appauvrie mais enrichie par l'apport, jamais égalé d'une pléiade d'écrivains, d'architectes et d'artistes.*

2.1.5   *Non-correspondence of the French and English present*

(i) The French present corresponds to a span of time covered by other tenses in English:

by the present progressive: 'I am working' = *je travaille*
by the perfect progressive: 'I have been working for the last two hours' = *je travaille depuis deux heures*
by the future and future progressive: 'this afternoon I shall work/be working' = *cet après-midi je travaille*
(in this case one could also use the present progressive in English and the future in French)
by the past (particularly in journalese): 'that was the good news from Whitehall today': *voilà* or *c'est là la bonne nouvelle qui nous vient de Whitehall aujourd'hui* (the use of *aujourd'hui* precludes the use of the imperfect except in its modal sense)

(ii) The English present corresponds to the French present in the following cases:

to express the eternal and the habitual: 'the sun sets in the west' = *le soleil se couche à l'ouest*

to express the punctual: 'X passes the ball to Y' = *X passe le ballon à Y*
to express the timeless: 'water boils at 100°' = *l'eau bout à 100°*

(iii) This extensive use made of the present tense may be illustrated by the following figures, which come from a study made in 1954 by E. Kahn of the speech of one Parisian.[4] The questionnaire was made up of some 2000 sentences. The use of tenses in the answers was as follows:

present:	66.89%
compound past:	22.98%
imperfect:	4.81%
future:	3.32%
aller + infinitive:	1.27%
pluperfect:	0.41%

(These figures are quoted by P. Imbs in *L'Emploi des temps verbaux en français moderne*.)

A study of the French spoken by workers in cafés in one of the poorest industrial districts in Lyons in 1978 also showed an extensive use of the present, since the latter appeared to be used in 52 per cent of cases (see F. Maretti, *Mémoire de maîtrise*, Université Jean Moulin, Lyon 1978).

2.2 The imperfect (for the modal imperfect see 4.2)

2.2.1 *Normal or basic meaning*

(i) The imperfect is the equivalent of the present in the past: the action is seen as happening, i.e. in progress, without reference to its beginning or end, hence the term 'imperfect':

hier je travaillais (ongoing action)

or

en 1960, Pierre était en Algérie (state of affairs)

In other words, the action − although in the past − is seen from within (this is called *l'aspect sécant* in French).

(ii) If the verb refers to an ongoing action − rather than to a state of affairs − it may combine with *être en train de* to stress the idea of progress: *hier à trois heures, j'étais en train de travailler*.

2.2.2 *The imperfect expressing the habitual*

(i) The imperfect may express the habitual in combination with suitable adverbials, e.g. *tous les jours, il quittait son bureau à six heures*.

(ii) If the verb refers to a noncontinuous action, the action will be seen either as limited in time or as habitual, depending on the presence or absence of a direct object:

il buvait un café (= one specific occasion)
cet homme buvait (= habitual : he was an alcoholic)

2.2.3 *The imperfect expressing the simultaneous*

The imperfect being the equivalent of a present in the past, when a passage contains a number of verbs in the imperfect, all the actions, processes or states of affairs referred to are simultaneous:

Lorsqu'il eut contourné l'aile sud, il aperçut soudain les roseaux, à perte de vue, qui formaient tout le paysage. L'eau des étangs venait de ce côté mouiller le pied des murs et il y avait, devant plusieurs portes, de petits balcons qui surplombaient les vagues clapotantes. Désœuvré, le promeneur erra un long moment sur la rive. (Alain-Fournier, *Le Grand Meaulnes*)

In this passage its use contrasts with that of the past historic, which refers to actions or states of affairs in their chronological order (see 3.1.1).

It is because the imperfect may refer to simultaneous actions and states of affairs that it is often referred to as *le temps de la description* or as *l'imparfait descriptif*. It is used in contrast with terms such as *l'imparfait dramatique* (see 2.2.5) and *l'imparfait modal* (see 4.2).

2.2.4   *The imperfect in subordinate clauses*

(i) It may express simultaneity in relation to the main clauses:

j'ai trouvé Paul en conversation avec Pierre qui rentrait du collège

(ii) It may also express the future in relation to the time referred to in the main clause, if the latter is in the past:

lundi dernier, nous avons acheté une valise pour Paul qui partait à Rome le lendemain

(iii) The imperfect and the temporal conditional form differ in their expression of the future seen from the past.

In the case of the imperfect the time of reference is the moment of speaking or writing:

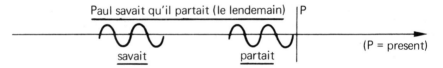

In the case of the *-rais* form, the point of reference is a point of time in the past:

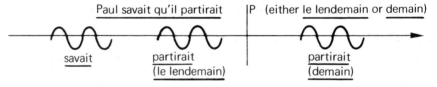

2.2.5   *Stylistic uses of the imperfect ('l'imparfait dramatique')*

(i) The following are examples of its use:

en 1944, les troupes alliées débarquaient en Normandie
à dix heures l'avion décollait

In both cases one would have expected either the compound past or the past historic. Using the imperfect replaces the reader in the middle of the action.

(ii) This use of the imperfect is common in two types of contexts; either within a narrative, to make the reader relive the story step by step, as in:

Une heure après il prenait le train pour Paris; vingt-quatre heures plus tard partaient des instructions adressées au Préfet du Rhône; et le lendemain il accourait à Lyon
(example borrowed from Schogt, *Le Système verbal du français contemporain*)

or to rivet the attention of the reader at the beginning of a story, as in:

Chateaubriand naissait à St Malo le 4 septembre

(If one took the imperfect at its face value it would mean that the birth of Châteaubriand had taken 24 hours; this is not the real meaning of the sentence!)
(iii) This kind of misuse of the aspectual connotations of the imperfect is only possible where no ambiguity could arise; in thrillers, however, the difference between the next two sentences could be crucial:

entre deux heures et trois heures, il a travaillé (travailla)
entre deux heures et trois heures, il travaillait

In the first case he has worked only between two o'clock and three o'clock; in the second case he was working both before two and after three.
(iv) Flaubert and then, to a far greater extent, Zola are said to have 'given the imperfect artistic overtones' which it had never had before. One may thus read in *Au Bonheur des Dames*:

Neuf heures sonnaient

and

elle s'animait, citait des exemples, se montrait au courant de la question, remplie même d'idées larges et nouvelles

In these cases the writer is referring either to actions which are punctual or seen in their totality: the past historic would be the normal tense to use and not the imperfect. But by using the imperfect, Zola places the reader in the middle of the action which he then relives step by step. The use of the imperfect also renders all of these actions simultaneous, which makes the description extremely lively. Indeed Zola often uses the imperfect in this way when describing a bustling scene, to give the idea that many actions are taking place at the same time: the past historic would have the drawback of describing them as happening in the order in which the verbs would appear.

2.2.6 *Other uses of the imperfect*

The imperfect may also express modality; it is then called the 'modal imperfect'. It may be used either to express a condition (*si j'étais riche* . . . . conditional), a regret (*si j'étais riche!*), politeness (*je voulais vous dire que*. . . .) etc. (see 4.2).

2.2.7 *Translation problems: French imperfect and English simple past*[5]

(i) The French imperfect sees the action midstream (*aspect sécant*) whereas the English past tense refers to a definite past. These two tenses are therefore in total contrast, thus 'he worked from two to six' becomes *il a travaillé de deux à six*, whereas *il travaillait de deux à six* becomes 'he was working between two and six' or 'he used to work between two and six', depending on whether the context makes clear whether one is referring to an ongoing or a habitual action. In other words, the French imperfect corresponds either to the past progressive or to the habitual form 'used to', except when it is used for stylistic effect, or as a mood.
(ii) Whereas the past may combine with the adverb 'today' in English, the same does not apply in French. Thus the past tenses in the following sentence have to be translated by a present and compound past in French:

The calculated risk taken in sacking X appeared to be backfiring today as thousands of workers walked out in protest.

Le risque calculé pris en renvoyant X semble aujourd'hui avoir été malencontreux vu que des milliers de travailleurs se sont mis en grève.

But pastness in relation to a point of time in 'today' may be expressed by the imperfect:

ce matin, je parlais à Jean quand Pierre est arrivé et nous a dit. . . .

2.3 The compound past

This tense is complicated because of its dual role: it may function either as a 'definite past' in place of the past historic (see 2.3.1) or it may function as a perfect, either to refer to a completed action or to anteriority (see 2.3.2). It may also sometimes replace the future anterior (see 2.3.3).

2.3.1   *The compound past replacing the past historic as a 'definite past'*

(i) The action is seen as completed. It may have taken place a long time ago (it is similar to the past historic), e.g. *il y est allé il y a dix ans*; or it may have taken place within the recent past, e.g. *il y est allé hier/ce matin . . .*

The compound past includes therefore both the period of time which used to be covered in classical French by the past historic and that which used to be covered by the compound past (see the 24 hour rule, 1.3.1 *iii*).

(ii) Although the compound past replaces the past historic in many contexts, its connotations are quite different: actions described in the compound past are felt to be relevant to the present (because the forms of the compound past are those of the present as far as the auxiliary is concerned), whereas actions in the past historic belong to 'story-telling'. It is this difference of perspective which explains why the past historic has survived in the written language (see 3.1.3). But in spontaneous French these nuances are lost, and only the compound past is productive.

2.3.2   *The compound past as a perfect*

(i) Used in a main or independent clause, the compound past describes the action as completed in relation to the present, and as therefore relevant to the present:

les cambrioleurs ont tout laissé dans un désordre effroyable

In this case one is faced with the result of the action.

(ii) In a subordinate clause, the compound past expresses anteriority, e.g. *dès qu'il a trop bu, il devient odieux.*

(iii) There are aspectual ambiguities. Compare the following:

il a lu ce livre (= *c'est fini, il ne le lit plus*)

il a beaucoup lu (= *il lit peut-être encore*)

In both cases one is dealing with a perfect, but in the first case it is a 'true perfect' since the action is truly completed; in the second case the action may continue into the present: its meaning is ambiguous. This is a 'false perfect'. These ambiguities only occur with verbs which refer to an action which implies duration.

2.3.3   *The compound past replacing the future anterior*

This may take place because the auxiliary is in the present (see 2.1.3 for 'the present stretching into the future'):

vous me direz quelle pièce vous aurez choisi d'aller voir (future anterior)

becomes

vous me direz quelle pièce vous avez choisi d'aller voir

2.3.4 *Stylistic use of the compound past*

(i) One can only speak of its stylistic use when the compound past is used in the written language instead of the past historic (see 3.1.3). In this case one has to use the concept of subjective and objective time: the past historic describes a past detached, psychologically speaking, from the present; it is therefore objective. But the past described by the compound past is still relevant to the present; it is therefore felt to be more subjective.

(ii) The device of using the compound past where the past historic could have been expected has been employed by Camus in *L'Etranger*. The effect is to destroy the concept of a logical sequence of events: the compound past brings all the actions near to the present without establishing links between them, whereas the past historic describes the actions chronologically (see 3.1.1 *iii* and 3.1.3).

2.3.5 *Translation problems involving the compound past*

The compound past will be translated differently depending on whether it is functioning as a perfect or as a definite past (i.e. instead of the past historic).
(i) When it functions as a perfect, it will be translated by the English perfect:

   il a lu ce livre = 'he has read this book'

but where a length of time is implied the present progressive is more likely:

   il a lu toute la journée = 'he has been reading all day'

(ii) Some English perfects are ambiguous and may be translated either by a compound past or a present:

   'he has lived in Paris for ten years'
   il a habité à Paris pendant dix ans (but he no longer does)

or

   il habite à Paris depuis dix ans (he still does)

A similar point may be made about the next example:

   'I have worked here all my life'
   j'ai travaillé ici toute ma vie (in this case *ma vie*
      is seen as a period which is complete at the time of speaking)
   je travaille ici depuis toujours (in this case the action is seen as continuing into the
      future)

(iii) When the compound past functions as a definite past, it may be translated by the simple past in English:

   il est venu nous voir lundi dernier ('he came to see us last Monday')

2.4 The future

2.4.1 *Basic meaning*

(i) The future refers to any future time as long as it does not overlap with the moment of speaking or writing:

   j'écouterai ton disque ce soir ('I shall listen to your record tonight')

but not:

   *maintenant j'écouterai ton disque

(whereas one can say, 'now I shall listen to your record'). Instead one has to use *aller +* infinitive:

 maintenant je vais écouter ton disque (see 2.4.3)

Aspectually the future is unmarked: aspect depends on the context:

 pendant ce temps-là je ferai les bagages (action in progress)

 ne t'inquiète pas, c'est moi qui ferai les bagages (action seen in its totality)

2.4.2   *The future as alternative to the imperative*

In this case it is used modally (see 4.3), e.g.

 tu iras demain

2.4.3   *Comparison between the future and 'aller' + infinitive*

(i)   Aller + infinitive is obligatory when referring to a future which is so immediate that it stems from the present (see 2.4.1), e.g. *maintenant je vais. . . .*
(ii) In all other cases there is a choice between these two forms:

 j'irai voir ce film la semaine prochaine
 je vais voir ce film la semaine prochaine

(iii) It is not true to say that the *aller +* infinitive form only refers to the immediate future:

 je vais passer l'année prochaine au Canada
 je passerai l'année prochaine au Canada

The difference between the two forms − if there is one − is that *vais* is modal in that it refers to an intention whereas *irai* simply expresses the concept of the future; *vais* is therefore more subjective and *irai* more objective. It is more usual, when speaking, to be subjective, hence the common use of the *aller +* infinitive form in preference to the future form.

2.4.4   *Replacement of the future tense by the temporal conditional*[6]

Whereas the form using the future has to refer to the future in relation to the moment of speaking, the temporal conditional refers to the future in relation to a point of time in the past:

 je te dis que Pierre écoutera ce disque avec plaisir (future)
 je te disais que Pierre écouterait ce disque avec plaisir (temporal conditional)

But used in combination with the compound past, there are two possible constructions because of the dual nature of the compound past:

je t'ai dit que Pierre écoutera ce disque avec plaisir
je t'ai dit (hier) que Pierre écouterait ce disque avec plaisir

Since the future time referred to by the temporal conditional could be situated either before or after the moment of speaking, this may be represented in the following manner:

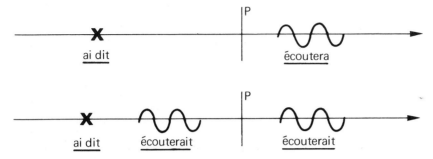

2.4.5 *Stylistic uses of the future: 'le futur historique'*

The future may be used in a historical context, in combination with the 'historic present' (see 2.1.4 *iii*), e.g. *Napoléon arrive à Sainte-Hélène où il mourra en 1821.*

2.4.6 *Translation problems*

(i) The choice between the future or *aller* + infinitive may present problems. Compare:

je vais lui dire que vous êtes là (= je me déplace pour lui dire que vous êtes là)
je lui dirai que vous êtes là (= quand il arrivera/quand je le verrai . . .)

This distinction has to be made lexically in English:

'I'll go and let him know you are here' (corresponds to *je vais*)
'I'll tell him you are here when he comes/when I see him' (corresponds to *dirai*)

(ii) If the future is seen as near to the present – particularly if there is an adverb such as *maintenant* in the clause – the English future equivalent will have to be translated in French by *aller* + infinitive (see 2.4.1).

(iii) Whereas 'when' is not usually followed by a future equivalent[7] in English, there are no such restrictions in French:

'I'll listen to your record when John arrives'
j'écouterai ton disque quand Jean arrivera (or *sera là*)

(Note, however, that although 'when' cannot be followed by a future equivalent when functioning as a conjunction, it may be followed by a future equivalent when it is used as the equivalent of a relative pronoun:

'be at my office at 5 pm, when (= at which time) I'll be back from the meeting.'

2.5 The pluperfect (or 'compound imperfect')

2.5.1 *Meaning of the pluperfect in main and independent clauses*

Whereas the compound past may indicate anteriority in relation to the present, the pluperfect indicates anteriority in relation to some point in the past. Thus:

j'avais déjà entendu le même cours le lundi précédent

is the equivalent in the past of:

j'ai déjà entendu le même cours lundi dernier

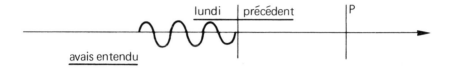

2.5.2   *Meaning of the pluperfect in subordinate clauses*

In the following example the action is seen as completed:

comme il avait fini son repas, il est allé faire un tour dans le jardin

but in subordinate clauses introduced by conjunctions expressing a notion of time, the pluperfect may refer to a habitual or repeated action (in which case the aspect is the iterative aspect and the term 'pluperfect' is a misnomer)

lorsqu'il avait fini son repas, il allait faire un tour dans le jardin

2.5.3   *The pluperfect expressing the distant past*

(i) Compare:

il lit le livre que tu lui as acheté (hier/l'année dernière)
il lit le livre que tu lui avais acheté l'année dernière

The use of the pluperfect emphasizes the fact that one is referring to a distant past.

2.5.4   *Modal use as a form of politeness*

j'étais venu vous dire que . . .

(See 4.2 *ii.*)

2.6   The future anterior (or 'compound future')

2.6.1   *Meaning in main and independent clauses*

Use of the future anterior implies that the action or state of affairs referred to is seen as completed:

j'aurai fini ce travail dans trois jours

2.6.2   *Meaning in subordinate clauses*

The future anterior refers to a past in relation to some point in the future (*le passé dans le futur*):

j'irai la voir quand j'aurai fini ce travail

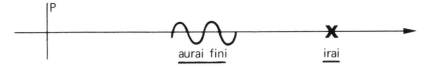

Note: One may contrast the future anterior, which may refer to a past seen in relation to some point in the future (*le passé dans le futur*), with the present conditional, which may when used temporally express a future in relation to some point in the past (*le futur dans le passé*):

il ira la voir quand il aura fini ce travail (past in future)
je savais qu'il irait la voir quand il aurait fini son travail (future in past)

2.6.3   *Modal use to express probability*

(See 4.4.)

elle aura tout entendu (= *elle a probablement tout entendu*)

2.7   The double compound forms

2.7.1   *General considerations of use*

(i) Within the General System only the double compound past is essential, since it may express anteriority in relation to the compound past, when the latter functions as a 'definite' or 'simple' past (see 2.3.1).
(ii) The other double compound forms, the compound pluperfect and the compound future anterior, are marginal to the system in the sense that they are used merely to emphasize either completion or speed of completion.

2.7.2   *The double compound past*

This may be used either to express anteriority (in which case it is used in the subordinate clause) or to stress completion.

2.7.2.1   *Expression of anteriority in subordinate clauses*   In this case the double compound past relates to the compound past in the same way as the past anterior relates to the past historic:

aussitôt que j'ai eu fait graver ce disque, le même est sorti dans le commerce

is the equivalent of

aussitôt que j'eus fait graver le[8] disque, le même sortit dans le commerce

The double compound past is rarely used in this kind of context however. One uses instead the compound past in both clauses:

aussitôt que j'ai fait graver ce disque, le même est sorti dans le commerce

(Note, however, that the use of the past historic, although grammatically correct, may appear odd to many present-day native speakers of French; this is because the past historic is associated both with the 3rd person and with an objective past unrelated to the present (see 3.1.4.1 and 3.1.4.2), whereas in this sentence the past historic is used in the 1st person, and in a modern context – i.e. that associated with records.)

2.7.2.2   *The double compound past stressing completion*   It is more usually used to stress completion than to express anteriority, hence its use with verbs which express lexically the idea of completion, such as *finir, faire, terminer, prendre*. . . .

je l'ai eu fait en un rien de temps
du Magalox, j'en ai eu pris beaucoup il y a quelques années (sentence heard by the author)

By stressing completion one may also imply speed of completion. This is the case in the first example; in the second example it is the fact that the action was completed in a past psychologically distant and separate from the present which is being emphasized.

2.7.2.3 *Stylistic restrictions on use*   The double compound forms were banned from all literary registers in the seventeenth century, but continued to survive in the spoken language, mainly in the *Langue d'Oc* areas.[9] For a long time it was typical of 'peasant speech':

des pommes de terre, j'en ai eu planté autrefois; ensuite j'ai fait du seigle et maintenant je fais du fourrage

In this case the double compound past expresses both anteriority and total completion (the implication is that this farmer is definitely not going to grow potatoes any more). The double compound reappears – although very rarely in literature – in the late nineteenth century in direct speech. Zola, for example, uses just one double compound past in *Au Bonheur des Dames*:

Quand j'ai eu passé mon bachot pour contenter ma famille, j'aurais pu devenir un avocat ou un médecin comme les camarades.

2.7.3   *The compound pluperfect (or 'double compound imperfect')*

The use of the compound pluperfect in Modern French is extremely rare; it is used mainly to express anteriority in relation to another action in the past:

Une certaine Jacqueline. . .avait épousé le duc Jean de Brabant. . .et auparavant avait eu épousé le comte de Ponthieu   (Mémoires de Pierre de Fénin (fifteenth century), *quoted by M. Foulet)*

But such constructions are either unacceptable or archaic in modern French; one tends to use instead a succession of pluperfects, the context indicating the chronology of the events described.

2.7.4   *The compound future anterior (or 'double compound future')*

The compound future anterior is used to stress the speed of the action, e.g. *il aura eu tout fait très vite*. It may also be used to stress the rapid succession of two events:
dès qu'il aura eu pris connaissance des résultats, il me les fera connaître
(This form appears to be used quite frequently in the south-eastern parts of France.)

2.7.5   *Summary of the expression of relative time in subordinate clauses in the General System*

(i)   verb in main clause: present
        reference to recent past: compound past
        reference to distant past: pluperfect
        e.g.   *il lit le livre que tu lui as acheté hier*
               il lit le livre que tu lui avais acheté l'année dernière
(ii) verb in main clause: compound past
        reference to recent past in relation to   compound past or double compound
           that point of time in past: past

reference to distant past: pluperfect

e.g.   *aussitôt que j'ai [eu] fait graver ce disque, le même est sorti dans le commerce*

il a lu, la semaine dernière, le livre que tu lui avais acheté lors de ton voyage en Espagne

(iii)   verb in main clause: imperfect

reference to recent or distant past in
    relation to that point of time in   pluperfect
    the past:

reference to very recent past: pluperfect or compound pluperfect[10]

e.g.   *lorsqu'il avait fini son repas, il allait faire un tour dans le jardin* (habitual)

à peine avait-il [eu] fini son repas qu'il allait faire un tour dans le jardin
(habitual)[11]

(iv)   verb in main clause: future

reference to a recent or distant past
    in relation to point of time in the   future anterior
    future:

reference to very recent past in
    relation to point of time in the   future anterior or compound future
    future: anterior

e.g.   *j'irai la voir quand j'aurai fini mon travail*

dès qu'il aura [eu] pris connaissance des résultats, il me les fera connaître

2.7.6 *Summary of the expression of aspect through tense forms alone*

The following table summarizes those aspects expressed by tense forms alone
(including the past historic):

Action to which the verb refers	Tense forms used	Examples
Completed action (Perfect)	Compound tenses Double compound tenses (stress completion and speed of completion)	*j'ai/j'avais/j'aurai mangé* (i.e. *j'ai fini de manger*) *en deux heures il avait eu fini son travail*
Continuous state of affairs	Simple tenses: imperfect, present and sometimes future (but not past historic)	*je pense y aller* *je pensais y aller*
Ongoing action (Progressive)	Simple tenses: present, imperfect and some-times future (but not past historic)	*je mange* (i.e. *je suis en train de manger*) *je mangeais* (i.e. *j'étais en train de manger*)
Permanent state of affairs	Present tense	*la terre tourne autour du soleil*
Action seen as a whole, without reference to its beginning or end (aspect of totality)	Past historic, and sometimes future	*il fit ses bagages*

We note the special case of the future tense, which can either indicate that the action is seen in its totality when used on its own or, when given a suitable context, may express the contrary aspect of non-completion.

3   The Narrative System

The Narrative System includes the past historic and the past anterior.

3.1   The past historic

3.1.1   *Use and meaning*

(i) As far as aspect is concerned, the past historic expresses the fact that the action is seen globally, in its totality, without any reference to its beginning, middle or end. This is why it is so suited to the expression of the punctual, e.g. *il sortit à six heures.* But it may equally well refer to an action or state of affairs which has gone on for a long time, in which case the whole of that period of time is seen as one unit, hence the term 'aspect of totality', e.g. *des milliards d'années s'écoulèrent avant l'apparition de l'homme.*
(ii) The past historic is a definite past in that it situates the action or state of affairs at some point in time in the past; it merely dates it: *il naquit à Paris le 22 décembre 1954.*
(iii) As such, it describes a succession of events in their chronological order (which is why this tense is so useful in story-telling: see 3.1.4):

> *elle se leva, écrivit quelques lettres, alla voir des amis et joua un moment du piano*

The actions in this sentence have to have taken place in the order in which they are presented whereas, were they in the compound past, there would be no way of knowing, grammatically speaking, the exact order in which they took place, since the compound past merely indicates completion.

Used in narrative the past historic pinpoints the various stages in the story:

> *La ville de Clément Marot marqua la fin du voyage et celle des ambitions du policier. Parce qu'Alice se plaisait* [state of affairs] *à Cahors, Neuvic refusa d'en bouger, fût-ce pour devenir commissaire divisionnaire. Leurs parents respectifs, dont ils étaient* [state of affairs] *les seuls héritiers, leur avaient laissé assez d'argent pour les garder à l'abri de soucis financiers trop pressants. Dès lors, ils purent vivre selon leur cœur.*
> (Exbrayat, *Qui veut affoler Martine*)

In this passage the three main actions or facts are *marqua, refusa d'en bouger* and *purent vivre*. The past historic describes them in their chronological order.

3.1.2   *The past historic in relation to the imperfect*

3.1.2.1   *Difference in aspect*
(i) Unlike the imperfect, the past historic describes a complete action seen from the outside, hence the difference of meaning between the following two sentences:

> *je savais à ce moment-là qu'elle reviendrait* (state of affairs)
> *je sus à ce moment-là qu'elle reviendrait* (punctual: 'I found out then (at that moment) that she would come back')

(ii) Since the past historic sees the action from the outside, it is objective, whereas the imperfect sees the action from within, which makes it suited to the expression of the subjective. This is why the implications of the following sentences are different:

> *il demeura silencieux* (= action seen in its totality)
> *il demeurait silencieux* (= action seen from within)

The first sentence implies that he remained silent for a specific length of time; the second sentence is ambiguous: 'he may or may not have remained silent for the whole length of time involved'. The action being seen from within, one does not know its outcome.

(iii) Both tenses may appear in the same sentence, the imperfect usually giving the time reference whereas the past historic marks a break, putting an end to a state of affairs:

Tout Paris dormait quand apparut le soleil (Flaubert)

3.1.2.2 *Translation problems due to aspectual connotations*
(i) The aspectual distinctions expressed by the imperfect and the past historic and their connotations are not always easy to translate into English, since the English translation may well be ambiguous where the French translation is not. Thus 'he remained silent' translates both *il resta silencieux* and *il restait silencieux*. If the distinction is important, it will have to be made lexically, and the solution to the problem will depend on the context.
(ii) The translation of *aller* when used in these two tenses illustrates this point further. Compare:

il alla se jeter dans la rivière (and he did so, i.e. he committed suicide through drowning)
sa décision était prise: il allait se jeter dans la rivière (declaration of intent)
il allait se jeter dans la rivière, lorsqu'un passant le retint (he was about to do so, but he was prevented from doing so)
tous les matins, il allait plonger dans la rivière (he did so every morning; *plonger* has replaced *se jeter*, in order to refer to 'swimming' rather than to 'drowning').

One therefore ends up with quite different translations in English:

'he went and threw himself into the river' *(il alla)*
'he would go and throw himself into the river' *(il allait)*
'he was about to throw himself into the river' *(il allait . . . lorsque . . .)*
'he used to dive into the river' *(il allait plonger)*

These various functions of the imperfect tie up with the modal use of the imperfect; see 4.2.*i*.
(iii) A historical note may be added. In present-day French, one may contrast *il dut se taire* (i.e. 'and he did') and *il devait se taire*, which is ambiguous, the action being seen from within. But one can sometimes write or say *il devait se taire* for *il aurait dû se taire*. This is in fact a latinism; Latin not having a conditional mood as such, the indicative imperfect of verbs with strong modal meanings such as *devoir, pouvoir* and *falloir* are sometimes used to express an unreal past: *il devait faire cela* means *il aurait dû faire cela* i.e. *il devait le faire mais il ne l'a pas fait.*

3.1.3 *The past historic in relation to the compound past*

3.1.3.1 *Difference in implication and connotation*
(i) From the seventeenth century onwards, the past historic came to be used only for actions which are no longer relevant to the present, the compound past taking its place in this respect. In Modern French, in contexts other than story-telling (see 3.1.4.2), the compound past has taken over completely from the past historic and therefore has a dual role: that of expressing the perfect and that of expressing the definite past (see 2.3). But the compound past has implications which the past historic has not.
Compare:

il a terminé son travail (= c'est fini, il ne travaille plus)
il termina son travail (no implications)

Similarly, the two following sentences have quite different implications:

> *il a fermé la porte (aussi je n'ai plus froid)*
> *il ferma la porte* (no implications)

In other words, the use of the compound past indicates that the action has some bearing on the present, the reverse being true for the past historic.

(ii) The past historic has acquired connotations which it never had in Classical French; since it is register bound (see 3.1.4.2), whenever it is used in different registers it becomes symbolic of another age. As such it may be used as a source of comedy; for example if one said to somebody, *mon mari et moi, nous allâmes en Corse cet été*, the effect would be ridiculous. (Its use is similar in this sense to that of the imperfect subjunctive.)

(iii) Use of the past historic as an indicator of an author's opinion.

This is illustrated by the fact that entries in dictionaries can be seen to illustrate the views of their authors, in that if the author writes about somebody famous in the compound past, it is felt that the author considers his contribution to history or knowledge or science of such importance that it still affects today's outlook, whereas the use of the past historic will indicate that the author considers the person described to be of historical interest only. The use of the present gives a universal touch to what is described, so that actions in the present are seen to be the most important of all. The following examples are borrowed from D. Leeman, I. Austruc and M. Sumpf, *Apprendre à rédiger*, Niveau 1.

Abercrombie (John), *médecin et psychiatre anglais* (Aberdeen 1780 Edinburgh 1844). *Précurseur de la psychologie physiologique et pathologique, il a publié . . .* (i.e. this work is still relevant)

Abernethy (John), *chirurgien anglais (Londres* 1764 − Enfield, *près de Londres,* 1831). *Chirurgien de l'hôpital Saint Barthélemy, à Londres, il exécuta le premier l'opération de . . .* (i.e. this work is of historical interest only)

Filatov (Vladimir Petrovitch), *médecin ophtalmologiste soviétique* (1875 − 1956). *Ophtalmologiste de la clinique des maladies des yeux d'Odessa, puis directeur de l'Institut ophtalmologique d'Ukraine, il entra à l'Académie des sciences de l'URSS en 1944* (i.e. this belongs to history). *Ses travaux portent sur la greffe de la cornée et sur les greffes cutanées, . . .* (i.e. this work is still of major importance)

3.1.3.2   *Chronological implications of the past historic*   The compound past and the past historic differ in their description of a succession of events, since the past historic describes them in the chronological order in which they happen, whereas the use of the compound past does not imply any specific order (see 3.1.1*iii*).

3.1.4   *Use and non-use of the past historic in modern French*

3.1.4.1   *Use of the 3rd person only*   There are two reasons for this avoidance of the 1st and 2nd persons.

The past historic, referring as it does to events of no particular relevance to present time, has become associated with the one person which can be viewed with some detachment, the 3rd.

The forms of the 1st person plural (in *-âmes* or *-îmes*) and of the 2nd person plural (in *-âtes* or *-îtes*) sound very different from the 1st and 2nd persons plural in other tenses; as a result, the less they are used, the more odd they sound.

This explains why the following sentence, when presented to a class of French students for translation into Latin, caused general hilarity:

UNIVERSITY OF ST. ANDREWS

With the Compliments of

DEPARTMENT OF FRENCH,
BUCHANAN BUILDING,
UNION STREET,
ST. ANDREWS.
Tel: (0334) 76161 Ext. 352
Fax: (0334) 74674

vous lui demandâtes pourquoi il était venu à Syracuse . . . (S. Deleani and J.M. Vermander, *Manuel d'initiation à la langue latine*)

To this one may add that forms in *-âtre* such as *marâtre* or *rougeâtre* have, in French, pejorative connotations which tend to be carried over into the 2nd person plural of the past historic (*-âtes*).

3.1.4.2 *Use of the past historic*

(i) Although the importance of the past historic has decreased over the past three centuries, one must talk in terms of its specialization rather than of its extinction.

The past historic is used in modern French for all narrative. As such it is used in novels, in all detective novels, and even in the editorials of children's journals. Indeed, children often invent different past historic endings for verbs which do not have different forms for the 3rd person singular from those for the indicative present – hence sentences such as: *alors le petit enfant *disa: 'Entrez!' et le loup entra*. The past historic does not therefore belong to 'elevated style' but to any kind of storytelling:

> *Les trois hommes avaient eu de légères nausées au début du voyage, mais ce n'avait été que passager. Ils ralentirent l'engin de 9.500 à 5.850 km/h., ce qui les porta à une altitude moyenne de 115 km au-dessus de la surface de la terre qu'il photographièrent sous toutes les coutures. (Le Journal de Mickey)*

This point is illustrated in the following extract from Robbe-Grillet's novel, *Djinn*:

> *Voilà. Un robot rencontre une jeune dame . . . .*
> *Mon auditrice ne me laisse pas aller plus loin. Tu ne sais pas raconter, dit-elle. Une vraie histoire, c'est forcément au passé.*
> *- Si tu veux. Un robot, donc, a rencontré une. . . .*
> *- Mais non, pas ce passé-là. Une histoire, ça doit être au passé historique. Ou bien personne ne sait que c'est une histoire.*

(ii) The past historic is not used as often as one would expect in historical works. The latter tends to be written nowadays using the present as point of reference: the author follows 'history' step by step. This is what is called *la nouvelle histoire* (see 2.1.4 *iv*).
(iii) The past historic is used fairly little in journalism, except for articles of a biographical nature and for articles on sport (the language used in sport is often very flowery since it is all about the exploits of heroes (see *L'Equipe*)).[12]
(iv) The use or non-use of the past historic may be a matter of editorial policy: some left-wing editors have been known to consider the past historic as 'bourgeois' and therefore undesirable. It is on these same grounds that others may wish to see it as a symbol of traditional values.

3.1.4.3 *Void left by non-use of the past historic*

(i) Although the past historic can no longer be used in all contexts, there is no real equivalent to take its place; the consequence of this is that the writer may find himself at a loss as to what form to use when referring to the punctual, the one being too specialized from the point of view of register, the other – the compound past – having such different connotations.[13]
(ii) The General System, unlike the Narrative System, has no tense which may convey the idea of a succession of events.
(iii) The General System has no way of expressing detachment from the past:

> *Nous arrivâmes au château. Le vieux donjon se reliait à la partie du batiment entièrement refaite sous Louis XVI . . . Je n'avais encore rien vu d'aussi original, . . . C'était monstrueux et captivant. En approchant, nous vîmes deux*

gendarmes qui se promenaient devant une petite porte ouvrant sur le rez-de-chaus-sée du donjon. (Leroux, *Le Mystère de la chambre jaune*).

In this case, the use of the past historic both indicates the sequence of events, and places them in a past totally detached from the present. The fact that forms such as *nous arrivâmes* and *nous vîmes* have now become slightly ridiculous (see 3.1.4.1) does not alter the fact that they were useful.

3.2   The past anterior

3.2.1   *Use and meaning in independent clauses*

(i) The past anterior is extinct in this context. It used to refer to an action completed with great speed:

Et le drôle eut lapé le tout en un moment (La Fontaine)[14]

It could not be used in this context without being accompanied by an adverb such as *vite, bientôt, en un clin d'œil* or *en un instant*.

3.2.2   *Use and meaning in subordinate clauses*

The past anterior expresses anteriority in relation to another verb in the main clause.
(i) The verb in the main clause may be in the past historic or pluperfect.
    The past anterior expresses a brief return to a past which precedes the point of time referred to by the verb in the main clause; it is from this preceding point in time that a new look is taken at what happened after it:

Un mois à peine après que les éléments avancés eurent touché la terre ferme, l'armée de Patch avait fait sa jonction avec celle de Patton. (Example taken from *Le Monde* 1966, and quoted by Mauger in *Grammaire pratique du français d'aujourd'hui*, 249)

(ii) The verb in the main clause may also be the 'historic present', which will not change the basic meaning of the sentence:

Après qu'il eut brouté, trotté, fait tous ses tours, Janot Lapin retourne aux souterrains séjours. (La Fontaine)

(iii) The verb in the main clause may be in the imperfect.
    This case is similar to the previous one, except that the verb in the imperfect refers to a state of affairs which both precedes and follows the point of time referred to by the past anterior:

Dès qu'on eut sur son front fermé le souterrain
L'œil était dans la tombe et regardait Cain.
    (Hugo, *La Conscience*)

('God's eye was there, in the tomb, both before and afterwards').
(iv) In modern French the past anterior is always used with subordinating conjunctions of time such as *dès que, sitôt que, après que* or *quand* which refer to a specific point in time:

Puis, quand il eut confié le sinistre colis au médecin légiste attaché à la rédaction de L'Epoque, il demanda à celui qui allait être bientôt Rouletabille ce qu'il voulait gagner pour faire partie, en qualité de petit reporter, du service des 'faits divers'.   (Leroux, *Le mystère de la chambre jaune*)

The example chosen here is one starting with *quand* because it is often assumed that the past anterior may only refer to an immediate past and may therefore only be used with conjunctions such as *dès que*. Although this is frequently the case, it is not necessarily so.

3.2.3 *Stylistic comment*

Use of the past anterior is very rare in modern French, even in stories written in the past historic. When it is used, in association with the past historic, its use is highly literary.

When used in less elevated literature, it tends to be used in association with the pluperfect to indicate anteriority:

> *Sitôt qu'il eut franchi le seuil de la vieille maison que les ans semblaient avoir bossuée, . . . le Commissaire avait oublié d'un seul coup ses préoccupations professionnelles et ses soucis familiaux.* (Exbrayat, *Qui veut affoler Martine?*)

The past anterior is used in this case because there is no other way of expressing anteriority – apart from the use of the compound pluperfect, since the use of the pluperfect would express the habitual. (In the General System, and in the spoken language, one would say *sitôt qu'il avait eu franchi*, which is the compound pluperfect).

3.3 Misuse of the past historic and past anterior

(i) These tenses differ from the past subjunctive and the pluperfect subjunctive, in the 3rd person singular, only by the absence of a circumflex accent:

past historic	past subjunctive
il fut	*qu'il fût*
past anterior	pluperfect subjunctive
il eut chanté	*qu'il eût chanté*

In many cases the accent is left out when it should not be and vice versa.

As a general rule, if the doubtful form may be replaced by a conditional or a modal imperfect it is a subjunctive and takes an accent; if it cannot, it is a past historic or a past anterior, in which case it does not take an accent:

> *Neuvic refusa d'en bouger, fût-ce pour devenir commissaire divisionnaire* (Exbrayat, *Qui veut affoler Martine?*, example quoted above) *fût-ce = même si c'était pour devenir* (= modal imperfect)

Since *fût* may be replaced by a modal imperfect, it takes an accent.

Similarly; *il l'eût avalé s'il l'eût pu* is the archaic equivalent of *il l'aurait avalé s'il l'avait pu*, hence the two circumflex accents.

(ii) The past anterior is often confused with the pluperfect subjunctive in the 1st person because of their morphological similarity:

past anterior	pluperfect subjunctive
j'eus chanté	*que j'eusse chanté*

Grevisse says the following on this point (*Le Bon usage*, 724):

> *Il faut se garder de confondre cette deuxième forme du conditionnel passé* [i.e. the subjunctive pluperfect] *avec le passé antérieur de l'indicatif.*

He then goes on to give two examples of such a confusion by two famous contemporary writers; one of these, by Sagan, reads as follows:

> **Je me demandais parfois . . . si je n'eus pas dû courir vers lui.*

instead of

Je me demandais si je n'eusse pas dû courir vers lui.

Grevisse condemns such slips with suitable vigour.

4 Modal differences between the indicative tenses

4.1 General considerations

4.1.1 *Definition of modality*

When referring to 'tenses' one is referring to specific, morphological forms. When referring to modality one is referring to the attitude of the speaker towards the action under consideration. One is therefore referring to meaning. We have seen that the indicative forms normally express time and aspect, but in some cases these forms function differently, indicating not so much time and aspect, but rather an attitude on the part of the person speaking or writing. Thus, in *si j'étais riche j'achèterais un bateau*, the imperfect does not refer to a real past but to an unreal present. The imperfect in *je voulais vous dire que je pars* does not refer to the past either, but expresses a kind of polite and considerate attitude in the present, the rest of the sentence indicating that the time referred to is, in fact, the present.

There are three kinds of tenses which may be used modally: the imperfect (4.2), the future and future anterior (4.3 and 4.4) and the conditional forms (Ch. 6). The most important of the indicative tenses is the imperfect in this respect.

4.1.2 *Expression of modality rather than time by certain tenses in certain contexts*

(i) It is not surprising that the future tenses should express modality: the future is doubtful by definition and there are varying degrees of likelihood as to whether events will take place.

(ii) The conditional forms are also easy to explain:

je pense que je chanterai si ma gorge est guérie

becomes in the past

je pensais que je chanterais si ma gorge était guérie

And if one suppresses *je pensais* one obtains:

je chanterais [maintenant] si ma gorge était guérie (mais elle ne l'est pas: this refers to an unreal present)

je chanterais [demain] si ma gorge était guérie (elle le sera peut-être: this refers to a hypothetical future)

In this case it is the other time references present in the context which determine the exact meaning to be attributed to each sentence.

See also Ch. 6, section 2.

(iii) The use of the imperfect as a mood is more difficult to explain. Various hypotheses have been put forward. Guillaume, for example, has written about the imperfect being the tense form used to express the *décalage*[15] or shift in time existing between the reality described and the time of speaking or writing. It is certainly true that children tend to use both the imperfect and the conditional to refer to the imaginary, although only the use of the conditional is acceptable in prescriptive terms. Children will thus say either *alors on était deux explorateurs* ('we would be two explorers') or *alors on serait deux explorateurs* ('let's be two explorers'); in the first case one is referring to a past state of affairs leading to an unpredictable present, whereas in the second one is referring to an imaginary present leading to an unpredictable future.

Since both the imperfect and the conditional have the same endings in *-ais*, the fact that these forms should have much in common is not altogether surprising. It is this ending which places the action in an imaginary world, and it is the presence of the *-r-* in the conditional form which displaces this imaginary world from the past (imperfect) into the present (the conditional form).

4.2 Modal uses of the imperfect

(i) The imperfect has been termed a 'second present', a present reflecting the imaginary, or a moment of doubt, or a possible future: *si j'étais riche j'achèterais un bateau*. This sentence applies to the present, but it is a present which is not realized, hence the use of a past tense to express it (see Ch. 6, section 3). But the imperfect may also refer to a possible present, even when used on its own. Compare:

on m'a dit qu'il est à la maison
on m'a dit qu'il était à la maison [maintenant]
on m'a dit qu'il était à la maison hier

The first sentence emphasizes the reality of the assertion (use of the present tense), the second refers to the present but with an element of doubt in the assertion. The third is a straightforward assertion relating to the past. The use of the second sentence without the adverb of time *maintenant* could give rise to doubts as to whether the reference is to a real past or a present containing an element of doubt.

This may lead to ambiguities, as in *cinq minutes plus tard et le train déraillait*. This could mean one of two things: that the train was actually derailed at some point in the past; or that the train would have been derailed if some other action had not prevented it from happening. The ambiguity is normally removed by the context.

(ii) The imperfect has a clearly different modal sense in certain contexts when used as a form or politeness; it is sometimes called *l'imparfait de discrétion*:

je voulais vous dire que je ne serais pas là mardi

In this case the use of the imperfect, instead of referring to a past point in time, refers to now; the imperfect translates the modality: 'I would like to do this or that, but I feel I should hesitate to do so.'

The pluperfect may also be used in this way:

j'étais venu vous dire que je ne pourrais pas être là la semaine prochaine

(iii) When talking to children or animals the imperfect is sometimes used in preference to the present, to express the entering or sharing of a different world (sometimes called *l'imparfait hypocoristique*, i.e. *l'imparfait de gentillesse ou d'affection*):

ah! il faisait des misères à sa maman!
ah! comme il était mignon le petit toutou!

4.3 Modal uses of the future

(i) The future may coincide with the present and be used to express a hypothesis:

Pourquoi n'est-il pas là?
Je ne sais pas. Il sera encore à Paris.

Here, reality is presented as only probable. This kind of use of the future has sometimes been called the 'conjectural' future.

(ii) The future may be used instead of the conditional. This was already the case in Old French. Thus Brunot and Bruneau (*Précis de grammaire historique de la langue française*) write:

Le futur, qui est l'Inconnu, n'offre guère de point de repère. En revanche il est souvent 'chargé' de notions diverses (idées de possibilité, d'obligation, etc.) et de sentiments (désir, crainte, etc.). Il a donc souvent une valeur suggestive. Nous n'en donnerons qu'un exemple. Un cuisinier, qui veut entrer dans le palais pour préparer le repas, trouve la porte fermée. 'Des or vorra le mengier conraer' (Charroi de Nîmes, v. 1250): voilà qu'il voudra préparer le manger. L'intensité du désir a transformé un conditionnel (il voudrait) en un futur.

A similar use is made of the future in Modern French: in the following sentence, *direz* stands for *pourriez me dire*:

> *vous me direz que ce que je vous demande n'est pas grand chose mais je serais ravie si vous pouviez le faire*

(iii) Since the point of time referred to by the future tense is vague, an adverbial − or the context − normally specifies more definitely the period of time referred to. If no adverbial is used, the future may be used instead of the imperative; this is particularly frequent in the 3rd person since the imperative has no 3rd person: *il ira!* The future is also frequently used as an imperative in the 2nd person: *tu iras t'excuser.* But in the 3rd person one can also use the subjunctive as an imperative: *qu'il aille se faire pendre!* (familiar).

The future can also function as an imperative when used in connection with adverbials of time, but in that case a distinctive intonation pattern is needed to differentiate the statement from one expressing simple futurity. In the written language an exclamation mark usually represents this special intonation:

il ira cet été (non-emphatic statement: 'he will go')
il ira cet été! (emphatic statement order: 'he shall go')

4.4 Modal uses of the future anterior (or 'compound future')

The future anterior normally refers to an action completed at a certain point in the future, as in: *j'aurai terminé quand il reviendra.* But it can also refer to a conjectural future: *je ne sais pas où il est; il sera allé sans doute au jardin* (i.e. 'this fact will be in the past by the time I find out whether or not it was true').

5 Auxiliaries of time, aspect and mood

5.1 Auxiliaries of time

There are three auxiliaries of time: *aller* + infinitive (see 2.4.3); *venir de* to refer to the immediate past (*je viens d'y aller/je venais d'y aller*); and *être sur le point de* (*j'étais sur le point d'y aller/je suis sur le point d'y aller/je serai sur le point d'y aller*).

5.2 Auxiliaries of aspect

(See section 2.7.6 for table of the aspects expressed by tense forms alone.)

Type or stage of action	Auxiliaries used	Examples
Beginning of the action(Inchoative)	*commencer à;* *se mettre à*	*je commence à travailler*
Progression of the action (Progressive)	*être en train de;* *continuer à*	*je suis en train de taper à la machine*

Type or stage of action	Auxiliaries used	Examples
Ending of the action (Terminative)	*cesser de; finir de; sortir de* (familiar)	*je finis de travailler* *il sort de dîner*
Action which lasts (Durative aspect)	*continuer à; ne pas cesser de; être à* (archaic)	*il continue à le faire* *(elle est à se préparer)*
Repeated action (Iterative aspect) (see Note below)	*ne pas s'arrêter de; ne faire que de*	*je n'arrête pas de travailler* *il ne fait que d'écrire des bêtises*
Habitual action (Habitual aspect)	*avoir l'habitude de*	*j'ai l'habitude de le faire*

Note: All French tenses may be used with an iterative sense, on condition that the sentence contains a temporal expression such as *toute sa vie, toujours, tous les matins*:

> *mon père fait/faisait/fera/a fait/aura fait/ferait/aurait fait tous les jours une demi-heure de gymnastique*

5.3 Auxiliaries of mood

The use of the following verbs enable one to express various moods lexically, whilst still using indicative forms.

5.3.1 *Main auxiliaries of mood*

The three main auxiliaries of mood are *devoir, pouvoir* and *vouloir*. They may take on different meanings depending on the context.
(i) Devoir
may indicate a necessity:

> *je dois y être avant cinq heures*

may indicate that the action is only probable:

> *elle doit être grande maintenant*

may be used to refer to a hypothetical future:

> *si cela doit se reproduire, j'agirai en conséquence*

(For the meaning of this verb when used in the imperfect, see 3.1.2.2 *iii*.)
(ii) Pouvoir
may indicate permission (can):

> *vous pouvez partir*

may express a probability (may):

> *elle peut avoir une trentaine d'années*

may indicate a possibility (to be able to):

> *Tu peux y arriver*

(iii) Vouloir
expresses the will of the speaker or subject:

je veux le faire

in the interrogative form, means 'are we ready/prepared to do something?':

voulons-nous vraiment étouffer notre économie à force d'impôts?

5.3.2   *Semi-auxiliaries of mood*

There are a number of verbs which function either lexically as full verbs or as auxiliaries of mood. These could be called 'semi-auxiliaries', since they do not always function as auxiliaries.

(i) There are two auxiliaries which indicate the immediate future plus an attitude on the part of the speaker towards the action: *être près de* and *être en passe de* indicate that the situation is favourable to the accomplishment of the action:

il est en passe de devenir célèbre (archaic)
il est près de réussir

(ii) *Être loin de*, on the other hand, expresses the opposition between the attitude of the speaker or writer and the action described:

je suis loin d'être satisfait de votre travail

(iii) *Être pour* indicates that one is favourably disposed towards the action:

ce qui m'arrive n'est pas pour me déplaire

(iv) *Faillir* and *manquer de* indicate that the action nearly took place:

j'ai failli me retrouver à la rue

(v) *Faire* translates the factitive: the subject is the agent and not the actor; it therefore expresses the will of the speaker or writer:

je le ferai venir à Paris

(vi) *Ne faire que* when used modally (and not as an iterative, in which case the expression is *ne faire que de*) has a privative meaning:

il ne fait que s'amuser ('he is only playing')

(vii) *Laisser* may indicate a permission:

je te laisse y aller tout seul

(viii) *Venir à* indicates a fortuitous action:

Un âne vint à passer . . . (La Fontaine) (archaic)

5.4   False auxiliaries of mood

Paraître and *sembler* are not semi-auxiliaries but stative verbs describing the appearance of a state. 'Appear' is often mistranslated into French by *apparaître*. This is because there is one verb 'appear' in English which corresponds to two verbs in French, *paraître* and *apparaître*. The difference between these two verbs is that *apparaître* means to appear physically, as in (1) below, whereas *paraître*, like *sembler*, refers to something mental (as does the English verb 'seem'), as can be seen in example (2):

(1) *elle a apparu dans l'encadrement de la porte*
(2) *elle paraît (= elle semble) fatiguée*

6 Tense Agreement or 'la concordance des temps'

6.1 General considerations

Much has been written on this subject by French grammarians. The concept itself was inherited from the Latin grammars which speak of 'consecutio temporum', by which term is designated the nearly mechanical sets of correspondences between the tense of the verb in the subordinate clause and that in the main clause, a change in the latter automatically entailing a change in the former.

Some grammarians maintain (see F. Brunot, *La Pensée et la langue*, 728) that there is, in fact, no such thing in modern French as *la concordance des temps*:

> *Le principe même en est mauvais. Ce n'est pas le temps de la principale qui amène le temps de la subordonnée, c'est le sens. Le chapitre de la concordance des temps se résume en une ligne: il n'y en a pas.*

From what has been described in this chapter it would appear that Brunot's point of view is the right one, in the sense that any combination of tenses may occur if it can be justified from a semantic point of view. On the other hand, there is a tendency in the language to try to maintain certain morphological harmonies; thus the first sentence below is usually preferred to the second:

> *je me disais que Paris était bien grand*
> *je me disais que Paris est bien grand*

It would appear that, where several forms are possible, the one using similar morphological constructions is felt to be the most harmonious, hence the *règles de concordance des temps*. But these rules belong to stylistics rather than to the description of the code of the language. The fact that there are no such rules within the code of the language may be illustrated by a quotation from Proust (*Du Côté de chez Swann*), in which the whole array − or nearly − of possible tenses is combined within the space of one paragraph:

> *. . . . elle l'entraînait avec elle vers des perspectives inconnues. Puis elle disparut. Il souhaita passionément la revoir une troisième fois. Et elle reparut en effet, mais sans lui parler plus clairement, en lui causant une volupté plus profonde: il était comme un homme dans la vie de qui une passante qu'il a aperçue vient de faire entrer l'image d'une beauté nouvelle qui donne à sa propre sensibilité une valeur plus grande, sans qu'il sache seulement s'il pourra revoir jamais celle qu'il aime déjà et dont il ignore jusqu'au nom.*

One may also quote Brunot and Bruneau (*Grammaire historique de la langue française*, 342) on this subject:

> *Des grammairiens modernes ont imaginé une prétendue règle de concordance des temps. Cette règle n'a jamais été observée par les bons écrivains. Un verbe principal au passé peut donc être accompagné de verbes secondaires au présent quand les propositions secondaires expriment une 'action' indépendante de celle de la principale: 'Je l'assurai que j'en connaissais qui sont aussi sévères que ceux qu'il me citait sont relâchés'* (Pascal, *Provinciales*, V).
> *'Etaient sévères' semblerait indiquer qu'ils ne le sont plus, ce qui est faux.*

It is also true that if a text is written in the historic present, the tenses in the subordinate clauses may or may not be in the past. Bruneau quotes the following sentence from *Fénelon*:

> *[Iris] voit de loin la querelle . . .; elle frémit à la vue du danger où était le jeune Télémaque; elle s'approche . . . .*

In this example, *était* could have been replaced by the present *est*.

6.2   The changing nature of 'la règle de la concordance des temps'

Although there are no *règles de concordance des temps* as such, there is a tendency for one tense to attract another if the meaning of the context allows it. But there have been different fashions in the ways these *attractions des temps* were realized. In this sense there are *règles de concordance des temps*. In the seventeenth century, for example, *l'attraction des temps* was different from that which is practised today.

(i) A compound past in the main clause often 'attracted' a past tense in the subordinate clause:

Le Roi n'a pas voulu que la Reine soit allée à Paris (Madame de Sévigné)

(*Soit allée* would become *aille* in present-day French.)
(ii) The past subjunctive was also normally used in the subordinate clause, even when the verb in the main clause was in the present or future:

Vous ne trouverez pas un seul homme qui pût vivre à porte ouverte (Malherbe)

Nowadays, this tense having ceased to be productive, a present subjunctive would take its place: *pût* would become *puisse* in present-day French.

The subjunctive imperfect was used to express the unreality of the action. It expressed *l'irréel* (the unreal). The subjunctive imperfect comes from the Latin subjunctive pluperfect and still retains the meaning of the latter in the seventeenth century. Hence the use of the imperfect and not of the present, which one could have expected but which would refer to something potentially possible.
(iii) Some forms of *attraction des temps* which were normal in the seventeenth century are no longer acceptable:

Il se pourrait bien que les Gascons l'y auraient apporté (Vaugelas)

In this case a conditional in the main clause has 'attracted' a conditional in the subordinate clause. In modern French one would write *aient apporté* for *auraient apporté*.
(iv) In contemporary French, the present and compound past in the subjunctive mood are used where an imperfect or a pluperfect subjunctive could be expected. In contemporary French one writes (and even more obviously says):

je ne pensais pas qu'il vienne/qu'il soit venu

instead of:

je ne pensais pas qu'il vînt/qu'il fût venu

Similarly the use of the conditional no longer entails using the imperfect or pluperfect subjunctive. One writes and says:

il se pourrait qu'il vienne/qu'il soit venu

instead of:

il se pourrait qu'il vînt/qu'il fût venu

In other words although there are no strict *règles de concordance des temps* as such, there are tendencies for certain tenses to attract others, when the context allows; it is those tendencies which have changed fairly dramatically over the last three centuries. (For the seventeenth century, see A. Haase, *Syntaxe française du XVIIe siècle*.)

Notes

1 There is still a gap in the system, however, since the compound past cannot replace the past historic in all its uses; see 3.1.4.3.

2 This table and what follows constitute 'sweeping generalizations', but the aim in this section is not to describe the verbal system in Old and Middle French per se, but to synthesize the various systems used throughout this period and throughout the country in order to give an overall picture of the way in which the verbal system has developed from one system into two systems today.

3 The terms 'general system' and 'narrative system' are adapted from those used by Benveniste (see in *Problèmes de linguistique générale*, vol. 1).

4 The reason why only one person was questioned was that in those days the speech of a single person was supposed to be representative of the potential of the language taken as a whole.

5 Only the temporal uses of the imperfect are covered in this section, not its modal use.

6 For a detailed study of the temporal conditional, see Ch. 6, 1.2.

7 The term 'future equivalent' is used, since English does not have a morphological future, but expresses the future through the use of modals such as 'will' and 'shall' and expressions such as 'going to'.

8 *Ce* becomes *le* because *ce* in this context refers to a present situation whereas *le* refers to a situation which need not be present.

9 These forms are still used far more often in these areas than elsewhere in France.

10 The compound pluperfect seems to be used, but very rarely.

11 If one wishes to refer to one specific occasion (i.e. the 'semelfactive') rather than to the habitual, one would have to use the past historic and past anterior (see section 3, e.g. *lorsqu'il eut fini son repas, il alla faire un tour au jardin*.

12 In this article, published in *Le Monde* in June 1980, the past historic is used, even in the first person plural, to emphasize the development of the story.

> *Bjorn Borg, qui s'est qualifié sans difficulté pour sa cinquième finale de Wimbledon, jeudi 3 juillet, aux dépens de l'Américain Brian Gottfried, réunit en sa personne tous les dons du champion des champions. Mais, comme la plupart des grands du sport, il a, en outre, le privilège d'être «chanceux». Tandis qu'il n'a plus qu'à attendre tranquillement celui que le sort voudra bien lui opposer – ils sont deux encore à se rencontrer : Connors et McEnroe, qui paient les contre-temps de la semaine, – l'adversaire qu'il craignait le plus, Roscoe Tanner venant d'être éliminé. Immense soulagement pour Borg.*
>
> *Quand sur le Centre Court à midi, heure de ce quart de finale retardé, nous vîmes ledit Tanner exécuter Jimmy Connors dans un premier set miraculeux (gagné 6-1) où il percutait ses premières balles de service comme au stand de tir, nous pensâmes un moment que nous allions vers une réédition pénible du match auquel nous avions assisté il y a quelques années en ces lieux mêmes. Mais le Connors de Wimbledon, cuvée 80 n'a aucun rapport avec celui qui besogna à Roland-Garros jusqu'à se faire éliminer par Gerulaîtis.*
>
> *Qui se serait sorti à sa place de cette mousqueterie? Nous nous le demandons. Car, à partir du deuxième set, nous avons retrouvé un tout autre homme : par la longueur inimaginable qu'il imprimait à ses balles de fond, par les retours foudroyants qu'il réussissait sur les balles-canons, par ses flexions à la limite de mettre le genou sur l'herbe et la délivrance de toutes ses forces de ripostes-éclairs, où sa propre impulsion profitait de celle de son adversaire, Connors nous rappela irrésistiblement le champion 1974 qui avait balayé Rosewall.*
>
> *A ce train-là, le deuxième set (6-2) vola dans sa poche à la vitesse grand V. C'est au milieu du troisième set, remporté 6-4 par Tanner, que les échanges furent les plus beaux. Après quoi, le tireur d'élite commença à «arroser» et Connors,*

enlevant le quatrième set par 6-2, ne rata plus une occasion de le pourfendre au filet. Au cinquième set, ce fut mieux encore : Connors monta délibérément à la volée, ne laissant plus aucune chance à Tanner, et l'emportant une nouvelle fois par 6-2. Aucun tie-break, *très peu d'égalités : comment, au rythme auquel les balles étaient frappées, aurait-ce été possible?*

13 Marouzeau (*Précis de stylistique française*, 124) writes the following on this point:
Le passé défini [i.e. the past historic] *n'a pas non plus de substitut exact; il en résulte quelque embarras lorsqu'on a besoin d'un passé historique: 'à minuit arriva la nouvelle que . . .'. On emploie alors parfois le passé indéfini* [i.e. the compound past] *qui se trouve ainsi conduit à jouer deux rôles très différents; celui d'exprimer le résultat d'une action passée: 'la voiture est arrivée', et celui d'affecter une action à un moment donné du passé: 'à minuit est arrivée la nouvelle que . . .'.*

14 Imbs writes as follows, basing his comments on this example:
En choisissant le passé dit antérieur, l'écrivain se place d'emblée à la sortie de la série début-milieu-fin, comme s'il n'avait pas le temps de l'évoquer, et ne relate que la situation qui résulte de l'accomplissement de cette série. Mais comme cette situation est elle-même évoquée comme privée de durée antérieure, (puisque l'auxiliaire est le passé simple perfectif-momentané), l'effet de rapidité est ainsi double, et en bon artiste qu'il est, La Fontaine clôt là-dessus la première partie de son récit, qu'il continuera d'abord au présent. (L'Emploi des temps verbaux en français moderne, 122)

15 This is a somewhat simple explanation of the phenomenon − but we hope not a simplistic one. Both Guillaume and Damourette and Pinchon have elaborated more complex theories on the subject.

Chapter 5

The subjunctive

0.1 The 'harmonizing' subjunctive

Some grammar books do not classify the subjunctive as a mood but as a tense, and include it under the *règles de concordances des temps* or 'tense agreement rules'. This is because in many cases the use of the subjunctive is determined by some structural feature contained in the main clause, in which case it is predictable and, therefore, noncontrastive (i.e. it carries no special meaning), as in *il faut qu'il vienne*. Here, the subjunctive is required in the subordinate clause because of the use of *il faut* in the main clause. This use of the subjunctive is sometimes called the 'amodal' subjunctive. It is said to be a *servitude grammaticale*, meaning that it is compulsory[1]. Here this is referred to as 'the harmonizing subjunctive' in order to emphasize its positive aspects (see 3.1 *iv, v* and *vi*).

0.2 The subjunctive as a carrier of meaning (or 'contrastive subjunctive')

(i) In opposition to this compulsory use of the subjunctive, one may quote a relatively small number of cases in which there is a contrastive choice between the use of the indicative and the subjunctive, as in:

nous comprenons que vous avez commis une erreur
   (plain statement of fact)
nous comprenons que vous ayez commis une erreur
   (implies sympathy and understanding)

The indicative and the subjunctive may also be used contrastively in certain cases in relative clauses; see 3.3.
Compare:

je cherche un étudiant qui sache le chinois (there may not be such a student)
je cherche un étudiant qui sait le chinois (there is such a student but I don't know
   who he is)

(See 3.3.2 for the influence on mood of the choice of determiner modifying the antecedent of the relative pronoun.)
This is sometimes called the 'modal' subjunctive.
(ii) In some cases there is disagreement as to whether the indicative is acceptable instead of a subjunctive:

je ne pense pas qu'il vienne demain
je ne pense pas qu'il viendra demain

For some prescriptive grammarians the second sentence is not, in fact, acceptable. At best they will consider it acceptable in the spoken language only. Descriptive grammarians will, however, list both sentences as acceptable in the spoken language whilst not allowing the second in the written language. One thus ends up with different rules for the spoken and written language.

Other grammarians maintain, however, that both sentences are acceptable and that their use is contrastive, with *je ne pense pas qu'il vienne demain* heavily emphasizing the element of doubt present in the mind of the speaker, and *je ne pense pas qu'il viendra demain*, on the contrary, not stressing the element of doubt. This kind of contrast may certainly be used in the following type of context:

(Comment) *Regardez! Je fais un dérapage* (skiier to skiing instructor)
(Response) *Ah oui! Et croyez-vous que vous le fassiez bien?* (subjunctive) or *faites bien?* (indicative)

In this case the indicative refers to the fact, whereas the subjunctive refers to the opinion the skiier may have on the fact.

The reason the indicative is used in this way in the spoken language, where the subjunctive would be expected, is as follows: the indicative gives reality to events (even if these do not take place) by situating them in time. The subjunctive, on the other hand, because it lacks temporal precision (cf. 1.2) shows the action at a kind of amorphous stage. The spoken language, however, prefers the precision given by the indicative as being more spontaneous; the kind of ponderings which go with the use of the subjunctive are, by definition, nonspontaneous, and therefore belong to the written language. Hence the natural tendency is to use the indicative rather than the subjunctive whenever possible in the spoken language (although where such strongly marked expressions as *il faut* occur, there is no choice but to use the subjunctive).

(iii) The subjunctive pluperfect may replace the compound conditional, in which case it is sometimes called *le conditionnel deuxième forme*; but the meaning of these two forms is not exactly the same, in that the subjunctive pluperfect refers specifically to a hypothesis which is gratuitous, i.e. to the unreal. (It is then called in French *le subjonctif de l'irréel*.) Thus:

Vous eussiez pu choisir un plus mauvais maître. (Couteaux, *Un monsieur de compagnie*)

refers to a gratuitous hypothesis. It is therefore the ideal mood to express the imaginary, making plain the fact that one is dealing with a dream world:

On eût dit [= aurait dit] une coupure pratiquée de main d'homme à travers l'épaisse muraille de la montagne. . . . (Gautier, *Le Roman de la momie*)

i.e. 'it looked as if the rock had been cut by a human hand, but, of course, this was just an impression': the pluperfect subjunctive makes very explicit this last point.

The pluperfect subjunctive may also be used to express the imaginary in combination with the conditional, in which case one ends up with two levels in this imaginary world (*l'imaginaire du deuxième degré*): the conditional expresses a first stage in the imaginary, and the subjunctive pluperfect a hypothesis which is even more remote or impossible, in relation to the first; see example in 4.4.1.

0.3   Different types of meaning carried by the subjunctive

The subjunctive may appear to express a large number of meanings, hence the numerous different schools of thought regarding its use. The truth of the matter is that there are a fair number of types of contexts in which the subjunctive may fit, in order to express a variety of meanings (cf. *iv* below). We shall however, enumerate first of all some of the generalities found in grammar books as to the meaning carried by the subjunctive, if only to point out some of the inadequacies of these definitions.

(i) Some see in the subjunctive a mood expressing a doubt, a wish or a feeling:

je veux qu'il parte (wish or order)
je doute qu'il parte (doubt)
je suis content qu'il parte (emotion)

(ii) For others, the subjunctive is the mood of subordination, since one rarely finds it in main clauses (except when the pluperfect is used as a *conditionnel deuxième forme* i.e., instead of a compound conditional) and one hardly ever finds it in independent clauses, except in fossilized expressions such as *vive le roi*. The subjunctive is therefore seen as describing an event which is the consequence of another, be it explicit or merely understood:

> *il faut qu'il s'en aille*
> *qu'il s'en aille!* (*il faut* is understood)

(iii) This interpretation does not, however, account for contrasting sentences such as:

> *il est certain qu'il l'a fait de bon cœur*
> *qu'il l'ait fait de bon cœur, c'est certain*

The difference between *qu'il l'a fait* and *qu'il l'ait fait* is that the indicative introduces new information whereas the subjunctive conveys the idea of a pre-existing notion. In this case one is speaking in terms of psychological subordination as well as grammatical subordination: purely grammatical subordination does not demand the use of the subjunctive, as can be seen in *il est certain qu'il l'a fait de bon cœur*, whereas the use of the subjunctive in *qu'il l'ait fait de bon cœur, c'est certain*, appears to express psychological subordination.[2]

(iv) Yet another attitude is to see the subjunctive as representing an intermediate phase in the thought process – the action as envisaged rather than as taking place. Time is not clearly expressed in this mood (see 1.2): the present and imperfect are simply oriented towards the future (or the future seen from the past, in the case of the imperfect), whereas the compound past and the pluperfect are oriented towards the past. In other words these tenses do no more than express the prospective and the retrospective. Since the action is merely envisaged, this mood is very suited to the interpretation of facts; hence the name sometimes given to the subjunctive of *le mode de l'interprétation*.

This interpretation has the advantage that it accounts for all the contrasts which can be achieved through the use and non-use of the subjunctive. It accounts for its use in relative clauses (see 3.3). It also accounts for sentences such as *je ne crois pas qu'il pleuve* and *je ne crois pas qu'il pleut*. In the first case the action is envisaged in the mind only, whereas in the second the indicative represents reality. This interpretation also accounts for both *il est possible qu'il vienne* and *il est possible qu'il viendra*, since the choice of one form rather than another will depend on whether the speaker sees the action as taking place, whether in the present, past or future, or as being still in the amorphous state of being envisaged. Another way of expressing this is to say that if one sees the action with clarity the indicative will be used, whereas the use of the subjunctive will imply a certain amount of opacity.

Examples of the type of *qu'il l'ait fait de bon cœur, c'est certain* may be explained similarly. This is not a simple case of inversion; the use of *'que'* in this position indicates the statement of a hypothesis. If one uses the subjunctive – which lacks definition – the event is seen as still amorphous, i.e. as still being a hypothesis. But if the indicative is used, the preciseness of the tense envisages the action as realized rather than as hypothetical – hence the fact that *qu'il l'a fait de bon cœur, c'est certain* is also acceptable.

This interpretation of the subjunctive may be represented in the following manner[3] (see diagram overleaf – the shaded areas are those of overlap of the moods):

(The nominal mood is made up of the infinitive, the participles and the gerund.)

(v) Another complicating factor is that the use of the subjunctive has varied through the centuries. *Croire,* for example, used to contain a much greater element of doubt than it does nowadays, hence sentences such as:

Thought processes involved in the conceptualization of time }

1st stage: nominal mood

2nd stage: subjunctive

3rd stage: indicative

La plus belle des deux, je crois que ce soit l'autre (Corneille)

It is for quite a different reason that Racine used an indicative instead of subjunctive in the following passage from Andromaque:

Oreste: *Souvenez-vous qu'il règne et qu'un front couronné . . .*
Hermione: *Ne vous suffit-il pas que je l'ai ordonné?*

Nowadays one would write *que je l'aie ordonné.* The use of the indicative rather than the subjunctive reflects the fact that Hermione's orders are so powerful as to represent reality, which removes from Oreste all freedom of manoeuvre.

1   Morphological considerations

1.1   The various tense forms

Unlike the indicative, the subjunctive system is very simple: two simple tenses, two compound tenses and one double compound tense:

present: (*que*) *je chante, que tu chantes . . .*
imperfect: (*que*) *je chantasse, que tu chantasses . . .*
compound past (or 'perfect'): (*que*) *j'aie chanté, que tu aies chanté . . .*
pluperfect (or 'past perfect'): (*que*) *j'eusse chanté,* (*que*) *tu eusses chanté . . .*
double compound past: (*que*) *j'aie eu chanté, (que) tu aies eu chanté . . .*

Although the subjunctive is indicated by suffixation there is also usually an anteposed conjunction, *que,* which illustrates the fact that the subjunctive, in most cases today, tends to appear in subordinate clauses. (*Que* does not of course have to be followed by the subjunctive; indeed in most cases it is followed by the indicative, as in *il dit qu'il vient.*)

1.2   Time and aspect

(i) The subjunctive does not represent time clearly. Its simple forms are basically oriented towards the future (i.e. prospective), while its compound forms are oriented towards the past (i.e. retrospective).

   It is the time referred to by the tense in the main clause and the context in general which indicate from what point in time the action in the subordinate clause is considered, either retrospectively or prospectively. In the following examples this point of reference in time is 'Noel':

prospective   *il faut qu'il finisse à Noël*
   viewpoint   *il fallait qu'il finît à Noël*
retrospective   *il faut qu'il ait fini à Noël*
   viewpoint   *il fallait qu'il eût fini à Noël*

It is because the compound forms are used to express the retrospective − by means of the idea of completion . that the double compound forms are needed, mainly in the spoken language, to stress the idea of completion itself, e.g. *il aurait fallu qu'il ait eu fini à Noël.*

(ii) Aspectually these tenses are similar to their indicative counterparts: the present and imperfect show the action seen in midstream; the compound forms see the action as completed, and the double compound form stresses completion.

1.3 Disappearance of the imperfect (or past) subjunctive and of the pluperfect (or past perfect) subjunctive

1.3.1 *The imperfect subjunctive*

(i) Of these two tenses, it is the imperfect which is least used in modern French; this is because it can no longer appear in as many hypothetical constructions as the pluperfect (see 2.3 and chapter 6, section 3). It has therefore survived largely for the purpose of morphological agreement only, and as such it does not usually carry meaning in modern French. It is often replaced by the subjunctive present (see 2.5).

(ii) Being a poor carrier of meaning, the imperfect subjunctive is a stylistic luxury; since most of its forms are rarely used, they appear strange to the ear when they are used. In a suitable register they may appear elegant, but in an informal context they will appear pedantic or even comic.[4]

(iii) Those forms which will shock most are those which resemble in nothing the phonology of other tenses: forms such as *'chantasse'* tend to appear 'ugly' because rarely used and resembling no other. But the 3rd person singular resembles the past historic; as such its forms are acceptable. *Qu'il eût, qu'il fût, qu'il fît* and *qu'il prît*, for example, are acceptable, being phonologically identical to the past historic (it is the circumflex accent which differentiates them in writing).

(See 1.4. For problems of agreement, see 2.5.)

1.3.2 *The pluperfect subjunctive*

The pluperfect differs from the imperfect in that it may be used not only for morphological agreement, but also as a carrier of meaning. It is used to refer to a purely gratuitous hypothesis, and as such it is often used to express the imaginary:

> *On eût dit les tas de cendres restés sur place d'une chaîne de montagnes brûlée au temps des catastrophes cosmiques dans un grand incendie planétaire.*
> (Gautier, *Le Roman de la momie*)

As such, it contrasts with the conditional which expresses both the hypothetical and the imaginary, without distinguishing between the two. This is, however, a subtle distinction, unnecessary in most contexts, hence the gradual disappearance of the pluperfect subjunctive which is replaced by the conditional.

1.3.3 *The imperfect subjunctive and the pluperfect subjunctive in 'si' clauses:*

Both tenses used to appear in *si* clauses (see chapter 6, section 3). They are normally replaced in modern French by the indicative imperfect or pluperfect, or by the conditional if no 'si' is present in the construction, e.g.

> *. . . . et le pauvre docteur allemand ne pouvait suffire à éponger l'eau de sa figure avec son mouchoir à carreaux bleus, trempé comme s'il eût été plongé dans l'eau [= comme s'il avait été plongé[5] dans l'eau].*
> (Gautier, *Le Roman de la momie*)

1.4 Misuse of the subjunctive and indicative moods from a morphological point of view

There are a number of mistakes made by French and English writers of French alike in relation to the morphology of the subjunctive.

(i) The most common mistake is to confuse the past subjunctive with the past historic in the 3rd person singular, since these two forms differ only in the use or non-use of the circumflex accent:

Past subjunctive	Past historic (indicative)
qu'il fût	*il fut*
qu'il eût	*il eut*
qu'il vînt	*il vint*

(ii) The case of *fassiez*

The following example was quoted in 0.2 *ii*:

Regardez! Je fais un dérapage
Ah oui! Et croyez-vous que vous le fassiez bien?/faites bien?

But one often hears from native speakers structures of the following type:

Ah oui! Et croyez-vous que vous le *faisiez bien?

This is because *faisiez* is thought (wrongly) to be a present subjunctive on the model of verbs of the 1st conjugation such as *chanter*: the present subjunctive 2nd person plural of this verb is *chantiez*, which form is common both to the present subjunctive and to the imperfect indicative.

Note that *faisiez* would be possible if one were referring to the past:

Vous avez vu mes dérapages tout-à-l'heure?
Ah oui! Et croyez-vous que vous les faisiez bien (i.e. tout-à-l'heure)?

2 Syntactic considerations

2.1 General considerations

The subjunctive is very rarely used in independent clauses. It survives mainly in exclamations expressing hopes, wishes, orders, etc., and it survives in only one construction forming a main clause '*je ne sache que*' (see 2.2). But the subjunctive is still used in hypothetical constructions (see 2.3) and in subordinate clauses (see 2.4).

Because of the gradual disappearance of the imperfect and pluperfect, agreement in the subordinated clause is a problem (see 2.5).

2.2 The subjunctive in independent clauses

(i) The subjunctive may be used to express a wish, an order, an exclamation or attitudes such as indignation, delight and so on:

vienne le printemps et tout semblera plus souriant (wish)
qu'il sorte tout de suite! (order)
Dieu soit loué! (exclamation)
que je le fasse, moi qui suis malade! (expression of indignation)

The subjunctive may also express a hypothesis, in which case it may be replaced by an imperative:

soit un triangle ABC (i.e. *prenons un triangle ABC*)

In all of these cases the speaker is expressing an attitude towards the action. As there is no 3rd person in the imperative, the subjunctive fills the gap, since the idea of order is very similar to that of will.

(ii) The subjunctive is used in paratactical constructions, i.e. constructions in which clauses are joined together without the use of conjunctions. In this case too one may talk of 'fossilized expressions'. Here there is normally inversion of subject and verb, e.g. *aucun être, fût-ce le diable, ne me ferait changer d'avis.*

(iii) In the fossilized expression *je ne sache*, as in *je ne sache pas de plus belle histoire*, the use of the subjunctive expresses the fact that it would be impossible for the speaker to know of a more beautiful story. In this sense the sentence contrasts with *je ne connais pas de plus belle histoire* ('I do not yet know a more beautiful story').

It has been pointed out (see Moignet, *Essai sur le subjonctif en latin post-classique et en ancien français*, 661-5) that attempts were made during the Old French period to establish the subjunctive in independent clauses, but without success. Only the odd expression *je ne sache* has survived from these attempts.[6]

2.3 Use of the subjunctive in hypothetical clauses

See Ch. 6, section 3.

(i) The imperfect subjunctive used to express the hypothetical did not survive much beyond the thirteenth century as a really creative form because of its ambiguity (see ch. 6, 3.2). But the imperfect subjunctive form was common up till the sixteenth century to express the unreal; indeed, one still finds the odd literary example in modern French:

Il semblait que nous demeurassions immobiles (Gide, *Amyntas*)

(ii) The pluperfect subjunctive appeared in hypothetical constructions in the thirteenth century but ceased to be productive in the seventeenth, having been condemned by Vaugelas. Its use has, however, survived in the literary system, mainly in the 3rd person singular, to refer to a hypothesis which is gratuitous or untrue (the pluperfect is still sometimes used in this way today):

Quand M. Hoveyda eût été le dernier des criminels, cela n'entamait en rien son droit à un procès public et régulier. (*Le Monde*, 10 March 1979)

It would have been more normal to write:

Même si M. Hoveyda avait été le dernier des criminels cela n'entamerait en rien son droit à un procès public et régulier.

The difference between the first example and the second example is that the first asserts that M. Hoveyda was not *le dernier des criminels*, whereas the second is ambiguous in this respect (see 6.0.*vii*)

(iii) Thus the code of the language allows one to contrast:

vous réussiriez si . . . .
vous auriez réussi si . . . .
vous eussiez réussi si . . . .

In the first case one is stating that success is possible if certain conditions − which are in fact possible − are fulfilled. In the second case one is referring to a real point in time in the past when success could have been possible. In the third case the conditions needed to ensure success have never been fulfilled. This is a mere hypothesis which is being put forward, the subjunctive being the form used to express a gratuitous hypothesis. This rather fine distinction is ignored in the spoken language.

2.4   Use of the subjunctive in subordinate clauses

2.4.1   *Features of the sentence entailing the use of a subjunctive*

These are so complex and numerous that they are discussed separately in section 3.

2.4.2   *Replacement of a subjunctive form by an infinitive*

(i) If the subject of the main clause is the same as that of the subordinate clause, and if it is in the 1st or 2nd person, the subjunctive must be replaced by an infinitive. Thus, **je veux que je vienne* must become *je veux venir*.

(ii) If the subject of both clauses is in the 3rd person, one may contrast:

> *il veut qu'il parte* (two persons involved)
> *il veut partir* (one person involved)

(iii) One may contrast:

> *j'ai ordonné qu'il parte* (order given to intermediary)
> *je lui ai ordonné de partir* (order given directly to the person)

2.5   The problem of agreement in subordinate clauses using the subjunctive

(i)   One can distinguish two systems of tense agreement: a General System, which is followed by most people when speaking or writing today, and a Literary System, which reflects the rules set up in Classical French. In the following tables, the examples which belong to the General System appear in one column, whereas the forms used in the General System appear in the other. The difference between the two systems is due to the disappearance from spontaneous language of the subjunctive imperfect and the subjunctive pluperfect, the present and the compound past being the only forms left to fill the gaps.

(ii) Simple forms:

Tenses/Sequence

	Literary System	General System
il faudra *il faut* *il a fallu* *il faudrait*	*qu'il finisse à Noël*	*qu'il finisse à Noël*
il fallut	*qu'il finît à Noël*	not used in General System
il fallait *il avait fallu* *il aurait fallu*	*qu'il finît à Noël*	*qu'il finisse à Noël*

(iii) Compound forms refer to an action completed before some point in time indicated in the context (in this case, before *Noël*):

	Literary System	General System (retrospective: see 1.2 *i*)
il faudra *il faut* *il a fallu* *il faudrait*	*qu'il ait fini à Noël*	*qu'il ait fini à Noël*
il fallut	*qu'il eût fini à Noël*	not used in General System
il fallait *il avait fallu* *il aurait fallu*	*qu'il eût fini à Noël*	*qu'il ait fini à Noël*

(iv) The double compound forms are used to stress the idea of completion. The same restrictions in terms of registers apply as for the double compound forms in the indicative. They belong more specifically to the spoken language, and certainly not to the Literary System.

il est parti bien qu'il n'ait pas encore eu fini son travail

The use of the double compound forms is never obligatory.

3 Features of the sentence entailing use of the subjunctive

3.1 General considerations

(i) It has been pointed out in 1.2 that the subjunctive is nontemporal in that it does not offer — as the indicative does — a tripartite conceptualization of time, but merely indicates whether the action is envisaged as prospective or retrospective (the latter being, however, fairly rare and register-bound). The event is thus deprived of the precision given to it through a clear expression of time and becomes an amorphous picture of something which is not quite seen as actualized. It has already been pointed out that this has nothing to do with the actual reality of the event or its non-reality, but refers only to the light in which this event is being considered.

(ii) In the spoken language there is a tendency to actualize rather than to envisage, and thus there will be a preference for the indicative whenever possible: *je ne pense pas qu'il viendra* will be preferred to *je ne pense pas qu'il vienne*, even though the event will probably not take place.[7]

(iii) Generally speaking, when using one or other mood one is distinguishing between the probable and the possible. A probable event is one which has more evidence for its happening than against its happening; a possible event is one which is not contrary to the nature of things. Thus we may contrast *il est probable qu'il viendra demain* with *il est possible qu'il vienne demain*. The subjunctive covers the range from the possible to the impossible, including the latter. But the dividing line between the probable and the possible can be a very fine one, and in some cases either mood could be used, depending on the light in which the action is being considered. Thus some speakers will say, *il est possible qu'il *viendra demain*, in which case the degree of probability of the assertion is greater than if the subjunctive had been used. (Such uses of the subjunctive are frequently heard but are still considered unacceptable in prescriptive terms.)

(iv) There are many cases in which one must use either one mood or the other because of some element in the main clause which makes clear that the action is seen as probable, possible or impossible, or translates an idea from which one of these categories may be deduced. In this case one is using the mood which agrees with this element, and this is a matter of semantic agreement. This could be termed 'the harmonizing subjunctive'.[8] Thus *il faut qu'il vienne* is a case of such a use: *il faut* refers to a necessity, but the action may or may not take place, hence the subjunctive.

(v) Although it is possible to set out a list of features which always require the use of the harmonizing or noncontrastive subjunctive, in some cases the matter is not clearcut, either mood being justifiable; in other cases the use of the mood may depend on the meaning to be attributed to the verb in the main clause, as in *je comprends que vous avez commis une erreur* (blunt statement of fact) and *je comprends que vous ayez commis une erreur* (implying that the mistake made was an understandable one). In this case the use of the subjunctive rather than the indicative alters the meaning of the sentence: it is a 'contrastive subjunctive'. When examining the list of features which may entail the use of one mood rather than the other, it will be necessary to distinguish those uses which are a matter of 'harmonizing' with the context and those which are 'contrastive'.

The features listed as requiring or allowing the use of the subjunctive do not form a closed system: the judgment of the writer plays a major role in this area, and interesting shades of meaning may be expressed by using the 'wrong mood' in terms of the rules in non-spontaneous language. Indeed the subjunctive can be said to be of major relevance to the written language, which is most suited to the expression of subtlety of thought.

(vi) There are three kinds of syntactical contexts in which the subjunctive may or must appear (i.e. the contrastive subjunctive versus the harmonizing subjunctive).

(a) Completive clauses introduced by the conjunction *que*: in this case the use of the subjunctive may be to harmonize with the verb in the main clause or with the imperative, interrogative or negative nature of the sentence taken as a whole (see 3.2)

(b) Completive clauses introduced by a relative pronoun: in this case the use of the subjunctive will be determined by the nature of the antecedent to the relative pronoun (see 3.3). Some problem cases relating to both types of clauses are listed in 3.4.

(c) Adverbial clauses: in this case it is the meaning of the conjunction introducing the adverbial clause which will entail the use of the subjunctive (see 3.5).

3.2 Completive clauses introduced by the conjunction 'que'

We shall distinguish four types of verb or verbal phrases which may entail the use of the subjunctive:[9] verbs of volition (or 'willing') in 3.2.1, imperative constructions in 3.2.2, verbs referring to the possible or impossible as against the probable in 3.2.3, and verbs of opinion and feeling in 3.2.4. The effect of having negative and interrogative constructions will be taken into account for these last two categories.

3.2.1. *Verbs of volition*

We are referring throughout to cases when the subjects of the two clauses are different, since if they are the same the subordinate clause will be an infinitival: **je veux que j'y aille* becomes *je veux y aller*.

(i) The following verbs take the subjunctive: *accorder que, désirer que,*[10] *demander que, défendre que, empêcher que, ordonner que, vouloir que* and *il faut que* (which is the expression which accounts for the majority of cases of use of the subjunctive, e.g. *j'ai ordonné qu'il y aille; il faut qu'il y aille*).

(ii) But if the decision is taken by an omnipotent authority which makes it impossible for the order not to be followed, the future indicative may be used, as is the case for *décider que, décréter que* and sometimes – but very rarely – *ordonner que*:

> *J'ai décidé qu'il ira*

> *Ordonné qu'il sera fait rapport à la cour*
> *Du foin que peut manger une poule en un jour*
> *(La Fontaine)*

Note: Prétendre que used to be used in the sense of *vouloir que* as in *je prétends qu'il soit couronné demain*, which meant *je veux qu'il soit couronné demain*. In contemporary French, *prétendre que* normally means *affirmer que*, as in *je prétends qu'il a été couronné*, which means *j'affirme qu'il a été couronné* (see 3.2.3 ii). This distinction can be important when reading Classical French.

(iii) Similarly, verbs expressing a promise or a resolution, such as *décider, dire, promettre,* are used with the indicative, e.g. *je te dis qu'il viendra.*

(iv) There is a difference between *décider que,* in which the action is seen as actualized and takes the indicative, and *être décidé à ce que,* which expresses volition and takes the subjunctive:

> *j'ai décidé qu'il viendra*
> *je suis décidé à ce qu'il vienne*

3.2.2 *Use of the imperative to indicate volition*

In this case the subjunctive is used in the subordinate clause: *attendez qu'il ait fini.*

3.2.3 *Verbs referring to the possible and the impossible rather than to the probable*

(i) Verbs indicating the probable take the indicative whereas those indicating the possible, the improbable, and the impossible, take the subjunctive. Thus *espérer que, croire que, penser que* are more positive than negative in terms of probabilities 'and, therefore, take the indicative. The same applies to *il est probable que, il est certain que* and *il est évident que*:

> *j'espère*
> *je crois*[11]   *qu'il viendra*
> *je pense*
> *il est certain*

In contrast *douter* and phrases such as *il est possible* or *il est peu probable que* are more negative than positive in terms of probabilities, and therefore take the subjunctive:

> *je doute*
> *il est possible*   *qu'il vienne*
> *il est peu probable*

Nier and phrases such as *il est impossible que* also take the subjunctive:[12] *je nie qu'il l'ait fait; il est impossible qu'il l'ait fait.*

(ii) Dire, comprendre, prétendre and *supposer* may be followed either by the indicative or by the subjunctive, but the choice of mood will affect the meaning of the sentence: in these cases the choice of mood is contrastive. Compare the following:

> *Jean a dit que Pierre aille le voir samedi prochain* (order)
> *Jean a dit que Pierre ira le voir samedi prochain* (factual)

> *je comprends que vous ayez commis une erreur* (sympathetic approach)
> *je comprends que vous avez commis une erreur* (blunt statement of fact)

> *je prétends que mon fils termine ses études avant de se marier* (= *je veux*)
> *je prétends que mon fils terminera ses études avant de se marier* (= *j'affirme, je suis sûr que*. . .)

> *je suppose que vous avez été surpris par l'orage* (i.e. 'this is what I think')
> *je suppose que vous soyez surpris par l'orage* (i.e. 'I imagine that you may have been . . .')

Il (me) semble que can take either indicative or subjunctive, but it is doubtful whether the choice in this case is really contrastive, *il me semble que* being on the borderline between the possible and the probable. Compare:

> *il (me) semble qu'il est gentil* (factual)
> *il (me) semble que cela soit bien* (possibility of error)
> *il (me) semble que cela est bien* (more positive than *il (me) semble que cela soit bien*)

Il est à craindre can similarly be interpreted differently depending on the mood used:

> *il est à craindre qu'il est arrivé trop tard* (probable)
> *il est à craindre qu'il ne soit arrivé trop tard* (possible – the 'expletive' *ne* expressing an idea of uncertainty)

But for many speakers these two sentences would not be felt to be contrastive; they would simply reckon that the first of these two sentences was 'wrong'.

(iii) In negative and interrogative constructions the idea of probability disappears from all these cases, hence the uniform use of the subjunctive:

je ne crois pas qu'il vienne
il n'est pas certain qu'il vienne
croyez-vous qu'il vienne?
est-il certain qu'il vienne?

But there are many people who no longer make this rather fine distinction between the probable or questioned probable: they use the indicative in both cases:

croyez-vous qu'il viendra?
est-il certain qu'il viendra?[13]

It is important to note that the subjunctive is dropped when the wording of the question is not based on the word-subject inversion but on *est-ce que?*, which is the normal interrogative form in the spoken language:

est-ce que vous croyez qu'il viendra?
est-ce qu'il est certain qu'il viendra?

It may be that when there is no inversion the sentence is felt to be more positive.

3.2.4   *Verbs expressing opinion and feeling*

(i) It is logical to use the subjunctive in these cases, since opinion or feeling are personal and not tied to time. But this section does not include verbs expressing opinions as to the probability or improbability of the action taking place. These come under the previous heading. Nor do these include verbs of judgement such as *savoir*, *affirmer*, *juger*, *penser*, which are followed by the indicative since they involve only intellectual activities, e.g. *je sais qu'elle viendra demain*.

(ii) These verbs may express personal attitudes: *aimer que, avoir envie que, avoir peur que, craindre que, consentir que, désirer que, se plaindre que, s'enorgueillir que, s'étonner que, être content que, être désolé que, être heureux que, préférer que, souhaiter que, se réjouir que.*

Note: The one verb expressing a personal attitude which takes the indicative is *espérer que*, e.g. *j'espère qu'il viendra*, because of its strong implication that this will indeed be the case.

(iii) A large number of impersonal verbal phrases also come under this heading, e.g. *il est dommage que, il est heureux que, il est fâcheux que*, e.g. *j'aimerais qu'il vienne; il est heureux qu'il vienne.*

(iv) Some verbal expressions in this category express moral criticism, e.g. *il est bien que, il est mal que, il est juste que*, e.g. *il est juste que les méchants soient punis.* Intellectual criticism also comes into this category, e.g. *il est logique que, il est fréquent que, il est rare que, il est incontestable que*: *il est logique qu'il faille employer le subjonctif dans ce cas. Il est exact que* normally takes the indicative, since it is felt to refer to a reality: *il est exact qu'il l'a fait.* But in literary works the distinction is sometimes made between the opinion expressed by *il est exact* and reality itself; it is this very fine distinction which enable some authors to write, *il est exact qu'il l'ait fait.*

3.3   Completive clauses introduced by a relative pronoun[14]

3.3.1   *General considerations*

(i) The problem only relates to restrictive relative clauses (*relatives déterminatives*) and not to nonrestrictive clauses (*relatives explicatives*) (see chapter 14), since the latter do not alter the determined or nondetermined nature of the antecedent and could be removed without the basic meaning of the sentence being impaired. Nonrestrictive relative clauses always take the indicative: the problem of mood only appears with the restrictive relative clauses.

(ii) The antecedent and the relative pronoun which stands for it make up a semantic whole, and hence the action will be seen either as actualized or only as envisaged, according to how clearly determined the antecedent is. If the antecedent is only envisaged, the subjunctive will be used.

3.3.2 *Influence on mood of the choice of article preceding the antecedent*

(i) The antecedent may be indeterminate because of the presence of an indefinite article. In the case of *je cherche une maison qui soit à vendre*, there may be no such house available at the time of speaking. On the other hand, if the antecedent really exists and is clearly defined, the indicative is called for: *je cherche la maison qui est à vendre*.

(ii) But the use of the indefinite article does not automatically imply the use of the subjunctive. Compare:

je cherche une maison qui soit à vendre (there may not be one)
je cherche une maison qui est à vendre (there is one: it is simply a question of finding it)

The use of the indefinite article may be due to the fact that the speaker knows the listener to have no previous knowledge of the existence of this house.

If the sentence is in the interrogative or the negative the same applies: if the existence of the house has not been attested one uses the subjunctive:

connaissez-vous une maison qui soit à vendre?
je ne connais pas de maison qui soit à vendre

But if the existence of this house has been previously attested in both sentences one would use the indicative:

connaissez-vous la maison qui est à vendre?
je ne connais pas la maison qui est à vendre

(iii) In the case of the examples in *(ii)* the use of the subjunctive is contrastive, since in both cases the determiner of the antecedent is indefinite. In all the other cases the use of the subjunctive is noncontrastive, i.e. harmonizing.

This contrastive use of the subjunctive seems in fact to be receding; many people do not distinguish between the examples in *(ii)*, since they use only the indicative. For them it is not possible to distinguish, except by the context, whether *je cherche une maison qui est à vendre* refers to a house which actually exists or not.

The French also often prefer an infinitival construction: *je cherche une maison à vendre*. But the latter is ambiguous, in that it could either mean that the person is looking for a specific house known to him but not to the listener (one for which he has the details for example) or that he is looking for a nonspecified house in a haphazard kind of way. But if this person were offered a house for rental, he may answer, *non, je cherche maison qui soit à vendre*, in order to make the distinction between these two different types of pursuits.

The degree of grammatical acceptability of the use of the indicative where the subjunctive would be expected varies from person to person; this area of the language is in a period of transition, with the subjunctive dying out.

(iv) The kinds of verb most commonly used in the main clause in this type of construction are *chercher, vouloir, il faut, demander, désirer, préférer, avoir envie* (verbs of volition and judgment):

il nous faut ⎤
j'ai envie d' ⎦ *une maison qui soit au bord de la mer*

But if the antecedent refers to an object which really exists, the indicative is used:

$\left.\begin{array}{l} \textit{il nous faut} \\ \textit{j'ai envie d'} \end{array}\right]$ *une petite maison blanche, très jolie, avec des volets verts*
     . . . qui est au bord de la mer

The use of the indicative implies that the antecedent is known to the speaker or writer, but not to the listener or reader.

3.3.3 *Influence on mood of the use of certain modifiers of the antecedent*

3.3.3.1 *The general rule*

(i) If the antecedent is modified by *seul, unique, premier, dernier, peu* or by a superlative phrase, the antecedent is then isolated from the group of objects or people to which it would normally belong; this establishes a gap between the object or person referred to and the group as a whole which calls for the use of the subjunctive. Hence:

Value judgement · qu'on

c'est le seul ami qui lui écrive
c'est l'unique objet qu'il ait rapporté
c'est le quatrième avion qui parte sur Paris (i.e. *il y en a eu quatre*)
il y a peu de personnes qui sachent le faire
c'est l'homme le plus bête que je connaisse

(ii) The nuance this use of the subjunctive carries is a fine one, hence the fact that it is frequently dropped, particularly in spontaneous speech:

c'est le seul ami qui lui écrit
c'est l'unique objet qu'il a rapporté
c'est le quatrième avion qui part sur Paris (meaning either *il y en a eu quatre* or *c'est le quatrième avion qu'il faut prendre pour aller à Paris*)
il y a peu de personnes qui savent le faire

These constructions are appearing more and more frequently in the spoken language, but their degree of acceptability varies from person to person.

But non-use of the subjunctive in constructions using a superlative appears to be far more rare, and therefore less acceptable:

* *c'est l'homme le plus bête que je connais*

3.3.3.2 *Apparent exceptions*

(i) Compare:

lundi dernier est la dernière fois que je l'ai vu (indicative) (or *la dernière fois que je l'ai vu, c'est lundi dernier*)
c'est la dernière hypothèse que je puisse envisager (subjunctive)

The reason for the use of the indicative in the first case is that *que je l'ai vu* is not a real relative clause but an adverbial clause: *que* is the semantic equivalent of *quand*, and indeed the corresponding question would be:

quand l'avez-vous vu pour la dernière fois?

(ii) Compare:

c'est la première/deuxième/dernière maison qui est à vendre ('it is the first/second/last house (of this street) which is for sale')
c'est la première/deuxième/dernière maison que soit à vendre ('it is the first/second/last house to come up for sale')

The difference between these two sentences, is that in the first case *premier* and *dernier* are used in a concrete sense whereas in the second sentence *premier* and *dernier* are used in an abstract sense.

3.3.4 *Use of a nondeterminate relative pronoun, acting as subject entailing the use of the subjunctive*

The nondeterminate relative pronouns are *qui que*, *quoi que* and *où que*:

je ne laisserai entrer qui que ce soit
je le ferai quoi qu'on en dise
je vous demande de me faire signe où que vous soyez

But *quiconque* (meaning *tous ceux*) takes the indicative:

quiconque le dit est mal renseigné sur la question

3.4 Problem cases

3.4.1 *Progression from a subordinate to a relative clause*

(i) The following sentence contains a subordinate clause introduced by *ce qui explique que* + subjunctive:

Née à la fin du Moyen-Age, l'assurance a pris son essor avec la société industrielle et commerciale, ce qui explique que les grands pays industriels soient aussi les grands pays d'assurances. (*Problèmes économiques*, 20 October 1976, 22)

In this case the subjunctive refers to an interpretation of facts. The latter could be rewritten without a subjunctive in the following manner:

Née à la fin du Moyen-Age, l'assurance a pris son essor avec la société industrielle et commerciale, ce qui explique pourquoi [or *le fait que*] *les grands pays industriels sont aussi les grands pays d'assurance.*

In this case the indicative refers to a statement of fact.
(ii) Similarly a subjunctive construction may become an indicative construction if one can build into it *de ce que* (= *de cela que*) even though the verb may otherwise call for the subjunctive:

je suis content que vous ayez fait ce travail si rapidement
je suis content de ce que vous avez fait ce travail si rapidement

See also 3.5.4 for a similar kind of problem.
(iii) For the case of a double hypothesis, in which the first element is introduced by *si* and the second by *et que*, see chapter 6 on the conditional, section 3.4.2.

3.4.2 *The case of 'l'idée que' and 'le fait que'*

Constructions of the following type may also take the subjunctive:

l'idée que ⎫
le fait que ⎭   + subjunctive + rest of main clause of which the first part is the subject

l'idée qu'elle parte me désole (but *l'idée qu'elle part* is also possible)
le fait qu'elle parte me désole (but *le fait qu'elle part* is also possible)

If it is the subjunctive which is used instead of the indicative, the speaker or writer is referring to the thought rather than to the fact. But this kind of distinction is usually ignored in contemporary French. Such a contrast is not possible with expressions such as *la crainte que*, *le désir que*, *l'espoir que*, because these necessarily refer to emotions; in these cases only the subjunctive is possible, e.g. *la crainte qu'elle parte me désole*.

3.5   Adverbial clauses

3.5.1   *General consideration*

As in the previously mentioned cases, the use of the subjunctive is the result of the kind of outlook of the speaker on the action; but in the case of adverbial clauses the outlook is expressed not by the verbal phrase but by the conjunction. Conjunctions may be of two types: simple or compound. The simple conjunctions always describe the action in the subordinate clause as taking place, and therefore always take the indicative. To have a subjunctive in a clause introduced by a simple conjunction one must have a verb or verbal phrase in the main clause requiring the use of the subjunctive mood; on their own the simple conjunctions never determine the use of the subjunctive.[15]

We shall therefore only deal with complex conjunctions. Conjunctions can rarely combine with both moods in order to express a shift in meaning; the only ones which can and are used regularly in this way are *de sorte que, de manière que* and *de façon que* (all three are near synonyms of each other). There is one problematic case which is that of *après que*, which is supposed to take the indicative but in fact often appears with the subjunctive – which is the reverse of the general trend (cf. 3.5.3 ii) – by analogy with *avant que*.

3.5.2   *Conjunctions requiring the subjunctive*

(i) If the action in the main clause is to take place after the one in the subordinate clause (i.e. if the action in the subordinate clause is anterior to the action in the main clause), the action in the subordinate clause is clearly seen as taking place and the mood used will be the indicative. This is the case for *lorsque, dès que, sitôt que, de la même manière que*:

> *j'irai à la plage dès que j'aurai fini mon travail*

But if the action in the main clause is to take place before the one in the subordinate clause (i.e. if the action in the subordinate clause is posterior to it) an element of doubt creeps in and the action is seen somewhat more hazily. Thus *avant que, jusqu'à ce que, en attendant que* take the subjunctive:

> *j'arriverai à la maison avant que l'orage n'ait éclaté*

(ii) If the conjunction introduces an idea of a purpose this is similar to an idea of volition, and this entails the use of the subjunctive.

The following come under this category: *afin que, pour que, de sorte que, de manière que, de façon que*:

> *je l'ai fait pour que cela lui fasse plaisir*

(iii) If the conjunction introduces an idea of supposition or conjecture the subjunctive is required. Hence the following conjunctions take the subjunctive: *à condition que, en admettant que, à supposer que, pourvu que* (hypothesis or necessary condition), *soit que . . . soit que, non que*:

> *je l'emmènerai[16] dans ma voiture pourvu qu'il soit à l'heure*

(iv) If the conjunction introduces an idea of judgment or criticism the subjunctive is required. This is the case for *quoique, bien que, à moins que, sans que, de crainte que,* de peur que, *quelque . . .* (adjective) *. . . que, si . . .* (adjective) *. . . que, pour . . .* (adjective) *. . . que, tout . . .* (adjective) *. . . que, encore que*:

> *je viendrai le voir bien qu'il soit pénible*
> *je viendrai le voir si pénible qu'il soit*
> *je viendrai le voir quelque pénible qu'il soit*

Note: Que is often used in elliptical constructions such as *viens ici, que je voie comme tu as grandi* (*que* = *pour que*). This was particularly frequent in the seventeenth century, e.g.

Fuyez, qu'à ses soupçons il ne vous sacrifie (Corneille)

in which case *que* stands for *de peur que*.

3.5.3 *Conjunctions allowing for both moods*

(i) The subjunctive and indicative are used contrastively in clauses introduced by *de sorte que, de façon que* and *de manière que*. Compare:

ils ont fermé la barrière de sorte que les cyclistes ne puissent pas passer (aim)
ils ont fermé la barrière de sorte que les cyclistes ne peuvent pas passer (fact)

In the case of the indicative we are dealing with actual cyclists who cannot get through because the barrier has been closed. In the case of the subjunctive the barrier has been closed to stop potential cyclists from getting through. In *ils ont fermé la barrière de sorte que les cyclistes ne peuvent pas passer*, the subordinate clause expresses a consequence (*subordonnée consécutive*), whereas in *ils ont fermé la barrière de sorte que les cyclistes ne puissent pas passer*, the subordinate clause expresses an aim (*subordonnée finale*).

(ii) Après que should normally take the indicative, since the action in the main clause is posterior to the action in the clause introduced by *après que*:

j'irai après qu'elle sera passée chez moi

There is a tendency, however, to use the subjunctive: one frequently hears:

j'irai après qu'elle *soit passée chez moi

This is usually explained in terms of the analogy with *avant que*:

j'irai avant qu'elle ne vienne

There is, however, according to Moignet (*Essai sur le subjonctif en latin postclassique et en ancien français*, 116-7) more to this phenomenon: this use of the subjunctive is not reserved to the spoken language, since he is able to quote from the Constitution of 1946 (which could hardly be called spontaneous speech) the following case:

Le Président du Conseil et les ministres ne peuvent être nommés qu'après que le Président du Conseil ait été investi de la confiance de l'Assemblée.

This he contrasts with the following:

Le vote sur la question de confiance ne peut intervenir qu'un jour franc après qu'elle a été posée devant l'Assemblée.

He points out that the use of the indicative points purely to the chronological order that the events must follow. The subjunctive, on the other hand, is referring not only to chronological order but to a necessary order. The different shades of meaning expressed by the two moods, unlike in (*i*) above, are very fine indeed and not felt by most. On the whole, in anything but extremely formal writings, the use of *après que* with the subjunctive is likely to be the result of analogy with *avant que*.

(iii) After *bien que* and *quoique*[17] the indicative is sometimes used instead of the subjunctive in the spoken language

**j'aimerais aller revoir ma maison d'enfance bien que
mes parent n'y sont plus*

The mistake is due to the fact that these conjunctions may refer to real facts: *mes parents n'y sont plus* is a true fact, hence the indicative. But the subjunctive alone is 'correct', since the idea expressed in the main clause is subjective and refers to the imaginary, which is timeless. But Moignet points out that the indicative can be used in rare cases not just by mistake but to express a fine shade of meaning. Thus he quotes Flaubert in *Madame Bovary*:

Quoiqu'il faudra pourtant suivre les autres

In this case the use of the indicative gives an idea of time to the sentence. It refers to a real future and not to the imaginary. Although such uses of the indicative are considered to be an error, these seem to be on the increase, particularly when *quoique* is separated from the verb by an adverbial, e.g. *tout devrait être terminé en juin, quoique vraisemblablement, avec les oraux, nous en aurons sans doute jusqu'au 5 juillet* (sentence spoken by a French lecturer in French).

3.5.4   *The hypothetical clause starting with 'si' and followed by another starting with 'que'*

The subjunctive no longer appears after *si*, despite the fact that one could expect it to do so. This is because in a clause such as *si j'étais riche, j'achèterais un bateau*, the hypothesis is imagined as taking place. The same does not apply to a hypothesis introduced by *que* + subjunctive, hence the possibility of contrast as seen in the following example:

si vous le faites (action seen as taking place) *et qu'un accident s'ensuive* (hypothesis) *vous le regretterez toute votre vie*

3.5.5   *Compound conjunctions including 'où'*

Compound conjunctions including *où* take the indicative, whereas their counterparts without the *où* may take the subjunctive.

Thus one must distinguish between:

jusqu'à ce que + subjunctive and *jusqu'au moment où* + indicative
avant que + subjunctive and *avant le moment où* + indicative
en attendant que + subjunctive and *en attendant le moment où* + indicative

This is because *où* can only refer to time if the latter is seen as taking place (be this in the present, past or future).

4   Stylistic considerations

4.1   A decline in the use of the subjunctive?

(i) There are two totally opposite points of view in this matter. Some have called the subjunctive *un fruit véreux* (a worm-eaten fruit):

Le subjonctif français à deux de ses temps n'est plus défendable: ses formes passent pour déplaisantes, pédantes, cocasses, ridicules. Qui oserait de nos jours signer, sinon par plaisanterie, une phrase comme celle-ci: 'le destin voulut que vous m'écrivissiez, que nous rompissions, et que je malmenasse le témoin. (Doppagne, Trois aspects du français contemporain, 154).

Doppagne goes on to say that the imperfect and the pluperfect subjunctive have completely disappeared from the spoken language, and that as far as the spoken language is concerned these tenses are dead. He then points out that all forms in *-asse, -usse* and *-isse* (which basically make up five out of six of the endings of the subjunctive) are frowned upon, and that only the 3rd person singular is retained because it sounds the same as the simple past, which makes it acceptable. He concludes:

> *Que conclure, cela paraît clair: faillite totale du subjonctif sur le plan morphologique — c'est à dire, dans le monde des formes. Le présent ne vit plus que par neuf formes irrégulières, et le passé dépend pour deux d'entre elles des auxiliaires 'être' ou 'avoir'.*
>
> *L'imparfait et le plus-que-parfait s'accrochent à leur dernier îlot de résistance, presque illusoire, une forme homonyme de l'indicatif, la troisième personne du singulier.* (155)

The author then goes on to illustrate his point by showing that with each generation of writers the subjunctive in five of its six forms becomes less and less acceptable and appears to be used consequently less and less often.

In the spoken language it is certainly easy to pick up many cases in which the harmonizing (see 3.1 *iv* and *v*) subjunctive has been replaced by the indicative.

(ii) On the other hand, Cohen (*Le Subjonctif en français contemporain*, 261) maintained that *Le subjonctif est encore plein de vitalité dans le parlé et non pas seulement dans l'écrit.* He — and others — have pointed out that it is now used with *après que, probable que* and *espérer que* (but see 3.2.3 *i* for the last instance). He even quotes a student news bulletin as saying:

> **espérons que la prochaine fois nous soyons* (for *serons*) *plus nombreux*

Glatigny goes so far as to wonder if the mistaken use of the subjunctive in the spoken language does not prove the need felt by the speakers to use a mood other than the indicative (*Le Français dans le monde* no. 122, 17).

(iii) The problem is that one cannot really count the number of subjunctives which are used or not used in a text, for as far as the three persons of the singular are concerned, verbs of the first conjugation sound and are written in the same way in the indicative and subjunctive in the present tense:

> *je chante une chanson* (= indicative)
> *il faut que je chante une chanson* (= subjunctive)

Therefore, in these cases — which in fact are particularly numerous — the opposition is completely neutralized from the morphological point of view.

It is also important to note that whereas some uses of the harmonizing subjunctive are disappearing, others show no sign of receding. For example *il faut que* always takes the subjunctive. But other types of harmonizing subjunctives seem on the way out: in particular subjunctives determined by negativity, as in *je ne crois pas qu'il viendra* instead of *je ne crois pas qu'il vienne*; and those determined by the use of certain modifiers of antecedents (*un, seul, premier, dernier*) as in *c'est la première maison qu'il a achetée* instead of *c'est la première maison qu'il ait achetée*. The degree of decline of the harmonizing subjunctive is extremely uneven and depends both on the feature which has called for it and on levels of education. The problem is to what extent the use of the subjunctive has now become a matter of style and to what extent it belongs to grammar.

4.2 The indicative used instead of the subjunctive

In some cases using an indicative tense rather than the expected subjunctive may change the meaning of the sentence. G. Price (*The French Language: present and past*) points out in this respect that one can contrast *je ne crois pas qu'il pleut* (which he translates as 'I'm pretty certain it isn't raining') with *je ne crois pas qu'il pleuve* (which he translates as 'I don't think it's raining but I'm not sure').

The replacement of the subjunctive by the indicative changes the emphasis of these sentences: the action, instead of being temporally defined, acquires sharpness by the definition given to it by the use of indicative tenses. Similarly one may read in a contemporary novel, in which the author uses the subjunctive whenever possible:

> *Il est à craindre qu'elle restera dans cette*
> *maison de repos toute sa vie* (F. Couteaux, *Un Monsieur de compagnie*)

instead of

> *Il est à craindre qu'elle ne reste dans cette*
> *maison de repos toute sa vie*

The indicative, by defining the action temporally, makes it seem more definite, more inevitable.

It may be because the subjunctive has become the *fruit véreux* where some of its harmonizing uses are concerned that it is acquiring a new lease of life as far as its contrastive uses are concerned: it is because its compulsory use no longer seems to preoccupy the native speaker to the same extent that it has regained some of its past freedom and, therefore, some of its meaningfulness as a mood.

4.3   Stylistic role of the subjunctive imperfect

4.3.1   *General considerations*

The use of the imperfect subjunctive does not usually change the meaning of the sentence (see 1.3), but — because its use is so rare[18] — it tends to change the 'tone of the passage'. This change of tone may be of two very different kinds (see 4.3.2 and 4.3.3)

4.3.2   *Use of the imperfect subjunctive in the Narrative System*

(i) Its use creates morphological harmony:

> *Mais enfin celle-ci encore, et ce devait être la dernière, avait quelque chose, si humble ce fût-il, qui était, au-delà de sa propre matière, une différenciation secrète. (Proust, A la Recherche du temps perdu)*

This kind of use of the imperfect subjunctive is typical of professional men of letters.
(ii) It may be used in order to emphasize a particular clause:

> *Mais vers 1900, il a fallu mener un fameux combat pour que les chirurgiens de l'époque acceptassent que leurs salles d'opération fussent dotées de lavabos. Se laver les mains avant d'opérer, diable, pourquoi faire?* (Extract from a report on the centenary celebrations of the Tenon hospital, taken from the daily newspaper *L'Aurore* in the late 1970s)

4.3.3   *Use of the imperfect subjunctive as a source of comedy*

The use of the imperfect subjunctive in a context other than an extremely formal one appears ridiculous. As such it is much used as a source of comedy (see note 18 to this chapter).

The following example is particularly striking, since the author has used the imperfect to create a comic effect, but his knowledge of the subjunctive is so poor that he has used the wrong form (namely **dusse-t-elle* for *dût-elle*):

> *Ce préambule pour vous dire que pendant plusieurs années j'ai suivi un traitement*

chez Mathieu où, sur le sièges voisins du mien, je recontrais régulièrement deux grands comédiens français, un très très grand couturier et plusieurs leaders d'entreprises industrielles ou Pdg de stations radio. Tous ont refusé de commenter leur traitement. Faute d'avoir pu les interviewer et ma modestie *dusse-t-elle en souffrir, je suis donc amené à m'auto-interviewer aujourd'hui. (*Vogue Hommes*, May 1979)

In the General System one would have written, *et même si ma modestie doit en souffrir . . .* (or *devait en souffrir*, in which case one would be using the modal imperfect).

4.4 Stylistic role of the pluperfect subjunctive

4.4.1 *The pluperfect subjunctive as a source of meaning*

(i) When expressing the hypothetical, the pluperfect subjunctive differs from the conditional in that the hypothesis expressed by the former is gratuitous or untrue (see example in 2.3. *ii*).
(ii) When used in conjunction with the subjunctive it may express *un deuxième degré de l'imaginaire* (i.e. it may refer to something imaginary which in turn is dependent on something else which is also imaginary, and expressed by the compound conditional:

A quoi songeait, dit-il, l'auteur de tout cela?
Il a bien mal placé cette citrouille là.
. . . . Hé parbleu! Je l'aurais pendu
A l'un des chênes que voilà!
C'eût été justement l'affaire!
Tel fruit, tel arbre, pour bien faire!
(La Fontaine, *Le Gland et la citrouille*)

In this case *c'eût été* is logically dependent on *aurais pendue*, which is itself dependent on an implicit *si* clause (i.e. *si j'avais été l'auteur de tout cela*).

4.4.2 *Use of the pluperfect subjunctive as a source of comedy*

The General System does not express nuances such as those described in 4.4.1. One simply uses the conditional in all cases. The use of a pluperfect subjunctive in the General System, for no particular semantic reason, creates a comic effect because it is so unexpected. This use of the pluperfect is very common with some contemporary writers such as Boris Vian, for example:

Vous eussiez pu (for *auriez pu*) *choisir un plus mauvais maître* (Vian, *L'Ecume des jours*)

In this case the sentence is uttered by a man speaking to his cook about the evening menu (the cook has declared his intention merely of copying a famous cook's recipe rather than inventing his own). The use of the pluperfect is meaningful, since it refers to a gratuitous hypothesis but such nuances clash with the subject matter and the context.

5 General conclusions

There are many different and contradictory attitudes adopted towards the use of the subjunctive, but the only way to describe the subjunctive in a way that accounts for all its uses seems to be in temporal terms: situated between the nominal mood (impersonal forms) and the indicative (which carries time according to a tripartite division), it represents the action either in a prospective manner or in a retrospective manner. As such the action lacks the precision of the indicative. It is its position in the system — more definite than the nominal or impersonal mood and less so than the indicative — which explains its many facets.

One can make the following general points about the various uses of the subjunctive:

(i) It may be used in independent clauses to express a wish, an order or a hypothesis. These cases are, however, very rare. The subjunctive is not used in main clauses with the one exception of *je ne sache que*, which constitutes a fossilized expression, a remnant of an unsuccessful effort to make the subjunctive function in such a manner. Thus the subjunctive is not really productive in this area.

(ii) The subjunctive may be substituted for the indicative in some subordinate clauses in order to achieve a change of meaning of the sentence. This is relatively rare since there are only a few cases in which the use of one or other mood is clearly contrastive. The change of meaning in the passage will consist of a change from something clearly stated with temporal precision (indicative) to something which is not clearly seen as taking place but only as conceptualized.

(iii) The subjunctive may be used to express a kind of semantic agreement between the clauses involved; in some cases this kind of agreement may not be felt to be necessary, in that both the indicative and the subjunctive could be justified — particularly the indicative in the spoken language, since in that mode the tendency is to actualize. Thus both *je ne pense pas qu'il vienne* and *je ne pense pas qu'il viendra* can be justified. In other more clearcut cases it is felt necessary to maintain semantic agreement, e.g. whenever one uses *il faut* or *bien que*.

(iv) The use of the past tenses is nearly always typical of very formal style. To use these tenses in nonformal contexts is a source of ridicule and pomposity, even though such a use may be contrastive where the pluperfect is concerned, because informal contexts do not make use of such fine shades of meaning. The use of these tenses being typical of literary French there are many cases where these forms are used purely for effect (this has been called *le subjonctif de snobisme*); these abound in present day writings, particularly in certain types of journalism. They may even sometimes appear in speech.

(v) Because language is always in a state of transition, there are a number of odd uses of the subjunctive which appear at irregular intervals in the language. These are sometimes fossilized expressions of the *dussé-je* type, or appear in proverbs; but there are also new uses and non-uses of the subjunctive which tend to appear first of all in the spoken language and then often to spread to the written language. Because of this phenomenon it is not always clear whether the use of an indicative instead of a subjunctive form is the expression of a different shade of meaning or is simply a result of the subjunctive being dropped — in which case its non-use is not relevant to the meaning of the sentence. Thus it is not always clear whether or not there is a difference between *croyez-vous qu'il vienne?* and *croyez-vous qu'il viendra?* There is therefore an area of uncertainty between what is clearly a contrastive use of a subjunctive or indicative form and its use as a harmonizing form, i.e. as a form of semantic agreement.

(vi) The subjunctive is a luxury in the language: it is only used in subordinate clauses, it is rarely contrastive and when it is it only carries shades of meaning. As such it is the most subtle stylistic tool in the language. It provides the writer with forms which are unfamiliar to eye and ear. Verlaine particularly appreciated the past subjunctive for this very reason:

> *Colères, soupirs noirs, regrets, tentations*
> *Qu'il a fallu pourtant que nous entendissions . . . .*
> (*Sagesse* XIX)

It provides the writer with rules which he may obey or flout; above all whenever he chooses to use a subjunctive, he is conveying to the reader or listener both his mood and his intentions without having to do so in so many words. Thus in the following article taken from *Le Monde* in 1979, the use of the subjunctive gives the passage both its tone and its very subtle meaning. There is, in particular, a lovely contrast between the present subjunctive *soit candidat* and the imperfect subjunctive *qu'il le fût* in the first sentence, the use of the imperfect subjunctive stressing the hypothetical nature of the assertion:

> *M. Mitterrand a déclaré qu'il y avait beaucoup de chances pour qu'il ne soit pas candidat à l'élection présidentielle de 1981, mais il a été tout aussi péremptoire en ajoutant qu'il y avait cependant quelques chances pour qu'il le fût.*
>
> *Comme, d'autre part, il y a quelques chances pour que M. Chirac ne nous annonce pas qu'il n'est pas candidat, quelques chances pour que M. Marchais nous laisse entendre qu'il pourrait l'être un jour s'il ne l'est pas encore, et beaucoup de chances pour que M. Giscard d'Estaing le soit tout à fait, on peut désormais parier que, dans le petit monde des candidats à l'élection présidentielle qui ne le sont pas tout en l'étant, il y a beaucoup de chances pour qu'on en parle un peu, et quelques chances pour qu'on y pense beaucoup.*

The *fût* at the end of the first paragraph is very logical. It is a direct result of the principle of tense agreement between clauses: the use of *avait* demands the use of a past subjunctive. The *soit* in the 1st line of the first paragraph, on the contrary, goes against the rules: logically one should have *fût* since it too has to agree with *avait* in the previous clause. It is the interplay between these two tenses which creates the comic effect of the passage.

Notes

1 This has led some grammarians to consider the subjunctive forms as mere fossils, since these uses are both determined by the context and declining in number.

2 There is another more mundane way of explaining *il est certain qu'il l'a fait de bon cœur* and *qu'il l'ait fait de bon cœur, c'est certain*, although less interesting than the former: the subjunctive is used because one does not know what the main verb is going to be; one uses it in case the main verb should require it. If, on the other hand, one uses the indicative, this necessarily will limit the type of verb possible in the main clause to verbs of perception or verbs expressing knowledge of the fact, in this particular case:

> *qu'il l'ait fait de bon cœur, je le veux bien/je me le demande . . . .*
> *qu'il l'a fait de bon cœur, je le sais/on me l'a dit . . . .*

3 Cf. Guillaume, *Temps et verbe.*

4 Marouzeau (*Précis de stylistique française*, 88-9) makes the following points concerning the use of the imperfect subjunctive:

> *La langue commune ne connaît guère que les formes monosyllabiques de la 3e personne du singulier de verbes fréquents: 'qu'il eût', 'qu'il fût', 'qu'il fît', 'qu'il prît'. . . . Pour le reste, les gens cultivés, soucieux de ne pas violer ouvertement la règle de concordance des temps en disant par exemple: 'j'aurais voulu qu'il entende', s'appliquent à tourner leur phrase de façon à éviter l'alternative ou d'appliquer une règle pédante ou de commettre une négligence; d'où en tout cas un élément de gêne réelle dans l'énoncé.*
>
> *Une question importante est celle des formations désuètes ou moribondes. Deux*

surtout, en français, nous apparaissent avec une physionomie marquée: le passé défini (ou passé simple) et l'imparfait du subjonctif. Nous sommes portés à trouver cacophoniques maintes formes de ces deux temps . . . . En fait, l'étrangeté des ces formes tient moins à leur consonnance qu'à leur rareté: 'que je crusse' n'est pas plus cacophonique que 'bleu de Prusse' et 'aimassiez' que 'émacié'; au XVIIe siècle, Vaugelas tenait l'imparfait du subjonctif pour 'un temps de verbe fort élégant' . . . . (aujourd'hui) l'emploi de l'imparfait du subjonctif confère à l'énoncé un caractère artificiel, sinon pédant ou même burlesque. Il nous paraît convenir excellemment à l'Oronte de Molière:

> *Je voudrais bien, pour voir, que de votre manière*
> *Vous en composassiez sur la même matière*

Ce qui n'empêche que certains écrivains modernes affectent de lui assurer une survie:

> *A supposer que je ne me trompasse pas* (M. Proust)
> *et que dans certains cas il trouve son excuse dans un souci de grandiloquence; ainsi quand V. Hugo fait crier au maréchal Ney en pleine bataille:*
> *Je voudrais que tous ces boulets anglais m'entrassent dans le ventre.*

5 In this case, it is a passive form which is being used.
6 *Si 'je ne sache' subsiste, il est littéraire, plus ou moins artificiel, sujet à provoquer des erreurs dans la parlure des semi-cultivés; en tout cas il n'a pas fait souche. Il reste en français moderne, une curiosité. C'est à peine si l'on sent en lui un subjonctif. Nous ne croyons pas forcer grandement les choses en disant que, pour beaucoup de Français, 'je ne sache' est à 'je ne sais' ce que 'je puis' est à 'je peux': une élégance un peu prétentieuse, rien de plus.*
7 This is what the French call the *valeur actualisante de l'indicatif.*
8 Grammarians usually use the term 'the noncontrastive subjunctive', which obscures its 'harmonising' quality.
9 In the seventeenth century there was much more freedom as to the use of one mood or the other; it was only during and after the seventeenth century that the use of one or the other mood with a particular verb became more or less set.
10 *Désirer que* can express either volition or judgment, hence its appearance under both headings.
11 Until the seventeenth century one could contrast *je crois qu'il viendra* and *je crois qu'il vienne.*
12 *Nier* and *douter* when used in a negative construction still take the subjunctive: *je ne nie pas qu'il l'ait fait; je ne doute pas.* Some linguists have expressed surprise at this, basing themselves on the false principle that two negatives equal a positive; this is not the case: *je ne nie pas* is not the same as *j'affirme*, nor is *je ne doute pas* the same as *je suis sûr.*
13 There seems to be some doubt as to the acceptability of these sentences.
14 Brunot and Bruneau (*Grammaire historique de la langue française*, 520) write:

> *En français moderne, c'est dans les relatives que la valeur modale du subjonctif apparaît le plus clairement; c'est là que l'orateur ou l'écrivain a le plus souvent l'occasion de faire un choix entre l'indicatif et le subjonctif. La raison en est claire. Le mode de la relative est plus 'libre' que le mode de la complétive, qui est imposé par le sens du verbe principal . . . . Ce n'est qu'après un relatif que nous pouvons, comme nos ancêtres du XVIIe siècle le faisaient dans la plupart des cas, exprimer la nuance de notre pensée par l'emploi d'un mode.*

15 *Quoique* – although spelt in one word – is similar to *bien que* and is classified here as a compound conjunction (= *quoi + que*); see 3.5.2 (*iv*).
16 The difference between *emmener* and *amener* is the following: *on amène quelque*

chose but *on emmène quelqu'un*. Thus one could say, *je viendrai déjeuner mardi; j'emmènerai ma tante Elisabeth et j'amènerai du bon vin*. But this is a rather fine distinction which has disappeared from most people's speech.

17 In Old French and up to the end of the seventeenth century it was still possible to use the indicative with these conjunctions (see A. Haase, *Syntaxe française du XVIIe siècle*, para. 83).

18 Its use in the General System is so rare that some people, when they hear it, may wonder what it is and think its use is a mistake. This was the subject of a recent skit, in which one of the comedians was supposed to be the Communist leader, M. Marchais, and the other the Conservative prime minister, M. Barre:

(The Communist leader): *Vous avez un ton doctoral qui ne passe pas, M. Barre. Vous parlez à des travailleurs. Faites des fautes de français qu'ils vous comprennent!*

(The Conservative leader): *M. Marchais, j'aurais voulu que vous m'expliquassiez . . . .*

(The Communist leader): *Ben voilà! Ce n'est pas difficile!*

Chapter 6

The conditional and the expression of the hypothetical

0   General considerations on the conditional's dual role as tense and mood

(i) The word 'conditional' gives rise to misunderstandings, since the conditional does not always express a condition. This is not the only complication involved. Although the conditional has been classified traditionally in France as a mood, present-day grammarians often tend to classify it as a tense. This is because morphologically it is akin to the indicative, in that it can carry temporality alone. In this case it expresses the future seen from the past, as in *je savais qu'il viendrait dimanche.* (see Ch. 4, 2.4.4).

(ii) On the other hand, the morphology of a form is not the only significant factor. There are many modal uses of the conditional which justify it being classified as a mood. In *il serait déjà arrivé que je n'en serais pas étonné*, the first use of the conditional indicates the arrival to be probable although not certain, and the second conditional expresses the dependency of the second action on the realization of the previous one which itself is uncertain. Given these factors it seems desirable to treat the conditional forms and uses under two headings: under the temporal conditional and under the modal conditional.

(iii) Whether the conditional functions as a mood or as a tense, is dependent on the syntactical context it appears in. As a general rule the temporal conditional only appears in subordinate clauses; the modal conditional is usually used in main clauses or independent clauses. There are, however, a number of cases in which the conditional may be used modally in subordinate clauses, namely if these are relative clauses or if the subordinate clause does not contain any time adverbials (see 1.3.2).

(iv) When the conditional is used as a mood, it always refers to the nonreality of the action considered; it is the mood of the imaginary. As such it is often ambiguous in its implications. In the following sentence, for example, the speaker is both asking and not asking for a favour:

je vous demanderais bien de le faire, mais cela me gêne

(v) The conditional contrasts modally with the indicative. One can normally choose between these two moods in any kind of clause considered (with the exception, in Modern French, of *si* clauses: in these neither the future nor the conditional are possible – see 4.2.2). In classical French even that restriction did not exist. Thus Brunot and Bruneau (*Précis de grammaire historique de la langue française*) quote Pascal as having written the following sentence with a conditional form in the first draft, and an indicative form in the second draft, thus achieving a shift in meaning from the action seen as hypothetical to the action seen as reality:

Je ne crois que les histoires dont les témoins se font égorger (Pensées XXIV 46, ed. Havet)

In the first draft Pascal had written *se feraient égorger*, which would have emphasized the hypothetical nature of the assertion, the hypothesis being *si cela était exigé d'eux pour prouver leur bonne foi*. Similarly, *est-il malade?* is a direct, unmarked question, whereas *serait-il malade*? has different implications. The implications in this last case are similar to those which could be expressed by the subjunctive: *est-il possible qu'il soit malade*? But when using the conditional it is simply an element of doubt which is being built into the sentence (a 'mild form' of the imaginary).

(vi) The conditional and the subjunctive may be used contrastively. The last two sentences demonstrate the fact that the conditional and the subjunctive are not in total contrast. The same applies in the following two sentences:

> *je cherche une maison qui soit assez grande pour nous tous*
> *je cherche une maison qui serait assez grande pour nous tous*

The subjunctive expresses the fact that such a house may not exist, whereas the conditional refers to an imaginary house. These two concepts are however very similar.

(vii) The conditional has taken over from the subjunctive in hypothetical clauses (see section 3).

The imperfect subjunctive is no longer used at all in this respect (see 3.2 for the reason for this). The pluperfect subjunctive is still sometimes used in hypothetical clauses to express the unreal (see Ch. 5, 1.3.2, 1.3.3, 2.3 and 4.4). But it is only used in this manner in certain registers. When used in this way it is also called *le conditionnel deuxième forme*. The conditional has a more general meaning than the *conditionnel deuxième forme*, in that it refers either to something which could or could not have taken place in the past, whereas the pluperfect subjunctive only refers to the latter. Thus *vous auriez réussi si . . .* implies, 'although you did not succeed you could have, had you taken the necessary steps to make this possible.' *Eussiez-vous réussi* means 'had you succeeded', but, does not imply, on the contrary, that any steps could have been taken to make this possible. It therefore refers to unreality or to a gratuitous hypothesis. This nuance is lost in the General System, but it is used in the Narrative System even in modern French.

(viii) The pluperfect subjunctive may be used to refer to the imaginary in relation to another imaginary expressed by a conditional (*le deuxième degré de l'imaginaire*) (see Ch. 5, 4.4.1).

1 Forms, time and aspect

1.1 Morphological considerations

(i) The conditional is formed in the same way as the future, i.e. on the infinitive form of the verb followed by an auxiliary, but whereas in the case of the future the auxiliary is in the present, in the conditional the auxiliary is in the imperfect. Thus the Latin form *portáre (ha)bébas* probably became *portáreas* (which form is not attested); the later then became *porteroies* and then *porterais*.

(ii) Both the conditional and the future (although in the case of the latter only to a lesser degree) have a dual function: one of expressing time and one of expressing mood. Both of these functions are attested in the very earliest texts in Old French.

(iii) There are three possible conditional forms (see (*v*) below):

> the present form (nonperfect), e.g. *je chanterais*
> the compound form or past conditional (perfect or past tense), e.g. *j'aurais chanté*
> the double compound form (stressing completion or anteriority), e.g. *j'aurais eu chanté*[1]

(iv) From a morphological point of view, the conditional includes one tense – the present – and two aspects – completed (or perfect) and not completed (action seen midstream or *aspect sécant*); the rarely used double compound form may stress either the completion aspect or modality (see 1.2.4 and 1.3.2 *iii*).

(v) The distinction between completion and noncompletion remains the same, whatever way the conditional is being used; but the time referred to by these forms depends on whether they are being used temporally or modally. We shall therefore have to examine separately the temporal conditional in respect to time in 1.2 and the modal conditional in respect to time in 1.3

1.2   The temporal conditional (the future seen from the past)

1.2.1   *General considerations*

This function of the conditional is dependent on its being used in conjunction with another verb in a past tense; the latter is normally the verb of the main clause, and the *-rais* form therefore normally appears in subordinate clauses. The simple and compound forms of the conditional correspond very exactly to the simple future and to the compound future or 'future anterior' in the indicative. We shall first examine the use of the present conditional (1.2.2) and then that of the compound forms of the conditional (1.2.3 and 1.2.4).

1.2.2   *The present conditional*

(i) The point of reference in the past is indicated by the verb in the main clause, and the conditional appears in the subordinate clause. Thus:

   je sais qu'il viendra

becomes:

   je savais qu'il viendrait

if the whole action is seen from a point of time in the past instead of in the present. If the action is seen as completed, the same parallel structures are used based on the compound forms:

   je sais qu'à huit heures il sera couché

becomes:

   je savais qu'à huit heures il serait couché

(ii) The temporal conditional describes an event which takes place in the future seen from the past, but this future could either be in the past in relation to Now (the moment of speaking or writing) or it could be in the future in relation to Now:

   je savais qu'il viendrait hier/aujourd'hui/demain

This may be represented in the following way:

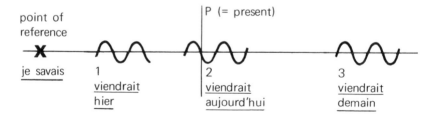

(iii) The temporal conditional can be used in the same way as the indicative future to express a succession of events:

nous avions décidé que nous nous lèverions très tôt, et qu'aussitôt après le petit déjeuner nous nous mettrions en route car nous éviterions ainsi toute la cohue

(iv) Like the indicative future, the temporal conditional describes an event or a series of events which may or may not take place. It is the context which normally resolves the ambiguity. Compare:

je savais qu'il viendrait (and he did come)
je croyais qu'il viendrait (and he did not come)

(v) The conditional could appear to be used in this way in a main clause in relation to a past tense used in a preceding clause, as in the following example (borrowed from Schogt, *Le système verbal français*):

Nous avions fini nos préparatifs. Jean entrerait par le trou de la haie et irait ensuite ouvrir le portail afin que nous puissions nous infiltrer sans bruit dans le jardin avec notre matériel.

In this case it is the word *préparatifs* which provides anchorage for the conditional forms which follow, for *préparatifs* implies *il était prévu que. . . .* In other words the sentence containing these conditional forms used to express time may be considered to be elliptical.

1.2.3 *The compound form of the conditional, or past conditional*

(i) The compound form may express a perfect aspect:

je pensais qu'il aurait fini son travail à midi

(ii) It may indicate anteriority as would a future anterior:

je pense qu'il viendra nous rejoindre quand il aura fini

becomes:

je pensais qu'il viendrait nous rejoindre quand il aurait fini

when seen from the past.

1.2.4 *The double compound conditional*

It stresses both completion and/or anteriority depending on the context, e.g.

je pensais qu'elle aurait eu fini plus tôt

Its use is rare, and belongs to the spoken language. It may be more frequently used in some regions than in others (mainly in eastern France). It is nearly always used with conclusive verbs (i.e. verbs expressing semantically the idea of completion).

1.3 The modal conditional

The conditional may be used modally both in main clauses and in subordinate clauses.

1.3.1 *The modal conditional in independent and in main clauses*

(i) The present form describes an action as yet not completed and which may be seen as either possible in the future, or impossible in the present.
    Compare the two following examples, in which the implications of the present conditional are different:

je viendrais tout de suite si je le pouvais ('but unfortunately I cannot come')

The next sentence, on the other hand, may be interpreted in two different ways:

je viendrais tout de suite si tu le voulais

This could refer either to a possible future (i.e. *si tu le voulais, et tu vas peut-être le vouloir*) or to an unreal present (i.e. *si tu le voulais, mais malheureusement tu ne le veux pas*). This is because of the two different meanings carried by the imperfect, both of which could fit into the context of this example. Note in this respect that the French language no longer distinguishes morphologically, as did Latin, between what is potentially possible and the unreal in the present.
Compare:

possim si velim (potential): contains two present subjunctives

and

possem si velem (unreal present): contains two imperfect subjunctives

The first sentence corresponds to *je pourrais si je voulais* (*et je voudrai peut-être*) whereas the second sentence corresponds to *je pourrais si je voulais* (*mais je ne veux pas*).
(ii) The compound conditional describes an action which is imagined as being completed, either in the future:

je serais venu te rejoindre cet après-midi (*si tu l'avais voulu*) (this action could still take place if the sentence is spoken in the morning, but not if it is spoken in the evening)

or in the past:

je serais venu te rejoindre hier après-midi (*si tu l'avais voulu*) (this action can no longer take place)

(iii) The double compound form stresses the modality:

la biche aurait eu passé tout l'hiver dans la vallée (i.e. *d'après ce qu'on dit, mais je ne garantis pas la vérité de l'assertion*)

But such uses of the double compound form are extremely rare and are probably confined both to the spoken language and to certain areas of France (this example was heared in a remote village in the Alps).

1.3.2   *The modal conditional in subordinate clauses other than hypothetical clauses*

(i) The present form of the modal conditional may be used instead of a present subjunctive: it expresses the prospective. Thus the following two sentences are both the same as far as their temporal connotations are concerned:

il faut que je trouve une maison qui soit près de mon travail
il faut que je trouve une maison qui serait près de mon travail

(See sections 0 *vi* and 2.3 for their modal differences.)
(ii) The compound form may be used instead of a subjunctive pluperfect to express the unreal, i.e. a gratuitous hypothesis (see also Ch. 5, 4.4.1):

il se disait en lui-même qu'il aurait fait n'importe quoi pour elle

corresponds to

il se disait en lui-même qu'il eût fait n'importe quoi pour elle

There is a difference in meaning, however, in that the compound conditional has a broader meaning than the pluperfect subjunctive since it encompasses both the possible and the impossible, whereas the pluperfect subjunctive only refers to the impossible. *Qu'il aurait fait* therefore refers to something which is no longer possible since it is in the past, but which may have been possible once upon a time, whereas *qu'il eût fait* does not refer to any specific reality; it is no more than a gratuitous hypothesis at the time of speaking or writing.

(iii) The compound past may either express modality or temporality, depending on the context. If the time at which the action described by a conditional in the subordinate clause is clear, as indicated by an adverb or an adverbial, the compound conditional will refer to a completed future seen from the past. If there are no temporal indications of this nature, the compound past will be expressing modality. Compare:

> *je savais qu'à dix heures il aurait fini* (future seen from the past)
> *il pensait en lui-même qu'il aurait fait n'importe quoi pour elle* (i.e. he would have done anything for her sake, whether she had asked him to do so in the past, or in the future, in relation to the time referred to in the main clause)

The difference in meaning of the conditional in these two sentences can be clearly seen if one tries to put both sentences in the present as far as the verb in the main clause is concerned:

> *je sais qu'à dix heures il aura fini* (compound future)
> *il pense en lui-même qu'il aurait fait n'importe quoi pour elle* (compound conditional: this tense remains unchanged)

In the first sentence the compound conditional has to become a compound future (or future anterior): the future seen from the past has become a future seen from the present. But in the second sentence the conditional form may remain unchanged: it is not expressing time.

1.4 Other ways of expressing the conditional

1.4.1 *Forms equivalent to the temporal conditional*

(i) It is sometimes difficult to separate the idea of futurity and that of modality, when the latter expresses an intention. This is why it is possible to replace the conditional by *devoir* used in the imperfect, since the imperfect can also be a mood (see Ch. 4, 4.2):

> *je savais qu'il viendrait ce jour-là*

may be replaced by

> *je savais qu'il devait venir ce jour-là*

Both sentences refer to the same time, but *devait venir* insists on the element of necessity contained lexically in *devoir*.

(ii) *Pouvoir* could replace *devoir*:

> *je savais qu'il pouvait venir ce jour-là*

In this case the modality is simply one of possibility.

(iii) *Falloir* may also be used with the subjunctive:

> *je savais qu'il fallait qu'il vienne ce jour-là*

This sentence is relatively similar to *je savais qu'il devait venir ce jour-là*.

(iv) One therefore gets the following system of correspondences:

> *je sais qu'elle viendra = je sais qu'elle doit venir*
> *je savais qu'elle viendrait = je savais qu'elle devait venir*

In other words:

a verb in the simple future = *devoir* in the present + infinitive
a verb in the present conditional = *devoir* in the imperfect + infinitive

1.4.2   *Forms equivalent to the modal conditional*

There is one form, *ne tenir qu'à* (*quelqu'un*) *de* + infinitive, which is the equivalent of a compound conditional. It expresses the idea that something which could have taken place in the past did not. Thus:

elle aurait pu y aller

could be rewritten as:

il ne tenait qu'à elle d'y aller

But this form emphasizes the responsibility of the subject in the matter referred to.

1.5   Some syntactic differences between the conditional in modern French and in classical French

In classical French *devoir, pouvoir* and *falloir* were used in the indicative imperfect to describe an eventuality in the past.
(i) J'aurais dû refuser used to be *je devais refuser, j'aurais pu refuser* used to be *je pouvais refuser*. This construction, extremely frequent in Old French, was still in frequent use in the seventeenth century. Thus La Fontaine (*Fables*) writes:

Je devais par la royauté
Avoir commencé mon ouvrage

instead of *j'aurais dû par la royauté avoir commencé mon ouvrage*. This construction is still used today in set expressions such as *elle pouvait le faire* (*elle aurait pu le faire*), *elle devait le faire* (*elle aurait dû le faire*), and *il fallait le faire* (*il aurait fallu le faire*). But these modal verbs are rarely used in this way with verbs other than *faire* and *aller*.
(ii) It used to be possible to use both the present and past or 'compound' conditional after the conjunction *si* in hypothetical clauses:

J'ai à vous dire . . . que si vous auriez de la répugnance à me voir votre belle-mère, je n'en aurais pas moins sans doute à vous voir mon beau-fils   (Molière, *L'Avare*)

These constructions may be considered to be elliptical, *s'il est vrai que* being implicit in each case:

j'ai à vous dire que si(*il est vrai que*) *vous auriez . . .*

But these constructions have not been possible in modern French since the end of the seventeenth century.

2   Meanings carried by the modal conditional in clauses other than hypothetical 'si' constructions

2.1   Meanings basic to the conditional

2.1.1   *The conditional used in independent declarative clauses*

(i) The conditional may be used in independent clauses to express make believe situations; this is particularly common in the context of a child's play, e.g. *je serais le gendarme et toi le voleur*.
(ii) It may also express wishful thinking and hence politeness (see 2.2.5):

je prendrais bien une tasse de thé maintenant (wishful thinking)
je voudrais vous parler (form of politeness)

(iii) The present conditional, by extension of its idea of eventuality, has come to express the idea of a present which is supposed to be true but where doubt is possible:

ils seraient actuellement en Espagne ('should be', 'are supposed to be')

Thus the conditional may be used to express unsubstantiated arguments, e.g. *nous serions au bord de la catastrophe; il y aurait eu plusieurs morts.*

It is for that reason that a conditional is often used in historical novels to express a 'doubtful general truth':

Que penser des prétentions de Tarakanova? D'après son récit, elle serait née d'un mariage secret qu'aurait contracté Elisabeth avec un certain Alexis Razoumovski. (Decaux, *Grands secrets, grandes énigmes*)

(This kind of nuance is particularly difficult to render in English.)

2.1.2   *The conditional used in exclamative sentences*

Exclamations such as *je ferais ça, moi*! and *j'aurais fait ça, moi*! are comparable to the use of the subjunctive in similar structures such as *que je fasse ça, moi*! and *que j'aie fait ça, moi*!

The form *que j'eusse fait cela, moi*! is grammatically possible, but archaic and ridiculous, since it uses a highly literary tense form – the pluperfect subjunctive – in an expression typical of informal spoken French (hence the stylistically necessary change of *ça* into *cela*). In these cases, the conditional expresses indignation. But it can also express delight, as in *tu me laisserais conduire ta voiture*! But with a suitable intonation this same sentence could also express disbelief, i.e. it could stress the unreality of the assertion. It is the context and the intonation pattern which determines the interpretation to be given to these sentences; the use of the conditional merely puts the assertion in the realm of uncertainty.

2.1.3   *The conditional used in interrogative sentences*

In these cases it is the doubtful nature of each question which is being expressed:

Serait-il malade? Est-ce qu'il serait malade?
Serait-il déjà arrivé? Est-ce qu'il serait déjà arrivé?

2.1.4   *The conditional in 'false' single-clause sentences*

riche, j'aurais acheté un bateau (= *si j'avais été riche, . . .*)
sans son aide, je n'aurais pas pu m'en sortir (= *si je n'avais pas eu son aide, . . .*)

In both cases a single word or phrase stands for a *si* clause, or else could be termed a 'reduced *si* clause'. The use of the conditional in main clauses, unlike that of the hypothetical subjunctive pluperfect, is always tied to a condition, but the latter may be implicit rather than explicit.

2.1.5   *The conditional in main clauses followed by a completive clause*

il ne voudrait pas que Jean y aille

In this sentence the conditional gives an idea of uncertainty as to the final outcome; whether the action is desirable or not is indicated lexically in this case. It is the verb in the main clause which usually expresses some kind of mood lexically (*j'aimerais, je vous serais reconnaissant, je voudrais, vous pourriez*).

2.1.6   *The conditional in completive clauses*

il n'y a rien que je ne ferais pour toi

In this case the conditional alone indicates the hypothetical nature of the statement.

2.1.7   *Use of the conditional in inverted clausal constructions*

There exists for the conditional a parallel to the subjunctive example mentioned in Ch. 5, 0.3 *iii*. The examples were:

il est certain qu'il l'a fait de bon coeur
qu'il l'ait fait de bon cœur, c'est certain

In this case the inversion of the two clauses requires a change in the mood used. The same applies to the conditional. Thus:

cela ne m'étonnerait pas qu'il soit déjà à Marseille

becomes

il serait déjà à Marseille que cela ne m'étonnerait pas

This is a particularly common type of expression in the spoken language, but the *que* is often omitted, in which case one ends up with a disjunctive construction, e.g. *il serait déjà à Marseille, cela ne m'étonnerait pas*).

The use of the conditional emphasizes that the speaker is only dealing with a possibility. The inversion of the clauses has to take place for the use of the conditional to be possible, however, since otherwise the use of the subjunctive is compulsory.

2.2   The conditional/indicative contrast

2.2.1   *The indicative future and the conditional*

These tenses are similar in that they usually refer to something which is not realized at the time of speaking. There is, however, a difference in nature between the uncertainty implied by the use of each of these forms. In the case of the conditional, realizability depends on a number of factors present or implicit in the context. With the indicative future, the uncertainty linked to the future is quite different in the sense that it is inherent to the human condition: one can never be totally certain that something one intends to do at a certain time and at a certain place will in fact get done. In other words the indicative future depends on a *si Dieu le veut* concept. The uncertainty is no longer verbal but philosophical. This being the case, the future is very much less uncertain than the conditional.

Thus one may contrast:

il sera déjà arrivé/il aura déjà fait ses bagages

and

il serait déjà arrivé/il aurait déjà fait ses bagages.

The second sentence implies 'according to 'X', or 'according to what he was planning to do'. The conditional refers basically to human conditions. In the first sentence on the other hand the speaker is convinced that the person spoken about has arrived at his destination; only something unforeseeable could get in the way of his arrival.

2.2.2   *Replacement of the conditional by the imperfect*

Les révolutionnaires durent se dire à ce moment-là qu'ils approcheraient/

approchaient (bientôt) de la fin de la guerre (example borrowed from Schogt, *Le Système verbal*)

There is a difference in time depending on whether the adverb *bientôt* is used or not; if it is used there is no difference in time, but if *bientôt* is not included, the imperfect refers to an action simultaneous with that in the main clause, whereas the conditional refers to the future in relation to the action in the main clauses. These two tenses may be contrasted in the following examples:

pour un peu je l'épousais (but I did not)
pour un peu je l'épouserais (and I may still do so)

In the first sentence, *pour un peu* indicates that the action did not take place, because it is used in conjunction with the imperfect, i.e. a tense referring to the past; in the second sentence on the other hand, it is used with a tense which refers to the future and therefore to the possible, which changes the implications of the adverbial *pour un peu*.

Thus it is only in certain contexts – namely in subordinate clauses and in conjunction with suitable adverbs or adverbials – that these tenses may be interchanged without the meaning of the sentence being changed.

2.2.3 *Replacement of the present indicative by the conditional in interrogative sentences*

(See also 2.2.5)

The use of the conditional attenuates the demand element of the question:

Avez-vous l'heure?
Auriez-vous l'heure?

2.2.4 *Replacement of the present indicative and imperative by the conditional in sentences giving orders*

These may both be used to give orders. As such they may be replaced by the conditional of politeness, provided that a new main clause is created which expresses semantically the idea of command:

tu rangeras ta chambre avant de sortir
range ta chambre avant de sortir

may become

je voudrais que tu ranges ta chambre avant de sortir

(But see 2.4 for the imperative/conditional contrast.)

2.2.5 *Use of the conditional to express politeness*

(i) First of all, politeness may be expressed by the use of the present conditional alone in a one-clause sentence: the idea of eventuality expressed by the conditional implying the possibility of a negative response, the statement automatically looses some of the bluntness it would have in the indicative, and therefore conveys an idea of politeness: *je voudrais une tasse de café* implies that I may not be given one.

We are dealing here in reality with an elliptical hypothetical structure: *je voudrais une tasse de café si vous pouviez/vouliez bien m'en donner une.* In some cases the *si* clause, instead of being understood, is plainly stated.

(ii) Another way of expressing politeness is to state first of all the degree of satisfaction/happiness which would be given, if the desire to be expressed were to be fulfilled:

je serais bien content si vous me donniez une tasse de café

Intensifiers are often used to emphasize the degree of contentment involved; modal auxiliaries are also used to achieve the same effect (for modal auxiliaries see Ch. 4, 5.3):

je vous serais bien obligé si vous vouliez bien me donner une tasse de café

In this case there are two clauses corresponding to the original one. This kind of construction is so obsequious that it could not be used without fear of ridicule in normal conversation. Such formulas are kept for contexts such as business letters:

nous vous serions infiniment obligés si vous vouliez bien donner suite à notre demande

Basically speaking, the longer the sentence the more formally polite it is, hence the possibility of sentences such as:

nous vous serions très reconnaissants si vous aviez l'obligeance de bien vouloir donner suite à notre demande

(iii) There is also a progression in the grammatical options open to the French speaker to express varying and increasing politeness. The principle of this progression is that the more imaginary the demand and the more remote it appears, the less the listener/reader will feel that the demands made upon him or her are aggressive. Compare the following structures:

(1) *si tu peux venir dimanche prochain, nous en serons ravis*
(2) *si tu pouvais venir dimanche prochain, nous en serions ravis*
(3) *si tu avais pu venir dimanche prochain, nous en aurions été ravis*

(1) refers to reality and therefore to the probable.

(2) refers to the imaginary: 'we are imagining that you are coming and how nice it would be'.

(3) refers to a point of time in the future posterior to that point in time when the person is expected to come; the speaker is therefore imagining that something he wanted to happen has not in fact taken place: the unreal past has become an unreal future. By speaking as if the outcome of the request were to be negative, less pressure is being put on the receiver of the message: he is being given the option of not coming on Sunday, however desirable his coming may be felt to be.

The pressure in (3) is therefore less than in (2) which, in turn, is less than in (1). Much use is made in nonspontaneous French − written or spoken − of these distinctions.

2.3   The conditional/subjunctive contrast

(i) One may contrast the conditional and the subjunctive forms in relative clauses. Compare:

il faut que je trouve une maison qui soit habitable toute l'année (= the subjunctive indicates doubt as to the availability of such a house)

and

il faut que je trouve une maison qui serait habitable toute l'année (= the conditional expresses the idea that so far, this house only exists in the speaker's mind).

Thus the conditional mood refers to a house which, so far, only exists in the speaker's imagination, whereas the subjunctive, harmonizing with the indefinite article in the nominal phrase acting as antecedent, stresses the uncertainty of finding such a house.

(ii) In the Literary System it is possible to contrast the compound conditional and the subjunctive pluperfect or *conditionnel deuxième forme* (see Ch. 5, 1.3.2, 1.3.3, 2.3

and 4.4): whereas the conditional is always tied to a specific condition which, even if it is not clearly stated, is nonetheless obvious from the context; the subjunctive pluperfect is not tied to any specific condition. Compare:

Mais cette démarche eût paru étrange à sa famille et aux gens du bourg, on aurait crié à la conversion (Mauriac, quoted by Wagner and Pinchon, *Grammaire du français classique et moderne*)

and

Mais cette démarche aurait paru étrange à sa famille et aux gens du bourg (si elle/il l'avait faite) et on aurait crié à la conversion (si elle/il avait fait la démarche)

The first sentence means *on aurait crié à la conversion s'il avait fait la démarche et cette démarche aurait paru étrange à sa famille et aux gens du bourg*. In other words, the compound conditional represents the first action to be imagined, the pluperfect subjunctive the second one, which is dependent on the first. In the second case, on the other hand, there is no emphasis on the dependency of the two facts: the idea of dependency is replaced by an idea of succession in time.

Note, however, that the pluperfect subjunctive does not always refer to a hypothesis, but may refer to a past which never happened (or an 'unreal' past) i.e.:

Une locution telle que 'ras le bol' eût mérité dans tout dictionnaire d'argot ou de langue populaire la mention 'vulg.' sinon 'obsc.'; 'bol' est synonyme de 'cul'; 'avoir du bol' c'est 'avoir du cul', c'est-à-dire avoir de la chance (Caradec, *Dictionnaire du français argotique et populaire*)

Eût mérité clearly indicates that one is referring to something which did not take place in the past. It is much stronger in expressing what is unreal than *aurait mérité*, for two reasons: on the one hand the subjunctive pluperfect does not automatically express an idea of an hypothesis as does the conditional, and on the other hand it stresses, from a morphological point of view, the idea of pastness (whereas the conditional has morphological ties with the future). The use of the pluperfect therefore stresses the 'irremediable' nature of the assertion.

2.4 The conditional/imperative contrast

One could also argue that the conditional is used in contrast with an imperative form, e.g. *je voudrais une tasse de café* for *donnez-moi une tasse de café*. But this implies changing lexical items (*vouloir* and *donner*) and changing the structuring of the message: instead of the subject being the first person singular it has to become a second person singular or plural. Thus although the message remains the same in its essence, the whole viewpoint is dramatically altered.

3 Moods used in 'si' clauses and in other constructions expressing the hypothetical

3.1 General considerations

A hypothetical construction is one in which somebody makes an assumption from which a conclusion is drawn. Thus, in *s'il pleut, je ne sortirai pas* the assumption is *il pleut* and the conclusion is *je ne sortirai pas*. A hypothetical construction is therefore always in two parts, although it sometimes happens that the assumption is understood, as in:

je viendrais bien (understood: *si je le pouvais*)

There are three types of assumptions corresponding to each of the three moods:

(i) The indicative refers to the probable: if a specific action takes place, and it probably will, another action will automatically take place as a result. It is reality which is being referred to:

> *s'il pleut je ne sortirai pas*

(ii) The conditional refers to the possible: if a specific action takes place (which it may not), another will follow automatically:

> *s'il faisait beau, je viendrais (mais il fera peut-être mauvais, dans lequel cas je ne viendrais pas)*

(iii) In the case of the subjunctive, the assumption may refer to a gratuitous hypothesis; in this case the assumption concerns the unreal (*l'irréel du passé*):

> *s'il eût fait beau, je fusse venu (mais il n'a pas fait beau, donc je ne suis pas venu)*

Such a sentence, however, although grammatically correct, would now appear ridiculous, given that the sentence belongs to the spoken language whereas the pluperfect subjunctive belongs purely to the Narrative System. It is the conditional which now expresses both the possible and the impossible or unreal: the compound conditional refers both to what could have taken place in the past (but did not), and to a gratuitous hypothesis − hence:

> *s'il avait fait beau, je serais venu*

which means exactly the same as its subjunctive counterpart above.

(iv) Combining both the subjunctive and *si* constructions happens mainly in poetry or in poetic prose:

> *Ils eussent, sans nul doute, escaladé les nues,*
> > *Si ces audacieux,*
> *En retournant les yeux dans leur course olympique*
> *Avaient vu derrière eux la grande République*
> > *Montrant du doigt les cieux.*

> > > > (Hugo, *Châtiments*)

The use of the pluperfect subjunctive, which clearly refers to an unreal past, makes it possible to put the main clause first, keeping the reader in suspense as to the hypothesis involved. The normal order, had the conditional been used, would have been:

> *si ces audacieux . . . avaient vu derrière eux . . . ils auraient . . . escaladé . . .*

The pluperfect subjunctive refers in this case to a visionary world.

There are many cases in French literature of the past in which such combinations of the pluperfect subjunctive with *si* constructions are used to emphasize the huge gap existing between real and imaginary worlds:

> *Elle n'eût jamais voulu toucher un sou, si l'on pouvait se divertir sans qu'il en coûte.*
> (Prévost, *Manon Lescaut*)

In this case the *si* + indicative imperfect construction refers to an unreal and permanent present, i.e. *l'on ne peut jamais se divertir sans qu'il en coûte* (use of the modal imperfect). Since this is the case, Manon was always in need of money: the ̣ubjunctive pluperfect refers to a desirable but unreal state of affairs.

Such a use of the pluperfect subjunctive has an attenuating effect on the reader: although Manon would have done anything for money, it was not really in her nature to do so; indeed, if the world had been a better one, she would not have needed a penny. One ends up, in this manner, sympathizing with the heroine despite her glaring shortcomings.

In contemporary French this dramatic gap between the real and the unreal may be expressed by the use of *si* + indicative pluperfect + indicative imperfect (instead of the conditional). Hence:

si j'avais fait un pas de plus, je serais tombée dans le trou

represents the norm in the expression of the hypothetical, whereas

si j'avais fait un pas de plus, je tombais dans le trou or
un pas de plus, et je tombais dans le trou

emphasize the dramatic nature of the situation (i.e. 'I very nearly did fall into the hole').

3.2 Historical development of hypothetical systems using 'si' clauses

The systems mentioned in 3.1 all existed in Old French; but there were two possibilities where the subjunctive was concerned, one (the original) based on the imperfect subjunctive, and one based on the pluperfect, the latter dating back to the thirteenth century. In Old French one therefore had five possibilities.
(i) Indicative + future, referring to reality:

s'il pleut je ne sortirai pas[2]

This system has survived unchanged.
(ii) Imperfect subjunctive + imperfect subjunctive: this system did not survive beyond the thirteenth century because of its ambiguity:

Si j'osasse parler, je demandasse (*Le Couronnement de Louis*)
(= either *si j'osais, je demanderais* (*et je le ferai peut-être*) or *si j'avais osé, j'aurais demandé* (*mais je n'ai pas osé*))
. . . *si Dieu n'aimât cette armée, elle ne pût pas tenir ensemble* (Villehardouin, *La Conqueste de Constantinople*[3])
(= either . . . *si Dieu n'avait pas aimé cette armée, elle*
n'aurait pas pu rester unie or . . . *si Dieu n'aimait pas*
cette armée, elle ne pourrait pas rester unie; in fact, given the context, it is the first interpretation which is the correct one[4])

It is the ambiguity contained in the imperfect subjunctive which led to its disappearance as a carrier of meaning: it only survived under the form of tense agreement.
(iii) The pluperfect subjunctive + pluperfect subjunctive. This appears in the thirteenth century for a hypothesis relating to the past, and refers to the impossible:

s'il eût plu, je ne fusse pas sorti

This kind of hypothetical construction ceased to be productive during the seventeenth century (it was condemned by Vaugelas). It is still sometimes used, however, in the 3rd person singular in the Literary System. But it tends to create a rather pedantic effect, as in, *si son père eût vécu, il ne fût pas tombé si bas* (see 3.3.2).
(iv) The indicative imperfect + the present conditional. This form is present in *Le Couronnement de Louis*, one of the oldest epic poems; it refers to the possible:

s'il pleuvait, je ne sortirais pas

This form remains unchanged today.
(v) The indicative pluperfect + the compound conditional. This appears in the sixteenth century. It is used to refer to the impossible, either because the possibilities were in the past or because one is dealing with a gratuitous hypothesis:

s'il avait plu, je ne serais pas sorti

This form remains unchanged today.

One is therefore left with *(i), (iv)* and *(v)* from the original system.

3.3   Expression of the hypothetical in modern French in 'si' clauses

3.3.1   *Two possibilities dependent on reference to time*

3.3.1.1   *No reference to time*

(1) *si* + Present + Future: *si tu viens, je serai content*
(2) *si* + Imperfect + Present conditional: *si tu venais, je serais content*
(3) *si* + Pluperfect + Compound conditional: *si tu étais venu, j'aurais été content*

(1) refers to a probable reality.
(2) refers to a possible future.
(3) refers to the impossible, either because although there was a possibility of realization at some time in the past this possibility is now over, or because one is dealing with a gratuitous hypothesis.

3.3.1.2   *Reference to time*

(1) *si tu viens dimanche, je serai content*
(2) *si tu venais dimanche, je serais content*
(3) *si tu étais venu dimanche prochain, j'aurais été content*
(4) *si tu étais venu dimanche dernier, j'aurais été content*

In this case the compound past may refer either to the impossible, as in (4), or to the improbable, as in (3). (1) and (2) remain unchanged.

3.3.2   *Survival of the pluperfect subjunctive in hypothetical constructions*

The pluperfect subjunctive survives in the Narrative System[5] but even then the use of the two subjunctives in a hypothetical construction is very rare, except in set expressions such as *s'il l'eût osé, il l'eût prié de faire telle ou telle chose* (see Ch. 5, 2.3).

On the other hand one sometimes finds a pluperfect subjunctive in a *si* clause, if the latter is coordinated to a previous *si* clause containing a conditional:

> *Ah! Si j'avais eu un but dans la vie, si j'eusse rencontré une affection, si j'avais trouvé quelqu'un. . . . Oh! comme j'aurais dépensé toute l'énergie dont je suis capable, j'aurais surmonté, brisé tout.*   (Flaubert, *Madame Bovary*, quoted by Brunot and Bruneau, *Précis de grammaire historique de la langue française*)

The pluperfect subjunctive expresses in this case the *second degré de l'imaginaire* mentioned in Ch. 5, 4.4.1. Note however that in contemporary French such constructions are acceptable only if in the 3rd person.

3.3.3   *The case of a double hypothesis*

In this case the second clause may either be a coordinated *si* clause or a *que* + subjunctive clause, which latter construction tends to be favoured from a stylistic point of view. One may thus write or say either:

> *si tu viens nous voir au bord de la mer et si tu as envie de faire du bateau, j'en louerai un à mon voisin* (stylistically poor)

or preferably:

> *si tu viens nous voir au bord de la mer et que tu aies envie de faire du bateau, j'en louerai un à mon voisin.*

3.4 Hypothetical clauses other than 'si' clauses

3.4.1 *Hypothetical clauses introduced by other conjunctions expressing a hypothesis*

(i) When the main clause is in the conditional, and the hypothetical clause is introduced by *que*, the latter will take the subjunctive:

> *cela ne m'étonnerait pas qu'il soit déjà parti*

But if the hypothetical clause is not introduced by *que* and appears in first position, the verbs in both clauses will be in the conditional:

> *il serait déjà parti que cela ne m'étonnerait pas*

(ii) *Selon que* and *suivant que* are followed by the indicative:

> *Selon qu'il fera beau ou mauvais, nous ferons un barbecue dans le jardin ou nous mangerons à l'intérieur*

(iii) *Au cas où, dans le cas où, pour le cas où, dans l'hypothèse où* are all followed by the conditional:

> *quand bien même il s'excuserait, je ne lui pardonnerais pas*

(iv) But *pourvu que, pour peu que, à supposer que, à moins que, en admettant que, pour autant que, pour peu que, à supposer que, à moins que* + expletive *ne* all take the subjunctive:

> *il s'en contenterait pourvu que/à condition qu'on lui écrive souvent*
> *pour peu qu'on lui écrive souvent, il s'en contenterait*
> *à supposer qu'on lui écrive souvent, il s'en contenterait*
>   (i.e. *de ne nous voir que de temps en temps*)

(v) *Comme . . . si* is used to introduce a comparison with something imaginary; it may combine with the same verbal forms as in the ordinary hypothetical *si* constructions:

> *il l'a traitée comme (il l'aurait traitée) si elle avait été son esclave*

It is however normal to leave out the section between brackets, which remains understood.

(vi) *Quand bien même* introduces the idea of something extremely improbable, and is followed by two conditional forms:

> *quand bien même il s'excuserait,[6] je ne lui pardonnerais pas*

(vii) *Ne serait-ce que parce que* is now a formalized expression which stands for 'if only because'; it functions simply as a subordinating expression:

> *nous n'irons pas ne serait-ce que parce que c'est trop loin*

This expression is commonly used in the spoken language. It takes the indicative.

3.4.2 *The case of a double hypothesis: the 'si . . . et que' construction*

(i) *Si* is normally followed by the indicative and *et que* by the subjunctive:

> *si tu viens à Londres cet hiver et que tu aies envie d'aller au théâtre, je te prendrai des places*

(ii) In some rare cases *et que* may also be followed by an indicative:

> *Si c'est vrai et que vous êtes venu pour servir . . . .* (Claudel)

or

Si vous arrivez par le fond du vallon, et que vous débouchez brusquement dans la cour . . . . (Schlumberger)

(Both of these examples are quoted by Grevisse, *Le Bon usage*.)

In these last two examples the use of the indicative after *que* is made necessary by the fact that the first hypothesis implies the second. Cases such as these are very rare; the norm is for *et que* to be followed by the subjunctive, since in most cases both clauses introduce a hypothesis.

3.4.3   *Hypothetical clauses not introduced by a subordinating conjunction ('asyndetic' clauses)*

(i) If there is inversion of the subject/verb word order in the hypothetical clause, the subjunctive is used in such a clause:

survienne le moindre obstacle (et) il est tout de suite découragé

This construction is literary and very rarely used in contemporary French.

(ii) The hypothetical may be expressed by an imperative construction followed by a clause containing a future tense:

taisez-vous, on vous le reprochera; parlez et on vous le reprochera de même (= *si vous vous taisez, on vous le reprochera et si vous parlez, on vous le reprochera aussi*).

In this case the imperative replaces a *si* + present construction.

(iii) Both clauses may be in the conditional, if there is no conjunction to introduce the hypothetical clause:

tu serais à sa place, tu ne ferais pas mieux

Sentences such as the latter are particularly common in the spoken language and tend to take on the overtones of proverbs.

(iv) A relative clause may contain a conditional; the verb in the main clause will normally also be in the conditional:

un homme qui ne serait pas énergique ne ferait pas l'affaire

3.4.4   *Other ways of expressing the hypothetical*

(i) By certain prepositional phrases followed by an infinitive:

After *à condition de, à moins de*, providing that there is identity of subject in both clauses:

vous y arriverez, à condition de vous y prendre à temps

(In certain cases the infinitive used on its own may express the hypothetical:

à vous écouter, on croirait qu'il s'agit du paradis!)

(ii) By a gerund at the beginning of the sentence:

en vous y prenant à temps, vous y arriverez

(iii) By an adjective in contrast with a noun or pronoun:

plus jeune, il aurait fait ce travail en un tournemain

(iv) By a noun preceded by *avec, dans, en, en cas de* or *sauf*:

je viendrai, sauf imprévu

(v) By a clause introduced by the adverbs *autrement* or *sinon*:

> *depêche-toi, autrement* (or *sinon*) *nous serons en retard*

(*Autrement* belongs more, in this case, to the spoken language, and *sinon* to the written.)

(vi) The hypothesis may be expressed in an elliptical construction containing a modal imperfect:

> *un peu plus, et je manquais mon train!*

In this case the 'imperfect' is used in a modal sense.

4 Translation problems

4.1 The problem of 'would', 'should' and 'could'

There are good reasons for these being a source of error, namely the very different meanings and functions which they may assume.

4.1.1 *The problem of 'would'*

(i) 'Would' can express willingness:

> 'I asked him for his advice but he would not give it'
> (= 'did not want to give it')

becomes

> *je lui ai demandé son avis mais il n'a pas voulu me le donner*

(ii) 'Would' can express the conditional:

> 'if I were rich, I would buy a boat'

becomes

> *si j'étais riche, j'achèterais un bateau*

(iii) 'Would' can express habit:

> 'my father would always walk to his office in summer'

becomes

> *mon père se rendait toujours à pied à son bureau en été*

The use of 'would' does not, therefore denote automatically the presence of a hypothetical clause.

4.1.2 *The problem of 'should'*

(i) 'Should' usually corresponds to the conditional, as can be seen in the following examples; but the use of the conditional is often combined with *devoir*. This is in fact the norm when 'should' is used with any person but the 1st person. Thus 'you should start at the beginning' becomes *vous devriez commencer par le commencement*. But where 'should' is used with the 1st person one does not use *devoir*: 'I should go to the doctor's if I were you' becomes *j'irais chez le médecin si j'étais vous*.

There are also cases in which 'should' means 'were to', e.g. 'if your car should (were to) break down, you could take mine'.

There are two translations possible, depending on the place of the stress in English:

si votre voiture tombait en panne, vous pourriez prendre la mienne
si votre voiture devait tomber en panne, vous pourriez prendre la mienne

The first translation given would correspond to an unstressed version of 'if your car should break down you could take mine' whereas the second translation corresponds to a stressed 'should'.

4.1.3 *The problem of 'could' and 'could be'*

It is important to distinguish between 'could' as a weak version of 'should' (which is translated in French by *pouvoir* + conditional); 'could be', meaning 'it is possible' (which is translated by *pouvoir* + present indicative); and 'could' as the past tense of 'can', meaning 'to be able to' (which is translated by *pouvoir* + imperfect).

(i) 'Could' usually corresponds to a weak form of 'should'; in this case it is translated by *pouvoir* + conditional:

'she could have told me she wouldn't be there' (a weaker form of 'she should')

becomes

elle aurait pu me dire qu'elle ne serait pas là (this implies she did not do so)

Similarly:

'she could do it all the same' (a weak form of 'she should')

becomes

elle pourrait le faire tout de même

(This implies that she may do so if someone convinces her to do so.) There is a tendency in French to use intensifiers in these cases, usually *bien*. Thus, 'it could be' becomes *cela se pourrait bien (i.e. que ce que vous dites soit vrai)*. (In the case of the compound conditional, *bien* is placed between the auxiliary and the lexical verb, e.g. *elle aurait bien pu me dire qu'elle ne serait pas là*.)

(ii) 'Could be' means 'it is possible that' or 'it may be that'. It is translated either by *il se peut que* or *peut-être que* (plus the indicative). Thus, 'he could be working' becomes *il se peut qu'il travaille* or *peut-être qu'il travaille*.

(iii) 'Could' may also be the past tense of 'can' in the sense of 'to be able to'; in this case it is translated by *pouvoir* + past tense:

'she could never remember our names' (= 'she was never able . . .')

becomes

elle ne pouvait jamais se rappeler nos noms

4.2 The problem of 'si' corresponding either to 'if' or to 'whether'

4.2.1 *The nonhypothetical 'si' (= 'whether')*

Normally *si* introduces a clause of a hypothetical type (i.e. of the 'if I were' type). In this case, the conditional should not appear in the *si* clause.

But there is another *si* clause to be considered which is not hypothetical: the interrogative *si*, which translates (or may translate) the English 'whether'. This interrogative *si* may be followed by a conditional form. Thus,

'I wonder if I should go there or not'

becomes

je me demande si je devrais y aller ou pas

There are therefore two contrasting constructions based on *si*:

(*si* + imperfect or pluperfect) + conditional: hypothetical sentence
indicative + (*si* + conditional): not hypothetical, but interrogative

Note that when *si* means 'whether', the *si* clause – which is interrogative – necessarily follows the main clause.

4.2.2 The hypothetical 'si' (corresponding to 'if')

This use of *si* excludes the possibility of using either the indicative future or the conditional. Thus none of the following is acceptable:

*je serai content s'il *sera là* (= *s'il est là*)
*je serais content s'il *serait là* (= *s'il était là*)
*j'aurais été content s'il *aurait été là* (= *s'il avait été là*)

and yet this kind of construction appears so logical that children and uneducated people may often be heard using the conditional in a *si* clause. Thus:

*Si *tu serais pas un ange, qu'est-ce que tu serais?*

asks a little girl of a man wearing wings in Lamorisse's film *Fifi la Plume*.

Another famous example is from Louis Pergaud's *La Guerre des boutons* in which the hero, a young boy nicknamed *Petit-Gibus* keeps on saying:

*Si j'aurais su, j'aurais pas v'nu!

Note that such constructions were possible in Old French.

Notes

1 Traditional grammarians have not usually included the double compound forms, all double compound forms having been banned as 'clumsy'. They have still ended up with three tenses, however: the conditional present, the conditional past and the pluperfect subjunctive, renamed *le passé deuxième forme* when the latter is used to express the conditional. But *le passé deuxième forme* is, nonetheless, morphologically a pluperfect subjunctive, which may in certain contexts serve to express a gratuitous hypothesis. This will merely be considered to be a special use of the pluperfect subjunctive; there seems no reason to classify this particular form under two different headings.

2 One could also write *s'il pleut je ne sors pas*, since verbs in the indicative present may refer to the future (see Ch. 4, 2.1.3). The latter could also refer to the habitual.

3 Both sentences have been rewritten in modern French; the examples are borrowed from Price, *The French language*.

4 S. Lamothe writes: 'The meaning of *si Dieu n'aimât cette armée, elle ne pût tenir ensemble* is either *si Dieu n'avait pas aimé cette armée, elle n'aurait pu rester unie*, or *si Dieu n'aimait pas cette armée, elle ne pourrait pas rester unie*. Given the context, it is the first possibility which is the correct one, since the full sentence is: *Or poez savoir, seignor, que, se Diex ne amast cest ost, qu'ele ne peüst mie tenir ensemble, a ce que tant de gent li queroient mal*. Blaise de Vigenère 'translated' this sentence in 1583 as *Dont on peult assez recueillir que si Dieu n'eust particulièrement assisté de sa saincte grace et amour à ce camp, il ne se fust peu [= pu] guere maintenir sans se rompre; puis que tant de gens qui estoient ainsi desloyaulx et mal-affectez leur manquoient*. In this case the two subjunctive imperfects have been translated by two

subjunctive pluperfects. Another translation, published in 1938, translates them by a normal hypothetical *si* construction using the indicative pluperfect and the compound (or 'past') conditional: *Or, vous pouvez savoir, seigneurs, que, si Dieu n'avait aimé cette armée, elle n'aurait pu rester réunie, alors que tant de gens lui voulaient du mal* (tr. E. Faral, *Les Belles lettres*, ed. G. Bude).'

5 For the difference between the Narrative and the General Systems see chapter 4 section 1.3.3. Roughly speaking the Narrative System is the more complex one, using all possible tenses. It is used in formal French particularly in Narration. The General System is simpler, not using certain 'literary tenses' such as the past historic. It is used in all other contexts.

6 In the seventeenth century use of the indicative was possible, in order to underline the possible reality of an assertion.

Chapter 7

The imperative mood

0 Preliminary remarks

Ce drôle de mode (J. Cellard)

Some grammarians maintain that there is no such mood as the imperative in French, because the imperative mood borrows all of its forms from other moods. This is why grammarians such as Baylon and Fabre only mention the imperative very briefly under *remarque* in their *Grammaire systématique de la langue française* (150–1). Martinet, on the other hand, states that there are four personal moods in French, one of which is the imperative (see *Grammaire fonctionnelle du français*, §3.15).

Although it is true that the imperative has no forms which are specifically its own – except for the 2nd person singular of verbs of the 1st conjugation (see 2.2.*ii*) – the manner in which these forms are used makes them unique: they are the only personal forms to be used without their being accompanied by an explicit subject. This unique way of using forms belonging to other moods also reflects a different attitude on the part of the speaker towards what he is saying: instead of stating a fact he is issuing an order. It is true that one can issue orders in the indicative for example, but that is not the normal function of the indicative, whereas it is the normal function of the imperative.

1 General characteristics

(i) Unlike the other moods, the imperative has only one function: that of issuing orders. It is true that this function is subdivided by some grammarians into 'order', as in *viens ici*, 'advice', as in *fais attention*, 'wish' as in *espérons qu'il en sera ainsi*, 'apology', as in *excusez-moi*, 'hypothesis', as in *supprimez l'échauffaudage et tout s'écroule*, but all of these may be considered to be subdivisions of the same function: the imperative mood is the mood of action in the sense that it is used to obtain a result.

(ii) The imperative is a personal mood but only includes three persons instead of six as in the other moods: it includes the 2nd person singular and plural and the 1st person plural.

(iii) Although it is a personal mood it is not a temporal mood. The action is not seen as realized: it refers to the completion of an action in the future, and as such it is prospective. The compound form of the imperative is also prospective, but it is aspectually different since it refers to the completion of an action in the future. Completion may also imply anteriority: if something must be completed before a certain date, it is also anterior to this date.

Note: The names given traditionally in France to the simple and compound forms of the imperative, *l'impératif présent* and *l'impératif passé*, are inaccurate, since the imperative is always prospective; in English one refers to the 'present' and 'present perfect', which is more defensible, but 'simple' and 'compound' forms seems preferable, since this makes no reference to time.

(iv) The imperative is not the only mood used for issuing orders: the indicative, the infinitive and the subjunctive may also fulfil this role (see section 3).

2 Morphology and syntax

2.1 The forms of the imperative

2.1.1 *The norm*

The simple forms are normally based on the present indicative forms, and the compound forms are all based on the present subjunctive:

The simple forms:	The compound forms:
lis/chante (2nd person singular)	*aie lu/aie chanté*
lisons/chantons (1st person plural)	*ayons lu/ayons chanté*
lisez/chantez (2nd person plural)	*ayez lu/ayez chanté*

(But see 2.2 *ii* and *iii* and 2.3 for the absence of -*s* from the 2nd person of 1st conjugation verbs and those verbs other than *être* which use the subjunctive to form their imperative.)

2.1.2 *The exceptions*

(i) *Avoir, être, savoir* and *vouloir* use the present subjunctive forms for the simple forms: *aie/ayons/ayez; sois/soyons/soyez; sache/sachons/sachez; veuille/veuillons/veuillez* (but see 2.3 for these verbs).

(ii) The reason for these exceptions is probably because they are not felt to be real imperatives, in the sense that they do not convey orders on their own: *avoir* and *être* because they are auxiliaries, *vouloir* because in the imperative it is no more than a form of politeness (*veuillez sortir*). As for *savoir*, the use of the subjunctive corresponds to a shift of meaning from *savoir* to *apprendre: sachez votre leçon pour demain* = *apprenez votre leçon pour demain* (but *sachez* insists on the result whereas *apprenez* insists on the process).

2.2 Morphological and syntactic differences between the imperative and other moods

(i) Since the imperative borrows its forms from other moods, it differs from these mainly by the absence of the subject. Thus *lis* is in opposition with *tu lis*, and *aie lu* is in opposition with *(que) tu aies lu*. The subject is implied by the form of the verb.

(ii) The 2nd person singular of the imperative mood may be distinguished by the absence of the 2nd person -*s* which characterizes the corresponding indicative and subjunctive forms. This applies to all verbs of the 1st group, to all compound forms of the imperative, and to those verbs other than *être* using the subjunctive to form their imperative. *Mange donc!* differs in this manner from *tu manges*, and *aie fini avant cinq heures* from *il faut que tu aies fini avant cinq heures*. This rule does not apply to the other conjugations when used in the simple form: e.g. *fais-le*[1] is spelt the same as *je le fais*.

The missing -*s* may reappear, however, in certain constructions, namely those including *en* or *y*, on condition that these are not followed by an infinitive:

achètes -en	but	*achète-le* (not followed by *en* or *y*)
vas-y	but	*va y mettre un peu d'ordre* (followed by an infinitive)

(In *vas-y, y* is the complement of *va*, whereas in *va y mettre un peu d'ordre, y* is the complement of *mettre* − hence no liaison.)

(iii) In Latin one could distinguish *cantas* (= *tu chantes*) from *canta* (= *chante*). In French this distinction is purely orthographic and only applies to verbs of the 1st

conjugation, and to those verbs other than *être* using the subjunctive to form their imperative (*aie/sache/veuille*). Verbs of the other conjugations take an -*s* both in the indicative and in the imperative (*tu prends* and *prends, tu fais* and *fais*). This complicates orthography exceedingly and one may wonder why no orthographic reform was proclaimed allowing **chantes* by analogy with *prends*. This is because the grammarians of the seventeenth century decided this should not be the case, since this would be a historical misrepresentation of the language, these verbs never having had an -*s* in the first place.

2.3 Historical considerations on the forms of the imperative

(i) Whereas in Latin the imperative had its own specific forms, in Old French it is the indicative forms which have taken over. But *être, avoir, savoir* and *vouloir* borrowed their forms from the subjunctive; even so, some of these (*sachiez* and *voilliez*) have lost the *i* of the -*iez* subjunctive endings which brings them into some kind of alignment with the indicative. The imperative forms of these four verbs in modern French are as follows:

sois	*soyons*	*soyez*
aie	*ayons*	*ayez*
sache	*sachons*	*sachez* (for *sachiez*)
veuille	*veuillons*	*veuillez* (for *voilliez*)

Apart from these four verbs, some others also appear in Old French in the subjunctive where the indicative could be expected, as in *oies, beaus niès* (= *écoute, cher neveu*) instead of *ois, beaus niès*.

(ii) In Old French it was possible to emphasize the imperative by using a pronoun subject: *or vous prenés garde au revenir* (= *prenez bien garde qu'il faudra revenir*).[2]

This was unambiguous in the case of the 2nd person when the -*s* was still omitted; thus one could contrast *tu chantes* and *tu chante*. This is no longer possible in modern French, except if the pronoun is in apposition and appears in its stressed form, as in *toi, prends garde*.

(iii) In Latin the 2nd person singular of the imperative did not include a final -*s*. The same holds for Old French: thus one wrote *connoy* for *connais, vien* for *viens* etc. It is towards the end of the fourteenth century that the -*s* was often added, probably by analogy with the indicative. Up till the seventeenth century this problem of the -*s* remains unsettled and both forms appear (see *iv*).

(iv) *Voici* and *voilà* are usually classified as 'verbal substitutes'. They were in fact originally proper verbs, *voi ci* and *voi là*, in which the *voi* is the 2nd person singular, without an -*s* as was normal in the imperative (see *iii*).

(From a semantic point of view, *voici* introduces something new, whereas *voilà* refers to something which has already been mentioned, a point often not appreciated by students.)

2.4 Ways of emphasizing the imperative

(i) It has already been mentioned that whereas in Old French one could emphasize the imperative by using a pronoun subject, this is no longer possible in modern French (see 2.3 *ii*). It is possible however to name the addressee by putting the latter in apposition, thus emphasizing the imperative nature of the clause. If a pronoun is used instead of a noun, it should appear in its stressed form:

Jean, viens ici!
toi, viens ici!

3   Other ways of expressing orders

3.1   Use of the future indicative

tu viendras demain à 10 heures

instead of

viens demain à 10 heures

(See Ch. 4, 4.3.)

3.2   Use of the subjunctive

The subjunctive is similar to the imperative since they both represent an action which is envisaged – however strongly this may be, as in the case of an order – rather than one which is 'seen' as realized. It is not surprising therefore that the subjunctive should supplement the imperative for those persons the imperative does not possess, namely the 3rd person singular and plural. Moreover, the subjunctive functioning as such normally appears in subordinate clauses; it is quite natural that when it appears in an abnormal syntactic environment, i.e. in an independent clause, it should take on a different function, that of issuing orders (see Ch. 5, 2.2).

There are two types of construction based on the subjunctive.
(i) The subjunctive may appear preceded by *que*:

qu'elle s'en aille!

In this case one is dealing with an order transmitted by a third party.
(ii) The subjunctive may appear without *que*:

périssent nos ennemis!

In this case the subjunctive is expressing more a wish than a direct order. The *que* is usually absent when the subject follows the verb. This kind of construction is most usual with modals of the *pouvoir* type, as in:

puisse-t-il arriver à temps!

This construction appears to be on the decline: it is mainly used in fossilized expressions such as *plût à Dieu; advienne que pourra; vaille que vaille; plaise à Dieu!*

Corneille, in *Horace*, contrasts both types of use of the subjunctive, i.e. with and without *que*, in the following passage:

Puissent tous ses voisins ensemble conjurés
Saper ses fondements encore mal assurés!
Et si ce n'est assez de toute l'Italie,
Que l'Orient contre elle à l'Occident s'allie!

3.3   Use of the infinitive

3.3.1   *Use of the infinitive to express an order*

When there is no specific addressee(s), it is possible to use the infinitive to express an order either positive or negative:

pour tout renseignement, s'adresser à M. X
ne pas se pencher à la portière (see chapter 8, 4.3.6 *ii*)

3.3.2   *Historical note*

This use of the infinitive for prohibitions was the same in Old French:

nel dire ja (= *il ne faut plus dire cela désormais*)

But for the infinitive to be used as an imperative in Old French in a positive sentence it had to be preceded by the adverb '*or*' meaning *maintenant* and the preposition *de* followed by the article, as in:

or del bien faire (example borrowed from Ménard, *Manuel d'ancien français*)

which means

maintenant agissons comme il faut

4 Limitations on the formation of imperatives

(i) There appear to be two types of verb where the imperative is concerned: those which refer to a voluntary action and which may be used in the imperative mood, and those which refer to involuntary actions and which cannot be used in the imperative for semantic reasons. There are, sometimes in both languages and sometimes in only the one, pairs of verbs which differ in this respect only:

entendre (involuntary) and *écouter* (voluntary) = to hear and to listen
voir (involuntary) and *regarder* (voluntary) = to see and to look at

but

connaître (involuntary) and *savoir* (volontary) = to know

(ii) Stylistic effects may be obtained by 'misusing' the members of these pairs of verbs in the imperative.

One may permute the verbs, using one for the other in a poetic context:

écoute les cloches dans le lointain (logically a volontary action)

may become *entends les cloches dans le lointain*. *Entends* refers to a totally passive person who simply perceives the sound of bells rather than listens out for them. Such a stylistic effect is used in

Entends, ma sœur, entends
La douce nuit qui marche (Baudelaire)

In familiar speech, too, this kind of permutation may occur, e.g. *entends comme il parle!* or *entends ça!*

The use of *entends* is emphatic in this case: it implies that the persons present cannot but help hearing something, even if they may wish not to.

The same effects may be achieved by using *voir* for *regarder*.

(iii) It is interesting to note the various dialectal differences which exist in this respect. The dialectal form *voya* (for *vois*), for example is used quite normally in the patois of Bresse, instead of *regarde*! The same applies to *vé* in Provençal. Similarly in the Massif Central, particularly in the Auvergne, *écouter* is often used for *entendre*. Thus, if somebody says on the telephone *je ne vous écoute pas*, in Standard French this would mean 'I will not listen to you', whereas in the Auvergne it would mean 'I can't hear you', i.e. 'speak up'.

Notes

1 For the use and non-use of the hyphen, see Ch. 3, 1.2.12.
2 Example borrowed from Brunot and Bruneau, *Précis de grammaire historique de la langue française*, 323.

Chapter 8

The nonfinite forms: the participles, the gerund and the infinitive

0   General considerations

(i) The infinitive, the participle and the gerund are different from the other 'moods' in that these forms do not always function as verbs, but may also function as nouns, where the infinitive is concerned, and as adjectives, where the participles are concerned; as for the gerund, it always functions as an adverb. In these cases, the verbs have become detached from the verbal system as such, and no longer refer to an action or a process situated in time. Because of this, they end up functioning differently than they would if they were retained in the verbal system.

(ii) These moods are characterized by the fact that they do not inflect for person – even when used verbally – but when the present participle is used adjectively it agrees in number and in gender with the noun modified. It is therefore important in the written language to distinguish between adjectival and verbal uses of these forms since the former are not invariable. Further complications occur when the past participle is used verbally: it sometimes agrees with the subject of the verb, sometimes with the object and sometimes it remains invariable.

(iii) These moods being nontemporal, the time referred to is automatically simultaneous with that expressed by the tense of the main verb, or by an adverbial. Thus *partir* could refer either to the present, as in *je dois partir*, or to the past, as in *je devais partir*, or to the future as in *il faudra partir*, or in *je dois partir à deux heures*. The terms 'past' and 'present' when applied to the nonfinite forms are therefore a misnomer – the gerund is not included here, since there is only one form of the gerund. The terms 'present' and 'past' are used to distinguish the simple and the compound forms (e.g. *chanter* v. *avoir chanté*) but the difference expressed by the presence or absence of an auxiliary does not in fact usually express time (although the compound infinitive may express anteriority) but aspect.

(iv) The participle and the infinitive both include a simple and a compound form, the former referring to an action seen midstream (*aspect sécant*) and the latter to the action seen as completed. Only the gerund has one form, the simple form, which shows the action to be in progress.

(v) From a historical point of view there are many differences between the use made of these forms in the past, as compared to modern French: the compound infinitive has become rare; the rules of agreement for the participles have changed – but stylistic effects may still be achieved by going back to former rules; and the gerund has changed in that nowadays it has to be preceded by the preposition *en*, which has not always been the case.

1   The present participle and the verbal adjective in '-ant'

1.1   The present participle

1.1   *Aspect*

(i) The simple form refers to an action or process and not to a quality, as does the

adjectival -*ant* form. The action is always seen midstream (*aspect sécant*) whether the action lasts as in:

j'ai connu Pierre conduisant une Jaguar

or whether it is of short duration as in:

j'ai vu Pierre sortant du cinéma

In its compound form the present participle indicates that the action or process is seen as being completed:

ayant fermé la porte, il remit la clé dans sa poche

(ii) The present participle was formerly used with *être* to express the progressive aspect:

*je suis chantant (= je suis en train de chanter)

but nowadays this form has been replaced by the simple present: *je chante* (or *je suis en train de chanter*, if one wants to emphasize the progressive aspect).

The present has thus acquired the possibility of expressing the progressive in place of the present participle, but the present participle is still sometimes used to express the progressive with the verb *aller*, e.g. *la criminalité va croissant* or *l'inquiétude allait grandissant*. In these cases the idea of progression is heavily emphasized. But such sentences are very rare in modern French, and are felt to be archaic, hence their use in certain literary contexts:

Un refrain qu'on s'en va chantant
Efface-t-il la trace altière
Du pied de nos chevaux marqué dans votre sang?   (Musset, *Le Rhin Allemand*)

but such a use of -*ant* is in imitation of its use in Old French, a use which survives in old folk songs, as in:

Le fils du roi s'en va chassant
Avec un beau fusil d'argent. . . .

1.1.2 *Voice*

Nowadays the present participle is always active; but in Old French it could also be Passive: *un vin buvant* meant *un vin qui se laisse boire*, i.e. *un vin qui est bon*. One can still say *un refrain chantant*, i.e. *un refrain agréable à chanter*; *une rue passante*, i.e. *où l'on passe beaucoup*.

1.1.3 *Syntactiç characteristics*

1.1.3.1 *General considerations* It is important to know whether one is dealing with the present participle or with the verbal adjective in -*ant*, since this determines whether there should be agreement or not (see. 1.1.4). The spelling of the participle and the adjective are also sometimes different (see 1.2.3).

1.1.3.2 *Syntactic potential* Unlike the adjectival form in -*ant*, the present participle may appear in the following typically verbal constructions:
(i) It may take a direct object:

quittant ma famille, je me sentais triste (comme je quittais ma famille. . . .)

(ii) It may take an indirect object:

c'est là une réponse équivalant à un refus (= qui équivaut à) (iii) It may be modified by an adverbial:

> *le chien, dormant dans sa niche, paraissait ne pas se soucier de la présence des voleurs*

(iv) It may be modified by an adverb; the adverb is normally placed after the participle as is the case for the verb:

> *l'enfant courant très vite, je n'ai pu le rattraper*

(v) It may be negated:

> *ne pouvant y aller moi-même, j'y ai envoyé mon frère*

(vi) It may take a specific subject different to that of the main clause, in which case one is dealing with a participial clause. This is the case in:

> *l'enfant courant très vite, je n'ai pu le rattraper*

L'enfant is the subject of *courant* and *je* the subject of *ai pu rattraper*. The same would apply to:

> *la pluie tombant à verse, le voyageur s'arrêta sous un hangar*

in which *pluie* is the subject of *tombant*.

1.1.4   *Invariability of the present participle in modern French*

(i) It was decided in 1679 by the French *Académie* to make the verbal form in *-ant* invariable, in order to distinguish it from the adjectival form in *-ant*. One could thus distinguish between *une mère aimante* (*une mère qui est affectueuse*) which refers to a nontemporal quality, from *une mère aimant son enfant* which refers to a process delimited in time.

Before 1679 the present participle had agreed in case and in number – but not in gender – with the noun acting as subject; then agreement in gender became frequent (although Vaugelas disapproved of it). There are many cases of such an agreement in gender in the works of the classics. Thus Racine writes:

> *La veuve d'Hector pleurante à vos genoux* (*Andromaque*)

Obviously such an agreement was still felt to be normal in Racine's day. Later, Rousseau and Lamartine still sometimes make the same kind of agreement, and even in the twentieth century writers such as Proust sometimes continue to do so. Nowadays, however, such an agreement being extremely rare, it is felt to be highly marked stylistically.

(ii) In law there are a number of set phrases which have kept the present participle agreeing in gender and number with the noun which acts as their subject: *des ayants-droit* and *une fille majeure usante et jouissante de ses droits* are examples of this.

(iii) In some cases the participle has become a noun, as is the case for *les assistants, les participants, les aspirants*. In other cases the older forms of participles have survived as adjectives or nouns only, whilst a new form of the participle has been created. Hence:

savant:	adjective/noun	as against *sachant* the participle
puissant:	adjective	as against *pouvant* the participle

(See also 1.2.3 for differences in spelling between the verbal adjective and the corresponding participle.)

1.1.5   *Stylistic considerations*

The present participle is very rarely used in the spoken language; it belongs nearly exclusively to the written language. In this it differs from the other *-ant* forms, and from the gerund in particular, since the latter is extremely frequent both in the written and in the spoken language. The present participle was frequently used in the past, however, particularly in the sixteenth century, when the language was nearer to Latin from a syntactic point of view. In those days there was also a conscious return to Latin usages, which explains the frequency of these forms, and also their having receded when the fashion of latinizing the language had passed. It is frequently used for stage directions, as in *Pierre, sortant à la dérobée. . . .*

1.2 The verbal adjective in '-ant'

1.2.1 *Generalities: the 'non-verbal' quality of the verbal adjective in '-ant'*

(i) Unlike the present participle, the verbal adjective does not normally refer to an action situated in time, but rather to a state or quality which is nontemporal. Thus *une robe ravissante* and *des enfants charmants* refer to the inherent qualities of *robe* and *enfants* and not to the actions of 'bewitching' or 'trying to charm'. They refer to inherent static properties, for in these cases − which represent the norm − the noun takes on the semantic value of the verb.

(ii) There are some cases, however, in which a certain verbal quality is retained by the verbal adjective: *un thé dansant* is *un salon de thé où l'on danse* (active voice); *une couleur voyante* may stand either *for une couleur qui se voit facilement* (pronominal form) or for *une couleur qui est vue facilement* (passive form).

(iii) There are cases in which one could use either the verbal adjective or the present participle, depending on whether one wants to emphasize the adjectival or the verbal quality or the word. One could thus write either *les eaux tourbillonnant au fond du gouffre* or *les eaux tourbillonnantes au fond du gouffre. Les eaux tourbillonnant* means either *qui tourbillonnent* or *parce que les eaux tourbillonnent*, but in either case it is an action which is being described. On the other hand *les eaux tourbillonnantes* stands for *les eaux qui sont tourbillonnantes* which refers to a quality of the water (temporary or permanent). The word *tourbillonnantes* could commute with any number of adjectives such as *sombres* for example: *les eaux sombres au fond du gouffre*. (Note that if the verbal form is used, a complement of some kind needs to follow *tourbillonnant*, to detach it from the noun with which one would expect it to agree: *des eaux tourbillonnantes* sounds all right, but *des eaux tourbillonnant* on its own seems either wrong, as if agreement had been forgotten, or incomplete.)

One could similarly contrast:

il y a une gitane errante dans le bois (= inherent characteristic of that person)
il y a une gitane errant dans le bois (= *en train d'errer*)

In the first case one is dealing with a 'vagrant' whereas in the second sentence the person referred to is imply 'wandering'. Similarly *une chienne errante* would be 'a dog which is lost', whereas *une chienne errant dans la rue* would be 'a dog wandering in the street'.

1.2.2 *Possible functions of the verbal adjective*

These are the same as for other adjectives (see Ch. 11).

(i) The verbal adjective agrees with the noun it modifies both in number and in gender, as would any other adjective, e.g. *une plaie suintante*.

(ii) It may also be modified by intensifiers, e.g. *une femme très attrayante*.

(iii) The adverb appears before the verbal adjective, and not after, as was the case for the present participle, e.g. *un remords quelquefois accablant*.

1.2.3   *Differences in spelling between the verbal adjective and the present participle*

There are a number of ways by which one may distinguish the verbal adjective from its corresponding present participle, in the written language. These constitute spelling subtleties which are difficult even for the French; they are also somewhat unrewarding, since they are not carriers of meaning as such.

(i) Some verbal adjectives differ from their verbal counterpart in that the adjective may end in -*ent* whereas the present participle ends in -*ant*:

adjective:	present participle:
différent	*différant*
précédent	*précédant*
excellent	*excellant*

Some of these adjectives may also be used as nouns: *président, différend* (the 'd' being no more than a spelling variant of 't').[1]

(ii) Verbs ending in -*guer* and -*quer* usually spell their participle with -*gu*- and -*qu*-, but their adjectival form with -*g*- and -*c*-:

infinitive:	participle:	adjective:
fatiguer	*fatiguant*	*fatigant*
naviguer	*naviguant*	*navigant*

(hence *le personnel navigant* as against *en naviguant, on apprend la géographie*). One also gets:

convaincre	*convainquant*	*convaincant*

which is very confusing.

Historical note: The present participle was not, in Latin, the same in all conjugations.

Verbs in -*are* such as *amare* and *cantare* had their present participle in -*ans*, -*antem*, and *cantantem* became, in French, *chantant* (*amantem* became in fact *amant*, which only survived as a noun, the present participle being reformed on the present indicative forms, hence *aimant*).

The other conjugations, on the other hand, formed their present participles in -*ens*, -*entem*; thus *excellere* gave *excellens*, *excellentem*. It would have been logical if the latter had given **excellent* as a present participle in French. It did not: it gave instead *excellant*: it would appear that from the start all present participles in French were formed in -*ant*, whatever the conjugation; indeed, there appear to be no traces of any other types of present participles in the development of the language. This meant that when at a much later date it became fashionable to coin new adjectives based on Latin verbs, these were made to correspond whenever possible to the -*ens*, -*entem* forms, since these had not yet been used up. It became in this manner possible to distinguish between the present participle *excellant* and the new adjective *excellent*. The effect of this decision has been to complicate French spelling beyond the threshold of what is bearable. What is more, the distinction between *excellent* and *excellant* cannot be made for verbs of the 1st conjugation (e.g. *ce sont des fleurs ravissantes* and *la pianiste, ravissant son auditoire, accepta de jouer un nouveau morceau*) and yet no confusions arise. It cannot therefore be said to be a very important distinction.[2]

2   The past participle

This may be used either adjectivally (see 2.1) or verbally (see 2.2)

2.1   The past participle used adjectivally

(i) As is the case for the present participle, the past participle may function as an

adjective (in which case it is sometimes called *la deuxième forme adjective du verbe*).
(ii) When the past participle is used adjectivally, it is similar in all ways with other adjectives. It agrees in number and gender with the noun modified, and its functions are the same: it may be epitheitic or attribute:

elle mangeait un bon melon mûri au soleil (epitheitic)
ma robe est finie (attribute)

The verbal adjective is always passive.

2.2 The past participle used verbally

2.2.1 *The past participle used to form all the compound forms of the verb*

These may be finite or nonfinite, as in *j'ai chanté* and *ayant chanté*.

2.2.2 *The past participle used to form participial clauses functioning as adverbials*

(i) The rule, which is the same in French as in English, is that, placed at the beginning of a sentence, the past participle must refer to the subject of the main verb; thus

assis sur la barrière, les enfants regardaient passer le train

is acceptable, but not

*assis sur la barrière, le train passa devant nous en sifflant

(ii) The rule above is not always followed, however. French children sometimes get this kind of sentence wrong and produce sentences such as the one above, or:

*arrivés à la maison, la pluie s'est mise à tomber

Both these sentences are unacceptable in modern French, since they would imply in the first case that the train was sitting on the barrier, and in the second case that it was the rain which had arrived home. But such constructions were possible in the sixteenth and even in the seventeenth century.

2.2.3 *Omission of the auxiliary*

There are two possibilities depending on which auxiliary is omitted.
(i) If the auxiliary to be omitted is *être* the sentence keeps the same meaning. Thus:

étant rentré plus tôt que prévu, j'ai surpris le voleur sur les lieux mêmes du cambriolage

may become:

rentré plus tôt que prévu, ...

(ii) If the auxiliary is *avoir* it cannot be omitted without changing both the syntax and the meaning of the sentences. Thus:
Ayant fini son travail, il se repose cannot become

*fini son travail, il se repose

One can write, however:

le travail fini, il se repose

but the latter stands for a passive construction:

le travail ayant été fini, il se repose

and not for the original sentence.

2.3   The problem of agreement

2.3.1   *Preliminary comments on obligatory and optional rules*

(i) The main problem where the past participle is concerned is that of agreement; and this problem belongs mainly to the written language, since in many cases agreement is orthographic and not phonological.

(ii) Some of the rules are simple and easy to cope with: these are the obligatory rules (see 2.3.2). Others are extremely complex and subtle and seem rather pointless in this day and age: these are the optional rules[3] (see 2.3.3). Both the obligatory and optional rules go back to Vaugelas.

2.3.2   *The obligatory rules*

(i) If the past participle is used with *être*, whether one is dealing with an intransitive verb or a passive construction, the past participle agrees in gender and number with the grammatical subject of the verb (as in *elles sont allées au cinéma* and *elle a été opérée ce matin*).

(ii) If the past participle is used with *avoir* and the verb is intransitive, the past participle remains invariable as in *elle a travaillé tout ce matin*.

(iii) If the past participle is used with *avoir* and the verb is transitive matters are relatively complicated, since agreement depends on a number of syntactic factors. Generally speaking there is agreement with the object if the latter precedes the past participle, e.g. *la lettre que j'ai écrite* (this rule goes back to Marot).

2.3.3   *The optional rules[4]*

They either constitute exceptions to the rule in 2.3.2 iii (see 2.3.3.1), or they apply to the case of the past participle followed by an infinitive (2.3.3.2) or they apply to pronominal verbs (see 2.3.3.3).

2.3.3.1   *The auxiliary 'avoir': exceptions[5] to the rule by which the past participle agrees with the object if the latter precedes it*
(i) Impersonal verbs normally remain invariable, as in:

>   *les inondations qu'il y a eu ont été catastrophiques pour les récoltes*

(ii) Some verbs may be used either transitively or intransitively; agreement in these cases may not be obvious: (*courir, coûter, dormir, peser, régner, valoir, vivre*):

>   *les efforts que ce travail m'a coûtés (il m'a coûté quoi? des efforts* = direct object)

but

>   *les trois mille francs que ce meuble m'a coûté (il m'a coûté combien? trois mille francs* = not a direct object)

(iii) There is no agreement if the object is *en (= de cela)* as in:

>   *j'ai cueilli des cerises et j'en ai mangé un plein panier*

or if it is the pronoun *le* representing a clause as in:

>   *la journée fut plus belle qu'on ne l'avait prévu*

2.3.3.2   *The past participle followed by an infinitive*
(i) The past participle followed by an infinitive remains invariable if the object preceding the past participle is in fact the object of the infinitive, e.g.

l'histoire que j'ai entendu raconter (i.e. *j'ai entendu raconter une histoire*)
la maison que j'ai fait bâtir (i.e. *j'ai fait bâtir une maison*)

In these cases the object follows the infinitive when the latter is replaced in a simple clause.

The same applies if the verb *faire* is understood:

vous n'avez pas fait les efforts que vous auriez dû (i.e. *faire*)

This kind of elliptical construction is frequent with *devoir, croire, pouvoir*, and *vouloir*.

(ii) If the object of the main verb is also the subject of the infinitive, there is agreement:

la cantatrice que j'ai entendue chanter (i.e. *j'ai entendu la cantatrice qui chantait*)[6]

2.3.3.3 *The case of the pronominal verbs*[7] One must distinguish those verbs which are 'essentially' (i.e. always) pronominal, such as *s'évanouir*, and those which are 'accidentally' (i.e. sometimes) pronominal, such as *baigner* and *se baigner*.
(i) If the verb is 'essentially' pronominal, the rules are as for *être*: there is always agreement:

elle s'est évanouie

(ii) If the verb is 'accidentally' pronominal, the rules are as for *avoir*: there is agreement if the pronoun is a direct object:

ils se sont baignés

but there is no agreement if the pronoun is an indirect object:

les rois qui se sont succédé

because the underlying structure of the latter is *succéder à quelqu'un*, i.e. *les rois qui ont succédé à des rois*.
(iii) Similarly there is no agreement when the pronominal form is attributive (see Ch. 9, 2.2.1 *iii*). Compare:

elle s'est coupée (reflexive: *elle a coupé elle*)
elle s'est coupé le doigt (attributive: *elle a coupé le doigt à elle*)

Similarly:

elles se sont serrées[8] (= *elles ont serré elles-mêmes*)
elles se sont serré la main (= *elles ont serré la main à elles*)

2.3.3.4 *Agreement where a compound infinitive is used* This seems to be one of the few areas of grammar where both agreement and nonagreement are allowed, although there seems to be a preference for agreement:[9]

la chanson qu'elle dit avoir appris(e) dans sa jeunesse

3 The gerund

3.1 Morphological considerations

3.1.1 *The form of the gerund*

(i) The form of the gerund is *en* + present participle, e.g. *en chantant*.
(ii) The use of *en* became the norm only in the eighteenth century; but in the seventeenth century Vaugelas notes that it is more common to find the gerund on its

own rather than preceded by *en*. A number of fossilized expressions still exist which contain this use of the gerund without *en*:

> *payer argent comptant* (= *en comptant l'argent*)
> *rencontrer chemin faisant* (= *en faisant son chemin*)

In La Fontaine's *Fables*, for example, the gerund is often used without *en*.
(iii) It was also possible in Old French to use prepositions other than *en* with the gerund, as in *à son corps défendant* (= *en défendant son corps*). *Après, sans, sur* and *avant* were the most commonly used.

3.1.2   *Historical explanation for the modern form of the gerund*

In the same way as the present participle comes from the Latin present participle, the gerund comes from the ablative form of its Latin counterpart, the other cases having disappeared. For both the present participle and the gerund, it was the ending of the verbs of the 1st conjugation which were used for all verbs. Thus all gerunds are formed on the model of *cantando*, which gives *chantant*. But the endings of the present participle and of the gerund developed in such a way that they became identical; the gerund having become morphologically the same as the present participle, it was decided that, for the sake of clarity, the gerund would be preceded by *en* in order to distinguish the two forms.

3.2   Function

3.2.1   *Function of the gerund in modern French*

The gerund functions essentially as an adverbial, i.e. it introduces an action or process which is secondary to that expressed by the main verb:[10]

> *il travaille en sifflant*

3.2.2   *Past functions of the gerund*

In Latin the gerunds were used to express the dative, ablative and genitive forms of the infinitive used as a noun. This use of the gerund as a nominalized infinitive is still to be found in Old French. Indeed it was perfectly possible to coordinate a gerund and an infinitive up to and including the seventeenth century:

> *Tout parfait en ouvrant, tout parfait au connoistre* (D'Aubigné, *Tragiques, Misères* quoted by Brunot and Bruneau, *Précis de grammaire historique de la langue française*)

3.3   Syntactic characteristics

(i) The gerund is invariable.
(ii) The gerund always refers in modern French to the subject of the main verb. But up to the seventeenth century the gerund could refer to any word in the main clause. Thus it was possible to write what is no longer possible nowadays:

> *Tout en parlant de la sorte*
> *Un limier le fit partir* (La Fontaine, *Fables*, VI 9, v. 11–12).

In this case it is not *le limier* who is 'speaking' but a deer (i.e. *le*). This use survives in modern French in notices such as *on paie en servant* (quoted by Brunot and Bruneau, *Précis de grammaire historique de la langue française*). In this case it is not *on* who 'serves' but 'the waiter', 'waiter' being understood. It also survives in proverbs such as:

> *la fortune vient en dormant (= pendant qu'on dort)*

in which case the gerund is independent of the main verb. It could even be used as a noun, as in *de mon vivant*, meaning *moi étant vivant*.

(iii) It is possible to emphasize the gerund by preceding the *en* by *tout*:

> *il travaille tout en sifflant*

(iv) Since the gerund functions as an adverb it may take on a variety of meanings, depending on context, e.g.

> *il travaille en sifflant* (manner)
> *il s'est foulé la cheville en tombant* (cause)
> *viens me voir en arrivant* (time)
> *en prenant son temps, il a tout de même fini le premier* (concession)

3.4 Similarities and differences between the present participle and the gerund

(i) Because the gerund refers to an action performed by the subject of the main clause, it may appear in different parts of the sentence without the meaning of the sentence being changed:

> *Pierre, en sortant du restaurant, a rencontré Paul*

is the same as

> *Pierre a rencontré Paul en sortant du restaurant*

In both cases *en sortant* refers to *Pierre*.

(ii) The same does not apply to the present participle, since the latter, when used verbally, refers to the nearest noun:

> *Pierre a rencontré Paul sortant du restaurant (i.e. Paul sort du restaurant)*

is not the same as:

> *Pierre, sortant du restaurant, a rencontré Paul (i.e. Pierre sort du restaurant)*

(iii) On the other hand, gerund and present participle may be similar in that

> *Pierre, en sortant du restaurant, a rencontré Paul*

is very similar to

> *Pierre, sortant du restaurant, a rencontré Paul*

The difference is that the adverbial quality of the gerund makes the sentence containing it mean *alors que Pierre sortait du restaurant il a rencontré Paul*, or *parce que Pierre sortait du restaurant il a rencontré Paul*, whereas the sentence containing the present participle means *Pierre, qui sortait du restaurant, a rencontré Paul*. There is therefore a difference at a 'deep level' but in most cases it would matter little which was used.

4 The infinitive

4.1 General considerations

The infinitive is in an ambiguous position since it can function either as a verb or as a noun, i.e. as either of the two basic elements necessary to form a sentence. It may function as a noun because it expresses neither person, number, mood nor time as such. But it may function as a verb, since it expresses aspect and it may express voice. Like a verb it may have complements and it may be the nucleus of clauses.

The infinitive is a particularly unstable element of the language, the extent of its nominal use having considerably changed through time – seventeenth-century French being still quite different in this respect from modern French. In its verbal uses it has changed as well, both in terms of the prepositions which specific verbs may be preceded by, and in terms of the verbs which may form the nucleus of 'real' infinitival clauses (see 4.3.3 and 4.3.6).

4.2   Nominal use

4.2.1   *Nominalization of infinitives in modern French*

The infinitive is no longer used exactly as if it were a noun, in the sense that it is no longer possible to use it in the same syntactic environment: it can no longer be used with either a determiner or an adjective, except in those cases in which the infinitive is no longer felt to be verbal in any way: thus *un souvenir, un dîner, un baiser* are no longer felt to be verbs, morphologically speaking; they are nouns in their own right and behave like other nouns. These nouns tend to be masculine in gender and may be singular or plural, depending on the context. They may be preceded by determiners, modifiers and intensifiers in the normal way, as in *un très bon souper*. But it is no longer possible to nominalize just any infinitive; thus constructions such as *un bon taiser*, meaning *une bonne occasion de se taire*, or *au traire de l'espée* meaning *au moment de tirer l'épée* are no longer possible in modern French, except as stylistic devices.

4.2.2   *The infinitive functioning as a noun*

(i) The infinitive may be the subject of a verb:

   lire tard le soir fait mal aux yeux

This is common in sentences of a proverbial nature. When used to refer to something particular rather than something general, the infinitive functioning as subject is often preceded by *de: de lire tard le soir me fait mal aux yeux*.
(ii) It may be attribute of the subject:

   vouloir, c'est pouvoir

(iii) It may be the complement of an adjective:

   cette robe est prête à porter

(iv) It may be the complement of a noun or pronoun:

   le plaisir de donner est plus grand que celui de recevoir

(v) It may be the direct object of a verb:

   j'aime m'amuser

A certain number of verbs may thus be followed by an infinitive without the use of a preposition being necessary. These verbs are mainly verbs of movement (e.g. *courir, envoyer, descendre*), of perception (e.g. *regarder, s'imaginer, se figurer, entendre, écouter*) and of opinion (e.g. *affirmer, croire, penser*) (see dictionary entries).
(vi) The infinitive may be an indirect object of a verb. In this case there are four possibilities.

The infinitive is preceded by *de*; this is usually so with transitive or pronominal verbs, as in *elle s'arrêta de parler*.

The infinitive is preceded by *à*; this is usually so with verbs which tend to express an idea of effort, desire or aim, e.g. *il cherche à réussir dans sa branche*.

Some verbs may take either *de* or *à* without there being a change in meaning, e.g. *ne continuez pas à/de le faire*

Some verbs may take either *de* or *à*, but the choice of the one or the other may alter the meaning of the sentence. Compare:

> *cela m'a décidé à me lancer dans cette voie* (i.e. *m'a poussé* – idea of external pressure)

and

> *j'ai décidé de partir tout de suite sur les lieux du désastre* (no idea of external pressure)

There are many cases in Classical French of different prepositions being used as compared to Modern French. This seems to have remained a relatively unstable area in the language. Different usages also prevail in different areas of France. Thus whereas one may say either *j'aime lire* or *j'aime à lire* throughout France, one may hear *j'aime de lire* in the Provence area. (See also Ch. 13.)

4.2.3 *The infinitive functioning as an adverbial*

(i) This function usually indicates a purpose. As such it may be preceded by *pour*:

> *je prends l'avion pour aller à Marseille*

But the *pour* may be omitted with certain verbs of movement:

> *je cours voir ma fille = je cours pour voir ma fille*

This is important where negation is concerned; see 4.3.2 *iv.*

(ii) When the infinitive is preceded by a preposition and is playing the part of an adverbial clause, it may occur at the beginning of a sentence rather than after the main verb. Thus, *je prends le train pour aller à Paris* (either *train* or *Paris* may be emphasized in speech) may become *pour aller à Paris, je prends le train*; but in the latter case the emphasis is necessarily on *train*.

(iii) It used to be possible to use other prepositions to introduce such adverbials: *avant, après, en, par, sur* were commonly used in the old language in this manner. This is no longer possible unless the infinitive has become a real noun; thus one may say *après dîner*, and *après boire* as in *Elle chantait de bien vilaines chansons après boire* (Daudet, *L'Elixir du Révérend Père Gaucher*). One does not however find in modern French phrases such as **après baigner*. One has to say instead *après la baignade*, or *après que je me suis baigné*. In this area the use of the infinitive has drastically receded.

4.3 Verbal uses

4.3.1 *Verbal uses from a morphological point of view*

(i) The infinitive is the form used to determine which group a verb belongs to, and how it is therefore going to behave, from a morphological point of view, in the various tenses and moods.

(ii) Like the other verbal forms the infinitive expresses aspect, the simple form *aimer* referring to the action seen midstream (*aspect sécant*) whilst the compound form *avoir aimé* refers to a completed action. But the infinitive on its own cannot express time.

(iii) Like the other verbal forms it exists in both a passive and an active voice, e.g. *aimer* and *être aimé*, and also in a pronominal form, e.g. *s'aimer*.

4.3.2   *Verbal uses from a syntactic point of view*

(i) It may take a subject:

je regarde passer le train or *je regarde le train passer*

In this case the subject of *passer* is *train*.

(ii) It may take an object:

je pense faire ce travail demain

(iii) It may take an adverbial:

il désire aller en Espagne

(iv) It may be negated, although it is more usual to negate the main verb rather than the infinitive: *je ne veux pas partir* would be the norm, whereas *je veux ne pas partir* would be a highly emphatic form (the same applies in English). There are cases, however, in which one may wish to negate the infinitive: *j'espère ne pas partir* ('I hope I will not be going') does not mean the same as *je n'espère pas partir* ('I am not hoping to go'). Again the same applies in English, and for the same reasons.

It is not possible, however, to negate in this manner infinitives which indicate a goal if *pour* is not stated explicitly. Thus, in:

Jean court voir Paul (= *Jean court pour voir Paul*)

one cannot negate *voir* directly: **Jean court ne pas voir Paul*, whereas *Jean court pour ne pas voir Paul* is perfectly acceptable (see also Ch. 12, 7).

(v) Where voice is concerned the infinitive is rather unstable: it is rarely used in the passive, or at least the auxiliary is rarely expressed: *j'ai vu un piéton (être) renversé par une voiture*.

There are however cases in which the passive is obligatory, e.g. *être aimé est bien doux, aimer l'est plus encore*. In this case the contrast between passive and active infinitive is essential to the meaning of the sentence. In the past, voice was made explicit less often than today; but even today the infinitive often has to be interpreted as active or passive depending on the context. Compare:

j'ai une nouvelle machine à laver (= *la machine lave* − active)
j'ai du linge à laver (= *le linge doit être lavé* − passive)

The voice of the infinitive has similarly to be worked out from the underlying structure of the phrase whenever it functions as the head of a compound noun:

machine à coudre = *la machine coud*
gomme à mâcher = *je mâche la gomme*
fil à coudre = *je couds avec le fil*
machine à écrire = *j'écris avec la machine*

(vi) In modern French the infinitive functioning as an adverbial must have the same subject as that of the main clause. This has not always been the case, thus *rends-le moi sans te fouiller* used to mean *rends-le moi sans que je te fouille*. Sentences of this type are no longer acceptable. But in the seventeenth century one still finds constructions of this type:

Le public m'a été trop favorable pour m'embarrasser du chagrin particulier de deux ou trois personnes (Racine, example borrowed from Wagner and Pinchon, *Grammaire du français classique et moderne*) (*pour m'embarrasser* = *pour que je m'embarrasse*)

4.3.3 *Verbal uses from a functional point of view: general considerations*

(i) The infinitive may be part of the main verbal group in two ways, either because it is preceded by an auxiliary of time, aspect, mood or voice, as in:

> *je vais le faire* (time/mood)
> *je commence à le faire* (aspect)

in which case the infinitive functions as the lexical element of the verbal phrase, the concepts of time, mood, voice, person and number being carried by the auxiliary; or because the infinitive is used as the object of the main verb, as in:

> *j'aime chanter en travaillant (= j'aime le fait de chanter en travaillant)*

in which case *chanter* merely refers to the fact of singing and the infinitive is functioning more nominally than verbally.

(ii) The infinitive may be the nucleus of an 'infinitive clause', if the infinitive has a subject. If this subject is also the direct object of the main verb, one is dealing with a 'real infinitival clause', 'real' in the sense that it corresponds to the Latin infinitival clause, as in *je regarde passer le train* (see 4.3.4).

If the subject of the infinitive is either the same as that of the main verb or an indirect object of the main verb, one may say that the infinitive is the nucleus of 'an abbreviated subordinate clause' (see 4.3.5):

> *je veux venir (= *je veux que je vienne)*
> *je lui ai ordonné de partir (= j'ai ordonné qu'il parte)*

(iii) The infinitive may also be the nucleus of an independent clause, as in *ne pas marcher sur l'herbe* (see 4.3.6).

There is much disagreement amongst grammarians as to what constitutes a 'real' infinitival clause. Some grammarians simply refuse to accept the existence of such clauses, or do not feel the distinction to be meaningful in modern French (see Wagner and Pinchon, *Grammaire du français classique et moderne*); others only accept those clauses in which the subject of the infinitive is also the direct object of the main verb – this being the prevailing attitude; whilst others such as Grevisse have a broader definition, since they include under 'infinitival clauses' clauses having the same subject as the main verb, on condition that the infinitive stands for a different tense or mood to that in the main clause. Thus Grevisse quotes *je savais revoir là ma famille (= je savais que je reverrais là ma famille)* as containing an infinitival clause, despite identity of subjects.

4.3.4 *The 'real' infinitival clause*

4.3.4.1 *Definition* The infinitive clause was a frequent occurrence in Latin; by definition it had to have a subject which was also the object of the main verb:

> *je regarde passer le train*

In this case the subject of *passer* is *train*, which is also the object of *regarder*. The expression 'real infinitival clause' refers to an infinitival clause in the Latin sense.

Note: This definition is due to the fact that in Latin the subject of the infinitive was in the accusative, which led to the assumption that the subject of the infinitive was also the object of the main verb. But it is simpler in modern French to consider that it is the whole infinitival clause which is the object of the main verb: in this case it is *passer le train* which is the object of *regarde*.

4.3.4.2 *Word order in real infinitival clauses*
(i) The subject of the infinitive may either precede it or follow it if the infinitive has no direct object of its own:

je regarde passer le train
je regarde le train passer

(ii) If the infinitive has an object, its subject must precede it:

j'écoute Paul jouer un morceau de Chopin

(iii) If the infinitive is passive in its meaning, one can place its subject after it on condition it is preceded by *par*:

j'ai déjà entendu jouer ce morceau par Paul

In some cases the subject of the infinitive may be indefinite, in which case it may remain unexpressed:

j'ai entendu (quelqu'un) jouer ce morceau l'autre jour

4.3.4.3   *Use made of the 'real infinitival clause' in French*
(i) This type of infinitival clause is possible in modern French in only a very few cases, namely with verbs of perception such as *écouter, entendre, regarder, voir, sentir* and with verbs expressing some idea of persuasion such as *mener, conduire, forcer à, disposer à, convaincre de, laisser*:

j'ai forcé les cambrioleurs à partir les mains vides

(ii) This has not always been the case. This kind of construction was frequent with other types of verb in the twelfth century and became more and more frequent in literature and legal texts up until the sixteenth century. After that the construction seems to have died a natural death despite the fact that many writers approved of it. Bossuet, for example, uses it quite frequently:

Vous reconnaissez ce défaut être une source de discorde (= *que ce défaut est une source de discorde*) (*Exhortation aux Ursulines de Meaux*)

The only type of infinitival clause of this kind to survive is in relative clauses introduced by que:

cette femme qu'elle dit avoir vu(e)[11]

which is less cumbersome than:

cette femme qu'elle dit qu'elle a vu(e)

This construction is quite frequent in modern French.
(See also Ch. 15, 4.2 for the stylistic unacceptability of a *cascade de 'que'*.)

4.3.5   *The infinitive as the nucleus of an 'abbreviated subordinate clause'*

4.3.5.1   *Identity between the subject of the main clause and the infinitive*
(i) Usually the use of an abbreviated subordinate clause is obligatory. Thus, **je veux que je vienne* must become *je veux venir*.
(ii) But with *avant* and *après* this is not the case, and two constructions are possible:

j'irai le voir avant de partir
j'irai le voir avant que je ne parte

(iii) If the main verb is a verb of movement, it may be necessary to use the preposition *pour* to introduce the infinitive:

je me précipite pour l'aider

In this case the *pour* is necessary, but in:

je cours l'aider (= je cours pour l'aider)

this is not the case. These two sentences function however in the same way; this becomes obvious if one pronominalizes the verb in each sentence:

je m'y précipite
j'y cours

4.3.5.2 *The impersonal main verb* In this case two constructions are possible if the subject of the subordinate is the second person pronoun *tu* or *vous*:

il faut que tu viennes
il faut venir

4.3.5.3 *The subject of the infinitive as the indirect object of the main verb* In this case the verb is usually a factitive verb such as *convaincre de, forcer à, disposer à, conduire*, and of course *faire*. These verbs may fit into two different kinds of construction:

je lui ai ordonné de partir
j'ai ordonné qu'il parte

These two sentences do not always have exactly the same meaning, since the one based on the infinitive presumes that the order is given directly by the subject of the main clause to the subject of the infinitive, whereas in the second sentence the order could have been transmitted by an intermediary.

4.3.6 *The infinitive as the nucleus of an independent clause*

This use of the infinitive is limited to the following kinds of cases:
(i) Exclamative clauses:

voir Naples et mourir!
moi, faire les premiers pas, jamais!

It is used in these cases to stress the strong emotional content of the sentence.
(ii) It is used as a variant of the imperative to give orders (see Ch. 7), e.g. *prendre deux comprimés matin et soir.* Used in its positive form it tends to appear mainly in the written language and in legal or medical contexts. It is often used in negative constructions in preference to the imperative on notice boards, e.g. *ne pas marcher sur l'herbe (= il ne faut pas marcher sur l'herbe*, hence the place of the negation which is different from that in the imperative construction *ne marchez pas sur l'herbe).*
(iii) It is used in questions: *que faire?* instead of *que pourrions-nous faire?* The impersonal and timeless quality of the infinitive make the question much more abstract.
(iv) The 'narrative' infinitive: in this case the infinitive is preceded by *de* and replaces a normally finite form. The impact due to the clash between the expected form and the one used heavily emphasizes the action:

et moi de rire tant que j'ai pu

This kind of construction is particularly frequent in La Fontaine's *Fables*; it belongs now mainly to the written language, and is essentially literary.

Notes

1 Unless the 'd' form comes from the Latin gerund: *ridendo* gives *en riant* and *ridentem* gives *riant*.

2 A French grammarian (private communication) on this point:

'Si j'étais ministre de l'Education, je tâcherais de faire voter une loi uniformisant ces subtilités orthographiques qui ne servent que de menues satisfactions aux cuistres. Mais je n'y arriverais sûrement pas! Il faudrait d'abord être convaincante pour mes collègues, en vainquant leur obstination . . . . et ce n'est pas demain la veille!' (S. Lamothe)

3 It is in the *Arrêté* of 28 December 1976 on *Les Tolérances grammaticales ou orthographiques* (see Appendix) that these rules have been declared optional, allowing therefore agreement or nonagreement as the writer may wish. Nonagreement is still, for some people, a sign of a lack of education. Brunot and Bruneau (*Précis de grammaire historique de la langue française*) write as follows on this point:

'Conclusion: La règle des participes est une règle artificielle, à laquelle les grammairiens logiciens ont attaché, depuis la fin du XVIIIe siècle, une importance excessive. Il est regrettable que l'Université, au XIXe siècle, ait repris cette tradition. Il serait sage de laisser toute liberté à l'usage, qui tend évidemment à considérer le participe construit avec 'être' comme un adjectif variable, et le participe construit avec 'avoir' comme une forme verbale invariable.'

4 'Optional' according to the *Arrêté* of 28 December 1976. For some people these may still be felt to be obligatory.

5 Or rather 'apparent' exceptions.

6 Example borrowed from Dubois and Lagane, *La Nouvelle grammaire française*.

7 See also Ch. 9, 2.2.

8 Example borrowed from Bonnard, *Grammaire des lycées et collèges*.

9 On the question of whether it should be *la femme qu'elle dit avoir vu* or *la femme qu'elle dit avoir vue*, S. Lamothe answers as follows:

'Le silence prudent des grammaires (j'en ai consulté douze) m'a laissée rêveuse. Même l'oreille n'est pas d'un grand secours ici: "c'est une décision que j'ai pris" et "c'est une décision que j'ai prise" semblent toutes les deux acceptables. Hier soir, j'ai fait compléter par différents membres de ma famille la phrase "C'est une chanson qu'elle dit avoir (appris) dans sa jeunesse." Tous ont dit: "apprise". A. Haase cite un exemple de Mme de Sévigné: "Cette fille qui chanta tout haut à l'église cette chanson gaillarde qu'elle se confessoit avoir chantée ailleurs . . ." (Syntaxe du XVIIe siècle); il la cite à propos de la construction infinitive après les verbes déclaratifs. Il ne fait pas même mention de l'accord du participe passé de l'infinitif composé. C'est donc qu'il le trouve normal.'

10 An amusing little story illustrates this point:

'Deux religieux sont en retraite et ne doivent pas fumer. Ils vont en demander la permission à leur supérieur. L'un a la permission et l'autre pas. . . . . Le premier avait demandé:
"Puis-je fumer en lisant mon office?"
Réponse: "Non!"
Le deuxième, plus malin:
"Puis-je lire mon office en fumant?"
Réponse: "Oui!"'

The point in this case is the *en*. In *fumer en lisant mon office, lisant mon office* is secondary to the main verb *fumer*; in *lire en fumant*, it is the smoking which is secondary to the reading of the service.

11 See note 9 above.

Chapter 9

Voice: the active voice, the pronominal form and passivization

0   General considerations

0.1   The active voice

(i) The active voice indicates that the grammatical subject is the actor, e.g.

le chat attrape la souris

Le chat is both the grammatical subject and the actor:
(ii) The active voice is the only morphological voice in French; the pronominal forms and the passive are all derived from the active voice.
(iii) The active voice is examined in terms of the different types of active constructions which may exist (see 1.1).

0.2   The pronominal forms

There are many different kinds of pronominal constructions, in the sense that the relationship involved between the object pronoun and the subject may vary considerably: in *je me lave* one is dealing with a reflexive, in *nous nous écrivons souvent* with the expression of reciprocity, in *je me coupe du pain* with an attributive, in *ce livre se lit facilement* with a passive substitute; and in *je m'abstiens de voter* the pronoun object does not play any specific role.

When functioning as a passive substitute, the pronominal form does not however always have the same implications. For all of these problems see section 2.

0.3   Passivization

(i) The passive uses the same forms as the active voice, but arranges them differently from a syntactic point of view, in order to express that the grammatical subject is the goal or sufferer and not the actor, e.g.

la souris est attrapée par le chat

La souris is both the grammatical subject and the sufferer.
(ii) Since the same forms tend to be used in such very different ways, there exists in the language a number of homonymic constructions:

la porte est ouverte (*ouverte* is an adjective)
la porte est ouverte par le concierge (passive voice)
il est sorti de bonne heure (active voice)

(The first example could be translated either by 'the door is open' or 'the door is opened', if it is considered to be the elliptical version of the second example.)
(iii) There are limitations on passivization: all transitive verbs may not be passivized (see 3.2).
(iv) Passivization is an important tool in the language: it may enable an easier flow

from sentence to sentence; it may make a complex sentence easier to plan; and it may enable the speaker or writer to shift the emphasis of the sentence from the actor to the sufferer.

For all these points see section 3.

1　The active voice

The type of construction is dependent on the type of verb used.

1.1　Transitive verbs

The verb may take one or more object complements. These verbs all form their compound forms with *avoir*.

(i) The object is not preceded by a preposition: it is a *transitive* verb, as in *je lis un livre*.

(ii) The object may be preceded by a preposition: this is an indirect transitive verb, as in *l'enfant parle de ses projets*.

(iii) There are two objects, one direct and one indirect: it is a ditransitive verb: *il donne une pomme à sa sœur*.

A sa sœur is also said to be 'an attributive complement'.

1.2　Complex transitive verbs

(i) Such verbs take both an object and an attribute of the object, as in *il a rendu sa femme heureuse*; *ils ont élu M. X président*. In the first case the attribute is an adjective: *heureuse* is the attribute of the 'object', *sa femme*. In the second case the attribute is a noun.

(ii) Main complex transitive verbs taking an adjective as attribute of the object are: *croire, juger, estimer, trouver, rendre, laisser*.

(iii) Main complex transitive verbs taking a noun as attribute of the object are: *appeler, nommer, élire, faire*.

1.3　Intransitive verbs

(i) The verb may take neither an object nor an attribute of the subject, as in *j'ai couru*.

(ii) Most intransitive verbs form their compound forms with *avoir*, except for a number of verbs expressing some idea of movement, which take *être*. The main verbs taking *être* are: *aller, arriver, décéder, devenir, éclore, entrer, mourir, naître, partir, rentrer, rester, retourner, sortir, tomber, venir, parvenir, revenir, survenir*.

(iii) Some transitive verbs may be used without an object and yet still be transitive, an object being understood:

> *cet homme boit trop* (i.e. *il boit trop d'alcool*)

(iv) In some cases a verb may be used either transitively or intransitively. The passage from intransitive to transitive is expressed by a change of auxiliary:

> *je suis sorti*
> *j'ai sorti la voiture*

But where the tense used is a simple tense, the same construction appears in both cases:

> *je sors*
> *je sors la voiture*

In Old French, many verbs could be used either transitively or intransitively, but later they tended to become one or the other. Vaugelas, for example, condemned *sortez ce cheval* in favour of *faites sortir ce cheval*. (see 1.5).

1.4 Intensive (or 'copulative') verbs

(i) These take a complement of the subject, the verb expressing the link between the two:

> *mon cousin semble riche*
> *mon père est comptable*

In the first case the complement of the subject is adjectival, in the second it is nominal.
(ii) The main intensive verbs are: *être (avoir été)*, *devenir (être devenu)*, *paraître (avoir paru)* and *rester (être resté)*. They normally refer to a process or state of affairs. The most important of these, *être*, may take on three meanings depending on the context: it may act as a linking verb, as in *il est riche*; it may indicate place as in *il est là*; it may express existence as in *je pense donc je suis*.

1.5 Causative (or 'factitive') verbs

(i) In this case the *grammatical* subject does not perform the action but causes it to take place:

> *je fais cuire les pommes de terre* (= *les pommes de terre cuisent*)
> *la fée a changé la citrouille en carrosse*[1] (= *la citrouille change*).

In both cases the 'real' subject is different from the grammatical subject; the grammatical subject is the Agent.
(ii) The main causative verbs are *faire*, *changer* and *transformer*.
(iii) In speech *faire* is sometimes dropped, hence prescriptively incorrect constructions such as? *je cuis les pommes de terre*.

1.6 The case of 'jaunir'

Some verbs express voice lexically, in which case the choice among the active voice, the pronominal form or passivization matters little: it merely shifts the emphasis in the sentence from one element to another, e.g.

> *le soleil jaunit le papier* (= *fait jaunir*: causative)
> *le papier est jauni par le soleil* (= passive)
> *le papier jaunit* (= *devient jaune*: active voice)
> *le papier se jaunit* (= *devient jaune*: pronominal form)

1.7 Impersonal verbs

1.7.1 *Definition*

A personal verb is a verb which is used in all three persons, as opposed to an impersonal verb (or 'unipersonal verb') which is used in the 3rd person only.

Although impersonal verbs inflect for the 3rd person singular, and are preceded by the pronoun *il*, this *il* is a purely grammatical subject, since these verbs cannot have a real subject, e.g. *il pleut*.

1.7.2 *Historical note*

(i) In Old French impersonal verbs did not have to be preceded by a 'pseudo subject'; fossilized expressions such as *n'importe* and *peu s'en faut* are survivals of this use of the verb on its own. In the spoken language constructions such as *faut pas y aller* or *faut pas le faire* are still frequently used, although they are frowned upon.

These impersonal verbs used previously without a subject were replaced at a later stage by a number of periphrastic constructions such as: *il est nécessaire*, *il faut*, *il s'agit*, *il est évident* and *il y a*. Thus *a* becomes *il y a* in the translation of:

bien a un an que t'eüsse lessié (= *il y a bien un an que je t'aurais laissée*)

(ii) Personal verbs were formerly used impersonally in order to insist on the action, e.g.

après, contreval le moustier, pendait bien chent[2] *lampiers* (= *Ensuite du haut des voûtes de la cathédrale, il pendait au moins cent lustres*) (Robert de Clari, *Conquêtes de Constantinople*)

Most impersonal verbs have disappeared from French: the action is nearly always seen nowadays as performed by a subject, even if there is no real subject.

2 The pronominal forms

2.1 Basic principles

(i) Most transitive verbs may be pronominalized, with the exception of *avoir*. They all form their compound form with *être*. There are some pronominal verbs which are intransitive, but these are not the result of pronominalization (see 2.2.4).

(ii) Pronominal forms are identical in the simple tenses to other active forms: it is simply that the pronoun object happens to stand for the subject. Thus, *je me coupe* (i.e. *moi*) is morphologically and syntactically the same as *je le coupe* (i.e. *le pain*).

(iii) The pronominalized forms are different from the corresponding active forms in the compound tenses, since pronominalization implies the obligatory use of *être* instead of *avoir*:

Non-pronominal forms:	Pronominalized forms:
je le coupe/je l'ai coupé	*je me coupe/je me suis coupé*
tu le coupes/tu l'as coupé	*tu te coupes/tu t'es coupé*
il le coupe/il l'a coupé	*il se coupe/il s'est coupé*

(iv) There is a similarity between the pronominalized forms and the passive forms but with a difference of emphasis (but see 2.3). Compare:

je suis lavé (passive)
je me suis lavé (pronominalized form of *j'ai lavé quelqu'un*, in which case *quelqu'un* = *moi*)

Both sentences imply *je suis propre*, but the difference in emphasis lies in the fact that in the first it is the result, 'washed', which is being insisted upon, whereas in the second it is the action, 'washing', which is being talked about.

Note: *Je suis lavé* is in fact grammatically ambiguous. Used without an agent *lavé* can be considered to be a past participle functioning as an adjective which is attribute of *je*, as in *je suis sage*. It is only if an agent is included, as in *je suis lavé par la pluie*, that one can say that one is really dealing with a present passive.

(v) When a sentence is pronominalized to obtain a passive substitute, the agent has to be omitted: *le marchand vend son blé cher cette année* becomes: *le blé se vend cher cette année* and not: **le blé se vend cher cette année par le marchand*.

This has not always been the case (see 2.5 *iii*).

(vi) The pronominal form expresses the continuous aspect in its simple forms and completion in its compound forms.

2.2   The different kinds of pronominal forms

2.2.1   *Equivalent of an active construction where subject is animate*

In this case the grammatical subject is also the actor.

(i) In the case of the reflexive pronominal form, the action is carried out by the actor on himself, e.g. *il s'est coupé en se rasant*. This is what is usually understood by the 'pronominal' voice.

(ii) In the case of the reciprocal pronominal form, the subject and object pronoun are in the plural, e.g. *nous nous voyons souvent*.

(iii) The action may be carried out not on the actor but for the actor, in which case the pronominal form is attributive, e.g. *je me suis acheté un livre*. In this case the 'deep structure' is different, since *me*, in this sentence, is an indirect object (or 'attributive complement'): *j'ai acheté un livre pour quelqu'un, et ce quelqu'un c'est moi.*

2.2.2   *Equivalent of a passive construction where subject is inanimate*

le blé se vend bien cette année (= *on vend bien le blé cette année*)

(But see 2.1v and 2.3.)

2.2.3   *Absence of both actor and agent*

In this case the pronominal form will refer to a state of affairs, e.g. *le Mont Blanc s'élève à 4.807 mètres.*

2.2.4   *The lexicalized pronominal verbs*

(i) Some verbs can only be used in their pronominal form: *s'évanouir*, *se repentir*, *s'abstenir*, *s'écrouler*, for example, cannot appear without the presence of the corresponding reflexive pronoun. These verbs are not different from active verbs, except that they are all intransitive and cannot therefore be passivized, e.g. *il se repent* (= *il regrette ses actions*).

(ii) Some verbs may be used either in their simple form or in a pronominal form: *résoudre* is transitive, whereas its pronominal form *se résoudre à* is intransitive; the latter is no more than a lexicalized pronominal verb, since its meaning is totally different from its transitive counterpart, e.g. *j'ai résolu le problème* ('I have solved the problem') and *je ne peux pas me résoudre à le faire* ('I cannot bring myself to do it'). In such cases the two verbs are clearly two different lexical entities and appear separately in the dictionary.

2.2.5   *Ambiguity of pronominal constructions with plural subjects*

One may not always know whether one is dealing with a reflexive or a reciprocal form, e.g. *je me lave les cheveux* (reflexive) but *nous nous lavons les cheveux* (reflexive or reciprocal form, depending on whether each person involved is washing his own hair or the people involved are washing each other's hair).

2.2.6   *The problem of agreement*

(i) Lexically (or 'essentially') pronominal verbs agree in the same way as any other verb taking *être* as an auxiliary, e.g. *elle s'est évanouie*; *ils se sont évanouis*.

(ii) But verbs which are not lexically pronominal (i.e. which are 'accidentally' pronominal) behave as do the verbs which take *avoir* as far as agreement with the object is concerned, e.g.

elle s'est coupée (= *elle a coupé elle*)
elle s'est coupé le doigt (= *le doigt à elle*)

(see Ch. 8, 2.3.3.3.)

2.3 The pronominalized forms v. passivization

(i) If the grammatical subject is not in a position to perform an action, as is the case in the following example, the pronominal form may express something which is similar, although not identical, to what is expressed by a passive, e.g. *ce livre se lit avec facilité* is similar to *ce livre peut être lu avec facilité* (= *on peut lire ce livre avec facilité*).

In this case, the subject needs to be nonhuman. But if this is not the case the sentence may have a completely different meaning, e.g.

le livre s'est bien vendu
Jean s'est vendu

In the first case, the book cannot do anything: the meaning of the sentence has to be passive. In the second case one is dealing with a reflexive: 'John sold out', literally 'John sold himself'.

(ii) If the action described in the passive construction is seen as an ongoing process (i.e. if it is imperfective), the meaning of the two constructions will be similar: *ce médicament doit être pris à jeun* means the same as *ce médicament doit se prendre à jeun.*[3]

This use of the pronominal as a passive substitute has developed considerably in modern French, particularly in sentences such as *ces matériaux se travaillent facilement*.

Such a construction may also have an impersonal *il* standing for *on* as its subject, e.g. *il se consomme, chaque année, tant de tonnes de blé.*

(iii) If the action described in the passive construction is seen as completed (i.e. if it is the perfective), the meaning of the two constructions will be different. Compare:

c'est une chose qui est faite (= *sur laquelle on ne peut plus revenir*: the action is completed, i.e. 'that has been done')
c'est une chose qui se fait (= *c'est une chose que l'on fait normalement et qui est acceptable*: the action is seen as repeated.)

2.4 The verbal phrases 'se voir' + infinitive and 'se faire' + infinitive

2.4.1 *Use with an agent*

The verbal phrases *se voir* + infinitive and *se faire* + infinitive, unlike other pronominalized constructions, may be used with an agent:

il s'est fait mettre à la porte (par le proviseur)
il se voit reprocher (par ses collègues) de ne pas avoir été assez vigilant.

There is a semantic difference between these constructions and the passive form: the pronominalized form implies total lack of control by the 'sufferer' or 'grammatical subject' over the events or actions described, i.e. it puts the subject in the position of an observer of what is happening to him.

2.4.2 *Use to passivize a construction based on an indirect object*

It has been pointed out (Price, *The French language*, 236–7) that *savoir* + infinitive and *se faire* + infinitive make possible semantic passivization based on an indirect object. Thus an English passive sentence such as 'her father was offered a book' cannot be passivized in French in the normal ways (see 3.2); but it can be translated

into French by a passive substitute such as *son père s'est vu offrir un livre*, or *son père s'est fait offrir un livre*. In the latter case there is a change in meaning, since it implies 'her father wanted a book', and *faire* is used in this case as a causative verb (see 1.5).
Price states in this respect:

> 'Though this construction is ignored by most grammars, it is first recorded in the seventeenth century and it is now in common use, particularly but not exclusively in journalistic style. . . . It is likely that the semantic value of *voir* is no longer felt in this construction and that the verb has become fully grammaticalized as an auxiliary of the passive. . . .'

2.5   Historical note

(i) The pronominal forms were used far more extensively in Old French than in modern French; they were used – or omitted – to express a variety of nuances which are lost in the modern language, and the exact meaning carried by the pronominal forms is often difficult to translate into modern French. For example, the pronoun was often omitted when used with verbs in the compound tenses; but in this case a stylistic effect was often achieved, the pronominal form emphasizing the action preceding the consequence or result and the nonpronominal form emphasizing a state of affairs: thus *armez s'est* contrasts with *armez est* (i.e. *il s'est armé* and *le voilà armé*.)
(ii) In Old French the pronoun *se* was often omitted with verbs used transitively in certain areas of France, particularly in the east; one can still hear *aller promener* for *aller se promener* for example. On the other hand intransitive verbs could be preceded by *se*: hence *se dormir* existed side by side with *dormir*. In the seventeenth century writers started hesitating between the pronominal and nonpronominal forms of verbs when these had basically the same meaning; then these forms tended to disappear except when the pronominal form became the carrier of a different meaning. Thus *mourir* and *se mourir* have acquired a different meaning in Bossuet's famous sentence: *Madame se meurt, Madame est morte. Se jouer de* and *se rire de* have also survived in modern French.
(iii) It used to be possible to use the pronominal form as a passive substitute whilst indicating the agent:

> *Cependant par Baucis le festin se prépare* (La Fontaine, *Philémon et Baucis*)

Bossuet also still uses this construction:

> *L'élection s'en faisait [i.e. des rois] par tout le peuple*

3   Passivization

3.1   The principle of passivization

3.1.1   *Basic principles of passivization*

(i) The passive voice being expressed syntactically in modern French, a certain number of conditions are necessary for it to take place: there needs to be an active construction containing a nominal phrase (NP1) acting as the grammatical subject of a verb (V) which has a direct object (NP2). Thus *le chat attrape la souris* may be passivized into *la souris est attrapée par le chat*. In this second case the goal or sufferer of the action expressed by the verb has become the grammatical subject of the sentence; the actor is not essential to the sentence, hence *la souris est attrapée* can stand on its own.
For French, passivization may be represented as follows:

NP1 + V + NP2 becomes NP2 + *être* + V (participle) + (par NP1)

– the parenthesis indicating that 'par NP1' is not essential for the sentence to be well formed. (NP1 stands for first nominal phrase and NP2 for second nominal phrase.)
(ii) Only those verbs which take a direct object may be passivized; this corresponds in semantic terms to the distinction between verbs expressing an action or a process and verbs expressing a state: only verbs indicating an action or process may be passivized.

Another way of stating this is by saying that only verbs which take *avoir* as their auxiliary may be passivized.

3.1.2 *Different types of passivization*

3.1.2.1 *Constructions containing a subject, a verb and an object*
(i) One may list the following possibilities:

Paul bat Pierre becomes
Pierre est battu par Paul

One could include an indirect object (or 'attributive complement'):

Paul donne un cadeau à Pierre becomes
un cadeau est donné par Paul à Pierre.

One could include an attribute of the object:

l'arbitre déclare Pierre vainqueur becomes
Pierre est déclaré vainqueur par l'arbitre

(ii) The agent is normally preceded by *par*, but there are some cases when *de* is also possible (see also Ch. 13), e.g. *il est aimé de tout le monde*. The agent is preceded by *de* instead of *par* in three cases:
   (a) when the agent is already 'part of the subject', or 'contained in the subject, as in *son visage était inondé de larmes*.
   (b) when there is a permanent quality about the action, as in *ce rocher est battu des flots* (*par les flots* is possible but more informal, whereas *des* is more poetic).
   (c) when one is dealing with fossilized expressions such as *couronné de succès* or *un bois mangé de vers*.

3.1.2.2 *Impersonal constructions*
(i) These forms are useful when one does not want to state the real subject or 'actor', whilst still retaining the original order of the sentence. The passive construction is then the equivalent of an active construction in which the subject would be *on*, e.g.

il est déclaré que Pierre est vainqueur instead of
on a déclaré que Pierre est vainqueur

(ii) This form may also be used in a construction in which the direct object is an infinitive preceded by *de*, e.g.

on a interdit de fumer becomes
il est interdit de fumer

This kind of construction is frequent in sentences such as *il a été procédé au vote* or *il sera mis fin à de tels abus*.
(iii) This kind of 'impersonal passive' was frequently used in Old French in order to emphasize the verb. Brunot and Bruneau (*Précis de grammaire historique de la langue française*) quote the following sentence to illustrate the fact that this still happens in modern French, as a stylistic effect:

   il fut très affectueusement et très solennellement bu à votre santé. (Boileau, in a
   letter written in 1703)

This use of the impersonal passive is no longer possible when one can state the real subject. It is only acceptable when used instead of *on*.

3.1.2.3 *Passive infinitival clauses* *Que* clauses, in which the object of the subordinate clause is the same as the subject of the main clause, can be transformed into passive infinitival clauses, if the verb in the main clause is one of the following (although this list is not exhaustive): *aimer, craindre, détester, espérer, préférer, regretter se réjouir, souhaiter* e.g.

Pierre craint que Paul ne le batte becomes
Pierre craint d'être battu par Paul

3.2 Limitations on passivization ('les blocages du passif')

3.2.1 *General considerations*

Students are sometimes told not to use the passive, since passivization is not always possible and can therefore be an area in which language mistakes can be made. This is however, an unfortunate attitude to adopt, since the non-use of the passive for this kind of reason can lead to a stilted and unsophisticated style. These limitations are not too difficult to deal with, since they tend to be similar in English and French; thus, although it is difficult to analyse in linguistic terms what the limitations are and why they exist, in practice they are not all that difficult to handle: most of the 'odd'-sounding passives in French sound equally odd in English.

There is however, one major difference between English and French: passivization cannot be based in French on an indirect object (or 'attributive complément'). Thus, 'I was taught French by M. Dupont' has no direct passive equivalent in French. An active form has to be used instead: *M. Dupont m'a enseigné le français* or *c'est M. Dupont qui m'a enseigné le français*. The word 'French', being a direct object, could however serve as a base for a passive construction: *le français m'a été enseigné par M. Dupont*. (See also 2.4.2.)

3.2.2 *Limitations on the passive due to the use or non-use of determiners:*

(i) Passivization is not possible when the 3rd person possessive adjective modifies the object: *Pierre m'a prêté son livre* cannot be passivized because *son* has to refer backwards, which would not be possible in the passive construction. The same applies to English.

(ii) Passivization is not normally possible when the verbal group is made up of a verb and a noun which is not preceded by a determiner, such as *prendre rendez-vous* or *rendre hommage*. When it does occur, however, the agent is not normally specified:

rendez-vous fut pris pour le lendemain
hommage a été rendu au héros

(iii) Passivization is not possible with *avoir* (see 3.2.4*i*).

3.2.3 *Constructions using personal pronouns*

In most cases the personal pronoun which has become the agent is dropped in passivization:

il (Napoléon) a propagé les idéaux des révolutionnaires dans toute l'Europe

becomes:

les idéaux des révolutionnaires ont été propagés dans toute l'Europe or, with the subject-verb inversion:

c'est par lui qu'ont été propagés dans toute l'Europe les idéaux des révolutionnaires

Note: Such constructions are desirable only when one wants to stress both the agent and the result of the action. In sentences such as:

j'ai trouvé un livre parmi toutes ces vieilleries

one would therefore have to use an active construction if one wished to stress the personal pronoun:

c'est moi qui ai trouvé un livre parmi toutes ces vieilleries

rather than:

?c'est par moi qu'a été trouvé un livre parmi toutes ces vieilleries

which is difficult to justify from a semantic point of view because of the excessive stress laid on the action of 'finding'.

3.2.4 *Transitive verbs which cannot be used in the passive form*

(i) Avoir cannot be passivized (except in the case of the slang expression *j'ai été eu*, 'I have been swindled', 'I have been had').
(ii) Comporter cannot be passivized.
(iii) Verbs used metaphorically cannot be passivized: *perdre* in *perdre son sac*, for example, is concrete and can be passivized, whereas *perdre* in *perdre ses parents* is used metaphorically; it cannot be passivized.
(vi) If passivization seems desirable where it is not normally possible, one replaces the problematic verb by one which is not used metaphorically and which is similar in meaning:

cette affaire regarde Paul (passivization not possible)
Paul est concerné par cette affaire
il a perdu ses parents très tôt (passivization not possible)
ses parents lui ont été enlevés très tôt

The same applies to English.
(v) In a rather similar manner some verbs cannot be passivized because they describe more a state or a general attitude than an action; in this case there is no real 'sufferer' of the action and passivization becomes difficult to accept on semantic grounds:

Paul aime les cerises (but not **les cerises sont aimées par Paul*)
Paul possède une maison (but not **une maison est possédée par Paul*)

The same applies to English.

3.2.5 *Impossibility of passivization where the subject is an infinitive used nominally*

Lire me fatigue les yeux cannot be passivized, but one can passivize if the infinitive can be nominalized: *mes yeux sont fatigués par la lecture*.

3.2.6 *Stylistic preferences*

(i) There appears to be a preference at the level of the sentence for the subject to be an animate and the object an inanimate, rather than vice versa; thus, although

une voiture a écrasé un piéton au passage clouté

is perfectly acceptable, the following passive construction seems to be the favoured form:

> *un piéton a été écrasé par une voiture au passage clouté*

(ii) There appears to be a preference to go from the singular to the plural rather than the other way round:[4]

> *six hommes ont enlevé un propriétaire*

is perfectly acceptable, but the following passive form seems to be the favoured form:

> *un propriétaire a été enlevé par six hommes*

English passive constructions are often nominalized in French:

> 'they are waiting for it to be published'
> *ils en attendent la publication*

rather than:

> *ils attendent que ce document/livre . . . soit publié*

One may have the choice among up to four possibilities:

> *on a décidé d'annuler les élections*
> *il a été décidé d'annuler les élections*
> *la décision a été prise d'annuler les élections*
> *l'annulation des élections a été décidée*

3.3 Stylistic role played by the passive

3.3.1 *Within the sentence*

The use of the passive may emphasise the sufferer of the action rather than the actor:

> *Pierre a battu Paul*
> *Paul a été battu par Pierre*

In the first case the emphasis is on *Pierre*. In the second case it has shifted to *Paul*. This kind of construction is frequently used in sport in order to emphasize whether certain results were predictable or not. Compare:

> *Nice a été battu par Bastia sur son propre terrain*
> *Bastia a battu Nice sur son propre terrain*

In the first case the emphasis is on the sufferer. In the second the emphasis is on the actor; it is therefore Nice having lost which is emphasized in the first case, and Bastia having won in the second.

3.3.2 *Use of the passive enabling the avoidance of 'on'*

The indefinite *on*[5] is usually felt to be typical of informal spoken French and to use it in the written language is often felt to be clumsy. The impersonal passive is therefore sometimes used to avoid this. *On a procédé au vote* thus becomes *il a été procédé au vote*.

3.3.3 *Passivization when the subject is modified by a clause*

A sentence should be passivized if the number of modifiers of the subject is such that the subject is too far from the verb for the sentence to be easily interpretable:

Aussi les avantages dont pourront bénéficier les partis légalisés seront compensés, dans le cas du parti communiste, par les avantages électoraux et politiques qu'il ne manquera pas de retirer de l'ostracisme officiel face à des rivaux socialistes qui font déjà figure de 'favoris du pouvoir'. (*Le Monde,* 25 February 1977)

An active form would be impossible in this case because of the very complex nature of the modifiers of the real subject (or semantic subject), *avantages électoraux et politiques*.

3.3.4 *The coordination of active and passive constructions*[6]

Although one normally has similar constructions on each side of the conjunction *et*, one can in fact have an active form on one side and a passive on the other. Thus the following two statements:

cet enseignement créé par le Conseil de l'université de Provence (Aix-Marseille I) dure deux années
un diplôme couronne cet enseignement

may be combined into one sentence:

cet enseignement, créé par le Conseil de l'université de Provence (Aix-Marseille I) dure deux années et sera sanctionné par un diplôme d'Université. (*Le Monde,* 25 February 1977)

3.3.5 *The cohesive role of the passive within the text*[6]

The use of the passive may help to ensure the flow of language by bringing the coreferent (*le référent*) nearer to its referent (*le référé*). Thus the first example below contains discontinuities at the organizational level which have been removed from the two following versions:

Le chien a mordu l'enfant; son père l'a transporté d'urgence à l'hôpital. Le père a déclaré qu'on devrait garder le chien à l'attache puisque de toute évidence il est dangereux.
Le chien a mordu l'enfant qui a été transporté de toute urgence à l'hôpital par son père qui a déclaré que la bête devrait être gardée à l'attache, puisque de toute évidence elle est dangereuse.
Le chien a mordu l'enfant qui a été transporté de toute urgence à l'hôpital par son père; celui-ci a déclaré que la bête devrait être gardée à l'attache puisque de toute évidence elle est dangereuse. (This version contains fewer relative clauses.)

The non-use of the passive makes for a jerky style, since the reader or listener can no longer progress smoothly from point to point.

3.3.6 *Conclusion*

One may conclude with Pinchon (*Le Français dans le monde*):

Tous ces facteurs interviennent dans le choix du passif, certains se cumulent, d'autres s'annulent, il semble difficile d'établir une hiérarchie. Ce qui paraît dominer, d'après les enquêtes de S. Granger, c'est l'organisation thématique de la phrase. Si l'on considère que la phrase comporte un thème qui est donné et un rhème qui apporte un élément nouveau, et l'ordre thème-rhème est l'ordre habituel, on constate que la phrase passive qui correspond à cette organisation correspond à 98,2% des cas.

3.4 Aspectual connotations

Whereas matters are relatively simple for pronominal forms used as passive substitutes there exists a certain amount of confusion where the passive proper is concerned.

3.4.1 *The pronominal form used as a passive substitute*

(i) The simple form:

  le blé se vend bien (continuous/progressive)

The progressive aspect could, in fact, be emphasized by *en train de*:

  le blé est en train de bien se vendre

(ii) The compound forms:

  le blé s'est bien vendu

In this case, the action is completed although it may have been continuous over a certain period:

  le blé s'est bien vendu pendant toute l'année

3.4.2 *Aspectual connotations of the passive: the general case*

(i) There is a simple passive form based on the use of one auxiliary which is imperfective or continuous (except when the auxiliary is in the past historic − see *(iii)* below):

  je suis aimée par Paul

(ii) There are also compound forms based on the use of two auxiliaries which indicate that the action is completed (perfective):

  j'ai été aimée par Paul (mais je ne le suis plus)

(iii) The simple passive form indicates completion when it is in the past historic:
  Juliette fut aimée par Roméo
(iv) The English speaker must not confuse:

  la porte est/était ouverte par le concierge

which implies that the opening of the door takes or took place regularly, with:

  la porte a été/fut/avait été ouverte par le concierge

which refers to one specific occasion on which the door was opened. See also 3.4.3.3 below.
(v) The passive sentence based on the future is ambiguous, since the future tense is ambiguous: being unmarked for aspect, it may refer either to a specific occasion or to a habitual action in the future.

  In this case it is therefore necessary to add an adverb or an adverbial phrase in order to make the aspect of the action explicit:
  la porte sera ouverte à 8 heures demain (one specific occasion)
  la porte sera ouverte tous les jours à huit heures (iterative)

3.4.3 *The case of lexically perfective verbs used without an agent*

3.4.3.1 *Aspectual ambiguity of lexically perfective verbs* Such verbs differ aspectually depending on whether or not they are accompanied by an agent. If no agent is expressed the participle may be felt to be either verbal or adjectival. This can be illustrated by the two possible interpretations to be given to the sentence *le blé est vendu*. This could mean either:

> *le blé est vendu* (= *je n'en ai plus à vendre*: completed action)

or:

> *le blé est vendu* (= *le blé qui est là est vendu, je ne peux donc pas vous en vendre*: a quality of the wheat)

It is the context which is crucial in this case: see 3.4.3.2

3.4.3.2 *Presence or absence of an adverbial* Lexically perfective verbs, used in the passive without an agent, may vary depending on whether or not they are accompanied by an adverbial. If they appear on their own, they refer to a completed action or state of affairs; but if they appear with an adverbial they may refer to a noncompleted action, i.e. one which is continuous, progressive or habitual:

> *les œufs sont vendus* (completed action)
> *les œufs sont vendus à la douzaine* (habitual action)

or:

> *le blé est vendu en ce moment au-dessous de son cours normal par les Etats-Unis* (ongoing action)

3.4.3.3 *Historical note on aspectual confusion in passive constructions* It is for historical reasons that confusion occurs in the case of lexically perfective verbs used in constructions not including an agent or an adverbial. In Latin there were two forms:

> *amor* (——➤*je suis aimé*): ongoing action or lasting state of affairs
> *amatus sum* (——➤*j'ai été aimé*): completed action or state of affairs which is over

The Latin auxiliary *esse* was explicit in making the action completed in the past. The forms based on *amor* having disappeared, these two aspects both came to be expressed by *être*. The problem, then, is that when no agent is present and the verb used is lexically perfective, the passive construction, based on the simple passive, is morphologically the same as the noun + *être* + attribute (or complement of the subject) construction, which obviously has different aspectual connotations: *la porte est ouverte* corresponds both to 'open' and to 'opened'.

3.4.3.4 *Expression of the progressive*
(i) Where the verb is lexically imperfective, the simple passive forms – with the exception of the past historic – may express the continuous and/or the progressive without having to add *en train d'être*, although the latter makes the expression of the progressive more explicit. But the use of *en train d'être* also makes the occasion referred to specific. Compare:

> *l'enfant est observé par le professeur (maintenant/au cours de l'année/d'une manière générale)*
> *l'enfant est en train d'être observé par le professeur (en ce moment)*

The active form would however usually be preferred to the passive for reasons of simplicity:

> *le professeur est en train d'observer l'enfant*

The passive would only be used in order to change the emphasis of the sentence (see 3.3.1).
(ii) Where the verb is lexically perfective, the simple passive forms cannot express on

their own the progressive. In this case it is necessary either to add *en train d'être*, or *en train de se* . . . , to avoid repetition of *être*, or to use the pronominal form:

> *le blé est en train d'être vendu/de se vendre*
> *le blé se vend bien/au quintal/sur la place du marché/*. . .

There is however a difference of meaning between these two sentences: the passive form indicates the specific, whereas the pronominal form tends to be used for generalizations. The passive presumes an agent even if the latter is not expressed explicitly, whereas the pronominal form precludes the idea of an agent.

The pronominal form is generally preferred to the passive in more formal registers, but if one uses the pronominal form to express what is meant by the passive, adverbs or adverbial phrases will be necessary to turn what is a generalization into something specific; hence *le blé se vend bien aujourd'hui*.

Notes

1 *En* introduces an 'indirect attribute'; in the example above, it is an indirect attribute of the object. It could however be an indirect attribute of a subject, e.g. *la citrouille a été transformée en carrosse par la fée*. In this case *en carrosse* is the indirect attribute of the subject.

  Traiter de may also introduce an indirect attribute of the object, e.g. *Pierre a traité Paul de lâche*. One could also write: *Paul s'est fait traiter de lâche par Pierre*, in which case *s'est fait* is the equivalent of *a été (traité de lâche)*; *de lâche* becomes the indirect attribute of the subject.

2 *Chent* is the Picard form of *cent*.

3 Example borrowed from Wagner and Pinchon, *Grammaire du français classique et moderne*.

4 Granger, *A contrastive study of the passive in French and English*.

5 The indefinite *on* is the *on* which refers to anybody, as against the *on* which stands for *nous*. See Ch. 3.

6 The examples in this section are borrowed from Pinchon, *Le Français dans le monde*, no. 132.

Chapter 10

The forms of the verb

0   General considerations

This chapter is concerned with the forms (or morphology) of the French verb, a much more complex matter in French than in English. This complexity is due to the fact that the French verb inflects for person, number, tense and mood, although there may not exist one unique form of the verb for each possible combination (e.g. *je chantais* and *tu chantais*, which do not differ in form despite the fact that the person referred to is different). See sections 2 to 6 for these variations. This complexity is also due to the fact that not all verbs follow the same pattern. French verbs are traditionally grouped into 'conjugations'. Thus verbs which inflect as does *chanter* belong to the 1st conjugation, verbs which conjugate as does *finir* to the 2nd conjugation, etc. Grammarians tend to disagree as to the number of conjugations existing in French (see section 7). In any case, whichever the system used, one still ends up with a large number of irregular verbs, which further complicates matters (see section 9). Derivation used to verbalize an item is another aspect of the already complicated morphology of the verb (see section 8).

Note: The forms of the reflexive verbs are not dealt with here, since they do not represent a distinctive set of verb forms (see Ch. 9).

1   Historical considerations

Having developed over a long period of time from the dialects of Latin spoken in Roman Gaul, French has preserved verb paradigms which are in many ways similar to those of Latin, but with marked simplifications. On the whole, French can be said to have kept the distinction existing in classical Latin of six different verb forms in each tense, indicating three persons and two numbers, although in modern French, and more especially in spoken French, the number of recognizable forms has been quite drastically reduced from six – sometimes even to three. In addition, French possesses a number of compound tenses formed by the appropriate tense of the auxiliary verbs *avoir* or *être* followed by the past participle of the lexical verb, e.g. *j'ai chanté* ('I have sung', 'I sang'), *j'étais allé(e)* ('I had gone'). These compound tense forms were not present in classical Latin but were slowly evolving in the various 'colonial' dialects of Latin such as that spoken in Gaul.

Certain tense forms in modern French (future and conditional) can also be regarded as compound tenses in derivational terms, as they derive from the late Latin constructions[1] infinitive of lexical verb + present indicative of *habere* ('to have') indicating future action, and infinitive of lexical verb + imperfect tense of *habere* indicating conditionality. Although no longer recognizable in modern French as compound tenses, the future and conditional have the useful property, from the learner's point of view, of possessing endings which are, in the case of the future, very similar to the present indicative tense of avoir:

je chanter-ai	*(j'ai)*	*nous chanter-ons*	*(nous avons)*
tu chanter-as	*(tu as)*	*vous chanter-ez*	*(vous avez)*
il chanter-a	*(il a)*	*ils chanter-ont*	*(ils ont)*

Only the 1st and 2nd persons plural do not follow the scheme exactly, as the first syllable of the verb form (*av-*) has disappeared.

In the conditional the endings are identical with those of the imperfect tense of *avoir*:

je chanter-ais	*(j'av-ais)*	*nous chanter-ions*	*(nous av-ions)*
tu chanter-ais	*(tu av-ais)*	*vous chanter-iez*	*(vous av-iez)*
il chanter-ait	*(il av-ait)*	*ils chanter-aient*	*(ils av-aient)*

2   General characteristics of verb formation in French

2.1   The conjugations

In the French verb, morphological changes take place in varying ways according to the class of the verb and its degree of regularity. By regularity we mean the extent to which a given verb conforms to a set pattern of change (a paradigm), which is normally called a conjugation. In general terms a verb may be considered more or less 'regular' to the extent to which it deviates from the pattern of the conjugation it most nearly follows. These changes may occur in three possible places in the verb:

(i) Changes in the ending (the most normal and most clearly interpreted kind of change).

(ii) Changes in the root (stem) of the verb. These are not present in the major 'regular' conjugations and are most prevalent in the auxiliary verbs *avoir* and *être*, in the modal verbs *pouvoir* and *devoir*, and in the highly irregular verb *aller*.

(iii) An infix may occur between the stem and the ending, this being either -*r*- as in future and conditional tenses,[2] e.g. *je chante-r-ai*, *il fini-r-ait*, or -*iss*-, which occurs only in verbs with an infinitive ending in -*ir* and which are conjugated like *finir*.

2.2   Possible ambiguity in the information carried by the verb forms

(i) Morphological changes in the verb can and often do indicate person, number, tense and mood; but there are many cases of homonymy between persons and even moods. In the following sentence, for example, *chante* functions first of all as an imperative, then as a present indicative in the 1st person and then in the 3rd person:

chante, chérie, et je chante avec toi, car lui, il ne chante plus

(ii) Similarly, there is no distinction between the forms of the present indicative and the present subjunctive, except in the 1st and 2nd persons plural, in regular verbs conjugated like *chanter*:

je chante une chanson provençale
il faut que je chante une chanson provençale

(iii) Confusion may also arise as to which tense of the indicative is intended by a form such as *il dit* − is this the present or the past historic tense? In fact it is only number which is in general clearly obvious from the verb form in written French in all cases; in the spoken form, possible ambiguities become much more numerous, since here there is no possible way − apart from contextual clues − of distinguishing between *il chante* and *ils chantent*.

(iv) Such ambiguity is greater than that which existed in the Latin verb. There each person in each number had a distinctive form in each tense, and on the whole only a small degree of ambiguity in tense was possible. Latin, however, did not know the obligatory use of pronoun subjects (where no noun subject was present), at least in its classical written forms, and it was therefore necessary for the verb form to carry all the relevant information about the way in which it was being used in a given sentence.

In English quite the reverse applies, since the form of the verb itself carries virtually no information of a grammatical kind except to indicate the tense, in a limited way (i.e. whether present or past), and to indicate when the subject is 3rd person singular (although that morphological change does not apply to all English verbs: 'he sings', but 'he can'). All other meaning, in terms of person or number, has to be conveyed by the word denoting the subject, while other information about tense or mood is normally carried by structural devices involving various auxiliary verbs and nonfinite parts of the verb.

The French verb appears to fall somewhere between these two extremes of Latin, which may be said to be almost completely dependent on morphology to make clear the function of the verb within the sentence, and of English, which, except in one person (3rd person singular) in one tense (present) of most verbs, has no morphological change denoting person or number of the subject, and only one possible change to indicate tense (past). Indeed, the sum total of other possible changes in the English verb is limited to those which produce the two participles, present and past, so that the English verb may be said to be totally dependent on the presence of an indicated subject (except in the imperative) to achieve grammatical meaning.

2.3 Redundancy in the French verb

Since the French verb has the same advantage (from the point of view of comprehensibility) as the English verb of having a stated subject, whether noun or pronoun, and at the same time a large measure of the morphological change which marked the Latin verb, it will be clear that the French verb, at least in the written form, carries more information than is strictly necessary to identify its grammatical role in a given context. Although this can be very helpful in assisting comprehension of a French text, it can also present serious difficulty for anglophone learners of the language. This surplus of information (or redundancy) presents its greatest difficulty in the production of correct written French, since many of the 'different' written forms are phonetically the same, e.g. *je chante/tu chantes, je chantais/il chantait* (see 2.4).

2.4 Difference in the number of forms used in the written and spoken language

(i) In spoken French the normal number of identifiable separate forms in each simple tense varies from three (in the present, present subjunctive, imperfect and conditional tenses of regular -*er* verbs) to four (in the future, past historic and imperfect subjunctive, although only one form of this last tense, the 3rd person singular, is now normally found in conversation). These compare with the five or even six different forms that may be found (e.g. the future indicative and imperfect subjunctive) in the written language. This can be illustrated in the following table, where repetition of the same numeral in each of the 'Written' and 'Spoken' columns indicates forms which are indistinguishable in that particular mode:

Written		Spoken	Written		Spoken
1	*j'aime*	1	1	*j'aimerais*	1
2	*tu aimes*	1	1	*tu aimerais*	1
1	*il aime*	1	2	*il aimerait*	1
3	*nous aimons*	2	3	*nous aimerions*	2
4	*vous aimez*	3	4	*vous aimeriez*	3
5	*ils aiment*	1	5	*ils aimeraient*	1

These patterns are not uniform for all classes of verbs, however, as the following tables of the present tense of *finir* and of *avoir* show:

Written		Spoken	Written		Spoken
1	*je finis*	1	1	*j'ai*	1
1	*tu finis*	1	2	*tu as*	2
2	*il finit*	1	3	*il a*	2
3	*nous finissons*	2	4	*nous avons*	3
4	*vous finissez*	3	5	*vous avez*	4
5	*ils finissent*	4	6	*ils ont*	5

From the last example, the present tense of *avoir*, it will be seen that this commonly used auxiliary verb is an exception to what has been said above, since it, together with the other common auxiliary *être*, presents the maximum variation of all in the present tense, having six different written forms and five different spoken forms.

From what has been said above it will be clear that the difference between the apparent number of verb endings in the written and spoken forms of the language is due to these endings having become silent in speech in many cases. Consequently it is the noun or pronoun subject which has, in these particular instances, taken over the information role of the verb ending which had existed in Latin or even sometimes in earlier forms of French, insofar as indication of person and number is concerned. Indication of the tense, however, usually remains clear: *chante* is always a present tense, although the mood could be either that of the indicative, the imperative or the subjunctive; *chantais* is always an imperfect although it may refer either to a first or second person. But there are some important exceptions to this: the first three persons of verbs in -*ir* such as *finir* are the same in the present indicative and in the past historic. It is the context which resolves the problem.

3   Formation of the simple tenses

3.1   General considerations

Traditionally this has been explained by positing the addition of certain characteristic tense endings to the stem of the verb, seen as that part of the verb form persisting when the typical infinitive ending is removed: *chant-er*, *fin-ir*, *vend-re* etc. In theory this allows a general rule to be applied (albeit with a few exceptions) by which the addition of sets of endings for the different persons in each tense produces the simple tense system. Reality is a little more complex, since not only does this simplistic formula fail to take account of unexpected changes in the stem itself of many irregular verbs, but also it does not work for the regular conjugation of verbs conjugated like *finir*. Verbs of this last conjugation take the infix -*iss*- (or -*ss*-, see footnote 3 below) in all three persons of the plural of the present (*nous finissons*, *vous finissez*, *ils finissent*), in the two plural persons of the imperative, in all persons of the imperfect and of the present subjunctive, as well as in all except the 3rd person singular of the imperfect subjunctive and in the present participle. For this reason it is more convenient to consider the verb stem of this group of verbs as that which is left of the infinitive form when the final -*r* is removed: to take the infinitive *finir*, *fini*- is the stem and -*r* is the ending. This stem persists in all forms of verbs in this group, although it is modified by a circumflex accent in three forms: the 3rd person singular of the imperfect subjunctive (*qu'il finît*) and the 2nd and 3rd persons plural of the past historic (*nous finîmes* and *vous finîtes*).[3]

Taking due note of the exceptions already stated, rules of morphology can be laid down for the formation of simple tenses. Unfortunately, however, a number of further exceptions must be taken into account, as indicated below, while it must also be stated that these rules do not cover certain changes arising from alterations which take place in the stems of some verbs.[4]

3.2 The indicative and conditional moods[5]

3.2.1 *The indicative present*

For verbs ending in *-er*, the following endings are added to the stem:

	Singular	Plural
1st person	*-e*	*-ons*
2nd person	*-es*	*-ez*
3rd person	*-e*	*-ent*

This rule also applies to the following verbs ending in *-ir*: *assaillir (j'assaille)*, *cueillir*, *couvrir*, *défaillir*, *offrir*, *ouvrir*, *souffrir*, *tressaillir*.

For all other verbs (apart from the exceptions below) the endings are: *-s, -s, -t, -ons, -ez, -ent*.

This is far from being a safe or helpful rule, however, since many verbs to which it applies undergo changes in their stem or the addition of infixes, as the following tables illustrate:

finir:	*sortir:*	*recevoir:*
je fini-s	*je sor-s*	*je reçoi-s*
tu fini-s	*tu sor-s*	*tu reçoi-s*
il fini-t	*il sor-t*	*il reçoi-t*
nous fini-ss-ons	*nous sort-ons*	*nous recev-ons*
vous fini-ss-ez	*vous sort-ez*	*vous recev-ez*
ils fini-ss-ent	*ils sort-ent*	*ils reçoiv-ent*

Verbs conjugated like *vendre* (including those with endings in *-endre*, *-andre*, *-ondre* and *-ordre*, e.g. *mordre*) come close to conforming to this model except for the 3rd person singular, which has a zero ending:

je vend-s	*nous vend-ons*
tu vend-s	*vous vend-ez*
il vend –	*ils vend-ent*

Pouvoir, *valoir* and *vouloir* have the forms *je peux* (or *je puis*)/*tu peux*, *je vaux*/*tu vaux* and *je veux*/*tu veux*. *Vaincre* has the form *il vainc*.

With the exceptions of the two auxiliary verbs *avoir* and *être* and the verb *aller*, all persons of the plural in all verbs have regular endings in this tense, even though there may be changes in the stem, except for the following:

faire: vous faites, ils font
dire: vous dites (redire: vous redites), but *maudire: vous maudissez*

avoir:	*être:*
j'ai	*je suis*
tu as	*tu es*
il a	*il est*
nous avons	*nous sommes*
vous avez	*vous êtes*
ils ont	*ils sont*

These forms cannot easily be fitted into any pattern. Similarly, the verb *aller* has a present tense with endings and also stem changes which defy classification:

je vais	*nous allons*
tu vas	*vous allez*
il va	*ils vont*

3.2.2   *The indicative imperfect ('l'imparfait')*

This tense is extremely regular in formation, being produced by the addition of the following endings to the stem of the infinitive: *-ais, -ais, -ait, -ions, -iez, -aient*, e.g. *je parlais, tu venais, il était, nous avions, ils disaient*. In the case of verbs like *finir*, however, the infix *-iss-* occurs: *je finissais, tu finissais, il finissait, nous finissions, vous finissiez, ils finissaient*.

Etre almost follows the standard pattern in this tense, except for the change of accent on the stem vowel from *ê* to *é*.

3.2.3   *The past historic ('le passé simple')*

There are a number of possibilities which make this tense morphologically complicated, and it is this complexity of form which some grammarians[6] feel to be partly responsible for its disappearance from the current spoken language.

(i) *-er* verbs have the following endings added to the stem of the infinitive: *-ai, -as, -a, -âmes, -âtes, -èrent* (*je chantai, tu chantas, il chanta, nous chantâmes, vous chantâtes, ils chantèrent*).

(ii) *-ir* verbs conjugated like *finir*, and all other *-ir* verbs except those conjugated like *venir* (*je vins*) and *courir* (*je courus*) take the following endings, but often with considerable changes in the stem in irregular verbs: *-is, -is, -it, -îmes, -îtes, irent* (*je finis, tu finis, il finit, nous finîmes, vous finîtes, ils finirent*).

(iii) *-re* verbs usually follow the above pattern also: *je vendis, tu vendis, il vendit, nous vendîmes, vous vendîtes, ils vendirent*.

(iv) *-oir* verbs (and those listed in *v* below) take the endings *-us, -us, -ut, -ûmes, -ûtes, -urent* (*je sus, tu sus, il sut, nous sûmes, vous sûtes, ils surent*). Both auxiliaries *avoir* and *être* follow this pattern.

(v) Certain verbs, almost all very irregular but which might be thought likely to follow the *-re* model, follow instead the pattern for *-oir* verbs: *boire, croître, conclure, repaître, résoudre, taire, vivre* (e.g. *je bus, tu bus, il but, nous bûmes, vous bûtes, ils burent*).

3.2.4   *The future*

Only one form of ending exists for each person and for all conjugations, but very considerable changes in verb stems occur in this tense in irregular verbs (see Verb Tables at the end of this chapter). Although the forms of this tense usually present little difficulty to anglophone learners of French, it is in fact not easily fitted into classificatory systems in spite of its apparent regularity.

As indicated in 2.1 above, the tense endings of the future, which are common to all French verbs, are the developed forms of what was formerly the present tense of the auxiliary verb derived from *habeo* in colloquial Latin. This auxiliary, together with the infinitive of the lexical verb (which preceded it) became telescoped into the future tense form of modern French, but the final *-r* of the Latin infinitive remained. On account of this it is convenient, especially with regular verbs, to regard the complete infinitive form as the stem on which the future tense is formed. To this are added the endings *-ai, -as, -a, -ons, -ez, -ont*, endings which are identical, for four persons (1st, 2nd and 3rd singular and 3rd plural), to the forms of the present of *avoir*:

je chanter-ai	*je finir-ai*
tu chanter-as	*tu finir-as*
il chanter-a	*il finir-a*
nous chanter-ons	*nous finir-ons*
vous chanter-ez	*vous finir-ez*
ils chanter-ont	*ils finir-ont*

In *-re* verbs, however, the *-e* of the infinitive ending drops: *je vendr-ai, tu vendr-as, il vendr-as, nous vendr-ons, vous vendr-ez, ils vendr-ont*.

3.2.5 *The simple or present conditional ('le conditionnel présent')*

The same general remarks apply to this tense as to the future. It is derived from the Latin infinitive plus the imperfect of Latin *habeo*. It is not surprising therefore that the endings of this tense are the same as those of the French imperfect tense, but added to the infinitive of the verb: *-ais, -ais, -ait, -ions, -iez, -aient*, e.g. *je chanter-ais, je finir-ais*, but *je vendr-ais*.

It is important to note that precisely the same variations of stem are found in this tense for irregular verbs as in the future tense.

3.3 The subjunctive mood

3.3.1 *The present subjunctive ('le présent du subjonctif')*

(i) There is only one set of endings for the present subjunctive of all verbs except *être*. These are *-e, -es, -e, -ions, -iez, -ent*.

(ii) They are normally added to the infinitive stem: *que je chante, que tu chantes, qu'il chante, que nous chantions, que vous chantiez, qu'ils chantent*. But in the case of verbs conjugated like *finir*, an *-iss-* (*-ss-*) infix occurs: *que je finisse, que tu finisses, qu'il finisse, que nous finissions, que vous finissiez, qu'ils finissent*. Some irregular verbs also change their verb stem, e.g. *recevoir/que je reçoive, conduire/que je conduise*.

(iii) *Etre* has a present subjunctive formed on the basis of a stem now found only in this tense and in the imperative: *soi-, soy-*, giving: *que je sois, que tu sois, qu'il soit, que nous soyons, que vous soyez, qu'ils soient*.

(iv) *Avoir*, although using the regular endings, albeit with some contraction in the first two persons plural, has a present subjunctive formed using the 1st person singular of the present indicative as the stem: *que j'aie, que tu aies, qu'il ait, que nous ayons, que vous ayez, qu'ils aient*.

3.3.2 *The imperfect subjunctive ('l'imparfait du subjonctif')*

(i) The forms of this tense are fairly closely linked with those of the past historic of the indicative, as both derive from Latin tenses based on the Latin perfect stem. Use is sometimes made of this fact in learning the forms of this tense, since it can be schematized as the addition of certain endings to the 2nd person singular of the past historic. This method has limitations, however, with regard to the 3rd person singular. It may be easier to think of the imperfect subjunctive in terms of the addition of one of the following sets of endings to the infinitive stem, depending on the type of ending of the past historic of the particular verb:

-asse	*-isse*	*-usse*
-asses	*-isses*	*-usses*
-ât	*-ît*	*-ût*
-assions	*-issions*	*-ussions*
-assiez	*-issiez*	*-ussiez*
-assent	*-issent*	*-ussent*
e.g. *que je chantasse*	*que tu finisses*	*qu'il reçut* (etc.)

(ii) Verbs conjugated like *venir*, however, take these endings without the distinctive vowel: *-sse, -sses, t, -ssions, -ssiez, -ssent*, added to the past historic stem: *que je vinsse, que tu vinsses, qu'il vînt, que nous vinssions, que nous vinssiez, qu'ils vinssent*.

(iii) To form the imperfect subjunctive tenses of *avoir* and *être*, it is essential to take the stem of the past historic form as a basis, rather than that of the infinitive:

avoir:	*être:*
que j'eus-se	*que je fus-se*
que tu eus-ses	*que tu fus-ses*
qu'il eût	*qu'il fût*
que nous eussions	*que nous fussions*
que vous eussiez	*que vous fussiez*
qu'ils eussent	*qu'ils fussent*

Although complete sets of morphological forms exist for most verbs for this tense, only the 3rd person singular is today in use, and this only in very formal French.

3.4   The imperative mood

3.4.1   *General considerations*

The imperative mood has no characteristic forms of its own but uses those of the present indicative or, in a few cases, those of the present subjunctive. Since the imperative is really a nontemporal mood (see Ch. 7) it is not strictly correct to talk of the 'tenses' of the imperative. It has two 'forms' which are better described as the simple and the compound forms of the imperative, although the compound form is very rarely used and is, indeed, semantically impossible for many verbs.

The imperative has only three persons: 2nd singular, and 1st and 2nd plural. No pronoun subjects (or noun subjects) are employed with the imperative.

3.4.2   *The simple forms*

(i) These are normally the same as those of the appropriate persons of the present indicative except that, for *-er* verbs and those *-ir* verbs (e.g. *ouvrir*) which are conjugated like *-er* verbs in the present indicative, the final *-s* of the 2nd person singular drops. But some base their forms on the present subjunctive (see *iii* below).

chante	*ouvre*	*finis*	*tends*
chantons	*ouvrons*	*finissons*	*tendons*
chantez	*ouvrez*	*finissez*	*tendez*

(ii) Verbs which drop the final *-s* of the 2nd person singular do however retain it in locutions such as *achètes-en*, *penses-y* (see Ch. 3).

Note: The 2nd person singular imperative of *aller* is *va*, but note the phrase *vas-y*. The imperative of *s'en aller* is *va-t-en*, *allons-nous-en*, *allez-vous-en*.

(iii) Verbs which follow the form of the present subjunctive in the imperative are: *avoir* (*aie, ayons, ayez*); *être* (*sois, soyons, soyez*); and *savoir* (*sache, sachons, sachez*).

Vouloir has the forms *veuille, veuillons* (both very unusual) and *veuillez*. The form *veuillez* is normally used as a formula of politeness, especially in letters. The indicative form *voulez-vous* is also used with curt imperative force at the end of a request or command – cf. English 'will you'.

3.5   The impersonal forms or 'nominal mood'

3.5.1   *The infinitives*

The characteristic infinitive endings of French verbs are *-er*, *-re*, *-ir*, *-oir*, and classification of the verb groups is made broadly according to the form of the infinitive endings. Irregularities abound, however, so that similarity of infinitive endings is no guarantee that any particular set of verbs can be classed together as conjugating in exactly the same way (see Tables of Conjugation at the end of this chapter).

3.5.2 *The participles*

(i) Present participles invariably end in *-ant*. The stem and infixes (if any) to which this ending is added are the same as those of the 1st person plural of the present indicative: *chantant (nous chant-ons), finissant (nous finiss-ons), vendant, apercevant*, etc.

(ii) Past participles have many and diverse forms which can be accurately predicted only by extremely complex rules based on phonological premises (see M.H. Gertner, *The morphology of the French verb*). Completely regular verbs of the main groups have past participle endings as follows:

> *chanter: chant-é*   *vendre: vend-u*   *finir: fin-i*

but various possible endings also exist outside those of the regular conjugations, either with or without inflexions of the stem, e.g. *mourir: mort, vivre: vécu*.

In addition the endings belonging to the regular conjugations can be found in verb forms not belonging to that conjugation, e.g. *naître: né, vêtir: vêtu*.

4 Formation of the compound tenses

4.1 General considerations

The French compound tenses can be said to consist of two components: a lexical component, the past participle, which defines the verb in terms of meaning, and a morphological component, the tense form of the auxiliary verb, which defines the compound form in terms of person, number and tense. The way in which this takes place should present little conceptual difficulty for the anglophone learner of French, since it is similar to the manner of production of tenses such as the perfect and pluperfect in English ('I have eaten', 'I had played') which consists of bringing together the appropriate tense of the auxiliary verb and the past participle of the lexical verb, e.g. *j'ai mangé, j'avais joué*.

Comparisons with English compound tense formation have only limited usefulness, however, since there are certain important differences.

(i) English uses only one auxiliary verb for compound tenses in the active voice ('have'), whereas French uses either *avoir* or *être*, the choice of auxiliary depending on semantic factors (see 9.2.3.5 below).

(ii) Whereas in English the past participle is invariable, in the French compound tense it may vary in both gender and number in certain circumstances.

Where the auxiliary used is *être (elle est arrivée, elles sont allées)*, the past participle agrees with subject in gender and number except in certain specific cases as set out in Ch. 9. In the passive voice this kind of agreement always takes place.

Where the auxiliary is *avoir* the past participle agrees in number and gender with a preceding pronoun object:

> *elles les ont achetées (les = les pommes de terre)*
but *elles ont acheté les pommes de terre* (no agreement of past participle)

See Ch. 9.

4.2 Compound forms in the indicative and conditional moods

4.2.1 *The compound past ('le passé composé')*

This is formed by the present indicative tense of the auxiliary verb and the past participle of the lexical verb:

j'ai chanté ('I have sung')	*je suis tombé(e)* ('I have fallen')
tu as chanté	*tu es tombé(e)*
il a chanté, elle a chanté	*il est tombé, elle est tombée*
nous avons chanté	*nous sommes tombé(e)s*
vous avez chanté	*vous êtes tombé(e)s*
ils ont chanté, elles ont chanté	*ils sont tombés, elles sont tombées*

The other compound tenses are formed in a similar way, using in all cases the past participle of the lexical verb with the appropriate tense of the auxiliary, as below.

4.2.2   *The pluperfect ('le plus-que-parfait')*

The auxiliary is used in the imperfect tense: *j'avais chanté*; *j'étais tombé(e)*.

4.2.3   *The past anterior ('le passé antérieur')*

The auxiliary is used in the past historic tense: *[quand] j'eus chanté*; *[quand] je fus tombé(e)*. Nowadays these are only used in subordinate clauses.

4.2.4   *The compound future ('le futur antérieur')*

The auxiliary is used in the future tense: *j'aurai chanté*; *je serai tombé(e)*.

4.2.5   *The compound conditional ('le conditionnel passé')*

The auxiliary is used in the conditional tense: *j'aurais chanté*; *je serais tombé(e)*.

4.3   Compound forms in the subjunctive

4.3.1   *The compound past subjunctive (or perfect subjunctive)*

The auxiliary is used in the present subjunctive: *que j'aie chanté*; *que je sois tombé(e)*.

4.3.2   *The pluperfect subjunctive*

The auxiliary is used in the imperfect subjunctive: *que j'eusse chanté*; *que je fusse tombé(e)*.

4.4   The compound forms of the imperative

These rarely found forms are made up of the imperative of the auxiliary and the past participle of the lexical verb:

aie chanté	*aie fini*
ayons chanté	*ayons fini*
ayez chanté	*ayez fini*

These forms are used to express anteriority in the future, as in *aie fini avant mon retour*.

4.5   Compound forms in the nominal or impersonal mood

4.5.1   *The infinitive*

This form is sometimes called the 'past infinitive', and is made up of the infinitive of the auxiliary and the past participle of the lexical verb: *avoir chanté*; *être tombé(e)(s)*.

4.5.2 *The compound participles*

These are made up of the present tense of the auxiliary and the past participle of the lexical verb, e.g. *ayant chanté; étant tombé(e)(s)*.

5 The double compound forms

5.1 General considerations

These are formed from the various compound tenses of the auxiliaries *avoir* and *être* plus the past participle of the lexical verb. There is no morphological equivalent to these forms in English. In French they not only exist but are also of some antiquity in the language, even though their existence has only relatively recently been accepted and recognized by all grammarians. From the morphological point of view there is no reason why any of the compound tenses of the auxiliaries should not be used for the formation of double compound tenses. In practice, however, this type of tense is only found with any frequency in the indicative mood, and only the double compound past and the double compound pluperfect are used at all commonly in modern written French. Since this tense form has a particular aspectual value of anteriority, it is not surprising that there is no surviving form of compound past anterior tenses.

5.2 Double compound forms in the indicative and conditional moods

In the seventeenth century these forms were banned by the *Académie*. They are:
(i) the double compound past (or *passé surcomposé*): *j'ai eu chanté; j'ai été parti(e)*.
(ii) the compound pluperfect (or *plus-que-parfait surcomposé*): *j'avais eu chanté; j'avais été parti(e)*.
(iii) the compound future anterior (or *futur antérieur surcomposé*): *j'aurai eu chanté; j'aurai été parti(e)*.
(iv) the double compound conditional (or *conditionnel surcomposé*): *j'aurais eu chanté; j'aurais été parti(e)*.

5.3 Double compound forms in the subjunctive mood

(i) the double compound past subjunctive: *que j'aie eu chanteé; que j'aie été parti(e)*.
(ii) the compound pluperfect subjunctive (this is no more than a morphological possibility): *que j'eusse eu chanté; que j'eusse été parti(e)*.

5.4 Double compound forms in the nominal or impersonal mood

Although rarely found in either the written or spoken forms of the language, these forms are morphologically possible and do occasionally occur:

    avoir eu chanté   *avoir été parti(e)*
    ayant eu chanté   *ayant été parti(e)*

6 Forms of the passive voice

6.1 General considerations

The passive voice is denoted entirely by compound forms. The simple passive forms which existed in classical Latin have disappeared during the evolution of French, leaving a straightforward (for the anglophone learner) compound system in which the forms of the various tenses of the auxiliary *étre* are followed by the past participle of the lexical verb. The tense of the auxiliary will, in each case, be the tense of the resulting passive form. The past participle of the lexical verb will in all cases agree in gender and number with the subject.

6.2 The indicative mood

present: *je suis aimé(e)* ('I am loved')
imperfect: *j'étais aimé(e)* ('I was loved')
past historic: *je fus aimé(e)* ('I was loved')
compound past: *j'ai été aimé(e)* ('I have been loved')
pluperfect: *j'avais été aimé(e)* ('I had been loved')
past anterior: [*quand*] *j'eus été aimé(e)* ('I had been loved')
future: *je serai aimé(e)* ('I shall be loved')
compound future: *j'aurai été aimé(e)* ('I shall have been loved')
conditional: *je serais aimé(e)* ('I should be loved')
compound conditional: *j'aurais été aimé(e)* ('I should have been loved')

6.3 The subjunctive mood

present: *que je sois aimé(e)*
imperfect: *que je fusse aimé(e)*
compound past: *que j'aie été aimé(e)*
pluperfect: *que j'eusse été aimé(e)*

6.4 The imperative mood

Although very rarely used, the passive imperative exists in French:

present: *sois aimé(e)!*   *soyons aimé(e)s!*   *Soyez aimé(e)s!*

6.5 The nominal or impersonal mood:

infinitive: present − *être aimé(e)*   past − *avoir été aimé(e)*
participle: present − *étant aimé(e)*   past − *ayant été aimé(e)*

7   Verb conjugations in French

7.1 Classification

(i) Verbs in French are conjugated according to a relatively small number of patterns (paradigms) broadly following a system of classification which depends on the form of the ending of the present infinitive of each verb. There are however a number of verbs of all types which do not accord completely with the pattern for the group to which they appear to belong. Where this departure from the norm is very small, affecting only one or two parts, e.g. the spelling of the past participle, the verb is usually regarded as belonging to the appropriate group or class but presenting minor irregularities. Where the differences are greater, affecting for example one or more whole tenses, then the particular verb is usually regarded as 'irregular', unless there are a few other verbs showing similar variations, in which case it may be convenient to regard them as a subgroup or subclass.
(ii) There are considerable differences among grammarians as to how French verbs should be classified, although it is universally accepted that this should be done according to the ending of the infinitive. Native French grammarians frequently adopt a scheme in which verbs are classified as belonging to one of three groups:

-*er* verbs, e.g. *donner, chanter*;

-*ir* verbs conjugated like *finir* (the so -called 'regular' -*ir* group), characterized by the occurrence of the infix -*iss*- or -*ss*- in the forms for the first two persons plural, the whole of the imperfect tense and the present participle, e.g. *nous finissons, vous finissez, je finissais. . ., finissant*;

all other verbs, which are thereby effectively considered to be more or less irregular, since there is really no common denominator of form among them except at such a level of generality as to be useless for classificatory purposes.

Various permutations of the above scheme will be found in different grammars, but they are all produced by subdividing group *c* above into varying numbers of subgroups.

(iii) Anglophone authors of French grammars have tended to use more detailed classifications of French verbs, and this tradition will be followed here, as it is considered more convenient for anglophone learners. It is also more accurate from a historical point of view: see 7.1.1 below. In the tables which follow the method of grouping verbs will be as follows:[7]

Group 1: -*er* verbs, e.g. *aimer, chanter*. This group includes several thousand verbs.

Group 2: -*ir* verbs (e.g. *finir*) having a present participle ending in -*issant*. This group includes several hundred verbs.

Group 3: -*ir* verbs (e.g. *sentir, mentir*) not having a present participle ending in -*issant*.

Group 4: -*re* verbs (e.g. rendre).

Group 5: -*oir verbs (e.g. recevoir)*.

Of the verbs in the last three groups, only a few are in constant use.

Other verbs not fitting these categories will be regarded simply as irregular. *Avoir* and *être*, because of their importance as auxiliary verbs, will be treated first, as special cases, in the verb tables.

(iv) It is important to realize that new verbs are constantly being added to the French language. Fairly recent examples of this are *interviewer, téléviser, polycopier, politiquer, alunir* ('to land on the moon'). All such new verbs which are formed in the language and eventually become accepted follow either the -*er* or the -*ir* (*finir*) paradigm. These two groups are therefore known in French as *conjugaisons vivantes* ('live conjugations'), since they alone are expanding by the addition of new verbs. In practice, however, the 2nd conjugation, -*ir* verbs like *finir*, acquires a very small number of new additions as compared to the 1st conjugation (-*er* verbs)[8] – but see 8.3.*iii* below. Since this is the conjugation to which the great majority of new verbs are assimilated as well as being that which contains by far the greatest number of existing verbs, it may be regarded as the standard or typical regular conjugation of French verbs. Unfortunately, however, for the ease with which correct French may be spoken or written, although the other and less 'regular' conjugations contain most of the verbs which are gradually dropping out of everyday usage, they also contain many of the verbs, especially the modal and the auxiliary verbs, which are most frequently used. In spite of this lack of regularity and the consequent difficult morphology, it is a happy fact that these latter verbs are so frequently used that their forms tend to become familiar through usage relatively rapidly.

7.1.1 *Historical note*

The English system of classification does indeed reflect the historical development of the conjugations:

The -*er* or Group 1 verbs go back to the Latin -*áre* verbs (*cantáre* > *chanter*).

The -*ir* or Group 2 and 3 verbs go back to the Latin -*ıre* verbs (*finíre* > *finir*), but these either had their 1st person singular in *-io* (*audio* > *j'ouïs*) or in *-esco* (*floresco* > **florisco*[9] > *je fleuris*).

The *-re* or Group 4 verbs go back to verbs ending in either a consonant or an accentuated vowel + *-ĕre* (*vivĕre* > *vivre*, *plángerĕ* > *plaindre*).

The *-oir* or Group 5 verbs go back to the Latin *-ére* verbs (*habére* > *avoir*).

M.K. Pope (*From Latin to modern French*, §§ 880, 881) writes the following on the 2nd and 3rd conjugations:

'Conjugation II, Infinitive termination *-ir*, was developed out of the Latin inchoative (inceptive) verbs, i.e. those verbs to which the use of the infix *-sc-* gave originally the significance of change of state or beginning of action. The infix was originally used with verbs of all conjugations, cf. *irascere*, *parescere*, cog*noscere*, *dormɪscere*, but in Gaul and some other parts of the Roman Empire it attached itself more and more exclusively to the present stem tenses of the 4th conjugation,[10] lost all significance and became a simple flexional element. When placed before the palatal vowels *e* and *i* (e.g. in *finiscebam*, *finiscentem*, *finiscis*) • /isk/ was palatalized to /iʃ/ (> /is/, § 315) and the palatalized form was generalized in all the parts of the verb in which the infix had secured a place, i.e. throughout the present indicative and subjunctive as well as in the imperfect indicative, gerund and present participle.

Conjugation II included: (1) the verbs of Latin origin that had adopted the infix, e.g. *florir* (> *fleurir*), *norrir* (> *nourrir*), *porrir* (> *pourrir*); (2) verbs of Germanic origin derived from verbs in **-jan* and occasionally others, e.g. choisir< **kausjan*, *honnir* < *honir* < **haunjan* etc; (3) derivative verbs (especially those formed from adjectives) and Latin loanwords from conjugations II, III, IV, e.g. *asservir* (*servum*), *blanchir*, *noircir* (Old French *nercir*) . . . *agir* etc.'

7.2   The irregular verbs

7.2.1   *'Avoir' and 'être'*

These two verbs, which may have a lexical or an auxiliary role, are the most commonly used of all French verbs and among the least regular. They are therefore usually treated as not belonging to any specific group or groups, although each of them has a number of apparently 'regular' features (e.g. the imperfect of *avoir* is perfectly regular if it is thought of as an *-oir* verb: *j'avais*, *tu avais*, *il avait*, *nous avions*, *vous aviez*, *ils avaient*). In the tables of conjugations which follow, *avoir* and *être* will be given separate treatment (see 9.1).

7.2.2   *Different forms of irregularity in other verbs*

(i) Irregularities may be readily apparent in both form and pronunciation, e.g. the present tense of *être* − *je suis*, *tu es* etc; or changes in spelling may be necessitated by phonetic factors, as in the verb *changer* − *nous changeons* (whereas **nous changons* would be expected according to regular formation of the present tense), or *froncer* − *nous fronçons* (not **nous froncons*). These changes are due to the fact that the consonants *g* and *c* are pronounced hard in French before *a*, *o* and *u* but soft before *e* and *i*.

(ii) In verbs such as *appeler*, *jeter* and *mener* a change of stress takes place between the radical (stem) and the ending in certain persons in the present tense. In all of these verbs it is the same persons which carry these changes of stress, those with which the radical is stressed being sometimes called the 'strong' persons (*je*, *tu*, *il*, *ils*) while the others, where the stress falls on the ending, are called 'weak' (*nous*, *vous*).

je mène	*je jette*	*j'appelle*
tu mènes	*tu jettes*	*tu appelles*
il mène	*il jette*	*il appelle*
nous menons	*nous jetons*	*nous appelons*
vous menez	*vous jetez*	*vous appelez*
ils mènent	*ils jettent*	*ils appellent*

(iii) More major irregularities in verbs can occur either in the radical or in the ending. Irregularities of stem can often be such as to make the affected parts of the verb no longer easily recognizable as related to the infinitive or indeed to other tenses or parts, e.g. the present tense of *aller: je vais, tu vas, il va, nous allons, vous allez, ils vont*. In this example only the forms of the so-called 'weak' persons (1st and 2nd plural) are clearly morphologically related to the infinitive. This is thought to be due to the fact that historically *aller* is a hybrid verb, derived from two or even three Latin verbs.[11]

Changes in the verb stem occur in a number of verbs in the present tense – changes which cannot be systematized in any way likely to be helpful to the learner of the language, although they can be more or less satisfactorily explained by reference to the historical development of French. The only really constant factor (except for *être*, *dire* and *faire*) is that the 'weak' persons of the verb (1st and 2nd plural) always have the same stem as the imperfect tense:

j'ai	*j'av-ais*	*je vois*	*je voyais*
tu as	*tu av-ais*	*tu vois*	*tu voyais*
il a	*il av-ait*	*il voit*	*il voyait*
nous av-ons	*nous av-ions*	*nous voyons*	*nous voyions*
vous av-ez	*vous av-iez*	*vous voyez*	*vous voyiez*
ils ont	*ils av-aient*	*ils voient*	*ils voyaient*

but: *vous êtes*; *vous dites*; *vous faites*.

Irregularities in the verb stem, as compared to other verbs of the same general type, also often occur in the whole of the past historic, e.g. *vivre: je vécus*; *croître: je crûs*; *lire: je lus*. Verbs having a different radical in the past historic are sometimes referred to as 'strong' verbs,[12] although this term is not so widely accepted in French as in other languages.

(iv) Irregularities in verb endings, where the stem remains regular, normally take the form of sets of endings other than those which would have been expected given the ending of the infinitive, e.g.

> *offrir* (present tense): *j'offre, tu offres, il offre, nous offrons, vous offrez, ils offrent*
> *cueillir: je cueille*, etc.

(v) Various verbs show considerable irregularity in their past participles, e.g. *craindre: craint*; *peindre: peint*; *asseoir: assis*; *naître: né*. *Vivre: vécu* shows the ending *-u* which is regular for a verb ending in *-re*, even though the stem can be seen to be very irregular.

(vi) A number of verbs show considerable irregularity in the form of their present participles, usually giving rise to similar changes in the 1st and 2nd persons plural of the present, the whole of the present subjunctive and the imperfect, e.g.

> *absoudre:* present participle *absolvant*; present *nous absolvons, vous absolvez*; present subjunctive *que j'absolve*; imperfect *j'absolvais*
> *peindre:* past participle *peignant*; present *nous peignons*; present subjunctive *que je peigne*; imperfect *je peignais*

There are however a number of exceptions to this, as in *savoir: sachant*; present *nous savons, vous savez*; present subjunctive *que je sache*; but imperfect *je savais*.

7.2.3   *Defective verbs*

A very different form of irregularity, affecting a small number of verbs, some of which may be otherwise quite regular, is the lack of certain tenses. A verb of this kind is the now obsolescent *ouïr*, which is usually thought to have only an infinitive, a past participle and the compound tenses.[13] *Paître*, on the other hand, is not used in the simple past, nor in the imperfect subjunctive, nor in the compound tenses. There are a number of such verbs, but there does not seem to be complete agreement among the various grammars and dictionaries as to which tenses of some of these verbs actually exist or are in use. The reason for this lack of unanimity must probably be sought in the lack of any generally agreed criterion for establishing what is normal usage in such cases, or indeed for deciding exactly what is meant by a term such as 'defective', since it could quite logically also be applied (although it rarely is) to the verbs usually referred to as the 'impersonal' verbs. These, as illustrated in 7.2.4, are clearly deficient in a number of parts, but this particular kind of deficiency is usually semantically determined in a very specific way.

7.2.4   *Impersonal verbs*

The main characteristic of these verbs is that they have only one person, the 3rd singular, and normally (although by no means invariably) they have as subject the pronoun *il* which is invariable. The subject *il* can be seen in various ways,[14] but for anglophone learners of French it can conveniently be regarded as analogous to the English impersonal pronoun 'it': *il pleut*, 'it is raining'; *il gèle*, 'it is freezing'. While this provides an easy way of understanding the grammatical function of the pronoun *il* in these verb forms, it must be clearly understood that English and French do not, apart from expressions relating to the weather and a few others formed with the verb *être* used impersonally (*il est bon de* . . . etc.), follow exactly the same usage with regard to style. Thus *il me faut* + infinitive, although frequently translated as 'it is necessary for me to . . .', should really be translated by expressions such as 'I have to . . .', 'I must . . .', the personal form often being the preferred form in English.

As stated above, *il* is not invariably the subject of these verbs, since in everyday popular speech *il* is very often replaced by *ça* – *ça pleut*, etc.[15] This use of *ça* does however belong to very informal speech, and indeed to what is referred to as *la langue négligée*.

Impersonal verbs are sometimes said to fall into two categories: those which are always impersonal, such as *il faut* and certain verbs relating to the state of the weather (*il pleut, il neige, il gèle* etc.), and those which are only sometimes impersonal, such as *être* (*il est possible de*. . .), *faire* (*il fait bon*), *sembler* (*il semble que*. . .), *convenir* (*il convient de*. . .). This is something of an oversimplification, since at least two verbs in the first category can be used with real subjects: *je gèle, nous gelons* etc. can be used to mean that the various personal subjects are very cold (similar usages exist in English), or, with *pleuvoir*, such expressions as *les coups pleuvaient* are not infrequent.

Avoir only occurs in the one impersonal form *il y a*, although some slight confusion may arise on this point since it also occurs naturally as the auxiliary in certain impersonal passive formulations which are relatively common, especially in various jargon registers, e.g. *il a été décidé que*. . . .

8   Verbal derivation in modern French

8.1   Defining derivation

In order to avoid possible confusion with the other use of the term 'derivation' which is common in the context of philology, we should make it clear that the term is here used to denote the process by which changes may be made in the class of a word, i.e. in its grammatical status, or in its meaning. This is different from the morphological changes which have so far been studied in this chapter, and which are known as inflections. Inflections express person, number, tense and mood, whereas derivation can be used to nominalize, verbalize, adjectivize or adverbalize a root morpheme or radical. It may consist of the addition of a morpheme to a word of a specific class in order to change that class or to change its meaning without changing its class, e.g. the morpheme *-ass-* can be added to a verb root (*rêver: rêvasser*). In this case one is dealing with an infix.

8.2 Derivation used to verbalize a given root

This type of derivation is not used to change the meaning of a word.

In this case suffixation is normally used. This process is however less straight-forward than it seems, since it immediately gives rise to the question, 'what derives from what?' The fact is that varying relationships may exist between the verb obtained through derivation and other words based on the same root, e.g.

(1) *chant-*
$\begin{cases} er \text{ (verb)} \\ (chant)\text{-}\emptyset \text{ (noun)} \\ (chan)\,son \text{ (noun)} \end{cases}$
(2) *famil-*
$\begin{cases} le \text{ (noun)} \\ ial \text{ (adjective)} \\ ier \text{ (noun or adjective)} \\ iariser \text{ (verb)} \end{cases}$

(3) *pacif-*
$\begin{cases} é \text{ (adjective)} \\ ique \text{ (adjective)} \\ ier \text{ (verb)} \end{cases}$
(4) *rouge* (adjective)
    rougir (verb)
    le rouge (noun − nominalization
              produced by article)

In (1) there seems no reason to conclude that either the verb or the noun takes precedence over the other. When there are two words derived from the same root and belonging to the same class, these have different meanings, either slightly different, as in *chant/chanson*, or very different as in *familial/familier*, *familial* meaning 'belonging or appertaining to the family', *familier* meaning 'familiar'.

In (2) the noun seems to be the basic term of the set; or at least it seems to have some kind of precedence, since the basic concept denoted by the noun appears to be fundamental for the other words of the set to have any semantic justification.

In (3) the verb means *rendre pacifique*, which gives obvious priority to the adjective (*pacifier = pacifique* + causative).

In (4) the verb appears to derive directly from the adjective.

In other words, where there is a full series of noun, verb, adjective based on a common root or morpheme, there does not seem to be any invariable precedence of verb over noun or vice versa.

Where the series is incomplete and the adjective describes a state, the adjective seems to have precedence. It is in these cases that generalizations can be made on how to derive a verb from an adjective.

8.3 Derivation from adjective to verb (and from noun to verb)

(i) Changing from one state to another is often expressed by adding *-ir* to the adjective to form the verb: *aigre:aigrir*; *rouge:rougir*. Phonetic changes sometimes take place during this process: *dur:durcir*; *vert:verdir*.

(ii) 'To make something (somebody)' + adjective is usually expressed by adding *-iser* (from Greek) or *-ifier* (from Latin): *aigu:aiguiser*; *légal:légaliser*; *égal:égaliser*; *intellectuel/intellectualiser*; *ample/amplifier*; *glorieux/glorifier*.

Similar verbalization may take place with *-iser*, *-ifier* or *-eler* from certain nouns, producing a result similar to that seen above for adjectives, in that the resulting verb

indicates the entry into a state: *scandale/scandaliser*; *bosse/bosseler*; *ficelle/ficeler*.
(iii) The idea expressed in *ii* above of causative + adjective may sometimes be rendered by the combination of a prefix + suffix *-ir*, as in *pauvre/appauvrir*; *ferme/affermir*.

Verbs such as *alunir*, *atterrir* and *amerrir* are different from verbs such as *appauvrir* and *affermir*, in that the latter come from adjectives, whereas the former come from nouns (*lune*, *terre*, *mer*). The semantics of these two types of formation are quite different: *appauvrir* = *rendre pauvre*; *affermir* = *rendre ferme*, whereas *atterrir* = *prendre contact avec la terre*, *alunir* = *prendre contact avec la lune*.
(iv) There are adjectives and nouns which cannot be verbalized, e.g. *malade*. *Piano* has no corresponding verb: to verbalize this concept one has to say or write *faire du piano*. The verb *pianoter* does exist, but means *s'amuser au piano, jouer sans habileté*.

8.4 Derivation from verb to verb

In these cases it is the meaning of the verb which changes. These changes are affected by adding the following suffixes to certain verbs: *-iner*, *-iller*, *-ocher*, *-onner*, *-eter*, *-asser*, *-ailler*, and also *-oter*, *-ouiller*, both of which usually express disapproval.
(i) *-ailler* and *-asser* are both basically pejorative: *crier/criailler*; *tourner/tournailler*; *traîner/traînailler*; *écrire/écrivasser*; *traîner/traînasser*; *tourner/tournasser*; *rêver/rêvasser*.
(ii) *-oter*, *-iller*, *-iner*, *-ouiller*, *-ocher*, *-onner*, *-oyer* indicate repetition of an action seen in terms of very small individual motions — actions which are merely repeated, which take place on a small scale — or they may indicate that a pejorative view is being taken of the action(s): *trottiner* = *trotter à petits pas*; *boitiller* = *boiter légèrement*; *pianoter* = *jouer du piano à petits coups légers, peu organisés*; *toussoter* = *tousser souvent et faiblement*; *pluviner* = *pleuvoir d'une petite pluie fine*; *tournoyer* = *tourner en faisant plusieurs tours sur soi-même*.

Most of these derivations belong to popular or familiar language, and their use seems to have been more frequent in the past than now.
(iii) In certain instances some of these suffixes appear to occur with no apparent change of meaning resulting from the verbalization so produced. *Batailler* is simply the verb which corresponds to the noun *bataille* — i.e. the suffix is *-er* and not *-ailler* — and is not therefore pejorative, although a pejorative version *bataillasser* could, for instance, be envisaged. *Chatouiller* and *chatoyer* similarly have no pejorative force.[16]

8.5 Derivation from noun to verb

This takes place by the addition of affixes to nouns (proper or common nouns): *balkan-iser*; *pasteur-iser*; *voitur-er*; *cloison-ner* (noun + verbal suffix); *em-barqu-er* (prefix + noun + verbal suffix).
(i) The first conjugation infinitive suffix *-er* (shortened to *-r* after a final *-e* in the noun) is the only suffix now commonly used to produce new verbal forms from nouns, but it has also been much used in this way during the previous development of the language: *polémique/polémiquer*; *frein/freiner*; *béton/bétonner*; *fraude/frauder*. Doubling of the final consonant before this suffix is a frequent phenomenon, when the final consonant is a nasal.
(ii) The ending *-er* is found forming part of more complex suffixes, e.g. *-iser* and *-ifier*, which usually produce verbs of a technical or learned nature (see also 8.3ii for the use of these suffixes with adjectives): *code/codifier*; *Pasteur/pasteuriser*; *climat/climatiser*; *Taylor/tayloriser*.[17]

-eler, *-ailler*, *-oyer*, *-oter* etc., as in 8.4, may be found added to nouns to form verbs: *bosse/bosseler*; *coude/coudoyer*; but many such forms may be no more than

neologisms produced for stylistic effect and which do not find wide acceptance.
(iii) The infinitive terminal suffix *-ir* (as in 2nd conjugation *finir*) is also sometimes used to produce verbs from nouns, particularly in the fields of aeronautics and astronautics, presumably by analogy with the accepted forms *atterrir* and *amerrir*. Such forms as *alunir* have not yet found complete acceptance (see 8.3*iii*).
(iv) The prefixes *dé-*, *em-* and *en-* are also commonly found in combination with the verbal suffix *-er*: *déferrer*, *dévaliser*, *embrancher*, *embrigader*, *entêter*, *entasser*.

8.6 Lexical creativity of verbal derivation

(i) In endocentric derivation (i.e. derivation which does not change the class of a word), the variables are the word used, the person using it, and the context. One can make new verbs by adding suffixes on condition that one does not change the class of the word (e.g. *crier*/*criailler*; see also 8.4 above). These will be clearly understandable even though they may not appear in the dictionary. They will be interpreted depending on the context, since a strong element of style is involved.[18]
(ii) Exocentric constructions (e.g. *code*/*codifier*; see also 8.5 above) occur when the derivation alone determines the class of the word; derivation is not personal but has to be part of the vocabulary of the language. The same kind of innovation is not possible in this case.

9 Morphological tables

9.1 The auxiliary verbs 'avoir' and 'être'

Although not typical of any one conjugation and frequently irregular in form, these two verbs are fundamental to the formation of the compound tenses of all other French verbs and will therefore be treated first in the following tables.

9.1.1 *The case of 'avoir'*

9.1.1.1 *The indicative mood*

Simple tenses: Compound tenses:

Present: Compound past:

j'ai	*nous avons*	*j'ai eu*	*nous avons eu*
tu as	*vous avez*	*tu as eu*	*vous avez eu*
il a	*ils ont*	*il a eu*	*ils ont eu*

Imperfect: Pluperfect:

j'avais	*nous avions*	*j'avais eu*	*nous avions eu*
tu avais	*vous aviez*	*tu avais eu*	*vous aviez eu*
il avait	*ils avaient*	*il avait eu*	*ils avaient eu*

Past historic: Past anterior:

j'eus	*nous eûmes*	*j'eus eu*	*nous eûmes eu*
tu eus	*vous eûtes*	*tu eus eu*	*vous eûtes eu*
il eut	*ils eurent*	*il eut eu*	*ils eurent eu*

Future:

		Compound future:	
j'aurai	*nous aurons*	*j'aurai eu*	*nous aurons eu*
tu auras	*vous aurez*	*tu auras eu*	*vous aurez eu*
il aura	*ils auront*	*il aura eu*	*ils auront eu*

Conditional:

		Compound conditional:	
j'aurais	*nous aurions*	*,j'aurais eu*	*nous aurions eu*
tu aurais	*vous auriez*	*tu aurais eu*	*vous auriez eu*
il aurait	*ils auraient*	*il aurait eu*	*ils auraient eu*

9.1.1.2   *The imperative mood*

Present:

aie, ayons, ayez

9.1.1.3   *The subjunctive mood*

Present:

		Compound past:	
que j'aie	*que nous ayons*	*que j'aie eu*	*que nous ayons eu*
que tu aies	*que vous ayez*	*que tu aies eu*	*que vous ayez eu*
qu'il ait	*qu'ils aient*	*qu'il ait eu*	*qu'ils aient eu*

Imperfect:

		Pluperfect:	
que j'eusse	*que nous eussions*	*que j'eusse eu*	*que nous eussions eu*
que tu eusses	*que vous eussiez*	*que tu eusses eu*	*que vous eussiez eu*
qu'il eût	*qu'ils eussent*	*qu'il eût eu*	*qu'ils eussent eu*

9.1.1.4   *The nominal or impersonal mood*
(i) The infinitives

Simple form:	Compound form:
avoir	*avoir eu*

(ii) The participles

Simple form:	Compound form:
ayant/eu	*ayant eu*

9.1.1.5   *The passive forms*   In its role as an auxiliary verb, *avoir* clearly cannot possess a passive voice, although it does play a part as the auxiliary of *être*, in the formation of the double compound tenses of the passive of other verbs. Although in its role as a lexical verb *avoir* can be thought of as possibly possessing passive forms, in practice these are virtually never encountered in written French, and in spoken French only in slang.

9.1.2   *The case of 'être'*

9.1.2.1   *The indicative mood*

Simple tenses:		Compound tenses:	

Present:

		Compound past:	
je suis	*nous sommes*	*j'ai été*	*nous avons été*
tu es	*vous êtes*	*tu as été*	*vous avez été*
il est	*ils sont*	*il a été*	*ils ont été*

Imperfect:

j'étais	*nous étions*
tu étais	*vous étiez*
il était	*ils étaient*

Pluperfect:

j'avais été	*nous avions été*
tu avais été	*vous aviez été*
il avait été	*ils avaient été*

Past historic:

je fus	*nous fûmes*
tu fus	*vous fûtes*
il fut	*ils furent*

Past anterior:

j'eus été	*nous eûmes été*
tu eus été	*vous eûtes été*
il eut été	*ils eurent été*

Future:

je serai	*nous serons*
tu seras	*vous serez*
il sera	*ils seront*

Compound future:

j'aurai été	*nous aurons été*
tu auras été	*vous aurez été*
il aura été	*ils auront été*

Conditional:

je serais	*nous serions*
tu serais	*vous seriez*
il serait	*ils seraient*

Compound conditional:

j'aurais été	*nous aurions été*
tu aurais été	*vous auriez été*
il aurait été	*ils auraient été*

9.1.2.2 *The imperative mood*

Present:

sois, soyons, soyez

9.1.2.3 *The subjunctive mood*

Present:

que je sois	*que nous soyons*
que tu sois	*que vous soyez*
que'il soit	*qu'ils soient*

Compound past:

que j'aie été	*que nous ayons été*
que tu aies été	*que vous ayez été*
qu'il ait été	*qu'ils aient été*

Imperfect:

que je fusse	*que nous fussions*
que tu fusses	*que vous fussiez*
qu'il fût	*qu'ils fussent*

Pluperfect:

que j'eusse été	*que nous eussions été*
que tu eusses été	*que vous eussiez été*
qu'il eût été	*qu'ils eussent été*

9.1.2.4 *The nominal mood*
(i) The infinitives

Simple form:	Compound form:
être	*avoir été*

(ii) The participles

Simple forms:	Compound form:
étant/été	*ayant été*

9.1.2.5 *The passive forms* Whether *être* is seen in its auxiliary role or in its lexical role, it will be obvious that passive forms would be semantically a nonsense.

9.2   Morphological tables for the regular verbs

9.2.1   *1st conjugation verbs taking the auxiliary 'avoir'*

9.2.1.1   *The indicative mood*

Simple tenses: Compound tenses:

Present: Compound past:[19]

je chante	*nous chantons*	*j'ai chanté*	*nous avons chanté*
tu chantes	*vous chantez*	*tu as chanté*	*vous avez chanté*
il chante	*ils chantent*	*il a chanté*	*ils ont chanté*

Imperfect: Pluperfect:

je chantais	*nous chantions*	*j'avais chanté*	*nous avions chanté*
tu chantais	*vous chantiez*	*tu avais chanté*	*vous aviez chanté*
il chantait	*ils chantaient*	*il avait chanté*	*ils avaient chanté*

Past historic: Past anterior:

je chantai	*nous chantâmes*	*j'eus chanté*	*nous eûmes chanté*
tu chantas	*vous chantâtes*	*tu eus chanté*	*vous eûtes chanté*
il chanta	*ils chantèrent*	*il eut chanté*	*ils eurent chanté*

Future: Compound future:

je chanterai	*nous chanterons*	*j'aurai chanté*	*nous aurons chanté*
tu chanteras	*vous chanterez*	*tu auras chanté*	*vous aurez chanté*
il chantera	*ils chanteront*	*il aura chanté*	*ils auront chanté*

Conditional: Compound conditional:

je chanterais	*nous chanterions*	*j'aurais chanté*	*nous aurions chanté*
tu chanterais	*vous chanteriez*	*tu aurais chanté*	*vous auriez chanté*
il chanterait	*ils chanteraient*	*il aurait chanté*	*ils auraient chanté*

Double compound tenses:[20]
(infrequently used, especially in the written mode)

Double compound past:

j'ai eu chanté	*nous avons eu chanté*
tu as eu chanté	*vous avez eu chanté*
il a eu chanté	*ils ont eu chanté*

Compound pluperfect:

j'avais eu chanté	*nous avions eu chanté*
tu avais eu chanté	*vous aviez eu chanté*
il avait eu chanté	*ils avaient eu chanté*

Double compound future:

j'aurai eu chanté	*nous aurons eu chanté*
tu auras eu chanté	*vous aurez eu chanté*
il aura eu chanté	*ils auront eu chanté*

Double compound conditional:

j'aurais eu chanté	*nous aurions eu chanté*
tu aurais eu chanté	*vous auriez eu chanté*
il aurait eu chanté	*ils auraient eu chanté*

9.2.1.2   *The imperative mood*

Simple form:	Compound form:
chante	*aie chanté*
chantons	*ayons chanté*
chantez	*ayez chanté*

9.2.1.3   *The subjunctive mood*

Present:

que je chante	*que nous chantions*
que tu chantes	*que vous chantiez*
qu'il chante	*qu'ils chantent*

Compound past:

que j'aie chanté	*que nous ayons chanté*
que tu aies chanté	*que vous ayez chanté*
qu'il ait chanté	*qu'ils aient chanté*

Pluperfect:

que j'eusse chanté	*que nous eussions chanté*
que tu eusses chanté	*que vous eussiez chanté*
qu'il eût chanté	*qu'ils eussent chanté*

Imperfect:

que je chantasse	*que nous chantassions*
que tu chantasses	*que vous chantassiez*
qu'il chantât	*qu'ils chantassent*

Double compound past:

que j'aie eu chanté	*que nous ayons eu chanté*
que tu aies eu chanté	*que vous ayez eu chanté*
qu'il ait eu chanté	*qu'ils aient eu chanté*

9.2.1.4   *The nominal mood*
(i) The infinitives

Simple form:	Compound form:	Double compound form:
chanter	*avoir chanté*	*avoir eu chanté*

(ii) The participles

Simple form:	Compound form:	Double compound form:
chantant	*ayant chanté*	*ayant eu chanté*

9.2.1.5   *Classification of the past participle*   Past participles usually belong to the passive voice. In the active voice there are basically three forms: *chantant, ayant* *chanté* and *ayant eu chanté*. In the passive voice there are also three forms: *chanté*, *ayant chanté* and *ayant été chanté*.

This does not apply to verbs which cannot take the passive (namely *avoir* and the intransitive verbs).

9.2.2   *The passive voice*

This uses the auxiliary *être* instead of *avoir*, e.g. *être aimé(e)(s)*. The change of example from *chanter* to *aimer* is because, although *être chanté* may be conjugated morphologically in all tenses and all persons, to do so in all but the 3rd person creates a semantic nonsense.

The tables given below show masculine gender only. Use of a feminine subject would of course entail agreement of the past participle, e.g.

je suis aimée	*nous sommes aimées*
tu es aimée	*vous etes aimées*
elle est aimée	*elles sont àimées*

Where a plural subject is made up of both masculine and feminine persons or things, the masculine form is used.

9.2.2.1   *The indicative mood*

Present:

je suis aimé	*nous sommes aimés*
tu es aimé	*vous êtes aimés*
il est aimé	*ils sont aimés*

Compound past:

j'ai été aimé	*nous avons été aimés*
tu as été aimé	*vous avez été aimés*
il a été aimé	*ils ont été aimés*

Imperfect:

j'étais aimé	*nous étions aimés*
tu étais aimé	*vous étiez aimés*
il était aimé	*ils étaient aimés*

Pluperfect:

j'avais été aimé	*nous avions été aimés*
tu avais été aimé	*vous aviez été aimés*
il avait été aimé	*ils avaient été aimés*

Past historic:

je fus aimé	*nous fûmes aimés*
tu fus aimé	*vous fûtes aimés*
il fut aimé	*ils furent aimés*

Past anterior:

j'eus été aimé	*nous eûmes été aimés*
tu eus été aimé	*vous eûtes été aimés*
il eut été aimé	*ils eurent été aimés*

Future:

je serai aimé	*nous serons aimés*
tu seras aimé	*vous serez aimés*
il sera aimé	*ils seront aimés*

Compound future:

j'aurai été aimé	*nous aurons été aimés*
tu auras été aimé	*vous aurez été aimés*
il aura été aimé	*ils auront été aimés*

Conditional:

je serais aimé	*nous serions aimés*
tu serais aimé	*vous seriez aimés*
il serait aimé	*ils seraient aimés*

Compound conditional:

j'aurais été aimé	*nous aurions été aimés*
tu aurais été aimé	*vous auriez été aimés*
il aurait été aimé	*ils auraient été aimés*

9.2.2.2   *The imperative mood*   This is rare in use and frequently difficult to accept semantically.

Simple form:

sois aimé
soyons aimés
soyez aimés

Compound form:

aie été aimé
ayons été aimés
ayez été aimés

9.2.2.3 *The subjunctive mood*

Present:

que je sois aimé	*que nous soyons aimés*
que tu sois aimé	*que vous soyez aimés*
qu'il soit aimé	*qu'ils soient aimés*

Compound past:

que j'aie été aimé	*que nous ayons été aimés*
que tu aies été aimé	*que vous ayez été aimés*
qu'il ait été aimé	*qu'ils aient été aimés*

Imperfect:

que je fusse aimé	*que nous fussions aimés*
que tu fusses aimé	*que vous fussiez aimés*
qu'il fût aimé	*qu'ils fussent aimés*

Pluperfect:

que j'eusse été aimé	*que nous eussions été aimés*
que tu eusses été aimé	*que vous eussiez été aimés*
qu'il eût été aimé	*qu'ils eussent été aimés*

9.2.2.4 *The nominal mood*

(i) The infinitives

Compound form (or 'basic form'):	Double compound form:
être aimé	*avoir été aimé*

(ii) The participles

Simple form:	Compound form:	Double compound form:
aimé	*étant aimé*	*ayant été aimé*

9.2.3 *1st conjugation verbs taking the auxiliary 'être'*

Only forms of the active voice can exist for these verbs.

The tables given below, as before, show masculine gender only (except in the imperative and nominal moods). However, the past participle of verbs conjugated with *être* agrees in all cases both in gender and in number with the noun or pronoun to which it refers, which is the subject in all finite forms, e.g.

je suis tombé(e)	*nous sommes tombé(e)s*
tu es tombé(e)	*vous êtes tombé(e)s*
il (elle) est tombé(e)	*ils (elles) sont tombé(e)s*

Where a plural subject is made up of both masculine and feminine persons or things, the masculine form is used.

9.2.3.1 *The indicative mood*

	Simple tenses:		Compound tenses:

Present:

je tombe	*nous tombons*
tu tombes	*vous tombez*
il tombe	*ils tombent*

Compound past:

je suis tombé	*nous sommes tombés*
tu es tombé	*vous êtes tombés*
il est tombé	*ils sont tombés*

Imperfect:

je tombais	*nous tombions*
tu tombais	*vous tombiez*
il tombait	*ils tombaient*

Pluperfect:

j'étais tombé	*nous étions tombés*
tu étais tombé	*vous étiez tombés*
il était tombé	*ils étaient tombés*

Past historic:

je tombai	*nous tombâmes*
tu tombas	*vous tombâtes*
il tomba	*ils tombèrent*

Past anterior:

je fus tombé	*nous fûmes tombés*
tu fus tombé	*vous fûtes tombés*
il fut tombé	*ils furent tombés*

Future:

je tomberai	*nous tomberons*
tu tomberas	*vous tomberez*
il tombera	*ils tomberont*

Compound future:

je serai tombé	*nous serons tombés*
tu seras tombé	*vous serez tombés*
il sera tombé	*ils seront tombés*

Conditional:

je tomberais	*nous tomberions*
tu tomberais	*vous tomberiez*
il tomberait	*ils tomberaient*

Compound conditional:

je serais tombé	*nous serions tombés*
tu serais tombé	*vous seriez tombés*
il serait tombé	*ils seraient tombés*

The double compound tenses are very rare; the verb *tomber* has been replaced by *rentrer* for semantic reasons.

Double compound past:

la table a été rentrée

Compound pluperfect:

la table avait été rentrée

Double compound future:

la table aura été rentrée

Double compound conditional:

la table aurait été rentrée

9.2.3.2   *The imperative mood*

Simple form:	Compound form:
tombe	⎡ *sois tombé(e)*[22] ⎤
tombons	⎢ *soyons tombé(e)s* ⎢
tombez	⎣ *soyez tombé(e)s* ⎦

9.2.3.3   *The subjunctive mood*

Present:

que je tombe	*que nous tombions*
que tu tombes	*que vous tombiez*
qu'il tombe	*qu'ils tombent*

Compound past:

que je sois tombé	*que nous soyons tombés*
que tu sois tombé	*que vous soyez tombés*
qu'il soit tombé	*qu'ils soient tombés*

Imperfect:

que je tombasse	*que nous tombassions*
que tu tombasses	*que vous tombassiez*
qu'il tombât	*qu'ils tombassent*

Pluperfect:

que je fusse tombé	*que nous fussions tombés*
que tu fusses tombé	*que nous fussions tombés*
qu'il fût tombé	*qu'ils fussent tombés*

Double compound past:

[*que j'aie été tombé*	*que nous ayons été tombés*]
que tu aies été tombé	*que vous ayez été tombés*
qu'il ait été tombé	*qu'ils aient été tombés*]

9.2.3.4 *The nominal mood*

(i) The infinitives

Simple form:	Compound form:	Double compound form:
tomber	*être tombé(e)(s)*	[*avoir été tombé(e)(s)*]

(ii) The participles

Simple form:	Compound form:	Double compound form:
tombant	*étant tombé(e)(s)*	[*ayant été tombé(e)(s)*]
tombé(e)(s)		

9.2.3.5 *Verbs taking 'être' in their compound forms* In addition to all the compound tenses of pronominal verbs[23] which take *être* as auxiliary, the following verbs also take *être*: *aller, arriver, décéder, devenir, échoir, éclore, entrer, mourir, naître, partir, repartir, rentrer, rester, retourner, sortir, tomber, venir, revenir, parvenir, survenir,* together with a number of less frequent derivatives of these verbs, e.g. *redevenir, ressortir, retomber.* It will be noted that these verbs are generally those indicating motion in some direction or a change of state.

Note: Some verbs taking *être* in their intransitive form may also be used transitively, in which case they are conjugated with *avoir*, e.g. *je suis sorti/j'ai sorti ma clé*; *je suis rentré/j'ai rentré les fauteuils.*

9.2.4 *2nd conjugation regular verbs with a present participle ending in '-issant'*

9.2.4.1 *The indicative mood*

Simple tenses: Compound tenses:

Present: Compound past:

je finis	*nous finissons*	*j'ai fini*	*nous avons fini*
tu finis	*vous finissez*	*tu as fini*	*vous avez fini*
il finit	*ils finissent*	*il a fini*	*ils ont fini*

Imperfect: Pluperfect:

je finissais	*nous finissions*	*j'avais fini*	*nous avions fini*
tu finissais	*vous finissiez*	*tu avais fini*	*vous aviez fini*
il finissait	*ils finissaient*	*il avait fini*	*ils avaient fini*

Past historic: Past anterior:

je finis	*nous finîmes*	*j'eus fini*	*nous eûmes fini*
tu finis	*vous finîtes*	*tu eus fini*	*vous eûtes fini*
il finit	*ils finirent*	*il eut fini*	*ils eurent fini*

Future:

		Compound future:	
je finirai	*nous finirons*	*j'aurai fini*	*nous aurons fini*
tu finiras	*vous finirez*	*tu auras fini*	*vous aurez fini*
il finira	*ils finiront*	*il aura fini*	*ils auront fini*

Conditional:

		Compound conditional:	
je finirais	*nous finirions*	*j'aurais fini*	*nous aurions fini*
tu finirais	*vous finiriez*	*tu aurais fini*	*vous auriez fini*
il finirait	*ils finiraient*	*il aurait fini*	*ils auraient fini*

Double compound tenses:

Double compound past:

		Compound pluperfect:	
j'ai eu fini	*nous avons eu fini*	*j'avais eu fini*	*nous avions eu fini*
tu as eu fini	*vous avez eu fini*	*tu avais eu fini*	*vous aviez eu fini*
il a eu fini	*ils ont eu fini*	*il avait eu fini*	*ils avaient eu fini*

Double compound future:

		Double compound conditional:	
j'aurai eu fini	*nous aurons eu fini*	*j'aurais eu fini*	*nous aurions eu fini*
tu auras eu fini	*vous aurez eu fini*	*tu aurais eu fini*	*vous auriez eu fini*
il aura eu fini	*ils auront eu fini*	*il aurait eu fini*	*ils auraient eu fini*

9.2.4.2   *The imperative mood*

Simple form:	Compound form:
finis	*aie fini*
finissons	*ayons fini*
finissez	*ayez fini*

9.2.4.3   *The subjunctive mood*

Present:

que je finisse	*que nous finissions*
que tu finisses	*que vous finissiez*
qu'il finisse	*qu'ils finissent*

Compound past:

que j'aie fini	*que nous ayons fini*
que tu aies fini	*que vous ayez fini*
qu'il ait fini	*qu'ils aient fini*

Pluperfect:

que j'eusse fini	*que nous eussions fini*
que tu eusses fini	*que vous eussiez fini*
qu'il eût fini	*qu'ils eussent fini*

Imperfect:

que je finisse	*que nous finissions*
que tu finisses	*que vous finissiez*
qu'il finît	*qu'ils finissent*

Double compound past:

que j'aie eu fini	*que nous ayons eu fini*
que tu aies eu fini	*que vous ayez eu fini*
qu'il ait eu fini	*qu'ils aient eu fini*

9.2.4.4 *The nominal mood*
(i) The infinitives

Simple form:	Compound form:	Double compound form:
finir	*avoir fini*	*avoir eu fini*

(ii) The participles

Simple forms:	Compound form:	Double compound form:
finissant	*ayant fini*	*ayant eu fini*
fini		

Note: Finissant and *fini* differ in aspect, *finissant* referring to the action seen midstream (*aspect sécant*) and *fini* referring to a completed action, when used verbally (see Ch. 8, section 2).

9.2.4.5 *The passive forms* Forms of the passive voice will not be shown separately for this and the remaining conjugations of verbs, as in all cases passive forms are the same for all verbs capable of being employed in this voice, except that in each particular instance the past participle of the appropriate verb is used; otherwise forms are the same as those for *aimer* (see 9.2.2).

9.2.5 *3rd conjugation regular verbs with a present participle without infix '-iss-'*

9.2.5.1 *The indicative mood*

Simple tenses: Compound tenses:

Present: Compound past:

je mens	*nous mentons*	*j'ai menti*	*nous avons menti*
tu mens	*vous mentez*	*tu as menti*	*vous avez menti*
il ment	*ils mentent*	*il a menti*	*ils ont menti*

Imperfect: Pluperfect:

je mentais	*nous mentions*	*j'avais menti*	*nous avions menti*
tu mentais	*vous mentiez*	*tu avais menti*	*vous aviez menti*
il mentait	*ils mentaient*	*il avait menti*	*ils avaient menti*

Past historic: Past anterior:

je mentis	*nous mentîmes*	*j'eus menti*	*nous eûmes menti*
tu mentis	*vous mentîtes*	*tu eus menti*	*vous eûtes menti*
il mentit	*ils mentirent*	*il eut menti*	*ils eurent menti*

Future: Compound future:

je mentirai	*nous mentirons*	*j'aurai menti*	*nous aurons menti*
tu mentiras	*vous mentirez*	*tu auras menti*	*vous aurez menti*
il mentira	*ils mentiront*	*il aura menti*	*ils auront menti*

Conditional:

je mentirais	nous mentirions
tu mentirais	vous mentiriez
il mentirait	ils mentiraient

Compound conditional:

j'aurais menti	nous aurions menti
tu aurais menti	vous auriez menti
il aurait menti	ils auraient menti

Double compound tenses:

Double compound past:

j'ai eu menti	nous avons eu menti
tu as eu menti	vous avez eu menti
il a eu menti	ils ont eu menti

Compound pluperfect:

j'avais eu menti	nous avions eu menti
tu avais eu menti	vous aviez eu menti
il avait eu menti	ils avaient eu menti

Double compound future:

j'aurai eu menti	nous aurons eu menti
tu auras eu menti	vous aurez eu menti
il aura eu menti	ils auront eu menti

Double compound conditional:

j'aurais eu menti	nous aurions eu menti
tu aurais eu menti	vous auriez eu menti
il aurait eu menti	ils auraient eu menti

9.2.5.2   *The imperative mood*

	Simple form:	Compound form:
	mens	*aie menti*
	mentons	*ayons menti*
	mentez	*ayez menti*

9.2.5.3   *The subjunctive mood*

Present:

que je mente	que nous mentions
que tu mentes	que vous mentiez
qu'il mente	qu'ils mentent

Compound past:

que j'aie menti	que nous ayons menti
que tu aies menti	que vous ayez menti
qu'il ait menti	qu'ils aient menti

Pluperfect:

que j'eusse menti	que nous eussions menti
que tu eusses menti	que vous eussiez menti
qu'il eût menti	qu'ils eussent menti

Imperfect:

que je mentisse	que nous mentissions
que tu mentisses	que vous mentissiez
qu'il mentît	qu'ils mentissent

Double compound past:

que j'aie eu menti	que nous ayons eu menti
que tu aies eu menti	que vous ayez eu menti
qu'il ait eu menti	qu'ils aient eu menti

9.2.5.4 *The nominal mood*

(i) The infinitives

Simple form:	Compound form:	Double compound form:
mentir	*avoir menti*	*avoir eu menti*

(ii) The participles

Simple form:	Compound form:	Double compound form:
mentant	*ayant menti*	*ayant eu menti*

9.2.5.5 *The passive form*   *Mentir* cannot be passivized since it is intransitive; but other verbs of this conjugation, such as *revêtir*, may be passivized in the manner indicated in 9.2.2.

The past participle of *mentir* is *menti*. Such a form may only be found in the compound tenses; it cannot be used adjectivally (**une parole mentie*, for example, is impossible).

9.2.5.6 *3rd conjugation verbs taking the auxiliary 'être'*   Certain verbs in this group – *sortir, partir* and their derivatives – are conjugated with *être* when used intransitively. The morphological pattern is the same as that for -*er* verbs conjugated with *être* but using, of course, the past participle of the appropriate verb, e.g.

Compound past:	Pluperfect:	Past anterior:	Compound future:
je suis sorti	*j'étais sorti*	*je fus sorti*	*je serai sorti*
etc.			

Compound conditional:	Past subjunctive:	Pluperfect subjunctive:
je serais sorti	*que je sois sorti*	*que je fusse sorti*

9.2.6 *4th conjugation regular verbs*

9.2.6.1 *The indicative mood*

Simple tenses: Compound tenses:

Present:

je rends	*nous rendons*	*j'ai rendu*	*nous avons rendu*
tu rends	*vous rendez*	*tu as rendu*	*vous avez rendu*
il rend	*ils rendent*	*il a rendu*	*ils ont rendu*

Imperfect: Pluperfect:

je rendais	*nous rendions*	*j'avais rendu*	*nous avions rendu*
tu rendais	*vous rendiez*	*tu avais rendu*	*vous aviez rendu*
il rendait	*ils rendaient*	*il avait rendu*	*ils avaient rendu*

Past historic: Past anterior:

je rendis	*nous rendîmes*	*j'eus rendu*	*nous eûmes rendu*
tu rendis	*vous rendîtes*	*tu eus rendu*	*vous eûtes rendu*
il rendit	*ils rendirent*	*il eut rendu*	*ils eurent rendu*

Future:

je rendrai	nous rendrons
tu rendras	vous rendrez
il rendra	ils rendront

Compound future:

j'aurai rendu	nous aurons rendu
tu auras rendu	vous aurez rendu
il aura rendu	ils auront rendu

Conditional:

je rendrais	nous rendrions
tu rendrais	vous rendriez
il rendrait	ils rendraient

Compound conditional:

j'aurais rendu	nous aurions rendu
tu aurais rendu	vous auriez rendu
il aurait rendu	ils auraient rendu

Double compound tenses:

Double compound past:

j'ai eu rendu	nous avons eu rendu
tu as eu rendu	vous avez eu rendu
il a eu rendu	ils ont eu rendu

Compound pluperfect:

j'avais eu rendu	nous avions eu rendu
tu avais eu rendu	vous aviez eu rendu
il avait eu rendu	ils avaient eu rendu

Double compound future:

j'aurai eu rendu	nous aurons eu rendu
tu auras eu rendu	vous aurez eu rendu
il aura eu rendu	ils auront eu rendu

Double compound conditional:

j'aurais eu rendu	nous aurions eu rendu
tu aurais eu rendu	vous auriez eu rendu
il aurait eu rendu	ils auraient eu rendu

9.2.6.2   *The imperative mood*

Simple forms:	Compound forms:
rends	aie rendu
rendons	ayons rendu
rendez	ayez rendu

9.2.6.3   *The subjunctive mood*

Present:

que je rende	que nous rendions
que tu rendes	que vous rendiez
qu'il rende	qu'ils rendent

Compound past:

que j'aie rendu	que nous ayons rendu
que tu aies rendu	que vous ayez rendu
qu'il ait rendu	qu'ils aient rendu

Pluperfect:

que j'eusse rendu	que nous eussions rendu
que tu eusses rendu	que vous eussiez rendu
qu'il eût rendu	qu'ils eussent rendu

Imperfect:

que je rendisse	que nous rendissions
que tu rendisses	que vous rendissiez
qu'il rendît	qu'ils rendissent

Double compond past:

que j'aie eu rendu	que nous ayons eu rendu
que tu aies eu rendu	que vous ayez eu rendu
qu'il ait eu rendu	qu'ils aient eu rendu

9.2.6.4 *The nominal mood*

(i) The infinitives

| Simple form: | Compound form: | Double compound form: |
| *rendre* | *avoir rendu* | *avoir eu rendu* |

(ii) The participles

Simple form	Compound form:	Double compound form:
rendant	*ayant rendu*	*ayant eu rendu*
rendu		

9.2.6.5 *The passive forms* These are formed as for all other verbs (see 9.2.2).

9.2.6.6 *4th conjugation verbs taking the auxiliary 'être'* There are no regular verbs of the 4th conjugation taking *être* as their auxiliary. Verbs with *-re* endings conjugated with *être*, e.g. *éclore*, *naître*, are very irregular but do follow the normal pattern as for *-er* verbs in this particular respect.

9.2.7 *5th conjugation verbs*

9.2.7.1 *The indicative mood*

Simple tenses: Compound tenses:

Present: Compound past:

je reçois	*nous recevons*	*j'ai reçu*	*nous avons reçu*
tu reçois	*vous recevez*	*tu as reçu*	*vous avez reçu*
il reçoit	*ils reçoivent*	*il a reçu*	*ils ont reçu*

Imperfect: Pluperfect:

je recevais	*nous recevions*	*j'avais reçu*	*nous avions reçu*
tu recevais	*vous receviez*	*tu avais reçu*	*vous aviez reçu*
il recevait	*ils recevaient*	*il avait reçu*	*ils avaient reçu*

Past historic: Past anterior:

je reçus	*nous reçûmes*	*j'eus reçu*	*nous eûmes reçu*
tu reçus	*vous reçûtes*	*tu eus reçu*	*vous eûtes reçu*
il reçut	*ils reçurent*	*il eut reçu*	*ils eurent reçu*

Future: Compound future:

je recevrai	*nous recevrons*	*j'aurai reçu*	*nous aurons reçu*
tu recevras	*vous recevrez*	*tu auras reçu*	*vous aurez reçu*
il recevra	*ils recevront*	*il aura reçu*	*ils auront reçu*

Conditional:

je recevrais	*nous recevrions*		
tu recevrais	*vous recevriez*		
il recevrait	*ils recevraient*		

Compound conditional:

j'aurais reçu	*nous aurions reçu*
tu aurais reçu	*vous auriez reçu*
il aurait reçu	*ils auraient reçu*

Double Compound Tenses

Double compound past:

j'ai eu reçu	*nous avons eu reçu*
tu as eu reçu	*vous avez eu reçu*
il a eu reçu	*ils ont eu reçu*

Compound pluperfect:

j'avais eu reçu	*nous avions eu reçu*
tu avais eu reçu	*vous aviez eu reçu*
il avait eu reçu	*ils avaient eu reçu*

Double compound future:

j'aurai eu reçu	*nous aurons eu reçu*
tu auras eu reçu	*vous aurez eu reçu*
il aura eu reçu	*ils auront eu reçu*

Double compound conditional

j'aurais eu reçu	*nous aurions eu reçu*
tu aurais eu reçu	*vous auriez eu reçu*
il aurait eu reçu	*ils auraient eu reçu*

9.2.7.2   *The imperative mood*

Simple forms:	Compound forms:[24]
reçois	*aie reçu*
recevons	*ayons reçu*
recevez	*ayez reçu*

9.2.7.3   *The subjunctive mood*

Present:

que je reçoive	*que nous recevions*
que tu reçoives	*que vous receviez*
qu'il reçoive	*qu'ils reçoivent*

Compound past:

que j'aie reçu	*que nous ayons reçu*
que tu aies reçu	*que vous ayez reçu*
qu'il ait reçu	*qu'ils aient reçu*

Imperfect:

que je reçusse	*que nous reçussions*
que tu reçusses	*que vous reçussiez*
qu'il reçût	*qu'ils reçussent*

Pluperfect:

que j'eusse reçu	*que nous eussions reçu*
que tu eusses reçu	*que vous eussiez reçu*
qu'il eût reçu	*qu'ils eussent reçu*

Double compound past:

que j'aie eu reçu	*que nous ayons eu reçu*
que tu aies eu reçu	*que vous ayez eu reçu*
qu'il ait eu reçu	*qu'ils aient eu reçu*

9.2.7.4   *The nominal mood*
(i) The infinitives

Simple form:	Compound form:	Double compound form:
recevoir	*avoir reçu*	*avoir eu reçu*

(ii) The participles

Simple form:	Compound form:	Double compound form:
recevant	*ayant reçu*	*ayant eu reçu*
reçu		

9.2.7.5 *The passive forms* These are formed as for all other verbs (see 9.2.2).

9.2.7.6 *5th conjugation verbs taking the auxiliary 'être'* The only verb in *-oir* to be conjugated with *être* is *échoir*, which is both defective and slightly irregular, but it does follow the same pattern as other verbs which take *être* in the compound tenses.

9.3 The irregular verbs

9.3.1 *General considerations*

The so-called irregularity of French verbs is a purely arbitrary creation of grammarians, depending entirely on what criteria they accept for 'regularity'. New categories or subclasses of 'regular' verbs can be created at will as long as consistent similarities of paradigmatic form can be perceived, but such a process merely becomes counterproductive after a certain point, since the only practical reason for such an operation in language-learning terms is to facilitate the acquisition of knowledge of these verb forms. Several important points should be noted, however, in the context of the following list.

(i) Many of the verbs given in the list form the basis of numerous derivatives. When these are verbs, they are normally conjugated as the root verb, e.g. *venir: devenir, intervenir, parvenir, prévenir, revenir, se souvenir*. Variations sometimes occur, however, in the conjugations of these derivations, as in the case of *prévenir*, which takes *avoir* as auxiliary.

(ii) Other verbs in the list can be seen as models for one or more others, e.g. *construire, cuire, déduire, détruire, enduire, induire, instruire, introduire, produire, réduire, reproduire, séduire* and *traduire*, as well as the derivatives *éconduire* and *reconduire*, are all conjugated like *conduire*, thus forming a sizeable subcategory. Similarly *craindre* is the model for a number of verbs ending in *-aindre* or *-eindre*.

(iii) Certain verbs, e.g. *aller, savoir, vouloir*, have irregular forms in the imperative. These are dealt with in Ch. 7.

(iv) A number of irregular verbs have a past participle which is monosyllabic, ending in *-û*, e.g. *devoir(dû), mouvoir(mû)*, but this is not universal, e.g. *voir(vu)*, nor does it extend to derivatives of such verbs, e.g. *promouvoir (promu), émouvoir (ému)*. Note also *croire (cru)* but *croître (crû)*.

9.3.2 *List of irregular verbs*

The following list does not claim to be comprehensive, but contains the more frequently encountered irregular verbs, showing the tenses in which irregularity occurs. Only the usual main meaning is given as a guide to the kind of context in which the verb is likely to occur. A blank indicates nonexistent verb forms for those verbs which are defective. It is interesting to note that dictionaries vary in the forms they quote for defective verbs. Larousse, for example gives two spellings for *échoir*, the second being *échéoir*; it also gives the form *échéait* for the imperfect. Le Micro-Robert, on the other hand, only gives *échoir* and makes no mention of a possible imperfect. Larousse gives *qu'il échée* as the subjunctive, whereas Mauger (*Grammaire pratique du français d'aujourd'hui*) gives *qu'il échoie*. This is an area of syntactic uncertainty.

   The list follows in very broad outline that used by G. Mauger (*Grammaire pratique du français d'aujourd'hui*). Further information may be found either in *Le nouveau Bescherelle* or in *Le dictionnaire des verbes français* by J. and J.P. Caput.

	Present indicative	Future	Imperfect	Compound past	Past historic	Present subjunctive	Present participle
acquérir (to acquire, purchase)	j'acquiers il acquiert nous acquérons ils acquièrent	j'acquerrai	j'acquérais	j'ai acquis	j'acquis	que j'acquière que nous acquérions qu'ils acquièrent	acquérant
aller (to go)	je vais tu vas il va nous allons vous allez ils vont	j'irai	j'allais	je suis allé	j'allai	que j'aille que nous allions qu'ils aillent	allant
apparaître (to appear, seem)	as for paraître			*Apparaître* is normally conjugated with *être* in the composite tenses whereas *paraître* takes *avoir*.			
assaillir (to attack, assail)	j'assaille nous assaillons ils assaillent	j'assaillirai	j'assaillais	j'ai assailli	j'assaillis	que j'assaille	assaillant
asseoir (cf. seoir) (to sit someone down)	j'assieds il assied nous asseyons ils asseyent or alternative forms (figurative sense): j'assois il assoit nous assoyons ils assoient	j'assiérai j'assoirai	j'asseyais j'assoyais	j'ai assis	j'assis	que j'asseye que j'assoie	asseyant assoyant
battre (to beat)	je bats il bat nous battons	je battrai	je battais	j'ai battu	je battis	que je batte	battant
boire (to drink)	je bois il boit nous buvons ils boivent	je boirai	je buvais	j'ai bu	je bus	que je boive que nous buvions que vons buviez qu'ils boivent	buvant

	Present indicative	Future	Imperfect	Compound past	Past historic	Present subjunctive	Present participle
bouillir (to boil)	*je bous* *il bout* *nous bouillons* *ils bouillent*	*je bouillerai*	*je bouillais*	*j'ai bouilli*	*je bouillis*	*que je bouille*	*bouillant*
braire (to bray – as of asses)	*il brait* *ils braient*	*il braira*	*il brayait*	*il a brait*		*qu'il braie*	*brayant*
bruire (to buzz, murmur)	*il bruit* *ils bruissent*		*il bruissait*	(*bruyant* is not a participle but an adjective)		*qu'il bruisse*	*bruissant*
choir (to fall)	*il choit* (no plural forms)	*il choira*		past participle *chu* is sometimes found	*il chut*		
circoncire (to circumcise)	*je circoncis* *nous circoncisons*	*je circoncirai*	*je circoncisais*	*j'ai circoncis*	*je circoncis*	*que je circoncise*	*circoncisant*
circonvenir (to circumvent)	(conjugated as *venir*, but with aux. *avoir*: *j'ai circonvenu*)						
clore (to close (a debate), end (a speech))	*je clos* *tu clos* *il clôt (no plural forms)*	*je clorai*		*j'ai clos*		*que je close*	
conclure (to conclude)	*je conclus* *il conclut* *nous concluons*	*je conclurai*	*je concluais*	*j'ai conclu*	*je conclus*	*que je conclue*	*concluant*
conduire (to drive – a car)	*je conduis* *il conduit* *nous conduisons*	*je conduirai*	*je conduisais*	*j'ai conduit*	*je conduisis*	*que je conduise*	*conduisant*
confire (to preserve, pickle)	*je confis* *il confit* *nous confisons*	*je confirai*	*je confisais*	*j'ai confit*	*je confis*	*que je confise*	*confisant*

	Present indicative	Future	Imperfect	Compound past	Past historic	Present subjunctive	Present participle
connaître (to know)	*je connais* *il connaît* *nous connaissons*	*je connaîtrai*	*je connaissais*	*j'ai connu*	*je connus*	*que je connaisse*	*connaissant*
contredire: (to contradict)	conjugated as *dire* with the single exception in the present Tense: *vous contredisez*						
contrevenir (to contravené – a rule, etc.)	both conjugated as *venir*, but *contrevenir* has auxiliary *avoir* while *convenir* has either *avoir* or *être* according to meaning (dictionary should be consulted for this)						
convenir (to agree to something)							
coudre (to sew)	*je couds* *il coud* *nous cousons*	*je coudrai*	*je cousais*	*j'ai cousu*	*je cousis*	*que je couse*	*cousant*
courir (to run)	*je cours* *il court* *nous courons*	*je courrai*	*je courais*	*j'ai couru*	*je courus*	*que je coure*	*courant*
craindre (to fear)	*je crains* *il craint* *nous craignons*	*je craindrai*	*je craignais*	*j'ai craint*	*je craignis*	*que je craigne*	*craignant*
croire (to believe)	*je crois* *il croit* *nous croyons* *ils croient*	*je croirai*	*je croyais*	*j'ai cru*	*je crus* *il crut*	*que je croie*	*croyant*
croître (to grow – in size)	*je croîs* *il croît* *nous croissons*	*je croîtrai*	*je croissais*	*j'ai crû*	*je crûs*	*que je croisse*	*croissant*
cueillir (to pick, gather – flowers etc.)	*je cueille* *il cueille* *nous cueillons*	*je cueillerai*	*je cueillais*	*j'ai cueilli*	*je cueillis*	*que je cueille*	*cueillant*

	Present indicative	Future	Imperfect	Compound past	Past historic	Present subjunctive	Present participle
déchoir (to demean oneself)	je déchois il déchoit nous déchoyons	je déchoirai		j'ai déchu je suis déchu (*déchoir* takes auxiliary *avoir* when it denotes an action but *être* when it denotes a state)	je déchus	que je déchoie	
devoir (to owe, or to have to do something)	je dois il doit nous devons	je devrai	je devais	j'ai dû	je dus	que je doive que nous devions que vous deviez qu'ils doivent	devant
dire (to say)	je dis nous disons vous dites	je dirai	je disais	j'ai dit	je dis	que je dise	disant
dissoudre (to dissolve)	(conjugated as *résoudre* except for the past participle *dissous* which has a feminine form *dissoute*)			je l'ai dissous je l'ai dissoute	(not used)		
dormir (to sleep)	je dors il dort nous dormons ils dorment	je dormirai	je dormais	j'ai dormi	je dormis	que je dorme	dormant
échoir also spelt *écheoir* (to fall to someone's lot, or share)	il échoit ils échoient	il échoira il écherra	il échéait	il est échu	il échut	qu'il échoie qu'il échée	échéant (le cas échéant)
éclore (to hatch, open out – of flower bud etc.)	il éclôt ils éclosent	il éclora	il éclorait	il est éclos		qu'il éclose	
écrire (to write)	j'écris il écrit nous écrivons ils écrivent	j'écrirai	j'écrivais	j'ai écrit	j'écrivis	que j'écrive	écrivant
envoyer (to send)	j'envoie il envoie nous envoyons	j'enverrai	j'envoyais	j'ai envoyé	j'envoyai	que j'envoie	envoyant

	Present indicative	Future	Imperfect	Compound past	Past historic	Present subjunctive	Present participle
faillir (to nearly do something)		*je faillirai*		*j'ai failli*	*je faillis*		*faillant*
faire (to do, make)	*je fais* *il fait* *nous faisons* *vous faites* *ils font*	*je ferai*	*je faisais*	*j'ai fait*	*je fis*	*que je fasse* *que nous fassions* *que vous fassiez*	*faisant*
falloir (impersonal) (to be necessary, to need to do something)	*il faut*	*il faudra*	*il fallait*	*il a fallu*	*il fallut*	*qu'il faille*	
frire (to fry)	*je fris* *tu fris* *il frit* (only these forms in use at present)	*je frirai*		*j'ai frit*			
fuir (to flee)	*je fuis* *il fuit* *nous fuyons*	*je fuirai*	*je fuyais*	*j'ai fui*	*je fuis*	*que je fuie*	*fuyant*
gésir (to lie dead)	*je gis* *il gît (ci-gît)* *nous gisons*		*je gisais*				*gisant*
lire (to read)	*je lis* *il lit* *nous lisons*	*je lirai*	*je lisais*	*j'ai lu*	*je lus*	*que je lise*	*lisant*
luire (to gleam, shine)	*je luis* *il luit*	*je luirai*	*je luisais*	*j'ai lui*	*je luisis*	*que je luise*	*luisant*
maudire (to curse)	*je maudis* *il maudit* *nous maudissons*	*je maudirai*	*je maudissais*	*j'ai maudit*	*je maudis*	*que je maudisse*	*maudissant*

	Present indicative	Future	Imperfect	Compound past	Past historic	Present subjunctive	Present participle
mentir (to (tell a) lie)	*je mens* *il ment* *nous mentons*	*je mentirai*	*je mentais*	*j'ai menti*	*je mentis*	*que je mente*	*mentant*
mettre (to put)	*je mets* *il met* *nous mettons*	*je mettrai*	*je mettais*	*j'ai mis*	*je mis*	*que je mette*	*mettant*
moudre (to mill, grind – coffee etc.)	*je mouds* *il moud* *nous moulons* *ils moulent*	*je moudrai*	*je moulais*	*j'ai moulu*	*je moulus*	*que je moule*	*moulant*
mourir (to die)	*je meurs* *il meurt* *nous mourons* *vous mourez* *ils meurent*	*je mourrai*	*je mourais*	*je suis mort*	*je mourus*	*que je meure* *que nous mourions* *qu'ils meurent*	*mourant*
mouvoir (to move)	*je meus* *il meut* *nous mouvons* *ils meuvent*	*je mouvrai*	*je mouvais*	*j'ai mû*	*je mus*	*que je meuve* *que nous mouvions* *qu'ils meuvent*	*mouvant*
naître (to be born)	*je nais* *il naît* *nous naissons*	*je naîtrai*	*je naissais*	*je suis né*	*je naquis*	*que je naisse*	*naissant*
ouvrir (to open)	*j'ouvre* *il ouvre* *nous ouvrons*	*j'ouvrirai*	*j'ouvrais*	*j'ai ouvert*	*j'ouvris*	*que j'ouvre*	*ouvrant*
plaire (to please)	*je plais* *il plaît* *nous plaisons*	*je plairai*	*je plaisais*	*j'ai plu*	*je plus*	*que je plaise*	*plaisant*
pleuvoir (impersonal) (to rain)	*il pleut* *(les coups pleuvent)*	*il pleuvra* *ils pleuvront*	*il pleuvait* *ils pleuvaient*	*il a plu* *ils ont plu*	*il plut* *ils plurent*	*qu'il pleuve* *qu'ils pleuvent*	*pleuvant*

	Present indicative	Future	Imperfect	Compound past	Past historic	Present subjunctive	Present participle
pourvoir (à) (to provide someone with something)	je pourvois il pourvoit nous pourvoyons ils pourvoient	je pourvoirai	je pourvoyais	j'ai pourvu	je pourvus	que je pourvoie	pourvoyant
pouvoir (to be able to do something)	je peux (je puis) il peut nous pouvons ils peuvent	je pourrai	je pouvais	j'ai pu	je pus	que je puisse que nous puissions que vous puissiez	pouvant
prendre (to take)	je prends il prend nous prenons ils prennent	je prendrai	je prenais	j'ai pris	je pris	que je prenne	prenant
résoudre (to resolve – a problem etc.)	je résous il résout nous résolvons	je résoudrai	je résolvais	j'ai résolu	je résolus	que je résolve	résolvant
rire (to laugh)	je ris il rit nous rions	je rirai	je riais	j'ai ri	je ris	que je rie	riant
rompre (to break)	je romps il rompt nous rompons	je romprai	je rompais	j'ai rompu	je rompis	que je rompe	rompant
savoir (to know)	je sais il sait nous savons	je saurai	je savais	j'ai su	je sus	que je sache que nous sachions que vous sachiez	sachant
seoir (to be proper, fitting or becoming)	il sied ils siéent	il siéra ils siéront	il seyait ils seyaient			qu'il siée rare qu'ils siéent	seyant
servir (to serve)	je sers il sert nous servons	je servirai	je servais	j'ai servi	je servis	que je serve	servant

	Present indicative	Future	Imperfect	Compound past	Past historic	Present subjunctive	Present participle
suivre (to follow)	*je suis* *il suit* *nous suivons*	*je suivrai*	*je suivais*	*j'ai suivi*	*je suivis*	*que je suive*	*suivant*
suffire (to suffice)	*je suffis* *nous suffisons*	*je suffirai*	*je suffisais*	*j'ai suffi*	*je suffis*	*que je suffise*	*suffisant*
surseoir (to delay, put off – usually in legal or administrative usage)	*je sursois* *il sursoit* *nous sursoyons* *ils sursoient*	*je surseoirai*	*je sursoyais*	*j'ai sursis*	*je sursis*	*que je sursoie*	*sursoyant*
taire (to be silent)	*je tais* *il tait* *nous taisons*	*je tairai*	*je taisais*	*j'ai tu*	*je tus*	*que je taise*	*taisant*
tendre (to tighten, stretch)	*je tends* *il tend* *nous tendons*	*je tendrai*	*je tendais*	*j'ai tendu*	*je tendis*	*que je tende*	*tendant*
tenir (to hold)	*je tiens* *il tient* *nous tenons* *ils tiennent*	*je tiendrai*	*je tenais*	*j'ai tenu*	*je tins*	*que je tienne*	*tenant*
traire (to milk)	*je trais* *il trait* *nous trayons* *ils traient*	*je trairai*	*je trayais*	*j'ai trait*		*que je traie*	*trayant*
vaincre (to conquer)	*je vaincs* *il vainc* *nous vainquons*	*je vaincrai*	*je vainquais*	*j'ai vaincu*	*je vainquis*	*que je vainque*	*vainquant*
valoir (to be worth)	*je vaux* *il vaut* *nous valons*	*je vaudrai*	*je valais*	*j'ai valu*	*je valus*	*que je vaille* *que nous valions* *qu'ils vaillent*	*valant*

	Present indicative	Future	Imperfect	Compound past	Past historic	Present subjunctive	Present participle
venir (to come)	*je viens* *il vient* *nous venons* *ils viennent*	*je viendrai*	*je venais*	*je suis venu*	*je vins*	*que je vienne*	*venant*
vêtir (to clothe)	*je vêts* *il vêt* *nous vêtons*	*je vêtirai*	*je vêtais*	*j'ai vêtu*	*je vêtis*	*que je vête*	*vêtant*

vêtir is often found conjugated as *finir*; its derivatives
dévêtir and *revêtir* always follow the pattern shown above

	Present indicative	Future	Imperfect	Compound past	Past historic	Present subjunctive	Present participle
voir (to see)	*je vois* *il voit* *nous voyons* *ils voient*	*je verrai*	*je voyais*	*j'ai vu*	*je vis*	*que je voie*	*voyant*
vivre (to live)	*je vis* *il vit* *nous vivons*	*je vivrai*	*je vivais*	*j'ai vécu*	*je vécus*	*que je vive*	*vivant*
vouloir (to want, wish)	*je veux* *il veut* *nous voulons* *ils veulent*	*je voudrai*	*je voulais*	*j'ai voulu*	*je voulus*	*que je veuille* *que nous voulions* *que vous vouliez* *qu'ils veuillent*	*voulant*

Notes

1 For a fuller discussion of this phenomenon, see Price, *The French language*, 199-200. The Latin antecedents of this formation are dealt with in more detail by Wagner in *Les Phrases hypothétiques commençant par 'si. . .'*, 79ff.

2 The theory of infixes to explain these phenomena, useful though it may be, is based purely on formal analysis and has little historical justification, as can be seen from 7.1.1 below: *-r-* in French future and conditional tenses is simply the survival of the *-r-* of Latin infinitives.

3 It follows from this scheme that the use of the infix *-iss-* becomes a logically untenable proposition and it must be modified to *-ss-* if the verb stem is to be taken as *fini-* etc.

4 M.H. Gertner/(*The morphology of the French verb*) has worked out a set of rules, based on transformational phonology, that can be applied to any French verb in order to generate all the forms of that verb. These are '55 morphophonemic rules [with which] we can generate all 51 forms of all regular conjugations in the language, without generating any incorrect forms.' The remaining irregular forms are accounted for by means of another 66 special rules which apply only to certain verbs. These rules relate to written French: spoken French, with its simpler system of verb forms, needs only 33 such rules.

5 See Ch. 5 for the reasons for regrouping these two moods.

6 See G. Mauger, *Grammaire pratique du français d'aujourd'hui*, 232.

7 According to Grevisse (*Le Bon usage*, 9th edn, 614), 'La tradition a longtemps maintenu pour les verbes français la classification latine en quatre conjugaisons caractérisées par les désinences de l'infinitif: *-er*, *-ir*, *-oir*, *-re*. Cette classification est à peu près abandonnée aujourd'hui: elle est purement historique, en effet, et ne saurait s'appliquer à la langue moderne, qui ne présente pas, en réalité, quatre systèmes de flexion différentes selon les quatre conjugaisons traditionelles.' While this is undeniably true, the old system had become well established, even if it was particularly perverse in not clearly making the distinction between the two groups of *-ir* verbs. The 3-group system which by and large seems to have replaced it (*-er*, *-ir* (like *finir*), and an undifferentiated 3rd group) seems to be singularly unhelpful to non-native learners of French, since it ignores such helpful traces of regularity as undoubtedly exist among the verbs of the so-called 3rd group. It is interesting to note that Grevisse himself, in his *Précis de grammaire française*, uses a 5-group classification very similar to that used in the present book.

8 Normally hardly any new verbs in *-ir* are now formed, *alunir* being an exception since the verb *aluner* (= *imprégner de dissolution d'alun*) already exists.

9 An asterisk, in historical linguistics, denotes a reconstructed form.

10 The latter, in Latin, being in *-ire*.

11 For amplification of this and similar points see Anglade, *Grammaire élémentaire de l'ancien français*, 8th edn, 112f.

12 See Anglade, *op. cit.*, 126f for an example of this treatment of French verbs in a historical context.

13 The present participle *oyant* and the imperative *oyez* would appear to be obsolete now. Harrap's *New Standard French and English Dictionary* allows the possibility that a future and a past historic tense of *ouïr* may exist, as in *les dimanches messe ouïras* (= *tu entendras*). But − despite Harrap's − this term is totally obsolete.

14 Wagner and Pinchon (*Grammaire du français classique et moderne*, 262) state: 'Dans ces emplois, le pronom *il* n'est pas un représentant. On ne peut l'analyser comme terme de phrase. Il n'est que l'indice morphologique de la 3e personne du singulier.'

15 For a discussion of the other obvious case in which *il* is not invariably used (*il est. . .* − *c'est. . .*) see Ch. 3.

16 The same idea can be expressed by saying that if the adding of the suffix gives an endocentric construction at word level the meaning will be changed, whereas in an exocentric construction it is the class of the word which will have changed.

17 *Tayloriser* – after the American time and motion expert Frederick Winslow Taylor (1856-1915). See *Nouveau Petit Larousse*: '*Tayloriser v.t. procéder à une taylorisation.*' This method of producing verbal forms by adding suffixes to proper nouns was clearly known and used in the time of Molière, at least for comic effect, as in the following from *Le Tartuffe*:

Non, vous serez, ma foi, tartuffiée.

18 Gertner (*The morphology of the French verb*) quotes hundreds of words produced by such suffixations, many of which are not in the dictionary, but each of which could, given the right context, fulfil a unique role. Gertner also quotes the following text illustrating the use which can be made of this creative type of derivation.

J'enumérais tout à l'heure la multitude des suffixes verboverbaux. Mais combien aiguëment un Français en sent-il la diversité sémantique quand on les applique au même verbe primitif! Dans la pièce commune d'une maison, l'enfant tournille, ça et là en des jeux inconsistants et gracieux, cependant que sottement la ménagère tournique sans rien faire d'utile, sans savoir à quelle occupation se donner; voilà qu'elle tournouille un coup la soupe qui cuit tranquillement sur le feu; elle regarde dans son placard un reste de lait qui a l'air d'avoir tournoché; elle tournicote autour de son mari et l'accable d'observations et de questions alors qu'il voudrait travailler tranquille. Au dehors se prolonge une fête foraine à demi-déserte: un pauvre manège de chevaux de bois tournote, presque sans clients; cependant une prostituée tournasse encore dans ces parages, obstinée, et des mauvais garçons tournaillent en quête d'un mauvais coup.

19 This is the form often misleadingly called the perfect tense (see Introduction to Part II, section 4).

20 Since these tenses follow exactly the same morphological pattern for all verbs, the double compound paradigms will only be shown for verbs of the 1st conjugation.

21 It will be apparent that all tenses of the passive voice are in reality compound tenses, and that those tenses which are compound in the active voice really become double compound tenses in the passive voice. There are no tenses in the passive voice when correspond to the double compound forms of the active voice.

22 There are some cases where verb forms are morphologically possible but semantically unlikely or impossible. Where these forms are shown, they are set within square brackets.

23 Although in general pronominal verbs are conjugated with *être* in a similar way to the verbs dealt with here, there are special rules relating to the agreement of the past participles of such verbs: such agreement does not invariably take place. This is dealt with in Ch. 8.

24 The periphrastic construction *tâche d'avoir reçu* is possible, however, as in *tâche d'avoir reçu ton passeport avant jeudi*.

Part III
The modifiers: adjectives and adverbs

(i) A modifier is a word which adds a complement of information to another word which dominates it within a syntactic group. Thus an adjective may modify a noun (as in *la robe rouge*); and an adverb may modify an adjective (as in *la couleur de cette robe est trop vive*), a verb (as in *il court vite*), another adverb as in (*il court trop vite*) or even a whole sentence (as in *sans doute viendra-t-il plus tard*). Generally speaking, adjectives modify nouns whereas adverbs may modify anything which may dominate them syntactically, but mainly verbs and adjectives.

(ii) The complement of information carried by the modifier may be essential or nonessential: it may limit the meaning of the word modified, in which case it will be restrictive; but if the information is nonessential, it will be nonrestrictive and the modifier will be detached from the rest of the clause by pauses, or by commas in the written language. Such a construction is said to be 'disjunctive'. Compare:

les enfants attentifs écoutaient la leçon
les enfants, attentifs, écoutaient la leçon (disjunctive)

In the first sentence only those children who were attentive were listening whereas in the second all the children were listening. In the first sentence the adjective delimits a subcategory of 'children', whereas in the second it does not. The term 'disjunctive' applies equally well to adverbs and to adjectives. Compare:

je vais y aller peut-être lundi
je vais y aller, peut-être, lundi (disjunctive)

In the first sentence the adverb modifies *lundi*; in the second the adverb is detached from what precedes and follows it: it modifies the clause as a whole.

(iii) The following problems are associated with the adjective:

(a) Although the principle of agreement is simple to understand, it is sometimes quite difficult to apply because of the many peculiarities involved (e.g. *joli/jolie* but *roux/rousse*; *bon/bonne, flatteur/flatteuse* and *consolateur/consolatrice*).

(b) The place of the adjective is problematic, because of the changes of emphasis and meaning which may be achieved by changing its position in the sentence. The place of the adjective has also changed considerably over time.

(c) As far as translation is concerned there is a shortage of adjectives in French compared to English; there is a particular shortage of relational adjectives, i.e. adjectives which correspond to nouns (i.e. *la chaleur solaire = la chaleur du soleil*). The fact that new relational adjectives are being created in great numbers at present only partly solves the problem.

(iv) Adverbs are particularly difficult to cope with because they may fulfil quite different functions and carry quite different meanings, depending on their position in the clause. They may modify a word in terms of quantity or quality (as in *il a trop mangé* and *il a bien mangé*); they may modify the modality of the clause or sentence (*peut-être viendra-t-il lundi*); they may refer to the manner in which the action has been carried out (*il a fait son travail soigneusement*), in which case it replaces a prepositional phrase functioning as an adverbial (i.e. *il a fait son travail avec soin*); finally the

adverbs of place and time are the direct equivalent of adverbials of place and time: there is no difference between the function of *demain* (which is usually classified as an adverb) and of *le lendemain* (which is a noun) in *il viendra demain* and *il viendra le lendemain*.

Adverbs are also used in comparative and superlative constructions (as in *il est plus petit que son frère* and *c'est le plus grand*). Negation too is expressed through the use of adverbs, as in *je n'ai ni pain ni vin* or *je n'ai pas pu le faire*. Finally, adverbs are used in some cases as syntactical links (cf. Ch. 15 on subordinators at the level of the clause and Ch. 16 on coordination).

It is the incredible flexibility of the adverb, its multiplicity of uses, which makes it one of the most versatile elements in the language.

Chapter 11

The Adjective

0 General considerations

(i) Adjectives are marked for both gender and number, which means that an adjective may have four forms: masculine singular and masculine plural, feminine singular and feminine plural. The choice of one form rather than another depends on the gender and number of the noun modified: *un petit garçon/des petits garçons; une petite fille/des petites filles*.

But although the categories of gender and number are both expressed in the written language, the category of number is only rarely expressed in the spoken language, since the final plural *-s* in modern French is no longer pronounced. For gender, number and agreement, see sections 1 and 2.

(ii) Adjectives may be basic or relational

Compare:

un chat noir = un chat qui est noir
la chaleur solaire = la chaleur du soleil

In the first example the adjective is 'basic': it refers to a quality of the noun. In the second, the adjective is 'relational': it corresponds to a *de* + noun construction and usually expresses possession, place of origin, or − as in this case − the psychological subject of the action represented by the noun (= *le soleil chauffe*) − see section 5. The distinction between these two types of adjectives is important because relational adjectives are syntactically restricted (see section 3) and because they present major translation problems from English into French (see section 5).

(iii) One of the difficulties related to the adjective in French is the flexibility of its place. Some must be placed before the noun, some must be placed after the noun, and some may appear in both positions; but choice of one or other position will have important stylistic and semantic consequences (see section 4).

(iv) There are numerous types of problems associated with the translation of adjectives from English into French and vice versa. Each problem has been examined under the section concerned: restrictions in terms of the number of adjectives which may be used to modify one noun and the order in which they may appear in 4.2.1.2, 4.2.2.2 and 4.2.3; the problem of the translation into French of English relational adjectives in 5.3; and the problems of the translation of nominalized French adjectives into English in 3.6.

(v) Ordinal adjectives such as *premier, second, troisième* function as do basic adjectives. They are however morphologically derived from cardinal numerals which function as determiners, and they are therefore examined in Ch. 2 under the heading 'Determiners'.

(vi) Whereas in English the adjective may be modified morphologically to express the comparative and the superlative (as in 'big/bigger/biggest'), the same does not apply to French: adverbs are used instead (*grand/plus grand/le plus grand*). Comparatives and superlatives are therefore examined in Ch. 12.

(vii) Past participles and present participles may be used adjectivally, as in *une*

personne affolée and *une nouvelle affolante*. Reference to these adjectival uses of the verb is made in Ch. 8.

1   Forms of the adjective

Adjectives vary in gender and in number; these changes may be simply orthographic, or they may be phonetic as well. But whereas these morphological changes are simple where number is concerned (see 1.2) they are extremely complex where gender is concerned (see 1.1 and table at the end of this chapter). The choice of one form rather than another is a matter of syntax, since adjectives agree with the noun they modify, whether their function is epithetic or attributive (see 3.1).

1.1   Changes due to gender

1.1.1   *The general rule*

(i) The general rule is that the feminine form of the adjective is obtained by adding an *-e* to the masculine form: *bleu/bleue; petit/petite; net/nette*. The addition of an *-e* will not affect pronunciation if the adjective ends in a vowel or a sounded consonant, e.g. *dur/dure; joli/jolie*.

(ii) The addition of an *-e* may entail certain changes.

It may entail changes in pronunciation (*fort/forte; brun/brune*) – see 1.1.2.

It may entail changes in both pronunciation and spelling: (*sot/sotte; blanc/blanche*) – see 1.1.3. Adjectives ending in *-eur* may follow three different patterns (*antérieur/antérieure; flatteur/flatteuse; consolateur/consolatrice*), so these are discussed separately in 1.1.4.

In some rare cases the feminine forms are based on archaic masculine forms (*beau/bel/belle*) – see 1.1.5.

In some rare cases the adjectives remain invariable (*snob, kaki*) – see 1.1.6. (1.1.7 is a note on spelling changes made in order to maintain certain specific pronunciations.)

1.1.2   *Changes affecting pronunciation*

(i) The end consonant becomes sounded: *fort/forte; haut/haute; petit/petite*.

(ii) Where the final consonant is *-n* preceded by the vowel *a, i* or *u* there is denasalization: *brun/brune* /brœ/bryn/;[1] *enclin/encline* etc. A similar phenomenon occurs with *-ain*: *lointain/lointaine* (for adjectives ending in *-on* see 1.1.3.1 *iii*).

(iii) Adjectives in *-er* pronounced /e/ in the masculine: the pronunciation of the previously unsounded /r/ entails a change in vowel quality: the *-é* (/e/) becomes *-è* (/ε/); *frontalier/frontalière; ménager/ménagère*. This fact is signalled by the presence of a grave accent.

1.1.3   *Changes affecting pronunciation and spelling*

(except adjectives in *-eur* and *-teur*)

1.1.3.1   *Doubling of final consonants*   This is a frequent phenomenon but one lacking in uniformity.

(i) Some adjectives ending in *-et* double the final consonant in the feminine, e.g. *net/nette; muet/muette; pauvret/pauvrette*; but *complet, incomplet, concret, désuet, discret, indiscret, inquiet, replet* and *secret* all have their feminine in *-ète*.

(ii) A few adjectives in *-ot* have their feminine ending in *-otte*: *boulot, bellot*,

maigriot, pâlot, sot, vieillot. Of these only *sot/sotte* and *vieillot/vieillotte* are encountered with any frequency.

(iii) Adjectives in *-on* and *-en* normally double their final consonant: *bon/bonne, ancien/ancienne, indien/indienne*. Denasalization of the final syllable also takes place. (*Note: lapon, letton* and *nippon* may either have their feminine forms with two consonants or with one: *lapone* or *laponne*; *lettone* or *lettonne*; *nippone* or *nipponne*.
(iv) The following adjectives in *-an* double their final consonant: *paysan/paysanne, rouan/rouanne, valaisan/valaisanne* (native to the Valais in Switzerland).
(v) Adjectives ending in *-s* (following a vowel) usually have regular forms: *gris/grise, clos/close, berlinois/berlinoise*. In these cases the *-s* − which is mute in the masculine form − becomes sounded as /z/ in the feminine form.

However, a certain number of adjectives in *-s* double their final consonant: *gras/grasse, las/lasse, épais/épaisse, gros/grosse, exprès/expresse*. In these cases the *-s* is pronounced /s/ cf. 1.1.7.*i* (*Note:* In the case of words such as *exprès*, the grave accent is always dropped in the feminine form, although pronunciation remains unchanged.)
(vi) Adjectives in *-x* (following a vowel) usually form their feminine in *-se: heureux/ heureuse, pouilleux/pouilleuse*. But *faux* and *roux* have feminine forms *fausse* and *rousse*. (*Note: doux* does not follow either pattern from an orthographic point of view since its feminine form is *douce*.)
(vii) Adjectives in *-el* and *-eil* double the consonant in the feminine: *cruel/cruelle, vermeil/vermeille*. *Nul* and *gentil* behave in a similar manner: *nulle, gentille*.

1.1.3.2 *Changes affecting final consonants*
(i) Adjectives ending in *-f* change *-f* to *-ve: vif/vive*; *agrégatif/agrégative*.
(ii) Adjectives ending in *-c* may change *-c* to *-che* in those cases in which the final *-c* is not sounded: *blanc/blanche, sec/sèche, franc/franche*. But where the *-c* is pronounced, only the orthography is changed (see 1.1.7), e.g. *public/publique*.
(iii) Special cases not fitting into any specific category are: *andalou/andalouse, tiers/tierce, frais/fraîche, doux/douce, coi/coite, bénin/bénigne, malin/maligne*. (There are, of course, historical explanations.)

1.1.4 *Adjectives ending in '-eur' '-teur'*

(i) Some follow the general rule; there are eleven of these, ten of which fall into pairs:

antérieur(e)	*postérieur(e)*
majeur(e)	*mineur(e)*
intérieur(e)	*extérieur(e)*
inférieur(e)	*supérieur(e)*
ultérieur(e)	*citérieur(e)* (an obsolete geographical adjective meaning 'on this side')
meilleur(e)	

(ii) Adjectives in *-eur* which clearly derive from verbs usually form their feminine in *-euse* (the open /œ/ becoming a closed /ø/:

tromp(er)	*trompeur/trompeuse*
flatt(er)	*flatteur/flatteuse*

In these cases it is normally possible to transform the adjective into a present participle simply by substituting the present participle *-ant* ending for the adjectival ending: *trompant* becoming *trompeur*, *flattant* becoming *flatteur* − but see *(iv)* below for exceptions.
(iii) There are however some rather archaic verbs which form their adjectives in *-eresse*

instead of *-euse*: *veng(er)*, *vengeur*, *vengeresse*; *enchant(er)*, *enchanteur*, *enchanteresse*; *péch(er)*, *pécheur*, *pécheresse*.

(iv) There are some exceptions to the rules described in *(ii)* and *(iii)* above. *Vainqueur* has no feminine: *victorieuse* is used instead. *Sauveur* has no feminine, and *salvatrice* is used instead. The feminine of *avant-courreur* is *avant-courrière*.

(v) Adjective in *-teur* form their feminine in *-trice*: *consolateur/consolatrice*, *créateur/créatrice*, *collaborateur/collaboratrice*, *directeur/directrice*.

Note: Some of these words may also function as nouns, in which case the latter will usually refer to some kind of agent:

un plan directeur (adjective)	*un directeur d'usine* (noun)
une roue motrice (adjective)	*une motrice de tramway* (noun)

(vi) It is not always clear whether one is dealing with the *-eur* suffix or the *-ateur* suffix: *flatteur/flatteuse*, but *consolateur/consolatrice*. If one can replace *-eur* by *-ant* to obtain the present participle one is dealing with the *-eur* suffix, e.g. *flatteur/flattant*; if one cannot, one is dealing with the *-ateur* suffix, e.g. *consolateur/consolant* and not **consolatant*. There is one exception to this rule – *persécuteur/persécutrice*, the present participle of which is *persécutant*.

1.1.5 *Cases in which the feminine form is based on an archaic masculine form*

(i) There are a few adjectives which have two masculine forms, one being archaic. *beau/bel*, *nouveau/nouvel*, *vieux/vieil*, *fou/fol* and *mou/mol*. In all five cases the feminine is formed on the second item in each pair, i.e. on the now archaic forms of the masculine: *bel/belle*, *nouvel/nouvelle*, *vieil/vieille*, *fol/folle*, *mol/molle*.

(ii) The archaic masculine forms are still used before a noun beginning with a vowel or a mute *h*: *un vieux livre* but *un vieil homme*; *un beau cadeau* but *un bel enfant*. (One of the reasons for this is that it helps to maintain the consonant/vowel succession which is typical of French syllabic structure).

1.1.6 *Adjectives which remain invariable for gender and number*

Adjectives invariable for gender are also invariable for number.

(i) Adjectives which are 'nouns in disguise' in that they refer to the colour of a specific object (e.g. *marron*, *cerise*, *crème* or *orange*, meaning 'of the colour of') remain invariable. This is because *des robes orange* is felt to be an elliptical structure corresponding to *des robes de la couleur de l'orange* (see section 2.1.2*i*). Similarly *des favoris poivre et sel* stands for *des favoris de la couleur du poivre et du sel*. In other words, these terms are used adjectivally but are not real adjectives.

(ii) A certain number of real adjectives do not change either in the feminine or in the plural: *angora* (*une chatte angora/des chattes angora*); *rococo*, *snob*, *kaki* (but *kakie* is occasionally found) and *gnangnan* (colloquial, meaning 'wet' or 'drip'). *Hébreu* is a special case since it has no regular feminine form. The form *hébraïque* serves as a feminine form, but only when referring to inanimates as in *la langue hébraïque*; for people one uses the term *juif/juive*.

(iii) *Grand* is a special case. It was traditionally invariable in *des grand-mères*, *des grand-tantes*, *des grand-messes* and *des grand-rues*, as against *des grands-parents*, *des grands-pères* and *des grands-oncles*. But the *Arrêté* of 28 December 1976 (see Appendix, section 21) now allows for *des grands-mères*, *des grands-tantes* etc.

Note: Many Latin adjectives had one form only for masculine and feminine: *grandem*, *fortem*, *mortalem*, *crudelem*. The same applies to their 'descendants' in Old French: *grant*, *fort*, *mortel* and *cruel*. But very early on there was a tendency to make these adjectives agree, on the same model as other adjectives; thus *grande* appeared next to *grant*, *forte* next to *fort*, and so on. But relics of the original forms still exist in compound nouns such as *grand-mère* and *grand-rue* and in names of places such as *Rochefort* (instead of *Rocheforte*). (See Price, *The French language*, 108.)

1.1.7 *Spelling changes made in order to maintain a specific pronunciation*

(i) According to the spelling conventions of French, the following combinations of letters represent the following sounds:

ge = /ʒ/ as in *garage*
ce = /s/ as in *douce*
Vowel + *s* + vowel = /z/ as in *rose*

In order to maintain the original sounds associated with g (/g/), c (/k/) and s (/s/), changes in spelling have to take place:

(a) A *u* is inserted to maintain the /g/ sound, as in *longue*.

(b) A *que* replaces the *c*, as in *traqué* (/trake/), meaning 'hunted', as against *tracé* (/trase/), meaning 'drawn' or 'marked out'.

(c) Two *s* symbols are used instead of one, as in *basse* (/bas/), 'low', as against *base* (/baz/), 'base'.

(ii) These rules affect the spelling of adjectives used in their feminine form in the following manner:

(a) *Long* and *oblong* have their feminine in *-gue* to maintain the original /g/ sound: *longue*, *oblongue*.

(b) Adjectives ending in *-c* have their feminine in *-que*, as in *publique*, or sometimes in *-cque*, as in *grecque*.

(c) *Aigu* and *ambigu* (pronounced /egy/ and ãbigy/) have in their feminine form a diaresis (or 'trema') in order to dissociate the feminine form from the ordinary ending in *-gue* which would be pronounced /g/ and not /gy/, hence the feminine forms *aiguë* and *ambiguë* (pronounced in the same way as the masculine forms).

1.2   Changes due to number

1.2.1 *The general rule*

The rule is the same as for nouns: adjectives take a plural -s which is added to the singular form. This final *-s* appears at the end of all feminine adjectives (*petite/petites, grise/grises, fausse/fausses*) and at the end of most masculine ones (*fort/forts, grand/grands*). Those which already end in *-s* remain unchanged (*clos/clos*). See also 1.1.6.

1.2.2 *Plurals in '-x'*

(i) A certain number of adjectives make their masculine plural form by adding an *-x* to the masculine singular form, namely: Adjectives in *-eau* (*nouveau/nouveaux, beau/beaux*) and *hébreu/hébreux*.

(ii) Those adjectives ending in *-x* in the singular remain unchanged (*heureux/heureux, ingénieux/ingénieux*).

(iii) Adjectives ending in *-al* usually have their plural in *-aux* (*normal/normaux, marginal/marginaux*). However, *bancal, fatal, final, natal* and *naval* take a final *-s* (*bancals* etc.). *Banal* has two plural forms, each one carrying a different meaning, e.g. *des fours banaux/des outils banals*. *Banaux* is a term of feudal law referring to certain communal facilities such as bakehouses, owned by the lord of the manor; *banals* simply means 'ordinary' or 'standard'.

(iv) Some *-al* forms may take two plurals, but this is an area of syntactic uncertainty; thus Larousse gives both *astrals* and *astraux*, *matinals* and *matinaux*, *pascals* and *pascaux*. Robert also gives *glacials* and *glaciaux* whereas Larousse only gives *glacials*. Lexis gives both *boréals* and *boréaux* whereas Larousse and Lexis only give *boréaux*. Some of these may sound odd to many native speakers.

2　Adjectival agreement

There are a number of cases to be examined: where the adjective modifies one noun only (2.1); where it modifies more than one noun (2.2); where a plural noun is modified by several adjectives (2.3); and where the adjective is a compound-adjective (2.5). In all of these cases agreement is made both on grammatical and semantic grounds.

2.1　Adjectival modification of one noun only

2.1.1　*The general rule*

(i) French adjectives agree in gender and number with the noun they modify, whether they function as epithets or as attributes, e.g. *les bons œufs; ils sont fatigués*.
(ii) Agreement with the pronouns *vous* and *on* functions as follows. Compare:

> *vous, messieurs, qui êtes pressés. . . .*
> *vous, madame, qui êtes pressée. . . .*

In this case the verb agrees with *vous* and the adjective with *messieurs* or *madame*. This contrasts with the next example which belongs to colloquial French:

> *? nous, on est égaux*

The verb agrees with *on*, but the adjective with *nous*. Such a sentence usually belongs to what the French call *un style négligé*. In Marivaux however one finds:

> *j'aime qu'on soit gaie*

because the addressee of this remark is a woman.
(ii) With *avoir l'air*, agreement is possible either with the subject or with *l'air*:

> *elle a l'air mécontente (= elle semble mécontente)*
> *elle a l'air mécontent (= elle a un air mécontent)*

2.1.2　*Exceptions to the general rule*

(i) Adjectives which are nouns in disguise remain invariable (see 1.1.6*i*), e.g. *des robes orange, des tailleurs marron*.
(ii) Adjectives used as prepositions remain invariable; *excepté* is often used in this way:

> *ils ont tous émigré, excepté les grands-parents*
> *les grands-parents exceptés, ils ont tous émigré*

In the first sentence *excepté* functions as a preposition meaning *à l'exception de*, whereas in the second *exceptés* modifies *grands-parents*. Similarly *ci-joint* agrees in postnominal position but not in prenominal position: *la somme ci-jointe*, but *ci-joint la somme* (but see Appendix section xiii for a more tolerant attitude).
(iii) Adjectives used as adverbs remain invariable:

> *les enfants crient trop fort*
> *j'ai grand faim (= très faim)*

(but see Ch. 12, 2.1.3.1 for the use of *très* instead of *grand*).
　Similarly, *possible* remains invariable when it reinforces intensifiers such as *le plus* or *le moins*, e.g. *il s'est attaqué aux travaux les plus durs possible* (although in practice one often finds *possibles* in such cases).
(iv) It is sometimes possible to confuse an adjective functioning as the modifier of a noun with an adjective functioning as part of a compound noun:

j'ai des nu-pieds (compound noun, no agreement)
j'ai les pieds nus (adjective modifying a noun)

Thus it is that traditionally one writes *nu-pieds* for the sandals of that type, and *demi-heure*. But the *Arrêté* of 28 December 1976 (see Appendix) now allows for *nus-pieds* and *demie-heure*.

(v) It sometimes happens that in infinitival clauses the subject is understood but not exactly expressed, except in terms of agreement, e.g. *il faut être sincère(s)*. In this case the presence or absence of the *-s* indicates whether the adjective refers to one person or several.

(vi) There is an archaism in the odd case of adjectives modifying the noun *gens*. *Gens* was originally feminine, and feminine agreement is still possible in a prenominal position, but not in a postnominal position. Compare agreement in the three following sentences:

Mes amis étaient de vieilles (fem.) *bonnes* (fem.) *gens pleins* (masc.) *de saveur antique et fruste.* (Henriot)

Plus telles (fem.) *gens sont pleins* (masc.) *moins ils* (masc.) *sont importuns.* (La Fontaine)

J'écris pour ces petites (fem.) *gens d'entre lesquels* (masc.) *je suis sorti.* (G. Duhamel)

Masculine agreement is now obligatory for the personal pronoun and for relative pronouns. What is more, if the adjective is prenominal but coordinated with another which is unmarked for gender, it will also be used in its masculine form. Compare:

quelles bonnes (fem.) *gens!*
quels bons (masc.) *et honnêtes gens!*

In other words, *gens* has become nearly entirely masculine, but not quite.

2.2 Adjectival modification of more than one noun

There are four possibilities:

noun + *et* + noun + adjective
noun + *ou/ni* + noun + adjective
noun, noun, noun . . . + adjective
noun + *de* + noun + adjective

2.2.1 *Noun + 'et' + noun + adjective*

(i) The basic rule is that plural takes precedence over singular, and that masculine takes precedence over feminine, e.g. *cette table et cette chaise sont anciennes*; *cette table et ce lit sont anciens*.

(ii) If nouns are of different genders, it is necessary to place the masculine noun nearest to the adjective for the sake of morphological harmony, particularly if one can 'hear' the agreement. Thus, although sentences such as:

on voyait des hommes et des femmes assemblés dans la cour

are not offensive because the agreement is inaudible, sentences such as the following one are quite unacceptable in formal French:

*on voyait des hommes et des femmes sportifs assemblés dans la cour

(iii) In principle, if agreement is made with one noun only, the one nearest to the adjective, this means that the adjective refers to that noun only. But in Classical French this was not always the case; some authors followed the Latin rule according to

which agreement was made with the nearest noun only, even though one adjective could modify several nouns. This is the case in the following sentence:

Armez-vous d'un courage et d'une foi nouvelle (Racine, *Athalie*)

In this case *nouvelle* modifies both *foi* and *courage*, since one could not simply write, **Armez-vous d'un courage.*

2.2.2   *Noun + 'ou'/'ni' + noun*

Modern usage tends towards general acceptance of the plural agreement:

ni la viande ni les légumes n'étaient assez cuits
il cherchait un magasin ou un restaurant ouverts

In certain cases such an agreement is not possible, however:

il cherchait une cabine téléphonique ou un café ouvert (telephone boxes are always 'open')

In some cases agreement may be chosen to give a different meaning to the sentence, e.g.

je cherche une voiture ou une motocyclette neuves (both are new)
je cherche une voiture ou une motocyclette neuve (only the motorbike is new)

2.2.3   *Noun, noun, noun . . . + adjective*

(i) Where the nouns are roughly synonymous and an effect of stress by simple repetition is aimed at, the adjective will be in the plural, e.g. *il y avait un bruit, un tintamarre, un vacarme épouvantables*
(ii) Where the aim is to build up to a final stressed word, the adjective will be in the singular, e.g. *il y avait un bruit, un tintamare, un vacarme épouvantable*

2.2.4   *Noun + 'de' + noun + adjective*

Agreement in such constructions is decided on semantic grounds. Compare:

les bains de soleil ne sont pas nécéssairement bons pour la santé
une bande d'étudiants bruyants était (or *étaient*) *descendue dans la rue*

In the first case the adjective is attributive of *les bains de soleil*; in the second case *bruyants* simply modifies *étudiants*.

Note: These agreements may also be justified on grammatical grounds. In the first sentence agreement has to be with *bains* because *bains de soleil* is a compound noun, whereas in the second sentence agreement has to be with *étudiants* because *bande d'étudiants* is not a compound noun. *Bains de soleil* is a compound noun for two reasons. First, no adjective may be interposed between *bains* and *soleil* (i.e. one cannot say **des bains prolongés de soleil* whereas one can say *une bande importante d'étudiants*). Secondly, *soleil* cannot be modified (one cannot say **des bains de soleil pâle*) whereas *étudiants* can be modified (*une bande d'étudiants bruyants*). Thus it is that one may say or write both *une bande d'étudiants bruyants* and *une bande bruyante d'étudiants*, but only *de bons bains de soleil* and not **des bains de bon soleil*.

2.3   Modification of a plural noun by several adjectives

The adjectives will always agree in gender; agreement in number will be made on semantic grounds. Compare:

les armées française, anglaise et américaine étaient en état d'alerte (if in the singular each nation has but one army, if in the plural this would mean each nation had several, there is choice between the singular and the plural forms.)

les dix-huitième et dix-neuvième siècles sont au programme (in this case there is no choice)

2.4 Agreement of the adjective in a superlative construction

(i) Where there is a complement in a superlative construction, the adjective agrees with the complement in gender: *à ce moment-là, le moteur à réaction était la plus récente des inventions.*

(ii) Adjectives preceded by *des plus* or *des moins* will normally be in the plural: *c'était une plante des plus exotiques.* There are however some exceptions to this, namely when agreement would be semantically absurd, e.g. *M. Coutre était des plus satisfait de sa femme* (*des plus satisfait* = *très satisfait, satisfait à un tres haut degré*).

2.5 Agreement of compound adjectives

2.5.1 *The compound adjective corresponding to two coordinated adjectives*

Examples are *sourd-muet*, which means *sourd et muet*, and *aigre-doux* (*aigre et doux*). In these cases both adjectives will agree with the noun modified: *des femmes sourdes-muettes*; *des vins aigres-doux.*

But if the first part of the compound adjective ends in *-o* or *-i* it remains invariable: *des traités franco-russes*; *des pièces tragi-comiques.*

2.5.2 *The compound adjective including an adjective functioning as an adverb*

(i) The normal rule is that the adjective functioning as an adverb remains invariable (see 2.1.2*iii*), e.g. *une dame haut placée; la couronne grand-ducale; des poupées grand-guignolesques.*

(ii) It is not, however, always clear whether the adjective is functioning as an adverb or as an adjective, hence the possibility in some cases of either making the adjective agree or not, e.g. *des chansons bas-bretonnes/des chansons basses-bretonnes*; *des mœurs petit-bourgeois/des mœurs petites-bourgeoises.*

(iii) Similarly, there are a number of compound adjectives having a past participle as their second term and an adjective functioning as an adverb as their first which continue to agree in both parts, e.g. *les nouveaux-mariés*; *notre dernière-née, des fenêtres grandes-ouvertes*; *une fleur fraîche-éclose.* (In all of these examples the first adjective could be replaced by a 'proper' adverb, e.g. *des personnes nouvellement mariées; des fleurs fraîchement écloses.*)

(Note however that one always says *une nouveau-née* and never *une nouvelle-née.*)

2.5.3 *The compound adjective including an adverb or a preposition + adjective*

In this case the preposition or adverb remains invariable:

des personnes bien intentionnées (*bien* = adverb)
des signes avant-coureurs (*avant* = preposition)

2.5.4 *Compound adjectives of colour*

These are invariable in both parts, even though the separate components may agree when used alone: *des gants jaune pâle; une robe vert-bouteille.* Thus both *des yeux bleus* or *des yeux clairs* are possible, but only *des yeux bleu clair* is acceptable. (This is because these constructions are felt to be elliptical: *des gants d'un jaune pâle, des yeux d'un vert clair*.)

3 Functions of the adjective

3.1 General considerations

(i) The distinction between basic and relational adjectives is important from a functional point of view, because basic adjectives may function in a much greater variety of ways than may relational adjectives.

Basic adjectives may be epithetic (3.2), may function as attributes (3.3), may have complements of their own (3.4) and may appear in elliptical constructions (3.5). They are easier to nominalize in French than in English – hence the translation problems (3.6).

Relational adjectives may only be epithetic, and only in restrictive constructions (3.2.1). They may only be placed after the noun (see section 4 for the place of the adjective) and they cannot be modified by an adverb as can the basic adjective (3.4.2).
(ii) A basic adjective is one which refers to an inherent characteristic of the noun (*la robe rouge* or *la grande maison*). The semantic relation between the noun and the adjective is of the *qui est* type: *la robe rouge* = *la robe qui est rouge*; *la grande maison* = *la maison qui est grande*. A relational adjective is one which is the equivalent of a *de* + noun construction (*la chaleur solaire* = *la chaleur du soleil*; *le voyage présidentiel* = *le voyage du président*). These are also sometimes called derivational adjectives. For more details, see section 5.

3.2 The adjective as epithet

When the adjective functions as an epithet (an adjective used to qualify a noun within the same noun phrase), one may distinguish restrictive and nonrestrictive constructions.

3.2.1 *Restrictive adjectives*

(i) A restrictive adjective is one which carries essential information, in that it restricts the range of meaning of the noun modified: *rouge* in *une robe rouge* excludes all dresses which are not red.
(ii) Both basic and relational adjectives may function as restrictive epithets – indeed it is the only function possible for relational adjectives:

> *la robe rouge est tâchée* (= basic adjective)
> *la chaleur solaire pourrait être une source d'énergie importante* (*solaire* = relational adjective)

(iii) Relational adjectives are always placed after the noun modified, but basic adjectives may appear either before or after: *la robe rouge*, but *la grande maison*. (Some of these may appear in either position, but adjectives of colour appear normally only after the noun. For the place of the adjective, see section 4.)

3.2.2 *Nonrestrictive adjectives*

(i) A nonrestrictive adjective is one which conveys information which is not essential, in that it does not restrict the range of meaning of the noun modified. These adjectives are normally placed between commas, hence the term 'detached adjectives' which is sometimes used for them. They are also said to be in apposition. Compare:

les écoliers, attentifs, écoutaient la leçon (all of the pupils were listening to the lesson; they were all attentive)
les écoliers attentifs écoutaient la leçon (only those which were attentive were listening to the lesson)

In the first sentence, *attentifs* does not restrict the meaning of *les enfants*; it is nonrestrictive. In the second sentence *attentifs* does limit the meaning of *les enfants*; it is restrictive.
(ii) This kind of construction is obligatory where two adjectives are opposed to one another, e.g. *ces enfants, si jeunes et pourtant si marqués par la vie, ...*
(iii) Relational adjectives cannot be used in this kind of construction.

3.3 The adjective as an attribute

(This category does not apply to relational adjectives.)

3.3.1 *Attribute of the subject*

In this case the adjective is linked to the subject by a verb expressing some kind of identity between the subject and what follows it, i.e. the attribute: *elle est intelligente*.
(ii) The adjective functioning as an attribute agrees in gender and in number with the noun or pronoun of which it is the attribute.
(iii) The most commonly used verb in this kind of construction is *être*, but there are others, e.g. *sembler, paraître, passer pour, être considéré comme*:

cette eau est/semble/a été reconnue/a été déclarée bonne pour la consommation

3.3.2 *Attribute of the object*

(i) In this case the adjective modifies the object:

je le devine impatient de partir (= *je devine qu'il est impatient de partir*: *impatient* modifies *le*)
je crois ma soeur heureuse (= *je crois que ma soeur est heureuse*: the adjective modifies *soeur*)

Note: There are areas in which there is an intermediary − namely a preposition − between the attribute and the adjective:

elle le traite d'imprudent (attribute of *le*)

But the *de* is part of the verb since the verb is *traiter quelqu'un de quelque chose*.

3.4 Adjectives with complements and modifiers

(This category does not apply to relational adjectives.)

3.4.1 *Adjectives with complements*

(i) The complement will be a noun, a pronoun or an infinitive. The link between the adjective and the complement will be expressed by the preposition *de*:

un homme plein de défauts (noun complement)
il est content de lui (pronoun complement)
il est content de partir (verb complement)

(ii) When an adjective has a complement it is said to be used 'transitively'; some adjectives such as *généreux*, *aimable* and *peureux* never seem to appear with a complement: these are said to be 'intransitive'.

Note: Adjectives may appear with prepositions other than *de*, however, e.g. *peureux devant le danger, aimable envers les autres*, but these prepositions are adverbial in their function.

3.4.2 *Adjectives modified by adverbs*

il est vraiment content de lui

See Ch. 12.

3.5 Adjectives used in elliptical clauses

The adjective used on its own may stand for *c'est* + adjective:

Nouveau, amusant: avec Arlequin, la chance rebondit — Loterie Nationale — tirage mercredi prochain (advertisement for the French national lottery)

Adjectives used in this way appear mainly in publicity texts. They usually appear at the beginning of the text, the syntax of which is often disjointed:

Exclusif: Paris — Oslo en Airbus (advertisement)

In this case the full sentence would be *Paris — Oslo: c'est un voyage exclusif* (the word *voyage* being implied by *Paris — Oslo*). It is the elliptical nature of the syntax and its disjointedness which gives the text its impact. The adjective often represents the most important element in the message, hence its being placed first and on its own: it is up to the reader to work out what it applies to.

3.6 Nominalization of the adjective: translation problems from French to English

It is extremely easy to nominalize a French adjective, whereas the same cannot be always said of English adjectives. One may distinguish three cases of nominalization:
(i) An adjective which refers to an inanimate attribute may be used in the singular, and preceded by the definite article, to refer to abstract concepts: *le beau* (beauty), *le vif du sujet* (the heart of the matter).
(ii) An adjective which refers to animate attributes may be used in the plural, and preceded by the definite article, to refer to a whole category: *les jeunes* (young people), *les grands* (the older ones), *les anciens* (the elders).
(iii) Adjectives may be used as anaphoric proforms[2] in their own right:

j'ai été regarder les fauteuils dont tu m'avais parlé; je préfère les petits aux grands (i.e. *fauteuils*).

4 The place of the adjective

4.1 General considerations

Only adjectives functioning as epithets present problems. This is because, although such adjectives are usually placed after the noun modified, there are cases in which either they may or they must be placed before.
There are three aspects to this problem: the distributional aspect (4.2) the phonological aspect (4.3) and the stylistic aspect (4.4). It is also important to note that the place of the adjective has changed through time (4.5).

4.2 The distributional aspect

4.2.1 *Adjectives preceding the noun*

4.2.1.1 *Cases in which adjectives precede the noun* There are only a few cases, the norm being for adjectives to be placed after the noun.
(i) Ordinal numerals precede the noun: *la quatrième chaise; le second rang.*
(ii) Some adjectives normally appear before the noun where the noun modified refers to inanimates: *beau, bon, faux, grand, gros, haut* (except in *marée haute*), *joli, mauvais, nouveau* (except in *vin nouveau*), *petit, vieux* (except in *vin vieux*), *vilain* and *vrai*: *un joli chien; une belle armoire; une grande table.*
   Exceptions such as *vin vieux* have become more or less compound nouns.
(iii) Where one is dealing with animates – especially humans – the adjectives above and many others may appear in both positions. When this is the case the adjective when placed before the noun takes on a figurative or abstract meaning: *un homme grand* (a tall man), but *un grand homme* (a great man (but *une grande femme*, a tall woman)); if two adjectives were used, however, *grand* would go back to meaning 'tall', as in *un grand homme sec*, 'a tall lean man'; *un pauvre homme* (a man to be pitied), but *un homme pauvre* (a man who is short of money); *une jeune fille* (a young girl between 17 and 25), but *une fille jeune* (a girl or woman who is young – no age implied); *une brave femme* (a kindly woman), but *une femme brave* (a courageous woman); *un homme vilain* (an ugly man), but *un vilain homme* (a nasty man).
(iv) Adjectives normally placed after the noun when the latter refers to inanimates may sometimes be placed before the noun if they take on a figurative meaning: *des livres chers* (expensive books), but *mes chers livres* (my dear books).
   The same sometimes applies to adjectives used with abstract nouns. Thus, *un problème difficile* only applies to mathematical or scientific problems, whereas *un difficile problème* although rare, is possible when referring to any other kind of problem, as in: *la question du Moyen-Orient pose un difficile problème.*
   In this case *difficile*, once it is placed before the noun, takes on a more general meaning than when placed after the noun. The effect achieved is one of emphasis. (See 4.4.) (Such cases of anteposition are extremely rare, however: see 4.2.2.1. *ii*).
(v) Adjectives normally placed after the noun may be placed before when they are used as quantifiers or intensifiers (see 4.3.2*iii*).

   un ennui mortel and *un mortel ennui* (= *un très grand ennui*)
   un effort immense and *un immense effort* (= *un très grand effort*)

But there are phonological restrictions to the anteposing of the adjective: see 4.3.1.

4.2.1.2 *Word order when several anteposed adjectives modify the same noun*
(i) One usually distinguishes four classes of adjectives in terms of word order:

Class 1	Class 2	Class 3	Class 4
the ordinal numerals, the indefinite adjective, (see Ch. 2, section 5)	*nouveau* *jeune* *vieux* *vrai* . . .	*mauvais* *faux* *bon* *beau* *joli* . . .	*grand* *petit* . . .

Examples:

   donnez-moi un autre joli petit livre
   c'est la deuxième fausse nouvelle de la journée

(ii) There are restrictions on the use of more than two anteposed adjectives.

It is not possible, stylistically speaking, to modify the noun by three or more adjectives in a row. Thus, although *le nouveau joli petit chat* is a theoretical possibility, such a noun phrase would be unacceptable to most French speakers. The syntax of the phrase would have to be changed in order to get rid of at least one of the adjectives preceding the noun; this could be done by saying, instead, *le joli petit chat nouveau-né*. Similarly although *les autres nouvelles grandes voitures américaines* is a theoretical possibility, it would not be considered acceptable by most French speakers; one would say instead something like *les autres grandes voitures américaines nouvellement sorties*.

(iii) When two adjectives which are normally placed before the noun are coordinated there are two possibilities:

> *une grande et belle femme*
> *une femme grande et belle*

4.2.2   *Adjectives which must follow the noun*

4.2.2.1   *Cases in which adjectives must follow the noun*
(i) Adjectives referring to colours:

> *des cheveux gris*, but not **des gris cheveux*

Note: One can say *de blonds cheveux,* but this has poetic connotations (see 4.3.2*ii* and 4.4*i* for the anteposing of adjectives of colour).

(ii) Adjective modifying an inanimate noun (but see 4.2.1.1*iv* for those used figuratively):

> *des fruits amers*, but not **d'amers fruits*
> *une porte basse*, but not **une basse porte*

(iii) Past and present participles used as adjectives:

> *une porte fermée*, and not **une fermée porte*
> *une jovialité affectée*, and not **une affectée jovialité*
> *un marchand ambulant*, and not **un ambulant marchand*

(iv) Relational adjectives:

> *la chaleur solaire*, and not **la solaire chaleur*
> *un exercice livresque*, and not **un livresque exercice*

(v) Adjectives followed by a complement:

> *un enfant bon à rien*, and not **un bon à rien enfant*

4.2.2.2   *Word order when several adjectives follow the noun*
(i) Where there is more than one adjective following the noun, the term felt to be closest semantically to the noun comes nearest to it:

> ·*une jupe plissée verte* (*plissée* is felt to be a more inherent quality than *verte*)
> *une jupe verte plissée* (*verte* is felt to be a more inherent quality than *plissée*)

(ii) If neither adjective is felt to be closer to the noun, the two adjectives may be coordinated by *et*: *un bateau à fond large et plat*.

(iii) Where one of the adjectives can be placed before the noun and one after there will be two possibilities, e.g. *un petit chien marron/un chien petit et marron*

(iv) when more than two adjectives follow the noun, these must appear in a nonrestrictive construction, i.e. in apposition; in this case their order of appearance will be in terms of *masses croissantes*, i.e. the shortest will appear first and the longest

last. The last adjective may well have a complement added to it in order to give it length:

il y avait là une petite plage abritée, souriante, tapie au pied de la falaise

4.2.3 Translation problems

These are due partly to the restrictions on the number of adjectives which may be anteposed (or placed before (the noun in this case)) and partly on the restrictions in terms of the order in which they may appear after the noun (see 4.2.1.2 and 4.2.2.2). The syntax of the original English sentence often has to be changed to make allowance for this:

'the countryside was divided into patches by a multitude of little old grey stone walls'

could be translated as:

la campagne était divisée en parcelles par une multitude de petits murs en pierre grise, fort anciens

In this case *anciens* has become a nonrestrictive adjective, *fort* has been added to give this rhythmic group greater length.

'she had a long, thin, pale face'
elle avait un long visage, maigre et pâle

One adjective has remained anteposed; two have been postposed instead of one, for the balance of the sentence.

Generally speaking, adjectives are less freely used in French than in English.[3]

4.3 Phonological aspects

There are a number of restrictions on the anteposition of adjectives. These are phonological (4.3.1), and the adjective may take on a different emphasis depending on its position within the intonation group (4.3.2).

4.3.1 Phonological restrictions on the anteposition of the adjective

(i) If the adjective is polysyllabic and the noun monosyllabic, the adjective must follow the noun:

un cas difficile, but not **un difficile cas*
un air satisfait, but not **un satisfait air*

This rule does not however apply in those cases in which the final *-e* of the feminine entails the pronunciation of an otherwise unsounded consonant: both *une nuit courte* and *une courte nuit* are acceptable.

(ii) If both the noun and the adjective are monosyllabic, the adjective will be postposed (or placed after (the noun in this case)) if it ends in a consonant:

un bruit sec, and not **un sec bruit*
un cri bref, and not **un bref cri*

But this rule does not automatically apply if the adjective ends phonetically with a vowel; in this case both positions are possible:

un long manche and also *un manche long*
. . . . le héron au long bec emmanché d'un long cou (*La Fontaine*)

(iii) An exception to both these phonological rules is that words referring to colours are normally postposed whatever their phonological structure (for cases such as *prairies vertes* and *vertes prairies*, see 4.4).

4.3.2   *Importance of the place of the adjective within the intonation group*

(i) The basic principle is that the position of the adjective within the intonation group determines its preeminence.

If a word is said in isolation, it is the last syllable which is stressed, but − unlike English − every word spoken in French is not automatically stressed: words are normally classed together in 'rhythmic' or 'intonation' groups, each of these corresponding to a grammatical unit such as the nominal phrase and the verb phrase (see Ch. 17, section 5). This means that a postposed adjective will be phonologically in a more preeminent position than an anteposed adjective, since the latter has no phonological identity. Compare:

> *elle a un nouveau pantalón*
> *elle a un pantalon trop lárge* . . .

(ii) The length of the last word of the intonation group may increase or decrease this effect. If the intonation group ends with a word which is monosyllabic, this precludes all possibility of the previous word bearing a secondary stress; if, on the other hand, the last word is polysyllabic the previous word may bear a secondary stress:

> *elle a des cheveux brúns* (= one stress only)
> *elle a des cheveúx chátáins* (= two stresses, a primary stress on *chátains* and a
>   secondary stress on *cheveux*)

This rule is particularly important in poetry.

It is also sometimes possible for other words to be stressed within the intonation group, as in:

> *elle avait de loñgues tresses brúnes*

In this case the 'mute *e*' has to be pronounced (because of the rule of the three consonants[4]), which lengthens the *on* (/õ/) in *longues* and the *e* (/ɛ/) in *tresses*, obliging the speaker to emphasize these words.

(iii) The position of the adjective may have semantic consequences. Since an anteposed adjective usually has no phonological identity of its own, it tends to refer to an inherent or permanent quality of the noun (noun + adjective = 1 semantic unit). A postposed adjective does have a phonological identity, and in this case it is the quality attributed to the noun which is stressed (noun + adjective = 2 semantic units). Compare:

> *un brave homme* (= a kindly man, which is an inherent permanent quality)
> *un homme brave* (= a brave man, in which case the quality may be less permanent,
>   since to be a brave man one must do brave things − i.e. one is not brave 24 hours
>   a day)

> *des amants heureux* (= refers to a state of affairs true at one particular point in time)
> *d'heureux amants* (= refers to a permanent state of affairs)

> *un ennui mortel* (*mortel* is the stressed element)
> *un mortel ennui* (*ennui* is the stressed element)

One can see from these examples that changing the place of the adjective in *un brave homme* and *un homme brave* changes its meaning completely, in *des amants heureux* and *d'heureux amants* there is a change of emphasis from the temporal to the more permanent and in *un ennui mortel* and *un mortel ennui* there is simply a change as to which element is stressed, but not basic change of meaning. See also examples in 4.4*iv*.

4.4 Stylistic considerations

Since the normal place of the adjective is after the noun, most writers try to achieve an effect by placing it before: an anteposed adjective tends to be more literary since less spontaneous (see *(i)* − *(iv)* below). When anteposing the adjective, the writer may be functioning within the rules of the language (*(i)* − *(iv)*) or he may be going against them (*(v)*).

(i) Anteposition of the adjective gives it a figurative or abstract meaning (see 4.2.1.1 *iii* and *iv*):

une dure épreuve (= a terrible hardship)
une épreuve dure (= a difficult task, exam, hurdle . . .)

A colour may also be used figuratively:

Elle se levait au milieu de la nuit comme une blanche vestale (Chateaubriand)

In this case *blanche* no longer refers to a physical reality but to a moral quality. But such examples of anteposition are only possible because they do not go against the phonological rules, (see 4.3.1; these would not allow for **un dur homme* for example).
(ii) Anteposition is used to refer to an inherent or permanent quality (see 4.3.2*iii*, and also examples in 4.4*iv*):

une praire verte and *une verte prairie*

Such a case of antepositioning of the adjective with an adjective of colour is possible only because 'green' may be considered to be a characteristic of all 'fields'. But one could not write in the same way *un chapeau vert* and **un vert chapeau*, since it is difficult to see how 'green' could be an inherent quality of all 'hats'.
   (Zola frequently changes the place of his adjectives in this way: he writes, for example, *l'étroite boutique* instead of *la boutique étroite*, since *étroite* may be said to be an inherent quality of *boutique*; it can also be understood figuratively in the sense of 'mean' in this context. Thus the adjective takes on two meanings instead of one.)
(iii) The adjective is often placed before the noun when it is used to quantify or to intensify the noun. This is particularly common in journalism: *une attaque remarquable* becomes *une remarquable attaque*; *un effort immense* becomes *un immense effort*.
   Writers such as Zola have also used this device:

Les travaux d'en face étaient un continuel tourment (*continuel* implying quantity)

(iv) Normally, anteposed adjectives may be postposed to express a different emphasis or shade of meaning. Compare the following sentences by Zola:

Il leva ses gros yeux embroussaillés, resta surpris de la voir
Ce jour-là, quand elle vit les yeux gros de ce dernier, elle le sermonna doucement

In the first case *gros* refers to an inherent quality of the person's eyes; in the second he is referring to the fact that the child referred to has 'swollen eyes' because he has been crying: here the adjective is referring to a temporary quality.
(v) There are cases in which writers 'go against the rules' in their antepositioning of adjectives. Compare the following lines by Verlaine and Hugo:

C'est par un ciel d'automne attiédi
Le bleu fouillis des claires étoiles. . . .

and

Les lutins, les hirondelles
Entrevus évanouis
Font un ravissant bruit d'ailes
Dans la bleue horreur des nuits

The names of colours normally follow the noun; here they precede it. In the first sentence the terms *bleu* and *fouillis des claires étoiles* are not incompatible, since 'night' is associated with the colour 'blue'. Therefore, although surprised by the place of the adjective, the reader will accept *bleu* as referring to an inherent quality of night. Anteposition in this case achieves an effect of what is called in French *un flou artistique*. In the second sentence the antepositioning of the adjective is more difficult to accept, despite the presence of the word *nuits*, mainly because it modifies *horreur*: it is difficult to see how the colour 'blue' could be inherent to 'horror'; anteposition in this case is therefore difficult to accept. On the other hand, if Verlaine and Hugo had written *fouillis bleu* and *horreur bleue* this would have meant that 'blue' would have been the word stressed in both cases, and not the more important words *fouillis* and *horreur* (see 4.3.2ii).

Whether anteposition in these examples is successful or not is a matter of taste and not of grammar, but the impact itself is partly grammatical and partly semantic. The degree of 'shock' is proportional to the difficulty felt by the reader in justifying in semantic terms the position of the adjective.

Note: Excessive use of the anteposed adjective tends to be typical of certain kinds of contemporary French prose; but repeated shifting of the adjective from its normal position may become extremely exasperating for the reader:

Sept heures, le lendemain matin. Merveilleuses secondes de l'aube, éphémère congé accordé aux malades pour contempler leur route du haut d'une colline bocagère (Rouanet)

In both cases anteposition is necessary because the adjective has a complement; but excessive use of structures requiring anteposition can also be disruptive.

4.5   Historical note

In Old French, word order was far more flexible than now, since the two-case system made the function of words less dependent on word order. There was, however, a tendency in those days to make the adjective prenominal. Even in the sixteenth century many adjectives which would now normally be postnominal were then prenominal:

Nageoit en parfonde eau (parfonde = profonde) (Rabelais)

On the other hand it was also normal to postpose adjectives which would normally be anteposed nowadays, particularly when forming part of compound nouns (*souris chauves* for *chauve-souris* for example). Adjectives such as *grand, petit, vieux* and *beau*, which are nearly always prenominal nowadays, often appeared after the noun (*enfants petits* for *petits enfants*). There was also more flexibility as to the construction of coordinated adjectives; thus Montaigne writes *d'une parfaite union très vive*. In contemporary French the two coordinated adjectives have to remain on the same side of the noun, whether before or after (*d'une parfaite et très vive union* or *d'une union parfaite et très vive*). Such constructions are attested as late as the seventeenth century; Madame de Sévigné writes, for example,

il vous dira s'il y a plus honnête homme à la cour et moins corrompu

By the end of the seventeenth century the adjectives occupied on the whole much the same place as in modern French. There were some exceptions such as *bon, grand* and the ordinal numbers, which could still be postposed, whereas *naturel, féminin, manifeste, tragique, public, natal* etc. could still be anteposed; but whereas in modern French changing the place of the adjective can modify the meaning of the sentence, this was not so clearly the case then.

The problem of the place of the adjective was a subject much debated by the grammarians of the seventeenth century: Estienne and Vaugelas, for example, both declared that *beau, bon, grand* and *petit* should be anteposed; Malherbe demanded that past participles should follow the noun qualified; and Thomas Corneille specifically made the point that *grand* referred to an objective quality when it followed the noun modified (as in *un homme grand et bien bâti*) whereas it could take on a figurative meaning when preposed (as in *c'est un grand homme*). In other words, the writers and grammarians of the seventeenth century, remarking on the flexibility of the place of the adjective, codified it with rules and principles which have survived intact up to this day.

5   Basic and relational adjectives

5.1   General considerations: reasons for distinguishing two types of adjective

One must distinguish relational adjectives from basic adjectives for a number of reasons:

(i) There are semantic differences between these two types of adjective (see 5.2*i-iv*).
(ii) There are syntactical differences (see 5.2 *v*).
(iii) Since there are fewer relational adjectives in French than in English − given that English does not make this distinction explicitly − there are a number of problems involving translation from English to French (see 5.3). On the other hand, adjectives may be nominalized far more easily in French than in English, and this gives rise to translation problems from French to English (see 5.3).
(iv) This distinction is important because a great number of new relational adjectives are being coined at present in French. Many of these are felt to be unacceptable to some, but totally acceptable to others, thus creating a problem as far as prescriptive grammar is concerned (see 5.4).

5.2   Defining relational adjectives

(i) A relational adjective may be defined as one which is the equivalent of a nominal construction of the *de* + noun type. Thus *le voyage présidentiel* stands for, or is the same as *le voyage du président*, and *un conseil paternel* stands for *un conseil de père*.
(ii) Relational adjectives usually express one of three types of relations:

> possession: *la voiture présidentielle (= du président)*
> place of origin: *un vase chinois (= qui vient de Chine)*
> the psychological subject of the action represented by the noun: *le voyage présidentiel (= le président a fait un voyage)*.

(iii) In many cases there is a difference in meaning between the *de* + noun construction and the basic adjective formed on the noun. Compare:

> *un camarade d'enfance* = a childhood friend
> *un camarade enfantin* = a childish friend

Usually the basic adjectives formed on the noun are abstract in their meaning, whereas in the *de* + noun construction the noun retains its original meaning.
(iv) In some cases there are two adjectives corresponding to the same radical, one basic and the other relational, e.g.

un homme alcoolique = an alcoholic man (= an inherent characteristic)
une boisson alcoolisée = an alcoholic drink (= which contains alcohol).

In other cases the same adjective may function either as a basic or as a relational adjective; but these are few in number, except in the fields of science and technology:

un enfant nerveux = *un enfant qui est nerveux*
le système nerveux = *le système des nerfs*

(v) There are syntactical restrictions on the use of relational adjectives (see section 3 above): they may only function as epithets and only as restrictive epithets. They cannot be attributes (**la chaleur est solaire*), they cannot be modified by adverbs or complements (**la chaleur très solaire*), and they cannot be used as nonrestrictive epithets (**la chaleur, solaire, présente des dangers*).

5.3   Translation problems from English to French

(i) There are fewer relational adjectives in French. In English this distinction is not so relevant: the same adjective may express either concept, i.e. it may either refer directly to the quality to be attributed to a noun or it may correspond to a 'preposition + noun phrase' type of construction: 'a musical evening' means a particular type of evening, an evening which is musical; but 'a musical instrument' means an instrument for the making of music.

In French, very few adjectives may be both basic and relational. There are relational adjectives in French, but there are fewer than in English in more or less all domains, except technology and science.

(ii) If the adjective used in English corresponds conceptually to a relational adjective, and if there is no corresponding relational adjective in French, it is necessary to go back to a *de* + noun construction, e.g.

'a musical evening' = *une soirée musicale*
'a musical instrument' = *un instrument de musique* (*un instrument musical* is also possible, but carries a different meaning, since in this case *musical* would mean 'melodious' and would refer to an instrument which produces a particularly beautiful sound)
'a medical student' = *un étudiant en médecine* (*en* replaces *de*)
'a medical product' = *un produit médical*
'a rural church' = *une église de campagne*
'an active church' = *une église active*
'a fishing village' = *un village de pêcheurs*
'a fishing boat' = *un bateau de pêche*

5.4   The new proliferation of adjectives, particularly relational adjectives

(i) French, when it emerged from Vulgar Latin, was extremely poor in adjectives, as tends to be the case with emerging languages. To compensate for this, innumerable 'new' adjectives were coined in Old French, using mainly Classical Latin as a base. This custom has continued uninterrupted till now. This potential source of adjectives has not, however, been tapped to the extent it could have been, because of an equally strong tendency in French to fight against the use of 'an excessive number' of adjectives. This goes back to the idea that nonessential information could obscure the message, i.e. that it would be against the principle of *la clarté française*. Thus it is that French Classical writers made a point of using adjectives very sparsely indeed.

Today this whole trend is reversed, partly because the ideal of *la clarté française* and similar ideals are no longer fashionable, and partly perhaps because of the influence of English, which contains a great number of adjectives, notably of the relational type.

(ii) A large number of relational adjectives have been coined during the last 20 years, and are continuing to be created. But many of these are frowned upon by purists. This is mainly because some of them could be ambiguous in their meaning. Thus *la campagne présidentielle* could mean either *la campagne faite pour le président* or *la campagne faite par le président*. Similarly *l'exemple parental* could mean either *l'exemple du père/l'exemple de la mère*, or *l'exemple du père et de la mère*. In each of these two cases, the construction could have more than one meaning; but this is contrary to the French Classical ideal of *la clarté française*.

Relational adjectives are however extremely economical, and their very ambiguity may be desirable in some cases; such constructions enable more than one thing to be said at a time. This explains their popularity nowdays, particularly in journalism, where speed is all important. One may thus read: ?*zone avalancheuse* for *zone d'avalanche*; ?*à titre informatif* for *à titre d'information*; ?*la campagne préparative* for *les préparatifs pour la campagne électorale*.

Sometimes several such expressions are competing for acceptance, as is the case for ?*rue piétonne* and ?*rue piétonnière* instead of the 'correct' *rue pour piétons*. A large number of such adjectives have been created, particularly in the fields of technology and science: *réforme agraire* for *réforme de l'agriculture*, *l'équipement sanitaire* (= *relatif à la santé*), *un objet métallique* for *un objet en métal*.

(iii) Newly coined technological and scientific relational adjectives are easily accepted as 'correct'. But those associated with the 'short-cuts' typical of journalism are not so easily accepted, although they may appear frequently in print. One may read, for example, **la tournée américaine du président* for *la tournée du président en Amérique*, but such constructions will be unacceptable to most French speakers. Given, however, the need for the language to coin new adjectives it is probable that most of these will become acceptable within a fairly short space of time. In the meantime, their use by anglophones has to be dependent on register: they are acceptable in informal registers, but to be avoided in very formal ones.

6   Summary of the morphological features of feminine forms of adjectives

(See also 1.1 above.)

6.1   Addition of final '-e'

The feminine form is normally obtained by adding an -*e*. Such an addition may entail:
(i) No change in pronunciation, e.g. *joli/jolie, dur/dure, mat/mate, nul/nulle*.
(ii) Changes in pronunciation:
  (a) the final consonant becomes sounded, e.g. *fort/forte*
  (b) there is denasalization, e.g. *brun/brune* (/brœ̃/ − /bryn/)
  (c) if the masculine form ends in -*er*, the /e/ becomes more open and the -*r* is sounded, e.g. *léger/légère*
(iii) Changes in both pronunciation and spelling:
  (a) doubling of final consonant:
    -*ot/otte*, e.g. *sot/sotte* (closed /o/ becomes open, i.e. /o/ becomes /ɔ/
    -*et/ette*, e.g. *muet/muette* (/e/ becomes /ɛt/)
    -*on/onne*, e.g. *bon/bonne* (/o/ becomes /ɔn/)
    -*ien/ienne*, e.g. *indien/indienne* (opening of vowel + denasalization)
    -*s/sse*, e.g. *gras/grasse* (pronunciation of consonant which is mute in the masculine form; but also very commonly -*s/se*, e.g. *gris/grise* (the -*s* becomes voiced, i.e. /s/ becomes /z/)
    -*x/sse*, e.g. *faux/fausse*, *roux/rousse*; but usually -*x/se*, e.g. *heureux/heureuse* (voicing of -*s*, i.e. /s/ becomes /s/)

(b) changes affecting the final consonant:
   -if/ive, e.g. *vif/vive* (voicing of the *-f*, i.e. /f/ becomes /v/)
   -c/che, e.g. *blanc/blanche* (/blã/ − /blãʃ/); *sec/sèche* (/sɛk/ − /sɛʃ/)
      odd cases: *andalou/andalouse, tiers/tierce, frais/fraîche, coi/coite*
(iv) In the case of adjectives ending in *-eur*, final consonant or suffix may be changed, in addition to the general rule of addition of a final *-e*, e.g. *antérieur/antérieure* (11 adjectives in this category):

   -eur/euse, e.g. *flatteur/flatteuse*
   archaic derivation, e.g. *vengeur/vengeresse*
   -teur/trice, e.g. *consolateur/consolatrice*

(v) Some adjectives have two masculine forms: *beau/bel/belle*; *nouveau/nouvel/nouvelle*; *vieux/vieil/vieille*; *fou/fol/folle*; *mou/mol/molle*. (The archaic forms *bel*, *nouvel*, *vieil* and *mol* are used before masculine nouns beginning with a vowel or a mute *h*, e.g. *un bel homme* but *un homme beau*.)

6.2 Adjectives which remain invariable

The most common invariable adjectives are *chic*, *impromptu*, *kaki* and *snob*. Some adjectives remain invariable because they have become prefixes. In this case they are often tied to the noun modified by a dash, e.g. *une demi-heure, la mi-carême, être nu-tête* (but *tête nue*).

Adjectives which are nouns in disguise remain invariable, e.g. *cerise, marron, orange*.

6.3 Spelling changes made to maintain pronunciation

   g = *gu*, e.g. *long/longue*
   s = *ss*, e.g. *bas/basse*
   ¨ is added to final *-e* to dissociate feminine ending from the rest of the word, e.g. *aigu/aiguë* (/egy/)

Notes

1 /. . ./ denotes phonetic transcription.
2 A proform is a part of speech which is used instead of another; for example, a pronoun is used instead of a noun and a pro-verb is used instead of a verb (e.g. 'I have done it', in which 'done' stands for an action mentioned previously). A word used anaphorically is one which refers back to another word already mentioned.
3 There is much disagreement among French writers as to the desirability of using adjectives. Marouzeau (*Précis de stylistique française*, 122-3) writes:
   'L'emploi de l'adjectif épithète fournit un des critères les plus propres à permettre une caractérisation du style. Maints écrivains ont une tendance à prodiguer l'épithète inutile, celle qui, n'étant pas indispensable au sens strict, fait figure dans l'énoncé d'une fantaisie ou d'un luxe.
   'Toute une échelle des valeurs peut être observée, depuis les qualificatifs quasi obligatoires et stéréotypés: "une *fine* allusion", "une *amère* déception", jusqu'à l'épithète inattendue qui réclame presque un commentaire: "ces impressions restaient douillettes" (J. Romains). . . . Louis Veuillot écrivait de Jules Favre: "Il ne va pas sans adjectifs; toujours il les étale par paires, souvent par triades, et même par grappes, n'omettant guère que celui qui conviendrait.". . . . et J. Giraudoux fait dire à un de ses personnages (dans *Juliette au pays des hommes*): "Déteste les adjectifs et chéris la raison. . . . Les adjectifs sont dans la langue française ce que les

parasites sont dans les caves ou les bateaux. . . . Quand les adjectifs sortent à la queue-leu-leu . . . c'est que le mot vogue à sa perte. . . . Entre deux épithètes, le nom crucifié meurt.'' '

And Marouzeau then quotes the following lines from Giraudoux's *Judith*:

Jean: Pour sauver ce peuple brutal, ces prêtres sans honneur, ces enfants sans beauté, tu pars?

Judith: Des adjectifs dans une heure pareille! Pour tenter de sauver ce peuple, ces prêtres, ces enfants, je pars.

4 The rule of the three consonants, or *la règle de Grammont*, is as follows:

if an *-e-* appears between three consonants, it is pronounced, e.g. *appartement;*
if an -e- appears between two consonants, it is dropped (at least in standard French), e.g. *j'irai d∉main*

The rule of the three consonants also applies within the larger framework of the 'rhythmic' or 'intonation' group (for a definition of 'intonation group', see Ch. 17, 5.2), e.g.

ferme la petite fenêtre = ferm∉lap∉tit∉fenêtr∉

Note that, in the previous example, the rule applies to all but the final 'mute' *e*: the latter is dropped in accordance with another rule which states that the final *e* of a word is not pronounced if it appears at the end of a rhythmic group, e.g. *la maison vast∉* but *la vaste maison*. For further details on these complex phenomena, see for example Peyrollaz and Bara de Tovar, *Manuel de phonétique et de diction françaises*, 76-82, from which the last example was borrowed.

Chapter 12

The adverb

0 General considerations

0.1 Variable position of the adverb

Adverbs may appear straightforward at first, since they are invariable (cf. section 1); but this apparent simplicity is misleading, for there are problems where the position of the adverb is concerned, in terms both of linguistic comprehension and of language production. Compare:

ce chiffon est plutôt sale ('this rag is rather dirty')
donnez-moi un chiffon propre, plutôt ('I would rather you gave me a clean rag')

In this case the place of the adverb actually changes its meaning in the sentence. It is also necessary to explain why sentences such as *il a beaucoup marché* are acceptable, whereas sentences such as **il a lentement marché* are not, (except in certain rare poetic contexts).

0.2 The position of the adverb determining its function

(i) An adverb may modify a specific word in a clause either by quantifying it: (*il a beaucoup mangé*) or by referring to its quality (*il a bien parlé*). These are the adverbs of quantity and quality; see section 2.
(ii) Adverbs may modify the modality of a sentence, either in terms of a specific word (as in *il viendra peut-être mardi*) or in terms of the sentence taken as a whole (as in *peut-être viendra-t-il lundi*). These are the modal adverbs; see section 3.
(iii) Some adverbs may refer to the manner in which the action has been carried out (e.g. *il l'a fait rapidement*). These are the adverbs of manner; see section 4.
(iv) Some adverbs function as if they were adverbial complements (or *compléments circonstanciels*): they do not modify anything, but add a complement of information as to the place or time of the action (as in *j'y suis allé aujourd'hui*, and *va chercher ton chandail en haut*). These are the adverbial adverbs of time and place; see section 5.
(v) All the problems related to the place of the adverb − including translation problems − are summarized in section 8.

0.3 Use in comparative and superlative constructions

Adverbs are used in most comparative and superlative constructions, (as in *il est plus grand que son frère* or *il est le plus grand*). Such constructions are examined in section 6.

0.4 Negative adverbs

The case of the negative adverbs (as in *je n'ai plus de pain*) is examined in section 7.

0.5 Translation problems

There are different kinds of translation problems associated with adverbs. These appear under the following headings:

(i) the noncorrespondence of adverbs between English and French, and the shortage of French adverbs in *-ment* in relation to English adverbs in '-ly'; see 1.2.7;

(ii) differences in terms of the cases in which English uses comparative and superlative constructions and in which French uses absolute constructions; see 6.4.

0.6 Adverbs functioning as conjunctions

Some adverbs combine with *que* to form compound subordinating conjunctions, e.g. *pendant que, ainsi que, alors que, encore que*. These are examined under 'Conjunctions' in Ch. 15. Others may function as coordinators, either in the same way as coordinating conjunctions do, e.g. *je suis fatigué, aussi je vais me coucher* (= 'therefore') or as transitional links ensuring the smooth flow of speech from one sentence to the next, e.g.

Ce problème sera bientôt résolu. Je suis allé, en effet, consulter la personne qu'il fallait, à ce sujet.

These are examined in Ch. 16.

1 Defining adverbs

Section 1.1 deals with the adverb as a part of speech; 1.2 deals with morphological considerations.

1.1 The adverb as a part of speech

1.1.1 *Basic definition*

Adverbs are words which are invariable. There are other types of words which are invariable, namely prepositions and conjunctions. But adverbs differ from prepositions and conjunctions in that they are intransitive, i.e. they do not introduce syntactically new elements. Prepositions and conjunctions, on the other hand, are transitive, since prepositions normally introduce nominal phrases and conjunctions normally introduce clauses.

1.1.2 *Functions*

The main function of adverbs is to modify some element in the clause, or in some cases the clause itself.

(i) They may quantify: these are the adverbs of quantity:

(a) they may quantify in absolute terms, e.g. *il a peu dormi* (see section 2);

(b) they may quantify in comparative terms, e.g. *il a moins dormi que la nuit précédente* (see section 6);

(c) they may refer to the quantity zero, e.g. *il n'a pas dormi cette nuit*; these are the negative adverbs − see section 7.

(d) they may function as determiners when followed by *de*: *peu de gens sont venus*.

(ii) They may define the action qualitatively; these are the adverbs of Quality, e.g. *il travaille bien* − see section 2.

(iii) They may modify the modality either of a specific word or of a sentence: these are the modal adverbs. Compare:

il mangera peut-être du caviar demain
il mangera du caviar peut-être demain
peut-être mangera-t-il du caviar demain

In the first sentence, the uncertainty is associated with *caviar*, in the second with *demain* and in the third with the whole sentence.

(iv) A pause or a comma may enable one to associate the adverb with the words forming a phonetic unit with it; hence the following types of opposition:

il mangera du caviar, demain peut-être (the adverb modifies *demain*)
il mangera du caviar demain, peut-être (the adverb modifies the whole sentence)

See section 3.

(v) They may refer to the manner in which the action is carried out:

il fait toujours son travail très soigneusement

in which case they are the equivalent of a prepositional phrase functioning as an adverbial:

il fait toujours son travail avec grand soin (or *de manière très soigneuse*)

but whereas the prepositional phrase functioning as an adverbial is felt to add a complement of information to the sentence, the adverb of manner modifies the verb, i.e. it is to the verb what the adjective is to the noun, hence the very term 'adverb' (see section 4).

(vi) They may function as if they were adverbials, i.e. as complements of the verb: they add a complement of information to the clause in terms of the circumstances in which the action takes place, either in terms of time or of place:

j'y vais demain (time)
il y a des jouets partout (place)

See section 5.

(vii) Adverbs are also used in comparative and superlative constructions (see section 6) and in negative constructions (see section 7) but both of these may be considered to represent special aspects of the 'adverbs of quantity'.

(viii) Adverbs may also be used as coordinators or link words: *je n'ai pas entendu le réveil, aussi j'ai été en retard* or *ai-je été en retard* in more formal French and they may also help to ensure a smooth flow of speech from one sentence to another; adverbs such as *en effet, cependant, pourtant* frequently function in this way. See 1.2.5 and Ch. 16.

1.1.3 *Classes of words upon which the adverb may depend*

(i) Whereas the adjective modifies the noun, adverbs may modify any of the non-nominal parts of speech:
the verb: *il travaille courageusement*
the adjective: *il est très sage*
the adverb: *il l'a fait très gentiment*
the preposition: *il se tenait tout contre le mur*
the clause: *il sortait de chez lui/juste [quand nous sommes arrivés]*.

(ii) There are a few cases in which the adverb may modify the noun directly, e.g. *des gens bien* and *les roues arrière*; in these cases although the adverb functions adjectivally it remains invariable.

(iii) Quantifying adverbs + *de* may however function as determiners of the noun: *peu de gens sont venus*.

(iv) Adverbial adverbs may sometimes complement the noun, as would an ordinary noun: *la mode de demain* (= *la mode de l'avenir*).

1.1.4 *Words usually classified under other parts of speech functioning as adverbs*

(i) Prepositions used intransitively[1] function as adverbs: *je partirai après* (preposition used intransitively). One may distinguish between:

Je prends mes vacances en août. Je reviendrai après (= adverb)

and

> *Je participerai à la cérémonie. Je reviendrai après* (= *après la cérémonie*: in this case there is an elliptical construction and *après* functions as a preposition)

(ii) An adjective used to modify anything else but a noun will be used adverbially:

parler à haute voix (adjective)
parler haut (adverb)

1.1.5 *The case of 'tout'*

The rule in this case is a rather pernickety one; one must distinguish between *tout/tous/toute/toutes*, meaning 'each one of them' and agreeing with the adjective modified, and *tout* the adverb, meaning 'completely' or 'very', which is invariable, except where the adjective modified is feminine and starts either with a consonant or an aspirated *h*, in which case there is also agreement. Hence the following possibilities:

ils sont tous émus, tous heureux, tous confus ('each one of them')
elles sont toutes émues, toutes heureuses, toutes confuses ('each one of them')
ils sont tout émus, tout heureux, tout confus ('completely', 'very')

but:

> *elles sont tout émues* (no agreement), *tout heureuses* (no agreement because of the mute *h*), *toutes confuses* (agreement because the adjective starts with a consonant), *toutes honteuses* (agreement because of aspirated *h*)

There is therefore ambiguity when the adjective modified is feminine and plural and starts either with a consonant or an aspirated *h*. However, the *Arrêté* of 28 December 1976 allows the agreement to be kept even when the adjective modified starts with a vowel or a mute *h*:[2] *tout (toutes) émues; tout (toutes) heureuses*;

In other words, the ambiguity which existed for feminine adjectives starting with a consonant or an aspirated *h* has now spread to all feminine adjectives.

1.2 Morphological considerations

1.2.1 *General considerations*

Adverbs may be formed by derivation; these are the *-ment* adverbs (1.2.2); they may exist as words in their own right, i.e. not as words obtained through derivation (1.2.3); some are obtained through borrowing (1.2.4); others are created through a word changing class from a syntactic point of view (1.2.5). Those adverbs which may also function as link words may have acquired in doing so a second meaning (1.2.6). On the whole there are fewer adverbs in French than in English, or at least there is no one-to-one correspondence between the two languages, and this gives rise to translation problems (1.2.7).

1.2.2 *Adverbs obtained through derivation: the '-ment' adverbs*

1.2.2.1 *Origin of the '-ment' suffix*
(i) The *-ment* suffix comes from *mente*, the ablative form of *mens*, Latin for 'mind'.

Since it is a feminine noun, the adjective was in the feminine form, hence *bona mente*, which gave *bonement* (written nowadays as *bonnement*), the unstressed vowel *a* of the feminine ablative becoming a mute *e* in adjectives of the 1st declension. But adjectives of the 3rd declension do not have an *e* derived from an *a*, since their form is the same in the feminine as in the masculine. Thus *forti mente* gave *forment* (nowadays *fortement*). It is at a later date that adverbs were remodelled on the feminine form of the French adjective; thus *forment* was rewritten as *fortement*, by analogy with *bonnement* (see 1.2.2.1).

1.2.2.2 *Formation of the '-ment' adverbs*   Although this suffix appears most frequently with adverbs of manner, it may also appear with adverbs of time, as in *prochainement*, and with adverbs of mood, as in *certainement*. The suffix is usually, but not always, added to an adjective. Several cases have to be considered.

(i) Originally the suffix *-ment* was added to the feminine form of the adjective if it was short (*bonnement, vraiement, forcéement*), but the *e* was later dropped from the spelling of these words when it did not affect their pronunciation, hence the present-day spelling (*vraiment, forcément*). Sometimes the disappearance of the *e* has been compensated for by the addition of a circumflex accent (*l'accent du souvenir*) as in *assidûment, crûment*. In some cases there are still, in principle, two possible spellings (for example *gaiement* and *gaîment*), but the second of these may now be considered obsolete.

(ii) Where the adjective was long, adverbs were no longer formed in French on the feminine form but on the masculine form: *méchamment* is formed on *méchant* and not on *méchante* (although *méchantement* used to exist). Similarly, *excellent* gives *excellemment*.

(iii) Adjectives ending in *-ent* or *-ant* take two *m*s: *indolent* becomes *indolemment*, *brillant* becomes *brillamment*. These adverbs come from adjectives which were participles.

(iv) The suffix *-ment* may also be added to past participles as in *aisément, aveuglément, conformément, précisément*. These cases give the false impression that the suffix is *-ément*: *expréssement, immensément, intensément, obscurément*. *Impuniment* was remade as *impunément* on this model. The existence of this second suffix enables one to contrast pairs of words such as: *aveuglément* (adverb = 'blindly') and *aveuglement* (noun = 'blindness' in the figurative sense as opposed to *cécité*, meaning 'blindness' in the physical sense). Adjectives formed on past participles only take one 'm' in contrast to those based on adjectives in *-ent*, which take two.

(v) The suffix *-ment* may be added to interjections: *bougrement, diablement, vachement* (vulgar).

(vi) The suffix *-ment* is sometimes added to nouns, but such adverbs are usually created for the need of a specific context: *chattement* for *à la manière d'un chat*, *hommement* for *à la manière d'un homme*. This area is largely one of personal lexical inventiveness; and the resulting adverbs are highly marked stylistically.

1.2.2.3 *The loss in modern French of adverbs ending in '-ons'*   There existed in Old French another adverbial suffix: *-ons*, as in *à tâtons* (= *à la manière de ceux qui tâtent*), *à chevauchons* (= *à la manière de ceux qui chevauchent* — no longer used), *à reculons*. This suffix is no longer productive.

1.2.2.4 *Adjectives upon which two adverbs may be formed*   There exist pairs of adverbs based on the same adjective, one ending in *-ment* and the other being the adjective which has become invariable: *haut/hautement; cher/chèrement; bas/bassement*. In these cases the adverb formed by derivation is used with a figurative meaning, whereas the adjective used adverbially is used in a concrete sense. Thus *parler haut* means 'to speak with a loud voice', whereas *parler hautement* means 'to speak highly' in the sense of quality. Similarly *cher* means 'expensively' whereas *chèrement* is used in a figurative sense.

1.2.3 *Adverbs not obtained through derivation*

These exist as words in their own right.

1.2.3.1 *Adverbs developing directly from Latin*

(i) These are usually simple adverbs such as: *bien, hier, là, loin, mal, mieux, moins, non, ne, ou, peu, pis, plus, si, sus, tant, tard, très.*

(ii) Because invariable words are often short, however, they are more subjected than other words to *l'usure phonétique*, and this gives rise to a tendency to use them with others, as in: (Latin) *ab ante = avant; ad satis = assez; ad retro = arrière; de retro = derrière.*

1.2.3.2 *Adverbs resulting from agglutination of French words rather than of their Latin counterparts*

(i) Agglutination may be complete: *bientôt, depuis, dessus, dessous, désormais, naguère, maintenant.*

(ii) Agglutination may be incomplete: *là-dessus, ci-devant, dès lors, en arrière, avant-hier, en face, côte à côte.* . . .

Note: The problem is to determine when a phrase is a compound adverb and when it is not. Should one, for example, classify *à la fin*, or *par-dessous* (as in *faire les choses par-dessous*), as a compound adverb or as a preposition plus a noun functioning as an adverbial? The criterion most usually used is the presence or absence of an article: if the article is absent it is a compound adverb; if it is present it is a prepositional phrase functioning as an adverbial.

1.2.4 *Borrowing*

(i) Borrowings are usually from Latin:

a posteriori (= après expérience)   *ipso facto (= per le fait même que)*
a priori (= avant l'expérience)   *intra muros (= dans les murs)*
in extremis (= à l'extrémité)   *passim (= çà et là)*
in extenso (= du début à la fin)   *sic (= ainsi, textuellement)*

In the spoken language one uses words such as *gratis* (free), *grosso modo (à peu près), vice versa (dans un sens comme dans l'autre), primo, secundo, tertio* and *idem (de même).*

(ii) There are a few borrowings from other languages, e.g. *piano* as in *aller piano* (= *aller doucement*), borrowed from Italian; *schuss* as in *descendre schuss (= comme d'un trait)* borrowed from German; and in slang, *bézef (= beaucoup)* usually in a negative construction *(il n'y en avait pas bézef)* borrowed from Arabic.

1.2.5 *Adverbs created through change of syntactic class*

(i) This applies to adjectives where there is no noun to modify: *boire sec, manger frais.*

(ii) This also applies to adjectives used to modify other adjectives: *court vêtu (= vêtu de manière courte), une fillette nouveau-née (= nouvellement née)*; but there is some hesitation as to whether certain words modifying adjectives should be considered as adjectives or adverbs (see Ch. 11, 2.5.2).

(iii) Adjectives are sometimes used to modify verbs. In some cases they become invariable, as in *habillez-vous pratique, votez utile, il gagnera facile* (for *facilement*). This tendency is on the increase, particularly in the media, and it is not new; du Bellay

recommended *il vole léger* for *il vole légèrement*, and Mme de Sévigné also used such constructions.

(*iv*) In some cases adjectives – whilst remaining adjectives in terms of agreement – may take on an adverbial type meaning. Compare:

> *les enfants tranquilles dorment* (normal use of the adjective: it is those children who are normally peaceful who are asleep)
> *les enfants dorment tranquillement* (normal use of the adverb: it is the sleeping which is peaceful)
> *les enfants dorment tranquilles* (both the children and the sleep are peaceful)

It is the postposition of the adjective in the third sentence which gives it quasi-adverbial qualities.

A disjunctive construction could also be possible in order to emphasize either the adjective or the adverb:

> *les enfants dorment, tranquilles* (referring only to the children)
> *les enfants dorment, tranquillement* (adverb referring to the whole clause)

(*v*) In some cases, adverbs and their corresponding adjectives may be used contrastively. Compare:

> *c'est un homme bon* ('he is a kind man')
> *c'est un homme bien* ('he is a respectable man')

In the second case *bien* applies not only to the man himself but to the opinion others have of him: the adjective tends to be used where agreement is easily possible, whereas the adverb tends to be used where gender and number are more difficult to determine. But one does sometimes hear people use the expression *c'est bon* for *c'est bien*, in which case *bon* is used adverbially.

1.2.6   *Adverbs with several meanings*

(*i*) Many adverbs have changed meaning since the sixteenth century, or at least have acquired a second meaning, because they have a 'conjunctive' function which has extended their meaning considerably, so that the context determines which meaning is applicable. Thus, in dictionaries, for certain adverbs such as *comme* at least two meanings are listed, depending on function:

> *comme* = conjunction meaning 'as', 'when' or 'because'; *comme* = exclamative adverb meaning 'how', 'to what point'
> *ce pendant* = adverb meaning 'during that time' (now archaic); *cependant* = conjunction meaning 'however'
> *aussi tôt* and *si tôt* = adverbs meaning 'so soon' and 'so early'; *aussitôt* and *sitôt que* = conjunctions meaning 'as soon as'

(*ii*) Some adverbs have changed their meaning during the course of the last few centuries. *Sitôt* used to mean *si vite* in Classical French:

> *Comment puis-je sitôt servir votre courroux?* (Racine)

Sitôt is no longer used as one word, except in set phrases such as *sitôt dit, sitôt fait*, and *pas de sitôt* (meaning 'not for a long time' or 'not in a hurry').

Jamais is dependent on its position in the sentence and on other syntactic features for semantic interpretation. Compare:

> *je n'y vais jamais* ('I never go there')
> *si jamais tu le vois, dis-lui de me téléphoner* ('if ever you see him, tell him to phone me')

In the first sentence the assertion is negative, in the second it is positive. *Jamais* and *ne jamais* thus correspond to 'ever' and 'never'.

Note: The positive interpretation which may be given to *jamais* is due to the fact that originally *jamais* was positive, since it comes from *jam + magis*, meaning 'from now on'. *Si jamais*, therefore, has the meaning of 'if ever'. It is the use of *jamais* in combination with *ne* which gives it its negative meaning of 'never': *ne . . . jamais = ne . . . quelque jour que ce soit*.

1.2.7 *Translation problems*

These problems are due to the shortage of adverbs in *-ment* corresponding to the English adverbs in '-ly', for the simple reason that there are more adjectives in English to which '-ly' may be added than there are adjectives in French which can take *-ment*.

In French one may therefore have to replace the English adverb by one of the following:

a preposition + noun: 'angrily' = *avec colère*; 'concisely' = *avec concision*
a preposition + noun + adjective: 'reliably' = *de source sure*; 'deservedly' = *à juste titre*
a preposition + clause: 'brightly' = *en brillant d'un vif éclat*; 'unaccountably' = *sans qu'on sache pourquoi*

For example:

'he decided to treat the patient surgically' = *il décida de passer par la chirurgie*

In some cases the *-ment* adverb exists, but its meaning is different from that of the corresponding '-ly' adverb:

'the stars shone brightly' = *les étoiles brillaient d'un vif éclat*

Vivement does exist, but it means *avec vivacité*, implying movement, which is not the case here. *Brillamment* also exists, but is only used in an abstract sense, as in *il réussit brillamment à ses examens*.

Note: Some francophone countries use adverbs in *-ment* which are unknown in France. The Belgians, for example, use *anticipativement, méritoirement* and *supplémentairement*, which do not appear in most French dictionaries.

2 Adverbs of quantity and quality

The quantifying adverbs are examined in 2.1, and the qualifying adverbs in 2.2.

2.1 Adverbs of quantity

Some adverbs of quantity may function as normal adverbs, whilst others may function as intensifiers and others as determiners when used in combination with the preposition *de*.

2.1.1 *The 'normal' quantifying adverbs*

(i) These may refer to 'amounts': *peu, assez, bien, beaucoup, fort, trop, par trop, comme, combien, autrement* (used in the sense of *bien plus que*) *très, surtout . . .: il est fort drôle; il mange beaucoup*.

(ii) They may be used in some cases in combination with an article. Compare:

il est peu serviable ('he is not very helpful')
il est un peu avare ('he is rather mean')

(iii) They may refer to time in terms of frequency or duration: *vite, quelquefois, souvent, longtemps, parfois, toujours, rarement, longuement: il a vite fait son travail.*
(iv) For clashes with the modal adverbs, see 3.2.1 *ii.*

2.1.2 *The intensifying adverbs*

(i) Sometimes adverbs may be used to intensify rather than quantify:

> *il mange beaucoup* (quantification)
> *il mange beaucoup mieux* (intensification)

The main intensifiers are: *très, bien, beaucoup, si, tellement, tant, trop, autrement* (in the sense of *bien plus* but used in this sense only in the spoken language), *surtout. Comme* and *combien* and the construction *si. . . . que cela* may also be used as intensifiers, but they modify the whole clause:

> *comme il fait chaud*
> *combien vous avez tort* (formal French)
> *il n'est pas si méchant que cela* (= *il n'est pas bien méchant*)

(*Combien*, being so very formal, tends to sound odd when associated with informal constructions, e.g. *combien tu as tort.*)

2.1.3 *Syntactic restrictions on the use of quantifying adverbs (including intensifiers)*

Some adverbs may modify only certain classes of words, whereas others are less restricted.

2.1.3.1 *Adverbs modifying verbs only* These adverbs are *tant* and *beaucoup*. But *très* is also used in verbal phrases of the *avoir très envie de, avoir très peur,* and *avoir très mal* type. Purists often reject *avoir très envie de*, on the grounds that a noun (*envie*) should be modified by an adjective and not an adverb; they suggest instead *avoir grande envie de; avoir très mal* is felt to be more acceptable since *mal* may be considered to be either an adverb or a noun, since the Latin forms *malum* (noun) and *male* (adverb) both give *mal* in French. Purists will therefore accept as equally correct *il ne s'est pas fait grand mal* (with *mal* as a noun) and *il s'est conduit très mal* (with *mal* as an adverb); but **il s'est fait grand mal* (i.e. the positive version of the first sentence) does not seem acceptable to anyone.

J'ai grand faim/grand soif/grand peur are nonetheless considered to be literary because archaic.

2.1.3.2 *Adverbs modifying adjectives and adverbs only* These are *si, très* (but see 2.1.3.1) and *tout* when the latter means *très. Beaucoup* can no longer be used to qualify adjectives (*je mange beaucoup* is acceptable but **il est beaucoup drôle* is not). This was not so in Classical French, hence sentences such as:

> *Leur savoir à la France est beaucoup nécessaire* (Molière)

Even today *beaucoup* is still used in the spoken language where one would expect *très*, hence the prescriptively unacceptable **j'ai beaucoup soif* for *j'ai très soif.*

2.1.3.3 *Expression of intensity in the spoken language* One may use intensifying adverbs, but one may also use other constructions to set up an emotional progression: *j'ai soif* (neutral); *j'ai très soif; j'ai une de ces soifs!* (informal); *je t'ai une de ces soifs!* (vulgar).

2.1.4   *Quantifying adverbs functioning as determiners*

(i) The quantifying adverbs differ from numerals in that they refer to quantities which are not exactly quantifiable: *peu (de), beaucoup (de), assez (de), bien (des), pas mal (de) trop (de), combien (de), moins (de), plus (de)*, e.g. *peu de gens sont venus; vous m'avez donné trop de vin.*

These quantifiers may be used on their own in elliptical structures, e.g. *peu sont venus; donnez m'en peu*

(ii) Quantifying adverbs may carry different meanings. *Peu (de)* refers to a quantity felt to be too small, as in *peu de gens sont venus*; but *un peu de* refers to a small but sufficient quantity. *Bien des fois* is used as a literary variant of *très souvent.*

nous y somme allés très souvent (informal, spoken French)
nous y sommes allés bien des fois (formal)

Bien (des) is also used instead of *beaucoup* in subjective statements: *nous avons eu beaucoup d'ennuis/bien des ennuis; nous avons eu beaucoup de chance/bien de la chance.*
Pas mal (de) and *un tas (de)* are informal variants of *beaucoup (de)*: *j'ai beaucoup de choses à vous raconter; j'ai un tas de choses à vous raconter.*

2.2   Adverbs of quality

(i) Adverbs of quality modify the verb or adjective in terms of its quality:

il a fort bien parlé (*bien* modifies *a parlé*)

(ii) The adverbs of quality do not form a morphologically cohesive class: they are made up of a number of unrelated adverbs such as *bien, mal* and a number of *-ment* adverbs, most of which may also function as adverbs of manner (see *(iv)* below).

Mal can no longer modify an adjective, although this use survives in adjectives such as *malhabile* and *maladroit*; but it can modify a participle: *mal reçu, mal connu, mal habillé. . . .*
(iii) When modifying an adjective, adverbs of quality may become at the same time adverbs of quantity:

il est horriblement pâle (= 'very pale', and a particular kind of paleness)

(iv) There are many adverbs ending in *-ment* which may function either as adverbs of quality or as 'manner adverbs', depending on their position in the sentence (see 2.3 for the place of the adverb of quality and 4.2 for the adverb of manner). Compare:

il a soigneusement ficelé le paquet (adverb of quality)
il ficèle soigneusement le paquet (adverb of quality)
il ficèle le paquet soigneusement (adverb of manner)

2.3   Position of adverbs of quantity and quality

(i) They precede the word modified, except when the word modified is a verb in a simple tense, in which case it follows the verb:

c'est très bien
nous avons beaucoup marché pendant les vacances
nous marchons beaucoup pendant les vacances

(ii) Where the present participle is concerned, there are two possibilities. Compare:

c'est un homme austère et peu souriant (= inherent quality)
c'est un homme austère, souriant peu et parlant rarement (in this case *souriant* is
    similar to *parlant* and is clearly felt to be verbal)

In other words, if the present participle is used adjectivally, the adverb precedes it, but if it is used verbally it follows it, as it would a verb in a simple tense.

3 Modal adverbs

3.1 Types of modal adverb

(i) Some modal adverbs indicate whether an action is likely or unlikely to take place, e.g. *peut-être, probablement, vraisemblablement, assurément, sans doute, certes*. These include *-ment* adverbs, unrelated adverbs such as *certes* and *volontiers*, and set phrases such as *peut-être* and *sans doute*. (But *sans doute* used to express far greater certitude than it does now; it therefore has to be reinforced by *aucun* as in *sans aucun doute* for it to regain its original meaning.)

(ii) Some have an emotional or an intellectual meaning, e.g. *heureusement, malheureusement, naturellement, apparemment*.

(iii) In other cases they may indicate an approximation, e.g. *en somme, en général*.

3.2 Function and position of modal adverbs

3.2.1 *Modal adverbs modifying one word only*

(i) The modal adverbs may modify a specific word, in which case they behave exactly as do the adverbs of quantity and quality:

> *il viendra peut-être lundi*
> *il va peut-être venir lundi*

In the first sentence *peut-être* modifies both *lundi* which it precedes and *viendra* which it follows. In the second sentence *peut-être* modifies *va venir* only.

(ii) If an adverb can function either as a quantifying adverb or as a modal adverb, the modal adverb will follow the adjective or the participle, and the construction will be disjunctive. Compare:

> *ce chiffon est plutôt sale* (a rather dirty rag)
> *donnez-moi un chiffon sale, plutôt* (a dirty rag, preferably)

(iii) Some adverbs in *-ment* may function either as modal adverbs or adverbs of manner, when the verb modified is in a compound tense. Compare:

> *j'ai franchement répondu* (= without hesitating)
> *j'ai répondu franchement* (= in a frank manner)

In the first sentence the adverb functions as a modal adverb, and in the second as an adverb of manner. In this case changing the place of the adverb has altered the meaning of the sentence.

One could contrast in a similar manner:

> *il lui a gentiment parlé* (= i.e. 'it was nice of him to speak to him')
> *il lui a parlé gentiment* (= *de manière gentille*)
> *il a malheureusement péri* (= 'he has unfortunately perished')
> *il a péri malheureusement* (= *d'une manière malheureuse*, i.e. 'in unfortunate circumstances')

In other words, when the adverb follows the verb it has to be interpreted objectively, and when it precedes it, it has to be interpreted figuratively; the position of the adverb is similar in this respect to the position of the adjective (see Ch. 11).

(iv) But in most cases changing the position of the adverb does not alter its meaning; in this case the change from the most normal place to a less normal place will simply emphasize the importance of the adverb:

Panzo lancera un défi. . . . à P. Le Joncour, le champion de France, très préoccupé malheureusement par des soucis musculaires. (L'Equipe)

In this case one would expect *malheureusement très préoccupé*, since the adverb used figuratively should precede the word modified; but since no 'concrete' meaning may be given to it in this context, its being postposed merely emphasizes it.

(v) Sometimes the place of the adverb is not due to functional or semantic but to phonological consideration: formal written French is organized in terms of *masses croissantes*, i.e. in terms of longer and longer rhythmic groups, or at least equal ones. An adverb may sometimes be used in an odd position from a syntactic point of view purely for reasons of phonological harmony, as is the case in 4.1.*iv*, for example.

3.2.2   *Modal adverbs modifying a whole clause or sentence*

Modal adverbs may either form an integral part of the clause (3.2.2.1) or may belong to disjunctive constructions (3.2.2.2).

3.2.2.1   *Modal adverbs as an integral part of the clause*
(i) Sans doute and *peut-être* may appear at the beginning of the sentence, e.g. *sans doute aura-t-il été retardé*. When used in this way, they are usually followed by an inversion of subject and verb.

(ii) But some modal adverbs other than *peut-être* and *sans doute* are usually followed by the conjunction *que*, thus making them into the equivalent of a modal clause, e.g. *heureusement qu'il a obtenu son visa à temps*.

3.2.2.2   *Modal adverbs as part of a disjunctive construction*   In this case the adverb will be separated from the clause by pauses (or by commas in the written language), and it may appear anywhere in the clause except between the subject and the verb or within a nominal phrase.

heureusement, il a obtenu son visa à temps
il a, heureusement, obtenu son visa à temps
il a obtenu, heureusement, son visa à temps
il a obtenu son visa, heureusement, à temps
il a obtenu son visa à temps, heureusement

Zola frequently used modal adverbs in disjunctive constructions:

Justement, une cliente se présentait. . . .
Justement, elle venait d'avoir une alerte (Au Bonheur des dames)

4   Adverbs of manner

4.1   General considerations

(i) These are the *-ment* adverbs formed simply by adding *-ment* to the adjective, e.g. *gentiment, orgueilleusement, modestement*. Not all adverbs in *-ment* are 'manner' adverbs, however.

(ii) The basic difference between adverbs of manner and the corresponding adverbials — when these exist — is that the adverb of manner focuses on the subject of the verb which it modifies, whereas the adverbial does not (see 9.3). Compare:

je garde cette lettre soigneusement
je garde cette lettre avec soin

Soigneusement refers to the intentions of the subject, whereas *avec soin* refers to the letter. Similarly:

il m'a totalement payé ce qu'il me devait
il m'a payé la somme due en totalité

In the first sentence *totalement* is all to the credit of the subject of the clause; *en totalité* simply refers to the sum of money involved.

Note: The 'manner' adverbs in -*ment* have often been considered 'heavy' and 'inelegant' because of their length. Some writers try to avoid them by using instead the corresponding adverbial phrase, e.g.

prudemment = avec prudence
travailler constamment = travailler avec constance (à un projet)

but this not only entails a shift in emphasis from the subject (in the case of the adverb) to the object (in the case of the adverbial), it may also entail a real change in meaning:

travailler constamment = to work all the time (could refer to a 'workaholic')
travailler avec constance = to show perseverance in one's work (usually refers to a specific task or occasion)

(iii) The adverb of manner may be contrasted with certain adverbs of quality, also in -*ment* (see 2.2 *iii*). In most cases there is no great difference in meaning between the two constructions:

il a correctement résolu le problème (adverb of quality)
il a résolu le problème correctement (adverb of manner)

These two types of adverbs are not interchangeable, however: we can write:

nous avons bien marché (adverb of quality)

but not:

**nous avons lentement marché*

which must be expressed:

nous avons marché lentement

In other words, if an adverb is purely an adverb of manner (= *d'une manière* X) it cannot appear before the verb as can the adverbs of quantity, quality and mood.
(iv) Phonological considerations may counterbalance functional considerations in deciding the position of these adverbs. Compare.

nous avons marché lentement (normal word order)
* *nous avons lentement marché* (unacceptable)
nous avons, lentement, remonté le cours du fleuve (acceptable)

The third sentence is possible because one is dealing with a disjunctive construction and, phonologically, with a succession of nearly equal intonation (or rhythmic) groups, the last one being the longest, which corresponds to the much favoured *organisation de la phrases par masses croissantes*:[3]

nous avons	*lentement*	*remonté le cours du fleuve*
3 syllables	3 syllables	7 syllables (or 3 + 4)

Euphony thus plays an important role, rendering acceptable some constructions which would not be so on other grounds.

4.2   Position of adverbs of manner

(i) If the verb is intransitive, the adverb of manner follows the verb, e.g. *nous avons marché lentement aujourd'hui.*
(ii) If the verb is transitive, the adverb of manner may follow either the verb or the direct object:

nous avons résolu correctement le problème
nous avons résolu le problème correctement

If the adverb of manner follows the verb rather than the direct object it is slightly emphasized.

5 Adverbial adverbs: adverbs of time and place

5.1 General considerations: the function of adverbial adverbs

These are adverbs in the sense that they are invariable, but instead of modifying a specific word of the clause as do the other adverbs, they function as would adverbials, i.e. they complement the verb in terms of the place or time of the action. The French sometimes call them *des compléments circonstanciels grammaticalisés* (i.e. circumstantial complements which have become a grammatical category in their own right). Compare:

j'irai le jeudi de la rentrée (adverbial or 'circumstantial complement')
j'irai jeudi (adverbial adverb, functioning in the same way)

5.2 Adverbs of time

5.2.1 *Types of adverb of time*

The adverbs of time referring to duration and frequency have already been mentioned under the quantifying adverbs (see 2.1.1). But there exist other types of time adverb, namely those referring to dates and specific points in time (see *(i)* and *(ii)* below).

One may sometimes contrast time adverbs referring both to time and to manner with the same adverbs expressing quantity (see *(iii)* below).

(i) Some adverbs 'date' the action. The point of reference is the time of writing or speaking, i.e. 'now': *aujourd'hui, hier, avant-hier, demain, après-demain*. If the point of reference is other than 'now', a series of nouns will correspond to the preceding adverbs: *ce jour-là, la veille, l'avant-veille, le lendemain, le surlendemain*.

(ii) Some adverbs refer to a specific point in time: *auparavant, aussitôt, désormais, ensuite, dorénavant, tantôt, tôt, tard* (but not adverbial phrases such as *en même temps*[4]).

(iii) Adverbs expressing frequency normally function as quantifiers (see 2.1.1) but in some cases they may function as adverbs of time and manner combined. Compare:

il s'est longuement promené dans le jardin (*longuement* = *beaucoup*; adverb of quantity)
il s'est promené longuement dans le jardin or
il s'est promené dans le jardin longuement (= *en prenant son temps, sans se presser*; adverb of manner + time)

One could also have a disjunctive construction:

il s'est promené dans le jardin, longuement

in which case *longuement* appears as an afterthought.

(iv) Some adverbs referring to time are felt to be 'quantifying adverbs' rather than adverbial adverbs, and vice versa. *Vite* and *souvent*, for example, sound better when used as adverbs of quantity, whereas adverbs in *-ment* such as *rapidement* tend to sound better when functioning as 'time + manner' adverbial adverbs. Thus, *il a vite fait son travail* (adverb of quantity) sounds better than *il a fait son travail vite* (adverbial adverb); but *il a fait son travail rapidement* (adverbial adverb) sounds better than *il a rapidement fait son travail* (adverb of quantity).

There is in fact a difference in meaning between these sentences. Compare:

il a fait son travail rapidement = il a été rapide dans son travail (i.e. j'admire le fait
   qu'il soit si rapide)
il a rapidement fait son travail = il a été vite parce qu'il était pressé

The preferred constructions, depending on the meaning to be expressed, are:

il a fait son travail rapidement = il a été rapide dans son travail (i.e. j'admire le fait
   qu'il soit si rapide)
il a rapidement fait son travail = il a été vite parce qu'il était pressé

5.2.2   *Position of adverbs of time*

(This section excludes those adverbs expressing frequency which function as would adverbs of quantity.)
(i) Adverbs of time normally appear at the end of the clause or sentence, after the direct object if there is one:

je me suis acheté ce disque hier
j'irai m'acheter ce disque demain

(ii) They are frequently used in disjunctive constructions, particularly in first position:

aujourd'hui, je me suis acheté un disque

They may also appear at the end of the construction:

je me suis acheté un disque, aujourd'hui

It is also possible to insert the adverb in a disjunctive construction between the verb and its object; such a construction is, however, emphatic and the rest of the sentence must semantically justify such emphasis:

je me suis acheté, aujourd'hui, un disque que je cherche depuis longtemps.

(iii) The adverb of time may sometimes be used to modify the verb alone:

quel rôle joue aujourd'hui l'enseignement privé en France?

In this case *aujourd'hui* limits the range of *joue*.
(iv) If the adverb of time is to be heavily emphasized (i.e. if it is to become the main information in the sentence) it will be introduced by a *c'est . . . que* construction:

c'est aujourd'hui que je me suis acheté ce disque.

5.3   Adverbs of place

5.3.1   *Types of adverb of place*

(i) The adverb of place may relate to a specific point in space, which may or may not be explicit in the context: *arrière, au-dehors, au-dedans, avant, ci-après, ci-contre, contre, dedans, dehors, dessus, dessous, en arrière, en haut, ici, là, loin, près*.
(ii) *-ci* and *-là* (*ci* corresponding to *ici*) combine with the demonstrative adjective for the location of objects (as in *ce meuble-ci* and *ce meuble-là* (see Ch. 2). The discontinuous *ce . . . ci* and *ce . . . là* correspond to 'this' and 'that' in English.
   Ci and *là* may also combine with other words to form compound adverbs such as *jusqu'ici, jusque-là, de-ci, de-là*. The adverb *çà* only survives in *çà et là, en deçà, deçà, delà*, or in interjections such as *Ah ça!* Note that there is a difference in the use made of *ici* and *là* and the corresponding English terms 'here' and 'there':

'he is here' (i.e. 'he has arrived') = *il est là*

Generally speaking, *là* is often used for 'here' when the latter is used in a rather global and general fashion.

(iii) Some adverbs of place may also function as adverbs of quantity or quality, and may therefore appear in the same place:

> *cette réflexion, partout entendue, est des plus inquiétantes* (adverb of quantity = *beaucoup entendue* + idea of place)
>
> *cette réflexion, entendue partout, est des plus inquiétantes* (adverbial adverb = *entendue dans tous les lieux*)

5.3.2   *Position of adverbs of place*

The same applies as for the adverbs of time.

(i) Adverbs of place normally appear at the end of the sentence or clause, e.g. *j'ai acheté mon disque ici*.

(ii) They are also used in disjunctive constructions, usually to express an idea of opposition, or to emphasize the point:

> *ici, on travaille* (implying *mais où vous êtes on ne travaille pas* = opposition)
>
> *Ici, le passé ne dort pas, il est mort* (emphasis)
>
> *Partout, des panneaux bilingues annoncent qu'il est verboten de se baigner, de stationner, de rire et d'être content* (emphasis)

(The last two examples are from P. Jardin, *La Guerre à neuf ans*.)

(iii) If the adverb of place is to be heavily emphasized it will be introduced by a *c'est . . . que* construction:

> *c'est ici que j'ai acheté mon disque*
>
> *C'est là que, dès le matin, il peint ses aquarelles, lit ses auteurs préférés, et sort de temps à autre faire un tour de pelouse* (P. Jardin, *La Guerre à neuf ans*)

(iv) Where the same clause contains both an adverb of time and an adverb of place, it is stylistically preferable to place the adverb of time at the beginning of the sentence or clause, and the adverb of place at the end, e.g. *hier, j'ai dormi ici*, but not **ici, j'ai dormi hier*, although one can write or say, *c'est ici que j'ai dormi hier*. The reason for this seems to be that the connection between verb and place seems stronger than that between verb and time.

(v) The rule in *(iv)* does not apply, however, if both adverbs are at the end of clause. Thus one may say or write either *j'ai dormi hier ici* or *j'ai dormi ici hier*.

6   Use of adverbs in comparative and superlative constructions

6.1   Comparative and superlative forms: derivation and use of adverbs

(i) In some cases, adjectives and adverbs may be modified by quantifying adverbs in order to express the intensity of the adjective or adverb modified. In these cases intensity is seen in absolute terms, i.e. without referring to a yardstick of any kind. But it is also possible to evaluate the intensity of an adjective or adverb by comparing it to the amount of that quality to be found in somebody or something else. Thus one may have *c'est joli, c'est assez joli, c'est très joli*, in which case one has a gradation from 'a little' to 'a lot' in absolute terms. But one could also have *ce garçon est plus intelligent que celui-là*, in which the amount of intelligence of the boy is seen in relation to the intelligence of another boy: this is comparative quantification.

(ii) A distinction is made between comparative and superlative constructions. A comparative construction expresses a higher or lower degree of a particular quality or attribute in relation to a reference point, i.e. a hotter day than yesterday, a more beautiful day than yesterday. A superlative construction expresses the highest or

lowest degree of a quality or attribute: 'it is the hottest day of the year', 'it is the most beautiful day we have had so far'.

(iii) In English both comparative and superlative degrees may be expressed either by derivation ('big/bigger/biggest') or by the use of adverbs: ('beautiful/more beautiful/most beautiful'). In French, however, the comparative and superlative are, in nearly all cases, expressed by adverbs: *grand/plus grand/le plus grand*. Equality is expressed in both languages by using an adverb in all cases: 'as big as' = *aussi grand que*. The normal way of expressing the comparative and the superlative, i.e. by using adverbs, is examined in 6.2.2, whereas the forms obtained through derivation are examined in 6.2.3.

6.2 Expression of degrees of comparison through use of adverbs

6.2.1 *Explicit or non-elliptical constructions*

(i) There are altogether five possibilities:

'least'	'less'	'as'	'more'	'most'
le moins	*moins*	*aussi*	*plus*	*le plus*

The comparative degree can be seen to be expressed by *plus* and *moins*, the superlative degree by *le plus* and *le moins*. Equality is expressed by *aussi*:

Jean est plus/aussi/moins grand que Pierre
Jean est le plus/le moins grand de la famille

(ii) Where it is the comparative degree which is expressed, the introduction of the reference point will be through the conjunction *que*. Where it is the superlative degree which is expressed there is no necessary second half to the comparison, in the sense that one is expressing the very highest or lowest degree of a quality in relation to a whole group, which may or may not be specified (see 6.2.2.*ii*):

Jean est le plus grand
Jean est le plus grand de la famille
Jean est le plus grand de la classe . . .

If the whole group referred to is specified, it will be introduced by the preposition *de*.

(iii) The superlative may be reinforced by the adverb *possible: achetez le moins cher possible*.

(iv) The comparative may be reinforced by the adverbs *bien, même* and *encore: il est bien/même/encore plus riche que son frère*

6.2.2 *Implicit comparisons*

(i) Where there is a comparative construction, i.e. *plus* or *moins* not preceded by an article, one expects a *que* complement to follow. When this is not the case, the sentence is felt to be elliptical and the speaker will try to fill in the missing information from what precedes:

Jean est grand mais Jacques est encore plus grand (i.e. *que lui*)

There are some cases however in which the second half of the comparison is not directly retrievable from the verbal context, but only deducible from the context, and which appear mainly in the spoken language:

il n'a qu'à travailler plus (i.e. *qu'auparavant* or *qu'à présent*)
lisez plus (qu'auparavant ou que maintentant)

Plus is, in this case, simply used in the sense of *davantage*. It may be reinforced in this case by *encore: lisez encore plus* (= even more).

Davantage in Classical French could mean either *le plus* or *de plus*, as in *que demander de plus?* In modern French it can only correspond to a comparative.

(ii) Similarly, where one finds a superlative construction, i.e. *plus* or *moins* preceded by a determiner, it is necessary to work out from the context over what group the referent has unqualified superiority or inferiority. The information may be found in the verbal context, but it may also be found in the situational context. One could for example point at a picture in a room in which there are several pictures and say *c'est celui-là le plus beau*.

6.2.3 *Other types of comparative construction*

(i) Comparative constructions may also be used to express a relation of cause and effect:

plus . . . plus: *plus il devient riche et plus il devient avare*
plus . . . moins: *plus il vieillit et moins il a envie de sortir*
moins . . . mieux: *moins vous mangerez et mieux vous vous porterez*
tellement . . . que and *si . . . que*: *il est si fort qu'il a tout transporté tout seul*

(ii) They may also be used to indicate that the degree of quality referred to is considered in relation to some other element; in this case one uses the expression *d'autant plus (que)*:

le fait qu'il ait si bien réussi est d'autant plus étonnant qu'il ne s'était donné aucun mal pour y arriver

6.2.4 *Position of comparative and superlative adverbs*

These constitute a particular kind of quantifying adverb; as such they always precede the word modified, e.g. *Jean est plus grand que Pierre; Jean est le plus grand*.

6.3 Forms obtained through derivation

6.3.1 *Survivals from Latin: comparative adjectives*[5]

(i) Ironically, these 'survivals' come themselves from abnormal cases in Latin. These are:

Adjective	Comparative	Superlative
bon(ne)	*meilleur(e)*	*le meilleur/la meilleure*
mauvais(e)	*pire*	*le pire/la pire*
petit(e)	*moindre*	*le moindre/la moindre*

These forms are not, in fact, a survival from Classical Latin directly, but a re-import into French from Latin via Italian in the sixteenth century (*pire* coming from *pejorem* and *moindre* from *minorem*).

(ii) Of these three adjectives, the use of *bon* and *meilleur* is fixed and unvarying (except in certain nonstandard forms of speech such as creoles).

Plus mauvais is found as often as *pire*, but with a semantic difference: *plus mauvais* tends to be used for less abstract meanings than *pire*. Compare:

la nourriture était encore plus mauvaise que celle de l'internat
la nourriture était pire encore que celle de l'internat

Plus mauvaise refers to its taste, whereas *pire* refers both to its taste and its quality; its meaning is more abstract.

Plus petit is used for concrete meanings in general, whereas *moindre* is kept for abstract meanings:

sa voiture est plus petite que la nôtre
ses chagrins sont moindres que les nôtres

6.3.2   Survivals from Latin: comparative adverbs

(i)

Adverb	Comparative	Superlative
bien	*mieux*	*le mieux*
mal	*pis*	*le pire/le pis*

(ii) Pis is rarely used in contemporary French, *pire* being used instead; thus *pire que* (as in *il est pire que moi en mathématiques*) has become the normal comparative, with *le pire* remaining as the superlative.

Mieux is sometimes used on its own as in *faites pour le mieux* (or *faites au mieux*). In this case the *mieux* has been nominalized; *pis* and *pire* may also be nominalized.

6.3.3   Lexically creative derivation in modern French

One suffix and several prefixes may be used to express the superlative.
(i) -issime, as in *richissime* = 'rich beyond belief'), is a superlative suffix. This form was borrowed from the Italian form, which came from the Latin *-issimus*. It was originally used for titles as in *Son Altesse Sérénissime*. When used with adjectives such as *grand/grandissime* or *savant/savantissime* the effect is ironic.
(ii) Of the superlative prefixes *archi-, extra-, super-, sur-, ultra-; extra* and *ultra* normally produce hyphenated compounds, whereas the others normally produce compounds written as one word: *extra-sec, ultra-royaliste* but *surfin, archifou* and *superfin.*

6.4   Different uses of comparative and superlative constructions in French and English

(i) A comparative or superlative construction may be used in English where it cannot be used in French:

'to be at one's best' = *être très en forme* (or *en pleine forme*)
'the lower part of the wall' = *le bas du mur*

In the first case a superlative is translated in absolute terms in French; in the second case it is a comparative construction which is also translated in absolute terms in French.
(ii) There are also many cases in which comparative or superlative constructions are possible in French but unlikely to be used, e.g. 'stays cleaner longer' may be translated by *est peu salissant* or by *n'est pas salissant* (*reste propre plus longtemps* is possible but stylistically improbable).
(iii) When *plus, moins* and *mieux* are used in combination with an idea of cause and effect, the English construction includes the use of the definite article, whereas the French construction excludes it:

'the hotter it gets, the happier he is' = *plus il fait chaud, plus il est content*

7 Negative adverbs

This type of adverb expresses the quantity zero.

7.1 Morphological and syntactic considerations

For the historical development of these adverbs, see 7.4.

(i) The negative adverbs may be used to negate verbs, nouns or adjectives, or whole statements. It is in the negation of verbs and statements that they are most important:

> *je ne veux pas y aller* (negation of verb)
> *je veux voir un médecin, et non un charlatan* (negation of noun)
> *je veux un pull-over bleu marine, et non noir* (negation of an adjective)
> *tu ne penses pas qu'il faut y aller? Non* (negative answer to a question; in this case the adverb is negating a whole sentence (see 7.4*i*))

(ii) The negative adverb is made up of one word, *non*, when negating a noun or an adjective, or when functioning as a negative answer to a question (for positive and negative answers to questions, see Ch. 19).

(iii) The negative adverb is made up of two words, when negating a verb:

> *j'y vais* and *je n'y vais pas* (total negation)
> *j'y vais souvent* and *je n'y vais guère* (often and rarely)
> *j'y vais encore* and *je n'y vais plus* (still and no longer)

Ne . . . pas therefore simply negates the verb, whereas the other negative forms negate a verb + adverb.

Ne becomes *n'* before a vowel (see examples above).

Note: Ne is still sometimes used on its own, i.e. without *pas* or *point*. This may happen in the following cases:

(a) in fossilized constructions such as proverbs (e.g. *il n'est pire eau que l'eau qui dort*) and set phrases (e.g. *à Dieu ne plaise*);

(b) in subordinate clauses containing a subjunctive dependent upon an interrogative or negative main clause (e.g. *y-a-t-il quelqu'un dont il ne dise du mal?, ce n'est pas qu'il ne soit de bonne volonté*);

(c) with *cesser, oser* and *pouvoir* followed by an infinitive complement (e.g. *il ne cesse de parler* as against *il n'arrête pas de parler*);

(d) with *depuis que, longtemps que, voilà que* and similar expressions (e.g. *voilà bientôt dix ans que je ne l'ai vu*). But it is the complete form *ne . . . pas* which is used if the verb introduced is in the present or imperfect tense (e.g. *cela fait longtemps que nous ne nous voyons pas* (or *plus*).

(e) after *que* used with the meaning of *pourquoi* (e.g. *puisque tu en es sûr, que ne le dis-tu pas?*)

(See 7.4 for historical note.)

(iv) Ne may also be used in combination with *nul, aucun, personne* and *rien*; in this case no *pas* is needed, since the second part of the negation is already contained in each of these four words:

> *nul n'est venu me secourir*
> *personne n'est venu me voir ce matin*

In the case of *personne*, it is the presence or absence of an article which changes its meaning from 'somebody' to 'nobody':

> *une personne m'a dit* ('somebody told me')
> *personne ne m'a dit* ('nobody told me')

(v) Ne is often dropped in informal speech: *je n'en ai pas* becomes **j'en ai pas*.

(vi) Ne . . . point is a variant of *ne . . . pas* still in use in modern French, but in two

very different kinds of context: either in very formal French, or in popular speech. In certain areas of France (in Lyon in particular) it is frequently used in shops in sentences such as *je n'en ai point*.

Note: Ne . . . point may only be used if the verb has a complement. One may thus give as an answer to the question *avez-vous des pommes aujourd'hui?* either *aujourd'hui je n'en ai point* or *aujourd'hui je n'en ai pas*. One cannot however say **je ne marche point* but only *je ne marche pas*.

The other variants of *ne . . . pas*, such as *ne . . . goutte* and *ne . . . mie* are no longer used; see 7.4.

(vii) The negative conjunction *ni* may signify *et . . . ne . . . pas*, and may therefore be classified either as a negative adverb or as a conjunction:

> *il ne veut ni boire ni manger* (= *il ne veut pas boire et il ne veut pas manger*) (*ni* may modify infinitives)
> *je ne veux ni soupe, ni fromage (= je ne veux pas de soupe et je ne veux pas de fromage)*

Note: In Classical French it was not necessary to repeat *ni*:

> *Le soleil ni la mort ne se peuvent regarder fixement (La Rochefoucauld)*

Today one would have to write:

> *Ni le soleil ni la mort ne se peuvent regarder fixement*

Ni comes from *ne* (*ne icelui* and *ne icelle* gave *ni celui* and *ni celle*); and we still find in the seventeenth century *ne plus que* and *ne moins que* instead of *ni plus que* and *ni moins que*, particularly in Molière's works – although Molière, in using such constructions, is being deliberately archaic.

7.2   The half-way negation: the use of 'ne' on its own or the 'expletive "ne"'

The expletive *ne* should not be confused with the purely negative *ne*: see 7.1*iii* Note.
(i) *Ne* is sometimes used on its own in a subordinate clause simply to highlight the underlying semantic opposition existing between the main clause and the subordinate clause. This idea of opposition may be expressed either by a phrasal conjunction expressing opposition or negation such as *sans que, à moins que, plus que* or *moins que*, or by the meaning of the verb in the main clause (verbs of fear such as *appréhender, avoir peur, craindre*), verbs expressing the idea of trying to stop something from happening (verbs such as *empêcher, éviter* or *prendre garde*) and verbs expressing the opposition existing between reality and what could have been (*il s'en faut que, peu s'en faut que*). In all of these cases there is a certain element of implicit negation, which the *ne* is there to emphasize:

> *j'irai avant que tu ne reviennes = quand tu reviendras je serai parti*, or *tu ne seras pas revenu quand je partirai*
> *j'irai à moins que son état n'empire = si son état n'empire pas, j'irai, mais si son état empire je n'irai pas*
> *tu vas vexer plus de gens que tu ne l'imagines = tu ne t'imagines pas combien de gens tu vas vexer*
> *je crains qu'il ne pleuve = je désire qu'il ne pleuve pas, mais je crains que la pluie arrive*

The use of this type of *ne* is not obligatory and is typical of careful speech or writing. Its use seems to be on the increase, but more as an automatic reflex than for the purpose of emphasizing the negative quality implicit in the sentence.
(ii) If one writes *il s'en faut de beaucoup qu'il ait réussi*, the expletive *ne* cannot be used, since in this case there would be little margin for doubt.

(iii) In Classical French the situation seems to have been extremely confused: the expletive *ne* was sometimes used as it is in modern French (as in the first example below), but it was sometimes replaced by a full negation (as in the second example):

> ... *cela aurait pu s'appeler leur portrait à bien plus juste titre que tout ce qu'ils ont fait ne peut être appelé le vôtre* (Molière) = *ce qu'ils ont fait ne peut pas être appelé votre portrait*
> *Vous avez plus froid que vous ne pensez pas* (Molière) = *vous ne pensez pas avoir aussi froid que vous avez froid en réalité*

The use of the full negation where it is unnecessary is extremely confusing to the modern reader. Sentences such as the second example are not considered acceptable in modern French. One has to write instead: *vous avez plus froid que vous ne le pensez.* The position in modern French is therefore much clearer than it used to be. Where opposition and implicit negation are present, *ne* may be used to emphasize both opposition and negation. Its use does not, however, change the polarity of the sentence as the full negation does, hence the possibility of dropping it, which is characteristic of informal speech.

Note: The precise rules are as follows:

(a) The expletive *ne* may be used with verbs such as *avoir peur que, craindre que* (and their corresponding phrasal conjunctions *de peur que* and *de crainte que*), *empêcher que, éviter que, prendre garde que* (but *not défendre que*), on condition the main clause is declarative and positive (e.g. *je crains qu'il ne se trompe* but *je ne crains pas qu'il se trompe*). It is important to note that *je crains qu'il ne se trompe* is quite different in meaning from *je crains qu'il ne se trompe pas*: in the first case the meaning is 'I fear he will make a mistake but I would like him not to' whereas the second case means 'I fear he may not make a mistake which I would like him to make'.

(b) The expletive *ne* may be used with *douter que, mettre en doute que, nier, disconvenir, désespérer, contester, méconnaître, dissimuler,* on condition that the main clause is declarative and negative (e.g. *je ne doute pas que ses intentions ne soient des meilleures*). With *nier* the same applies if the sentence is an interrogative (e.g. *nierais-tu qu'il ne soit malhonnête?*).

(c) The expletive *ne* is used with *avant que, sans que, à moins que* (e.g. *je serai de retour avant que tu ne sois parti*).

(d) The expletive *ne* is used with *moins que, plus que, meilleur que, pire que, plutôt que,* on condition that the main clause is both declarative and positive (e.g. *il est plus malin que je ne le pensais*).

In all of these cases the use of *ne* is optional, at least in the spoken language; its use is however one of the niceties of the written language.

7.3 Position of negative adverbs

7.3.1 *Negation of noun, adjective or infinitive*

In these cases the negative adverb precedes the word negated, as do other adverbs:

noun adjective infinitive	+	*(et) non* *non pas* *mais pas*	+	noun adjective infinitive

Examples:

> *j'aime les chats, mais pas les chiens* (stylistically unmarked)
> *j'aime les chats, (et) non les chiens* (slightly more emphatic)
> *j'aime les chats, non pas les chiens* (literary)

In spoken French one would usually say:

j'aime les chats, pas les chiens

In this case the construction may be considered the elliptical version either of the *non pas* or the *mais pas* construction. One could thus write:

c'est Racine, et non La Fontaine qui fut historiographe du roi Louix XIV

but not:

*c'est Racine pas, La Fontaine qui fut historiographe du roi Louis XIV

for stylistic reasons: there would be a clash between the context which is formal and this construction which is informal.

7.3.2　*Negation of verb in main or independent clauses*

7.3.2.1　*Tense of negated verb*　There are four cases to be considered.
(i) If the verb is in a simple tense, *ne* precedes the verb and *pas* follows it:

je ne chante pas

(ii) If the verb is in a compound tense, *ne* precedes the auxiliary and *pas* follows it:

je n'ai pas chanté

(iii) If the verb is in a double compound tense, *ne* precedes the first auxiliary and *pas* follows the first auxiliary:

je n'ai pas eu fini mon travail avant six heures

(iv) Ne pas precedes the infinitive:

je lui ai dit de ne pas chanter

But note the contrast:

je lui ai dit de ne pas chanter = 'I told him not to sing'
je ne lui ai pas dit de chanter = 'I did not tell him to sing'

Similarly:

je ne peux pas partir = 'I cannot leave'
je peux ne pas partir = 'I could very well not leave'

7.3.2.2　*Archaic rules of position of negation with infinitives*　Vaugelas declared that *ne pas tomber* was preferable to *ne tomber pas*, but the 'banned' version, far from totally disappearing, became a literary variant:

je vous conseille de ne pas y penser (normal word order)
je vous conseille de n'y penser pas (archaic and literary)

(Montherlant and Aymé are particularly fond of this construction.)

7.3.2.3　*Reinforcement of the second element of the negation*　The second element may be modified by adverbs such as *jamais, presque, même, encore, toujours* and so on. The modifying adverb precedes the second element of the negation:

je n'arrive presque plus à le faire (*presque* modifies *plus*)
je ne l'ai même pas vu (*même* modifies *pas*)

In some cases it is semantically possible to change the modifying adverb into the modified adverb, thus achieving a change either in emphasis or in meaning (see 8.4.*iv*).

7.3.3 *Negation in completive clauses*

(i) If the main clause expresses modality, the negation of the completive clause is in the main clause:

je ne veux pas qu'il y aille

rather than:

je veux qu'il ne parte pas

The second sentence is however possible if the first negated completive clause is followed by a second coordinated positive completive clause, as in:

je veux qu'il ne parte pas et qu'il obéisse

Similarly the presence of an adverbial complement could make such a construction acceptable:

je veux qu'il ne parte pas avant mon retour

(ii) If there are two non-coordinated completive clauses, the negation will be in the negated clause and not in the main one carrying modality:

il faut qu'il n'ait pas de mémoire pour qu'il ait pu oublier cette insulte

7.3.4 *Negation in interrogative sentences*

The rules of the place of the negative adverb remain unchanged in interrogative sentences:

vient-il? ne vient-il pas?
est-il venu? n'est-il pas venu?
est-ce qu'il vient? est-ce qu'il ne vient pas?

7.4 Historical note on morphological aspects of the negative adverbs

The Latin negative adverb *non* survived in Old French in two forms; a strong form *non*, and a weak form *nen*.
(i) The strong form *non* survives in the negation of nouns, adjectives and infinitives, when there are two in opposition: *je veux ceci, et non cela* (see 7.3.1). It also survives in the conjunction *sinon* which comes from Old French *se . . . non*. (This adverb has become a conjunction, as in *tais-toi sinon je me fâche*.) *Non* has also survived in negative words such as *un non-lieu, un non-sens, le non-être* (the latter coined in the eighteenth century). *Non* used on its own negates a whole preceding sentence: *Viens-tu? Non.*
(ii) The weak form *nen*, which became *ne*, could be used on its own to negate the verb up till the seventeenth century. This use of *ne* survives in expressions such as *je n'ose, je ne puis, n'empêche que* etc. (see also 7.1*iii* Note and 7.2)
   The weak *ne* used to be frequently reinforced by other adverbials such as *jamais, guère, plus: je n'ai jamais faim/je n'ai guère faim/je n'ai plus faim.*
   It was also possible to insist on the negative aspect of the sentence by reinforcing *ne* with *pas, goutte, mie, grain, point*; all of these were originally nouns. A distinction was made between these according to meaning:

je ne mange mie (pas une mie de pain)
je ne vois goutte dans la cave (in the cellar)
je ne vois grain dans le grenier (in the attic/granary)
je ne veux pas y aller (process: 'I'm not making one step in that direction')
je ne veux point d'argent (negated object: 'I do not want the tiniest bit (point) of
   money')

By the seventeenth century only *pas* and *point* survived, both having lost their original meaning and having become purely negative words.

In modern French it is *pas* – and more rarely *point* – which are felt to be the negative elements in a sentence; *ne* is therefore disappearing from the informal spoken language, although it appears to be more firmly entrenched when used in combination with *nul, aucun, personne* and *rien. Ne* remains indispensable in the written language and in formal spoken French.

8   The position of adverbs (summary)

8.1   General considerations

(i) Adverbs occupy slightly different positions in the sentence depending on whether they are functioning as adverbs of quality or quantity, as modal adverbs, as adverbs of manner, or as adverbs of place or time. Adverbs expressing negation are in a category of their own.

(ii) In some cases the same adverb may function as an adverb of quality, as an adverb of mood, or as an adverb of manner. It is its position in the sentence which will define its exact function; in these cases changing the place of the adverb – and hence its function – may either change its meaning or may entail a shift in its emphasis only. It is therefore important to understand what the implications are when placing an adverb at one point in the sentence rather than at another, when several positions are possible.

8.2   Normal rules

8.2.1   *Adverbs of quantity and quality*

The rule is that these adverbs precede the word modified, unless the latter is a verb used in a simple tense, in which case they follow it:

il a trop mangé but *il mange trop*
il a bien mangé but *il mange bien*

Note, however:
If an adverb could be either an adverb of quantity or a modal adverb, the latter will be used in a 'disjunctive' construction in order to differentiate it from an adverb of quantity. Compare:

voilà un chiffon plutôt sale (adverb of quantity)
donnez-m'en un propre, plutôt (modal adverb)

In most cases the meaning of two such constructions is more or less the same.

8.2.2   *Modal adverbs*

The modal adverbs may modify either a word or a sentence.

8.2.2.1   *Modification of a single word*
(i) If they modify a word they behave exactly in the same way as the adverbs of quantity and quality: they precede the word modified, unless it is a verb in a simple tense:

il va peut-être venir lundi
il vient peut-être lundi

(In this last case *peut-être* modifies both *vient* and *lundi*.)
(ii) See 8.2.1 for disjunctive constructions to differentiate certain modal adverbs from certain adverbs of quantity.

(iii) Some adverbs in *-ment* may function either as modal adverbs or as adverbs of manner, depending on their position in the clause:

> *il lui a gentiment parlé* (modal adverb: 'it was nice of him to talk to him')
> *il lui a parlé gentiment* (adverb of manner: 'he spoke to him in a kindly fashion')

In other words, if the adverb appears before the verb it expresses mood, and if the adverb follows the verb it is used in its concrete or objective sense.

8.2.2.2 *Modification of a clause or sentence* In this case there are several possibilities.
(i) The modal adverb sometimes appears at the beginning of the clause or sentence: *sans doute aura-t-il été retardé par ses amis.* (*Sans doute* and *peut-être* are usually followed by subject/verb inversion.)
(ii) But if the modal adverb appears at the beginning of the sentence, it will usually combine with *que*, thus becoming the equivalent of a modal clause: *sans doute qu'il aura été retardé par ses amis* (no inversion in this case).
(iii) In this case, however, disjunctive constructions are the most usual:

> *heureusement, il a obtenu son visa à temps*
> *il a, heureusement, obtenu son visa à temps*
> *il a obtenu son visa, heureusement, à temps*
> *il a obtenu, heureusement, son visa à temps*
> *il a obtenu son visa à temps, heureusement*

(i.e. the adverb may appear between two pauses between any two grammatical units, except between those functioning as subject and verb).

8.2.3 *Adverbs of manner*

(i) If the verb is intransitive, adverbs of manner follow the verb: *nous avons marché lentement*.
(ii) If the verb is transitive, the adverb of manner may appear either before or after the direct object:

> *nous avons résolu le problème correctement*
> *nous avons résolu correctement le problème* (slight emphasis on the adverb)

8.2.4 *Adverbs of time and place*

8.2.4.1 *Adverbs of time*
(i) Adverbs of time normally appear at the end of the clause or sentence, after the direct object if there is one:

> *je me suis acheté ce disque aujourd'hui*

(ii) They are frequently used in disjunctive constructions, particularly at the beginning of sentences:

> *aujourd'hui, je me suis acheté un disque*

but also within the sentence:

> *je me suis acheté, aujourd'hui, un disque que je cherche depuis longtemps*

(See 5.2.2*ii*.)
(iii) Adverbs of time may sometimes be used to modify the verb alone, in which case they follow the verb:

> *quel rôle joue aujourd'hui l'enseignement privé en France?*

(iv) If the adverb of time is to be heavily emphasized, it will be introduced by a *c'est . . . que* construction:

c'est aujourd'hui que je me suis acheté ce disque

8.2.4.2   *Adverbs of place*
(i) Adverbs of place normally appear at the end of the clause or sentence, after the direct object if there is one: *j'ai acheté mon disque ici.*
(ii) They may appear in disjunctive constructions, but when appearing at the beginning of a sentence, they are used to express an idea of opposition:

ici, on travaille (mais pas là-bas)
là-bas, il fait beau (mais pas ici)

(iii) Where the same clause contains both an adverb of time and an adverb of place, it is usual to place the adverb of time at the beginning of the sentence and the adverb of place at the end: *hier, j'ai dormi ici*, but not **ici, j'ai dormi hier*. The reason for this is that the connection between verb and place seems stronger than that between verb and time. But *j'ai dormi hier ici* and *j'ai dormi ici hier* are both acceptable.
(iv) Adverbs of place may however appear at the beginning of a sentence in a *c'est . . . que* construction: *c'est ici que j'ai dormi hier.*

8.2.5   *Comparative and superlative adverbs*

These are quantifying adverbs and therefore precede the word modified: *il est plus grand que son frère; c'est le plus grand.*

8.2.6   *Negative adverbs*

8.2.6.1   *Negation of noun or adjective*   If the word modified is a noun or an adjective, the negative adverb precedes the word modified as do the other adverbs:

j'aime les chats, mais pas les chiens
j'aime les chats, et non les chiens
j'aime les chats, non pas les chiens (literary)

8.2.6.2   *Negation of verb and several nouns or adjectives*   In this case *ne* precedes the verb and *ni* each noun or adjective negated:

je n'aime ni les chats, ni les chiens
il n'est ni intelligent ni travailleur

8.2.6.3   *Negation of verb in main or independent clause*
(i) The verb is in the simple tense: *ne* precedes the auxiliary and *pas* follows: *je ne chante pas.*
(ii) The verb is in a compound tense: *ne* precedes the auxiliary and *pas* follows it: *je n'ai pas chanté; il n'a pas eu fini à temps.*

8.2.6.4   *Negation of infinitive*   In this case *ne pas* normally precedes the infinitive:

je lui ai dit de ne pas chanter ('I told him not to sing')

But this construction may be contrasted with the following:

je ne lui ai pas dit de chanter ('I did not tell him to sing')

8.2.6.5   *Negation in completive clauses*
(i) If the main clause expresses modality, negation of the completive clause will be

contained in the main clause: *je ne veux pas qu'il y aille*.
(ii) But if the completive clause is followed by a coordinated clause which is not negated, negation will appear in the completive clause being negated instead of in the main clause: *je veux qu'il ne parte pas et qu'il obéisse*.

8.2.6.6 *Interrogative sentences* In interrogative sentences, the rules regarding the negative adverb remain the same as those described above.

8.3 Stylistic considerations

Adverbs of manner may appear in a different position from that expected, for emphasis, on condition that this does not change the meaning of the adverb:

Il pourrait vivre de ses rentes richement (Bourget)

instead of:

il pourrait vivre richement de ses rentes (*richement* modifies *vivre*)

(ii) Modal adverbs and adverbs of time and place appearing in disjunctive constructions are emphasized, since they are 'detached' from the rest of the clause or sentence. Compare:

. . . *une éducation classique l'attendait, sans surprise, sans doute* (Jardin *La guerre à neuf ans* (back cover))
instead of
. . . *sans doute qu'une éducation classique sans surprise l'attendait*

Disjunctive constructions of this kind are typical of journalese and reviews.
(iii) Sometimes the position of the adverb is changed for phonological reasons: to ensure that the written language is organized in terms of *masses croissantes*, i.e. in terms of rhythmic or intonation groups of increasing or at least equal length. In these cases the construction must be disjunctive:

nous avons,	*lentement, remonté le cours du fleuve*
3 syllables	3 syllables 3 + 4 syllables
	(or 7, depending on how this is read)

instead of

nous avons remonté	*lentement*	*le cours du fleuve*
6 syllables	3 syllables	4 syllables

8.4 Different position of the adverb in English and French

(i) It is possible in English, but not in French, for an adverb to precede a verb in a simple tense:

'John strongly objects to that idea'
Jean s'oppose violemment à cette idée

(ii) In French, adverbs of quality normally follow the verb if it is in a simple tense, or come between the auxiliary and the verb if the latter is in a compound tense. The same does not apply in English. Compare:

vous avez très mal répondu à cette question
'you have answered that question very badly'

One could also say or write in French, *vous avez répondu très mal à cette question*; but in this case the adverb occupies the place of an adverb of manner. The effect is to emphasize the adverb.

(iii) English adverbs do not always correspond to adverbs in French:

'you could get a pass on that answer alone'
vous pourriez être reçu grâce à cette seule question

(iv) The position of adverbs modifying *pas* in *ne . . . pas* is not usually the same as the position of adverbs modifying 'not'; indeed different adverbs, in French, may behave quite differently in this respect.

(a) Même normally precedes *pas: il ne m'a même pas téléphoné* ('he did not even telephone' – the 'me' being understood in English); but *même* may follow *pas* in highly emphatic constructions: *il ne m'a pas même téléphoné* (in this case the *même* is heavily emphasized).

(b) Encore normally follows *pas: il ne m'a pas encore téléphoné* ('he has not yet telephoned' or 'he has not telephoned yet'); but *encore* may precede *pas*, in which case the meaning of the sentence is changed: *il ne m'a encore pas téléphoné* means 'yet again he has failed to telephone'.

(c) Toujours normally precedes *pas: il ne m'a toujours pas téléphoné* ('he has still not telephoned'); but *toujours* may follow *pas*, in which case the sentence takes on a different meaning: *il ne m'a pas toujours téléphoné* ('he did not always telephone').

(v) Some written English sentences containing adverbs may be ambiguous, whereas their French counterparts may not. Thus 'John only phoned Mary today' could correspond to the following sentences, depending on which word is stressed in English:

Jean a téléphoné à Marie aujourd'hui seulement ('only today')
Jean n'a téléphoné qu'à Marie aujourd'hui ('only Mary')
Jean a seulement téléphoné à Marie aujourd'hui ('only phoned')

9   Stylistic considerations other than those relating to position

9.1   Adverbs of manner ending in '-ment'

These have been described as *des adverbes qui font plouf* (Veuillot). Molière, for example, uses such adverbs to create a comic effect in *Les Femmes savantes*, in the following poem written for 'a princess suffering from a fever':

> *Votre prudence est endormie*
> *De traiter magnifiquement*
> *Et de loger superbement*
> *Votre plus cruelle ennemie*

On hearing this poem Philaminte exclaims:

J'aime superbement et magnifiquement. Ces deux adverbes joints font admirablement.

Excessive use of these adverbs tends therefore to be avoided. Thus, in some cases, one may wish to rewrite a sentence such as *il partit finalement* as *il finit par partir*, or expressions such as *s'exprimer ironiquement* as *s'exprimer en termes ironiques*. On the other hand, when these are used in writing, they do tend to be emphatic. Gautier and Zola, in particular, have obtained interesting effects from their use.

9.2   Adverbs of quantity

Adverbs such as *beaucoup, peu, trop, très, plus, moins, assez* and *combien* are sometimes considered typical of relatively informal registers. It is therefore sometimes suggested that in formal written French one would replace sentences such as *je vous dirai combien il faut de chaque ingrédient* by sentences such as *je vous indiquerai la dose pour chaque ingrédient*; similarly *je ne sais pas combien je vous dois* could be replaced by *j'ignore le montant de ma dette*, if the context permits (the latter being very formal). On the same theme, *un vent très froid* could become *un vent glacial* and un *agriculteur qui a beaucoup de terre* could become *un agriculteur riche en terre*. It is certainly important to be aware of the possibilities of substitution of one form for another, since although one form may not be intrinsically better than another, one may fit into a particular context rather better.

9.3 Choice between adverbs and corresponding adverbial phrases

(English and French tend to behave in the same way in this respect.)
(i) In some cases the two constructions may differ in nuance, since the adverb tends to be more subjective in its implications than the corresponding adverbial phrase. Compare:

je vais ranger ces papiers soigneusement (refers to the intention of the speaker)
je vais ranger ces papiers avec soin (refers to the result of the action)

Similarly, *il m'écoute attentivement* refers to the fact that the listener is making an effort, whereas *il m'écoute avec attention* refers to a state of affairs from an objective point of view.
(ii) The use of one or the other form may imply whether or not the action is deliberate:

il pose son journal lentement ('slowly', i.e. no implication of deliberate action)
il pose son journal avec lenteur (refers to a deliberate action, implying that the person is purposely not hurrying)

(iii) In other cases there may be a more definite change in meaning. One may thus contrast *il est venu en personne* and *il en est personnellement responsable*. The first of these sentences means 'he came in person', whereas the second means 'he is personally responsible for it'. In other words, *en personne* refers to a concrete reality, whereas *personnellement* is used in an abstract sense.
     One may similarly contrast:

il a exécuté mes instructions à la lettre
il a exécuté mes instructions littéralement

The first of these sentences means 'he followed my instructions precisely', whereas the second means 'he took what I said literally'. Again, the adverb is used in an abstract sense.
     Finally, if somebody is told something *en confidence*, this means that strictly nobody is to be told (i.e. *sous le sceau du secret*), whereas something told *confidentiellement* merely refers to something which is not to be broadcast (i.e. *à ne pas crier sur tous les toits*).

9.4 Comparison between positive and negative constructions

(English and French behave in the same way in this respect).
     In some cases a single positive lexical item may correspond to a negative construction:

ne pas tenir compte d'un avis = négliger un avis
ne pas reconnaître un droit = contester un droit

The positive construction tends to be more emphatic than the negative one which is why the negative form may sometimes be used as an attenuated version of the corresponding positive construction. Thus, *mon entreprise n'a pas réussi* is less harsh than *mon entreprise a échoué*; similarly, the statement *mes parents ne sont pas riches* implies that they have more money than if one had said *mes parents sont pauvres*. Such negative constructions are sometimes used to express euphemisms, as in the case of *cette personne n'est plus jeune*, meaning *cette personne est âgée*.

Notes

1 A preposition used transitively introduces a complement; one used intransitively does not introduce anything.
2 For a definition of a mute *h* see Ch. 2, section 1.1.2 Note.
3 *Organisation de la phrase par masses croissantes* means that the sentence is organized in such a way that the rhythmic groups becomes longer as the sentence progresses. (For a definition of rhythmic groups, see Ch. 17, section 5.)
4 Expressions such as *en même temps* function as adverbial phrases – or *compléments circonstanciels* – and do not normally appear at the beginning of sentences, as adverbs of time may do:

> *ces progrès de la technique ont fait naître en même temps la peur de nouveaux licenciements*

but probably not

> **en même temps, ces progrès de la technique ont fait naître la peur de nouveaux licenciements.*

5 These adjectives appear under this heading rather than under that of adjectives because they are so few in number. The normal way of expressing the comparative and the superlative in modern French is through the use of adverbs; these adjectives are no more than survivals.

Part IV

Link words

0.1 Defining link words

There are a certain number of words which are used mainly to express the kind of grammatical relationship existing between two items, either within a clause (prepositions and coordinating conjunctions), between clauses (coordinating conjunctions, subordinating conjunctions and relative pronouns) or between sentences (coordinating conjunctions and other coordinators).

0.2 Terminological problems concerning prepositions, subordinating conjunctions and coordinating conjunctions

(i) Traditional terminology distinguishes between the following categories:

(1) Conjunctions   *(a)* coordinating conjunctions
                                 (b) subordinating conjunctions
(2) Prepositions

This classification obscures the fact that subordinating conjunctions and prepositions are both 'subordinating words', albeit at different grammatical levels. This classification also links together two quite different types of words, namely coordinating and subordinating words. Various twentieth-century French grammarians have tried to remedy this by creating a new terminology (e.g. Damourette and Pichon in the 1930s, and Baylon and Fabre in the late 1970s); but none of these new terminologies seems capable of replacing the traditional one. The following one, for example would better reflect linguistic reality:

(1) Coordination: coordinating conjunctions and other coordinators (see 0.5)
(2) Subordination:
    (a) at the phrase level: prepositions
    (b) at the clause level: subordinating conjunctions or 'subjunctions', and relative pronouns or 'subordinating pronouns'

There is a defect, however, where the word 'subjunction' is concerned: the adjective derived from 'subjunction' would be subjunctive, which could lead to confusion with the name for that mood. Given the pedagogical aims of this book, we shall keep to the traditional terminology, bearing in mind, however, its imperfections.

(ii) Traditional terminology also has problems in distinguishing between adverbs, conjunctions and prepositions: different grammars give widely differing lists of the words belonging to these various classes. Thus although most link words belong rather more to one class than another, this classification cannot be said to be absolute.

0.3 Historical note

As the Latin system of prepositions and conjunctions had partly disintegrated during the passage from Latin to French (mainly for phonetic reasons, but also because only those link words which belonged to the spoken language were likely to survive), new items were needed to take the place of those that had disappeared, particularly when French became a written language. Adverbs played a major role in filling the gaps, being used both as prepositions and as subordinating conjunctions when used in combination with *que*. Adverbs were also used, to compensate for the loss of many of the Latin coordinating conjunctions. Adverbs had in any case always been used as linking words, even in Latin. It was therefore quite natural in Vulgar Latin and then in Old French for words such as adverbs to belong to several word classes. But during the later periods of the development of French, the tendency was to separate the word classes as much as possible; this was done in the case of the adverb/preposition overlap by creating doublets of the *dans* (preposition)/*dedans* (adverb), *sous/dessous, sur/dessus* type. In other cases words came to belong to one category rather than the other, instead of belonging to both as before. Thus *avec* came to be classified only as a preposition, although it may still function as an adverb in the spoken language (as in *je joue avec*). It is the duality of role of some of these link words which explains some odd uses in certain dialects even today.

0.4   General characteristics of link words

(i) All link words are transitive, i.e. their function is to introduce new elements.
(ii) Words which are purely link words, i.e. those words which have no other function but to subordinate or coordinate, are invariable. Thus prepositions, subordinating conjunctions and coordinating conjunctions are invariable. Relative pronouns, on the other hand, are both link words − they subordinate − and pronouns, which means they have a nominal function in the clause. They are not invariable.
(iii) Prepositions, subordinating conjunctions and relative pronouns are all subordinators, i.e. they introduce items which are dependent on others. They differ in that prepositions introduce new elements within the clause (see Ch. 13) whereas subordinating conjunctions and relative pronouns introduce new clauses. The relative pronouns differ from other link words in that they fulfil a syntactic function of their own within the clause they introduce; and this function is normally similar to that of a noun (see Ch. 14 for relative pronouns and Ch. 15 for subordinating conjunctions).
(iv) Coordinating conjunctions and transitional adverbs (see 0.8.iv) are coordinators, i.e. they introduce items which function on the same syntactic level as the preceding one; they may function both within the sentence and between sentences (see Ch. 16).

0.5   Defining subordination

Subordination is the relationship between a dependent grammatical structure and that upon which it is dependent. Only those described in *(ii)* and *(iii)* below are relevant to this section.
(i) In an endocentric construction there is one constituent which is the head or centre, which is modified by one or more constituents which are dependent and therefore subordinated to the head. In 'the very old house', 'house' is the head and 'very' is an intensifier which modifies either 'old house' or 'old', depending on one's grammatical framework.
(ii) Another kind of subordination is the one involving prepositional phrases: the preposition introduces an element which is subordinate to or dependent on a preceding item. Thus in 'the buttons on his uniform', 'on' introduces 'his uniform' which is subordinate to 'the buttons', which it determines (see Ch. 13).
(iii) Subordination may also occur at the level of the clause: a subordinate clause is one which is dependent on another for its full meaning and which is joined to it by means either of a subordinating conjunction or of a subordinating relative pronoun (see Chs. 14 and 15). In:

il lisait quand je suis entré dans la pièce

the subordinate clause *quand je suis entré dans la pièce* is linked to the main clause *il lisait* by the subordinating conjunction *quand*. In:

Il lisait le livre que je lui avais donné

the relative clause *que je lui avais donné* is subordinated to the noun *le livre* which it determines. *Que* stands for *le livre*.

0.6 Defining coordination

Coordination, on the other hand, may be defined as the linking together of syntactic units of equal rank or status, as is the case when two nouns are joined by 'and' as in 'pencils and paper', or when two clauses are joined in a similar fashion, as in 'he came and put everything right' (see also 0.8).

0.7 Grammatical v. semantic coordination and subordination

(i) The distinction between coordination and subordination is not always an easy one: it sometimes happens that two clauses are grammatically coordinated but that one clause is semantically subordinated to the other:

cherchez et vous trouverez (= *si vous cherchez, vous trouverez*)

In this case the second clause is semantically the main clause although both clauses are syntactically of equal status and behave as coordinated clauses (i.e. one cannot change the order in which they appear as one could with the *si* + clause version). (See also Ch. 16, section 0.2.)
(ii) There are cases in which there may be a clash between the concept of grammatical subordination and semantic subordination:

Je découpais tranquillement mon pain, quand un bruit très léger me fit lever les yeux
(Baudelaire)

In this case the important information from a semantic point of view is contained in the subordinate clause *quand un bruit très léger me fit lever les yeux*.

0.8 Coordinating conjunctions and other coordinators

(i) Coordination is associated with 'coordinating conjunctions', these being *mais, ou, et, or, ni, car* and *donc*. These function mainly within the clause (except for *car* and *or* which function at the clause level).
(ii) Coordinating conjunctions are not the only words to function as coordinators between clauses and sentences: adverbs such as *aussi, alors*, prepositional phrases such as *par exemple, en effet*, even clauses such as *c'est pourquoi* may also coordinate either independent clauses or sentences. Hence the term 'coordinators' for all such words or expressions when these express coordination. Coordinating conjunctions are therefore merely a subset of this class, a subset defined by the fact that its items may have no other function than to coordinate, whereas the other coordinators may fulfil other functions.
(iii) Coordinators can only appear between the two elements linked, and belong to neither: in *mon père et ma mère*, the *et* does not belong to the second noun phrase any more than it does to the first.
(iv) If a coordinator appears within a clause or sentence rather than at its beginning, it functions as a transitional link or adverb. As such it functions as a modifier of the

second element, and the link with the first one will be due only to the anaphoric qualities of the transitional link used. For example:

> *J'achèterai ton livre après-demain. Ce jour-là, en effet, je dois aller au centre de Londres.*

In this case *en effet* establishes a logical or transitional link between the second sentence and the first.

Chapter 13

The prepositions

0 General considerations

(i) Prepositions are words (or groups of words, in the case of phrasal or compound prepositions) which are invariable and whose function is to subordinate the words or phrases they are 'pre-posed to' to those which precede them.

j'ai le livre de Pierre ('Peter's book')
j'ai le livre pour Pierre ('the book for Peter')
j'ai le livre sur Pierre ('the book about Peter')

(ii) Their use is determined both by what precedes them and by what follows them.
The element which precedes the preposition is the 'supporting element'. The element which follows the prepositions is 'the introduced element'.

Supporting element	Preposition	Introduced element
passer	*pour*	*malhonnête*
travailler	*en*	*chantant*
la maison	*de*	*son père*
sa maison	*à*	*lui*

The use of one preposition rather than another depends both on its support and on the element to be introduced.

(iii) The main function of the preposition is to introduce nouns (as in *la maison de mon père*), but it may also introduce verbs, adjectives and adverbs: for example *utile à savoir*, *passer pour intelligent* and *revenir de loin*. The introduced element may also be a clause, as in *nous parlions de quand nous étions enfants (= de notre enfance)*.

The supporting element is usually a noun or a verb (*le frère de mon ami* and *tenir à quelqu'un*) but it may also be an adjective or an adverb (*riche en vitamines* and *loin de la ville*).

(iv) In most cases the use of the preposition is clearly semantically determined, each preposition expressing a different kind of relationship between the subordinated element and its support:

je vais
- *à la campagne*
- *dans l'eau*
- *sur le bateau*
- *en haut*

In cases where the support is a verb, it often happens that the use of one preposition rather than another alters the meaning of the verb:

tenir	=	to hold
tenir à	=	to be fond of somebody
tenir de	=	to take after somebody
tenir pour	=	to regard as (as in *tenir quelqu'un pour un ami*)

In these cases the verb + preposition forms a lexical unit similar to prepositional verbs in English. The problem of the choice of the preposition in these cases is lexical rather than grammatical, i.e. the solution to these problems is to be found in dictionaries rather than in grammars.

(v) As far as anglophone speakers are concerned, prepositions present two main problems (apart from the one listed above):

English and French prepositions are very similar in terms of dictionary entries, but they may nonetheless function in widely differing contexts (see section 4).

Infinitive complements are introduced in English by 'to', whereas in French they may be introduced by *à, de* or nothing in ways which are difficult to predict (see 2.1.3.3). Another problematic area is that of the use of prepositions with geographical names (see 3.2.5).

1 Morphological considerations

1.1 The different types of prepositions

1.1.1 *General considerations*

There are no specific morphological features by which prepositions may be recognized out of context, since they are all invariable and are made up either of one word or several depending on their origin. There are however different types of prepositions. The first distinction which may be made is between those prepositions directly inherited from Latin and those which were created during the development of French.

Amongst the 'French' prepositions one may distinguish between the simple prepositions which are the result of 'improper derivation' i.e. a word from one class coming to be used as a word from another class, and phrasal prepositions.

1.1.2 *The 'inherited' prepositions*

These are *à, de, en, entre, sans, par, pour, sur,* and 'indirectly' *jusque, sous,* and *dans.*

Amongst the 'French' prepositions one may distinguish between the simple prepositions which are the result of 'improper derivation' i.e. a word from one class coming to be used as a word from another class, and phrasal prepositions.

1.1.3 *Prepositions due to changes in word class*

The preposition may have been originally:

a noun phrase or a noun: *malgré* (= *mal gré*)
a verb used in its present or past participal form: *excepté, vu, passé/durant, suivant, pendant*
an adverb: *avant*
a prepositional phrase: *devant* (from '*de ab ante*'), *derrière* (from '*de retro*'), *avec* (from '*apud hoc*')

1.1.4 *Phrasal prepositions*

(i) Phrasal prepositions are groups of words which form an expression fulfilling the same function as a preposition and which have acquired lexical status in the language. One may wish to distinguish within this group those phrasal prepositions which include a noun and those which do not. In addition one may make a further division between phrasal prepositions which contain a definite article and those which do not:

No noun	Noun without an article	Noun with an article
jusqu'à	*en face de*	*aux alentours de*
d'entre	*par rapport à*	*au lieu de*
lors de	*grâce à*	*le long de*
quant à	*à force de*	*à l'insu de*

One of the newest and most commonly used phrasal prepositions is *au niveau de* as in *la situation est assez bonne, sauf au niveau des prix,* or *je me débrouille bien en français, mais pas trop bien au niveau des mathématiques. Au niveau de* is used with the meaning of *en ce qui concerne.*

(ii) The construction *il y a* may function as a preposition:

elle est venue me voir il y a deux jours ('two days ago')

Il y a deux jours forms an adverbial complement similar to *avant-hier.*

1.1.5 *Syntactic uncertainties*

There appears to be a process at work in the language which tends to eliminate prepositions from prepositional phrases.[1] Compare:

en face de l'église
*en face l'église
*face l'église

This process is common with a number of prepositional phrases:

par manque de (moyens)	**manque de (moyens)*
du côté de (la rivière)	**côté (rivière)*
à la fin de (juin)	**fin (juin)*
à cause de (du départ)	**cause (départ)*

The omission of the preposition is frequent in the spoken language. In some cases this omission is an archaism or a regionalism *(face/en face l'église* is particularly frequent in Provence); in other cases it is the language of the theatre which has been extended to other areas (for example *côté cour, côté jardin);* in other cases it is due to the influence of the language used in classified advertisements (for example *Vends cause départ appartement bien situé).*

The subject has been widely reported on in the various *grammaires des fautes* published during this century (see for example Frei's *Grammaire des fautes* of 1929).

1.1.6 *Confusion between prepositions and other parts of speech*

(i) Prepositions differ from subordinating conjunctions only in that they function at a different syntactic level: subordinating conjunctions subordinate clauses to other clauses, whereas prepositions function at the level of the word or phrase. But it is often quite easy to turn a preposition into a conjunction: one simply adds the conjunction *que:* thus the preposition *pour* becomes the subordinating conjunction *pour que,* and the preposition *dès* becomes the subordinating conjunction *dès que:*

preposition: *avant mon arrivée*
conjunction: *avant que j'arrive*

(ii) Confusion with adverbs is something more fundamental, and was already a cause of concern to grammarians of the French Classical age. This is due to the fact that in Vulgar Latin many words could function either as adverbs or as prepositions. Later specialization took place. For example *avec* became purely a preposition; in

other cases two forms were created: *dedans* was kept as an adverb and *dans* as a preposition. But even so there are cases in modern French in which prepositions may
function as adverbs and vice versa. *Avant, avec, devant, derrière* in particular,
although normally used as prepositions, may appear in contexts in which they are
clearly adverbial in the sense that they do not introduce a complement of any kind:

> *prenez donc du vin avec* (adverb)
> *prenez du vin avec le fromage* (preposition)
> *qu'est-ce qu'il y a derrière?* (adverb)
> *qu'as-tu derrière ton dos?* (preposition)

1.1.7 *Historical comment*

(i) Although Classical Latin was a highly inflected language in which many relationships (between nouns in particular) were indicated by inflected endings, there existed
nevertheless a clearly recognizable group of around 40 prepositions which comple-
mented the case system, since these prepositions were able to express many more
nuances of meaning than could the inflectional system. In Vulgar Latin, some of these
prepositions could combine with each other; thus *de ex* gave *dès* in modern French,
and *de ab ante* gave *devant*. Many also combined with adverbs; thus *de foris* was to
give *defors* in Old French and *dehors* in modern French, *de subtus* gave *dessous*, and
de intus gave *denz* and later *dans*.[2]
(ii) Vulgar Latin brought prepositions into ever more frequent use because of the
gradual collapse of the case system (only two cases remained in Old French). In
addition there were a number of new prepositions and prepositional phrases which
came into use in Vulgar Latin and continued their development over the centuries into
modern French, such as, for example, *de usque* which gives *jusque*, *de retro* which
gives *derrière* and *apud hoc* with gives *avec*. Others disappeared as free prepositions
but survived in specific lexical items: *ex*, for example, survives in *exil* and *cum* in
convenir. There have even been a number of quite recent creations such as *conurbation*
(Latin *cum* + *urbs*) which have revived the use of Latin prepositions in the domain of
lexical creativity.
(iii) One may note the increasing use of phrasal prepositions: the simple prepositions
such as *de* and *à* were used far more often on their own in Classical French than in
modern French.
(iv) The complement of the comparative, nowadays introduced by *que*, used to be
introduced by *de*, which would have seemed more logical, at least from the point of
view of prepositions, since their very role is to indicate such functions of complementa-
tion. Thus one used to write:

> *n'i ot meillor vassal de lui*

for

> *il n'y avait pas meilleur guerrier que lui*

although the construction with *que* is also found in Old French.

2 Syntactic considerations

2.1 Main functions of prepositions

2.1.1 *General considerations*

The sequence 'preposition + noun/verb/adverb/infinitive' makes up a prepositional
phrase. This may function either as a determinative complement (2.1.2), as an object
complement of the verb (2.1.3), as an agent in passive constructions (2.1.4), or as an

adverbial complement (2.1.5). A preposition is also required to form the equivalent of a gerund (2.1.6).

2.1.2 *Determinative complements*

(i) The role of these complements is to narrow down or 'determine' the scope of the word which they complement. These may be nouns, adjectives or adverbs. The prepositional phrase may be the complement of:

a noun:	*le frère (de mon ami)*
an adjective:	*un fruit riche (en vitamines)*
	c'est utile (à savoir)
an adverb:	*beaucoup (de pain)*
	cette question a été étudiée indépendamment (des autres)

(ii) In most cases determinative complements complement nouns. Such constructions often have adjectival qualities, and indeed may be translated by an adjective in English (see relational adjectives, Ch. 11, section 5):

un instrument de musique = 'a musical instrument'

2.1.3 *Object complements of the verb*

2.1.3.1 *Direct and indirect objects* Transitive verbs are verbs which take an object complement; but some verbs are classified as direct transitive verbs and others as indirect transitive verbs.

A direct transitive verb is one in which no preposition is needed to indicate the relationship of verb to object; word-order suffices. An indirect transitive verb is one which uses a preposition to link the object to the verb; the object is often called an 'indirect object'. Compare:

direct construction: *l'ennemi prend la ville*
indirect construction: *l'ennemi s'empare de la ville*

There is however no real difference of function between *la ville* and *de la ville* in this case. One could in fact argue that in both cases one is dealing with a 'direct object', the verb being a simple verb in the case of *prendre* and a 'prepositional verbal phrase' in the case of *s'emparer de*. In other words the use of the preposition in the case of indirect transitive verbs is a lexical matter, the preposition being considered not as a link word at all but as part of a lexical unit larger than the word, i.e. as part of a 'prepositional verb' (see also 2.2).

One thus finds in the dictionary that some verbs always 'take' or rather 'include' *à* (*parvenir à, procéder à*) whilst others always include *de* (*se réjouir de, abuser de, se souvenir de*). There are usually semantic reasons for this (see section 3.2) In most cases the 'prepositional verbal phrase' may take either a noun or an infinitive as an object:

il est parvenu à des résultats satisfaisants
il est parvenu à se faire aimer de sa belle-mère

But it may sometimes happen that a verb may be transitive direct when the object is a noun and transitive indirect when the object is an infinitive:

elle essaie une robe (transitive direct)
elle essaie de marcher (transitive indirect)

Se rappeler is a direct transitive verb and *se souvenir de* an indirect transitive verb:

je me rappelle mes dernières vacances
je me souviens de mes dernières vacances

But many French native speakers say **je me rappelle de mes dernières vacances* although the latter is unacceptable in prescriptive terms.

There are considerable differences in this respect between modern French and Old and Middle French. One used to say *marcher l'herbe* instead of the modern French *marcher sur l'herbe*; one used to say *favoriser aux vassaux* where one now says *favoriser les vassaux*. In some cases the speaker may hesitate between two forms as is the case for *aider*: on *aide le fermier* (animate) but on *aide à la moisson*. Some people end up saying, by analogy, the 'incorrect' form *aider au fermier*. This is an area of syntactic uncertainty.

2.1.3.2 *The second complement of transitive verbs: the indirect or attributive complement*   Direct transitive verbs may take two objects, the second being normally the recipient of the action, hence the name 'attributive complement' sometimes given to this type of complement. The preposition used is *à*:

il donne une pomme à l'enfant

2.1.3.3 *The infinitive as object*

il aime peindre ('he likes to paint', 'he likes painting')
il a permis à Pierre de partir ('he has allowed Peter to go')
il hésite à le faire ('he hesitates to do it')

Whereas in English the infinitival complement in invariably introduced by 'to' – unless an '-ing' form is being used – in French it may be preceded either by nothing, or by *à* or *de*. Matters in French are extremely complex.

(i) There may be no preposition: *je veux vous voir/je pense partir*.

(ii) In some cases the same verb may or may not be followed by a preposition, without much change of meaning: *j'aime lire* is not very different from *j'aime à lire*.

(iii) A few verbs take *à* or *de* without any change of meaning: *commencer à/de, continuer à/de*.

(iv) Some verbs only take *à*; these usually refer to an idea of effort in a specific direction: *s'acharner à, s'amuser à, s'appliquer à, se préparer à*.

(v) Some verbs only take *de*. The *de* often seems to be semantically 'empty': *prendre la ville* and *s'emparer de la ville* mean much the same.

(vi) Some verbs may or may not take a preposition, the use of a preposition entailing a complete change of meaning:

je viens te voir = 'I have come to see you'
je viens de te voir = 'I have just seen you'
tenir quelque chose = 'to hold something'
tenir à quelqu'un = 'to be fond of somebody'
tenir de quelqu'un = 'to take after somebody'

(vii) In some cases the change of preposition entails a shift of emphasis from an action seen actively to one seen passively, *de* referring to an active action and *à* to a passive one; the verb is sometimes used in its pronominal form with *à*:

refuser de partir = 'to refuse to leave'
se refuser à partir = 'to be unable to bear to leave'
décider de partir = 'to decide to leave'
se décider à partir = 'to make up one's mind to leave'
demander à quelqu'un de faire quelque chose = 'to ask somebody to do something'
demander à faire quelque chose = 'to ask permission to do something'

(viii) Some verbs sometimes take *à* sometimes *de*, and sometimes no preposition, depending on whether the subject of the main verb is also the subject of the infinitive or not:

il aime rêver (one subject)
il donne à rêver (two subjects)
j'admets de rester ici (one subject)
les autorités admettent Pierre à faire valoir ses droits (two subjects)

To find out, one has to consult the examples given in dictionary entries with this point in mind.

2.1.4 *Expression of the agent in a passive construction*

The agent is normally linked to the verb either by *par* or, more rarely, by *de*:

cette maison a été construite par mon frère
il a été abandonné de tous ses amis

De cannot be used in all passive constructions, however: whereas *par* refers to an activity, *de* refers to the ensuing state of affairs. What is more, *de* is not possible if the agent is modified in any way:

il a été blessé d'une balle à la tête

but

il a été blessé par une balle ennemie

When the passive voice is expressed by the factitive *faire*, the animate/inanimate concept may interfere:

il s'est fait accompagner
$\begin{cases} \text{\emph{par son frère}} \\ \text{\emph{de son frère}} \end{cases}$

In this case both *par* and *de* are possible. But in the next examples only *de* is possible:

j'ai fait servir un lapin accompagné de sauce à la moutarde
je l'ai fait garnir de fleurs fraîches

It is probably because *de* is the 'emptier' of the two prepositions that it is felt to be preferable to *par* in the case of inanimates. Where animates are concerned, although in the cases quoted both prepositions are acceptable they do not always have exactly the same meaning:

il est venu accompagné de son frère (they both came)
il est venu accompagné par son frère (his brother escorted him)

2.1.5 *Adverbial complements*

(i) Prepositional phrases frequently function as adverbials:

j'y vais dans deux jours (time)
je vais à Paris (place)
elle a tué par jalousie (cause)
il a écrit son devoir au crayon (means)
il travaille avec application (manner)

But adverbials are not always prepositional phrases:

il vient nous voir tous les dimanches (time)

The main area of difficulty is that of the use of prepositions with geographical names. For this problem see 3.2.5.

(ii) In all the previous examples the adverbial complements the verb. This is not always the case:

tous, sauf Pierre, sont venus
outre Pierre, elle invita Paul

In these two sentences the relationship is not between the adverbial and the verb but between the adverbial and the rest of the clause. Similarly, the adverbial in the following sentence complements the whole clause rather than the verb:

on peut tout juste acheter une bicyclette avec cette somme

Avec cette somme does not narrow down the meaning of *on peut acheter* but of *on peut acheter une bicyclette*; and since it complements the whole clause rather than the verb it may appear in various positions in the clause:

avec cette somme on peut tout juste acheter une bicyclette
on peut tout juste, avec cette somme, acheter une bicyclette
on peut tout juste acheter, avec cette somme, une bicyclette

These adverbials which modify the clause rather than the verb are similar in function and in syntactic behaviour (i.e. in terms of the positions they may occupy) to adverbial adverbs (see Ch. 12, 5).

2.1.6   *The gerund*

The gerund may be the equivalent of an adverbial:

il s'est fait mal en tombant (cause)
il travaille en chantant (manner)
je l'ai aperçu en arrivant (time)

It may also be the equivalent of a hypothetical *si* clause:

en mangeant moins, vous vous porteriez mieux = si vous mangiez moins vous vous
    porteriez mieux

The gerund is always introduced by *en*.

2.2   Direct v. indirect constructions

A direct construction is one in which no preposition is used; an indirect construction is one which uses a preposition. In most cases one has to use either one or the other; there are however some cases of choice.
(i) The choice may be a lexical choice: the use of one verb may or may not entail the use of a preposition (see 2.1.3.1). The element introduced is either the direct or the indirect object of the verb:

direct construction: *l'ennemi prend la ville*
indirect construction: *l'ennemi s'empare de la ville*

The element introduced may function as a direct or indirect adverbial:

direct construction: *il travaille la nuit*
indirect construction: *il travaille pendant la nuit*

In these two cases there is no great difference in meaning between the direct and indirect constructions.
(ii) The choice may entail syntactic consequences other than the choice of preposition. The element introduced may function as attribute of the subject:

direct construction: *on dit que Paul est menteur*
indirect construction: *Paul passe pour menteur*

The indirect construction corresponds in this case to a much longer direct construction.

The element introduced may function as an epithet:

direct construction: *y a-t-il une place libre (= qui est libre)?*
indirect construction: *y a-t-il une place de libre (= qui soit libre)?*

In this case the indirect construction corresponds to a difference of mood. This distinction is not made in English.

The element introduced may be the 'real' or semantic subject. Compare:

direct construction: *mentir est honteux* (no preposition)
indirect construction: *il est honteux de mentir* (preposition)

In this case the prepositional phrase is the 'real' subject of the clause.

2.3 Repetition and ellipsis

(i) Where a noun is followed by two determinative complements which are not coordinated, it is preferable to use different prepositions in order to distinguish more accurately from a semantic point of view the different relationships existing between the supporting elements on the one hand and the introduced elements, or 'complements', on the other. Thus un *portrait de la reine* and un *portrait d'Annigoni* when combined gives: *un portrait de la reine par Annigoni*; and *la passion de sa femme* and *la passion de la bouteille* gives *la passion de sa femme pour la bouteille* (Simenon). Thus it is the second instance of *de* which tends to be replaced by a semantically 'fuller' preposition. *Hériter* is a special case:

j'ai hérité d'une maison + j'ai hérité de mon oncle = j'ai hérité une maison de mon oncle

(ii) Where two prepositional phrases starting with the same preposition are coordinated, the preposition is normally repeated (French differs in this from English):

il était sans amis et sans argent

This is particularly true where the semantically empty prepositions *à*, and *de* are concerned.

Exceptions occur:

(a) when the two prepositional phrases form a set phrase, e.g. *à vos risques et périls*
(b) when the second phrase is in apposition to the first, e.g. *parlez-en à Jean, votre associé*
(c) when the second phrase is an extension or explanation of the first and does not represent a separate idea, e.g. *j'ai acheté un dériveur pour mes enfants et leurs amis.*

But when the preposition used is in fact made up of two prepositions, it is normal to drop one of these, and retain only the *de* which is part of it:

auprès de ma sœur et de mon frère

(iii) The preposition is repeated after the comparative *que*, but not after *que* preceded by a prepositional phrase including *autre* + noun:

il a plu davantage à Pierre qu'à moi (preposition repeated)

but

j'ai pris part à d'autres réunions que celles-ci (preposition not repeated)

(iv) If the coordinated prepositional phrases are made up of different prepositions but identical nouns, it is not necessary to repeat the noun:

il s'agit de savoir si vous êtes pour ou contre moi

2.4   Prepositions and personal pronouns

(i) Where the prepositions *de* and *à* introduce an indirect object, both preposition and complement may be pronominalized as follows:

je me souviens de lui
je m'en souviens
je m'applique à cela (à le faire)
je m'y applique

In other words the sequence *de* + *lui/elle, eux, elles, cela* is replaced simply by *en*; and the sequence *à* + *cela* is replaced by *y* (*en* and *y* are always placed immediately before the verb).

(ii) Where the preposition introduces an adverbial complement, the latter may be pronominalized in the following manner. Compare:

tu cours après moi
tu me cours après
je cours après toi
je te cours après

but:

je cours après lui (or *après elle*)
je lui cours après

Compare also:

vous courez après nous
vous nous courez après
nous courons après vous
nous vous courons après

but:

nous courons après eux
nous leur courons après

This change is due to the fact that the pronouns when placed after the verb are stressed, whereas when they are placed before they are unstressed. Thus *moi* becomes *me*, *toi* becomes *te*, *eux* becomes *leur*, and *elle* becomes *lui*; but *lui*, *nous* and *vous*, being the same in both their stressed and unstressed forms, remain unchanged.

3   Semantic considerations

3.1   'Full' and 'empty' prepositions

It is customary to distinguish between 'full' and 'empty' prepositions, i.e. between those which have both syntactic and lexical meaning and those which have syntactic meaning only. Thus all phrasal prepositions have both syntactic and lexical meaning (*à l'abri de*, *à la faveur de*, *par rapport à*); but prepositions such as *de* and *à* may appear in so many different contexts that it is difficult to attribute a specific lexical meaning to them independent of their syntactic meaning. Compare:

le pied de la table ('of')
il tient de sa mère ('after')
il finit de faire son travail (no preposition in English)
il arrive de Paris ('from')

De in these examples functions as a 'grammatical tool', i.e. as a word used to introduce an element which is subordinate to the preceding one. It does not appear to have − at first sight at least − specific lexical content. The most frequently used prepositions, or at least those used in the most varied syntactic contexts, are necessarily the ones which have the least specific lexical content. The following prepositions, being the most commonly used, are also the most abstract (the following figures refer to their percentage frequency in relation to other prepositions[3]):

de: 50.6   *à*: 14.6   *en*: 6.7   *dans*: 5.6   *sur*: 3.7   *par*: 3.6

These figures show *de* to be by far the most abstract of French prepositions. The same applies to English, but what differs is the degree of abstraction achieved by the most commonly used prepositions: *De* is far more abstract than its English equivalents 'of', 'after', 'from' etc.: it functions at a higher level of abstraction, since its meaning encompasses all the meanings of its English contextual equivalents, and this can cause major translation problems (see 4.1.1). The constant use of 'empty' prepositions may entail difficulties; a need may be felt to be more explicit. It is this need which explains the existence of numerous phrasal prepositions in modern French. Thus *de la part de* usually corresponds quite simply to 'from', and *écrivez à l'adresse ci-dessous* will usually correspond to 'write to' (see 4.1.2).

3.2 General meanings attributed to the more abstract prepositions

3.2.1 *The case of 'de'*

3.2.1.1 *The meaning of 'de'*   *'De'* is usually said to refer to an origin of some kind; it comes from the Latin *de* meaning either 'from' or 'concerning'. Its meaning in present-day French is much broader, however: it simply indicates a point of reference, hence apparently 'illogical' constructions. *S'approcher de Paris* is illogical compared to the unacceptable but logical **s'approcher à Paris*. But if one considers *de* as indicating a point of reference or as a psychological point of departure, the construction appears logical:

s'approcher   *de Paris*[4]

(point of reference)

It is clearly the idea of 'point of reference' (which resembles the idea of 'concerning') which is expressed by the *de* in prepositional verbs such as *se réjouir de, abuser de, se souvenir de*.

3.2.1.2 *Specific uses of 'de'*
(i) 'De' may introduce the complement of a noun (determinative), e.g. *le livre de mon frère*, particularly of nouns which could correspond to relational adjectives in English: 'a marble statue' = *une statue de marbre*.
(ii) It may introduce the subject of an indirect (or impersonal) construction, e.g. *il est honteux de mentir*.
(iii) It may introduce an epithet in an indirect construction: *quelqu'un de grand*.
(iv) It may introduce the object of a verb in an indirect construction (i.e. an intransitive verb), e.g. *s'emparer de la ville*.
(v) It may combine with certain verbs when these are followed by an infinitive, e.g. *finir de travailler, essayer de chanter*.

(vi) It may introduce the comparative complement after the adverbs *moins, plus* and *assez*, e.g. *moins de trente, plus de vingt, assez de pain*.

(vii) De (referring to origin) was used to express 'a part of' i.e. it played the role of a partitive article: *boire du vin* (in Old French *boire de vin*); formerly used without the article, it is now used with it.

3.2.1.3 *Historical note*　The use of *de* on its own has receded since the seventeenth century mainly because of its lack of lexical content which makes it too vague. Instead *de* is combined with other words to form phrasal prepositions which may express a more or less limitless range of lexical meanings whilst still expressing the syntactic meaning of *de*.

3.2.2　*The case of 'à'*

3.2.2.1 *The meaning of 'à'*　*A* has two Latin origins: *ad* (goal) meaning 'to', and *ab* ('from'), meaning 'out of'. It is this double origin which explains certain sentences which could appear odd, such as *puiser de l'eau à la rivière* in which the *à* corresponds to the Latin *ab* meaning 'out of'. The most usual meaning of *à* is to express movement. It may be used to express physical movement: *je vais à la gare* ('I am going to the station'); or it may express figurative movement, in which case it is often not translated into English: *plaire à*, 'to please (somebody)', *se fier à* 'to trust (somebody)', *ressembler à* 'to resemble (somebody)'. *A* contrasts in this respect with *de*, since *de* indicates a point of reference: *abuser de; se réjouir de; se souvenir de*.

3.2.2.2 *Specific uses of 'à'*
(i) It may introduce indirect or 'attributive' objects: *j'ai donné un livre à mon frère*.
(ii) It may introduce the verb complement of certain adjectives: *c'est facile à faire*.
(iii) It may introduce many adverbials: *je vais à la campagne* (place); *je l'ai regardé à la dérobée* (manner).
(v) It may combine with certain verbs when these are followed by an infinitive: *commencer à, se mettre à, parvenir à, ressembler à*.
(vi) It may express possession, either when the possessor is an indirect object or when it is a personal pronoun, functioning as a determinative complement: *la maison est à Paul; sa maison à lui est grande*.

3.2.2.3 *Historical note*
(i) A used to be used in all cases where the idea of possession was to be expressed. Thus one used to say *la maison à Paul*, and such constructions survive in various dialects and in set phrases such as *un fils à papa*. In the seventeenth century grammarians decided that such constructions were vulgar and therefore unacceptable and the concept developed from possession being expressed by the idea of movement towards an owner to its expression by the idea of origin implied by the use of *de*.

A is sometimes used instead of *chez*, as in the following 'unacceptable' sentence: **je vais au médecin* instead of *je vais chez le médecin*. *Chez* is considered more accurate since it means 'in the house of' whereas *à* simply indicates the goal.
(ii) A has receded for the same reasons as *de*, but to a lesser extent, the idea of a goal being more specific than a simple point of reference. It has often been replaced in modern French by *dans, sur* and *pour*. Thus one used to say in the seventeenth century *monter au trône*, instead of *monter sur le trône*. Racine also writes *à cette fois* for *pour cette fois* and *mourir à milliers* for *mourir par milliers*.

3.2.3 *Main uses of the seven principal prepositions*

de
origin: *il vient de Paris*
possession: *le livre de Pierre*
agent: *il est aimé de tous* (there are syntactic and semantic restrictions on this use)
matter: *une statue de marbre* ('a marble statue')
price: *Une robe de 500 francs* ('worth')
contents: *Une tasse de café* ('a cup of coffee')
point of reference: *il se réjouit du succès de sa sœur*

à
place: *il va à Paris*
time: *il ira à trois heures*
attribution: *il donne un livre à sa sœur*
container: *une tasse à café* ('a coffee cup')
price: *Une robe à 500 francs* ('priced at')
possession: *la maison est à lui/la maison est à Jean* (?*la maison à Jean* is dialectal and
    considered 'ungrammatical')
destination or use: *une machine à laver*

Note: En is sometimes used instead of *à* or *dans* on invitations and notices of various
kinds:

vous êtes invité à un vin d'honneur en la mairie de Toulouse
1864 – 24 novembre naissance de Henri de Toulouse-Lautrec en la maison
    familiale de l'hôtel du Bosc à Albi

en
comparison: *agir en adulte* (= *comme un adulte*)
place: *il est en France*
matter: *une statue en marbre* ('a statue made out of marble')
duration: *il a fait le voyage en trois heures*
means: *il est venu en voiture*
gerund: *en arrivant, il a pris une douche*
transformation: *il s'est déguisé en clown*; *elle a changé la citrouille en carrosse*

Note: In the case of *il agit en adulte* or *il se conduit en enfant*, *en* introduces an
attribute of the subject, and in *elle a changé la citrouille en carrosse*, *en* introduces an
attribute of the object.

dans
place: *il s'est perdu dans la forêt*
time: *il arrivera dans deux jours*
approximation (numbers): *cela coûte dans les 300 francs*

sur
place: *le livre est sur la table*
approximation in the future: *il va sur ses quarante ans*

par
agent: *il a été renvoyé par son patron*
place (through which one goes): *il est passé par Lyon*
means: *voyager par avion*
distribution: *une portion par personne*

pour
place (destination): *le train pour Paris*
duration: *partir pour huit jours*
aim: *travailler pour réussir*
price: *il a eu cet appartement pour une bouchée de pain* (= *pour pas cher*)

3.2.4 *Summary of the use of 'de' in relation to other prepositions*

(i) Place:

de (stresses point of reference):	*à* (stresses goal):	*pour* (stresses immediate departure):	*chez* (used for animates):	*dans* (used for inanimates):
je viens de Paris	*je vais à Paris*	*je pars pour Paris*	*je vais chez le médecin*	*je vais dans la tente*
je m'approche de Paris	*il est au Mexique* (also *en*: *il est en Espagne* see 3.2.5.3)			

(ii) Time:

de (refers to the beginning of a clearly defined period of time):	*en* (duration):	*à* (goal)
j'irai de deux heures à quatre heures	*j'irai en deux heures*	*j'irai à deux heures*

(iii) Price:

point of reference: *une robe de 500 francs* (i.e. worth 500 francs)	goal: *une robe à 500 francs* (i.e. priced at 500 francs)

(iv) Origin v. material:

de (origin): *une statue de marbre* ('a marble statue')	*en* (material): *une statue en marbre* ('a statue made out of marble')

(v) Contained v. container:

contained: *une tasse de café* ('a cup of coffee')	container: *une tasse à café* ('a coffee cup')

(vi) Possession:

complement of the noun: *la maison de Jean*	indirect object/complement of the noun if a possessive pronoun: *la maison est à Jean* *sa maison à lui* (emphasis of the idea of possession)

(vii) Passive:

de (many semantic and syntactic restrictions apply): *il a été abandonné de ses amis*	*par* (a few restrictions apply): *il a été abandonné par ses amis*

3.2.5 *Use of prepositions with geographical names*

The difficulties which arise in this area are mainly due to the presence or absence of the definite article in association with the preposition, to the gender of the place name itself, and to whether the place name starts with à consonant or a vowel. Its status as the name of a town, a province, a departement or a country also plays a part.

3.2.5.1 *The use of 'à' on its own*   The use of *à* without the definite article indicates motion towards a place or presence within it.
(i) A may be used before the names of towns: *je suis/vais à Bordeaux/à Londres/à Moscou*; but the article is retained in those cases when the name of the town includes an article: *je vais à La Haye/au Havre/aux Aubrais.*
(ii) It may also be used before the names of islands which are masculine and do not have an article: *je vais à Cuba/à Madagascar/à Malte/à Chypre/à Jersey.*

3.2.5.2 *The use of à with the definite article*   This indicates motion towards a place or presence within it, and is used before the names of countries which are masculine and start with a consonant, or plural names starting with a vowel: *je suis/vais au Japon, au Canada, au Chili, aux Etats-Unis.*

3.2.5.3 *The use of 'en'*   This indicates motion towards a place or presence within it, and is used:
(i) before the names of countries and provinces which are feminine: *je suis/vais en Espagne/en Angleterre/en Bretagne/en Aquitaine*;
(ii) before the names of islands which are feminine: *je suis/vais en Corse/en Sicile/en Crète/en Australie*;
(iii) before the names of countries which are masculine singular and start with a vowel (these behave as if they were feminine): *je suis/vais en Iran/en Israël* (but the latter cannot be said to have a gender, since it cannot take a definite article).

3.2.5.4 *The use of 'dans' with the definite article*   This indicates motion towards a place or movement within it.
(i) Dans with the definite article is used before the names of French *départements* (British counties are usually treated in the same way): *je suis/vais dans le Var/dans le Gers/dans le Lot-et-Garonne/dans la Lozère/dans le Surrey.*
    En is sometimes found with the following: *je suis/vais en Lozère/en Lot-et-Garonne/en Corrèze.*
    There are some general rules in this matter:
    (a) Dans is obligatory with plural compound nouns (*dans les Deux-Sèvres/dans les Pyrénées-Orientales*), where the name of the *département* is monosyllabic (*dans l'Ain/dans le Doubs*), and where it is a compound noun containing a preposition (*dans le Puy-de-Dôme*).
    (b) En is the norm where the name of the *département* is made up of two coordinated nouns (*en Saône-et-Loire, en Seine-et-Marne*).
    In all other cases either *dans* or *en* is possible, although *dans* is the norm (*c'est en Corrèze, c'est dans la Corrèze*).
(ii) Dans with the definite article is used before the names of masculine provinces: *je suis/vais dans le Berry/dans le Poitou. En* is sometimes found, however: *je suis en Berry/en Poitou.*
    Note: The use of *en* instead of *dans* + article is somewhat archaic; traces of this once much greater use of *en* can be found on official invitations. See examples in note in 3.2.3.

4   Contrastive problems

4.1   Semantic problems

4.1.1   *The scope of 'de'*

The French preposition *de* is more semantically empty than any English preposition. There is a tendency, therefore, for English students to use, in French, prepositions which are 'fuller' than those probably used by the French. Compare:

'the buttons on his uniform': *les boutons de son uniforme* (and not *sur*)
'his house in London': *sa maison de/à Londres* (and not *dans*)
'a cheque for twenty pounds': *un chèque de vingt livres* (and not *pour*)
'a bend in the road': *un tournant de la route* (and not *dans*)
'with annotations by the teacher': *avec les annotations du professeur* (and not *par*)

The problem for the English student is to get back to the 'empty' *de*.

4.1.2   *The need to use phrasal prepositions in French*

As *de* is so empty, it is often necessary to 'pad' it with other items, thus turning it into a phrasal preposition; the same may also apply to *à*:

c'est au sujet de votre voiture: 'it is about your car'
un écart par rapport à la norme: 'a variation from the norm'
je l'ai su par l'intermédiaire de ma sœur: 'I found out about it through my sister'
c'est de la part d'un ami: 'it is from a friend'
écrivez à l'adresse ci-dessous: 'write to . . .'

4.1.3   *Different 'world views'*

(i) One may use different prepositions in the two languages:

'to leave the key in the door': *laisser la clé sur la porte*
'to meet somebody on the train': *rencontrer quelqu'un dans le train* (*sur le train* would mean 'on top of the train')

(ii) One may use a preposition in one language and not in the other:

je joue du piano, du violon, de la guitare: 'I play the piano, the violin, the guitar'
je joue au tennis, au rugby, au bridge: 'I play tennis, rugby, bridge'

In other words 'to play' may correspond either to *'jouer de* + article' or to *'jouer à* + article', depending on whether one is referring to a musical instrument or to a game. These differences have to be learned individually; language interference problems are particularly insidious in this area.

4.2   Use of the prepositional construction to compensate for the lack of lexical equivalents in French

4.2.1   *Lack of relational adjectives in French*

The lack of relational adjectives in French may make a prepositional construction necessary in French where it is not necessary in English:

'a musical instrument': *un instrument de musique*
'a medical student': *un étudiant en médecine*

(See Ch. 11.)

4.2.2   *The lack of certain verbs of movement or perception: the 'chassé croisé'*

The term *chassé croisé* refers to the fact that an English preposition − when part of a verbal phrase − is often translated by a verb in French and vice versa:

'to swim'

'across (a river)'

traverser (une rivière)

à la nage

In this case the English preposition 'across' has been translated by the French verb *traverser*, and the English verb 'swim' has been translated by the French prepositional phrase *à la nage*. This phenomenon is very common with verbs of movement and verbs of perception. Thus a bird may:

'fly into a room': *entrer dans une pièce (en volant)*
'hop into a room': *entrer en sautillant*

A person could:

'hobble into a room': *entrer en boitillant* . . . etc.

(The *en volant* in *entrer en volant* would be left unsaid in French since birds normally fly: the prepositional phrase is added only where the information it gives is essential.)

4.3   Syntactic differences

4.3.1   *Repetition of the preposition in coordinated constructions*

In French the preposition must be repeated, particularly if it is an empty preposition. The same does not apply to English:

cela dépend de vous et de moi: 'it is up to you and me'

For those cases when it is not strictly necessary to repeat the preposition in French, see 2.3.

4.3.2   *Translation of infinitival complements*

In English the construction 'verb + infinitive complement' always follows the same pattern ('verb + to + infinitive'), e.g. 'I want to sing', whereas in French there are various possibilities (see 2.1.3.3).

4.3.3   *The French infinitive and the '-ing' form*

It is sometimes but not always possible to translate the French 'verb + infinitival complement' by an equivalent English construction:

il commença de parler ('he started to talk/talking')

but

il a fini de parler ('he has finished talking' (and not *'to talk'))

and

j'ai fini de lire ('I have finished reading')

Notes

1 See L.C. Harmer, *The French language today*, 138 – 9.
2 *Dans* only appears in the thirteenth century; it does not appear to derive directly from *denz*, but from a compound form *dedenz* (from the reconstructed form *de intus*). *Dedans* appears in the eleventh century, and comes from the reconstructed form *de de intus*.
3 Figures obtained from *Le Grand Larousse de la langue française*, 4583 – 4, under the heading '*Préposition*'.
4 The French (but not the Belgians, nor the Swiss nor the Canadians) hesitate as to the meaning of the expression *le train de Paris*: does it mean *qui va à Paris* or *qui vient de Paris*? It should mean *qui vient de*, whereas *le train qui va à Paris* should be *le train pour Paris*. This may be due to the very central role played by Paris in French life, since this use of *de* does not appear to be so frequent with other towns: *le train pour Lyon*, *le train pour Bordeaux*.

Chapter 14

The relative pronouns

0 General considerations

0.1 Definition

(i) A relative pronoun is a pronoun which acts as a link between a noun (or pronoun) and a following subordinate clause. The relative pronoun differs from subordinating conjunctions in that it has a function of its own within the subordinate clause which it introduces:

le livre qui est sur la table est à moi

Qui stands for *le livre* and introduces the subordinate clause, and is the subject of the verb in the subordinate clause.

(ii) The relative clause is similar in its function to an adjective. It may narrow down the meaning of the noun modified:

le chat qui est noir m'appartient =
le chat noir m'appartient

and it may add a complement of information:

dans ce tableau, le chat, qui est noir sur un fond blanc, semble prêt à bondir = dans ce tableau, le chat, noir sur fond blanc . . .

When it narrows down the meaning of the noun it is said to be restrictive; when it adds a non-essential complement of information it is said to be nonrestrictive.[1]

(iii) Whereas the subordinating conjunctions are associated with the verb, the relative pronouns are associated with the noun.

0.2 Contrastive problems of the relative pronoun as a grammatical category

When translating from French into English, there may be an element of choice in English which does not exist in French (e.g. 'the book which I bought' 'the book that I bought' for *le livre que j'ai acheté*).

Also in some cases a participial clause may replace a relative clause in English ('I saw John who was driving his new car' = 'I saw John driving his new car'). Finally, the zero relative pronoun is much used in English but impossible in French (e.g. 'the book Ø I bought'). For all these problems, see 5.1.

It is also possible for a French relative pronoun to appear not to correspond to an English relative pronoun:

'I do not know when he is coming' *= je ne sais pas quand il vient*
'this directory is valid until 1 January, when it will be replaced by a new one' *= cet annuaire est valable jusqu'au 1er janvier, date à laquelle il sera remplacé par une nouvelle édition*

In the first example 'when' is translated in French by the conjunction *quand*; in the second, it is translated by the relative pronoun *à laquelle*, which means that an antecedent − in this case *date* − has to be built in. This problem is examined in 5.2. The reason for this is that French morphology makes a clearer distinction between relative pronouns and conjunctions than English morphology, with the exceptions of *où* (see 5.2.2.2) and *que* (see Ch. 16), which may function either as relative pronouns or as conjunctions within similar contexts. Finally, stylistic considerations are the subject matter of section 6.

1   Morphology

1.1   The two series of relative pronouns

There are two series of relative pronouns: one is made up of pronouns which have been directly inherited from Latin (1.1.1); the second series was created alongside the inherited one, during the development of the French language, which is why they are sometimes called the 'specifically French pronouns'. Since these are compound, they are also called the 'compound' pronouns (see 1.2 for tables). The two series overlap considerably, which is a source of syntactic uncertainty, even for the French.

1.1.1   *The inherited or 'Latin' series: 'qui', 'que', 'quoi', 'dont', 'où'*

(i)   Qui, que and *quoi* come from the corresponding Latin relative pronouns (see *iii*); *dont* and *où* come from the interrogative adverbs *de unde* (reconstructed form), 'whence' and *ubi*, 'where'. These always have an antecedent: they are 'definite relative pronouns' (see 1.2.1.1). It is also possible to use the relative pronouns without an antecedent: in this case they become 'indefinite relative pronouns'. The indefinite relative pronouns are: *qui que*, *quiconque* and *quoi que* (see 1.2.1.2 for further comments). *Où* may also be used on its own as an interrogative pronoun as in *où vas-tu?* or *je vais lui demander où il va*.

(ii)   Pronouns in this series are invariable for gender and number but marked for case:

> *la table qui est dans le coin fera l'affaire*
> *les tables qui sont dans le coin feront l'affaire*
> *la table dont tu m'as parlé est très ancienne*
> *les tables dont tu m'as parlé sont très anciennes*

(iii)   The historical development of *qui*, *que* and *quoi* − both as relative and interrogative pronouns − is as follows.

The relative pronoun *qui* comes from the Latin relative pronoun *qui* in its singular nominative form.

The interrogative pronoun *qui* also comes from the Latin relative pronoun *qui*; it became confused with *cui*, which was the ancient form for the singular dative, which had survived until then as an oblique case − hence the possibility of using *qui* preceded by prepositions. *Qui* appears to have been used as an interrogative from the tenth century onwards.

The relative pronoun *que* stands for the three unstressed forms of the Latin singular dative *quem/quam/quid*, *quid* having replaced *quod* in Vulgar Latin. This form was used from the ninth century onwards. The interrogative pronoun *que* comes from *quid*, the Latin neuter interrogative pronoun, and was used from the eleventh century onwards.

The relative pronoun *quoi* comes from the Latin *quid* when used in a stressed position. Its use developed during the twelfth century.

Note: The conjunction *que* probably comes from the reconstructed Latin form *qui*, a simplified version of the Latin conjunction *quia*, and was often confused with its homonym, the relative pronoun *que*.[2] Its use seems to date back to the tenth century.

1.1.2 *The specifically French or 'compound' series ('la série romane')*

(i) These pronouns developed from the combination of the definite article and the interrogative adjective *quel*, giving *lequel, laquelle, lesquelles*. When preceded by the prepositions *à* or *de* they may form either one word (*auquel, duquel*) if they are used in the masculine, or two words if they are used in the singular feminine form (*à laquelle, de laquelle*).

(ii) These pronouns are marked for gender and number but unmarked for case (which is the opposite of the Latin series):

> *la personne à laquelle je pense n'est pas là* (indirect object)
> *les personnes auxquelles je pense ne sont pas là*
> *j'ai recontré une amie, laquelle m'a parlé de toi* (subject)

See 1.2.2 for the table of the complete forms.

1.2 Tables of morphology and corresponding functions of the relative pronouns

1.2.1 *The Latin series*

1.2.1.1 *The definite relative pronouns*
The inherited or 'simple' forms:

	Subject	Direct object	Indirect object	Adverbial
animates:			*à qui, de qui*	
	qui	*que*		*où, d'où*
inanimates:			*à quoi, de quoi*	

1.2.1.2 *The indefinite relative pronouns* The indefinite relative pronouns are based on the inherited pronouns.

A distinction must be made between those which can refer to person, and which begin with *qui*, and those which can only refer to things or abstract notions and which begin with *quoi* (resembling in this the interrogative pronouns):

	Personal	Inanimate
Subject	*qui que ce soit qui. . . .*	*quoi que ce soit qui. . . .*
Object	*qui que . . .*	*quoi que . . .*
(direct or indirect)	*qui que ce soit (que)*	*quoi que ce soit que*
Either function	*quiconque*	

(i) Note the difference between the indefinite relative pronoun *quoi que*, written in two words, and the subordinating conjunction *quoique*, written as one word:

> *quoi qu'il fasse, il aura toujours tort*
> *quoiqu'il fasse des efforts, il aura toujours tort*

In the first sentence *quoi que* means *quelle que soit la chose que*; in the second, *quoique* means *bien que*.

(ii) *Qui que ce soit* and *quoi que ce soit* may stand on their own as a unit and are not, in that case, followed by *que* when they function as the object − direct or indirect − of the verb:

je ne veux pas qu'on touche à quoi que ce soit (indirect object)
il ne veut voir qui que ce soit (direct object)

(iii) Quiconque has two meanings, that of 'whoever', and that of 'all those' or 'anybody'. The reason for this is historical: *quiconque* comes from *qui conque*, which derived from *qui qu'onque(s)*, meaning *qui jamais* (the *onque* comes from the Latin *unquam* meaning *jamais*). But *qui conque* became confused with the Latin *quicumque*, meaning *tous ceux qui*, hence its two meanings, e.g.

Il est l'esclave, né de quiconque l'achète (Boileau) (*quiconque* = 'whoever')
Quiconque est capable de mentir est indigne d'être compté au nombre des hommes (Fénelon) (*quiconque* = 'anybody' in the sense of 'all those')

Quiconque is always singular and nearly always masculine.

1.2.2   *The 'French' or 'compound' relative pronouns:*

		Subject/ Direct object	Complement of the noun	Indirect object
Singular:	Masculine	*lequel*	*duquel*	*auquel*
	Feminine	*laquelle*	*de laquelle*	*à laquelle*
Plural:	Masculine	*lesquels*	*desquels*	*auxquels*
	Feminine	*lesquelles*	*desquelles*	*auxquelles*

(This table used to be learned by heart in French primary schools, chanted as quickly as possible.)

2   Syntactic functions of the relative pronouns

2.1   Syntactic functions of the simple or inherited relative pronouns

2.1.1   *Function determined by grammatical case*

Relative pronouns, according to their grammatical case, function as subjects, direct or indirect objects or complements of the noun
(i)

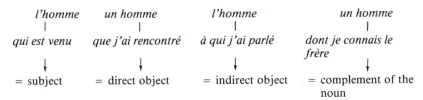

Relative pronouns may also function as adverbials:

le berceau
|
dans lequel dormait le bébé
↓
= adverbial

They may also function as attributes, but usually only in poetry or 'elevated' style (see the last of the following set of examples).

(ii) The following are examples of the use of relative pronouns in more complex sentences.

Subject:

Tu étais semblable au boxeur qui . . . entend les secondes tomber une à une dans un univers étranger, jusqu'à la dixième qui est sans appel. (Saint-Exupéry, *Terre des hommes*)

Direct object:

Alors dans le plus intelligent, dans le plus raisonnable pays de la terre, chacun, corps et âme, fut confié à la puissance de quelques mystérieuses médailles que sa mère lui suspendit au cou dans un sachet et, comme Malbrough, partit en guerre. (J. Guéhenno, *Journal d'un homme de 40 ans*)

Indirect object:

Mais ces hommes à qui je devais parler, demander leur vie, leur mort, quelle part réelle, quel intérêt profond avaient-ils dans ce drame dont il fallait qu'ils fussent les victimes? (Ibid.)

Attribute:

Ta douceur, ton langage et simple et magnanime,
Leur apprit qu'en effet, tout puissant qu'est le crime,
Qui renonce à la vie est plus puissant que lui
(Chénier, *A Charlotte Corday*)

In this case the relative pronoun refers to an adjective or an adjective equivalent such as a past participle. It is the *que* in *tout puissant qu'est le crime* which is the attribute.

2.1.2 *The case of 'dont': equivalent of 'de' with relative pronoun*

Dont is equivalent to *de qui/de quoi* and *duquel* (and its morphological variants *de laquelle, desquels* and *desquelles*):

$$\text{la personne (animate)} \left\{ \begin{array}{l} \textit{dont} \\ \textit{de qui} \\ \textit{de laquelle} \end{array} \right\} \textit{je parle}$$

but:

$$\text{le village (inanimate)} \left\{ \begin{array}{l} \textit{dont} \\ \textit{duquel} \end{array} \right\} \textit{je vois les maisons}$$

and:

$$\text{il n'y a rien (whole clause)} \left\{ \begin{array}{l} \textit{dont} \\ \textit{de quoi} \end{array} \right\} \textit{je ne puisse parler}$$

(*?Il n'y a rien dont je ne puisse pas parler* may also be heard, although the use of *pas* is not acceptable in prescriptive terms. Many people in everyday speech prefer to say *je peux parler de tout*, in order to avoid the possibility of a mistake.)

2.1.3 *The case of 'où'*

(i) *Où* is used when the relative clause functions as an adverb of place or of time: *la ville où j'habite/d'où je viens*; *le jour où il est venu*.

(ii) But when the relative clause functions as a time adverbial, *où* may be replaced by *que*: *le jour qu'il est venu*.

(iii) The antecedent of *où* may be a noun or the adverb *là*:

> *c'est la maison où je passe mes vacances*
> *c'est là où je passe mes vacances*
> *c'est là que je passe mes vacances*

2.1.4　*The case of 'quoi'*

(See 3.2.2 for syntactic uncertainties.)

　　Quoi is frequently used with a preposition at the beginning of a clause: *après quoi, il partit/sur quoi il partit*; *à quoi il répondit*. In this case *quoi* refers to all that precedes.

2.2　Syntactic functions of the 'French' or compound relative pronouns

2.2.1　*General considerations*

It is necessary in this case to distinguish between restrictive and nonrestrictive relative clauses because of certain syntactic restrictions which apply, depending on the type of construction used.

(i) A restrictive (*déterminative*) structure is one which specifies an antecedent in a way which narrows down its meaning:

> 'the boy on the coach was sick'

In this case 'on the coach' narrows down the range of the noun phrase 'the boy'. Such restrictive structures are essential to the meaning of the sentence, and are not usually set off from the rest of the sentence by commas or intonation.

(ii) The opposite is a nonrestrictive structure (*une structure explicative*):

> 'the boy, exhausted by the journey, fell asleep'

In this case 'exhausted by the journey' adds a complement of information but does not narrow down the meaning of 'the boy'.

　　Relative clauses may be restrictive or nonrestrictive:

> *prends le livre qui est sur la table*

In this case the relative clause determines which book is being referred to. It is a restrictive relative clause.

> *le film, qui a eu sa première à Paris, a surtout eu un succès de scandale*

In this case the relative clause does not determine which film is being referred to: it is a nonrestrictive relative clause. Nonrestrictive relative clauses are usually marked off from the rest of the sentence by commas or intonation.

2.2.2　*Compound relative pronouns in restrictive constructions*

These may only be used if preceded by a preposition

(i) Where the antecedent is animate and human, the use of the compound relative pronoun is optional: *la personne à qui j'ai parlé/à laquelle j'ai parlé*

(ii) Where the antecedent is inanimate, if the preposition used or implied is *de* there is a choice between *dont* and *duquel* (or its morphological variants):

> *l'association de ski dont je fais partie (= je fais partie de quelque chose)*
> *l'association de ski de laquelle je fais partie*

Similarly one may say or write:

l'outil dont je me suis servi
l'outil duquel je me suis servi

If the preposition used is other than the simple *de*, the use of the compound relative pronoun will be obligatory; since *dont* cannot be preceded by a preposition:

la boîte à l'intérieur de laquelle je l'avais mis a disparu
je ne retrouve plus le banc auprès duquel je l'avais posé

2.2.3 Compound relative pronouns in nonrestrictive constructions

(i) Lequel (and its morphological variants) may be used as a subject in nonrestrictive constructions (but not in restrictive constructions, in which it is always preceded by a preposition, see 2.2.2):

j'ai rencontré son frère, lequel m'a dit . . .

But *lequel* cannot refer to an indefinite or neuter form:

ce de quoi vous parlez
*ce duquel vous parlez

Lequel cannot be used after a coordinating conjunction such as *et*, *ou* or *ni*.
(ii) Lequel may also be used as a relative adjective; i.e. with repetition of the antecedent:

j'ai vu un ami, lequel ami m'a dit . . .

Such a construction is very rare except for emphasis or to achieve a humorous effect, since this kind of construction belongs to legal and administrative registers.
(iii) Lequel and its morphological variants may be used in nonrestrictive constructions to avoid ambiguity. They are very frequently used in situations in which the antecedent does not immediately precede the relative pronoun (whether subject or complement). In other words, they are used where the antecedent is one of two nouns in a noun phrase, and where ambiguity is possible. Compare:

il y a une nouvelle édition de ce livre, laquelle se vend très bien (laquelle = une
  nouvelle édition)
il y a une nouvelle édition de ce livre, lequel se vend très bien (lequel = ce livre)

The use of this type of relative construction is largely confined to the written language; in the spoken language one would say, for example:

c'est le frère de mon amie, celui qui habite à Bordeaux, qui me l'a dit
c'est le frère de mon amie, celle qui habite à Bordeaux, qui me l'a dit

rather than:

C'est le frère de mon amie, lequel/laquelle habite Bordeaux . . .

which sounds ridiculous.
(iv) Lequel may be used to avoid the repetition of *qui*:

. . . les changements radicaux qui sont absolument imprévisibles, sinon dans un
  avenir lointain, lequel ne relève pas de la politique (*Le Monde* (1965), quoted by
  Mauger, *Grammaire pratique du français d'aujourd'hui*)

(v) Archaic and ossified use of *lequel* may occur in legal and administrative documents:

on a entendu trois témoins, lesquels ont dit . . .

or a stylistic device to produce a humorous or satirical archaic effect using *lequel* adjectivally:

> *pour se donner une contenance le commissaire avait mis son chapeau, lequel chapeau ne lui allait pas très bien*

3   Morphosemantic difficulties

3.1   Morphosemantic oppositions between the various relative pronouns

3.1.1   *'Qui'/'lequel'*

(i) Both *qui* and *lequel* are possible if the antecedent is human and they are preceded by a preposition:

> *la personne à qui j'ai parlé*
> *la personne à laquelle j'ai parlé*

The latter tends to be the favoured form.
(ii)   Lequel/lesquels etc. is always used if preceded by a preposition and referring to an inanimate:

> *les vacances auxquelles je pense*

and not:

> **les vacances à qui je pense*

(iii)   Lequel may be used without being preceded by a preposition, i.e. as subject, in order to avoid ambiguity (see 2.2.3 *iii*):

> *il y a une édition de ce livre, laquelle . . .* (= *l'édition*)
> *il y a une édition de ce livre, lequel . . .* (= *le livre*)
> *il y a une édition de ce livre qui . . .* (= *l'édition* or *le livre*)

3.1.2   *Preposition with 'qui' and preposition with 'quoi'*

The contrast is essentially between animate (*qui*) and inanimate (*quoi*), but it is also between a pronoun which must stand for a definite antecedent (*qui*) and one which may stand either for an indefinite antecedent or for a whole clause (*quoi*):

> *il pêcha, après quoi il s'en alla*

The preposition + *quoi* construction tends to be limited to literary language.

3.1.3   *Preposition with 'quoi' and preposition with 'lequel'*

The preposition + *lequel* construction must have a definite antecedent:

> *je pense à une chose à laquelle je tiens beaucoup*
> *tu ne sais pas ce à quoi je pense*

3.1.4   *'Dont', 'duquel' and 'de qui'*

(i)   Dont is used instead of *de qui* when referring to inanimates (see 2.1.2) or animals (see *(iii)* below).
(ii)   Dont cannot be used if it is preceded by a preposition (since it contains the idea of *de*). One may thus write:

> *la grammaire dont je me sers est incomplète* (i.e. *je me sers de quelque chose*)

but not:

*la rivière au bord de dont je me promène

but instead:

la rivière au bord de laquelle je me promène

the preposition being the compound preposition *au bord de* (see 3.2.3 for further restrictions).

(iii) De qui is normally used for a person, although *dont* is also possible: *la personne dont tu parles*, or *la personne de qui je parle*; but *le chien dont je parle*, and not **le chien de qui je parle*.

(iv) Duquel may be used instead of *dont*: *l'outil dont je me suis servi/l'outil duquel je me suis servi*; but *duquel* is obligatory when preceded by a preposition; see example of *dont/duquel*, i.e. *la rivière au bord de laquelle je me promène*, in *(ii)* above.

3.2 Areas of grammatical and semantic uncertainty

3.2.1 *'Que' used instead of 'où' or 'dont'*

(i) One used to say:

c'est à vous à qui je parle

This was replaced by:

c'est vous à qui je parle

Now the accepted version is:

c'est à vous que je parle

probably by analogy with sentences such as *c'est vous que je vois* (see Deloffre, *La Phrase française*).

(ii) Que was formerly used instead of *où* and *dont*:

Du temps que (= *où*) *les bêtes parlaient* (La Fontaine)
Me voyait-il du même œil qu'il [= dont il] me voit aujourd'hui (Racine)

The use of *que* for *dont* is still frequent in popular speech, but it is completely unacceptable from a prescriptive point of view:

*et la dame que (= dont) j'ai retrouvé le sac, elle n'est même pas venue me remercier
(heard in the street)

3.2.2 *The use of 'quoi' with masculine and feminine nouns*

(i) Quoi has been replaced by *lequel* in referring to inanimates since the beginning of the eighteenth century. Thus one must say and write: *la table sur laquelle j'écris est branlante*, and not: **la table sur quoi. . . .* (The latter may still be heard, however, in uneducated speech.)

(ii) But *quoi* may still be used either with the neuter pronoun *ce*, or with *chose*, *rien* or *quelque chose* as an antecedent, since these are semantically neuter: *je vais vous dire ce à quoi je pense*.

Some writers do however sometimes use *quoi* in an 'incorrect' manner to achieve a stylistic effect (in which case they appear archaic) or if they want to create an impression of something neuter:

. . . une vieille bicyclette achetée d'occasion et sur quoi Jasmin nous faisait quelquefois monter (Alain Fournier)

In this case *sur quoi* implies *drôle de bicyclette* (i.e. that the bicycle is rather an odd one) (example borrowed from Larousse, *Grand dictionnaire de la langue française*). Similarly:

> *Prosper n'avait pas voulu quitter sa maîtresse à quoi l'attachait un lien inconnu de lui-même* (Bordeaux)

A quoi = à la maîtresse, i.e. *l'objet aimé* (also quoted by Larousse).
(iii) There is also a tendency to use *quoi* with *raison* and *motif*:

> *C'est une des raisons pourquoi j'ai eu quelquefois du plaisir à la guerre* (Montherlant)

In this case the preposition and *quoi* are written as one word only. Such a use of *pourquoi* is to be avoided by anglophone students, since it would be presumed to be an anglicism (see 5.2.2.3).

3.2.3   *The case of 'dont'*

(i) Dont may be the complement of several nouns in the relative clause:

> *Il plaignit les pauvres femmes dont les époux gaspillent la fortune* (Flaubert, quoted by Deloffre, *La Phrase française*)

In this case *dont* is the complement of *époux* and of *fortune*.
(ii) For some grammarians, however, it is unacceptable to have *dont* as complement of several nouns which are complement of one another:

> *?une femme dont la fraîcheur du visage était merveilleuse* (example borrowed from Deloffre, *La Phrase française*)

But *une femme dont la fraîcheur de visage était merveilleuse* is possible, because the absence of an article (use of *de* instead of *du*) changes the function of *visage* from a complement of a noun into the equivalent of a relational adjective (see Ch. 11 for relational adjectives and their equivalent in French). This now seems an over-purist rule.
(iii) It is also unacceptable to have the same noun represented both by *dont* and by another anaphoric term, be it a possessive adjective or a personal pronoun. Thus Deloffre quotes as 'incorrect' the following sentence:

> *?Un petit étang dont la robe de lentilles vertes semblait le revêtir comme un glacis de pistache* (Huysmans)

A better version would have been *un petit étang que sa robe de lentilles semblait revêtir comme un glacis de pistache*.
    This seems a little pedantic where repetition of the antecedent by a personal pronoun is concerned: the *le* could be said to help avoid ambiguity. But this rule always holds where the possessive adjective is concerned. One could not write or say:

> **un petit étang dont ses rives étaient bordées de jonquilles*

Dont resembles 'whose' in that the use of 'whose' also precludes the use of the possessive adjective.

4   Use of relative pronouns in relation to word-order

4.1   Position of the relative pronoun in relation to its antecedent

4.1.1   *The 'rule of the maggoty apple' ('la règle de la pomme véreuse')*

The definite relative pronoun introducing a restrictive relative clause (see 2.2.1 *i*) refers to the noun phrase which immediately precedes it, which is known as its antecedent.

Bonnard (*Grammaire des lycées et collèges*, 166) gives the following example to illustrate this rule:

j'ai mangé chez ma tante une pomme qui était véreuse ('I ate at my aunt's an apple which was maggoty')

One cannot however write or say:

*j'ai mangé une pomme chez ma tante qui était véreuse

for in this case it would be the aunt who was maggoty. These restrictions do not apply in English to the same extent (i.e. 'I ate an apple at my aunt's which was maggoty' is acceptable).

4.1.2 *Exceptions to the 'rule of the maggoty apple'*

(i) This rule does not apply to nonrestrictive relative clauses (see 2.2.1 *ii*):

j'ai mangé une pomme, chez ma tante, qui était véreuse

In this case intonation in the spoken language and punctuation in the written language make ·it plain that the antecedent of *qui* is not the word which precedes it, as is the norm. The two commas or pauses effectively 'bracket' *chez ma tante* from the rest of the sentence, and *qui* has to refer to the noun phrase immediately preceding it, i.e. *une pomme*. Such constructions tend to be avoided, however, as being stylistically clumsy.
(ii) Since the relative clause has the same function as an adjective (i.e. it modifies a noun), a relative clause may follow an adjective, providing the latter modifies the same noun:

c'était un enfant jeune, gai, agréable (et) qui charmait tous ceux qui le rencontraient

(iii) It is possible to find cases in literature of relative pronouns separated from their antecedent when the latter is *celui-là*:

Que celui-là lui jette la première pierre qui n'a jamais péché. (*Nouveau Testament*)

(iv) Similarly, one may separate the relative pronoun and its antecedent to obtain a stylistic effect:

Le passant n'avait rien vu, qui s'en tenait à ce premier regard. (Gide)

In this case the relative clause is heavily emphasized.
(v) The relative pronoun may have as an antecedent a noun already modified by another relative clause, although this is often considered to be poor style (see section 5):

c'est la partie qui s'est jouée ce matin qui a été la plus passionnante

(vi) But it is not possible in French for a relative to have as an antecedent a whole clause rather than a noun phrase whereas this is possible in English. 'He admires him, which surprises me' is translated by *il l'admire, ce qui m'étonne* (with *ce* as a dummy antecedent) and not by **il l'admire qui m'étonne*, which is totally unacceptable.
Note however that it was possible, in Classical French, to use *qui* to stand for a whole clause:

Madame de Dreux . . . fut admonestée, qui est une légère peine (Mme de Sévigné)

In this case *qui* stands for *ce qui*.

4.2 Word-order in the relative clause

4.2.1   *The relative pronoun as subject*

If the relative pronoun is a subject, the word order will be subject (= relative pronoun) + verb + complement (which may be optional):

mon père a acheté une maison qui se trouve en Normandie

4.2.2   *The relative pronoun as direct object, with no other complement*

In this case there are two word-orders possible: relative pronoun + verb + subject, and relative pronoun + subject + verb:

la maison (qu'a achetée mon père) est très grande
la maison (que mon père a achetée) est très grande

4.2.3   *The relative pronoun as direct object, with an indirect or 'attributive' complement*

In this case the normal word-order is relative pronoun + subject + verb + attributive complement', e.g.

la maison (que mon père a achetée à son voisin) est très grande

The following is probably not acceptable:

la maison (qu'a achetée mon père à son voisin) est très grande

The reason the latter is not totally acceptable is because there is a rule in French which states that one should not place side by side (or one after the other) two phrases which are not grammatically linked: since *mon père* and *à son voisin* are not grammatically dependent one on the other, they should not be contiguous. But such constructions do occur in spontaneous spoken French.

4.2.4   *The relative pronoun as attributive complement*

(i) In cases where the relative pronoun functions as an attributive complement and no other complement is included, there are two possible word-orders: relative pronoun + verb + subject, or relative pronoun + subject + verb:

la personne (à qui parle mon père) est un voisin
la personne (à qui mon père parle) est un voisin

(In this particular case, however, the first sentence is the best one from a stylistic point of view, partly because of the rule mentioned in 4.2.3 (*à qui/parle/mon père* as against *à qui/mon père/parle*), and partly because it avoids the need to pronounce two similar syllables one after the other (*père parle*), which sounds rather unpleasant to the French ear).

(ii) Where the relative pronoun is an attributive complement and an indirect object is also included, only one word-order is possible: relative pronoun + subject + verb + indirect object:

la personne à qui mon père parle d'affaires est un voisin

and not:

*la personne à qui parle mon père d'affaires est un voisin (for the reason given in 4.2.3).

4.3   Influence of the relative clause on word-order in the main clause

If the subject of the main clause is modified either by a long relative clause, or by several relative clauses, or by both participial clauses and relative clauses, the subject/verb word-order will be reversed, so that the subject may still remain contiguous to the verb:

> *Dans les flancs du rocher s'ouvraient çà et là des bouches noires entourées de blocs de pierre en désordre, des trous carrés flanqués de piliers historiés d'hiéroglyphes, et dont les linteaux portaient des cartouches mystérieux où se distinguaient dans un grand disque jaune le scarabée sacré, le soleil à tête de bélier, et les déesses Isis et Nephtys agenouillées ou debout.* (Gautier, *Le Roman de la momie*)

The subjects of *s'ouvraient çà et là* are *des bouches noires* and *des trous carrés*; *et dont* refers to *piliers historiés d'hiéroglyphes*; and *où* refers to *cartouches mystérieux*.
This kind of construction is typical of extremely elaborate written language.

5   Contrastive problems

5.1   Correspondence of the French relative pronoun to a possible English relative pronoun

The translation of French relative pronouns into English presents stylistic problems.
(i) It has already been mentioned (see section 4) that the relative pronoun must immediately follow its antecedent. In English the same does not necessarily apply.
(ii) The zero relative pronoun is extremely frequent in English whenever the relative pronoun is the object; but the zero relative pronoun does not exist in French:

> 'this is the colour of paint (= which) we want' = *voici la couleur de peinture que nous voulons*

(iii) There is often more than one relative pronoun which may be used in a particular context in English, whereas there will be only one in most cases in French (the exception being the areas of overlap between the Latin series and the French series).

			who				*l'homme qui est resté*
'the	{	man	that	}	remained'	=	
		table					*la table qui est restée*
			which				

			who(m)				*l'homme que j'ai vu*
'the	{	man	that	}	I saw'	=	
		table	Ø				*la table que j'ai vue*
			which				

(iv) Where the relative pronoun *qui* stands for the preceding clause (i.e. where it is neuter), it must be preceded by the neuter *ce* in French, although the same does not apply in English:

> *la lettre que j'attendais n'était toujours pas arrivée, ce qui m'empêchait de pouvoir faire quoi que ce soit* = 'the letter I had been expecting had still not arrived, which made it impossible for me to take any action'

(v) In English, participial clauses are often preferred to relative clauses: 'we saw John driving his new car' is often preferred to 'we saw John who was driving his new car'. The same does not apply in French: *nous avons vu Jean conduisant sa nouvelle voiture*

is possible but unlikely; *nous avons vu Jean qui conduisait sa nouvelle voiture* or *nous avons vu Jean en train de conduire sa nouvelle voiture* are far more likely.

5.2   Apparent absence of corresponding English relative pronoun

5.2.1   *Defining the problem*

The problem differs according to whether one is translating from French to English or from English to French. If one is translating from English to French, one may be dealing with a word which looks very much like a conjunction but which has to be translated by a relative pronoun:

'this directory is valid until January 1st, when it will be replaced by a new one'

can be translated by:

cet annuaire est valable jusqu'au 1er janvier, date à laquelle il sera remplacé par une nouvelle édition

or by:

cet annuaire est valable jusqu'au 1er janvier, (date) où il sera remplacé par une nouvelle édition

The first translation is the more formal one, but the *où* construction is becoming more and more common.

In this case one could have expected 'when' to be translated by *quand*, but such a translation would be unacceptable in prescriptive terms. With translation from French to English the problem is different: in this case being too literal will result in a stilted translation, i.e. one which is unacceptable on stylistic rather than grammatical grounds. Thus:

la période de Noël est celle à laquelle on échange des vœux (or *celle où on échange des vœux*)

can be translated as:

'Christmas is when people exchange greetings'

A direct equivalent of the French construction is possible but oddly formal, and therefore unsuitable in many contexts:

'Christmas is the time at which people exchange greetings'

The problem arises from the fact that the morphological categories of relative pronouns and conjunctions are not clearly separate in English: 'when', 'where' and 'why' may function either as conjunctions or as relative pronouns ('when' = 'the time at which'; 'where' = 'the place where'; 'why' = 'the reason why') and 'how' may stand for 'the way in which'. But since they are usually thought to be conjunctions the tendency is to translate them as conjunctions into French, leading to grammatical mistakes in French and stylistic mistakes in English.

5.2.2   *Items which may or may not be translated by relative pronouns in French depending on their grammatical function*

5.2.2.1   *'When'*   'When' may function as an interrogative adverb, a conjunction or a relative pronoun:
(i)   as an interrogative adverb:

'when will you see him?' = *quand le verrez-vous?*

(ii) as a conjunction:

'it was in 1968, when everyone least expected it, that the Six Day War broke out' = *c'est en 1968, alors qu'on s'y attendait le moins, que la Guerre des Six Jours a éclaté*

(*Quand* and *au moment où* could also be used.)

(iii) as a relative pronoun:

'Christmas is when (= the time at which) people exchange greetings' = *la période de Noël est celle à laquelle on échange des vœux*
(or *Noël est le jour où l'on échange des vœux*)

but not:

*la période de Noël est quand on échange des vœux

This is an extremely common mistake made by anglophone students. The rule is that when *quand* is preceded by a word which could be an antecedent it must be replaced by a relative pronoun. But see *(iv)*.

(iv) The 'relative pronoun/*quand*' alternative is an area of syntactic uncertainty: French speakers are tending to use *quand* in the same way as the English use 'when' with ever increasing frequency, particularly in *c'est quand* constructions:

?*Noël, c'est quand on échange des cadeaux·*
?*une imprudence c'est quand on ne fait pas attention au danger*

Such constructions used to be associated with the speech of children and uneducated adults; but they are now quite frequently heard in educated speech when the speakers are speaking spontaneously in an informal context.

This type of construction is still considered a 'mistake', in the sense that it goes against the French desire to explain a noun by a noun, a verb by a verb, and an adjective by an adjective and so on. The mistake itself is not surprising, however, since all the subordinating conjunctions – with the exception of *si* – come from the same Indo-European root, as do the relative, interrogative and indefinite pronouns *qui*, *que* and *quoi*.

5.2.2.2 *'Where'* 'Where' may function as an interrogative adverb, a conjunction or as a relative pronoun.

(i) as an interrogative adverb:

'where is he?' = *où est-il?*

(ii) as a conjunction (or 'relative adverb' according to Grevisse, *Le Bon usage*):

'there was nothing but ashes where the house had been' = *il n'y avait plus que des cendres (là) où il y avait eu la maison*

(iii) as a relative pronoun;

'the house where (= in which) I was born had remained unchanged' = *la maison où j'étais né était restée inchangée* or *la maison dans laquelle j'étais né était restée inchangée*

Où is similar to 'where' in that it may take on different functions, but *où* used without an antecedent is less formal than *où* used with an antecedent. The use of *où* does not present any grammatical problems as such.

5.2.2.3 *'Why'* 'Why' may function either as an interrogative adverb or as a relative pronoun.

(i) as an interrogative pronoun:

'why did you leave?' = *pourquoi êtes-vous parti*?

(ii) as a relative pronoun:

'he told us why he left' = *il nous a dit les raisons pour lesquelles il est parti* or *il nous a dit pourquoi il est parti*

but not:

*il nous a dit les raisons pourquoi il est parti

This is an extremely common mistake made by anglophone students.

5.2.2.4 *'How'* 'How' may function as an interrogative or exclamative adverb, as a conjunction, or as a substitute for the relative construction 'the way in which'.

(i) as an interrogative adverb:

'how did he paper his room?' = *comment a-t-il tapissé sa chambre?*

(ii) as an exclamative adverb:

'how he snores!' = *comme il ronfle!* (or *qu'est-ce qu'il ronfle!*)

(but see Ch. 19)

(iii) as a conjunction (conjunction being used in the sense of 'link word'):

'he does not know how she will take it' (= 'in what way') = *il ne sait pas comment elle le prendra* (*comme* in the seventeenth century)
'he told us how he loved her' (= 'how much') = *il nous a dit combien il l'aime* (*comme* is informal)

(iv) as a substitute for the relative construction 'in the way in which':

'it is the story of how a man became famous' = *l'histoire décrit comment un homme est devenu célèbre* or *l'histoire décrit la manière dont un homme est devenu célèbre* or *l'histoire décrit de quelle façon un homme est devenu célèbre*

In this case there is a choice between a construction based on an interrogative adverb, a relative pronoun and an interrogative adjective.

6 Stylistic considerations

6.1 Varying attitudes towards the use of relative clauses

(i) Relative pronouns and the clauses they introduce enable the expression of subtle subdivisions of thought. As such their use is typical of philosophical texts: Descartes, Pascal and others used them whenever they felt them to be useful to the expression of their thoughts.

(ii) In the past they were also used in descriptive passages:

Le cardinal de Lorraine, son frère, était né avec une ambition démesurée, avec un esprit vif et une éloquence admirable, et il avait acquis une science profonde dont il se servait pour se rendre considérable en défendant la religion catholique qui commençait d'être attaquée. (Mme de La Fayette, *La Princesse de Clèves*)

Nowadays, however, this would be considered clumsy. The accumulation of a number of relative clauses within the same sentence is also felt to be clumsy according to Legrand: *ils font un bruit de rocaille.*[3] Such an image is somewhat ridiculous, but it illustrates the attitude which has prevailed in France for over a century as regards the use of relative pronouns.

Marouzeau (*Précis de stylistique française*) writes in this respect:

> *On notera que le français moderne est très chatouilleux en ce qui concerne la multiplication des relatifs et conjonctifs. La langue classique l'était moins.*

And he quotes (83) an example from Racine:

> *Britannicus est seul; quelque ennui qui le presse,*
> *Il ne voit à son sort que moi qui s'intéresse,*
> *Il n'a pour tout plaisir, Seigneur, que quelques pleurs*
> *Qui lui font quelquefois oublier ses malheurs.*

6.2 Ways of avoiding relative clauses

Legrand (*Stylistique française*) lists the following ways of avoiding the use of relative clauses:

(i) replacing the relative clause by a noun in apposition (the latter may or may not be followed by a complement):

> *Racine qui a composé cette tragédie = Racine, auteur de cette tragédie*

(ii) replacing it by an adjective (the latter may be followed by a complement):

> *les accidents qui se sont produits auparavant = les accidents antérieurs*
> *cet homme qui tient ses promesses = cet homme fidèle à ses promesses*

(iii) replacing it by a possessive adjective followed by a noun:

> *les chagrins qu'il éprouve = ses chagrins*
> *les buts que vous visez = vos buts*

(iv) replacing it by a preposition followed by a complement:

> *un travail qui doit durer plusieurs jours = un travail de plusieurs jours*
> *des enfants qui ont le même âge = des enfants du même âge*

(v) replacing it by a main clause (but in this case the hierarchy of the thought process is no longer respected):

> *tu me payeras cher les beaux fruits que tu m'as volés = tu m'as volé de beaux fruits,*
> *mais tu me les payeras cher*

Legrand concludes with these amazing words:

> *Reconnaissons-le, notre langue offre à cet égard* (i.e. eliminating relative clauses) *des facilités trop souvent méconnues ou du moins négligées. Chateaubriand, dit-on, tenait à l'honneur d'avoir écrit des paragraphes entiers sans un seul 'qui'. Tour de force si l'on veut mais parfaitement imitable.* (Legrand, *Stylistique française, livre du maître*, 140)

Ridiculous as this may seem, it is nonetheless true that an excessive number of relative clauses is no longer acceptable in modern French, particularly in narratives; since relative clauses are a way of expressing modifications of one's thoughts, they seem particularly odd and out of place in this context. It is true however, that some writers such as Gautier and Proust, for example, have rebelled against such 'stylistic rules' and used relative clauses with such consummate skill as to have made them their trademark.

Notes

1 In French these are called *déterminatives* ('restrictive') and *explicatives* ('nonrestrictive').

2 Brunot and Bruneau trace *que* back to *quid, quod* and *quem, quid* (the *quid* being unstressed), depending on its function in the sentence (*Précis de grammaire historique de la langue française*). Dubois and Mitterand (*Dictionnaire étymologique*), however, trace it back to *qui* which replaced *quod* in the fourth century; the recent dictionary *Lexis* traces it back to *quid*; and *Le Grand dictionnaire Larousse de la langue française* traces it back to *quia*. Bourciez does not commit himself on the matter. The origins of this conjunction are therefore far from easy to determine.

3 Legrand writes under the heading '*Incorrections*' in *Stylistique française*:

Ces dangereux pronoms, sous la plume d'un élève inattentif et peu ferré sur la syntaxe, donnent lieu à des fautes matérielles de plus d'un genre.

On fait dépendre une proposition relative d'une autre relative. Grave irrégularité. Par fois même on offre à son lecteur une véritable cascade de 'qui':

'J'ai vu mon cousin qui m'a donné des nouvelles de ma tante, qui est malade depuis l'accident qui lui est arrivé en allant à la représentation qui a eu lieu vendredi dernier.'

Ces relatifs se heurtent avec un bruit de rocaille.

Chapter 15

The subordinating conjunctions and subordinate clauses (excluding relative clauses)

0 General considerations

0.1 Definition

(i) Subordinating conjunctions are invariable words; they introduce a clause which will be subordinate to another, in the sense that it will fulfil a specific function within the clause to which it is subordinated. In the case of *j'ai demandé qu'il vienne, j'ai demandé* is the main clause and *qu'il vienne* is the subordinate clause, the direct object of *j'ai demandé (j'ai demandé quoi? − qu'il vienne)*. For a definition of the clause, see Ch. 17.

(ii) Subordinating conjunctions only introduce a subordinate clause: they function as link words and do not have a function of their own. (It is this which differentiates subordinating conjunctions and relative pronouns. The latter function as would nouns: they may be subjects, objects or adverbial complements.)

Note: It is sometimes necessary to distinguish grammatically subordinate clauses from semantically subordinate clauses. See Introduction to Part IV, 0.7.

0.2 Problems of classification

(i) There are cases in which it is not clear whether a particular item is functioning as a relative pronoun or as a conjunction. For example, some grammarians may consider *du moment que* analytically, classifying *que* as a relative pronoun standing for *du moment*. Others will see such an expression globally, i.e. as forming just one lexical unit which functions as a compound conjunction, since it is interchangeable with other compound conjunctions, e.g.

du moment que tu y vas, j'y vais aussi = puisque tu y vas . . .

The use of *où* without an antecedent also presents problems of classification: see Ch. 14, 5.2.2.2.

(ii) It is also true that not all subordinated clauses are introduced by subordinating conjunctions as such: indirect interrogative sentences contain subordinate clauses which may be introduced either by interrogative adverbs, interrogative adjectives or interrogative pronouns (see 2.5). Such subordinate clauses function in the same way as nominal or 'completive' subordinate clauses, see 2.5.

0.3 Problems for anglophones

These are mainly semantic: the 'same' conjunction may take on different meanings in different contexts. *Comme* for example, may introduce a subordinate clause expressing a cause, in which case the subordinate clause will come first; it may also express an idea of time, i.e. of simultaneity, in which case it may either precede or follow the main clause. Compare:

comme il est déjà tard, je préfère ne manger qu'un sandwich (comme = puisque)
<u>*comme je partais,*</u> *il est arrivé (comme = alors que)*
il est sorti en courant, juste <u>*comme j'arrivais*</u> *(comme = quand)*

See section 5.

1 Morphology

1.1 Problems of definition

(i) If one defines as 'subordinating conjunctions' only those conjunctions which may fulfil that one function, there are but two simple conjunctions *que* and *si*; but to these one must add all the new 'French' conjunctions based on *que* such as *excepté que*, *ainsi que, pour que*.

(ii) There are also a number of words which may function either as subordinating conjunctions or as other parts of speech: *quand* (which may also be an interrogative adverb); *où* (which may also be a relative pronoun and an interrogative pronoun); *combien*, *comment* and *pourquoi* (which may also be interrogative or exclamative adverbs). These are the 'conjunctive adverbs'.

1.2 Subordinating conjunctions inherited from Latin

Most of these have disappeared (they became what is colourfully called in French *des mutilés phonétiques*), leaving but four 'conjunctions' in modern French which come directly from Latin conjunctions or adverbs:

si (Old French *se* and Latin *sǐ*, *sī* in classical Latin)
comme (*com* in Old French, *quomo* in Vulgar Latin for *quomodo*)
quand (*quando* in Latin)
que (which corresponds to *quid*, *quo*, *quia* and perhaps to *quiam*)

1.3 The new 'French' or 'compound' conjunctions

These are all based on a first element (which is variable) + *que*.
(i) The first element may be an adverb, e.g. *ainsi que, alors que, aussitôt que, bien que, encore que, loin que, non que, outre que, sitôt que, tandis que, tant que.*
(ii) The first element may be a combination of a preposition and an adverb, e.g. *à moins que, de même que, pour peu que.*
(iii) The first element may be a preposition, e.g. *après que, depuis que, dès que, malgré que, pour que, sans que, sauf que, selon que.*
(iv) The first element may be a preposition + *ce* (*que* being originally a neuter relative pronoun), e.g. *à ce que, de ce que, jusqu'à ce que, parce que* (which used to be written *par ce que*) and *pour ce que* (until the beginning of the seventeenth century).
(v) The first element may be a past participle, e.g. *attendu que, excepté que, hormis que, pourvu que, supposé que.*
(vi) The first element may be a present participle or a gerund, e.g. *pendant que, suivant que, en attendant que, en supposant que.*

1.4 Historical note on 'que' and the compound (or 'French') conjunctions

(i) Since *que* is a grammatical tool with no lexical content other than the expression of subordination, it was often omitted in Old French, whereas in modern French this is not possible:

nous lui promîmes (que) nous vous dirions que vous allassiez chasser en cette forêt (modern version of a sentence taken from *Aucassin et Nicolette* (anon. – probably written in the early thirteenth century – the *que* is absent from the original)

(ii) Since the *que* could be omitted when it had no lexical content other than the expression of subordination, when it was used it could take on a variety of meanings, such as *à savoir que, afin que, de crainte que*, depending on the context:

> *es-tu aveugle que tu ne me voies pas? (que = pour que* in the sense of *puisque*, indicating a cause)
> *viens que je t'embrasse (que = pour que*, indicating a goal)

2   Syntactical functions of the different kinds of subordinate clause

There are three types of subordinate clauses: nominal or completive clauses, which are introduced by the simple *que* (see 2.1); adverbial or 'circumstantial' clauses, introduced by conjunctions other than the simple *que* (see 2.2); and indirect interrogative clauses (see 2.5). Section 2.3 deals with the repetition of conjunctions and 2.4 with the various uses of *que*.

2.1   Nominal or completive subordinate clauses[1]

These are introduced by the simple *que* and function as would a nominal phrase.

2.1.1   *The subordinate clause as subject*

In the example *qu'il soit sincère ne fait aucun doute*, the subordinate clause is the subject of *fait*. This kind of construction is rare, however; it is more normal to place the subordinate clause in the object position using an impersonal verb, e.g. *cela ne fait aucun doute qu'il est sincère.* (This entails a change of mood; see Ch. 5.)

Another way of avoiding this kind of construction is to use a disjunctive structure:

> *qu'il soit sincère, voilà qui ne fait aucun doute*
> (or *qu'il soit sincère, cela ne fait aucun doute* in a less formal style)

2.1.2   *The subordinate clause as object*

This is the most usual case, hence the name 'completive clause' given to all these types of clauses.

(i) The verb may be transitive direct, e.g.

> *je te dis que tu te trompes*

In this case the verb used will be either a declarative verb (*dire, affirmer*), a verb of opinion (*penser, croire*) or a verb of emotion (*souhaiter, craindre*). See Ch. 5 for the moods which 'harmonize' with these verbs.

The use of *que* with declarative verbs may change direct speech into indirect speech (see 4.1.1).

> Direct speech:
> *Jean m'a dit: 'Pierre vient/viendra à cinq heures'*
> Indirect speech:
> *Jean m'a dit que Pierre vient/viendrait à cinq heures*

(ii) The verb may be transitive indirect, in which case one may use *à ce que* or *de ce que*. The subordinate clause is an indirect object:

> *je m'attends à ce qu'il soit en retard (s'attendre à quelque chose)*
> *je profite de ce qu'il est en retard pour finir mon travail tranquillement (profiter de quelque chose)*

Note that where the *que* is used on its own it is a conjunction; but when it is used with a preposition + *ce* which is a demonstrative it is similar to a relative pronoun, since it has an antecedent in *ce*. In this case the *ce* is cataphoric (i.e. refers forward to the subordinate clause to come).

2.1.3   *The subordinate clause as attribute of a noun*

la vérité est qu'il est souvent trop sûr de lui (= attribute of *la vérité*)

2.1.4   *The subordinate clause as complement of a noun*

elle était hantée par la crainte qu'il ne lui arrive un malheur (= complement of *la crainte*)

2.1.5   *The subordinate clause as complement of an adjective*

je suis heureux que tu sois là

But one can also write:

je suis content de ce que tu sois là (= du fait que, de cela que)

This second construction is becoming increasingly frequent.

2.1.6   *The subordinate clause as complement of an adverb:*

heureusement que je suis là
bien sûr qu'il viendra

2.1.7   *The subordinate clause in apposition*

Cette idée, que vous passiez nous prendre au retour, nous semble excellente

In this example, the *que* could be seen to be a relative pronoun standing for *cette idée*; but it is the whole clause introduced by *que* which stands for *cette idée*, and not *que* alone. What is more, *que* fills no specific function within the clause introduced, as would a relative pronoun: it is, therefore, a conjunction.

2.2   Adverbial or 'circumstantial' subordinate clauses

These are introduced by compound conjunctions and function, as would a prepositional phrase.

2.2.1   *Définition*

(i) Some subordinate clauses function as would 'adverbial complements' (also called 'circumstantial complements' in French):

il viendra te voir avant son départ
il viendra te voir avant qu'il ne parte

The prepositional phrase in the first sentence and the subordinate clause in the second sentence both function as time adverbials (or 'circumstantial complements of time'). *(ii)* Some of the adverbial conjunctions have been inherited from Latin (namely *quand* and *comme*), but most of them are 'French' conjunctions − i.e. phrasal conjunctions such as *de façon que* (goal), *de telle façon que* (conséquence), *pour que, afin que, bien que* − in which case the meaning is carried by the lexical elements which are turned into conjunctions by the presence of the ubiquitous *que*:

j'irai quand/aussitôt que tu auras fini (time)
je l'ai fait parce qu'on me l'a demandé (cause)

ils ont fermé la barrière de façon que les voitures ne peuvent pas passer
(consequence)
ils ont fermé la barrière de façon que les voitures ne puissent pas passer (goal)
bien qu'il aient fermé la barrière, les voitures sont quand même passées (concession)

2.2.2 Subclassification of adverbial clauses according to semantic criteria

(i) Adverbial clauses cannot be further subclassified according to syntactic function. They are however usually subclassified according to semantic criteria, according to whether they express time, place, cause, consequence, goal, concession, condition, comparison, opposition, addition or exception. One of the problems which arises from such a classification is that it is purely impressionistic. This is why the same semantic spectrum has been divided up somewhat differently by different grammarians. Some, for example, have a category called 'adversative conjunctions', while others put these under the heading 'concessive' conjunctions. Others do not have 'place' as a category because these phrasal conjunctions are relative constructions in disguise.

The reason for retaining such an imperfect system of classification is that what is known about adverbial conjunctions is unwieldy and amorphous. This classification does make the material easier to deal with; and students are used to these divisions, and usually find them helpful.

(ii) It will be noted from the following table that each concept may be expressed by a number of subordinating conjunctions. This is due to the fact that many may express a 'core' concept of time, cause etc. together with some other additional concept. For example, *une fois que* expresses posteriority + inchoative aspect (i.e. beginning of the action), whereas *jusqu'à ce que* expresses posteriority + terminative aspect. The conjunctions set in small capitals in the following tables represent those which correspond most exactly to the core concept to be expressed; the other conjunctions will represent that core concept plus other concepts (such as aspect, for example). It is the distinguishing of the differences of meaning existing among the various items figuring in the same column which is difficult for anglophone students (see 5).

Types of adverbial clauses classified according to semantic criteria

I Time		
Time	*avant que, en attendant que, jusqu'à ce que,* QUAND, LORSQUE, *comme, pendant que, tandis que, chaque fois que, après que, aussitôt que, dès que*	*je viendrai dès que j'aurai fini mon travail*

II Goal, Cause, Consequence, Concession and Opposition		
Goal	*afin que,* POUR QUE, *de crainte que, a cette fin que, de peur que, de façon que, de sorte que* (all of these take the subjunctive)	*je fais les bagages ce soir pour que nous puissions partir tôt demain matin*
Cause	PARCE QUE, *puisque, vu que, attendu que, comme, du moment que, dès lors que, d'autant que*	*je viens parce que tu insistes/je viens puisque tu insistes*
Consequence	*de manière que, de sorte que, de façon que, si bien que, si . . . que* (all of these take the indicative, whereas the same conjunctions expressing the idea of goal take the subjunctive)	*j'ai agi de sorte qu'il ne s'est aperçu de rien*

Concession (+ opposition)	*alors que,* BIEN QUE, *encore que, au lieu que, même si, quoique, tandis que, quand bien même, sans que* (+ subjunctive)	*il a réussi bien qu'il ait peu travaillé*
Opposition	*quand, alors que, pendant que,* TANDIS QUE, *au lieu que, si bien que*	*je travaille pendant qu'il se repose*

III Condition

Condition	SI, *au cas où, à condition que, à moins que, à supposer que, en admettant que, pour peu que, pourvu que, si tant est que, selon que . . . ou (que) . . . (si* takes the indicative; all the others take the subjunctive except for *selon que*)	*si j'étais riche, j'achèterais un bateau*

IV Comparison

Manner	COMME, *ainsi que, de même que, tel que, à mesure que, pour autant que . . . comme si* (hypothetical comparison)	*il m'a reçu comme si j'avais été un de ses meilleurs amis*
Quantity/ Quality	MOINS . . . QUE, AUSSI . . . QUE, PLUS . . . QUE, *au point que, mieux que, plutôt que*	*il est aussi gai que son frère est triste*

V Addition and Exception

	outre, hors que, sans compter que, excepté que, SAUF QUE, *sauf si, hormis que*	*tout va bien, sauf qu'il fait mauvais temps*

2.2.3 *Other types of clause which may function as adverbials*

There are other subordinate clauses which may function as adverbials and which are not introduced by subordinating conjunctions. They are:

(i) Infinitival clauses:

c'est bête à pleurer (= c'est bête au point qu'on en pleurerait)

(ii) The gerund:

il travaille en sifflant (= il siffle quand il travaille)

(iii) Participial clauses:

Present participle: *ne sortant guère de chez lui, il ne pouvait pas savoir ce qui s'était passé (comme il ne sortait guère. . . .)*
Past participle: *le repas fini, ils allèrent s'installer au salon (= quand le repas fut fini, . . .)*

(iv) Relative clauses:

nous attendrons le temps qu'il faudra

2.3 Repetition of conjunctions in coordinated subordinate clauses

(i) If there are several *si* clauses in a sentence, it is normal to replace all but the first by *que*:

si tu viens demain et s'il fait beau, nous irons à la campagne = si tu viens demain et qu'il fasse beau, nous irons à la campagne

Note that *que* should be followed by the subjunctive in this case, but in the spoken language the latter is often 'forgotten'. In the written language, however, such 'forgetfulness' is frowned upon.

(ii) In fact *que* tends to replace most conjunctions when these are repeated:

comme il faisait beau et que j'avais le temps, je l'ai raccompagné
quand vous serez vieux et que vous ne travaillerez plus, vous pourrez profiter davantages des joies de la lecture
bien que sa fille ait beaucoup d'enfants et qu'elle soit très occupée, elle rend de nombreux services à ses voisins

In this case the mood used after *que* is the same as that which one would use with the conjunction it replaces.

2.4 Uses of 'que'

2.4.1 *Normal use of 'que'*

The normal use of *que* is to introduce a nominal clause (see 2.1) or, when it combines with prepositions, adverbs or participles to form compound subordinating conjunctions, to introduce adverbial clauses (see 2.2).

2.4.2 *Other uses of 'que'*

(i) The simple *que* may be used emphatically to express an idea of opposition:

il avait six ans, qu'il savait déjà lire (= il savait lire alors qu'il n'avait que six ans)
j'étais déjà loin, qu'il hésitait encore (= il hésitait encore alors que j'étais déjà loin)

In this case the clause introduced by *que* is semantically the main clause and the main clause is semantically the adverbial clause.

(ii) In some cases the relative *que* becomes a 'conjunctive' *que*:

après tant d'années que nous ne nous étions pas vus, le contact a été difficile à rétablir (= pendant lesquelles . . .)
chaque fois qu'il rit, il m'énerve (= quand . . .)

Que may be used instead of a complex subordinating conjunction (see 1.4):

enlève ton manteau que je voie ta robe (= pour que . . .)

(iv) *Que* may be used as an empty introducer, i.e. as an introducer devoid of meaning:

que si nous considérons l'administration du palais, nous observons sous Philippe ler une importante transformation (Funck-Brentano)

(Que si is a structure which imitates the Latin rhetorical *quod si.)*

In this case *que* is devoid of lexical meaning and could be dropped. (This use of *que* is similar to that of the preposition *de* used before an infinitive, as in *de trop boire peut faire mal).*

This use of *que* belongs to the written language, being both formal and literary.

(v) *Que* may be used in informal speech for emphasis without having to introduce a subordinate clause:

Un soir, tout le monde couché, on a grimpé sur les toits, et que je te miaule . . . de quoi réveiller tout le quartier (Bernanos, *Journal d'un curé de campagne).*

2.5   Indirect interrogative subordinate clauses

2.5.1   *Definition*

The indirect interrogative sentence is made up of a main clause, which introduces the interrogative element lexically, and a subordinate clause, which introduces the actual question. The subordinate clause is the object of the main clause; indirect interrogative clauses are, in this way, similar to nominal or completive clauses when the latter function as the direct object of a transitive verb. But they do differ, however, in that nominal clauses are introduced by *que* whereas the subordinate clause in the indirect interrogative sentence may be introduced either by an interrogative adverb (see 2.5.2 i), by an interrogative adjective (see 2.5.2 *ii*), or by an interrogative pronoun (see 2.5.2 *iii*). Sometimes there is the possibility of choice amongst these structures (see 2.5.2 *iv*). In other words, these subordinate clauses are not introduced by subordinating conjunctions as such, although some of these (such as *quand*, for example) may in other contexts function as conjunctions:

> *je ne sais pas quand il viendra* (interrogative adverb)
> *j'irai quand il fera beau* (subordinating conjunction)

2.5.2   *Items which may introduce indirect interrogative clauses*

(i)   These items may be words which function as interrogative adverbs in independent clauses: *si, quand, où, comment, combien*. In this case the main verb is lexically interrogative (*se demander*) or expresses uncertainty of knowledge (*ne pas savoir, ne pas voir comment*):

> *je me demande s'il viendra/quand il viendra/comment il viendra/où il ira/combien il devra payer*

(ii)   These items include the interrogative adjective:

> *je me demande quel prix il paiera*

(iii)   These items include the interrogative pronouns (see Ch. 19):

> *je me demande qui viendra/lequel viendra*

(The interrogative pronouns are identical to the corresponding relative pronouns from a morphological point of view but not from a morphosyntactic point of view, since the interrogative *qui* may only refer to persons, and the interrogative *que* only to inanimates).

(iv)   There may be a choice as to which of these constructions to use:

> *je me demande quand il viendra* (interrogative adverb)
> *je me demande à quel moment/à quelle heure il viendra* (interrogative adjective)

3   Syntactical considerations of mood and word-order

The problem of mood and word-order depends on whether the subordinate clause is nominal (see 3.1) or adverbial (see 3.2). Indirect interrogative clauses come under the same heading as nominal clauses.

3.1   Mood and word-order in nominal subordinate clauses

3.1.1   *Mood*

Modern French differs from the original Latin system in that, whereas Latin possessed a limited number of conjunctions which entailed the use of specific moods, these have been replaced in modern French by just one conjunction – *que* – which is very general, and the compound conjunctions which are very precise. The consequence is that *que* may be followed by differing moods depending on the context (see Chs. 4, 5 and 6).

Generally speaking the indicative is normally used after verbs expressing a statement of fact (*dire, raconter, affirmer*), of judgement (*penser, croire, supposer*) or of knowledge (*savoir, apprendre*). The subjunctive is used after verbs, nouns or adjectives expressing doubt (*douter, ne pas croire*), fear (*craindre, avoir peur*), or a desire or some kind of order (*vouloir, désirer, souhaiter, admettre, interdire, il faut*). In some cases a different meaning may be expressed by using one or other mood; in this case the use of mood is contrastive.

je lui ai dit qu'il est à l'heure (statement of fact)
je lui ai dit qu'il soit à l'heure (order)

The mood may also depend on whether the subordinate clause comes in first or second position:

il est certain qu'il l'a fait exprès
qu'il l'ait fait exprès, c'est certain

3.1.2 *Word-order and clause-order*

The word-order within the subordinate clause is the normal one of subject/verb/object/adverbial. Since the nominal subordinate clause stands for a nominal phrase, it occupies the same place as would a nominal phrase: at the beginning of the clause if it is the subject, after the verb if it is object or attribute:

je vous annonce que vous êtes reçu (object)
le problème est que je n'en sais rien (attribute)
elle est obsédée par la crainte qu'il ne lui arrive un malheur (complement of the noun)
qu'il soit sincère ne fait aucun doute (subject)

This last word-order is rather rare; the more usual one is to have a dummy subject *il* or *cela* at the beginning, in order to have the completive or nominal clause at the end:

cela ne fait aucun doute qu'il est sincère (*cela* + noun)
il est certain qu'il est sincère (*il* + adjective)

3.2 Mood and word-order in adverbial clauses

3.2.1 *Adverbial clauses and the problem of mood*

(For more details see Ch. 5.)
(i) In adverbial clauses expressing time, the subjunctive is used with *avant que* and *jusqu'à ce que*. It is used in the spoken language with *après que*, but such usage is considered incorrect by prescriptive grammarians. The indicative or conditional are used with the other subordinating conjunctions.
(ii) In clauses expressing a goal, the subjunctive is used with *pour que* and *afin que*, with *dans l'intention que*, and with any other compound conjunction expressing a goal.
(iii) In clauses expressing cause, the indicative or the conditional is used in most cases (e.g. *parce que, puisque*), but *non que* is followed by the subjunctive.
(iv) In clauses expressing concession or opposition, the subjunctive is used in most cases (e.g. *bien que, quoique*). *Tout que* may take either the subjunctive or the indicative (e.g. *tout grand qu'il est* or *tout grand qu'il soit*).

However, the indicative or conditional is used with *même si, alors que, tout* . . . *que*, and sometimes with *au lieu que*. The conditional is normally used with *quand bien même*; the indicative is rare but possible.

(v) In clauses expressing consequence, the subjunctive is used with *trop (assez)* . . . *pour que* and sometimes with *de manière (façon) que* and *au point que*.

The indicative or the conditional are used in all other cases.

(vi) In clauses expressing conditions, the indicative is used after *si, selon que* and *suivant que*. The use of the hypothetical *si* excludes the use of the conditional. (See Ch. 6, 4.2.1 for the nonhypothetical *si*, and Ch. 6, section 3 for moods used in *si* clauses and other clauses expressing the hypothetical.) The conditional is used after *au cas où*.

3.2.2   *Word-order and clause-order*

It is important to distinguish between logical order and grammatical order.

(i) In adverbial clauses of time, the adverbial clause may precede or follow the main clause. Compare:

quand la pièce a commencé à m'ennuyer, je suis parti (chronological order)
je suis parti quand la pièce a commencé à m'ennuyer ('normal' grammatical order, i.e. the main clause comes first)

In the subordinate clause itself, subject and verb may be inverted in the same way as in relative clauses (see Ch. 14, 4.2):

Je les lui promettais tant qu'a vécu son père (Racine)

(ii) In adverbial clauses expressing cause, grammatical order demands that the main clause precede the subordinate clause. But a cause normally precedes an effect in real life: it is therefore also possible to put the subordinate clause first. This is particularly common when the subordinate clause is part of a reasoned argument: *puisque* is often placed at the beginning of the sentence, and *comme* is always in first position when expressing a cause:

je l'ai acheté parce que j'en avais envie
puisque j'en avais envie, je l'ai acheté
comme j'en avais envie, je l'ai acheté

(iii) In adverbial clauses expressing consequence, both grammatical and logical order demand that the main clause appear first and the subordinate clause second:

nous allons procéder de la façon suivante, de manière (à ce) que tout le monde soit content

(iv) In adverbial clauses expressing a goal, both grammatical and logical order demand that the main clause appear first and the subordinate clause second:

je fais les bagages ce soir, pour que nous puissions partir tôt demain matin

The goal may however also be seen as an explanation for an action, in which case the subordinate clause may be placed first; but this is rare in contemporary French:

Afin qu'il fût plus frais et de meilleur débit
On lui lia les pieds, on vous le suspendit

(La Fontaine)

(v) In adverbial clauses expressing concession, both orders are possible:

je lui confierai ce travail, bien qu'il soit très jeune
bien qu'il soit très jeune, je lui confierai ce travail

In the first case the concession is a kind of afterthought. In the second case the emphasis is on the concessive element.

(vi) In clauses expressing opposition, in the case of complete opposition the order is main clause/subordinate clause:

il l'a fait sans qu'elle le sache

When the opposition is expressed by adverb + adjective + *que*, the normal order is subordinate clause/main clause:

tout bête qu'il est, il réussira

(vii) Conjunctions expressing a condition
It is normal for the clause expressing the condition to precede the clause describing the hypothetical action or state of affairs:

si j'étais riche (condition), *j'achèterais un bateau* (hypothetical action)

It is possible to invert this order, but such an inversion is rare and highly emphatic:

j'achèterais un bateau, si j'étais riche!

In this case the hypothesis has exclamative overtones.
(viii) In adverbial clauses expressing comparison in terms of manner, it is usual to follow the order main clause/subordinate clause:

il m'a reçu comme si j'avais été l'un de ses meilleurs amis

But the order may be inverted in poetry. In this example *comme* has the meaning of *de la même manière que:*

> *Comme de longs échos qui de loin se confondent*
> *Dans une ténébreuse et profonde unité,*
> *Vaste comme la nuit et comme la clarté*
> *Les parfums, les couleurs et les sons se répondent*
> (Baudelaire)

In the case of comparison in terms of quantity and quality, the order is main clause/subordinate clause:

il est plus grand que (ne l'est) son frère

(ix) In clauses expressing addition or exception, where there is progression in importance between the subordinate clause and the main clause, the adversative clause normally comes first:

Outre qu'il était riche, il descendait en ligne directe de Jean sans Terre (Aymé)

Where the subordinate clause limits the meaning of the main clause it usually follows the main clause:

il s'est bien conduit dans l'ensemble, sauf qu'il aurait dû demander de l'aide plus tôt

4 Stylistic considerations

There are two areas in which choice may be made. One may wish to choose amongst direct, indirect and semi-indirect speech (see 4.1). And one may wish to get rid of a particular subordinate conjunction: the same taboos operate for subordinate clauses introduced by subordinating conjunctions as for relative clauses (see Ch. 14, section 5). This is dealt with under 4.2.

4.1 Direct, indirect and semi-indirect (or free indirect) speech

English and French behave in much the same way.

4.1.1   *Direct and indirect speech*

elle me dit: «Venez me voir ce soir»
elle m'a dit que j'aille la voir or *d'aller la voir ce soir-là*

From the sentences above, one may see that the change from direct to indirect speech implies that:

(i)   the quote becomes a nominal subordinate clause;
(ii) the subject of the quote must be changed;
(iii) the tenses must be changed;
(iv) there may have to be lexical changes, such as *venir/aller* and *ce soir/ce soir-là*.

One of the defects of direct style is that constant quotes break up the syntax of a written text and make it less formal; but the defect of indirect speech is that it entails using many cases of *que* (see 4.2). It is also impossible in indirect speech to have a lively style, since the use of these *que* clauses precludes certain inversions, the use of imperatives, any form of interruption, and exclamations. In other words, direct speech gives drama to the text, whereas indirect speech is closer to straightforward reporting. It is because of these inconveniences that at the end of the fifteenth century and at the beginning of the sixteenth a new type of sentence appeared for reported speech called 'free indirect speech' (*le style indirect libre* or *semi-indirect*).

4.1.2   *Free indirect speech: characteristics*

(i)   Free indirect speech is half way between direct and indirect speech, since it includes neither the use of *que* nor the use of direct quotes:

Direct speech: *elle me dit: «Venez me voir ce soir et je vous préparerai un bon repas»*
Indirect speech: *elle m'a dit d'aller la voir ce soir-là et qu'elle me préparerait un bon repas*
Free indirect speech: *selon elle, je devais aller la voir ce soir-là et elle me préparerait un bon repas*

Coordinating an infinitival clause and a clause in a personal mood, as in the sentence quoted under 'indirect speech' above (*d'aller . . . et qu'elle . . .*), was the norm in seventeenth-century French. Such a construction is however now felt to be clumsy and heavy, and this is another reason for using free indirect speech instead.

In free indirect speech, the speaker manages to suggest that what follows is a 'kind' of quote. There is a change of person compared to direct speech, and usually a change of tense and of adverbs of time, as with indirect speech. Free indirect speech is however made up of independent clauses.

(ii) This kind of reported speech has a kind of 'unreal' quality about it. This is partly due to the changes made in the tenses: there is a backshift from the present tenses into the imperfect and conditional, i.e. into tenses with strong modal connotations. This air of unreality is also due to the fact that the listener/reader is not told directly that he is dealing with a kind of quote: he has to deduce this from the context.

This explains why this kind of construction is frequently used for internal monologues.

(iii) Two of the most famous users of free indirect speech are La Fontaine and Flaubert. In the following passage (quoted by Deloffre in *La Phrase française*), La Fontaine switches from direct speech to free indirect speech to direct speech. The passage from the one (the most solemn) to the other two (each less formal and more lively than the previous one) corresponds to the author warming to the subject and expressing his ideas (or those of his character) in more lively terms:

> *La dame au nez pointu répondit que la terre*
> *Était au premier occupant*   Indirect speech
>
> *'C'était un beau sujet de guerre*
> *Qu'un logis où lui-même il n'entrait qu'en rampant!*   Free indirect speech
>
> *Et quand ce serait un royaume,*
> *Je voudrais bien savoir, dit-elle, quelle loi*
> *En a, pour toujours, fait l'octroi*   Direct speech
> *A Jean, fils ou neveu de Pierre ou de Guillaume*
> *Plutôt qu'à Paul, plutôt qu'à moi.'*
> > (La Fontaine, *Le Chat, la belette et le petit lapin*)

Deloffre quotes another example, this time from Flaubert:

> *Frédéric balbutia, chercha ses mots et se lança enfin dans une longue période sur l'affinité des âmes. Une force existait qui peut, à travers les espaces, mettre en rapport deux personnes, les avertir de ce qu'elles éprouvent et les faire se rejoindre.*

In this case the first sentence expresses the fact that what follows is a kind of quotation. The sentence that follows is the quotation, but the tense used is the past tense instead of the present (the present used in the subordinate clauses expresses the non-temporal). This avoids subordinating the second clause to the first.

4.2   Avoidance of subordinate conjunctions

4.2.1   *Reasons for avoiding the use of subordinate conjunctions*

4.2.1.1   *Phonological reasons*
(i) A succession of subordinate conjunctions is considered unacceptable from a stylistic point of view:

> *Le professeur a dit à Paul qu'il allait le punir parce qu'il avait été trop impertinent alors qu'il faisait son cours.*

Such a sentence is stylistically unacceptable.
Legrand writes in his *Stylistique française, livre de l'élève* (135):

> *Incapables soit de flatter l'oreille, soit de parler à l'imagination elles se montrent, pour la couleur et l'harmonie du style, les dignes émules des pronoms relatifs. Reconnaissons-leur toutefois l'avantage de marquer fortement les rapports logiques des idées, mais hâtons-nous d'ajouter qu'on obtient le même résultat par d'autres procédés moins incommodes.*

Such an attitude may seem ridiculous, but it does illustrate the attitude which has prevailed in France, at least in schools, over the last century.

4.2.1.2   *Avoiding a choice between indicative and subjunctive*   The use of conjunctions may involve a difficult choice of mood:

> *il ne réfléchit pas que vous pouvez lui nuire*

but: *il ne croit pas que vous puissiez lui nuire*
> *il paraît qu'il vient souvent*

but: *il importe qu'il vienne souvent*

4.2.1.3   *Avoiding the use of the imperfect subjunctive*   Subordinate conjunctions may demand the use of the imperfect subjunctive which could sound ridiculous:

> *ce livre que vous n'avez pas voulu que je lusse, passe pour très intéressant*
> *la leçon que vous avez voulu que j'étudiasse est difficile*

These uses of the past subjunctive are no longer acceptable in contemporary French.

4.2.2   *Methods of avoiding the use of subordinating conjunctions*

4.2.2.1   *Methods nonspecific to a particular adverbial conjunction*   There are three general ways of avoiding subordinating conjunctions which are not specific to a particular conjunction.
(i) The subordinate clause may be replaced by a noun:

> *ce livre pourra vous divertir lorsque vous n'aurez rien à faire (= ce livre pourra vous*
> *divertir pendant vos loisirs)*

The construction using the noun is generally more abstract.
(ii) An infinitival clause may be used:

> *il arrive que le patron se mette en colère (= il arrive au patron de se mettre en colère)*

(iii) Juxtaposition may replace subordination:

> *dépêche-toi puisqu'on t'attend (= dépêche-toi, on t'attend)*

4.2.2.2   *Methods specific to the adverbial conjunction*   There are a number of ways of avoiding subordinating conjunctions which are specific to the kind of adverbial conjunction used.
(i) Time conjunctions such as *quand*, *lorsque* and *dès que* can be replaced by the preposition *lors* + noun:

> *j'irai lorsqu'ils seront arrivés (= j'irai lors de leur arrivée)*

(ii) Conjunctions indicating a cause may be replaced by *à, par, grâce à* + noun:

> *nous sommes ici parce que nos parents le veulent bien (= nous sommes ici grâce à*
> *nos parents)*

(iii) Concessive conjunctions may be replaced by prepositions such as *contre, malgré, en dépit de* + noun, or by *avoir beau* + infinitive:

> *bien que j'aie insisté, il n'a pas voulu rester = j'ai eu beau insister, il n'a pas voulu*
> *rester.*
> *il a décidé d'y aller bien que je sois contre = il a décidé d'y aller contre mon avis.*

(iv) *Si* and *pourvu que* may be replaced by *en cas de*, or by *à* + infinitive, or by a participle:

> *si jamais j'étais en retard, attendez-moi = en cas de retard, attendez-moi*
> *si l'on en juge par les résultats, la solution est bonne = à en juger par les résultats, la*
> *solution est bonne*
> *il ne reviendra finir les travaux qu'une fois qu'on l'aura payé = il ne reviendra finir*
> *les travaux qu'une fois payé*

But *si* itself does not obey the same stylistic rules as *que* in the sense that it is not considered to be an 'inelegant' way of subordinating one idea to another.

5 Some semantic problems for anglophones

Many conjunctions may appear under more than one heading: *comme*, for example, may appear under time and under cause. Others may appear to be synonymous, at least according to the often circuitous definitions given by dictionaries (for example *comme = parce que/puisque*). In the following list it is the semantic differences between the conjunctions which are highlighted.

5.1 Subordinating conjunctions of time[2]

5.1.1 *Posteriority*

(i) Posteriority is normally expressed by *après que* (+ indicative).
(ii) Immediate posteriority is expressed by *dès que, aussitôt que, sitôt que, sitôt après que* (in spoken French, the prescriptively unacceptable **tout de suite que* may be heard).
(iii) Posteriority with an inchoative aspect may be expressed by *une fois que, depuis que, maintenant que, à present que, du jour où, du plus loin que, d'aussi loin que*.
(iv) Posteriority with a terminative aspect may be expressed by *jusqu'à ce que, d'ici à ce que, d'ici que*.
(v) Posteriority with a terminative aspect and duration may be expressed by *en attendant que*.

5.1.2 *Simultaneity*

(i) Simultaneity is generally expressed by *quand* and *lorsque*, which indicate simultaneity or near simultaneity:

> *ne m'interromps pas quand/lorsque je parle*

Lorsque is more formal than *quand*.
(ii) To express the idea that one action is progressing when another takes place, *comme, pendant que, tandis que* and *alors que* are used:

> *il est arrivé comme je partais* (punctual aspect)
> *il lit pendant que je travaille* (durative aspect)
> *il lit tandis que je travaille* (durative aspect + idea of opposition)

5.1.3 *Repetition*

> *toutes les fois que* (simple repetition)
> *aussi longtemps que, tant que* (repetition + duration)
> *à mesure que* (progression)

5.1.4 *Anteriority*

(i) Anteriority is generally expressed by *avant que* + subjunctive.
(ii) Anteriority may also be associated with other aspects:

> *le temps que* (anteriority = duration + aspect of totality − used mainly in spoken French)
> *d'ici que* (anteriority = duration + terminative aspect − used mainly in spoken French)
> *jusqu'à ce que* (anteriority = duration + terminative aspect)

The difference between these terms is as follows:
Le temps que and *d'ici que* are subjective, hence their frequent use in the spoken language.

> *le temps qu'il arrive, j'aurai terminé* (i.e. 'according to my assessment of the situation')
> *d'ici qu'il arrive, j'aurai terminé* (i.e. 'he will take a certain time to arrive, which will give me plenty of time to finish what I am doing')

Jusqu'à ce que, on the other hand, has no particular subjective connotations. It simply introduces a clause indicating when the action in the first clause will end:

> *je travaillerai jusqu'à ce qu'il arrive*

Note that the subjective quality of *le temps que* and *d'ici que* is further emphasized by the tendency to place these clauses at the beginning of the sentence, thus giving them phonological preeminence. The same does not apply to clauses introduced by *jusqu'à ce que*. *Jusqu'à tant que* used to be used with the same meaning, but is now felt to be archaic.

5.1.5   *Time and infinitival clauses*

Anteriority and posteriority may be expressed by a preposition + infinitival clause if there is identity of subject. *Avant de* is used with a simple infinitive; *après, aussitôt après* and *sitôt après* are used with a compound infinitive.

> *j'ai fini mon travail avant de t'écrire (= avant que je ne t'écrive)*
> *j'ai fini mon travail après t'avoir écrit (= après que je t'ai écrit)*

5.2   Conjunctions expressing cause

5.2.1   *Expression of simple cause*

Some conjunctions express a reason, a purpose or an effect (e.g. 'he did it *because* he had to').
(i) The most usual conjunctions of cause are *parce que* and *puisque*. *Parce que* introduces an explanation – an objective statement of fact, with no emotive overtones:

> *je le fais parce que cela me fait plaisir*

Puisque introduces a justification, often with emotive or subjective connotations. The clause introduced by *puisque* often precedes the main clause:

> *je vais te le faire tout de suite puisque tu es là*
> *puisque tu es là, je vais te le faire tout de suite*

Parce que and *puisque* may be used without a verb:

> *il a, parce que trop fatigué, rénoncé à venir*

Note: In some areas the expression *à cause que* is used instead of *parce que*; in prescriptive terms this is considered to be incorrect. *A cause que* is in fact an archaic term which was used in Classical French: *Et tous disoient qu'ilz estoient traistres: à cause qu'il y avoit deux maisons* (Commines). *A cause que* was considered to be more emphatic and precise than *parce que*.
(ii) *Etant donné que* is similar to *puisque*, with the additional idea of rigorous argumentation.
(iii) *Comme* introduces some new idea in the course of an argument. In this case it appears at the beginning of the sentence.
There may sometimes be a choice between *comme* and *puisque*:

> *comme/puisqu'il est question de politique, saviez-vous qu'il a été battu aux élections?*

In this case the first subordinate clause corresponds semantically to the expression *à propos de*: *à propos de politique*. *Puisque* implies some form of justification.

5.2.2 *Cause and time*

Comme, *dès lors que* and *maintenant que* are used to express cause and time. The context determines whether it is the temporal or the causal aspect which is highlighted.

Note that *du moment que* no longer has a temporal value. It introduces a clause justifying the main one, e.g. *du moment qu'il est parti, je peux en faire autant*.

5.2.3 *Cause and effect*

(i) *Vu que* was originally used in legal texts, and is now frequently used in all registers:

il n'a pas pu l'acheter vu qu'il avait oublié son portefeuille

(ii) *Du fait que* introduces the cause objectively − the cause is seen as evidence. This term is in frequent use in contemporary French.

(iii) *Attendu que* and *surtout que* indicate the reason for a judgement. The latter is used in the spoken language only.

(iv) *Sous pretexte que* introduces a false cause, and *faute que* (now rarely used) indicates that the action in the main clause took place because another did not. *Faute que* is followed by the subjunctive:

le vin est peu abondant cette année, faute qu'il ait plu suffisamment

Faute de is however often preferred stylistically to *faute que*:

le vin est peu abondant cette année, faute de pluie

(v) *Non parce que* and *non que* introduce a negated cause:

je ne vais pas la voir non parce que je n'en ai pas envie mais parce que je n'en ai pas le temps
je ne vais pas la voir non que je n'en aie (subjunctive) *pas envie, mais parce que je n'en ai pas le temps*

Que may also introduce a negated cause when used on its own (in the spoken language only):

il est malade, qu'on ne le voit plus?

Que used on its own is followed by the indicative, since it links two clauses of which one follows the other. *Non parce que* is also followed by the indicative, since it refers to reality. But *non que* is normally followed by the subjunctive, since in this case a hypothesis is being rejected:

il a été réformé, non qu'il soit malade, mais seulement un peu dépressif

5.3 Goal (or aim)

Expression of goal or aim implies the use of the subjunctive. There are two main conjunctions used: *pour que* and *afin que*.

(i) *Pour que* is the most neutral of the two terms; it is used to introduce the inevitable consequence of an action:

amène-moi à la gare en voiture pour que je ne manque pas mon train

As such it is used more and more in contemporary French. It may also be used to indicate a cause; in this case the subordinate clause comes first:

pour qu'il soit si méchant, il faut bien qu'il y ait une raison

(ii) Afin que indicates not so much an inevitable consequence but rather a goal. It now belongs to the written language only; it may be intensified by *seule*: *à seule fin que* (one used to say instead *à celle fin que* and *à cette fin que*).

5.4   Consequence

A consequence is less strong than a goal: whereas a goal is an aim, a consequence may be a by-product of the aim.

5.4.1   *Consequence of an aim*

The conjunctions used to indicate the consequence of an aim are *de sorte que, de telle sorte que* and *en sorte que* (which is usually used with *faire*: *j'ai fait en sorte que tout le monde était là*).

5.4.2   *Consequence due to manner in which the action is carried out*

Conjunctions used to indicate this type of consequence are *de (telle) manière que* and *de (telle) façon que*. In the spoken language one also hears *de manière à ce que* and *de façon à ce que*. These two expressions are becoming more and more frequently used.

Note that there is a difference between *de manière que* and *de telle manière que*, and between *de sorte que* and *de telle sorte que*. Compare:

> *j'ai placé les tableaux de telle manière qu'ils sont éclairés de biais* (use of the indicative after *de telle manière que*)
> *j'ai placé les tableaux de manière qu'ils soient éclairés de biais* (use of the subjunctive after *de manière que*)

In other words, *de telle manière que* refers to reality (acting in a certain manner in this case), whereas *de manière que* refers to a goal, which may not be fulfilled (it is possible that the pictures are still not getting indirect lighting in a satisfactory manner).

5.4.3   *Consequence due to degree of intensity expressed by the verb, adverb or adjective in the main clause*

The following conjunctions are used to indicate this type of consequence. They are followed by the indicative except where the adverbs in *(iii)* are concerned.
(i) Au/à ce point que, à tel point que and *tant et si bien que* refer to the intensity expressed by the verb or adjective:

> *leur situation financière s'est aggravée au point qu'ils ont du hypothéquer leur maison*

(ii) The discontinuous constructions *si/tant/tellement . . . que* and the nowadays rare *tant et tant . . . que* refer to a consequence due to the intensity of the quality expressed by an adjective, an adverb of manner or a verb (*si* only modifies adjectives and adverbs, *tant* only modifies verbs, whereas *tellement* may modify all three grammatical categories, see Ch. 12, 2.1.3):

> *il avait tellement couru qu'il n'arrivait plus à retrouver son souffle*

Note: Si bien que may take on two different meanings, depending on whether *si bien* is a modifying adverb or part of the phrasal conjunction *si bien que*:

> *il a travaillé si bien/qu'il a obtenu le prix* ('he has worked so well that he got the prize': the stress is on *bien*)

il a travaillé/si bien qu'il a obtenu le prix ('he has worked and as a consequence he got the prize': the stress is on the last syllable of *travaillé*)

(iii) The adverbs of quantity *assez/suffisamment/trop . . . pour que* are followed by the subjunctive, since they indicate a judgement:

il n'y avait pas assez de livres pour que chaque étudiant puisse en avoir un

5.4.4 *Infinitival clauses*

If the subject of both clauses is identical, one may replace the subordinate clause by an infinitival clause introduced by *de manière à, de façon à, au point de* or *jusqu'à* (meaning 'to the point of'):

il a réorganisé son emploi du temps de manière à libérer son vendredi (instead of *de manière à ce qu'il libère . . .*)

5.5 Concession

A concessive conjunction introduces a state or condition in spite of which the truth or validity of the main clause holds good; most involve the use of the subjunctive:

'we went out, although it rained'
nous sommes sortis, bien qu'il ait plu

(i) The main concessive conjunctions are *quoique* and *bien que*. *Bien que* is sometimes used discontinuously in literary texts, but such a use is extremely rare: *Bien, je le répète, qu'avec l'esprit le plus juste . . .* (P. Morand).

The concessive conjunctions may also be used without a verb: *quoique fatigué, il terminera ce travail.*

(ii) *Malgré que* is often used in this sense, although this is considered unacceptable in prescriptive terms. There is however one use of *malgré que* which is considered correct (although it is now extremely rare): *malgré qu'il en ait,* in the sense of *quel que soit le mauvais gré qu'il en ait,* i.e. *quel que soit son déplaisir, son mécontentement.*

Encore que in this sense used to be purely literary but it is now coming to be used more and more in the spoken language.

(iii) *Alors que* and *tandis que* are also used to express concession, particularly *alors que*. These take the indicative.

5.6 Opposition

(i) Opposition may be expressed by conjunctions referring to time: *quand, alors que, lorsque, pendant que, tandis que.* Most of these conjunctions take the indicative, e.g.

je travaille tandis que/pendant que/alors que tu t'amuses

(ii) Opposition may be expressed by compound conjunctions such as *au lieu que* or *loin que* (but *loin que* usually takes the subjunctive):

Loin que le besoin ait dégradé l'homme, c'est éloignement de la société qui le dégrade (Voltaire)

All of these are fairly rarely used in contemporary French. But *au lieu de* + infinitive is in frequent use:

il préfère se reposer au lieu de travailler

(iii) *Si* may be used to express opposition; in this case it tends to be used with *c'est que*:

si je suis triste, c'est (parce) que son départ me prive d'un grand ami

(iv) Opposition may be expressed by adverb + adjective + *que*:

si maladroit qu'il soit, il réussira

In this case the subordinate clause highlights the opposition between the two clauses. (A subjunctive must be used in this case because one is dealing with a judgement.)

5.7   Addition and exception

5.7.1   *The expression of addition*

Addition may be expressed by *sans compter que* + indicative, *non sans que* + subjunctive, and *outre que*. If *outre que* is used, the subordinate clause comes in first position, because *outre que* expresses the addition of two elements, implying a progression in importance:

Outre qu'il était riche, il descendait en ligne directe de Jean sans Terre (Aymé)

5.7.2   *The expression of exception*

(i) Exception is expressed through the use of conjunctions such as *sauf que*, *excepté que* and *sinon que* + indicative, and *sans que* + subjunctive: *il l'a fait sans qu'elle le sache*.
   Note: Classical French used conjunctions such as *hors que*, *à la reserve que* and *excepté que*; *si ce n'est que* had the meaning of *à moins que* when followed by the subjunctive.
(ii) Exception is expressed through the use of conjunctions expressing a hypothesis: *sauf si*, *excepté si* + indicative, and *à moins que* + subjunctive:

j'irai cet après-midi à moins qu'il ne pleuve

5.8   Expression of a condition and other uses of 'si'

5.8.1   *Uses of 'si'*

(i) *Si* may express a hypothesis:

si j'étais riche, j'achèterais un bateau

(ii) It may express a possibility:

excusez-moi si je vous dérange

(iii) It may be used interrogatively. If *si* means 'if', it cannot be followed by the conditional:

je me demande s'il est là ('I wonder if he is in')

If *si* means 'whether', it may be followed by the conditional:

je me demande si je dois rentrer tout de suite ('if I ought to')/*si je, devrais rentrer tout de suite* ('if I should')

5.8.2   *Phrasal conjunctions based on 'si'*

(i) *Si tant est que* introduces an undesirable hypothesis, or one which is highly unlikely; its use is rare.
(ii) *Si ce n'est* and *si ce n'est que* introduce a restriction to what has been stated; they are frequently used with infinitival clauses:

vous ne risquez rien, si ce n'est de vous mouiller

The same applies to *sinon* and *sinon que*.

(iii) In the case of *comme si*, the hypothesis is there to express a comparison:

il courait comme s'il avait la police à ses trousses

5.8.3 *Other hypothetical conjunctions*

(See Ch. 6, section 3.)

(i) The hypothetical conjunctions *quand, quand (bien même, lors même que* and *alors même que* have emotive overtones (which *si* has not). They all belong to the written language and are literary, or at least formal, in style. They are normally followed by the conditional, being very similar in meaning to *même si*:

quand tu serais député, je ne te soutiendrais pas

(ii) Some of these conjunctions – *en cas que, au cas où, dans le cas où* and *pour le cas où* – indicate that the action referred to in the main clause will take place only if the event in the subordinate clause takes place. (Most of these conjunctions include the relative pronoun *où*, but they are felt to function nevertheless as conjunctive 'units'.)

Au cas où, dans le cas où and *pour le cas où* are followed by the conditional, whereas *en cas que* is followed by the subjunctive.

Pourvu que expresses the idea of the minimum required for an event to take place; it is followed by the subjunctive.

Pour peu que limits the possibility of the action in the main clause taking place; it is followed by the subjunctive.

A moins que presents the action in the subordinate clause as being exceptional (hence its use to express opposition.) It is followed by the subjunctive.

(iii) Some conjunctions do not introduce a hypothesis but a condition: *à condition que, à la condition que, ne . . . que si, seulement si*:

je ne viendrai que si la voiture est prête

A condition que and *à la condition que* are followed by the subjunctive, but *ne . . . que si* and *seulement si* are followed by the indicative.

(iv) Some conjunctions introduce an idea of supposition. *En admettant que* indicates an improbable supposition, *à supposer que* an unlikely supposition. These take the subjunctive.

Note: *Quelquefois que and *des fois que, meaning *au cas où*, are considered unacceptable in prescriptive terms, but *des fois que is heard particularly often. The latter is a sociolinguistic marker to the point that educated speakers sometimes use it for fun: *des fois que tu m'offrirais une petite cigarette, je ne dirais pas non* (heard in university circles). In literary language up until the end of the nineteenth century, the expression *moyennant que* was used with the meaning of *à condition que*.

Notes

1 Neither of the terms 'nominal' or 'completive' is without problems. 'Nominal clauses' may be confused with 'nominal sentences', i.e. verbless sentences. On the other hand, the term 'completive clause' has been said to be misleading, since it makes one think of subordinate clauses functioning as the object of the verb, whereas in fact they may also function as subject or as attribute; in these last two cases the term 'completive' has been said to be a misnomer. It can be argued, however, that the use of the term in its semantic sense rather than its functional sense

is perfectly acceptable: a completive clause is one which is not necessarily the complement of the verb, but one which is essential to the semantic interpretation of the main clause. Thus, in the examples shown below, the subordinate clause fulfils each time a different function, but is essential to the meaning of the sentence:

j'aime que l'on obéisse (the subordinate clause is the object of *aime*)
il est évident qu'elle rentrera tard (the subordinate clause is the 'real' subject of *est évident, il* being an impersonal pronoun)
la vérité est qu'il devient tous les jours plus pénible à supporter (the subordinate clause is the attribute of *il*)

2 For the concept, of aspect referred to throughout this section see the introduction to Part II.

Chapter 16

Coordination and coordinators

0 Problems involved in defining coordination and coordinators

0.1 Defining coordination and coordinators

(i) Two items are said to be coordinated if they fulfil the same function within the same syntactic unit. They normally follow one another, with a linking word – a coordinator – making explicit the logical link existing between them, although sometimes the coordinator may be omitted (see *iii*) The coordinated items are sometimes called the 'conjoins'.

(ii) Coordination may take place at all syntactical levels: at the phrase level:

les livres et les cahiers sont sur la table

(*les livres* and *les cahiers* are both subjects of *sont*); at the clause level between subordinated clauses:

je sais qu'à l'origine il était en faveur du projet mais que, depuis, il a changé d'avis

(in this case both subordinate clauses are the object of *sais*); at the clause level between independent clauses:

je pense, donc je suis

(in this case neither clause is dependent on the other); and at the level of the sentence:

Il pleut. Donc je n'y vais pas.

(intersentential coordination is very similar to the coordination of independent clauses).

(iii) Coordination is said to be 'syndetic' if specific coordinating words are present and 'asyndetic' if no specific coordinator is present but one could be supplied. This is also called coordination by juxtaposition (or parataxis).

je suis venu, j'ai vu, j'ai vaincu (asyndetic)
les crayons, cahiers et livres étaient tous sur la table (syndetic)

(iv) For a word or phrase to function as a coordinator, it must be placed between the items being coordinated. There are several types of words which may fulfil this function:

(a) Coordinating conjunctions. These form a closed set, *mais, ou, et, or, ni, car*, to which many grammarians add *donc*. Others maintain that, as *donc* can appear within the second element to be coordinated, it is an adverb.

(b) Certain adverbs and adverbial phrases such as *aussi*.

(c) Certain prepositional phrases such as *par exemple, en effet*.

(d) Certain clauses such as *c'est pourquoi*.

(v) When certain adverbs appear within the second element instead of between the two elements to be coordinated, they function as adverbs and their meaning may be quite different in the two cases:

(1) *Le réveil n'a pas sonné. Aussi a-t-il été en retard.*
(2) *Le réveil n'a pas sonné. Il a été en retard lui aussi.*

In (1) *aussi* means 'therefore', whereas in (2) it means 'also'.
(vi) Whereas coordinating conjunctions and some coordinating set phrases must be placed between the coordinated items, all other types of coordinators (adverbs and adverbial and prepositional phrases) are mobile: they may either function as a syntactic coordinator, or they may figure within the second element, in which case they help to ensure the flow of language from a semantic point of view, since most of these are anaphoric, lexically speaking; (e.g. *ensuite* implies *avant*, *en effet* introduces an explanation of what precedes). They do not coordinate but act as cohesive ties. It is in this capacity that they are called 'transitional links': see 2.3.

0.2   Coordination v. syntactic subordination

(i) Coordinators link items which have the same function in relation to the same word, whereas subordinators link items which have a different function:

(1) *j'ai connu Marie à l'université mais elle n'était pas encore mariée*
(2) *j'ai connu Marie à l'université avant qu'elle ne se marie*

In (1) the two clauses are coordinated since neither is dependent on the other; in (2) the second clause is dependent on the first: it is subordinated to it. (It is the adverbial complement of time of the verb in the main clause.)
(ii) There are cases in which the construction appears to be coordinated from a syntactic point of view, but subordinated from a semantic point of view:

cherchez et vous trouverez

This sentence is made up of two syntactically coordinated clauses, but it is the equivalent of a conditional construction:

si vous cherchez, vous trouverez

A slightly different problem occurs with the following sentence:

Comme une colonne dont la masse solide paraît le plus ferme appui d'un temple ruineux, lorsque ce grand édifice fond sur elle sans l'abattre, ainsi la reine se montre le ferme soutien de l'Etat. (Bossuet, *Oraison funèbre d'Henriette d'Angleterre*)

In this case neither clause is syntactically dependent on the other, but the first clause is clearly semantically dependent on the second. (This type of sentence is rare, and belongs to the style of oratory only. It is in fact a 'Latinism', since the *comme. . . ainsi* construction is the direct equivalent of the *ut . . . sic* construction.)

0.3   Coordination v. apposition and asides

The difference between coordination and apposition is that whereas coordination links items which are different, in apposition the second item − the 'apposed' item − has the same coreferent as the first item. This means that, where verbal agreement is concerned, in coordination agreement is made with both items, whereas in apposition agreement is made with the first:

Pierre et Paul sont venus (coordination)
Pierre, mon frère, est venu (apposition)

(ii) As may be seen from the previous example, there is an element of subordination in appositive constructions, the apposition helping to define some other item in the sentence. (In this case the apposition specifies which *Pierre* is being referred to.)

(iii) Asides are half way between appositive and coordinated constructions: they are semantically subordinate, but in terms of agreement they behave as do coordinated constructions:

> *ce livre, et ceux qui lui ressemblent, sont très à la mode*
> * *ce livre, et ceux qui lui ressemblent, est très à la mode*

thus the second of these two sentences is unacceptable.

Asides are normally indicated either by commas, dashes, parentheses or brackets (appositive constructions normally use pairs of commas):

> *Les grammaires scolaires, et même des grammaires plus approfondies, considèrent parfois qu'il n'existe de proposition que s'il existe «un verbe à un mode personnel».* (Deloffre, *La Phrase française*, 21)
> *il m'a fallu beaucoup de patience – une patience incroyable même – pour faire aboutir ces démarches.*

1 Morphological considerations

1.1 The traditional method of defining coordinators

(i) There appear to be two ways of defining coordinating conjunctions, neither of which is totally satisfactory.

The narrow list of coordinators classifies *et, ou, ni, mais, car, or* as coordinating conjunctions mainly because they can only appear in one position in the coordinated construction – namely between the elements which are linked – and because they cannot combine with one another. (Since *donc* fails on both criteria, some grammarians have relegated it to the class of adverbs; see Wagner and Pinchon *Grammaire du français classique et moderne*, 431).

There is also a 'broad' list of coordinators which classifies as a coordinating conjunction any item which may 'coordinate', independently of any idea of word class. Thus Grevisse in *Le Bon usage* lists more than 30 coordinators; so does *Le Grand Larousse*, but they are not always the same ones. This means that within this broad 'functional' definition there are discrepancies. This is because the 'broad' definition allows the same words to belong to several classes; thus adverbs such as *ainsi* and *aussi* are also classified as conjunctions; similarly set phrases such as *en effet, c'est pourquoi* and *c'est-à-dire*, all of which express addition plus extra lexical content. These 'conjunctions' may in fact combine with one another when their lexical meanings are compatible.

(ii) It would seem preferable to keep the general term 'coordinator' for all words or phrases which may function as linking words placed between items fulfilling the same function within a syntactical context. Those which have no other functions in the language are 'coordinating conjunctions'; those which may function as coordinators are 'coordinating adverbs' or 'coordinating phrases'; those which function within the second element – rather than being placed between the two and belonging to neither – do not function as coordinators; they may however function as a cohesive tie because of their lexical implications: these are 'transitional adverbs'.

1.2 The main coordinators (those having no other function)

The disappearance of all but three of the conjunctions of Latin origin (namely *et, ou* and *ni*) led to the creation of alternative items, most of which came from adverbs. Most of these function both at the levels of the clause and the sentence.

1.2.1   *The French coordinating conjunctions: 'et', 'ou', 'ni', 'mais', 'car', 'or'*

Et comes from the Latin *et*, *ou* from the Latin *aut*. The development of *ni* was more complex: the Latin *nec* gave *ne* in Old French, and then *ne* combined with the *-i-* of the stressed forms of the demonstrative pronoun *iceluy*: *ne + iceluy* became *n'iceluy* which became *ni celui*. The other French coordinating conjunctions came from other parts of speech in Latin: *mais* comes from *magis*, *or* from *hac hora* (*à cette heure*), whilst *car* comes from a relative construction *qua re*. *Soit . . . soit* originally comes from the subjunctive form of the verb *être*, but it functions in exactly the same way as *ou . . . ou*.

1.2.2   *The other coordinators (those which may have other functions)*

Unlike the coordinating conjunctions, these are not part of a closed set. The following list is therefore not exhaustive; the classification given is an *ad hoc* semantic one, since they cannot be classified in a strict morphological fashion.

(a) Addition (either simultaneity or succession): *puis, ensuite, alors, bien plus, comme, ainsi que, aussi bien que, de même que, non moins que, avec.*

(b) Alternative: *soit . . . soit, tantôt . . . tantôt, ou bien, au contraire.*

(c) Opposition: *au contraire, mais au contraire, au demeurant, cependant, toutefois, néanmoins, pourtant, d'ailleurs, aussi bien, au moins, du moins, au reste, du reste, en revanche, par contre, sinon, encore, seulement.*

(d) Cause: *en effet, effectivement.*

(e) Consequence: *donc, aussi, partant, alors, ainsi, enfin, par conséquent, en conséquence, conséquemment, par suite, dans ces conditions.*

(f) Explanation: *savoir, à savoir, c'est-à-dire, soit.*

1.2.3   *Agreement*

All coordinators are invariable.

2   Syntactic considerations

Coordinators may function within the sentence (see 2.1), between sentences (see 2.2), or as transitional links (see 2.3). The case of coordinated independent clauses is examined under the same heading as coordinated sentences.

2.1   Coordination within the sentence (excluding coordinated independent clauses)

2.1.1   *Coordinators functioning at this level*

(i) Coordination may involve nouns, adjectives, verbs and adverbs. Coordinators functioning within the sentence include *et, ainsi que* and *comme* (when meaning *et*), *mais, ou, ni, soit . . . soit*, and all the adverbs of time indicating a succession of events in time since these are similar to *et* + time (e.g. *puis, ensuite*)

> *je veux des pommes et des poires*
> *je veux ou des pommes ou des poires*
> *je ne veux pas des pommes, mais des poires*
> *je veux soit des pommes soit des poires*
> *je ne veux pas de pommes ni de poires*
> *je ne veux ni des pommes ni des poires*
> *je veux des pommes, puis des poires*
> *je veux des pommes, des poires, des pêches et du raisin*

(ii) Coordination may involve subordinate clauses:

je veux qu'il vienne et qu'il parte ensuite.
je veux ou qu'il vienne ou qu'il parte, mais qu'il se décide
je veux soit qu'il reste soit qu'il parte, mais qu'il se décide

2.1.2 *Agreement*

There has been a considerable slackening of the 'rules' of agreement in recent years. The *Arrêté* of 28 December 1976 (see Appendix) proclaims the following points in this respect:

(i) L'usage (i.e. that prescribed by the *Académie Française* and the *Ministère de l'Education Nationale*) used to require that where a verb has several juxtaposed subjects which are near synonyms and which are in the 3rd person, the verb should be in the singular:

la joie, l'allégresse s'empara de tous les spectateurs

A plural agreement is now tolerated:

la joie, l'allégresse s'emparèrent de tous les spectateurs

But the plural is obligatory if a coordinator is used:

la joie et l'allégresse s'emparèrent de tous les spectateurs

(ii) Where there are several subjects which are coordinated by *ni . . . ni* or *ou . . . ou*, both the singular and plural agreement are acceptable:

ni l'heure ni la saison ne conviennent pour cette excursion
ni l'heure ni la saison ne convient pour cette excursion

(iii) L'un et l'autre used either as pronouns or as adjectives will be considered as being singular or plural depending on the intended meaning:

l'un et l'autre document m'a paru intéressant ('equally interesting')
l'un et l'autre documents m'ont paru intéressants ('both are interesting')

But in:

l'un et l'autre se taisaient

the plural agreement is obligatory since *l'un et l'autre* are both refraining from speech.
Note: This has not always been so. La Fontaine wrote *L'un et l'autre approcha* (*Fables* VII, 16) instead of *approchèrent*. This is no longer possible in modern French.
(iv) L'un ou l'autre and *ni l'un ni l'autre* are supposed to take the singular:

de ces deux idées, ni l'une ni l'autre ne m'inquiète

The plural, however, is now tolerated in both cases, but the use of the plural is accompanied by a shift in meaning:

de ces deux idées, ni l'une ni l'autre ne m'inquiètent

The plural corresponds to both ideas taken together, whereas the singular corresponds to both ideas taken separately.

2.1.3 *Repetition of coordinators*

2.1.3.1 *'Et'* *Et* is not normally repeated between the items of an enumeration, but is simply used between the last two items, the others being juxtaposed:

je veux des pommes, des poires, des pêches et du raisin

But *et* may be repeated for emphasis:

je veux et des pommes, et des poires, et des pêches et du raisin

Note: In Old French *et* was normally repeated before each item of the enumeration; repetition of *et* in Old French was therefore not emphatic.

2.1.3.2 'Ni'

(i) *Ni* is the negative version of *et*, and can in some cases be replaced by *et*, namely when it is the action expressed by the verb which is being negated:

je ne veux pas le dire à Pierre et Jean
je ne veux le dire ni à Pierre ni à Jean

Ni in this sentence fulfils the role of *pas*. But the meaning of these two sentences is not identical: in the first *Pierre* and *Jean* are seen as forming a set or a unit, whereas in the second they are seen as separate entities since the negative element is repeated for each name.

Ni may also combine with *pas*, but in this case the construction is disjunctive:

je ne veux pas le dire, ni à Pierre ni à Jean

and the comma is obligatory. In this case both the process and the complements are negated, whereas in:

je ne veux le dire ni à Pierre ni à Jean

only the complements are negated.

(ii) *Ni* is normally repeated before each of the terms negated, but it is sometimes omitted in literary texts, particularly in Classical French. If the coordinated construction includes the intensifier *si*, the first *ni* is omitted:

jamais il n'a fait si froid ni si humide

If the coordinated construction is introduced by the preposition *sans* the first *ni* is left out:

il agit sans rime ni raison

(iii) The differences between the uses made of *ni* today and in Classical French are as follows:

(a) *Ni* was not necessarily repeated in front of each of the terms negated:

Le soleil ni la mort ne se peuvent regarder fixement (La Rochefoucauld)

instead of *Ni le soleil ni la mort. . . .*

(b) In Classical French *ni . . . ni* could be used with the full negation *ne . . . pas* or *ne . . . point*:

> *Ni les éclairs ni le tonnerre*
> *N'obéissent point à vos yeux*

(Malherbe, cited in Wagner and Pinchon, *Grammaire du français classique et moderne*)

(c) Instead of *ni . . . ni* it was possible in Classical French to use *ni . . . et*:

> *De mes emportements elle n'est point complice,*
> *Ni de mon amour même et de mon injustice*
> (Racine, cited in Wagner and Pinchon)

(d) *Ni* could be used in constructions which are implicitly negative:

Patience et longueur de temps font plus que force ni que rage
(La Fontaine, cited in Wagner and Pinchon)

Note: Before the seventeenth century it was possible to use *ne* (then *ni*) as a coordinator whenever there was an idea of doubt or questioning:

> *Ah, dis-moi où, n'en quel pays*
> *Est Flora la belle Romaine . . .*
> (Villon, *Ballade des Dames du temps jadis*)

which means, *Ah, dis-moi où, et en quel pays. . . .*

2.1.3.3 *'Ou'* *Ou* needs to be used only once in order to express an alternative:

tu rentres ou tu sors?

It may be repeated for emphasis:

ou tu rentres ou tu sors!

Ou may be emphasized by the adverb *bien*:

ou bien tu rentres ou bien tu sors!

The article determining the second item is dropped when the latter is explanatory of the first:

un bic ou stylo à bille

2.1.3.4 *'Soit . . . soit'*
(i) Soit . . . soit marks a stronger opposition than *ou . . . ou*, and *soit* has to be repeated before each alternative:

Soit tu rentres, soit tu sors!

(ii) In Classical French *soit . . . ou* could also be found:

Soit raison ou caprice, j'ai toujours la croyance (Molière)

2.2 Coordinators functioning between sentences or independent clauses

2.2.1 *General considerations*

Coordination at this level differs from coordination within the sentence (excluding sentences made up of independent clauses) in that, within the clauses, the coordinated phrases or the coordinated subordinate clauses have the same function in relation to the specific word, whereas, at this level, the coordinated clauses and sentences do not have a function in relation to a word but only in relation to the whole 'text' ('text' meaning a stretch of language forming a cohesive whole). The link between the coordinated clauses or sentences is therefore much weaker than within the sentence. A consequence of this is that far more 'coordinators' may function at this level than within the sentence.

2.2.2 *Similarity of coordination between clauses and coordination between sentences*

Coordination within the sentence between independent clauses and coordination between sentences is very similar. Compare:

je pense, donc je suis
je pense; donc je suis
Je pense. Donc je suis.

Whether there is a break in the form of a comma, a semicolon or a full stop is not so much a matter of grammar as of style: thus the third example, being the least expected version, is the most 'dramatic', given that the sentences are so short. But when the coordinated clauses are long and complex, the pauses represented by semicolons and full stops will make for clarity and not for emphasis.

2.2.3   *Coordinators linking sentences and independent clauses*

(i) This category includes all those coordinators which can function within the sentence:

> *Je cherche du regard un bouton électrique, un commutateur, ou quelque chose d'autre pour donner de la lumière. Mais je ne vois rien de ce genre.* (Robbe-Grillet, *Djinn*)

(ii) There are two conjunctions which can function at this level only − *car* and *or*:

> *Je me mis tout de suite à la tâche. Car il allait bien falloir que je m'habitue à ce nouvel état des choses. Je n'aime pas m'occuper d'une affaire dont il s'est avéré qu'elle est l'œuvre d'un fou. Or ce ne peut être qu'un fou qui a commis ces deux crimes.* (San Antonio, *Votez Bérurier*)

(iii) A great many adverbs may function as coordinators, either between sentences within the same paragraph (see example 1), or between paragraphs (see example 2 below).

> (1) *Cette pauvre Gladys vivait tellement sur les nerfs qu'elle dramatisait tout. Toutefois, par mesure de précaution, le journaliste marcha au milieu de la rue, l'oreille aux aguets. . . . . . (Exbrayat, Les Dames du Creusot)*
> (2) *Ensuite, Marie a voulu savoir comment vivaient les gens à Moscou, puisqu'elle venait de m'attribuer la nationalité russe.* (Robbe-Grillet, *Djinn* − this sentence starts a new paragraph)

(iv) A number of set phrases may also function as coordinators between sentences, *c'est pourquoi* being the most frequently used:

> *Je ne vous ai pas vu. C'est pourquoi je ne suis pas resté.*

(*C'est pourquoi* could be replaced by the coordinating adverb *donc*.)

2.3   Transitional links between sentences and independent clauses

2.3.1   *Transitional links v. coordinations*

(i) The type of link expressed by a coordinator is a strong link of the 'additive' type. The link set up by transitional links is one of cohesion via anaphora, since the use of these adverbs, adverbials and set phrases implies lexically the existence of a previous clause or sentence. The transitional links do not therefore constitute syntactical ties but lexical ties, the latter being felt to be weaker than the former.

(ii) The difference between the two is in terms of the positions they may occupy: coordinators used as such come between the items coordinated, whereas the transitional links appear within the second item. (One of the tendencies of non-French-speaking students is to place all transitional links at the beginning of the clause, thus making unacceptable coordinators of them.)

(iii) In some cases the same word may function in either way, this change of function being sometimes accompanied by a change of meaning (see 2.3.2).

(iv) The favoured place for transitional links is either after the verb or between the auxiliary and the verb. Compare:

> *il parut, enfin, émerger de son état de torpeur*
> *Enfin, il parut émerger de son état de torpeur*

In the second case *enfin* functions as a coordinator, i.e. as a strong link: *enfin* means *finalement*, and the element of time is important in the description of the development of the action. In the first case no *et* is implied, and the importance of the time factor is heavily stressed.

The following two examples can be similarly contrasted:

Il parut se ressaisir. Il venait, en effet, de voir son frère passer.
Il parut se ressaisir. En effet il venait de voir son frère passer.

In the second sentence the position of *en effet* underlines the fact that the relation of cause and effect is being emphasized, whereas in the first sentence the causal element is no longer emphasized. In the second *en effet* could be replaced by *et c'est parce qu'*; this is not the case of the first sentence. This illustrates the different functions of the adverb in each case.

2.3.2   *Variation in meaning of certain linking adverbs according to context*

2.3.2.1   *'Donc'*

(i) Used as a coordinator, *donc* introduces the conclusion to an argument:

je lui ai promis de le faire, donc je dois m'exécuter

(ii) Used as an adverb, *donc* may provide emphasis:

dites-nous donc comment cela s'est passé ('do tell us what happened!')

(iii) In the spoken language *donc* may refer back to a previous point in the conversation, e.g. *donc je disais* or *je disais donc*, the latter being more probable.

2.3.2.2   *'Aussi'*

(i) *Aussi* may function in association with *que* to indicate equality:

c'est un homme aussi bon qu'intelligent

meaning *c'est un homme dont la bonté égale l'intelligence.*
(ii) It may indicate equality in a non-comparative construction:

il est intelligent lui aussi

(iii) It may function as a coordinator:

il est travailleur, aussi a-t-il réussi ('therefore, that is why')

When used as a conjunction it must be followed by the inversion of verb and subject:

Jean est travailleur, aussi ses parents l'ont-ils récompensé
Jean est travailleur, aussi a-t-il été récompensé

Note: Aussi + negative used to be used in place of *non plus* before the seventeenth century:

non, je ne le comprends pas ni mon fils aussi

2.3.2.3   *'Ainsi'*

(i) *Ainsi* may function as an adverb:

faites ainsi (= *de cette manière:* 'do it this way')

(ii) It may function as a coordinator:

venez à huit heures; ainsi nous pourrons bavarder (= *et comme cela*)

2.3.2.4   *'Mais'*   *Mais* is nearly always used as a coordinator, but there are still traces of its adverbial uses in expressions such as:

il n'en peut mais (*il n'y peut rien*) (archaic)
ah mais, ça suffit (spoken language)

2.3.2.5 *'Et'*   *Et* is the coordinator *par excellence*; but it may function as an adverb to emphasize a point if there is nothing to coordinate:

et tu crois t'en tirer comme ça? ('so you think you can get away with it so easily?')

2.3.2.6 *'Pourtant', 'pourquoi'* and *'par quoi'*   All three were used to introduce a conclusive element (*par* and *pour* were relatively interchangeable in Old French). This is no longer the case. (See Haase, *La syntaxe de XVIIe siècle*, 390.)

2.3.2.7 *'Alors'*   *Alors* may take on a number of meanings according to the context:

alors, je lui ai dit (= *à ce moment là, je lui ai dit*)
alors, je lui ai dit (= *je lui ai dit par conséquent*)

et alors ('so what?')
alors tu viens? ('so', 'well then')

Alors used with the meaning of *par conséquent* is typical of the spoken language or a fairly informal and lighthearted written style:

Le vin est bon à Beaune. Alors, on en boit plus que de raison et une ivresse légère donne toutes les audaces. . . . (Exbrayat, *Les Dames du Creusot*)

2.3.2.8 *'En effet'* and *'en fait'*   Anglophone students tend to confuse *en effet* with *en fait*. *En effet* usually introduces something which follows quite naturally from what precedes; *en fait* normally introduces an idea of opposition or contrast between what is and what appears to be.

En fait usually corresponds to 'in fact' or 'as a matter of fact'. *En effet*, on the other hand, may be translated in a number of ways. The Robert-Collins French-English Dictionary gives the following examples:

cette voiture me plaît beaucoup, en effet elle est rapide et confortable (in this case *en effet* may be translated as 'because')
cela me plaît beaucoup en effet (may be translated as 'yes, I like it very much' or 'indeed I like it very much')
Etiez-vous absent mardi dernier? En effet j'avais la grippe (the translation of *en effet* may be 'yes' or 'that's right': 'that's right, I had flu')
c'est en effet plus rapide ('it's actually (or in fact) faster')

There are thus many cases in which *en effet* may not be translated as 'in fact'.

3   Use of the comma in coordinated constructions

(See also Ch. 20.)
The comma separates items in lists, coordinated clauses, and initial adverbial clauses and phrases. The same general usage exists in both English and French, but with some differences of application.

(i) Whereas in English a comma cannot separate subject from verb, it sometimes can in French: the comma may or may not be used where juxtaposition alone is used:

L'Inde, la Perse, l'Asie Mineure, L'Afrique (,) sont représentées par des meubles, des stores, des tentures. . . . (Bazin, cited by Grevisse, *Le Bon usage*)

(ii) Whereas it is possible in English to have a comma before the 'and' ending an enumeration, the same is not true for French where none of the items is to be given particular emphasis:

'the farmer owned sheep, cattle, pigs, and poultry'
il possédait des moutons, du bétail, des cochons et de la volaille

(iii) Although it is not usual to have a comma before *et*, *ou* or *ni*, this may occur if each item in the enumeration is preceded by one of these conjunctions for emphasis:

prends et ton manteau de pluie, et tes bottes en caoutchouc

The use of the comma is also possible where more than two items are being coordinated:

un bon financier, dit La Bruyère, ne pleure ni ses amis, ni sa femme, ni ses enfants (Grevisse, *Le Bon usage*)

(iv) A comma may also be used when the coordinated clauses do not have the same subject, or when they express contrasting ideas (as is also the case in English):

l'ennemi est aux portes, et vous délibérez! (Grevisse, *Le Bon usage*)

Et must be preceded by a comma where it is linking discontinuous elements:

je suis allée en ville, ce qui ne m'arrangeait pas, et je suis allée voir mon avocat

(v) When coordinated constructions are discontinuous, they are usually so because of the insertion of an appositive construction, as is the case in the previous example. Appositive constructions in both languages are 'bracketed' by commas, dashes or parentheses. These are used to indicate that a construction is in apposition; if the writer uses commas, the appositive element is still felt to be part of the main text; with dashes, the appositive construction becomes more an 'aside'; parentheses indicate merely a detail inserted. French uses dashes rather less readily than English; also, both parenthetical constructions and constructions between dashes tend to appear towards the end of the sentence rather than in the middle, in order to be less disruptive.

4   Stylistic considerations

(i) Some coordinators express such fine nuances of thought that they are rarely used in spontaneous language, being typical of literary or formal French. *Or* and *car* are typical examples.
   Car indicates that the element introduced will be explanatory:

j'ai hésité à lui demander ce service, car je sais qu'il est actuellement surchargé de travail.

This would be 'careful' spoken French; in less careful French the use of *parce que* is more probable − or even the use of nothing (parataxis).
   Car may be emphasized by the adverb *en effet*: *car en effet je sais.* . . . It is useful in that it does not automatically introduce an explanation of the *parce que* or the *puisque* type; *car* combines the meanings of *parce que* + *puisque*.
   Note: In the days of the *Précieuses ridicules* a great campaign was launched against *car*; but Voiture defended it and won Vaugelas's praise.
   Or is also fairly subtle in its meaning. It introduces a new element in a sequence of events which will have further consequences; as such it is typical of 'syllogisms', and introduces the second element in such an argument:

tout homme est mortel, or Socrate est un homme, donc Socrate est mortel

Or used to be combined with *donc* (this construction is now archaic):

or donc nous étions à nous reposer quand un grand bruit retentit

In this example the original meaning of *or, ores (heure)*, is present, although combined with its present meaning (i.e. that of introducing a new element in an argument).

Or and *car* are typical tools of rhetorical speech.

(ii) Other coordinators have become archaic: *conséquemment* for example. Archaic coordinators and transitional links tend to have literary overtones.

(iii) Still other coordinators have become register bound. *Nonobstant* is typical of legal and administrative language; in any other register it is used as a caricature of *le langage gendarme*.

5 Translation problems

These translation problems belong to stylistics rather than to grammar, in the sense that a direct translation of coordinators from English into French and vice versa is usually grammatically possible, although not always desirable.

(i) In the following example 'and' is translated by *ainsi que*:

> 'a dilute solution of up to five per cent carbolic acid was used to clean the wound *and* to disinfect the hands and the instruments of the surgeon and his helpers'
> *une solution de moins de 5% d'acide carbolique servait à désinfecter les plaies* ainsi que *les mains et les instruments du chirurgien et de ses aides*

If *et* were used instead of *ainsi que*, this would imply that the wounds were those of the surgeon and his helpers: *et* may only be used to add together items which 'go together'.

(ii) In translations from French into English, English sentences and clauses are often linked by 'and', where in French they are simply juxtaposed:

> *Pradel représente la vindicte publique. C'est l'accusateur officiel, il n'a rien d'humain.* (Charrière, *Papillon*)

becomes in P.O'Brian's translation:

> 'Pradel stood for the vindication of society. He was the official prosecutor *and* there was nothing human about him.'

(iii) There is a verbal construction in English in which 'and' refers to a time sequence in which the second element is the goal:

> 'come *and* help me in the kitchen'
> 'go *and* get the shears'

In both cases 'and' means 'in order to'. Such a use of 'and' is not possible in French, the expression of goal being usually expressed by an infinitive:

> *viens m'aider dans la cuisine*
> *va me chercher les cisailles*

(iv) Sentences rarely start in the written language with *et*; this is also the case in English, but to a far lesser extent. The following example, borrowed from J. Guillemin-Flescher (*Syntaxe Comparée du français et de l'anglais, problèmes de traduction*) contains all three types of use of 'and':

> '*And* whenever he walked down the street in his high hat everyone would say, 'There goes the Doctor! – he's a clever man.' *And* the dogs *and* the children would all run and follow behind him; *and* even the crows that lived in the church-tower would caw *and* nod their heads.' (Lofting, *Doctor Dolittle*)

The English text contains six cases of 'and'.
Translation by S.Pairault:

> *Chaque fois qu'il descendait la grande-rue,*[1] *coiffé de son chapeau haut de forme,*

tout le monde disait: 'Ah! voilà le docteur! un homme bien capable!' Les chiens et
les enfants se précipitaient pour le suivre, même les corbeaux qui nichaient dans le
clocher de l'église hochaient la tête en croassant. (one *et* only).

(v) The same often applies to 'but', 'then' and other coordinators: one may well wish
to add them to a translation from French into English, whereas one may wish to delete
them when going from English into French J. Guillemin-Fischer gives an example of
this (*Syntaxe comparée* . . ., 85):

Charles attacha son cheval à un arbre. Il courut se mettre dans le sentier; il attendit.
Une demi-heure se passa, puis il compta dix-neuf minutes à sa montre (Flaubert,
Madame Bovary)

G. Hopkins's translation reads as follows:

'Charles tied his horse to a tree. *Then* he ran to the footpath and waited. Half an
hour passed, *after which* he counted another nineteen minutes by his watch.'

The translation contains an extra 'then' and the French *puis* has in fact been translated
as 'after which'.
Similarly, *et* is often translated by 'and then', as in:

il attendit un moment et *s'en retourna*
'he waited a while, *and then* turned back'

One may similarly quote from Charrière's *Papillon*:

Le président, puis cinq magistrats, toque sur la tête. Devant la chaise du milieu
s'arrête le président, à droite et à gauche se placent ses assesseurs.

becomes

'The president of the court and then five other lawyers with their official hats, their
toques, on their heads. The presiding judge stopped at the seat in the middle *and* his
colleagues arranged themselves to the right and to the left.' (P.O'Brian's
translation)

(vi) For the repetition and non-repetition of coordinators in French, see 2.1.3 above.

Note

1 Pairault should in fact have written either *grand-rue* or *grande rue* (without a
hyphen). *Grande-rue*, as quoted by J. Guillemin-Flescher, is incorrect.

Part V
The clause, the sentence and textual organization

(i) The clause and the sentence are made up of all the elements described in the previous sections. In Part V these elements are merely replaced, and discussed, within the context in which they function – hence frequent references to the previous sections.

(ii) A clause which may stand on its own, i.e. which is independent from any other from a grammatical point of view, constitutes a 'simple sentence'. Complex sentences are sentences which are made up of more than one clause. Thus, *la voiture est en panne* is a simple sentence, whereas *la voiture est au garage/parce qu'elle est en panne* is a complex sentence.

Clauses and sentences are defined in Ch. 17 with specific reference to French.

(iii) There are different types of sentence depending on their communicative functions: some are used for making statements ('declarative sentences'), some are used for asking questions ('interrogative sentences'), and some are used for giving orders ('imperative sentences'). The following are examples of different 'sentence types':

> *vous avez acheté un magnétophone* (declarative)
> *avez-vous acheté un magnétophone?* (interrogative)
> *achetez un magnétophone* (imperative)

Declarative sentences are the subject of Ch. 18, imperative and interrogative sentences of Ch. 19.

(iv) All three types of sentence may at the same time be 'exclamative'. An exclamative sentence is one which contains a strongly emphasized opinion, question or order. This strong emotional content is expressed mainly by specific intonation patterns or, in the written language, by an exclamation mark; but other elements such as exclamative adverbs may also be called into play:

> *la voiture est en panne!* (intonation)
> *est-il nigaud!* (intonation + inversion)
> *quelle horreur!* (intonation + *quelle*)
> *qu'il est bête!* (intonation + *qu'*)
> *fais-le tout de suite!* (imperative sentence + intonation)

Although the exclamative variant of each sentence type could be examined under its own heading, all three categories have been grouped together under the heading 'exclamative sentences' and dealt with in Ch. 19 along with imperative and interrogative sentences.

(v) Although intonation belongs to phonology and not to grammar, there are cases in which intonation patterns may express grammatical concepts:

> *la voiture est en panne* (declarative sentence)
> *la voiture est en panne?* (interrogative sentence)
> *la voiture est en panne!* (exclamative sentence)

In this example intonation alone is sufficient to express different sentence types.

Intonation patterns are therefore referred to whenever they have a grammatical function.

(vi) Texts are not simply made up of individual sentences strung together. They are organized into paragraphs, which in turn make up various kinds of texts. French textual organization is the subject of Ch. 20.

(vii) Ch. 21 is concerned with the spoken language. It deals with the organization of clauses into utterances (the utterance being defined as a stretch of speech between two periods of silence), and of utterances into various types of discourse (conversations, interviews, etc). The chapter is therefore concerned with the spoken language above the clause level.

Ch. 21 is not concerned with indicating the various constructions most favoured in the spoken language; this area has been covered independently within each section of the book.

Chapter 17

Defining clauses and sentences, with special reference to French

1 The basic clause

1.1 Basic elements making up the clause

(i) A basic clause is made up of a nominal phrase, which functions as a grammatical subject, and of a verbal phrase, which functions as a predicate. For example, in *le chat mange*, *le chat* is the subject and *mange* is the predicate (or *mange* is the verb, and *le chat* is the subject of that verb).

This may be represented symbolically in the following manner:

(ii) The predicate may also be made up of the verb and its complement – a direct object, for example:

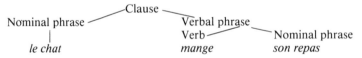

(iii) In an active construction, the subject usually states the actor, whereas in a passive construction the subject refers to the goal:

> *le chat boit le lait* (active construction)
> *le lait a été bu par le chat* (passive construction)

In some grammars, the subject of a passive construction is labelled the 'grammatical subject' to avoid ambiguity, given that the word 'subject' is very often associated with that of actor.

The 'actor' in a passive construction is called the 'agent' or the 'logical subject'.

The term 'topic' of a clause is often used when the latter is not the grammatical subject:

> *ce livre, je ne l'ai pas encore lu* (the 'topic' is *ce livre*)

This happens basically in clauses in which some item is to be emphasized.

(iv) the predicate contains the verb and any complement which may go with it; thus, in *le chat mange son repas*, *mange son repas* is the predicate.

1.2 The different kinds of clause structure

Clause structure depends on the kind of verb used, i.e. on whether the verb is 'intensive' or 'extensive' on the one hand, and whether it is 'intransitive' or 'transitive' on the other. If the verb is transitive it may also depend on whether it is 'monotransitive', 'ditransitive' or 'complex transitive'. (See Ch. 9, section 1 for an explanation of these terms. The term 'extensive', which is not mentioned in the above chapter, refers to any verb which is not intensive, i.e. to transitive and intransitive verbs. An intensive verb is one which takes a complement of the subject.)

The following diagram shows the different kinds of clause structures possible depending on the kind of verb used (based on Quirk *et al.*, *A University grammar of English*, 16):

Verb intensive:
- Cs: *il est sage*
- A place: *il est à Paris*

Verb extensive:
- Verb intransitive (± Adverbials): *il court (vite)*
- Verb transitive:
  - Monotransitive:
    - Od: *il prend la ville*
    - Oi: *il s'empare de la ville*
  - Ditransitive:
    - Od + Ac: *il donne le livre à sa sœur*
  - Complex transitive:
    - Od + Co: *ils ont nommé M. X président*

Note on the terminology and conventions used above:

(i) The parentheses indicate that the element is optional.

(ii) Cs = complement of the subject; A = adverbial; Od = direct object; Oi = indirect object; Ac = attributive complement (or indirect object in some grammars); Co = complement of the object.

(iii) The terms 'complement of the subject' and 'complement of the object' mean exactly the same thing as 'attribute of the subject' and 'attribute of the object'. In French only the term 'attribute' may be used with this meaning. Quirk uses the term 'complement', hence its use here. In other sections of the book the term 'attribute' has been favoured. Similarly, 'complement of the subject' could be called 'attribute of the subject'. There is no difference of meaning between these two sets of terms.

1.3 Expression of function in the clause

(i) Since French no longer inflects for case, word order has become essential in determining the function of a phrase within a clause. The French clause is therefore similar to a chain of functions. There are four main types of possible 'chains of functions':

Subject + verb + (adverbial): *il court vite*
Subject + verb + complement of the subject (+ adverbial): *il est sage*
Subject + verb + direct object: *il prend la ville*
Subject + verb + direct object + attributive: *il donne le livre à sa sœur*

The chain 'Subject + verb + direct object + complement of the object' also exists, as in *ils ont élu Monsieur X. président*, but is quite rare as there are very few complex transitive verbs.

Most of these points apply to English, for the same reasons.

1.4 Agreement in terms of gender and number

Agreement in terms of gender and number acts as a cohesive force in French, binding the various elements of the nominal phrases together; there is agreement between subject and verb, subject and complement of the subject, and – sometimes – between object and past participle.

Agreement is much more extensive in French than in English.

1.5 Exceptions to the word-order rule: subject + verb + complement

(i) There are obligatory exceptions to the word-order rules given above. These rules do not apply where pronouns are used as complements, e.g. *il le voit / j'y vais / je lui en parlerai*.

Word-order may also be changed to create different types of sentence. Thus a declarative clause may be transformed into an interrogative one: *tu y vas* becomes *y vas-tu?* Similarly, by the removal of a subject, a declarative sentence may be transformed into an imperative: *chantons* as against *nous chantons*.

(ii) There are optional exceptions to the word-order rules, when the clause is introduced by certain elements, e.g. *le réveil n'a pas sonné, aussi a-t-il été en retard*. Further, in certain subordinate clauses the subject may appear after the verb, e.g. *le livre que mon frère a écrit* may become *le livre qu'a écrit mon frère* without any change in meaning.

(iii) A change in word-order may have to be accompanied by other changes: this happens when there is a need to emphasize an element in the clause, e.g. *ce livre, je l'ai déjà lu*. In this case the first word is no longer the subject but the object; it is however separated from the rest of the clause by a comma/pause, and it reappears in the clause in the shape of a pronoun so that the structure of the clause may be complete (French differs from English in its insistence on the clause remaining syntactically complete).

2 The sentence

2.1 Simple and complex sentences

(i) A simple or minimal sentence is one which is made up of one clause only. It is a clause which can stand on its own both from a syntactic and a semantic point of view.

This independence is represented in the written language by the fact that such a clause starts with a capital letter and is terminated by a full stop. There are neither of these in the spoken language, although there are pauses of different lengths and different intonation patterns. The term 'sentence' therefore applies specifically to the written language and only marginally to the spoken language – certainly in so far as the development of a framework for the analysis of the spoken language is concerned (see Ch. 21).

(ii) A complex sentence is one which is made up of more than one clause. The clauses which make up a complex sentence may either function on the same syntactical level, in which case they are 'coordinated', or they may function on different levels, one clause being dependent on (i.e.) subordinate to another.

In a sentence in which there are two clauses, one being dependent on the other, the 'supporting clause' is called the main clause and the clause dependent upon it the 'subordinate clause':

[Il est venu faire le travail] et [ensuite il est parti] (coordination)
Il est parti [parce qu'il a fini son travail] (subordination)

2.2 The simple or minimal sentence

The simple sentence may be made up of a 'basic clause' (see 1.1.) or a complex clause. A complex clause is one in which one of the basic elements has been modified. The element modified is mainly the noun in the nominal phrase(s), e.g.

le chat mange son repas (basic clause)

In this case there are two nouns which may be modified, *chat* and *repas*:

$$
\left.\begin{array}{l}
\textit{le chat noir} \\
\quad \textit{affamé} \\
\quad \textit{de mon voisin}
\end{array}\right] \quad \textit{mange} \left[\begin{array}{l}
\textit{un repas copieux} \\
\textit{son repas du soir}
\end{array}\right.
$$

The verb could also be modified, but only by an adverb at this level:

le chat noir mange gloutonnement un repas copieux

In other words, a complex clause is one which contains a complex noun phrase; and the structure of the complex phrase will be made up of the core elements (the determiner + noun) and the modifying elements (adjectives, participles functioning as adjectives, and complements of the noun). Adjectives may be further modified by intensifying adverbs such as *très, tout,* e.g. *le tout petit chat noir*.

2.3 The complex sentence

A complex sentence may include a subordinate clause (see 2.3.1), coordinated clauses (see 2.3.2) or inserted clauses (see 2.3.3).

2.3.1 *Complex sentences including subordinate clauses*

There are two possibilities.
(i) The noun in the noun phrase may be modified by a relative clause functioning adjectivally, as in *le chat qui est noir est à moi* — the relative clause being *qui est noir*.
(ii) One of the noun phrases, usually the one contained in the predicate, may be replaced by a whole clause, as in *je veux que tu me ramènes un chat noir*, in which *que tu me ramènes un chat noir* is the object of the main verb.

The following is an example of a complex sentence (borrowed from Abbadie *et al.*, *L'Expression française, écrite et orale*, Presses Universitaires de Grenoble, 1976):

Complex nominal phrase: Complex verbal phrase:

$$
\left.\begin{array}{l}
\textit{ces hautes montagnes} \text{ (head} \\
\quad \text{noun)} \\
\quad \textit{avec leurs bois de} \\
\quad \textit{pins et de melèzes} \\
\textit{ces petits chalets} \\
\quad \text{(2nd head noun)} \\
\quad \textit{qui se ressemblent} \\
\quad \textit{tous} \\
\textit{ces cimes} \text{ (3rd head noun)} \\
\quad \textit{couvertes de neige} \\
\quad \textit{surgissant de la brume} \\
\quad \textit{dans un ciel hivernal}
\end{array}\right\} \quad \textit{rappelaient} \left[\begin{array}{l}
\textit{souvent} \\
\textit{à Pierre} \\
\textit{ces images de la Suisse dont il} \\
\quad \textit{avait parfois rêvé quand il} \\
\quad \textit{faisait ses études}
\end{array}\right.
$$

The structure of the complex sentence involving subordination may therefore be represented as follows:

Complex nominal phrase:	Complex verbal phrase:

Head noun
    + determiners, adjectives, participles, complements of the noun, relative clauses
	Verb
	    + complex nominal phrases (as in example above) or subordinate clauses introduced by subordinating conjunctions

(iii) The degree of complexity found in a sentence depends:
(a) on the register in the written language: complicated sentences belong to the more

formal types of language (literature, legal and administrative texts etc.);

(b) on stylistic fashions: it has been fashionable to use complex sentences and it has been equally fashionable to use simple sentences. (Complex sentences tend to be frowned upon in schools, since they are far more difficult to construct on the principle that *ce qui se pense clairement s'énonce aisément*.)

2.3.2 *Complex sentences made up of two or more coordinated clauses*

In this case each clause is independent of the other, at least from a grammatical point of view:

> *je suis passé te voir mais tu n'étais pas là* (explicit coordination)
> *je suis venu, j'ai vu, j'ai vaincu* (implicit coordination, also called either 'coordination by juxtaposition' or 'parataxis')

2.3.3 *Inserted clauses*

(i) These may be parenthetical, in which case they will be in parentheses or placed between two dashes, or sometimes two commas:

> *le bruit (la cloche venait de sonner) le réveilla en sursaut*
> *le bruit − la cloche venait de sonner − le réveilla en sursaut*

(ii) They may be in the text to introduce a quotation:

> *ça ne fait rien, lui dit-il*

These are usually associated with very simple constructions but this need not be the case:

> *Qu'avez-vous? se mit à lui dire*
> *Quelqu'un du peuple croassant.*

(La Fontaine − who should have written *coassant* and not *croassant*, since he is referring to frogs and not crows).

3 The different types of sentence

3.1 Social function and grammatical construction

In any given language it is possible to give orders, make comments or statements, ask questions or exclaim. These are social functions but they may be expressed grammatically, through the use of specific constructions. There are, therefore, the following set of correspondences both in English and in French between social function and grammatical construction:

Social function:	Corresponding grammatical construction:
to make a comment or statement	declarative sentence
to give an order	imperative sentence
to ask a question	interrogative sentence
to exclaim	exclamative sentence

It is important to note, however, that it is not always necessary to use the grammatical construction corresponding to the desired function; orders are in fact rarely expressed by imperative sentences, since these tend to sound abrupt and rude. Also, exclamative sentences are special forms of the declarative, imperative and interrogative sentence types. The declarative sentence is sometimes said to be the 'unmarked sentence', whilst the interrogative, imperative and exclamative sentences are said to be 'marked'.

3.2 Choice in terms of polarity and voice

Two other choices have to be made at the level of the clause or sentence:

It is necessary to choose between a 'positive' and a 'negative' sentence, the positive sentence being the 'unmarked' one; this is sometimes referred to as 'polarity'.

It is necessary to choose between the 'active' and the 'passive' voice, the active voice being the 'unmarked' one.

One is therefore faced with the following possibilities[1]:

Type of sentence	Voice	Polarity	
Declarative	Active	Positive:	*le garagiste a réparé ma voiture*
		Negative:	*le garagiste n'a pas réparé ma voiture*
	Passive	Positive:	*ma voiture a été réparée par le garagiste*
		Negative:	*ma voiture n'a pas été réparée par le garagiste*
Interrogative	Active	Positive:	*le garagiste a réparé ma voiture?* (+ intonation)
		or	*est-ce-que le garagiste a réparé ma voiture?*
			le garagiste n'a pas réparé ma voiture? (+ intonation)
		Negative:	*le garagiste n'a-t-il pas réparé ma voiture?*
		or	*est-ce que le garagiste n'a pas réparé ma voiture?*
	Passive	Positive:	*ma voiture a-t-elle été réparée par le garagiste?*
		or	*est-ce que ma voiture a été réparéé par le garagiste?*
		Negative:	*ma voiture n'a-t-elle pas été réparée par le garagiste?*
		or	*est-ce qu ma voiture n'a pas été réparée par le garagiste?*
Imperative	Active	Positive:	*réparez ma voiture!*
		Negative:	*ne réparez pas ma voiture!*
Exclamative	Active	Positive:	*le garagiste a réparé ma voiture!* (+ intonation)
		Negative:	*le garagiste n'a pas réparé ma voiture!* (+ intonation)
	Passive	Positive:	*ma voiture a été réparée par le garagiste!* (+ intonation)
		Negative:	*ma voiture n'a pas été réparée par le garagiste!* (+ intonation)

3.3 Different methods of changing the basic unmarked positive active declarative sentence in French

(i) The ways of changing the type of sentence are:

by using special intonation patterns (interrogative, imperative and exclamative)
by changing the word-order (interrogative)

by omitting the subject and using the imperative form of the verb (imperative)

by using interrogative or exclamative markers (such as certain adverbs) in the case of exclamatives (as in *ma voiture n'a même pas été réparée!*).

(ii) Polarity is changed by adding the discontinuous negative adverb *ne . . . pas* to express negation.

(iii) Voice is expressed by using the passive form, changing the place of the subject and object, and adding a preposition such as *par* to indicate the agent: (NP1 + V + NP2) becomes (NP2 passive V *par* NP1), e.g. *le chat a attrapé la souris* becomes *la souris a été attrapée par le chat*. The positive, active declarative sentence is dealt with in Ch. 18; the marked sentences are dealt with in Ch. 19.

4 Explicit and implicit sentences or clauses

An explicit sentence or clause is normally made up of two elements: a noun phrase and a verb phrase, functioning respectively as subject and predicate.

There are, however, exceptions to this:

(i) The utterance may be made up of one element only: it is called a *monorhème* in French:

à la porte!
bien joué!
formidable!

These 'implicit' clauses or sentences are usually marked emotionally, and are usually 'exclamative' sentences.

Monorhèmes may also be imperative constructions, e.g. *sortez!*

(ii) The utterance may be made up of two elements but no verb:

drôle d'idée! (= cette idée est drôle)
excellent, ce café! (= ce café est excellent)

Verbless sentences are called 'nominal sentences'. Nominal sentences are typical of the spoken language, since the intonation patterns supply most of the missing information; but they may also be used in the written language for stylistic effect.

(Constructions including two elements are called *dirhèmes* in French.)

5 The role of intonation in French grammar

5.1 Intonation as part of grammar

The study of intonation does not belong to grammar proper but to phonology. But in French, as in other languages, it is possible to express certain grammatical concepts simply by using specific intonation patterns: at this level, phonology becomes part of grammar:

tu aimes le café (declarative sentence)
tu aimes le café? (interrogative sentence)
tu aimes le café! (exclamative sentence)

In this example, all three sentences have the same syntax as far as word-order and moods are concerned, but the use of different intonation patterns (represented by different punctuation marks in the written language) transforms them into three different sentence types.[2]

5.2 Characteristics of French intonation

(See 5.3)

(i) French sentences are divided into 'rhythmic' or 'intonation' groups; these are sometimes also called 'sense-groups', since they correspond to units of meaning:

passez-moi/le gros dictionnaire/qui est sur la table/s'il vous plaît/

This sentence may be seen to be made up of four rhythmic groups, each group corresponding to either an NP, a VP or a very short sentence. In hurried speech the number of rhythmic groups could be reduced.

(ii) The words within the rhythmic group 'run into' one another (the phenomenon of 'liaison'). The word itself does not normally have a stressed syllable once it is integrated within the rhythmic group, unless it is the last word of a rhythmic group. In this case, the last sounded syllable of the word is emphasized, mainly by a slight change of pitch:

passez-moi/ le gros dictionnair(e)/ qui est sur la tabl(e)/ s'il vous plaît/

French differs in this respect from English, since in English each word retains its individual stress patterns within the intonation group.

(iii) There are three basic intonation patterns, indicative of sentence type in French.

The declarative intonation pattern is complex since it depends on the number of rhythmic groups in the sentence. Generally speaking, the final group is said on a 'rise-fall pattern', the rise being very slight; the nonfinal groups are said on a 'level-rise pattern', the rise being again very slight and on the last syllable:

je vais prendre / le gros dictionnaire / qui est sur la table /

The interrogative pattern is similar to the nonfinal declarative pattern — the 'level-rise' sequence:

est-ce que tu y vas?

The imperative intonation pattern corresponds to a 'falling pattern', but the interval of pitch between the highest and lowest syllable is somewhat more marked than in the preceding cases. Furthermore the variation of pitch is achieved by pronounced 'steps' rather than by way of a 'glide' on the last sounded syllable.

n'y va pas!

The exclamative patterns are all exaggerated versions of the three preceding cases plus others; the greater the degree of emotion to be expressed, the greater the variation in pitch (see Ch. 19, 2.2).

(iv) Since phonology is only marginally a part of grammar, and since little of a real scientific nature is known about intonation patterns in French, the points made are necessarily of a general nature. This is particularly true where exclamative intonation patterns are concerned, where there are many variations on the same basic theme.

5.3 Comparative 'pitch patterns' of French, American English, German and Spanish

The following is taken from Pierre Delattre, *Comparing the phonetic features of English, French, German and Spanish* (Harrap 1965).

Realizing that it was necessary in teaching foreign languages to complement the use of pitch *levels* with actual *shapes*, we have undertaken to study, by objective means, the most characteristic pitch shapes of [American] English, German, Spanish and French for the expression of basic attitudes such as continuation, finality, command, interrogative question, informative question, implication and parenthesis.

At present we have results to report concerning the pitch shapes of declarative intonations in the four languages under study. They were obtained by spectrographic analysis of at least five minutes of spontaneous speech by cultivated natives of each country. . . .

The following are examples of the results obtained:

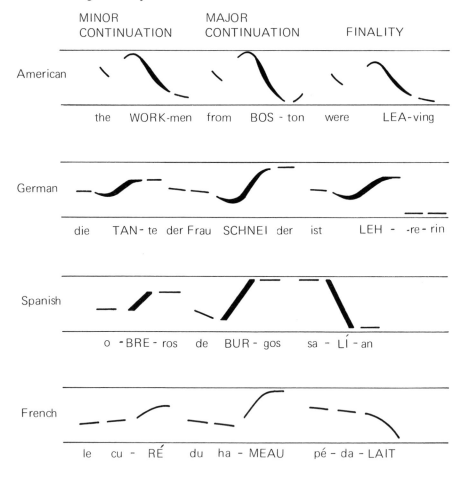

MINOR CONTINUATION	MAJOR CONTINUATION	FINALITY

American
the   WORK-men   from   BOS - ton   were   LEA-ving

German
die   TAN- te der Frau   SCHNEI der   ist   LEH - -re- rin

Spanish
o -BRE - ros   de   BUR - gos   sa - LÍ - an

French
le   cu - RÉ   du   ha - MEAU   pé - da - LAIT

Notes

1 This table is adapted from Dubois and Lagane's *La nouvelle grammaire du français*.
2 Actors are capable of conveying many more subtle implications to a sentence, simply by changing its intonation pattern. But from a grammatical point of view, only declarative, imperative, interrogative and exclamative patterns are relevant.

Chapter 18

The declarative sentence

In this chapter, section 1 examines the structure of the simple sentence, and section 2 the various transformations a sentence may undergo, whilst section 3 deals with stylistic considerations.

1 The simple (or minimal) declarative sentence

1.1 Structure of the basic simple sentence

(*i*) The diagram on p. 404 gives a symbolic representation of the various structural possibilities. (*Note*: These representations are in terms of surface structure only.)

In S1 the verb is intransitive; in S2 it is intransitive but requires an adverbial of place; in S3 the verb is intensive or copulative; in S4 it is transitive.

S4 may be more complex if the verb is not simply transitive but ditransitive (S5), or complex transitive (S6).

(ii) From these symbolic representations of the structures involved, it may be noted that the function of an item may be dependent upon two elements. Usually it is dependent upon word-order, but this may be supplemented by prepositions where word-order on its own would be an insufficient means to express structure.

Word-order in the basic declarative sentence is as follows (the numbers indicate sentence position):

(1) subject + (2) intransitive verb (± (3) adverbial of place)
(1) subject + (2) intensive verb + (3) complement of the subject[1]
(1) subject + (2) transitive verb + (3) direct (or indirect) object
(1) subject + (2) ditransitive verb + (3) direct object + (4) attributive object
(1) subject + (2) complex transitive verb + (3) direct object + (4) complement of the object[1]

There are of course some rare exceptions to these rules (see 3.1).

(iii) There is agreement in number and in person between the subject and the verb (*je chante/ nous chantons*); there is agreement in gender and number between the past participle and the subject when the auxiliary used is *être* or another intensive verb (*il est content/ elle est contente /elles sont contentes*). There may also be agreement between the past participle and the object in certain well-defined circumstances (*la lettre que j'ai écrite*) (see Ch. 8, 2.3).

1.2 Optional elements in the simple sentence

1.2.1 *The adverbial complements*

Except in the case of certain intransitive verbs such as *aller*, the adverbial complements are optional. They correspond to what the French call 'circumstantial complements'. They refer to the time, place or manner in which the action may take place.

The adverbial complements normally appear at the end of the clause, i.e. after all the other obligatory items. There are, however, some exceptions to this (see Ch. 12).

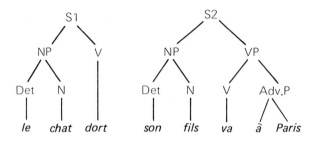

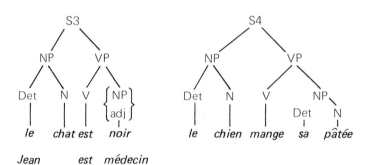

1.2.2　*Inclusion of modifiers in the noun phrase*

(i) The noun phrase may include modifiers; see the following diagram.

If the noun is modified by a relative clause, the sentence becomes a complex sentence.

The adjective may itself, in turn, be modified by an adverb, the latter always remaining invariable, e.g. *un très vieux livre*.

The adverb normally precedes the adjective modified (but see Ch. 12 for the place of the adverb).

le	*chat*	*noir*	adjective
		effrayé	participle
		de ma voisine	complement of the noun
		qui est dans la cuisine	relative clause

(ii) Word-order in the noun phrase is as follows:

Most adjectives follow the noun, but there are numerous exceptions (see Ch. 11). The complement of the noun follows the noun.

The relative pronoun immediately follows the noun modified, i.e. its antecedent. (But see 3.1 for possible exceptions.)

(iii) There is agreement in terms of gender and number between the noun, its determiner and its modifiers:

le petit livre / les petits livres
la petite table / les petites tables

Many of these forms of agreement are written but not oral.

(iv) Where a relative clause is concerned, the use of certain adjectives or determiners to modify the noun functioning as the antecedent may entail the use of the subjunctive in the relative clause. Compare:

c'est la première maison qui est à vendre (indicative)
c'est la première maison qui soit à vendre (subjunctive)

(See Ch. 5.)

1.2.3 *Replacement of the noun phrase by a subordinate clause*

In this case the sentence becomes a complex sentence.

(i) There are two possibilities: the clause may function as would any noun phrase:

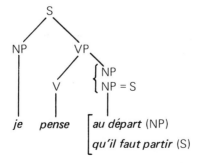

In this case the clause is the direct object of *penser* whereas *au départ* is the indirect object of *penser* since it includes a preposition.

(ii) But the clause could also function as an adverbial complement:

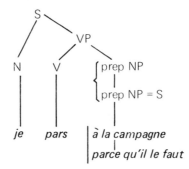

Note: The two adverbials in this case are not mutually exclusive: one could use both.
(iii) The use of certain constructions in the main clause may entail the use of specific moods and tenses in the subordinate clauses. The use of certain conjunctions introducing the subordinate clause may also entail the use of certain moods (subjunctive). (See Ch. 5.) Compare:

j'irai parce que tu le veux (indicative)
j'irai quoiqu'il en dise (subjunctive)
je sais qu'il y va (indicative)
je veux qu'il y aille (subjunctive)

1.3   Intonation pattern of the declarative sentence

The break-up of the declarative sentence into rhythmic groups (see Ch. 17, 5) has important consequences in terms of grammar (see 2.4 below). It is necessary, therefore, first of all to describe these intonation patterns, and then to examine their grammatical consequences.

1.3.1   *Description of intonation patterns used in declarative sentences*

The intonation sequence of the basic simple declarative sentence is the rise-fall. The syllable pronounced on the highest pitch is the *acmé* (which is very important in poetry). In the following examples the underlined syllables are those said on the highest pitch.

la Renault 9 me fait envie

(*Neuf* is the *acmé*.)
   The same pattern may be seen in the simple declarative sentence, even though the sentence may be more complex (i.e. longer):

la nouvelle Renault que j'ai vue au Salon me fait envie

(The-*on* of *Salon* is the *acmé*.)
   On the other hand, a long sentence may be broken down into smaller units, called 'rhythmic' or 'intonation' groups:

la nouvelle Renault que j'ai vue au Salon me fait envie

(The *-on* of *Salon* is the *acmé*.)

It is important to note that the rise in pitch is minimal in French, particularly between nonfinal syllables. Indeed, the rising intonation patterns only 'rise' on the last word of the rhythmic group, and mainly only on the last syllable, which sees its vowel lengthened. It is more often a glide than a rise.

A rhythmic group normally corresponds to a noun phrase or verb phrase, or to a basic simple sentence.

(ii) The general rules which apply when reading aloud are therefore as follows:

If the declarative sentence is said as one rhythmic group, the intonation pattern will be rise-fall.

If the declarative sentence is said as several rhythmic groups, the intonation patterns used will be rising intonation for the nonfinal rhythmic groups and rise-fall for the final rhythmic group.

1.3.2 *Grammatical implications*

(i) Since the rhythmic groups are separated by slight pauses, the only words which stand out are those at the end of each rhythmic group, e.g.

le gros dictionnaire / que j'ai acheté hier / est sur la table

In this case *dictionnaire, hier* and *table* are given the same weight. But in:

le gros dictionnaire que j'ai acheté hier / est sur la table

no emphasis is placed on *dictionnaire*, which is phonologically 'lost' or 'drowned' within the rhythmic group (see Ch. 17).

(ii) Rhythmic groups are delimited by pauses in the spoken language and by commas in the written language; but there is only a rough correspondence between pauses in the spoken language and commas in the written, partly because of hesitations in the spoken language and 'verbal crossing out', and partly because punctuation in French must also be grammatical.

An example of the 'clash' between phonological and grammatical punctuation occurs in the following example:

j'ai acheté des pommes, / des poires, / des bananes / et des fraises

No comma is possible before *et* in this case, even though there may well be a pause at this point.

(iii) Since it is necessary for a word to be in a certain position in order for it to stand out or to be emphasized, it may be necessary to make syntactic alterations in order to achieve that position. For example, in order to stress the *je* in *que j'ai acheté hier*, the whole syntax of the sentence must be changed so that *je* – which now becomes *moi* – occurs at the end of a rhythmic group:

c'est moi / qui ai acheté hier / le gros dictionnaire / qui est sur la table

See also 2.4

2   Possible transformations

2.1   Pronominalization

(See also Ch. 3.)

A noun phrase may be replaced by a pronoun, usually in order to avoid repetition of the noun phrase. In this case, pronominalization will entail a change of word-order unless the pronoun is functioning as subject, e.g. *le chat dort* becomes *il dort;* but *je donne du lait au chat* becomes *je lui en donne*.

2.2   Negative transformation

(See also Ch. 12, 7)

(i) There may be a wish to negate a part of a sentence only:

je veux du beurre et non de la margarine pour cette recette

(ii) It is more usual to negate the whole clause:

je ne veux pas de margarine pour cette recette, je veux du beurre

2.3   Passive transformation

2.3.1   *Basic passive transformation*

(See also Ch. 9.)

(i) In this case the subject becomes the agent, and the object the grammatical subject. In other words, NP1 + active verb + NP2 becomes NP2 + passive verb + *par* NP1. This implies a number of morphological and syntactical changes:

the verb must change voice which implies the addition of *être*;
the agent must be introduced by a preposition, usually *par* and sometimes *de* (see Chs. 9 and 13);
the verb will agree with the new 'grammatical'subject.

(ii) Passivization affects the whole basic clause, e.g. *le chat a attrapé la souris /la souris a été attrapée par le chat* but adverbial phrases remain unchanged. Compare:

le chat a attrapé une souris dans la cuisine
une souris a été attrapée par le chat dans la cuisine

(iii) The passive clause often lacks an explicit agent; in this case it often corresponds to an active declarative sentence having *on* as a subject, e.g. *on a annoncé un changement de programme* becomes *un changement de programme a été annoncé*.
(iv) The passive transformation is not always possible even when the verb is transitive (see Ch. 9).

2.3.2   *Impersonal transformation*

(See also Ch. 9.)

(i) Impersonal transformation is similar to the passive transformation in the sense that it may correspond to an active declarative sentence using *on* as a subject:

on a trouvé une paire de gants
une paire de gants a été trouvée
il a été trouvé une paire de gants

(ii) As in the case of the passive transformation, there is a change in the word-order:

des grêlons tombent
il tombe des grêlons

In this case, however, the verb is intransitive.
Impersonal transformation is rarely possible (see Ch. 9).

2.4 Emphasizing a specific element in the sentence

2.4.1 *Use of a disjunctive construction*

Whereas in English any word in a sentence may be emphasized merely by stress, in French only the last word of a rhythmic group may be stressed. It may be necessary to make structural changes to the sentence in order to bring the word to be stressed into the correct position:

'I love my wife'	=	*j'aime ma femme*
'*I* love my wife'	=	*j'aime ma femme, moi*
'I *love* my wife'	=	*je l'aime, ma femme*
'I love *my* wife'	=	*c'est la mienne que j'aime*, or *j'aime ma femme à moi*
'I love my *wife*'	=	*c'est ma femme que j'aime*

The emphasis is due to the fact that there is a rise in intonation on the last word of the non-final rythmic group which is represented in the written language by a comma − except in the last case, in which it is the introducer *c'est . . . que (qui)* which enables the positioning of the noun *ma femme* at the *acmé*, i.e. at the point in the sentence where pitch is highest.

Disjunctive constructions imply a change in word-order, the use of a personal pronoun in order to replace the displaced noun, and possibly, as in the last case, the use of an 'introducer' to highlight the item being introduced (see 2.4.2 below). There is also the breaking-up of the original rhythmic group into several groups, with the exception of cases using an 'introducer'.

2.4.2 *Use of an introducer*

2.4.2.1 *Constructions based on a relative pronoun*
(i) *Voilà . . . qui; voilà . . . que*:

   j'aime beaucoup ce livre becomes *voilà un livre que j'aime beaucoup*

(ii) *Il y a . . . qui; il y a . . . que*:

   un client attend dans l'antichambre becomes *il y a un client qui attend dans l'antichambre*

(iii) *C'est . . . qui; c'est . . . que*:

   je vous recommande ce produit becomes *c'est un produit que je vous recommande*

2.4.2.2 *Constructions based on the subordinating conjunction 'que'*
(i) *Voilà . . . que; il y a . . . que* (referring to time):

   Voilà bientôt deux mois que le conseil interministériel a décidé de réduire la vitesse à 100 km/h et de rendre obligatoire le port de la ceinture de sécurité. (La Vie ouvrière)

This sentence could have otherwise commenced: *il y a presque deux mois que. . . .*
(ii) *C'est . . . que* (referring to some circumstances in which the action takes place):

   c'est en Bretagne qu'il y a le moins d'autoroutes
   c'est à deux heures qu'il est finalement arrivé

2.5   The exclamative declarative sentence

(See Ch. 19, 3.3.1.)

2.6   Nominalization of the clause

It is sometimes possible to transform a clause into a nominal phrase. In this way, either a complex sentence may be reduced to a simple sentence, or two sentences reduced to one:

> *la voiture publicitaire a annoncé que les coureurs allaient bientôt passer* (complex sentence: two clauses)

becomes:

> *la voiture publicitaire a annoncé le proche passage des coureurs* (simple sentence: one clause)

> *La voiture démarre. Cela fait du bruit* (two simple sentences)

becomes:

> *le démarrage de la voiture fait du bruit* (one simple sentence)

Nominalization is not always possible, since the nominalized clause may have a slightly different meaning from the original.

3   Stylistic considerations

There are three areas to be examined: 3.1 deals with possible changes in word-order to achieve an effect, 3.2 with the stylistic uses made of nominal sentences, and 3.3 with the stylistic uses of different kinds of subordination.

3.1   Possible changes in word-order

3.1.1   *Changes in the norm through time*

(i) Word-order has replaced case endings as an indicator of function. This means that, in French, word-order is relatively inflexible. It is normally SVC (S standing for subject, V for verb, C for complement – this term being used in its broadest sense and including direct and indirect objects and complements of the subject). This sequence did not always apply to the same extent in Old French, since the presence of a case system enabled morphological distinction between subject and complement. Thus there were two possible word-order sequences at that time; SVC and CVS. There remain a few cases in modern French when the sequence CVS is still possible (see 3.1.2 below). Alternatives to the old CVS construction have also developed over the centuries (see 3.1.3 below).

(ii) The most mobile elements in the French clause are the adverbial complements or *compléments circonstanciels*.

The order sequence ASVC (A standing for adverbial complement) has become increasingly more frequent, particularly when the adverbial refers to time, since this often enables the author to establish a link between the new sentence and the preceding one. Glanville Price quotes Froissart in this respect:[2]

> *Apres disner le conte de Foeis emmena les chevaliers en ses galleries.*

3.1.2 *Cases of inversion of subject and verb*

3.1.2.1 *Inversion as a relic of the past*   Inversion is sometimes a relic of the CVS order possible in Old French due to the case system.

Inversion may take place:

(i) when the first position is occupied by an adjective which functions as a predicate, on condition S is a noun and not a personal pronoun:

Heureux est l'écrivain qui peut faire un beau petit livre (Joubert)
Combien différent du vôtre est l'enseignement que j'écoute dans le livre de la nature. (Gide)

(ii) when the first position is occupied by *quel* + noun functioning as a predicate, on condition S is a noun and not a personal pronoun:

Quel plaisir m' ont fait les boutiques! (Romains)

(iii) after certain adverbs such as *aussi, à peine, peut-être, sans doute* (see Ch. 12):

A peine Françoise était-elle descendue que. . . . (Proust)
Sans doute eut-il regret de ses paroles (Proust)

But if the first position in the clause is occupied by something other than one of the elements listed under *(i)*, *(ii)* and *(iii)*, then a disjunctive structure is called for: **la souris le chat a mangé*, for example, is not acceptable, whereas the disjunctive construction *la souris, le chat l'a mangée* is acceptable.

3.1.2.2 *Inversion for stylistic considerations*   Inversion may take place for two reasons:

(i) The aim, generally, is not to end a sentence with a verb used in a personal form. Thus Proust preferred to write (2) rather than (1) below:

(1) *Rappelez-vous ce que le docteur vous a dit.*
(2) *Rappelez-vous ce que vous a dit le docteur.* (Proust)

The inversion renders the sentence more elegant and more formal.

(ii) There is a tendency to organize the sentence into rhythmic groups of equal or increasing length. Thus Mauriac preferred to write (2) rather than (1) below:

(1) *Le chien gémissait toujours,/ quoique tout bruit de pas/ eût cessé.*
                 6 syllables   3 syllables.
(2) *Le chien gémissait toujours,/ quoiqu'eût cessé / tout bruit de pas.* (Mauriac)
                 4 syllables   4 syllables

3.1.2.3 *Inversion of the subject serving as psychological predicate*

(i) In this case it is the subject which is the most important part of the clause or sentence from an information point of view:

et ne voilà-t-il pas que sur ces entrefaites arrive le mari!

In this example *le mari* is emphasized, and the sentence would be said with an exclamative intonation pattern.

(ii) Alternatively, it may be that the subject is to be commented on further:

peuvent être envoyées sans autorisation spéciale les marchandises suivantes

This is typical of administrative and legal texts, but not exclusively so:

*Suivit une âpre discussion en russe, à laquelle je ne
pouvais prendre aucune part.* (Duhamel, cited by Price, *The French language*, 262)

This kind of inversion is on the increase in modern French, particularly in the written language.[3]

(iii) It is normal to use *a-t-il dit* instead of *il a dit* when referring to a quote:

> *nous amorçons la descente, nous a-t-il dit*

3.1.3   *Alternative constructions to the CVS order of Old French*

(i) Expressions such as *c'est . . . que* are used to emphasize certain elements by placing them at the beginning of the sentence (see 2.4.1 and 2.4.2), as in *c'est Jean que j'ai vu au supermarché*.

(ii) Disjunctive constructions enable a CSV word order to continue to be employed, on condition that a personal pronoun is used to indicate the function of what came before:

> *Jean, je l'ai vu au supermarché*

This kind of construction is typical of the spoken language.

3.2   The nominal sentence

A nominal sentence is one which does not include a verb. The nominal sentence may include one element only:

> *O rage! O désespoir! O vieillesse ennemie!*
> *N'ai je donc tant vécu que pour cette infamie?*
> (Corneille)

In this case the intonation patterns will be exclamative.

In other cases the verb may be felt to be simply unnecessary. In such cases the nominal sentences are frequently based on nouns indicating some idea of action or movement:

> *J'ai été à cette noce de Mlle Louvois: que vous dirai-je? Magnificence, illustration, toute la France, habits rabattus et rebrochés d'or, pierreries, brasiers de feu et de fleurs, embarras de carrosses, cris dans la rue, flambeaux allumés, reculement et gens roués; enfin le tourbillon, la dissipation, les demandes sans réponses, les compliments sans savoir ce qu'on dit, les civilités sans savoir à qui l'on parle, les pieds entortillés dans les queues.* (Mme de Sévigné, 29 November 1679).

The effect created by such sentences is one of speed and also one of disjointedness, since the construction is incomplete. Some writers, such as Victor Hugo, have used them extensively. Sainte-Beuve once said of Michelet, *Aujourd'hui Michelet a le style vertical; il ne met plus de verbes*.

The basic advantage of the technique is the lightening of the construction by leaving out what is not, strictly speaking, necessary.

3.3   Subordination and style

3.3.1   *Stylistic appeal of the simple declarative sentence*

Some writers have made the simple declarative sentence their ideal: *Ma phrase de demain*, said Jules Renard, *le sujet, le verbe, et l'attribut* and French schoolchildren, at least at first, are encouraged to write in simple declarative sentences.

Where the writer uses simple declarative sentences, they tend to be juxtaposed, leaving the reader to establish the link between them.[4] The final effect is one of jerkiness, or a *pointilliste* effect. Renard uses this technique extensively:

L'orage éclatait. La pluie tombait en rayons blancs. Les carreaux pleuraient comme des yeux. De petites gouttes jaillissaient par les fentes des croisées. Dehors le cheval courbait la tête. (Example cited by Marouzeau, *Précis de stylistique française* 134)

La Bruyère also frequently uses successions of simple declarative sentences in his portraits:

Phédon a les yeux creux, le teint échauffé, le corps sec et le visage maigre: il dort peu et d'un sommeil fort léger; il est abstrait, rêveur; et il a, avec de l'esprit, l'air d'un stupide: il oublie de dire ce qu'il sait, ou de parler d'événements qui lui sont connus; et s'il le fait quelquefois il s'en tire mal. . . .

Eight more sentences follow, limited by semi-colons, before one gets to a full stop. As may be seen from the above example, La Bruyère makes an extensive use of sentences separated by semicolons. He also consistently uses the colon as a means of introducing an explanation without having to make explicit the fact that it is an explanation.

3.3.2 *Stylistic appeal of the different kinds of subordinate construction*

3.3.2.1 *Subordinate clauses:*

Relative clauses and subordinated clauses introduced by conjunctions have known varying degrees of popularity throughout the ages (see Ch. 14, 16.1 and Ch. 15, 4.2).

3.3.2.2 *Parallel constructions* These are constructions which fulfil the same function in relation to the same element:

Ce jardin . . . était une broussaille, c'est-à-dire quelque chose qui est impénétrable comme une forêt, peuplé comme une ville, frissonnant comme un nid, sombre comme une cathédrale, odorant comme un bouquet, solitaire comme une tombe, vivant comme une foule (Hugo)

Flaubert also uses successions of parallel constructions:

Il voyagea: il connut la mélancolie des paquebots, les froids réveils sous la tente, l'étourdissement des paysages et des ruines, l'amertume des sympathies interrompues.

(This is an example of what Proust called *le grand rythme de Flaubert*. This type of construction is typically used for descriptive passages where the author displays his imagination.)

3.3.2.3 *Concatenated constructions* These are 'chainlike' successions of clauses which are dependent on one another, and are frowned upon (see Ch. 15). Thus sentences such as the following are considered stylistically unacceptable:

il pense qu'il lui faudra aller voir l'avocat qui pourra le conseiller sur ce qu'il devrait faire

The same criticism may be made of constructions using *de* repetitively:

la sœur de la belle-fille de sa voisine

Marouzeau (*Précis de stylistique française*) points out that whereas Flaubert avoided expressions such as *une couronne de fleurs d'oranger*, the Goncourt brothers did not hesitate to write, *Les filles de la nostalgie des pays de soleil de leur père*. Such sentences are not easily acceptable.

Similarly, a succession of adjectives modifying the same noun are frowned upon:

les cendres du vieux révolutionnaire diplomate soviétique émérite qui a combattu pour la paix (cited by Marouzeau from a newspaper article, *Précis de stylistique française*)

3.3.2.4 *A succession of embedded clauses*   These are clauses contained within other clauses, and are inadvisable since they make the sentence difficult to follow. Marouzeau cites the following as an example:

Il apprit que ce n'était pas parce qu'il le lui avait demandé qu'elle s'était abstenue de dire ce qu'il savait qu'elle avait déjà entendu raconter, mais parce que. . . . (translation by E. Coindreau of a sentence by Faulkner)

A certain degree of 'embeddedness' was, however, more acceptable in Classical French:

Les meilleurs livres sont ceux que ceux qui les lisent croient qu'ils auraient pu faire. (Pascal)

Such sentences are unacceptable in modern French, except when used to comic effect:

Un auteur que je prie qu'on croie que je ne calomnie pas. (Faguet)

In the following example, on the other hand, embedded constructions are used to convey the imponderable:

C'est ici où ceux qui de ce qui de ce monde est fait sont las ne parlent plus (Claudel)

(*Ici* refers to a cemetery.) In modern French such a sentence should be rewritten as:

C'est ici où ceux qui sont las de ce qui est fait de ce monde ne parlent plus.

But Claudel chose to use a Latin construction no longer possible in French in order to produce an impression of obscurity.

3.3.2.5 *Inserted clauses*   These are independent clauses which are inserted in sentences as asides. They do not, as such, complicate the structure of the main sentence to the same extent as embedded clauses, since they are not grammatically subordinated to the main sentence. Nevertheless, constant insertions are disruptive. On the other hand, these insertions or asides do tend to give a sentence a certain informality which may be suitable in particular contexts, e.g. an internal monologue. The effect will be to give the sentence an air of improvisation, as in the following passage by Proust:

Toujours est -il que chaque fois que je pense à ce salon que Swann (sans que cette critique impliquât de sa part l'intention de contrarier en rien les goûts de sa femme) trouvait si disparate − parce que, tout conçu qu'il était encore dans le goût . . . de l'appartement où il avait connu Odette, elle avait pourtant commencé à remplacer dans ce fouillis nombre des objets chinois . . . par une foule de petits meubles tendus de vieilles soies Louis XIV (sans compter les chefs-d'œuvre apportés par Swann de l'hôtel du quai d'Orléans), − il a au contraire dans mon souvenir, ce salon composite, une cohésion, une unité, un charme individuel que n'ont jamais même les ensembles les plus intacts que le passé nous ait légués. . . .

When the technique is used in an exaggerated fashion it may create a comic effect, as in the following passage by Cendrars:

C'était mon bon ami Colon, qui n'était pas Bas-de-cuir, malgré ses apparences (il était en tenu de cavalier de la prairie . . .), mais le plus riche droguiste (retiré des affaires) de la bonne ville de Winnipeg, avait trois jeunes filles à marier (Colon était âgé de 53 ans), une femme charmante (comme sont souvent les Canadiennes qui . . .), du bien au soleil (mon ami était gentleman-farmer, et c'est chassant, pêchant, montant à cheval . . . que j'avais passé quelques semaines dans son domaine la dernière fois que je l'avais vu deux ans auparavant et que . . .), était parti se battre pour la France (comme ça, me disait-il, et aussi parce que . . .) et qui a perdu une jambe en Champagne.

(Examples borrowed from Marouzeau, *Précis de stylistique française*)

3.3.2.6 *The periodic sentence*   The rhetorical concept of the 'periodic sentence' has remained far more alive in French stylistics than in English stylistics. Its use was fairly typical of certain types of writing in Classical French.

In English, a periodic sentence is usually one which builds up to the main idea. Compare the following sentences, the second being the periodic counterpart of the first:

'every candidate holds meetings at which he tells you, all the things he hopes to get done through his Party, if only you will return him to the Commons as your representative'

'so that he can tell you all the things he hopes to get done through his Party, if only you will return him to the Commons as your representative, every candidate holds meetings'

(Example borrowed from Ridout, *English today*, 141)

There are two, rather different, definitions given of the periodic sentence in French. On the one hand it may be defined as a circular complex sentence with the introduction of the main idea at the beginning and its conclusion at the end of the sentence:

Il part puissamment du silence, anime peu à peu, enfle, élève, organise sa phrase, qui parfois s'édifie en voûte, se soutient de prépositions latérales distribuées à merveille autour de l'instant, se déclare et repousse ses incidentes qu'elle surmonte pour toucher enfin à sa clé, et redescendre après des prodiges de subordination et d'équilibre jusqu'au terme certain et à la résolution de ses forces. (Statement made by Valéry about the periodic sentence used by Bossuet; this statement is itself in the form of a periodic sentence, fugue-like in nature; example borrowed from Duprès, *Gradus, les procédés littéraires*, 33)

Another definition of the periodic sentence is based on the fact that the Latin *peri* means 'around' and the Greek *odos* means 'road': the main clause which contains the main idea is both preceded and followed by subordinate clauses.

Quoique ce fussent des choses propres à donner de l'étonnement et à être écoutées avec attention, Mme de Clèves les entendit avec une froideur si grande qu'il semblait qu'elle ne les crût pas véritables ou qu'elles lui fussent indifférentes. (Mme de La Fayette, *La Princess de Clèves*)

Si, au lieu d'avoir remporté dix victoires, tué vingt mille ennemis, ramené deux mille vierges choisies parmi les plus belles, rapporté cent charges de poudre d'or, mille charges de bois d'ébène et de dents d'éléphant, sans compter les productions rares et les animaux inconnus, Pharaon eût vu son armée taillée en pièces, ses chars de guerre renversés et brisés, et se fût sauvé seul de la déroute sous une nuée de flèches, poudreux, sanglant, prenant les rênes des mains de son cocher mort à côté de lui, il n'eût pas eu, certes, un visage plus morne et plus désespéré. (Gautier, *Le Roman de la momie*)

Whatever the definition, such a sentence is syntactically complicated and suited only to literary registers.

Notes

1 Complement of the subject and of the object mean exactly the same as 'attribute' of the subject and of the object. It is a question of choice which term grammarians prefer to use. In French, however, the term *attribut* is used exclusively.
2 Price (*The French language*, 260) makes the following comments on the functions of the first position:

'The first position in a sentence may serve one of two functions:
(a) it may be occupied by an element that serves to link the sentence with what has gone before . . . ("for that reason", "next", "amongst those present"); or
(b) it may be occupied by something unconnected with what has gone before, in which case the element in question is thrown into relief.
The distinction between the two functions may be simply illustrated:
(a) "When I entered the room, John and Peter were sitting at the table; John was reading the paper"; here "John" links the sentence to what has gone before, "was reading the paper" is new information conveyed by the sentence.
(b) "When I entered the room, one of my brothers was reading the paper, and one was writing a letter; John was reading the paper"; here "John" conveys new information (whereas "was reading the paper" links the sentence to the previous one) and so is thrown into relief.'

In French a Gallicism would be used in this second case, namely, *c'est Jean qui lisait le journal*.
3 See Le Bidois, *L'inversion du sujet dans la prose contemporaine (1900 – 1950)*, and Clifford, *Inversion of the subject in French narrative prose from 1500 to the present day*.
4 The joining together of sentences or clauses by juxtaposition, without the use of conjunctions, is called parataxis, as opposed to hypotaxis, which is the joining together of sentences or clauses using conjunctions.

Chapter 19

The marked sentences: imperative, interrogative and exclamative sentences

Although the exclamative sentences figure in this chapter in the same way as the imperative and interrogative sentences, there is a difference between them: the exclamative sentence is often simply a marked variant of the declarative, imperative and interrogative sentence. All of these variants have been grouped together under one heading for reasons of convenience.

1 The imperative sentence

The term 'imperative' applies both to a mood and to the type of sentence this mood is associated with. Most of the points in this section may also feature under the chapter on the imperative mood (see Ch.7).

1.1 Semantic function of the imperative sentence

The imperative sentence can correspond to:

an order: *ferme la porte!*
advice: *fais attention, surtout!*
an apology: *excusez-moi*
an hypothesis: *continue, et tu auras un accident!*

1.2 Different types of imperative sentence

There are two types of imperative sentence:
(i) those which use the imperative mood (see Ch. 7), in which case the subject is not explicitly expressed:

prends une pêche/ prenons une pêche/prenez une pêche

(ii) those which use the subjunctive mood (see Ch. 5), in which case the subject is explicitly expressed; this mood is used for the 3rd person only:

que tout le monde fasse très attention à ce que je vais dire!
vienne le beau temps, et la ville se videra de sa population

(The subjunctive in the second example constitutes a fossilized expression. Its meaning is complex since it stands for both *si le beau temps vient* and *dès que le beau temps viendra*.)

1.3 Position of personal pronouns in the imperative sentence

(See also Ch. 3.)
    The position of the pronoun is dependent upon whether the sentence is positive or negative:

(i) If the sentence is negative the personal pronouns, functioning as complements, follow the same rules as in declarative sentences:

> *tu ne le fais pas/ne le fais pas!*

(ii) If the sentence is positive the personal pronouns, functioning as complements, are placed after the verb and appear in their stressed form:

> *il me regarde/regarde-moi!*
> *il te regarde/regarde-toi!*

If several complements are used the order will be the same as for the declarative sentence, except that the succession of pronouns will appear after the verb:

> *tu le leur envoies/envoie-le leur!*
> *tu lui en donnes/donne-lui-en!*

1.4 Exclamative potential of the imperative sentence

1.4.1 *Exclamative imperative sentences*

The imperative may be written with or without an exclamation mark, the punctuation corresponding to differences in intonation patterns. The difference between the sentences given below is that between the 'softened' order (1) and a straightforward order (2):

(1) *pardonnez-moi de vous déranger* (on entering a room where there are already several people)
(2) *sortez tout de suite d'ici!*

In the first case the intonation pattern used will be similar to that used for a statement i.e. it will include some kind of rise-fall pattern. In the second, the intonation used is the falling intonation normally associated with the imperative. The second sentence clearly has 'exclamative' overtones since the 'imperative concept' is expressed twice.

pardonnez-moi de vous déranger

sortez d'ici tout de suite!

1.4.2 *Reinforcing imperative sentences*

The exclamative nature of an imperative sentence may be reinforced in several ways.
(i) By the use of an emphatic exclamative intonation pattern − in this case a major falling intonation, i.e. one in which the first syllable is at a much higher pitch than for the normal imperative falling intonation. The intervals of pitch between each syllable are also greater. (See 3.2 below.)
(ii) By the addition of the adverbs *donc* and *quand même*:

> *dépêche-toi donc!*
> *dépêche-toi quand même!* (informal style)

(iii) By the addition of the personal pronoun *moi* in informal speech:

> *regarde-moi ça!*

(iv) By the use of a name in apostrophe:
> *Pierre, viens ici!*

1.5 Verbless or nominal imperative sentences

Expressions such as *à la soupe, à table* are imperatives in the sense that they correspond to the explicit constructions *allons à la soupe, allons à table*, or *allez à la soupe, allez à table*.

2 The interrogative sentence

2.1 Direct v. indirect speech: 'yes'/'no' questions v. 'wh-' questions

(i) An interrogative sentence is one which is used to ask direct questions. If the question is not put in a direct manner, it is an indirect question:

> *comment faut-il y aller?* (direct question: interrogative sentence)
> *je me demande comment il faut y aller* (indirect question: the question is contained in the subordinate clause)

Indirect questions are dealt with under subordinate clauses, Ch. 15, 2.5.
(ii) There is a distinction made between 'yes'/'no' questions (which the French call 'total' questions) and 'wh-' questions (which the French call 'partial' questions).
A 'yes'/'no' question is one which calls for either 'yes' or 'no' as an answer:

> *tu y vas maintenant? oui/non*

A 'wh-' question is one which asked for information on an element in the sentence:

> *qui y va? Pierre, Paul, Jeanne . . .*
> *où vas-tu? à Paris, Londres, Tombouctou . . .*
> *quand iras-tu en vacances? la semaine prochaine, . . .*

'Wh-' questions are so called in English because they usually begin with interrogative words starting with those two letters: 'who?', 'which?', 'where?', 'why?'. 'Yes'/'no' questions are examined in 2.2 and 'wh-' questions in 2.3.

2.2 'Yes'/'no' interrogative sentences

A distinction is made between interrogative sentences which are interrogative because of their word-order and those sentences which are interrogative for other reasons.

2.2.1 *Interrogative sentences based on a verb + subject word-order*

(i) Where the subject is a pronoun there is a simple inversion of verb and subject: *tu chantes* becomes *chantes-tu?*
(ii) Where the subject is a noun the order becomes subject + verb + pronoun subject: *ta sœur chante* becomes *ta sœur chante-t-elle?*
     In both cases the intonation pattern normally used is the level/rise pattern, although there are exceptions to this.

2.2.2 *Interrogative sentences retaining the normal subject + verb word-order*

(i) The intonation pattern used is an interrogative pattern, i.e. a level/rise sequence:

tu aimes la télévision?

This interrogative pattern is represented in the written language by a question mark. This kind of interrogative sentence is typical of relatively informal spoken French.
(ii) Est-ce-que is added at the beginning of the sentence:

est-ce que tu aimes / la télévision?

In this case the intonation pattern used is usually, but not always, an interrogative pattern, i.e. a level-rise sequence.

2.2.3 *Answers to 'yes'/'no' questions*

2.2.3.1 *The use of 'oui', 'si' and 'non'*
(i) A positive answer to a positive question is expressed by *oui* (which is a 'pro-sentence'):

   vous en voulez? oui

(ii) A negative answer to a positive question is expressed by *non* (which is a 'pro-sentence'):

   vous en voulez? non

(iii) A positive answer to a negative question is expressed by *si*:

   vous n'en voulez-pas? si

(iv) A negative answer to a negative question is expressed by *non*:

   vous n'en voulez-pas? non

2.2.3.2 *Historical note on the creations of 'oui', 'si' and 'non'*
(i) The word *oui* first came into existence in Old French, Latin having no equivalent. In its first form it was simply *o* from the latin *hoc*, meaning *cela*:

   ferez-vous cela? O je ferai (= *cela je ferai*)

This became shortened to *O je*. Other forms were also used: *o je, o tu, o il, o nous, o vous, o ils*. Since *o il* was the most commonly used it displaced the other forms and became *oil*, which in turn became *oui*.[1] *Si* was also used in combination with other items: *si est, si a, si fait*. These forms were shortened to the present day *si*. *Si* comes from the latin *sic*, meaning 'so' or 'thus'. The same type of development also applied to *non*.
(ii) Non comes from the latin *non* which was a negative adverb. In the seventeenth century a negative sentence could be negated by using *non* instead of the present day *oui mais*:

> Laodice: *Ne parlez pas si haut: s'il est roi, je suis reine;*
>   *Et vers moi tout l'effort de son autorité*
>   *N'agit que par prière et par civilité.*
> Attale: *Non; mais agir ainsi souvent c'est beaucoup dire.*
>   (Corneille, *Nicomède*)

S'il est roi, je suis reine means *il est roi, oui, mais je suis reine*; Attale's *non* also means *oui mais*, but the *non* would be said on a rising tone and not on a falling one in this case (see Brunot and Bruneau, *Précis de grammaire historique de la langue française*, 467). Such a use of *non* is no longer possible in modern French, and sentences such as the one above are likely to give rise to misunderstandings.

2.3 'Wh-' questions

2.3.1 *The interrogative markers*

Since these questions may concern the identity of the subject or the object, or the nature of the circumstances, the markers may be of three types: pronominal (*qui, que, lequel*); adjectival *(quel(le))*; or adverbial (*quand, comment, pourquoi.*)

qui va là?
quelle heure est-il?
pourquoi est-il venu?

These markers are examined under 2.4, 2.5 and 2.6.

2.3.2 *Word-order in 'wh-' interrogative sentences*

(i) The word-order is verb + subject: *qui as-tu vu hier?*
(ii) But this inversion tends to be avoided in the spoken language:
    (a) By the use of *est-ce que*: *qui est-ce que tu as vu hier?* (see 2.4.2.3)
    (b) By replacing the word asked for by its interrogative counterpart: *tu as vu qui hier?* (informal speech)
    (c) By placing the interrogative element at the beginning of the sentence: *qui tu as vu hier?* or *qui t'as vu hier?* (very informal)
    (d) By using ellipsis or interrogative tags, see Ch. 21, 3.2.1.

2.4 The interrogative pronouns

2.4.1 *Morphology*

There are basically two types of interrogative pronoun, the simple and the compound forms. It is even possible to identify a third variety, the complex compound form. All three types are identical in form to the corresponding relative pronouns; but there are important differences between them as regards function (see 2.4.2 below).

(i) The simple forms are:

qui? (subject)	*que?* (object) (cannot be preceded by a preposition)	*quoi?* (object) (not interchangeable with *que* – often preceded by a preposition)

(ii) The compound forms are:

Singular		Plural	
Masculine	Feminine	Masculine	Feminine
lequel? *duquel?* *auquel?*	*laquelle?* *de laquelle?* *à laquelle?*	*lesquels?* *desquels?* *auxquels?*	*lesquelles?* *desquelles?* *auxquelles?*

(iii) The complex compound forms are:

Subject	Direct object
qui est-ce qui? (human) *qu'est-ce qui?* (nonhuman)	*qui est-ce que?* (human) *qu'est-ce que?* (nonhuman)

Qui may also be used with those animals which may be personified.

2.4.2   *Syntactic use of the interrogative pronouns*

2.4.2.1   *The simple forms*
(i) Qui refers only to humans whereas the corresponding relative pronoun is not limited in this way.
Qui may function as:

>   subject: *qui es-tu?*
>   direct object: *qui as-tu vu?*
>   indirect object: *à qui as-tu parlé?*
>   attribute (complement of the subject): *qui est-elle?*

Qui is grammatically singular but may be semantically plural:

>   *nous serons nombreux ce soir*
>   *ah! qui vient?*

If an explicit plural is required a different construction is necessary:

>   *qui sont les gens qui sont là?*

In this example *qui* is the attribute of *les gens*.
(ii) Que refers to inanimates of all kinds and to the mental and physical states of persons:

>   *que voulez-vous? que dit-il?*

Que is the object of the verb. When used with *être* it may function as the attribute or function of the subject:

>   *qu'est-il sans son grade?*

(iii) Quoi is used for inanimates.
    (a) Its normal use is in interrogative sentences which do not contain a verb, or which contain only an infinitive:

>   *quoi de neuf?*
>   *quoi faire? (que faire?* is also found − see below)

    (b) Quoi and *qui* may be contrasted as follows:

>   *je m'appelle Pierre*
>   *Pierre qui?*
>   *Pierre Durand*

but:

>   *c'est la saint quoi?*
>   *c'est la Saint Médard*

In the first example *qui* refers to a person, whereas in the second example *quoi* refers to an abstract concept, that of a feast-day, and not to the Saint that feast-day commemorates. In informal speech, *quoi* could be used in both cases.
    (c) Que may be contrasted with *quoi*. These were originally the unstressed and stressed versions of the same word. They are not interchangeable, however, since *quoi* is restricted in use to the stressed position and *que* to the unstressed.

que dire?	*dire quoi?*
que faire?	*faire quoi?*
que manger?	*manger quoi?*

Sometimes *quoi* is used instead of *que* for emphasis; *quoi faire?* is more emphatic than *que faire?* The use of *quoi* is also more informal.
(d) Quoi is used whenever there is a preposition: *à quoi penses-tu?*

(e) Quoi is also used in fossilized expressions such as *quoi de neuf?* ('what's new' or 'what's the news?'), and *à quoi bon?* ('what good would it do?').

2.4.2.2   *The compound forms*

lequel as-tu pris? (i.e. *quel livre as-tu pris parmi ceux qui étaient là?*)
lequel est venu? (i.e. *quel homme est venu parmi ceux qui auraient pu venir?*)
auquel t'es-tu adressé? (i.e. *à quel homme t'es-tu adressé parmi ceux auxquels tu aurais pu t'adresser?*)

The compound forms may refer either to animates or to inanimates. They mean 'which one' or 'to which one', i.e. they pick out one or several items from a group.

Note that, in the spoken language, the compound forms are sometimes used as interrogative adjectives, although this is not acceptable in prescriptive terms:

prends ton chapeau! ? lequel chapeau?

2.4.2.3   *The complex compound forms*

(i) Those forms based on *est-ce que* used to be used for emphatic questions only; now, however, they are commonly used for any kind of question:

(a) If *qui* is the subject, the first element will be either *qui* or *que*. Where *qui* is human, the first pronoun will be *qui*: *qui est-ce qui vient?* Where *qui* is nonhuman, the first pronoun will be *que*, and the *qui* will be the subject of an impersonal verb: *qu'est-ce qui se passe?*

(b) If *que* is a direct object, the first element will again be either *qui* or *que*, depending on whether *que* represents a human or a nonhuman:

qui est-ce que vous cherchez?
qu'est-ce que vous cherchez?

(c) The same applies if *que* is an attribute:

qui est-ce que c'est?
qu'est-ce que c'est?

(ii) The *qui est-ce qui/qui est-ce que* forms are no longer emphatic, given their constant use in the spoken language. Consequently, a new set of even longer compound forms, *qu'est-ce que c'est qui/ qu'est-ce que c'est que*, has been coined in informal spoken language:

? qui est-ce que c'est que vous cherchez?
? qu'est-ce que c'est que vous cherchez?
? comment est-ce que c'est qu'on joue de cet instrument?
? quand est-ce que c'est que tu dois arriver?

(iii) Apart from these forms a number of alternatives exist in popular spoken language which are also regarded as unacceptable in prescriptive terms and which are regarded as sociolinguistic markers. These are based on *c'est qui?* and *c'est quoi?*, as in:

? c'est qui, qui vient?
? c'est quoi qui se passe?
? c'est qui que vous cherchez?
? c'est quoi que vous cherchez?

The very long forms given in *(ii)* above tend to be shortened to *qui que, quand que, pourquoi que*:

* qui que tu cherches?
* comment qu'on joue de cet instrument?
* quand que tu dois arriver?

These forms of the interrogative will shock a great many people who will regard them as examples of *la langue négligée*. (S. Lamothe prefers to say that they belong to *le musée des horreurs*.)

2.5 The interrogative adjectives

(i) There is just one interrogative adjective, *quel*, which varies for gender and number (*quelle, quels, quelles*). It may be epithetic: *quel journal as-tu acheté?* or it may be an attribute: *quelle sera ta situation dans dix ans?*
(ii) When *quel* functions as an attribute, a choice may exist between *quel* and *que*:

> *quelle sera la situation dans dix ans?*
> *que sera la situation dans dix ans?*

The meaning of these two sentences is roughly identical; the only difference is that the first anticipates an adjectival response (e.g. *la situation sera mauvaise*) whereas the second anticipates a noun (e.g. *ce sera le chaos*).
(iii) A choice can also exist between the use of *quel* and *qu'est-ce que c'est*:

> *quel est ce livre?* ('which one is it?')
> *qu'est-ce que c'est que ce livre?* ('what on earth is this book?')

Here, as can be seen from the translations, there is a great difference of meaning resulting from this change.

2.6 The interrogative adverbs: 'où', 'quand', 'pourquoi', 'comment', 'combien' and 'que' (adverb)

This category also includes the above adverbs in their compound forms:

> *où allez-vous? jusqu' où ira-t-il? d'où vient que tu boites? quand iras-tu? jusqu'à quand peux-tu rester?*

(i) In Classical French *comme* could be used as an alternative to *comment* but only *comment* survives in this function in Modern French.
(ii) *Combien* may be used with or without the gallicism *est-ce que*:

> *combien cela coûte-t-il?* (or *combien ça coûte?* or *ça coûte combien?*)
> combien est-ce que cela (or ça) coûte?

In formal French it is advisable to avoid the use of the gallicism; it is frequently used, however, in spontaneous spoken French.
(iii) *Que* corresponds to the Latin *quid*; in this context its use is now restricted to formal French (*la langue soignée*):

> *que ne me l'avais-tu dit plus tôt?*
> *qu'avait-il besoin d'aller chercher cela?*

but there is a tendency for it to be replaced by *pourquoi*:

> *pourquoi ne me l'avais-tu pas dit plus tôt?*
> *pourquoi était-il allé chercher cela?*

However, it is still commonly used in the fossilized expression *qu'importe?*

> *qu'importe qu'il soit en retard?*
> *que vous importe?* (this would become *qu'est-ce que ça peut vous faire?* in informal speech)

2.7   Possible transformations

2.7.1   *The negative interrogative sentence*

(i) If the word-order is subject + verb, nothing is changed in relation to the corresponding declarative sentence: *Jeanne ne chante pas* becomes *(est-ce que) Jeanne ne chante pas?*
(ii) If the word-order is subject + verb + pronoun subject, the second element of the negation follows the pronoun subject: *Jeanne ne chante pas* becomes *Jeanne ne chante-t-elle pas?*

2.7.2   *The passive interrogative sentence*

(See Ch. 9.)
(i) If the word-order is subject + verb, nothing is changed in relation to the corresponding declarative sentence: *le travail a été bien fait* becomes *(est-ce que) le travail a été bien fait?*
(ii) If the word-order is changed, the pronoun subject appears between the two auxiliaries: *le travail a-t-il été bien fait?*

2.7.3   *The exclamative interrogative sentence*

All interrogative sentences may become exclamative interrogative sentences if the interrogative pattern is exaggerated (see 3.2), and if there is no inversion of subject and verb:

tu y vas?   *tu y vas?*   *tu y vas?*

This is sometimes represented in the written language by a combination of an interrogative and an exclamation mark: *tu y vas?!* Use of repeated punctuation signs in this way is frequently found in cartoon strips (see 3.2.iii).

3   Exclamative sentences

3.1   Semantic function of the exclamative sentence

Exclamative sentences correspond to the expression of strong emotion, be it horror, amazement or delight: *c'est un désastre! c'est incroyable! c'est merveilleux!* They belong essentially to the spoken language (see 3.2 *iii*).

3.2   Exclamative intonation patterns

Intonation is the most important element in an exclamative sentence.
(i) The intonation patterns used in exclamative sentences may have the same pitch contour as the basic declarative, interrogative and imperative intonation patterns, but in a much more exaggerated form. The rising intonation typical of the interrogative intonation pattern rises far more, and there is a bigger pitch interval between the last two syllables:

il y est allé?   *il y est allé!*

The falling intonation typical of the imperative intonation pattern also covers a much greater pitch range — the interval:

n'y vas pas   *n'y vas pas!*

The rise-fall typical of the declarative sentence also covers a much greater pitch interval:

Pierre aime le café   *Pierre aime le café!*

Another alternative is for this pattern to end on a higher note, thus introducing an interrogative element into the sentence due to surprise:

Pierre aime le café?

Whereas in nonexclamative sentences rises and falls are often gradual 'glides' rather than 'steps', in exclamative sentences the speaker proceeds in large steps.

Exaggeration and steps are the key words to exclamative intonation patterns; a further detailed breakdown would take the subject into the field of phonology. It is important to remember, however, that only the most basic exclamative patterns have been described. In particular, no mention is made of stress, although it plays a large part in exclamative sentences.

(ii) Given that a rising intonation, a falling intonation and a rise-fall have different connotations, both in terms of syntax and semantics, the choice of one or the other in their exclamative (i.e. exaggerated) form also has different implications:

(1)   *ce n'est pas possible!*   (2)   *ce n'est pas possible!*

(3)   *ce n'est pas possible!*

In (1) the implications are 'can't you do something about it?' (slight touch of hysteria); in (2) the implications are 'quite definitely nothing can be done about it'; in (3) the implication is one of surprise (see *(i)* above).

There is also an alternative to (1) in terms of implications: the principle in this case is that, given that it is normal to stress the last syllable of the stressed word, one may express extra emphasis by stressing a different one. This applies mainly where the word to be stressed is made up of at least three syllables. Compare:

il fait un froid épouvantable   *il fait un froid épouvantable*

(There is a break in the level-rise pattern in the first case partly to give emphasis to *froid* and partly because of the length of this particular intonation group.)

(iii) As has been indicated, although the three different types of intonation pattern have different implications, all are represented in the written language by the same exclamation mark. This means that in the written language the meaning of the exclamation mark can only be determined by the context. The exclamative sentence is therefore difficult to represent in the written language and is more typical of the spoken language. There is a tendency in written styles such as the comic strip to use more than one exclamation mark to express stronger forms of exclamative sentence, and to use larger print to indicate a louder voice. In an example from *Astérix*, the Roman centurion, speaking of the druid Panoramix, says, *Nous allons torturer le Druide; il parlera!* In the next illustration, the druid is seen tied to a bed undergoing torture and being asked by the centurion, *Tu parles?*, to which the reply is *Tu parles!!!* The various meanings of these sentences would be as follows:

il parlera! 'we'll make him talk'/'then he'll talk . . .'
tu parles? 'Now will you talk!'
tu parles!!! 'not likely!'/'you must be joking!'

(*Parler* is used metaphorically in the third case.)

3.3 Syntax of the exclamative sentence

3.3.1 *Exclamatives based on intonation alone*

For exclamative imperatives and exclamative interrogatives, the syntax remains unchanged (see 1.4 and 2.7.3). Where the exclamative declarative is concerned, there are three possibilities:

(i) The basic sentence may be a complete declarative sentence:

il a fait cela! (*ça* in more informal speech)

(ii) More often, however, the basic sentence is a nominal sentence: (see Ch. 17):

bien joué!
excellent, ce café! (= *ce café est excellent!*)

(iii) In some cases the exclamative corresponds to either a nominal declarative sentence or to an exclamative imperative:

silence! (= meaning either *taisez-vous!* or *je veux le silence*)

Unlike in English, exclamatives cannot be based upon an interrogative verb/subject inversion:

'isn't it a shame!' *quel dommage!*
'was he furious!' *ce qu'il était furieux!* (but *était-il furieux!* used to be the norm, up to the end of the 19th century)

3.3.2 *Exclamatives using exclamative markers*

3.3.2.1 *Exclamative adverbs* The exclamative adverbs are *que, comme, comment, combien* and *qu'est-ce que*.
(i) *Que* refers to quality or quantity, and is frequently used in the spoken language:

que de pluie!
qu'il est grand!

Note that the *que* is often reinforce by *ce* in the spoken language if the sentence includes a verb:

> *? ce qu'il a plu!*
> *? ce qu'il est grand!*

This form is considered incorrect in prescriptive terms.
(ii) Comme refers to intensity and corresponds to *très*:

> *comme cette coupe de cheveux te va bien!* (= *cette coupe te va très bien*)
> *comme c'est cher!* (= *c'est très cher*)

(iii) Combien may either express intensity, in which case it corresponds to *beaucoup*:

> *combien vous avez dû vous amuser!* (= *vous avez dû beaucoup vous amuser*)

or it may refer to quantity, in which case it functions as a pronoun:

> *combien vont souffrir de cette décision!* (= *combien de personnes*)

In this case *combien* is the subject of the verb. But when *combien* determines the object from which it is separated by the subject and verb, the subject may be repeated after the verb, in its pronominal form:

> *combien ce pauvre homme a-t-il fait d'efforts!*

(See Wartburg and Zumthor, *Précis de syntaxe du français contemporain*, 41.) Such a use of *combien* belongs to formal written French only, and is somewhat archaic.
(iv) Comment is rarely used as an exclamative adverb in modern French, except in fossilized expressions such as *Et comment donc! Comment* in expressions such as **et comment que j'irai!* is used to express emphasis the spoken language, but the construction *et comment que* is considered incorrect in prescriptive terms.
(v) Qu'est-ce que is the most commonly used exclamative adverb in spoken French, particularly in informal spoken French. It may be used in all the preceding cases, except in the first (*que de pluie!*) because there is no verb. Its use is however considered incorrect in prescriptive terms and is often considered to be a sociolinguistic marker.

> *? qu'est-ce qu'il a plu!*
> *? qu'est-ce qu'il est grand!*
> *? qu'est-ce que cette coupe de cheveux te va bien!*
> *? qu'est-ce que vous avez dû vous amuser!*

It cannot be used, however, where the exclamative sentence uses an exclamative pronoun (*combien vont souffrir de ces décisions!*). In this example *combien* means *beaucoup de personnes*. To use *qu'est-ce que* it would be necessary to restructure the sentence along these lines:

> *? qu'est-ce qu'il y a comme gens qui vont souffrir de ces décisions!*

A typical example of such a use of *qu'est-ce que* is the following:

> *? qu'est-ce qu'il y a comme chômeurs qui prient le bon Dieu pour pas trouver de travail!* (the *ne* of *ne pas* is also missing in this example)

3.3.2.2   *The interrogative/exclamative adjective 'quel'*
(i) In *quelle horreur!* or *quel homme détestable!* the exclamation refers to the nominal element in the sentence.
(ii) If the noun modified in this fashion is the object of the verb, this will entail a change in the word order:

> *quelle belle maison vous avez!* (= *vous avez une bien belle maison!*)

Note

1 The *oil* form is characteristic of the dialects spoken in the northern parts of France, whereas *oc* (which developped from *hoc ille*) was the form used in the south. The *langue d'oc* and the *langue d'oil* are often contrasted with the *si* languages, i.e. the other romance languages, in which there is no *si/oui* distinction. But German has the same distinction (*ja/doch*).

Chapter 20

Textual organization in written French

0 General considerations

The written language is governed by conventions; the more formal the written language, the more rigidly these conventions will be adhered to. The conventions governing written French and written English are, for the most part, quite similar. There are however some differences which, when not clearly understood, are enough to make a text written in French by an English person seem 'unFrench' − in spite of an absence of actual grammatical or lexical errors.

These conventions are of several types. Some are purely formal − punctuation, the use of capital letters and general layout. Others are in terms of the approach to the organization of the content: French and English paragraphs and texts tend to have slightly different characteristics. It is the ability to reproduce these characteristics when writing in French which will ensure an authentic feel to the finished product.

1 The formal conventions: punctuation and other typographical conventions

1.1 Punctuation

1.1.1 *General considerations*

Punctuation has been described as 'the breathing apparatus of the sentence' and as playing the role of a 'signpost'. Both of these assertions are true. Punctuation serves as a breathing apparatus insofar as it indicates pauses in the flow of speech, e.g. commas in an enumeration; whereas it operates in a signposting capacity insofar as punctuation may serve to indicate inserted material (e.g. a parenthesis) and to indicate the function of a stretch of language (e.g. question and exclamation marks).

Punctuation has therefore a phonological and a grammatical role.

1.1.2 *Punctuation indicating the function of the whole sentence*

1.1.2.1 *Normal types of punctuation, excluding direct speech*
(i) The full stop (*point*) indicates the end of a declarative sentence.
(ii) The question mark (*point d'interrogation*) indicates the end of an interrogative sentence.
(iii) The exclamation mark (*point d'exclamation*) indicates the end of an exclamative sentence (see Ch.19).
(iv) Several full stops (*points de suspension*) indicate that a declarative sentence is unfinished, either grammatically or semantically. As regards intonation they indicate a level-rise intonation sequence, typical of nonfinal rhythmic groups.

1.1.2.2 *Punctuation to indicate direct speech*   There are two distinct circumstances in which direct speech may arise in the written language: in written dialogue (in plays,

novels etc.) and where direct speech is inserted as a quotation in the body of the text. In both cases the punctuation is quite different in English and French (see example text at end of chapter).

These differences can be dealt with under the following heads.

(i) Dialogue: indicating a change of speaker:

There are two different conventions, depending on whether the work is a novel or a play. In the novel a dash will be used to indicate a change of speaker:

> *Il faut bien dire tout de suite que Sonia a une façon de prendre les médecins qui ne leur convient pas toujours. Tandis que celui-là m'auscultait ne voilà-t-il pas qu'elle risque:*
> *– Dis donc au docteur ce qu'il a pris, Robert, qui lui a fait tant de bien. . . . Ah! oui, de l'Agrippine 52. . . . Tu te rappelles? Vous voyez ça docteur?*
> *– Une minute, mon petit, dit le médecin.*
> (Daninos, *Tout Sonia*)

In a play, the layout is usually quite different. The French tend to write the name of the speaker in the middle of the page with his dialogue set out below. The dash is not used:

PANISSE

Allons, Elzéar, pose-moi des questions.

ELZEAR, <small>solennel</small>.

Honoré, toute confession est grave. C'est pourquoi il convient de donner à cette cérémonie amicale, un caractère de solennité.

<small>Un peu de temps. Panisse rit.</small>

PANISSE

Tu veux que je mette un chapeau melon?

ELZEAR, <small>brutalement</small>.

Je veux que tu cesses de plaisanter.

(Pagnol, *César*)

(ii) The use of *guillemets* or quotation marks in dialogue:

Whereas in English there is a very necessary and very liberal use of quotation marks, in the form of inverted single and double commas above the writing line, the French position seems both less definite and more sparing.

Thus in the example cited under *(i)* above (Daninos, *Tout Sonia*) no *guillemets* are used at all to introduce the dialogue. In contrast to this other books use the *guillemets*:

> *Quand la porte s'ouvrit et que la maigre lumière découpa la silhouette de Fanchon sur le seuil, Vincent s'approcha d'un air gauche.*
> *« Où allez-vous donc, Fanchon?*
> *– Donner de la paille aux vaches.*
> *– Je peux vous aider?*
> *– Ce n'est pas de refus, Vincent. »*
> (Marseille, *Une famille de paysans du moyen-âge à nos jours*)

Here the passage of dialogue is opened and closed by *guillemets*.

Where *guillemets* are used to introduce dialogue, and where a passage of direct speech continues for more than one paragraph, the *guillemets* will be used to open and close each paragraph even where there is no change of speaker (see extract A at end of chapter).

The use of the *guillemets* in this way would seem to indicate a more formal approach to punctuation.

(iii) Inserting a dialogue quote:

(a) The French use the *guillemets* – the equivalent of quotation marks. Whereas in English the quotation marks are placed above the writing line, in French they are on

the line. Also, they are different in shape from the English quotation mark which is shaped like a comma: in French they are either semicircular: ((. . .)) or triangular: « . . . ».

In keeping with the rather variable approach general in this area, it is possible to find exceptions to this rule in certain cases. Thus there are examples where the publishers will use the English style of quotation marks for inserting a dialogue quotation:

> « *Passa un gros monsieur qui avait un chapeau brodé, avec un manteau rouge, un habit rouge, des culottes rouges, des bas et des souliers rouges, monté sur une grosse jument noire comme de l'encre. Le monsieur dit à la petite fille: "Qu'est-ce que tu as donc à pleurer, la petite? – Hélas! monsieur! j'ai perdu ma marraine qui me nourrissait."* » (Marseille, *Une famille de paysans du moyen-âge à nos jours* . . .)

(b) Single and double inverted commas:
In English it is possible to use single and double inverted commas as quotation marks; in French there is no equivalent to the single inverted comma, e.g.

> 'I heard "Keep out" being shouted,' he explained (Quirk *et al.*, *A University Grammar of English*, 460)

becomes in French:

> – *Je l'ai entendu qui criait: « Recule-toi », m'expliqua-t-il.*

In French a colon is necessary to introduce the quotation.

In French, punctuation indicating the end of a sentence between quotation marks usually precedes the closing quotation mark:

> « *Tout ce que vous dites, s'exclama-t-il, est exact.* »

Note: The French use the *guillemet* in cases where the English would use the single inverted comma to emphasize a particular word or phrase, usually because it belongs to a different register or dialect or even to a different language:

> *Il s'agit d'un appartement* « *grand standing* »

But double inverted commas are also used – see example in *(iii)* above.

1.1.3 *Punctuation within the sentence*

1.1.3.1 *Punctuation indicating syntactic structure of the sentence*
(i) The full stop is used to indicate an abbreviation as in *P.T.T.* (*Postes, Téléphone et Télégraphe*) or the shortening of a word, as in *l'apéro.* for *l'apéritif.* If an abbreviation such as *U.N.E.S.C.O.* becomes much used in the language it may become a word in its own right. In this case the way of writing it will change from the one given above to *UNESCO* and even to *Unesco*. All three ways of writing such terms are used in newspapers and books. The extreme form of development will only be possible where the 'word' produced is pronounceable. Thus *P.T.T.* can only develop into *PTT*, it cannot become a full word such as *Unesco*.

A similar development can be seen in English, e.g. 'N.A.L.G.O.' becomes 'NALGO', then 'Nalgo'.

(ii) There are important differences between French and English as regards the use of the comma (see Ch. 16). It can be used in French in the following ways:

(a) To separate the elements in an enumeration, as in English. In such a case *et/ ou/ ni* may not be preceded by a comma if they are linking what immediately precedes them with what immediately follows (see Ch. 16, 3).

(b) It is used to separate adverbial phrases or clauses from the rest of the sentence, when they appear in first position in the sentence:

hier, il a fait particulièrement froid
quand vous serez parti, alors je rangerai

(c) It is used in disjunctive constructions, the word before the comma being in an emphatic or stressed position:

un coureur épuisé s'écroule (*épuisé* restricts the meaning of *coureur*)
un coureur, épuisé, s'écroule (= *parce qu'il était épuisé*) (in this case *épuisé* is nonrestrictive; one could also write *un coureur s'écroule, épuisé*).
les soldats marchaient sans se plaindre (manner)
les soldats marchaient, sans se plaindre (= *et/mais ils ne se plaignaient pas*) (in this case the second element is as important as the first)

(d) It may be used to indicate that what follows does not modify what precedes:

la statue représente Charlemagne sur son cheval, tenant une épée à la main

Here the comma indicates that it is Charlemagne, and not the horse, holding the sword.

(e) The comma is used in a completely different way from in English where numbers are concerned, e.g. 'twelve thousand pounds' is written '£12,000' in English, but *12.000 livres* in French.

The English comma corresponds to the full stop in French. On the other hand, the decimal full stop in English corresponds to a comma in French: 'three and a half' is written '3.5' in English, but *3,5* in French.

(f) A pair of commas may serve to indicate insertions. These may be of the *dit-il* or the 'vocative' type:

pourquoi, dit-il, n'êtes-vous pas venus?
veuillez agréer, Monsieur, l'expression de mes sentiments distingués

(iii) The semicolon indicates a pause which is shorter than the full stop. It indicates the syntactic completeness of the sentence which it terminates, but stresses the semantic ties of that sentence with what follows:

Les livres ont été mes oiseaux et mes nids, mes bêtes domestiques, mon blé et ma compagne; la bibliothèque, c'était le monde pris dans un miroir; elle en avait l'épaisseur infinie, la variété, l'imprévisibilité. (Sartre, *Les mots*, cited in Grunewald and Mitterand, *Itinéraire grammatical*)

The semicolon is frequently used within a complex sentence where the two subjects are different:

cette lettre doit partir immédiatement; tout retard serait fâcheux

Note that this makes it a particularly useful punctuation mark when translating from English into French. It sometimes happens that the fairly flexible English syntax cannot be rendered directly into French: the semicolon enables the translator to end up with two syntactical sentences whilst making it clear that semantically they are but one. Thus

'De Efteling is the only picture-book in the world that you can walk through. You can see, hear, and even touch the fabulous tales.' (direct translation from Dutch in a tourist guide)

becomes:

De Efteling est le seul livre d'images que vous puissiez parcourir à pied. Vous pouvez y voir et entendre les merveilleux personnages des contes; vous pouvez même les toucher.

Similarly, in another guide book:

'There is a mild climate here with frequent rainfall and in winter the hills over 1000m attract many skiers.'

becomes:

De climat tempéré, la Forêt-Noire est riche en précipitations atmosphériques; au-dessus de 1000m, elle est devenue une région de sports d'hiver particulièrement fréquentée.

In this last case, a word-for-word translation would be possible, but the 'and' link is felt to be illogical in French, coordinating as it does two items which do not go together from a semantic point of view, i.e. 'mild climate' and 'many skiers' — hence the use of the semicolon instead of 'and'.

(iv) The colon is used to link two sentences which are related to one another logically:

Je me lançai dans d'incroyables aventures: il me fallait grimper sur les chaises, sur les tables, au risque de provoquer des avalanches qui m'eussent enseveli. (Sartre, *Les mots*).

The logical link may be one of cause and consequence (as in the above example), one of opposition or one of coordination. The colon is useful in that it can express all of these types of link simultaneously, since none of them is made explicit. (This is called parataxis.)

   The colon can also be used to introduce a quote (see 1.1.2.2 *iii*); it may also introduce an enumeration (see example in 1.1.3.2. *i* below).

(v) The comma-dash combination is used to indicate a slightly lengthier pause than the comma: *j'irai, — parce que j'en ai décidé ainsi*. By indicating a longer pause, the second element is emphasized.

1.1.3.2 *Punctuation indicating inserted material: parentheses, square brackets, dashes*[1]

(i) In the case of parentheses or round brackets (*parenthèses*), the inserted material does not represent information essential to the message. The inserted material is said on a different intonation pattern, normally fall-rise, and on a lower tone:

Le ciel grouille de choses passionnantes à observer: Saturne (on ne sait pas à quoi sert son anneau), la végétation de Mars (qui change de couleur avec les tempêtes de poussière et de sable), les cratères de la Lune, les galaxies lointaines (habitées), etc. (Paris-Match)

(ii) Square brackets (*crochets*) are basically the same as parentheses, but used less frequently. They are usually used to bracket information which already includes a parenthetical element, e.g. [*cf. Le Bon usage, M. Grevisse (1969)*].

   The main use of the square bracket, as in English, is in mathematical formulae.

(iii) Dashes (*tirets*) are also used to indicate inserted material (for the use of dashes in dialogue see 1.1.2.2 above). They resemble parentheses except that the inserted material is no longer felt to be nonessential:

Tout autant ou plus encore que la réponse à son problème, la lectrice attend une marque d'intérêt de son journal. Bien souvent elle pourrait fort bien donner son adresse; mais la récompense est de se voir répondre dans le journal. Car si l'anonymat que permet de garder le courrier est la raison même de son extra-ordinaire fortune — l'anonymat invitant à la confession — il faut y ajouter le trouble plaisir de 'se-voir-imprimé-dans-le journal' sous un pseudonyme: sentiment de participer au journal, de sortir, grâce à lui, de la masse et de la solitude. (E. Sullerot, *Le courrier de cœur: La presse féminine*)

In this example the element between the dashes is relevant since it gives an explanation, but it has to be separated from the rest of the sentence since it interrupts its syntactic and semantic development. The intonation pattern used will be a fall-rise sequence.

It is also possible to replace a full stop by a dash, and add the extra material which will be followed by a full stop:

> *le père Desbois commençait à avoir des cheveux blancs, oh! quelques uns à peine − mais c'était une indication*

In this example the inserted material is essential and is indeed emphasized by the construction.

1.1.4 *Historical comment*

Punctuation is a relatively recent development in the art of writing. There was, for example, no punctuation in Classical Greek. It was invented by one Aristophanes in Byzantium in the second century BC. He used three full stops: one above the line, one on the line and one below. The one above the line corresponded to our full stop, the one on the line to our semicolon, and the third to our colon. In Latin inscriptions a full stop is often used simply to separate the different words.

Punctuation, as we know it, started to be used around the ninth century. By the sixteenth century the comma, full stop, colon and question mark were all in use. The hyphen and the double inverted commas were added, followed in the seventeenth century by the semicolon and the exclamation mark. Dashes and brackets date from the nineteenth century only. (See Grevisse, *Le Bon usage*).

1.2 Typographical conventions

1.2.1 *The hyphen or 'trait d'union'*

(i) The hyphen serves to link several words in a compound expression: see example in 1.1.3.2 *iii*: − *le trouble plaisir de 'se-voir-imprimé-dans-le journal'*.

Hyphens have the effect of binding together all the elements of the construction to make them into one single indivisible concept (i.e. the new concept is synthetic instead of analytic).

(ii) The hyphen also has a key role to play in the layout of material. When a hyphen is used at the end of a line, it indicates that part of the word will be on the next line. English and French differ in this respect in that French only allows for syllabic division, whereas English allows for both syllabic and morphological division. Compare English 'struc-ture', 'repu-tation/reputa-tion' (syllabic) but 'answer-ed' and 'sing-ing' (morphological); and French *struc-ture, répu-tation/réputa-tion, répon-dait* but not **répond-ait, chan-tant* but not **chant-ant*.

1.2.2 *Typography*

A different type (italic or the heavier type of bold/extra-bold) may be used to emphasize a word or expression. French editors are rather fonder than their English counterparts of indulging in a great variety of type and size. This is true mainly of nonfictional works, particularly educational books, and is due to the need to emphasize the 'plan' followed by the author (see 2.3.4 below).

1.2.3   *Capital letters*

1.2.3.1   *General use of capital letters*   Capital letters are used in two ways. They are used to indicate that the word which starts with a capital is the first word in a sentence; and they are used to give a special significance to a word, indicating that it belongs to a particular category. It is in this second use that differences exist between English and French.

Words starting with a capital letter, whatever their position in the sentence, normally refer to something which is either unique or different from others in some way: the name of a person (*Mme Dupont*), the name of a people (*les Belges*, *un Belge*), the name of a place (*la France*) or of a company (*Peugeot-Citroën*). These do not present problems for English speakers.

Problems do occur, however, when more than one word is being used to refer to an institution or a title; although there are no hard-and-fast rules in this area, there are preferences and these seem to be changing, with France (but not Quebec) realigning itself on Anglo-American lines.

1.2.3.2   *Traditional preferences*
(i) A capital letter is usually used for the first word only in French: *la Fédération des médecins spécialistes de Québec*, but 'the Federation of Medical Specialists of Quebec'; *l'Office franco-québécois pour la jeunesse*, but 'the Franco-Québécois Office for Youth'.
(ii) There are exceptions to the rule that only the first word has a capital letter:

L'Ecole polytechnique (any such school)
L'Ecole Polytechnique (the famous one in Paris)
L'Organisation mondiale de la santé, but
L'Organisation des Nations unies

In other words, a second capital may be used if the modifying term also refers to a unique concept.
(iii) Sometimes it is not the first word which starts with a capital letter: *l'observatoire de Greenwich*; *l'université Jean Moulin*; *le laboratoire Pasteur*.
The following should also be contrasted:

le Président du conseil d'administration
le président du conseil, Jean Dupont

M. le Ministre sera là
M. Dupont, le ministre de l'agriculture, sera là

If the title alone is used it will normally be written with a capital letter; but, if the name of the person is included, it will not. Generally speaking, fewer capitals are used in French than in English, e.g.

'a French man' =   *un homme français*, but
                      un Français

(Contrary to English usage, adjectives referring to nationality are not usually written in French with a capital letter, e.g. *un étudiant français*, as against *un jeune Français*; *un Canadien français* follows the same rule since in this case *Canadien* is a noun and *français* is an adjective. When referring to the name of a language, the same rule is supposed to apply, i.e. one should write *le français*, *l'anglais* as in *je parle français*, but nowadays more and more people seem to be using capitals in this case).

1.2.3.3   *New preferences*   There is a tendency in France today to follow the Anglo-American custom of using capitals for all nouns, hence *l'Organisation Mondiale de la Santé*, instead of *l'Organisation mondiale de la santé* (see 1.2.3.2).

2   Semantic and grammatical characteristics of texts

A text is made up of sentences which are grouped into larger units – paragraphs; these may be regrouped under one or more headings or form one or more parts. This section will first of all consider the paragraph (2.1), then some of the differences between French and English paragraphs (2.2), and finally textual organisation (2.3).

2.1   The paragraph

2.1.1   *Definition of the paragraph*

A paragraph is a set of sentences which are linked to one another both semantically and grammatically. When a paragraph comes to an end, the writer switches to a new line of writing which is often indented. Thus paragraphs are separated by at least part of a blank line on a page.

An *alinéa* – a term and concept more typical of French than English – is a paragraph which is very short, often no more than one sentence.

2.1.2   *Semantic unity of the paragraph*

(i) The simplest form of paragraph corresponds to one idea. This idea may be expressed in a variety of ways. The most usual way in French is for the basic idea to appear in the first sentence and then to be developed in the rest of the paragraph (see examples in *(ii)* below). But it is also possible for the main idea to derive by implication from the juxtaposition of sentences expressing apparently quite different meanings:

> *L'avant-veille de ma naissance, l'équipe de la Teste vainquit celle de Gujan, en un match de rugby amical. Sur les huit blessés qu'il fallut transporter d'urgence à l'hôpital d'Arcachon, cinq étaient le fait de mon père.* (example borrowed from Cocula and Peyroutet, *Didactique de l'expression,* Delagrave, *1978*)

What is important in this extract is not the actual description of the match but what may be inferred from this description: the implications in this case are that the father of the author was not very interested either in his son's imminent birth or in his wife's welfare at the time; he also seems to have had a very violent nature. In other words he is indirectly described as being both irresponsible and insensitive. In this case what is important is expressed through connotation.

(ii) A distinction must be made between 'tight' and 'loose' paragraphs.

A tight paragraph is one in which every sentence is relevant to the subject, which demands rigid selectivity. The first sentence will contain the topic, the second will derive from the first, the third from the second and so on. In this case relevance, order and inclusion are the keywords to the organization of the paragraph. As such, it is carefully planned in a formal manner. Administrative texts fall into this category, as do scientific texts and most other 'formal' texts.

A loose paragraph is one in which the topic is more diffuse. The subject is the centre around which the paragraph evolves. In the following example, taken from *Tout Sonia* by Daninos, the first paragraph is an example of a tight paragraph (this paragraph is also argumentative – see 2.3.4) whereas the second is a loose paragraph:

> *Quant à mon incapacité technique, je m'en console en me disant que si je savais exactement ce qu'est un moteur, ce qui se passe dans une tête de bielle ou dans une tige de soupape, comment l'essence se transforme en gaz, et l'huile en rien, je ferais perdre beaucoup d'argent à une foule de braves (ou pas) garagistes qui vivent de mon ignorance. Mais puisque ma carence dans la technique de l'automobile est patente, pourquoi faut-il que ces spécialistes me regardent avec un dédain mêlé de pitié?*

> *Il paraît que l'enfance de l'art pour un automobiliste, c'est de savoir déboucher le gicleur. Il faut croire que je ne suis pas un enfant de l'art. Je trouve simplement stupide, et tout à fait indigne de notre époque, que l'on n'ait encore rien trouvé pour empêcher que s'obstrue le trou minuscule de cet appareil. N'ayant jamais pu démonter un carburateur sans en égarer sur-le-champ la moitié, je préfère depuis longtemps le laisser tel qu'il est: bouché mais entier. D'ailleurs, je ne possède jamais la clef qui convient. J'ai renoncé à la chercher. Je préfère avoir le complexe du gicleur. Quand je suis en panne à travers la campagne, je fais une petite prière pour que ce soit tout, sauf le gicleur. De façon à ne pas m'entendre dire par la première personne qui me dépannera (vous savez, le premier garagiste sur la droite, après avoir monté la troisième côte):*
> *– C'était pourtant simple . . . il suffisait de déboucher votre gicleur!*

(iii) In French transitions between paragraphs are *de rigueur*. These are usually achieved by allowing for an overlap of material between the end of one paragraph and the beginning of the next.

The transition in the example in *(ii)* above is the phrase *l'art pour un automobiliste*, which overlaps with *la technique de l'automobile* in the previous paragraph.

2.1.3   *Formal linking of sentences in paragraphs*

Sentences must be bound together to ensure cohesion. This may be achieved in a number of ways.

(i) It is possible to refer to some other sentence within the paragraph, thus creating a tie with it. This reference can be made by:

(a) the use of certain pronouns;

(b) the use of certain determiners.

These will indicate that the noun determined has already been defined: *la table / sa table / cette table*; they may also create contextual synonyms:[2]

> *L'administration centrale est représentée par les ministères qui, chacun dans un domaine particulier, ont une compétence qui s'étend à l'ensemble du territoire. Ces administrations ont pour rôle de donner aux ministres des avis techniques. . . .* (*L'Organisation administrative* (government booklet) in this case *ces administrations* is a contextual synonym for *Les ministères*.)

Reference is normally anaphoric, i.e. backwards. Although both languages use the same anaphoric referents, there are many differences in their use; and English students of French make many mistakes in the use of both personal and demonstrative pronouns and articles at the level of the paragraph (see Ch. 3).

(ii) Intersentence reference can be by means of an elliptical construction, i.e. the omission of items indispensable to the meaning of one sentence, those items being retrievable from other sentences. The retrieval of those items then acts to link the sentences. Ellipsis of a noun is possible in French with certain words expressing quantity (*un/ plusieurs/ beaucoup*); ellipsis of the object is possible with certain verbs (*vous ne comprenez pas? je vais vous expliquer*, i.e. *ce que vous ne comprenez pas*). On the whole, however, this process is rarely used in French. It is, however, frequently employed in English, and French texts written by English students are often rendered unacceptable by being syntactically elliptical.

An example of this is to be found in 1.1.3.1*iii* in the third example: *De Efteling est le seul livre d'images que vous puissiez parcourir à pied. Vous pouvez y voir et entendre. . . .* The French text contains an *y* not paralleled in the English text (nor indeed in the original Dutch text). (In the following example in that section, 'here' is translated by *la Forêt-Noire*; this is not a problem of ellipsis, but of differing referential elements.)

(iii) Some coordinating conjunctions and many adverbs are used as links between sentences. Differences between the use of these items in English and French will be found in Ch. 16.

(iv) Tense sequences and time adverbs act as cohesive forces. Thus an inaccurate use of tense will cause a whole paragraph to collapse into meaninglessness. This can present problems, since the French tense system does not correspond with the English one (see Part II).

2.2 Differences between French and English paragraphs

(i) In terms of paragraph structure, the French favour tight paragraphs in a formal context. The planning of the paragraph tends to be very rigid in terms of order, relevance and inclusiveness of the material included (but see 2.3.4).

(ii) In terms of length, French paragraphs are often shorter than English paragraphs, certainly in nonfiction. Unlike the English, the French do not hesitate to write paragraphs of no more than a couple of sentences, sometimes even one. This tends to be characteristic of journalism and it can be taken too far:

> *Aujourd'hui, sous l'influence du journalisme, on tend à abuser de l'alinéa et à diviser le paragraphe. Ne cédez pas trop souvent à cette tentation.*
> *Evitez, en tout cas, l'excès de zèle très pénible pour le correcteur qui consiste à aller à la ligne à chaque phrase. La copie du candidat qui va sans cesse à la ligne est aussi pénible à corriger que celle du candidat qui n'y va jamais.* (Desalmand and Tort, *Du Plan à la dissertation,* Hatier, 1977)

Here the authors are guilty of the very crime against which they are warning the reader: there is no good reason to justify making these three sentences into two paragraphs instead of one.

An examination of translations from French into English, including even scientific articles, will further reveal that the number of paragraphs has been greatly reduced in the English version. The English tend to regard the French multiplicity of paragraphs as being 'bitty'; the French feel that, by clearly isolating the parts which make up the whole, they are making the complete work more understandable; (for an example of this see extract A at the end of this chapter, where seven paragraphs of French become one paragraph of English).

2.3 Textual organization

2.3.1 *General considerations*

In both the spoken and the written language there is the constant need to select from alternatives both in terms of vocabulary and grammar. These choices are made mainly on the basis of register (2.3.2) and on the function of the text being written (2.3.3) or of the stretch of language (see Ch. 21).

French textual organization differs quite dramatically from that of English. This is largely due to the French tendency to follow the rules laid down by rhetoric governing writing *plans*. These rules were originally applicable to certain kinds of text only, but have come to be generally applied (2.3.4).

2.3.2 *The importance of register*

(i) The term 'register' is used to refer to a variety of language defined in terms of subject matter, medium (e.g. printed material, handwritten letter, message on tape) and the level of formality (e.g. formal, casual, intimate, off-hand). Register affects many choices in grammar, an example being the use or nonuse of the subjunctive, e.g.

je ne pense pas qu'il vienne and *je ne pense pas qu'il viendra* (generally acceptable in spoken language but see Ch. 5 for further details).

Other examples are the use or nonuse of the past tenses of the subjunctive (depending on degree of formality and whether the text is literary or not); and the use or nonuse of the past historic. Many constructions in other sections preceded by an asterisk or question mark are limited in terms of the registers in which they may be used. They are possible in informal spoken French but not so easily in the written language which is, by definition, more bound by conventions.

2.3.3   *Different types of text*

(i) Texts may vary according to their social function and their length. There is a tendency for there to be corresponding identifiable linguistic characteristics. Thus advertisements tend to use nominal sentences and elliptical constructions, whereas the objectivity of abstracts and reports tends to be reflected in the use of the impersonal forms. Newspapers use the General system of verb tenses (see Ch. 4) since they deal with the 'news', whereas books, depending upon whether they are fiction or non-fiction will have prose which is in turn narrative, descriptive, argumentative or in the form of dialogue, each one of these prose types being characterized by the use of certain tenses, pronouns and types of construction. The study of most of these choices has been covered under the relevant section headings but only in an *ad hoc* manner, since the systematic study of the linguistic characteristics of prose types properly belongs to general stylistics rather than to grammar. See extract B at the end of this chapter.

(ii) It is only the textual organization of argumentative prose which differs in the two languages; however, since argumentative prose is not restricted in use to argumentative texts alone, there tend to be more general divergences in textual organization between French and English (see 2.3.4 below).

(iii) Poetry has so far not been mentioned since it is a very specialized form of writing. It is based on the principle of patterning: phonological, lexical and syntactical patterning is characteristic of poetry. A study of these patterns belongs properly to poetics or stylistics.

2.3.4   *The organization of argumentative prose in French*

The differences are largely due to the greater influence of the Rhetorical Tradition[3] in France. In England the teaching of the subject ceased in the eighteenth century, whereas it continued to be taught as a subject until the end of the nineteenth century in France, where it remains indirectly in the teaching syllabus today in the form of *la dissertation* and *la contraction de texte*.

Larousse defines *la dissertation* as follows:

> *Examen détaillé sur quelque question scientifique, historique, artistique, etc. Exercice littéraire, en latin ou en français, sur un sujet donné.*

Nowadays this exercise is restricted to French, and the subjects for which it is used have been updated. The method, however, remains the same: a specific form of plan is required;[4] all points raised must be illustrated by examples (*un gramme de concret vaut mieux qu'une tonne de généralités*[5]); the arguments must be set forth in the clearest manner possible:

> *Une bonne dissertation est l'expression d'une réponse personnelle à un problème donné, formulée avec rigueur et clarté, et se référant constamment au réel.*
> (Desalmand and Tort, *Du Plan à la dissertation*)

Such principles are enshrined in the *Instructions officielles* which establish what is required of candidates doing such an exercise for an examination. *Dissertations* are required not only for the *Baccalauréat* but for most *concours*, the competitive examinations sat by all people aspiring to enter the civil service, banking or indeed any organization of any size, at whatever level. Innumerable books exist on the subject. *La contraction de texte* (précis writing) is another major exercise in the curriculum at all levels:

> *De plus en plus pratiquée, surtout dans l'enseignement court . . . et aux concours d'entrée aux grandes écoles, cet exercice implique les aptitudes intellectuelles suivantes: aptitude à la compréhension; aptitude à la hiérarchisation; aptitude au choix des idées essentielles; aptitude à l'analyse et à la synthèse; aptitude à la « traduction ».* (Cocula and Peyroutet, *Didactique de l'expression*)

This constant effort to break down and classify material and to present it in an agreed acceptable format has left its imprint on French writing. (See example 4 in extract B, at the end of this chapter.) It is this factor for example which distinguishes editorials in the quality English press from those of *Le Monde*.

Extract A (See 2.2 above.)

Il se penche un peu vers moi pour me dominer mieux. Il a l'air de me dire: « Mon gaillard, si tu penses pouvoir m'échapper, tu te trompes. On ne voit pas que mes mains sont des serres, mais leurs griffes qui vont te déchiqueter sont bien en place dans mon âme. Et si je suis redouté par tous les avocats, et coté dans la magistrature comme un avocat général dangereux, c'est parce que jamais je ne laisse échapper ma proie.

« Je n'ai pas à savoir si tu es coupable ou innocent, je dois user seulement de tout ce qu'il y a contre toi: ta vie de bohème à Montmartre, les témoignages provoqués par la police et les déclarations des policiers eux-mêmes. Avec ce fatras dégoûtant accumulé par le juge d'instruction, je dois arriver à te rendre suffisamment repoussant pour que les jurés te fassent disparaître de la société. »

Il me semble que, très clairement, je l'entends réellement me parler, à moins que je ne rêve, car je suis vraiment impressionné par ce « mangeur d'hommes » :

« Laisse-toi faire, accusé, surtout n'essaie pas de te défendre: je te conduirai sur le « chemin de la pourriture ».

« Et j'espère que tu ne crois pas aux jurés? Ne t'illusionne pas. Ces douze hommes ne savent rien de la vie.

« Regarde-les, alignés en face de toi. Tu les vois bien, ces douze fromages importés à Paris d'un lointain patelin de province? Ce sont des petits-bourgeois, des retraités, des commerçants. Pas la peine de te les dépeindre. Tu n'as tout de même pas la prétention qu'ils les comprennent, eux, tes vingt-cinq ans et la vie que tu mènes à Montmartre? Pour eux, Pigalle et la place Blanche, c'est l'Enfer, et tous les gens qui vivent la nuit sont des ennemis de la société. Tous sont excessivement fiers d'être jurés aux Assises de la Seine. De plus ils souffrent, je te l'assure, de leur position de petits-bourgeois étriqués.

« Et toi, tu arrives, jeune et beau. Tu penses bien que je ne vais pas me gêner pour te dépeindre comme un don juan des nuits de Montmartre. Ainsi, au départ, je ferai de ces jurés tes ennemis. Tu es trop bien vêtu, tu aurais dû venir humblement habillé. Là, tu as commis une grande faute de tactique. Tu ne vois pas qu'ils envient ton costume? Eux, ils s'habillent à la Samaritaine et n'ont jamais, même en rêve, été habillés par un tailleur. »

(Charrière, *Papillon*)

He leant over a little so as to dominate me all the more, and he looked as though he were saying, 'If you think you can get away from me, young cock, you've got it wrong. My hands may not look like talons, but there are claws in my heart that are going to rip you to pieces. And the reason why all the barristers are afraid of me, the reason why the judges think the world of me as a dangerous prosecutor, is that I never let my prey escape. It's nothing to do with me whether you're guilty or innocent: all I'm here for is to make use of everything that can be said against you – your disreputable, shiftless life in Montmartre, the evidence the police have worked up and the statements of the police themselves. What I am to do is to take hold of all the disgusting filth piled up by the investigating magistrate and manage to make you look so revolting that the jury will see that you vanish from the community.' Either I was dreaming or I could hear him perfectly distinctly: this man-eater really shook me. 'Prisoner at the bar, just you keep quiet, and above all don't you attempt to defend yourself. I'll send you down the drain, all right. And I trust you've no faith in the jury? Don't you kid yourself. Those twelve men know nothing whatsoever about life. Look at them, lined up there opposite you. Twelve bastards brought up to Paris from some perishing village in the country: can you see them clearly? Small shopkeepers, pensioners, tradesmen. It's not worth describing them to you in detail. Surely you don't expect *them* to understand the life you lead in Montmartre or what it's like to be twenty-five? As far as they're concerned Pigalle and the Place Blanche are exactly the same as hell and all night-birds are the natural enemies of society. They are all unspeakably proud of being jurymen at the Seine Assizes. And what's more, I can tell you that they loathe their status – they loathe belonging to the pinched, dreary lower middle class. And now you make your appearance here, all young and handsome. Do you really suppose for a moment that I'm not going to make them see you as a night-prowling Montmartre Don Juan? That will put them dead against you right away. You're too well dressed: you ought to have come in something very modest indeed. That was a huge tactical error of yours. Can't you see how jealous of your suit they are? They all buy their clothes off the peg – they've never even dreamt of having a suit made to measure by a tailor.'

(Translated by P.O'Brian)

Extract B: Different types of texts (See 2.3. above.)

(1) This extract is descriptive: the tenses are in the imperfect, which is the ideal tense for describing actions or states which are simultaneous.

Lorsque la ville de Grenoble n'était *encore qu'une toute petite agglomération, des lavoirs* s'élevaient, *au-delà de la porte de Bonne, dans un quartier d'appellation curieuse: le quartier de la femme sans tête . . . Les laveuses, leur travail accompli,* étendaient *leur linge sur l'herbe rase des terrains vagues. Après quoi, le crépuscule venu, elles se* hâtaient *de retourner vers leurs demeures, craignant de rencontrer les monstres qui, la nuit tombée,* hantaient *cet endroit dangereux.*

Ces monstres redoutés étaient *des serpents ailés, à tête lumineuse et comme couronnée d'un diadème de pierreries. Ils* arrivaient *en volant sur le bord des lavoirs et, afin de pouvoir se désaltérer,* déposaient *à côté d'eux la pierre précieuse d'une valeur fabuleuse qu'ils* portaient *dans leur gueule entrouverte.*

(Rivière-Sestier, *Au Fil de l'alpe*)

(2) This extract is narrative: the main tense is the past historic, which describes actions or states in their chronological succession; this tense is typical of the narrative style.

Un garçon eut *un jour l'idée ingénieuse, afin de dérober une de ces gemmes, de se cacher sous un cuveau renversé. Il* observa *l'arrivée de l'animal en regardant à travers l'ouverture creusée dans l'une des douves de cette sorte de tonneau. Soulevant prestement le cuveau pendant que le serpent se désaltérait, il* s'empara *de la pierre précieuse. Ceci fait, il* se referma *dans son abri. Irrité, le serpent ne pouvant soulever le cuveau,* répandit *de telles vapeurs et de telles odeurs, que, asphyxié par ces émanations*

méphitiques, le pauvre garçon mourut. *Le lendemain, venant au lavoir, les femmes* trouvèrent *son cadavre complètement desséché. Quant au diamant, il avait disparu.*
(Ibid.)

(3) This extract is a dialogue; the use of tenses, moods and personal pronouns is different, since everything is seen in relation to the present, which is the moment of speaking in the play.

LE MÉDECIN. − *Majesté,* vous avez fait *cent quatre-vingts fois la guerre. A la tête de vos armées,* vous avez participé *à deux mille batailles. D'abord, sur un cheval blanc avec un panache rouge et blanc très voyant et vous n'avez pas eu peur. Ensuite, quand* vous avez modernisé *l'armée, debout sur un tank ou sur l'aile de l'avion de chasse en tête de la formation.*
MARIE. − *C'était un héros.*
LE MÉDECIN. − Vous avez frôlé *mille fois la mort.*
LE ROI. − Je la frôlais *seulement. Elle n'était pas pour* moi, je le sentais.
MARIE. − Tu étais *un héros,* entends-tu? Souviens-toi.
MARGUERITE. − Tu as fait *assassiner par ce médecin et bourreau ici présent . . .*
LE ROI. − *Exécuter, non pas assassiner.*
LE MÉDECIN, *à Marguerite.* − *Exécuter, Majesté, non pas assassiner.* J'obéissais *aux ordres.* J'étais *un simple instrument, un exécutant plutôt qu'un exécuteur, et* je *le faisais euthanasiquement.* D'ailleurs, je le regrette. *Pardon.*
(Ionesco, *Le Roi se meurt*)

(4) This extract belongs both to descriptive and to argumentative prose, since it contains a number of ideas which are developed and led to a conclusion.

Les éléments de la création artistique sont répandus *à profusion autour de nous: formes, couleurs et rythmes.* On peut *dire que tout est formes, couleurs et rythmes. Tout ce qui* est *donné par la nature ou ajouté par la main de l'homme. Cette main, en s'affairant dans un dessein de pure efficacité, ne* manifeste *le plus souvent que sa négligence ou son indifférence. Ainsi* s'élèvent *partout les villes industrielles, les banlieues,* courent *les voies de chemin de fer, se* tendent *les lignes électriques, se* dressent *les clôtures à travers la campagne. Autant d'entreprises inconscientes d'enlaidissement et de destruction de l'harmonie naturelle. Mais dès que quelqu'un, dans le mince univers personnel qui lui* appartient *en propre, sa maison, son jardin, sa chambre,* dispose *la moindre chose en trouvant qu'elle « fait bien », alors il* sort *du domaine utilitaire où se* passe *la plus grande partie de sa vie matérielle, pour entrer dans celui de la recherche esthétique.*
(Guichard-Meili, *Regarder la peinture*)

All four extracts are taken from Grunewald and Mitterand, *Itinéraire grammatical, classe de troisième,* F. Nathan, 1976.

Notes

1 The examples in this section are mainly borrowed from Grunewald and Mitterand, *Itinéraire grammatical, classe de troisième.*
2 Contextual synonyms are words which may be synonymous in one context but not in another; these may be words belonging to different registers and having different connotations ('boy' and 'lad'); or the one may be the superordinate of the other

('child' is the superordinate of 'boy'); or they may become synonyms by virtue of the text alone (e.g. 'idiot', when referring to a particular person).

3 Rhetoric, originally an offshoot of logic, was based on the principle that a correctly formed system does not cramp the natural powers of expression. The rules discovered and elaborated by the rhetoricians tried to do many things, but basically they tried to help the speaker and the writer communicate their ideas to an audience. The rules applied both at the level of the thought process (planning a speech) and at the level of 'technique' (presentation, gestures of the speaker: notations found on the manuscript of a sermon delivered in 1500 indicate that the preacher should 'sit down' . . . 'stand up' . . . 'mop his brow' . . . 'ahem! ahem!' . . . 'now shriek like the devil!').

The four different components of rhetoric were:

(i) Invention: the discovery by thought of what, for example, makes a cause probable.

(ii) Disposition: the arrangement of the argument invented, i.e. definition of the problem, comparison between thesis and antithesis, climax and conclusion.

(iii) Elocution: this nowadays refers to delivery but originally it referred to what is now called style, i.e. the wording of the discourse.

Elocution in the rhetorical sense deals with the problem of applying the right words and sentences to the invention. This is sometimes referred to as the clothing of thought with language. Different types of style have been analysed by generations of rhetoricians (the judicial, the sermon, the exhortative (political eloquence) etc.).

(iv) Memory and pronunciation (delivery): improving one's memory, making the right gesture at the right time, etc. All this was considered extremely important.

Disposition is obviously the part of rhetoric most relevant to the writer, since it deals with the order or method in which thoughts are arranged. It is the art of selecting them, disposing them and combining them in such an order as shall make them the most suitable to the writer's or speaker's design. 'Disposition is to the orator what tactics or the disposition of armies are to the military art.'

4 Different kinds of plans include *le plan dialectique* (*thèse − antithèse − synthèse* (disrespectfully referred to by generations of students as *le plan oui − non − merde!*); *le plan comparatif* (the description of one element in the comparison and then a description of the other, followed by the considerations arising from the comparison). *Le plan inventaire* involves one in listing the advantages or inconveniences of the point under discussion; although in this case there is no problem to be solved, a progression is required in the presentation of the facts and ideas. The same is true for *le plan explication-illustration*, which involves the explanation of a quotation followed by comment. The most frequently adopted plan is *le plan dialectique*; note however that *le plan* for a legal topic is required to be in two parts only. It is worth stressing the formality of the *dissertation*; to quote Desalmand and Tort (*Du Plan à la dissertation*): *Une dissertation est une construction; ce n'est pas une collection de remarques présentées en vrac.* The *plan* is regarded as so crucial that a student, given a subject to deal with, may be told to hand in the plan with only the introduction and the conclusion written out in full (for example, at the *Ecole des Sciences Politiques* in Paris and at many *Grandes Ecoles*).

5 This is a quotation from Henry James, as cited by Desalmand and Tort in *Du Plan à la dissertation*.

Chapter 21

The organization of spoken French

0   General considerations on the problems related to the description the spoken language

(i) There are two main types of spoken language: spontaneous and nonspontaneous. Conversations and some monologues are examples of the former, while speeches and language spoken from a prepared script are examples of the latter. Interviews fall somewhere between the two.

Nonspontaneous speech is organized along the same lines as the written language and can be analysed in the same way; only spontaneous speech, therefore, is relevant to this chapter.

(ii) There are 'extralinguistic' factors which considerably complicate a description of the spontaneous spoken language. Speech itself is not the only means of communication used in conversation; gestures, signs, posture, gaze etc. are all complementary to speech. Thus speech is but one element in the broader study of the processes and conventions, not all of them intrinsically linguistic in character, governing conversation.

(iii) The importance of intonation both in grammatical and semantic terms has already been stressed in this section. And, while the study of intonation belongs properly to phonology, to ignore its importance would be to leave out one of the essential components of spoken communication.

(iv) Spontaneous spoken language represents 'natural' language; the written language represents 'codified' language. Thus punctuation is a grossly simplified representation of intonation. It is therefore illogical to attempt to describe the spoken language in terms of the written language. There are for example no exact equivalents of the capital letter and the full stop in the spoken language, and while it is true that there are pauses which correspond to these to a certain extent, there is no known direct correspondence between the various pause lengths and full stops, colons, semicolons etc. These are all inventions for the convenience of written communication only. It is therefore necessary to set up a separate framework for the description of the sequential organization of the spoken language. The framework adopted recognizes the utterance (section 2); the unit (section 3); and the unit complex (section 4). Section 1 deals with the various factors affecting the choice of different grammatical structures in the spoken language.

(v) The framework used to analyse the spoken language was developed in the context of a PhD thesis (Judge 1975) aimed at defining and describing cohesion in spoken French. The linguistic model was established since no other model existed and proved adequate for the purpose. The material cited in the chapter was recorded in connection with the 'Orléans Project' (Blanc and Biggs 1971).

(vi) Relatively few studies have been made of spoken French; but it is a developing field of research. Because of this the material in this chapter must not be seen as 'the last word' on the topic. Research in this field is largely centred on the University of Aix-en-Provence and the *Groupe Aixois de Recherches en Syntaxe*. Their publication is called *Recherches sur le Français parlé*.

1   Different varieties of spoken French: factors affecting choice of grammatical structure

1.1   Differences between the written and the spoken language

These two forms of French, the 'natural' and the 'codified', while they are obviously the same language, have different choice criteria relating both to vocabulary and grammar. This is due to several factors.

(i) The absence of intonation in the written language sometimes has to be compensated for by the use of extra words or different structures. The absence of the situational context in the written language also needs to be compensated for by verbal description, once again resulting in increased length.

(ii) The range of registers available is different for the spoken and the written language; many things which can be said would not be acceptable in the written form. The spoken language is generally more informal than the written; the element of permanence of the latter encourages greater care.

(iii) The spoken language is relentlessly 'linear' whereas the written language is organized in 'discrete units' − sentences, paragraphs, sections etc. which can be seen as a whole.

1.2   Varieties of spoken French

1.2.1   *Geographical variations*

(i) French is one of the most 'standardized' languages known − in other words, one in which there are fewest geographical variations, apart from accent. This standardization has been the goal of all French governments. The absolute monarchs were in favour of standardized French in their desire to achieve a centralized France; the Revolutionaries were of the same opinion on the grounds that the existence of different dialects gave rise to inequality in society. Various French governments, for a variety of reasons, have therefore legislated to produce a standardized language, and this has always been considered a subject of importance. An example of such government interference can be seen in the Appendix in the form of the *Arrêté* of 28 December 1977 on *Les tolérances grammaticales ou orthographiques*.

(ii) Despite this programme, some minor differences in the forms of French in various parts of the country remain, relating to both vocabulary and grammar. This is in addition to the many different regional accents with which we are not really concerned here. There are two kinds of deviation from the standard norm (or *français neutralisé*) at which the government legislation is aimed.

There are constructions (or words) which are regarded as unacceptable because they are grammatically 'incorrect'. For example, in the Paris region there is a tendency to replace *lui* by *y*: ** j'y ai dit* instead of *je lui ai dit*. In Lyon there is a tendency to use *y* in place of *le/la* when these are direct objects: **je sais pas y faire* instead of *je ne sais pas le faire*. Such expressions are considered unacceptable in standard French. Other deviations from the norm are simply cases where certain forms are more favoured in certain regions. For example, the past historic is still supposed to be used in the spoken language in certain parts of southern France. Similarly, the use of the double compound tenses appears to be more frequent in the southeast of France. In spite of this, it is nevertheless true that there are comparatively few geographical variations in the spoken language as against other languages spoken over a similarly large area.

1.2.2   *Registers and levels in the spoken language*

(i) It is not possible to set up a strict 'number' of registers for the spoken language, given the infinite variations in terms of subject matter, speaker and situation. It is pos-

sible, however, to construct a system of classification which recognizes five levels of spoken language (as against the three for written French: formal, neutral and informal). The greater number for the spoken language is due to the need to distinguish between spontaneous and nonspontaneous language.

	Level of language	Characteristics	Context
Spontaneous	Very informal (*relâché/ négligé*)	No effort to control use of regional variants or to avoid mistakes; possible use of slang	Amongst friends who are also equals
	Informal (*familier*)	Controlled, but with some 'mistakes'	Between friends or equals
	Neutral (standard)	Standard or neutral French; careful speech/no mistakes	Media, serious discussions with nonequals, also educated equals
Nonspontaneous	Formal (*soutenu*)	Deliberate selection of vocabulary and grammatical constructions suited to subject matter and audience	Lectures, presented papers; no sense of equality/ inequality
	Very formal (*oratoire*)	Stylistic effects used *per se* in order to 'carry the audience'	Speeches and sermons

Thus a doctor may speak about a disease to a colleague, to the parent of the patient, to the sick person, or to a small child: on each occasion his choice of words and constructions will be different.

(ii) One of the peculiarities of French has been the pre-eminence of the written code and the general condemnation of the spoken language insofar as it varies from this code. Spoken French has often been regarded as 'poor French' at best and 'incorrect French' at the worst. The spoken language is 'corrected' in relation to the written language and is itself completely devalued.[1] (This of course applies to grammar and not to style: *l'art de la conversation* has never been expected to follow that of *l'art de bien écrire*).

(iii) The neutral style in the written language (*style standard*) and formal style are examples of carefully used standard language; not surprisingly, these styles lack vividness and a certain kind of spontaneous emotion. The written language often borrows from the spoken language in order to introduce an element of humanity into such a purified – and therefore somewhat sterile – form of language.

(iv) The points made in *(ii)* and *(iii)* were certainly true of the past and are still true to a large extent in the present, it is however reasonable to suppose that this might not always be true, in view of the constant increase in the use of the spoken language. The invention of printing brought in the period of supremacy of the written language; but modern inventions – the telephone, radio, television etc. – have dramatically increased the consequence of the spoken language. This has resulted in the gradual disappearance of certain expressions and constructions typical of some written registers; many conjunctions have become obsolete or linked with a specialized register only (*nonobstat* and *conséquemment* are limited to administrative style); and some tenses have almost completely disappeared, for example the imperfect subjunctive. On the

other hand, many specifically 'spoken' constructions are used more and more frequently in the written language. This has resulted in written French becoming less and less formal; and people are also more willing to accept the spoken language as it stands and not to see it as a debased form of the written language. Thus sentences such as : *je sais pas* instead of *je ne sais pas* are becoming used more and more frequently in educated speech, at least in informal contexts. In any case one could argue that the incorrectness of the former is due to speed, for although *je sais pas* becomes *chai pas* in comic strip, style, the *ne* is rarely dropped in slow speech.

2   The utterance[2]

2.1   Definition of the utterance

An utterance can be defined as a stretch of language limited by two blanks. These blanks, from the speaker's point of view, indicate his initial assumption and final relinquishment of the role of speaker. Where there are interruptions which the speaker ignores, the utterance will continue unbroken; but where he responds to the interruption, a new utterance will begin.

2.2   Relationships involved in the organization of the utterance

(i) The utterance is made up of a succession of clauses which tend to be linked together, but with the occasional break in the chain. More impressionistically, it appears to be self-generating, each clause leading to the production of the next one, with an occasional breakdown. Where there is a breakdown, the process tends to start up again with the use of such expressions as *pour revenir à ce que je disais tout-à-l'heure* or *pour passer maintenant à*. . . . The utterance can therefore be seen as chain-like in construction.

(ii) Within this chain there may be either coordination or subordination, although neither may be present where the unity of thought of the speaker or the presence of other cohesive ties – e.g. grammatical and lexical referents, ellipsis – make them unnecessary. In these cases the clauses or groups of clauses will be simply juxtaposed.

(iii) The chain-like structure does not imply simplicity of structure. Continuity of structure does not automatically mean coordination, as is often assumed; it may entail an extremely complex form of subordination (see 2.3. below).

(iv) The analysis of the utterance leads to the establishment of different levels of subordination. The first level corresponds to an absence of subordination; the others correspond to increasing levels of subordination. But not all clauses in the spoken language can be classified as either main or independent: some act as introducers or starters of a chain, while others act as a verbal closure to it. Some clauses may contain several verbs, although generally people tend to associate one verb with one clause. Furthermore, it can also happen that the speaker may have to make several attempts before managing to express what he wants to say, as in:

> *j'ai mis le pied sur la j'ai mis la main j'ai mis les mains sur la j'ai attrapé la table du poste* (see example in 2.3.1)

This type of construction counts as one clause only.

(v) An analysis of interviews and conversations shows the existence of the following relationships between clauses making up the utterance:

> *(a)* coordination through conjunctions and coordinating phrases;
> *(b)* subordination either through conjunctions, or through phrases or clauses functioning as conjunctions, or through relative pronouns introducing relative clauses;
> *(c)* insertion of certain clauses into the main stream of the utterance, either as asides

or to give extra information on some secondary point; these could also be referred to as 'parenthetical structures';

(d) juxtaposed clauses − in other words clauses which are not linked formally in terms of coordination or subordination;

(e) quotations, e.g. *il m'a dit je vais venir dimanche*. Here one clause announces the following one; intonation plays a major part in setting up all of these constructions. For examples see 2.3 below.

2.3 Examples of different possible types of sequential organization of the utterance

2.3.1 *Elements ensuring cohesion of the text*

In the first example below, the speaker, a dressmaker, was not aware that she was being recorded. This was not true for the interviewee in the second example, a union representative. The first example is taken from a lively spontaneous discussion, whereas the second is part of an interview and represents 'careful' speech. Neither speaker is particularly educated and their speech does not reflect the influence of a highly literary education. The aim of the analysis is to ascertain the degree of subordination used by the speaker.

In each example the words shown in italics are those which connect the various clauses. The clauses are numbered to facilitate the diagrammatic representation of the linguistic relationship within these utterances (see 2.3.2).

Example 1 is typical of spontaneous spoken language:

1   2
ah non je l'ai pas fait exprès (vous savez) / on se casse jamais la figure exprès [rires] /

3   4   5
non on passe sur ces planches / je passe sur ces planches / je ne peux pas vous dire

                      6   7
combien de fois par jour / *et* je fais très attention / *mais alors* là mon pied s'est mis sur

                   8   9   10   11
le bout de la planche / la planche s'est relevée / *et* / *depuis que* je suis malade / on a mis

                  12   13
le poste de télévision là / *parce que* en principe je me couche le soir / *parce que* je suis

        14   15   9
fatiguée / *alors* je me couche / *et pis* je vois j'écoute le je regarde la télé / *alors* la

                  16   17   18
planche s'est relevée / *elle* s'est empêtrée dans mes pieds / j'ai perdu l'équilibre / *et* /

19   18
pour me rattraper / j'ai mis le pied sur la j'ai mis la main j'ai mis les mains sur la j'ai

              20   21   22
attrapé la table du poste / *et* j'ai basculé le poste de television / *alors* / *quand* le maçon

        23   24   25   24
m'a dit hier / *mais* vous saviez pas / *que* / *si* votre poste votre tube avait éclaté / vous

              26
faisiez tout éclater / à ce qui paraît que si / . . .

Example 2 represents careful speech.

1   2   3
bien on a l'avantage / d'être assez près de Paris / *et* des industriels *s'en* sont aperçus /

4   5
d'autre part nous étions un département agricole / *et* autour d'Orléans il y a beaucoup

                                                                                                6
de il y avait beaucoup de fermes beaucoup d'ouvriers agricoles / *ce qui veut*

                                                                                                            7
dire – avec la mécanisation – il y avait des ouvriers en perspective / *qui*

                                                                     8
inévitablement seraient sans travail du fait de la mécanisation / *et alors* les industriels

                                    9   10
ont fait des études / *et* ils se sont aperçus / *que* dans la région orléanaise notamment du

                                       11   10
fait de sa place stratégique / euh on est très près de Paris / il y a des communications

                   12   13
faciles / il y a des grandes routes / c'était donc intéressant de construire [ ] de

                                 14
décentraliser des usines / ce qui fait que depuis une dizaine d'années Orléans est com-

                                 15   16
plètement transformée / *autrefois* c'était une ville de camp bourgeoise / un temps en a

                                                          17   18
fait même une ville de garnison Orléans / il *y* en avait des régiments / *maintenant* ça ne

              19   20
l'est plus / *maintenant* il y a des usines / *ce qui fait que* ces usines se décentralisant nous

                                 21
ont amené beaucoup de travail / *je crois en gros* il y avait trente-cinq mille salariés de

                                                          22   23
l'industrie à la libéra euh à la libération / il y a vingt ans / *et maintenant* on a cent

                                             24   25
quarante mille salariés et retraités [ ] / vous voyez la différence qu'il y a / *ce qui fait que*

                                                          26
économiquement jusqu'à maintenant on était favorisé / *ce qui a aidé* pour avoir des

              27   28   29   30
salaires / *parce que* / *quand* il y a une industrie nouvelle / *qui* s'installe / pour avoir des

              31   27
ouvriers / pour faire une sélection / on donne un petit salaire légèrement supérieur que

              32
le voisin / pour avoir les meilleurs ouvriers / . . .

2.3.2 *Diagrammatic representation of the linguistic relationships within utterances*

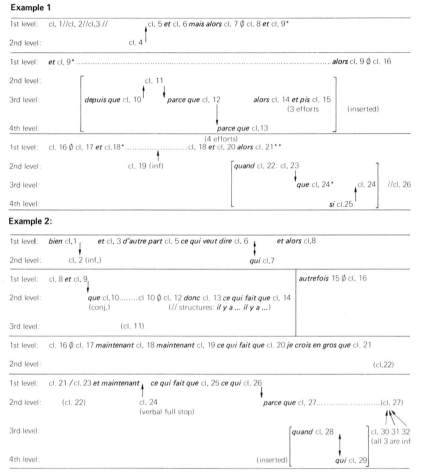

Example 1

Example 2:

Note: * indicates that only the connecting word has been said so far and no other part of the clause has yet been introduced
** indicates that although the connecting word is uttered the rest of the clause is never completed
'inf.' = infinitival clause

(i) The text is divided into numbered clauses, and these numbers then appear on different lines according to their status in terms of degrees of subordination.

Thus the first line represents the first level, i.e. that of main or independent clauses; the second line represents the first degree of subordination, i.e. clauses subordinate to main clauses; the third line represents second-degree subordination, i.e. clauses which are subordinated to clauses on the second level; and so on. The degree of subordination is proportional to the number of levels.

(ii) Within each level it may be desirable to indicate whether the clauses are coordinated, subordinated, inserted or juxtaposed, or whether they are quotations. This is represented as follows:

In cases of coordination the clauses are indicated on the same level, and the element marking coordination is indicated (many elements not generally classified as coordinators will be found to function as such). Ø indicates the absence of formal ties and indicates that it would be possible to insert an *et* at this point.

In cases of subordination, subordinate clauses introduced by conjunctions may occur either before or after the clause upon which they depend. If the main clause precedes the subordinate clause, an arrow pointing downwards indicates that the subordinate clause depends on the clause which precedes it. If, on the contrary, the subordinate clause precedes the main clause, an arrow pointing upwards will indicate that the subordinate clause depends on the clause which follows.

Relative clauses may only follow the antecedent for which the relative pronoun stands, i.e. they may only follow the clause upon which they depend. Furthermore, the relative pronoun has a dual role since it functions both as a referential and a subordinating element. To reflect this dual role it will be represented by an arrow with two heads.

In cases of insertion, these parenthetical structures are not formally linked to the main stream by subordinators or coordinators of any kind, although they usually contain cohesive elements linking them to other clauses. These are represented by square brackets.

Juxtaposed clauses are separated by two oblique strokes.

In case of quotations, both clauses function on the same level. This type of relationship is represented by a colon, e.g. Clause 1: Clause 2.

2.3.3 *Conclusion*

One of the standard presumptions about the spoken language is that, in contrast to the written language, there is a greater use of coordination in preference to subordination. The extreme complexity of the spoken language can, however, be seen from the examples cited. Spoken French, far from being a succession of clauses vaguely coordinated to one another, involves the same degree of complex subordination found in the written language, allowing for three and possibly more levels of subordination.

3 Organization of utterances into units

3.1 Definition and description of units

3.1.1 *Definition*

A unit is made up of stimulus + response, one at least of these being verbal. The combination question + answer is a typical unit; statement + comment is another.

A unit need not be limited to two responses, since a response may in turn function as a stimulus for another response, thus setting off a chainlike reaction. (See below.)

3.1.2 *The question + answer unit*

(i) Certain utterances are closely linked to – or dependent upon – one another. Thus a question and its answer form both a semantic and a syntactic whole:

Q (question): – *c'est aujourd'hui que ça s'est passé?*
A (answer): – *non, ça s'est passé dimanche*

In this case, the first utterance acts as a stimulus to which the second utterance is a response. Both utterances are obligatory and form a whole. Such a unit may be expressed by the formula Q + A.

(ii) The answer given above could in turn act as a stimulus for another response, in the shape of a comment on the answer:

C1 (comment): – *ça tombe mal un dimanche*

Such a unit may be expressed by the formula $Q + A \pm C$, the plus or minus signs indicating that this is an optional element.

This last comment could in turn act as a stimulus for another comment:

C2: − *oh! il y a toujours quelqu'un de garde vous savez*

Such a unit may be expressed by the formula $Q + A \pm C1 \pm C2$.

3.1.3   *Units based on statements*

(i) The verbal stimulus, instead of being a question, may be a statement which triggers off a comment on the part of a second speaker:

St (Statement): − *alors tu l'as fait exprès*: (the addressee has broken her leg)
C1 (comment): − *ah non − je ne l'ai pas fait exprès − on ne se casse jamais la figure exprès*

This unit may be expressed by the formula $St + C$.
(ii) A third person could comment on the first comment:

C2: − *je lui avais pourtant dit de faire attention*

In this case the comment is directed to the person who made the statement since the pronoun used is *lui*. This unit can be represented by the formula $St + C1 + C2\ (St)$ (i.e. statement + first comment on statement + 2nd comment on statement).

If the pronoun used had been the second person, the structure of the unit would be different:

C2: − *je t'avais pourtant dit de faire attention*

In this case the use of the second person *t'* indicates that the comment is directed at the speaker of the previous comment, hence the unit $St + C1 + C2\ (C1)$ (i.e. statement + first comment + 2nd comment on first comment).

One verbal stimulus may thus trigger off a response which may in turn act as a stimulus for a further response, and so on.

3.1.4   *Units including a nonverbal element*

Either stimulus or response may be nonverbal, represented by the letter G, standing for 'gesture'.
(i) The stimulus may be nonverbal, e.g. *ne fais pas ça!* may be a response to someone doing something. In such a situation the unit is made up of a nonverbal stimulus (G) and a verbal response (C): $G + C$.
(ii) The stimulus may be verbal and the response nonverbal, e.g. *passe-moi le sel* may be a stimulus and the resulting action would be its nonverbal response: $St + G$.
(iii) These basic patterns may be further complicated if either the verbal or the nonverbal response triggers off further utterances:

G: − (child wants to touch object on display in exhibition)
C1: − *ne touche pas!*
C2: − *tu rouspètes toujours!*

The second comment is, in this case, a comment on the first: $G + C1 + C2\ (C1)$ (i.e. gesture + comment 1, + comment 2 on comment 1). The 2nd comment could however have referred back to the original nonverbal stimulus:

C2 (St): − *mais je ne fais rien de mal!*

This unit may be expressed by the formula G + C1 + C2 (St).

Note: The difference between statements and comments is that comments always start off as responses, even though they may in turn become stimuli. Statements on the other hand start off as stimuli. (They may be triggered by psychological needs etc., but this does not belong to the domain of grammar, at least grammar as defined in this book.)

3.1.5   *Interruptions*

There are three types of interruptions depending on whether the interruption involves completing what the other person is saying (3.1.5.1.), or commenting on what is being said without effecting the flow of the original utterance (3.1.5.2.); interruptions may also seek clarification on some point raised by the original utterance (3.1.5.3.)

3.1.5.1   *Interruptions completing the other speaker's utterance*
(i) Some interruptions are due to the addressee guessing what the speaker is about to say. In this case he may interrupt the speaker and finish his utterance for him, thus indicating his full understanding of the material and showing that he is on the same wavelength. These interruptions have a 'contact function'; they fulfil a similar role to that of bridging elements (see 3.1.6 below). Thus in the following example the interruption (Int) is there to 'help the other speaker along':

Q: – *vous croyez que* –
Int. (interruption) – *ça ira?*
Q: – *ça ira pire le salaire?*

This kind of interruption is often used in situations in which the speaker is finding it embarrassing to say something. This aspect of a unit is expressed as Q . . . + int. (Q) + . . . Q (i.e. question + interruption completing the question + end of question).
(ii) The original speaker often tries to complete his own utterance even though his addressee has already done so for him:

St – (. . .) *alors Guy a été chercher du sable- il a-*
Int – *il a rempli-*
St (cont.) – *il a comblé un peu le trou*

It would appear that speakers are not always grateful for interruptions even when these mean approval and understanding on the part of the addressee; their reaction is to finish what they are trying to say regardless, as in the case above.
(iii) In some cases, however, a speaker will allow the other person to finish off what he was saying. This is particularly common amongst people living together or sharing the same experiences and then recounting them to a third party. In this case one has one 'semantic utterance' uttered by several people, as in:

Q (speaker 1): – *vos enfants se considèrent enfin toujours rattachés à votre milieu?*
A1 (2nd speaker): – *ah oui oui même étant mariée avec un ingénieur même- d'ailleurs lui-même n'est pas* – *c'est un fils d'ouvrier- et l'autre- le professeur*
Int1 (3rd speaker): – *lui ses parents étaient riches mais enfin-*
Int2 (2nd speaker) (continuing Int1): – *ses parents étaient riches mais- il a une situation de famille assez drôle-alors ça-*
Int3 (3rd speaker) (continuing Int2): – *ça l'a marqué un peu- alors vraiment il n'est pas il reste de notre côté quoi-*

This may be expressed: Q + A1 . . . + Int1 cont. A1 + Int2 cont. Int1 + Int3 cont. Int2 (i.e. question + answer + 1st interruption continuing the answer + 2nd interruption continuing the first + 3rd interruption continuing the 2nd).

Such patterns of speech are typical of many couples.

3.1.5.2 *Parenthetical interruptions* An interruption may comment on some aspect of what is being said, without the speaker who has been interrupted altering his utterance in any way as a result of this comment. In other words, a parenthetical interruption is a comment which fails to act as a stimulus for the person whose utterance is interrupted. This kind of interruption is extremely common where there are more than two speakers. There are two possibilities, depending on whether the comment passes totally unnoticed *(i)*, or acts as a stimulus for another comment by another person present, without either comment affecting the flow of the original utterance interrupted *(ii)*:

(i) The comment may pass totally unnoticed:

St: (a TV has been knocked off a table) − *mais enfin comme solidité il a été mis à l'épreuve- hein- parce qu'il est quand même tombé-*
C: − *et puis vous aussi-*
St (cont.): − *tombé de la table* − *euh par terre hein-*

In this case the comment has not given rise to a response, nor has it interrupted the flow of the statement; this interruption may be expressed: St . . . (+ C) . . . St (i.e. statement + ignored interruption + statement continued).

(ii) The comment may be stimulus for a response from a third party, without either affecting the flow of the original utterance:

St: − *mais enfin comme solidité il a été mis à l'épreuve* − *hein- parce qu'il est quand même tombé-*
C1 (2nd speaker): − *dire qu'il était tout neuf!*
C2 (3rd speaker): − *ne le lui rappelle pas!*
St (cont): − *il est tombé de la table- euh par terre hein* −

In this case the interruption may be expressed: St . . . [+ C1 + C2 (C1)] . . . St.

3.1.5.3 *Embedded interruptions* These are interruptions seeking clarification on some point made by the speaker. As such, they are not very frequent; they appear to be most frequent in near-monologues when one speaker is holding the floor trying to explain something complex to another, or when people are trying to do a difficult task together. Further clarification may be required either on statements, answers, comments or questions:

St (= Q: the latter is an implicit question): − *une autre chose qui frappe les Anglais c'est la façon dont les Français s'embrassent* − *le matin* − *le soir-*
Q c1 St (question asking for clarification of statement) − *sur les joues* − *entre camarades- ou bien quoi-*
A c1 Q (answer clarifying question) − *chez eux- entre amis surtout-*
A (to original implicit question) − *à chaque fois qu'on se sépare- voyez le matin quand je quitte ma femme on s'embrasse* − *je reviens le midi- on s'embrasse le midi- oui le matin midi et soir-*

This passage may be expressed St/Q1 + Q2 c1 Q1 + A1 c1 Q2 + A2 (Q1) (i.e. statement equivalent to a question + 2nd question seeking clarification on the 1st + answer to the second question + answer to the first). In this case the interruption is not optional, in that it cannot be ignored by the speaker interrupted. It is 'embedded' the unit.

3.1.6 *Bridging elements*

These are extremely brief utterances, sometimes no more than expressions such as *je vois* or *hé bien*, which are used as an alternative to a disruptive pause, or as a form of encouragement to the speaker. They fulfil what has been termed a 'phatic' or 'contact' function (see also 3.1.5.1 above).

(i) Bridging elements may act as an encouragement to the speaker:

> St: − *ah j'étais contrariée- alors moitié tremblant moitié pleurant j'ai été chercher monsieur Berthelot et pis monsieur Berthelot a appelé Bernard parce que c'est quand même assez lourd-* (the speaker is referring to a TV set)
> Br (bridging element: − *oui-*
> St (cont): − *pour qu'on le remette sur la table-*
> Br: − *ah oui évidemment-*
> St (cont) − *enfin je me suis demandé (. . .)*

Repetition of the words pronounced by the speaker is another way of fulfilling this function:

> St: − *alors le plâtrier m'a dit hier- qu'il fallait voir monsieur Ferry pour quand même le faire réviser* (i.e. the TV set) -
> Br: *-oui oh oui il faut le faire réviser-*
> St (cont): − *de façon parce que si il y avait eu quelque chose qui n'était pas cassé tout de suite et qui se casserait par l'avenir en fait ce serait contrariant-* (. . .)

(ii) Bridging elements may function as silence fillers:

> A: − *ça me déplaît pas-* (i.e. life in the provinces)
> Br: − *-oui-*
> A (cont.): − *oui heu j'ai vécu à Paris- quoi- ça me plaît assez Paris- mais hein* − *les conditions de vie sont assez- heu* − *ingrates hein- oui- surtout lorsqu'on est tout seul quoi- hein- enfin si vous si vous êtes à Paris heu-hein- hé-*
> Br − *oui ça c'est dur-*
> A (cont.): − *j'ai un emploi ici heu- qui me fait gagner ma vie enfin à peu près quoi- dans la mesure du possible hein-*

(iii) Bridging elements may fill a pause while the speaker is searching for a word:

> A: (. . .) *comment on appelle ça le mot-*
> Br: − *concours-*
> A (cont.): − *un concours voilà le mot que je cherchais* −

3.2 Constructions used for questions, answers, statements, comments and bridging elements

3.2.1 *Constructions used for questions*

There are three main constructions used:
(i) Interrogative constructions (see Ch. 19, section 2); it should be noted however that the interrogative construction using a subject verb inversion (e.g. *y vas-tu?*) is very rare; the most common forms involve the use of interrogative words (e.g. *est-ce que tu y vas?* or *quand est-ce que tu y vas?*) or the declarative form said with an interrogative intonation pattern (e.g. *tu y vas?*).
(ii) Declaratives followed by interrogative interjections or 'tags':

> St/Q: − *il vaut mieux faire comme ça- tu ne crois pas?*

(St/Q means that the utterance starts off as a statement and becomes a question.)
(iii) Incomplete or 'elliptical' sentences may also function as interrogatives:

> St/Q: − *et vous y allez le-?*
> A: − *j'y vais jeudi prochain-*

In this case the incomplete construction will be said with an interrogative intonation pattern.

3.2.2 *Constructions used for answers, statements and comments*

As could be expected, answers, statements and comments are all in the declarative form, although they may include interrogative tags *(i)* exclamative tags *(ii)* and although they do not always follow the word order one could expect *(iii)*.

(i) Interrogative tags usually seek approval from the listener and serve to check that the information is clear and fully understood:

> *c'est pas grand chose mais- voyez- vous l'avez eh- alors si vous l'avez pas eh ben-négative hein?*

The most commonly used types of interrogative tags are *hein, oui, non, n'est-ce pas* and other similar expressions said with a rising intonation pattern:

> *on a mis un atelier d'émaux − vous savez des émaux de bijouteries- oui?-*

An interrogative tag may be followed by a phrase or clause justifying semantically the present of the interrogative tag:

> *ce qui peut arriver à nous avoir encore une guerre ou quelque chose hein? on peut pas savoir-*

(ii) Exclamative tags or interjections are added to declarative constructions for emphasis. These are usually expressions such as *voyez, vous voyez, hé hé, hein quoi*. Other expressions such as *en quelque sorte, mettons* and *disons* and frequently used to attenuate what is being said. As for *alors voilà*, it is sometimes used as a kind of verbal full stop, indicating that the speaker has finished at least one aspect of the topic under discussion:

> A: − *je trouve pas ça normal heu heu vu les responsabilités pas tellement y a pas y a pas le choix c'est ça ou c'est rien d'autre et puis c'est tout vous comprenez hein alors voilà-*

(iii) Answers do not automatically follow the normal word order expected of them in that they sometimes begin with adverbial phrases qualifying and limiting the possible interpretation of what follows:

> Q: − *croyez-vous que le rôle de la femme surtout le rôle de la mère a beaucoup changé depuis la guerre d'après vos expériences ici?* − (to a social worker)
> A: − *moi il n'y a que deux ans que je suis ici à Orléans- mais mettons une expérience personnelle quoi-* (. . .)

3.2.3 *Constructions used for bridging elements*

Bridging elements are always responses; they are informative in that they signify approval, understanding, surprise, indignation and so on at what has just been said. There are two types of bridging elements: those which have no effect on the utterance interrupted *(i)* and those which are acknowledged by the main speaker *(ii)*.

(i) Bridging elements which are verbally ignored are in the declarative form and are usually adverbs or adverbial expressions such as *oui, non, évidemment, voilà*, or else they may repeat some element mentioned by the main speaker. For examples of all three cases see 3.1.6.

(ii) Bridging elements which are interrogative or exclamative may become a stimulus to which the main speaker responds. This acknowledgement usually takes the form of the repetition of the bridging element, to which is added *oui* or *non*:

> A: − (. . .) *parce que Guy n'était pas là*
> Br: *il n'était pas là?/!*
> A: − *non il venait de partir* . . .

(?/! indicates that the utterance could be said either with an exclamative or an interrogative intonation pattern.)

Where the bridging element fills a gap left by the speaker when searching for a word, there is also acknowledgement on the part of the main speaker (see 3.1.6*iii* for an example).

3.3   Structural ties linking the utterances forming a unit

(i) Answers are linked to questions both semantically and structurally: a question is not complete without an answer in the same way that a nominal phrase is not normally complete without a verbal phrase. Comments are similarly dependent upon that which is being commented upon. Statements alone stand on their own.

(ii) Although the unit forms a semantic and structural unit, it is also held together by cohesive ties, i.e. elements in one utterance which refer back to others (see 4.3). Thus, in the same way in which there are loose and tight paragraphs (see Ch. 20, 2.1), there are units in which the utterances are more or less tightly linked. In the following unit, for example, there are many links between the various utterances:

> St: − *ça a fait un bastringue* (a TV set has been knocked over) −
> Q (St): − *alors le poste il il est cassé il est quoi non?-*
> A: − *eh bien c'est-à-dire que le − il est pas il marche mais alors euh ça fait un cliquetis là-dedans épouvantable vous savez-*
> Br1: − *ah bon-*
> A (cont.): − *alors le plâtrier m'a dit hier − qu'il fallait voir monsieur Ferry pour quand même le faire réviser-*
> Br2: − *oui oui il faut le faire réviser-*
> A (cont.): − *de façon parce que si il y avait eu quelque chose-*

In this case *alors* acts as an extra link between the statement and the question, *il* stands for *le poste* in the answer, *là-dedans* and *le* also stand for *le poste*, and *il* reoccurs in the second bridging element and again in the last part of the interrupted utterance. This is an example of a 'tight' unit.

In the following example however, cohesion is maintained purely structurally and cohesiveness is not increased by the use of cohesive ties:

> A: − *vous voyez alors je suis patient-*
> C1: − *tu commences par rouspéter − mon Dieu!*
> C2 (C1): − *avoue que je suis patient- je recommence-*
> Br: − *je veux bien-*
> C2 (cont.): − *je me fous pas en colère- j'envoie pas tout dans les roses-*

This is an example of a 'loose' unit.

(iii) The cohesive ties which may occur at this level are mainly the same as those used at the unit complex level. For cohesive ties, see therefore 4.3 below.

4   Organization of units into unit complexes

4.1   Definition of the unit complex

When a discourse is broken down into units it becomes apparent that certain units are linked through the use of cohesive ties, i.e. devices which link two stretches of language (for cohesive ties see 4.3). Thus a unit may contain a pronoun which stands for something said in a previous unit − or indeed, in the case of *cela/ça*, the pronoun may stand for the whole preceding unit:[3]

> (Unit 1) Q: − *quarante-huit?* (i.e. *vous faites quarante-huit heures?*)
> A: − *quarante-huit voyez enfin nous faisons les trois − huits − hein*

> *les trois huits alors hé six jours enfin nous faisons six jours de travail et deux jours de repos et puis on repart les équipes comme ça (. . .) on a un salaire de base qui est de 1 100 francs moins la Sécurité Sociale et enfin toutes les charges quoi (. . .)-*

(Unit 2)   Q: *et ça vous suffit?-*
            A: *ah ça vous suffit mon Dieu si je pouvais trouver à gagner davantage (. . .)-*

In this case *ça* stands for *1 100 francs* and acts as a link between the two units.

Demonstrative adjectives, certain uses of the definite article, and certain words such as *autre* which refer lexically to other items may all act as 'ties' between units (see 4.3). Ellipsis (i.e. the use of incomplete constructions) may also make a unit dependent on a previous one:

(Unit 1)   Q: – *vous pensez vous marier bientôt?*
            A: – *oui oui oui oui bientôt-*
unit 2   Q: – *vous croyez que ça ira pire le salaire?*
            A: – *bah du fait que* – *le siècle veut que la femme travaille quoi-*

ça ira implies *quand vous serez marié*, retrievable from the previous unit.

Interrelated units can be defined as forming a unit complex; seven, eight or even more units may thus be related, forming one large unit complex. On the other hand, single units exist which are not linked to other units. The more coherent the conversation, the more likely it will be that the unit complexes will be large; the more 'choppy' the conversation, the fewer the units per unit complex.

4.2 Relations between units in a unit complex

(i) The most simple link, and the one most commonly found, is that linking a unit to the previous one (see examples in 4.1).

If one represents unit complexes as 'boxes', and indicates by arrows which units are linked with which others, this may be represented as follows:

unit complex 1

(ii) There are cases, however, in which a unit is linked not to the one immediately preceding it but to a previous one:

(Unit 1)   Q: – *comment ça se passe ici* – *quelle proportion des ouvriers sont membres des syndicats* – *au fait je devrais peut-être vous demander avant quels sont vos rapports entre différents syndicats* –
            A: – *en général ils ne sont pas mauvais (. . .)* – *on a pas toujours les mêmes points de vue* – *(. . .)* – *mais la période des heurts entre les syndicats est terminée (. . .)*
(Unit 2)   Q: – *est-ce que ces ces heurts se seraient produits euh à cause de questions syndicales ou plutôt politiques?* –
            A: – *disons* – *notre réponse était toujours parce qu'on avait pas la même position syndicale mais la différence de position syndicale venait aussi des options et orientations politiques (. . .)?*
(Unit 3)   Q: – *alors pour en revenir donc à cette question des effectifs* – *quel serait le pourcentage grosso modo d'ouviers syndiqués?* –

The link between units 2 and 1 is ensured by the demonstrative adjective *ces* in *ces heurts*; the link between units 3 and 1 is ensured by the linking phrase *pour en revenir* and by the demonstrative adjective *cette* in *cette question des effectifs*, *effectifs* being a synonym in this context for *proportion des ouvriers qui sont membres des syndicats*.

unit complex 1

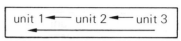

(iii) It is possible for one unit within a unit complex to interrupt another unit within the same unit complex:

(Unit 1)   St: – *elle est malade (. . .) ce qui est moche alors – préparer un baptême tout ça – y a la famille de mon gendre qui va arriver du Nord etcétéra alors – (. . .) – alors on va les avoir à la maison – c'est pareil il va falloir s'occuper d'eux –*

(Unit 2 inserted)

Q: – *mais ils sont de Munster ou est-ce que –*
A: – *non non ils sont de Nackenheim à côté de Mayence –*
Br: – *ah oui –*

(Unit 1 continued)

St: – *alors faut quand même s'occuper d'eux – ça fait des dérangements – (. . .)*

In this case the interruption is linked with the unit interrupted through the use of *ils*, which refers to *eux* in the interrupted unit.

unit complex 1

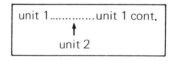

(iv) In some cases there may be a separate unit complex which interrupts a unit in another unit complex:

Unit complex 1:

(Unit 1)   St1(1st speaker): – *ben y a qu'un plat en général euh-en Allemagne vous allez même en Alsace vous allez à l'hôtel et ben-*

Unit complex 2, interruption (beginning of a unit)

St2(2nd speaker): – *on devait toujours aller à Munster-*

Unit complex 1 continued

(Unit 1)   St1(1st speaker): – *y a un plat qui est très bien garni mais y a qu'un plat-*
Br1(2nd speaker): – *ah oui –*
Br2(1st speaker): – *oui oui –*

Unit complex 3, interruption (1 unit only)

St3(2nd speaker): – *Michel correspond avec une Munstéroise-*
Br1(1st speaker): – *ah oui?-*
Br2(2nd speaker):-*oui-*

Unit complex 1 (unit 1 continued)

St1(1st speaker) cont: *oui ben c'est très agréable remarquez c'est c'est marrant –*

(It is remarkable in this case how speaker 1 never loses track of what she had meant to say in the first place). Such cases of interruptions are typical of informal conversations, in which dfferent people are competing for the floor. No cohesive ties are used in this case, since the second speaker keeps wanting to start on a quite different topic.

unit complex 1

4.3 Different cohesive ties

It is possible to distinguish among grammatical referents, lexical referents, linking words and ellipsis. A referent is an item which refers to another lexical item, its coreferent. If it refers back in the text or discourse it is said to be anaphoric; when it is anaphoric it is also cohesive. Cohesive lies function at all levels of language, but in this section only those functioning at the unit complex level are to be examined.

4.3.1 *Grammatical referents*

4.3.1.1 *Pronouns functioning as grammatical referents* These include the 3rd person pronouns, the demonstrative pronouns *c'(est) cela* and *ça* and the 3rd person possessive pronouns.
The personal pronouns are constantly used in this manner:

Q: – *quand est-ce que tu l'as vu*
Q: – *à quelle heure est-ce qu'il est arrivé?*
Q: – *tu y vas alors?*

In each case the pronouns *l'*, *il* and *y* are dependent for interpretation on what precedes.
Cela and *ça* are also very commonly used since they may stand either for a preceding nominal phrase or for all that has been said previously (see Ch. 3, section 2). Thus, in the first example quoted in 4.1, *ça* stood for *1 100 francs*, but a third unit followed which was linked to both units 2 and 1 through the use of *ça*:

(3rd unit) Q: – *vous trouvez ça normal?-*
A: – *je trouve ça normal heu heu vu les responsabilités pas tellement y a pas le choix c'est ça ou c'est rien-*

In this case *ça* stands for *1 100 francs* and for the fact that the person concerned works for 48 hours a week; it also refers to *si je pouvais gagner davantage je le ferais*, which implies *je ne le peux pas*. In other words *ça* stands for all that was said in the two previous units.
The possessive pronoun needing two coreferents, namely a possessor and a possessed, is the most cohesive but also the most difficult to use. Its use at this level is mainly theoretical since it tends to overload the communicative system.

4.3.1.2 *Determiners functioning as grammatical referents* There are three types: the definite article, the demonstrative adjective and the possessive adjective; but only definite articles and demonstrative adjectives appear to be used extensively at this level.
(i) The demonstrative adjective usually modifies a general noun, thus creating a contextual synonym. These general nouns are normally words such as *idée, mouvement,*

conditions, *domaine*, *chose*, *question*, *affaire*, *problème* and so on (see 4.2 *ii* for an example).

(ii) The definite article is less cohesive than the demonstrative adjective, since it may either particularize or generalize the noun (see Ch. 2, 1.1.3). The definite article is cohesive only when it particularizes the noun, but there are many cases of ambiguity in this respect:

> *-est-ce qu'il y a des crèches pour les enfants?* –

In this case one does not know whether the speaker is referring to a specific group of children or to the class of individuals called children.

Although not as cohesive as the demonstrative adjective, the definite article nevertheless plays an important cohesive role in elliptical structures since, in this case, it indicates the elliptical nature of the construction:

> *tu as vu la grande?*

Here the use of the definite article nominalizes the adjective *grande*.

4.3.2   *Lexical referents*

(i) These are lexical items which contain within their meaning some idea of reference. Thus, whereas grammatical referents have a referential function, lexical referents have a referential meaning.

Lexical referents may be adjectives, adverbs or interjections.

(ii) Referential adjectives include *autre*, *différent and même*:

> *est-ce que c'est comme ça dans d'autres régions?*
> *vous avez l'impression qu'ailleurs c'est différent?*

Other referential adjectives are *semblable, analogue, supplémentaire* and *égal*. These may all be anaphoric.

Adjectival referents often combine with general nouns (see 4.3.1.2*i*), e.g. *c'est toujours la même chose.*

(iii) Certain referential adverbs operate in conjunction with both the demonstrative pronouns and adjectives. The most commonly used is *-là* as in *ce que vous dites-là.* *Tout-à-l'heure,* which used to mean 'earlier on', is also frequently used referentially, as is *ailleurs* (see example under *(ii)*).

(iv) *Alors* is used particularly frequently, with the meaning either of *dans ce cas* or *d'après ce que vous dites*, or *à ce moment-là* or *tout-à-l'heure*. In the first two cases, *alors* refers to an idea of consequence and it is in this guise that it most frequently appears. In the other cases it refers to time, but its use in this case is infrequent.

(v) *Quand même* and *malgré tout* are used at the inter-unit level as strongly cohesive lexical referents. Other adverbs used are: *autrement, inversement, aussi, également, enfin, finalement, justement, précisément, à propos, en effet*. These also appear in formal written French.

4.3.3   *Connecting or 'linking' words and phrases*

(i) The coordinators most commonly used are: *mais, et, mais enfin, alors* and *donc*. It is noticeable that *et* is used in a different way at this level: whereas in a sentence or at the clause level it links two similar structures and is the equivalent of a plus sign, at this level in the spoken language it tends to mean 'what about?' In this role it appears at the beginning of the utterance:

> *et avant?-*
> *et vous-les femmes et les maris de vos enfants vous les tutoyez?*

As in the case of the English 'yes but', *mais* combined with *oui* to give *oui mais* often serves to introduce a contradiction in such a way as to make it less rude than a more direct negation.

Donc and *alors* are less frequently used at this level:

> *d'après vous se serait donc une question d'attitude . . .*
> *alors vous aviez là du flair* an alternative to this is *vous aviez donc du flair* (note changed place of adverb)

(ii) The only two subordinators which appear to be used at the level of the unit complex are *parce que* and *alors que*, the latter retaining its full meaning of time. There is a slight difference of meaning between *parce que* used at this level and *parce que* used within the sentence. The dictionary definition of *parce que* is *par la raison que*. In fact at the inter-unit level *parce que* can mean *dans ce cas* and *mais alors*:

> Q: *à qui est-ce que vous dites vous à qui est-ce que vous dites tu* – *ça m'intéresse beaucoup* –
> A: (. . . .)
> (Comment on A): *c'est très compliqué pour les Anglais* – *il n'y a pas* – *c'est très spécial* –
> Q: *parce qu'eux c'est quoi* – *c'est comment* –

Here *parce que* corresponds to something like *mais alors dans ce cas*.

(iii) A number of set phrases or clauses are used to express anaphora in the spoken language. The most frequently used in interviews are: *pour revenir à cette question; qu'est-ce que vous voulez dire par; d'après ce que vous disiez tout-à-l'heure; ça expliquerait ce que vous disiez tout-à-l'heure.* They all contain words expressing anaphora either grammatically or lexically or both.

As these connecting phrases contain a real battery of referential elements, they are extremely cohesive and are often used to refer to points which appeared several units previously.

4.3.4 *Ellipsis*

(i) Whereas ellipsis is rarely used at the sentence level in the written language or at the utterance level in the spoken language, it is greatly used at the unit complex level.

It is possible to distinguish between unfinished and incomplete utterances (see *(ii)* and *(iii)*). An unfinished utterance is one which is not complete when the speaker finishes speaking and which will be felt to be incomplete by the listener. The incomplete utterance, as its name suggests, will also have something missing, but not necessarily at the end. Indeed the incomplete utterance may well appear well formed to the listener. In this case there will be clues indicating that it is incomplete. Another kind of ellipsis is that which allows for words to be upgraded:

> *prends la grosse* (missing element = *orange*)
> (in English: 'take the big *one*')

(ii) Unfinished utterances can be left unfinished at any point; they will remain open to interpretation as long as the missing information is retrievable or deducible from the previous unit. The cut-off point gives the listener syntactic clues as to what is missing:

Thus, NP + *et* . . . indicates that the missing element is another retrievable NP since *et* in this position links identical structures:

> *alors quelle est la différence entre un ouvrier spécialisé et* . . . (missing element = *un ouvrier professionnel,* retrievable from the previous unit)

In the case of *et* + NP . . ., the missing element is a VP; in this case *et* means 'and what about':

et les filles? (missing element = *ont quel âge*)

Note the different function and meaning taken on by *et* depending on its position within the utterance and in relation to the cut-off.

In the case of a modal + . . ., the lexical part of the VP is missing; it may be either retrievable or deducible:

pourquoi à votre avis il n'y a pas de personnes dans les autres classes qui pourraient. . . . (missing element = *changer cela*)

In the case of *et/mais* + adverb such as *avant*, *pourquoi* or *depuis*, the missing element is the whole or part of the previous utterance:

et pourquoi?
et avant?
mais depuis?

In the case of *et* + NP + VP . . ., the missing element is an adverbial phrase or clause.

ils sont pas trop yéyés. . . . (missing element = *pour aimer ça* (i.e. *les opérettes d'autrefois*, retrievable from previous unit)

In the case of *et* or *aussi* or intonation + indirect object, a missing NP + VP are deducible from the context:

et le théâtre? (missing element = *vous y allez quelquefois?*)
quarante-huit! (missing element = *vous faites tant d'heures que ça!*)

(iii) Clues to the incompleteness of the utterance are:
(a) the cataphoric use of the definite article:

et comment ça s'est passé ici à Orléans sur le plan ouvrier – quelles ont été les répercussions?

The missing element here is *des grèves de mai et juin*. The definite article can be either generic[4] or specific, in which case it may be anaphoric (i.e. it may refer backwards) or cataphoric (i.e. it may refer forwards). In this instance it is necessarily cataphoric, and the NP in which it figures has to be elliptical: a prepositional phrase must be missing. (The way of checking whether the definite article is being used anaphorically or cataphorically is to see whether it is replaceable by the emphatic demonstrative adjective *ce . . . là*. If so, it is being used anaphorically.)
(b) the use of certain tenses and moods:

ça ira pire le salaire? (missing element = *quand vous serez marié?*)
qu'est-ce que vous auriez fait? (missing element = *si vous n'étiez pas devenu policier?*)

In the first example the use of the future begs the question 'when?'; while in the second example the use of the hypothetical conditional implies the need for two clauses, one starting with *si*.
(iv) The clue to the existence of an elliptical structure may be found within the semantic structure of individual words. This is particularly frequent with transitive verbs which require an object:

il n'a pas encore pigé (missing element = *le sens du mot bicharion*[5]; (*piger* is slang for *comprendre* and is transitive)

Similarly, *j'étais contrarié* (missing element = *par quelque chose*).
(v) Elliptical structures based on comparatives and superlatives:

ça ira pire le salaire?

This is doubly elliptical, i.e. *ça ira pire que quand?* and *ça ira pire que quoi?* The tense gives the clue to the first case of ellipsis, while the comparative *pire* gives the clue to the second.

It should be noted that *aller pire* is not acceptable in prescriptive terms, since *pire* can only be used with verbs which refer to a state of affairs – statives – such as *être, sembler, devenir, paraître*.)

Notes

1 When asked why she used an 'unacceptable' form in spoken French, a lecturer in French language answered, *'Parce que je parle mal, moi!'* This was despite a degree in French, the *agrégation* and a university post, all of which leads one to ask, *'Qui parle bien, alors!'*
2 The material in this section has been previously presented in *Discourse and style II*, ed. J. P. Petit (Publications de l'Université Jean Moulin, Lyon, L'Hermès, 1980).
3 Although the examples from this section are genuine, they have sometimes had to be shortened.
4 Generic: general, not specific.
5 *Bicharion* comes from *bicher* (*faire un petit baiser*) in the Orléans area; *bicharion* is used to mean 'affectionate'.

Appendix

TOLÉRANCES GRAMMATICALES ou ORTHOGRAPHIQUES

Arrêté du 28-12-1976

(B.O. n° 9 du 10-3-1977)

Article premier. — La liste annexée à l'arrêté du 26 février 1901 susvisé est remplacée par la liste annexée au présent arrêté.

Art. 2. — Le directeur général de la Programmation et de la Coordination, le directeur des Lycées, le directeur des Collèges et le directeur des Ecoles sont chargés, chacun en ce qui le concerne, de l'exécution du présent arrêté.

Le ministre d l'Education,

René HABY.

Annexe

Tolérances grammaticales ou orthographiques.

Dans les examens ou concours dépendant du ministère de l'éducation et sanctionnant les étapes de la scolarité élémentaire et de la scolarité secondaire, qu'il s'agisse ou non d'épreuves spéciales d'orthographe il ne sera pas compté de fautes aux candidats dans les cas visés ci-dessous.

Chaque rubrique comporte un, deux ou trois articles affectés d'un numéro d'ordre. Chaque article comprend un ou plusieurs exemples et un commentaire encadré.

Les exemples et les commentaires se présentent sous des formes différentes selon leur objet.

Premier type:

Dans l'emploi de certaines expressions, l'usage admet deux possibilités sans distinguer entre elles des nuances appréciables de sens.

Il a paru utile de mentionner quelques-unes de ces expressions. Chaque exemple est alors composé de deux phrases placées l'une sous l'autre en parallèle. Le commentaire se borne à rappeler les deux possibilités offertes par la langue.

Deuxième type:

Pour d'autres expressions, l'usage admet une dualité de tournures, mais distingue entre elles des nuances de sens; le locuteur ou le scripteur averti accorde sa préférence à l'une ou à l'autre selon ce qu'il veut faire entendre ou suggérer.

Les rubriques qui traitent de ce genre d'expressions conservent, pour chaque exemple, deux phrases parallèles, mais le commentaire se modèle sur un schéma particulier. Dans un premier temps, il rappelle les deux possibilités en précisant que le choix, entre elles, relève d'une intention; dans un second temps, il invite les correcteurs à ne pas exiger des candidats la parfaite perception de tonalités parfois délicates de la pensée ou du style. La tolérance est introduite par la succession des deux formules: «L'usage admet, selon l'intention, ...» et: «On admettra... dans tous les cas».

Troisième type:

La dernière catégorie est celle des expressions auxquelles la grammaire, dans son état actuel, impose des formes ou des accords strictement définis, sans qu'on doive nécessairement considérer tout manquement à ces normes comme l'indice d'une défaillance du jugement; dans certains cas, ce sont les normes elles-mêmes qu'il serait difficile de justifier avec rigueur, tandis que les transgressions peuvent procéder d'un souci de cohérence analogique ou logique.

Dans les rubriques qui illustrent ces cas, chaque exemple est constitué par une seule phrase, à l'intérieur de laquelle s'inscrit entre parenthèses la graphie qu'il est conseillé de ne pas sanctionner. Selon la nature de la question évoquée, le commentaire énonce simplement la tolérance ou l'explicite en rappelant la règle.

Parmi les indications qui figurent ci-après, il convient de distinguer celles qui précisent l'usage et celles qui proposent des tolérances. Les premières doivent être enseignées. Les secondes ne seront prises en considération que pour la correction des examens ou concours; elles n'ont pas à être étudiées dans les classes et encore moins à se substituer aux connaissances grammaticales et orthographiques que l'enseignement du français doit s'attacher à développer.

I. — Le verbe

1. Accord du verbe précédé de plusieurs sujets à peu près synonymes à la troisième personne du singulier juxtaposés:

La joie, l'allégresse s'empara (s'emparèrent) *de tous les spectateurs.*

L'usage veut que, dans ce cas, le verbe soit au singulier.
On admettra l'accord au pluriel.

2.

2 *a*. Accord du verbe précédé de plusieurs sujets à la troisième personne du singulier unis par *comme, ainsi que* et autres locutions d'emploi équivalent:

Le père comme le fils mangeaient *de bon appétit.*
Le père comme le fils mangeait *de bon appétit.*

L'usage admet, selon l'intention, l'accord au pluriel ou au singulier.
On admettra l'un et l'autre accord dans tous les cas.

---

2 *b*. Accord du verbe précédé de plusieurs sujets à la troisième personne du singulier unis par *ou* ou par *ni*:

Ni *l'heure ni la saison ne* conviennent *pour cette excursion*.

Ni *l'heure ni la saison ne* convient *pour cette excursion*.

> L'usage admet, selon l'intention, l'accord au pluriel ou au singulier.
> On admettra l'un et l'autre accord dans tous les cas.

3. Accord du verbe quand le sujet est un mot collectif accompagné d'un complément au pluriel;

A *mon approche, une bande de moineaux* s'envola.

A *mon approche, une bande de moineaux* s'envolèrent.

> L'usage admet, selon l'intention, l'accord avec le mot collectif ou avec le complément.
> On admettra l'un et l'autre accord dans tous les cas.

4. Accord du verbe quand le sujet est *plus d'un* accompagné ou non d'un complément au pluriel:

Plus *d'un de ces hommes* m'était *inconnu*.

Plus *d'un de ces hommes* m'étaient *inconnus*.

> L'usage admet, selon l'intention, l'accord au pluriel ou au singulier.
> On admettra l'un et l'autre accord dans tous les cas.

5. Accord du verbe précédé de *un des... qui, un de ceux que, une des... que, une de celles qui*, etc.:

La Belle au bois dormant *est un des contes qui* charment *les enfants*.
La Belle au bois dormant *est un des contes qui* charme *les enfants*.

> L'usage admet, selon l'intention, l'accord au pluriel ou au singulier.
> On admettra l'un et l'autre accord dans tous les cas.

6. Accord du présentatif *c'est* suivi d'un nom (ou d'un pronom de la troisième personne) au pluriel:

Ce sont *là de beaux résultats*.

C'est *là de beaux résultats*.

C'étaient *ceux que nous attendions*.

C'était *ceux que nous attendions*.

> L'usage admet l'accord au pluriel ou au singulier.

7. Concordance des temps.

J'avais souhaité qu'il *vînt* (qu'il vienne) *sans tarder*.

Je ne pensais pas qu'il *eût oublié* (qu'il ait oublié) *le rendez-vous*.

J'aimerais qu'il *fût* (qu'il soit) *avec moi*.

J'aurais aimé qu'il *eût été* (qu'il ait été) *avec moi*.

> Dans une proposition subordonnée au subjonctif dépendant d'une proposition dont le verbe est à un temps du passé ou au conditionnel, on admettra que le verbe de la subordonnée soit au présent quand la concordance stricte demanderait l'imparfait, au passé quand elle demanderait le plus-que-parfait.

8. Participe présent et adjectif verbal suivis d'un complément d'objet indirect ou d'un complément circonstanciel:

La fillette, obéissant *à sa mère, alla se coucher.*
La fillette, obéissante *à sa mère, alla se coucher.*

J'ai recueilli cette chienne errant *dans le quartier.*
J'ai recueilli cette chienne errante *dans le quartier.*

> L'usage admet que, selon l'intention, la forme en - *ant* puisse être employée sans accord comme forme du participe ou avec accord comme forme de l'adjectif qui lui correspond.
> On admettra l'un et l'autre emploi dans tous les cas.

9. Participe passé conjugué avec *être* dans une forme verbale ayant pour sujet *on:*
On est resté (restés) *bons amis.*

> L'usage veut que le participe passé se rapportant au pronom *on* se mette au masculin singulier.
> On admettra que ce participe prenne la marque du genre et du nombre lorsque *on* désigne une femme ou plusieurs personnes.

10. Participe passé conjugué avec *avoir* et suivi d'un infinitif:
Les musiciens que j'ai entendus (entendu) *jouer.*
Les airs que j'ai entendu (entendus) *jouer.*

> L'usage veut que le participe s'accorde lorsque le complément d'objet direct se rapporte à la forme conjuguée et qu'il reste invariable lorsque le complément d'objet direct se rapporte à l'infinitif.
> On admettra l'absence d'accord dans le premier cas. On admettra l'accord dans le second, sauf en ce qui concerne le participe passé du verbe *faire.*

11. Accord du participe passé conjugué avec *avoir* dans une forme verbale précédée de *en* complément de cette forme verbale:
J'ai laissé sur l'arbre plus de cerises que je n'en ai cueilli.
J'ai laissé sur l'arbre plus de cerises que je n'en ai cueillies.

> L'usage admet l'un et l'autre accord.

12. Participe passé des verbes tels que: *coûter, valoir, courir, vivre*, etc., lorsque ce participe est placé après un complément:
Je ne parle pas des sommes que ces travaux m'ont coûté (coûtées).
J'oublierai vite les peines que ce travail m'a coûtées (coûté).

> L'usage admet que ces verbes normalement intransitifs (sans accord du participe passé) puissent s'employer transitivement (avec accord) dans certains cas.
> On admettra l'un et l'autre emploi dans tous les cas.

13. Participes et locutions tels que *compris (y compris, non compris) excepté, ôté, étant donné, ci-inclus, ci-joint:*

13 *a. Compris (y compris, non compris), excepté, ôté:*

J'aime tous les sports, excepté la boxe (exceptée la boxe).

J'aime tous les sports, la boxe exceptée (la boxe excepté).

> L'usage veut que ces participes et locutions restent invariables quand ils sont placés avant le nom avec lequel ils sont en relation et qu'ils varient quand ils sont placés après le nom.
> On admettra l'accord dans le premier cas et l'absence d'accord dans le second.

13 *b. Etant donné:*

Etant données *les circonstances…*

Etant donné *les circonstances…*

> L'usage admet l'accord aussi bien que l'absence d'accord.

13 *c. Ci-inclus, ci-joint:*

Ci-inclus (ci-incluse) *la pièce demandée.*

Vous trouverez ci-inclus (ci-incluse) *copie de la pièce demandée.*

Vous trouverez cette lettre ci-incluse.

Vous trouverez cette lettre ci-inclus.

> L'usage veut que *ci-inclus, ci-joint* soient:
> invariables en tête d'une phrase ou s'ils précèdent un nom sans déterminant;
> variables ou invariables, selon l'intention, dans les autres cas.
> On admettra l'accord ou l'absence d'accord dans tous les cas.

II. — LE NOM

14. Liberté du nombre.

14 *a:*

De la gelée de groseille.

De la gelée de groseilles.

Des pommiers en fleur.

Des pommiers en fleurs.

> L'usage admet le singulier et le pluriel.

14 *b:*

Ils ont ôté leur chapeau.

Ils ont ôté leurs chapeaux.

> L'usage admet, selon l'intention, le singulier et le pluriel.
> On admettra l'un et l'autre nombre dans tous les cas.

15. Double genre:

Instruits (instruites) *par l'expérience, les vieilles gens sont très prudents* (prudentes): *ils* (elles) *ont vu trop de choses*.

> L'usage donne au mot *gens* le genre masculin, sauf dans des expressions telles que: *les bonnes gens, les vieilles gens, les petites gens*.
>
> Lorsqu'un adjectif ou un participe se rapporte à l'une de ces expressions ou lorsqu'un pronom la reprend, on admettra que cet adjectif, ce participe, ce pronom soient, eux aussi, au féminin.

16. Noms masculins de titres ou de professions appliqués à des femmes:

Le français nous est enseigné par une dame. Nous aimons beaucoup ce professeur. Mais il (elle) *va nous quitter*.

> Précédés ou non de *Madame*, ces noms'conservent le genre masculin ainsi que leurs déterminants et les adjectifs qui les accompagnent.
>
> Quand ils sont repris par un pronom, on admettra pour ce pronom le genre féminin.

17. Pluriel des noms:

17 *a*. Noms propres de personnes:

Les Dupont (Duponts). *Les Maréchal* (Maréchals).

> On admettra que les noms propres de personnes prennent la marque du pluriel.

17 *b*. Noms empruntés à d'autres langues:

Des maxima (des maximums). *Des sandwiches* (des sandwichs).

> On admettra que, dans tous les cas, le pluriel de ces noms soit formé selon la règle générale du français.

III. — L'ARTICLE

18. Article devant *plus, moins, mieux:*

Les idées qui paraissent les plus *justes sont souvent discutables.*

Les idées qui paraissent le plus *justes sont souvent discutables.*

> Dans les groupes formés d'un article défini suivi de *plus, moins, mieux* et d'un adjectif ou d'un participe, l'usage admet que, selon l'intention, l'article varie ou reste invariable.
>
> On admettra que l'article varie ou reste invariable dans tous les cas.

IV. — L'ADJECTIF NUMÉRAL

19. *Vingt* et *cent:*

Quatre-vingt-dix (quatre vingts dix) *ans.*

Six cent trente-quatre (six cents trente quatre) *hommes.*

En mil neuf cent soixante-dix-sept (mille neuf cents soixante dix sept).

> On admettra que *vingt* et *cent*, précédés d'un adjectif numéral à valeur de multiplicateur, prennent la marque du pluriel même lorsqu'ils sont suivis d'un autre adjectif numéral.
>
> Dans la désignation d'un millésime, on admettra la graphie *mille* dans tous les cas.
>
> *N.B.* — L'usage place un trait d'union entre les éléments d'un adjectif numéral qui forment un ensemble inférieur à cent.
>
> On admettra l'omission du trait d'union.

V. — L'ADJECTIF QUALIFICATIF

20. *Nu, demi* précédant un nom:

Elle courait nu-pieds (nus pieds).

Une demi-heure (demie heure) *s'écoula*.

> L'usage veut que *nu, demi* restent invariables quand ils précèdent un nom auquel ils sont reliés par un trait d'union.
>
> On admettra l'accord.

21. Pluriel de *grand-mère, grand-tante*, etc.:

Des grand-*mères*.

Des grands-*mères*.

> L'usage admet l'une et l'autre graphie.

22. *Se faire fort de...*:

Elles se font fort (fortes) *de réussir*.

> On admettra l'accord de l'adjectif.

23. *Avoir l'air:*

Elle a l'air doux.

Elle a l'air douce.

> L'usage admet que, selon l'intention, l'adjectif s'accorde avec le mot *air* ou avec le sujet du verbe *avoir*.
>
> On admettra l'un et l'autre accord dans tous les cas.

VI. — LES INDÉFINIS

24. *L'un et l'autre:*

24 *a. L'un et l'autre* employé comme adjectif:

1. *J'ai consulté l'un et l'autre document.*

   J'ai consulté l'un et l'autre documents.

2. *L'un et l'autre document m'a paru intéressant.*

   L'un et l'autre document m'ont paru intéressants.

> 1. L'usage admet que, selon l'intention, le nom précédé de *l'un et l'autre* se mette au singulier ou au pluriel.
>
> On admettra l'un et l'autre nombre dans tous les cas.
>
> 2. Avec le nom au singulier, l'usage admet que le verbe se mette au singulier ou au pluriel.

24 *b.* *L'un et l'autre* employé comme pronom:

L'un et l'autre se taisait.

L'un et l'autre se taisaient.

> L'usage admet que, selon l'intention, le verbe précédé de *l'un et l'autre* employé comme pronom se mette au singulier ou au pluriel.
>
> On admettra l'un et l'autre nombre dans tous les cas.

25. *L'un ou l'autre, ni l'un ni l'autre:*

25 *a.* *L'un ou l'autre, ni l'un ni l'autre* employés comme adjectifs:

L'un ou l'autre projet me convient.

L'un ou l'autre projet me conviennent.

Ni l'une ni l'autre idée ne m'inquiète.

Ni l'une ni l'autre idée ne m'inquiètent.

> L'usage veut que le nom précédé de *l'un ou l'autre* ou de *ni l'un ni l'autre* se mette au singulier; il admet que, selon l'intention, le verbe se mette au singulier ou au pluriel.
>
> On admettra, pour le verbe, l'un et l'autre accord dans tous les cas.

25 *b.* *L'un ou l'autre, ni l'un ni l'autre* employés comme pronoms:

De ces deux projets, l'un ou l'autre me convient.

De ces deux projets, l'un ou l'autre me conviennent.

De ces deux idées, ni l'une ni l'autre ne m'inquiète.

De ces deux idées, ni l'une ni l'autre ne m'inquiètent.

> L'usage admet que, selon l'intention, le verbe précédé de *l'un ou l'autre* ou de *ni l'un ni l'autre* employés comme pronoms se mette au singulier ou au pluriel.
>
> On admettra l'un et l'autre nombre dans tous les cas.

26. *Chacun:*

Remets ces livres chacun à sa place.

Remets ces livres chacun à leur place.

> Lorsque *chacun,* reprenant un nom (ou un pronom de la troisième personne) au pluriel, est suivi d'un possessif, l'usage admet que, selon l'intention, le possessif renvoie à *chacun* ou au mot repris par *chacun.*
>
> On admettra l'un et l'autre tour dans tous les cas.

VII. — «MÊME» et «TOUT»

27. *Même:*

Dans les fables, les bêtes mêmes *parlent.*
Dans les fables, les bêtes même *parlent.*

> Après un nom ou un pronom au pluriel, l'usage admet que *même*, selon l'intention, prenne ou non l'accord.
> On admettra l'une ou l'autre graphie dans tous les cas.

28. *Tout:*

28 *a.* *Les proverbes sont de* tout *temps et de* tout *pays.*
   Les proverbes sont de tous *temps et de* tous *pays.*

> L'usage admet, selon l'intention, le singulier ou le pluriel.

28 *b.* *Elle est* toute *(tout) à sa lecture.*

> Dans l'expression *être tout à...*, on admettra que *tout*, se rapportant à un mot féminin, reste invariable.

28 *c.* *Elle se montra* tout *(toute) étonnée.*

> L'usage veut que *tout*, employé comme adverbe, prenne la marque du genre et du nombre devant un mot féminin commençant, par une consonne ou un *h* aspiré et reste invariable dans les autres cas.
> On admettra qu'il prenne la marque du genre et du nombre devant un nom féminin commençant par une voyelle ou un *h* muet.

VIII. — L'ADVERBE «NE» DIT EXPLÉTIF

29. *Je crains qu'il* ne *pleuve.*
Je crains qu'il pleuve.

L'année a été meilleure qu'on ne *l'espérait*
L'année a été meilleure qu'on l'espérait.

> L'usage n'impose pas l'emploi de *ne* dit explétif.

IX. — ACCENTS

30. Accent aigu:
Assener (asséner); *referendum* (référendum).

> Dans certains mots, la lettre *e*, sans accent aigu, est prononcée [*é*] à la fin d'une syllabe.
> On admettra qu'elle prenne cet accent — même s'il s'agit de mots d'origine étrangère — sauf dans les noms propres.

31. Accent grave:

Evénement (évènement); *je céderai* (je cèderai).

> Dans certains mots, la lettre *e* avec un accent aigu est généralement prononcée [é] à la fin d'une syllabe.
>
> On admettra l'emploi de l'accent grave à la place de l'accent aigu.

32. Accent circonflexe:

Crâne (crane); *épître* (épitre); *crûment* (crument).

> On admettra l'omission de l'accent circonflexe sur les voyelles *a, e, i, o, u* dans les mots où ces voyelles comportent normalement cet accent, sauf lorsque cette tolérance entraînerait une confusion entre deux mots en les rendant homographes (par exemple: *tâche/tache; forêt/foret; vous dîtes/vous dites; rôder/roder; qu'il fût/il fut*).

X. — TRAIT D'UNION

33. *Arc-en-ciel* (arc en ciel); *nouveau-né* (nouveau né); *crois-tu?* (crois tu?); *est-ce vrai?* (est ce vrai?); *dit-on* (dit on); *dix-huit* (dix huit); *dix-huitième* (dix huitième); *par-ci, par-là* (par ci, par là).

> Dans tous les cas, on admettra l'omission du trait d'union, sauf lorsque sa présence évite une ambiguïté (*petite-fille/petite fille*) ou lorsqu'il doit être placé avant et après le *t* euphonique intercalé à la troisième personne du singulier entre une forme verbale et un pronom sujet postposé (*viendra-t-il?*).

OBSERVATION

Dans les examens ou concours visés en tête de la présente liste, les correcteurs, graduant leurs appréciations selon le niveau de connaissances qu'ils peuvent exiger des candidats, ne compteront pas comme fautes graves celles qui, en dehors des cas mentionnés ci-dessus, portent sur de subtiles particularités grammaticales.

Bibliography

A select bibliography of published works, with subjective comments, aiming at illustrating the very wide range of works in this field. (Reference is made to the place of publication only where it is not Paris or London.)

Section 1: Works referring to Modern French, either in terms of grammar or style, from a synchronic point of view:

ATKINSON, J.C. 1973: *Two forms of subject inversion in Modern French*. Mouton (A descriptive study of academic interest).

BAILLY, C. 1909: *Traité de stylistique française* (2 vols.). Klincksieck (Old-fashioned but a pioneering work).

BAYLON, C. and FABRE, P. 1978: *Grammaire sytématique de la langue française avec des travaux pratiques d'application et leurs corrigés*. Nathan (A good useful book for students; the section on tenses and moods is particularly well done; other sections are incomplete. Constitutes a modern approach to grammar).

BJORKMAN, S. 1978: *Type 'avoir besoin': étude sur la coalescence verbo-nominale en français*. Uppsala, Sweden (A doctoral thesis of academic interest).

BONNARD, H. 1950: *Grammaire française des lycées et collèges*. SUDEL (An excellent traditional grammar for French school children).

_____ 1981: *Procédés annexes d'expression*. Magnard (This book, along with a *Livre d'exercices* complements the previous one, but whereas *Le code du français courant* refers mainly to grammar, *Procédés annexes d'expression* refers to style. Very useful for teaching).

_____ 1982: *Code du français courant*. Magnard (An up-dated version of the previous one, using modern documents)

BOONS, J.P. 1976: *Structures des phrases simples en français: constructions intransitives*. Droz, Geneva (A very theoretical work linking grammatical and lexical matters).

BUREAU, C. 1978: *Syntaxe fonctionnelle du français*. Presses de l'Université de Laval, Quebec (An application of Martinet type functionalism to French; of theoretical interest only).

CATHERINE, R. 1946: *Le style administratif*. Albin Michel (Old-fashioned, but still used by some French administrators as a hand-book).

CELLARD, J. 1979: *Vie du langage: ensemble des chroniques 1971 – 1975 dans Le monde*. Le Robert (Good entertaining reading for students; many interesting insights).

CHEVALIER, J.C., BLANCHE BENVENISTE, C., ARRIVE, P., and PEYTARD, J. 1964: *Grammaire Larousse de français contemporain*. Larousse (Quite a good grammar, but without the insights of the newer Baylon and Fabre).

COHEN, M. 1963: *Nouveaux regards sur la langue française*. Editions sociales.

_____ 1965: *Le subjonctif en français contemporain*. SEDES.

_____ 1970: *Toujours des regards sur la langue française*. Editions sociales (All three books are a little dated; they are journalistic in their approach).

CRESSOT, M. 1947, (new edition 1976): *Le style et ses techniques*. PUF (Useful although somewhat heavy going).

DAMOURETTE, J. and PICHON, E. 1911 – 1940: *Des mots à la pensée: essai de grammaire de la langue française*. Editions d'Artrey (A fascinating effort to rethink the whole concept of French grammar; not suitable for undergraduates).

DANELL, K.J. 1973: *Emploi des formes fortes des pronoms personnels pour désigner des choses en français moderne*. Acta Universitatis, Uppsala, Sweden (An Interesting detailed description of a minor topic).

DELOFFRE, F. 1967: *La phrase française*. SEDES (Very useful at undergraduate level).

_____ 1981: *Eléments de linguistique française*. SEDES (A good introductory work).

DESIRAT, C. 1976: *La langue française au XXe siècle*. Bordas (A good straightforward work on the characteristics of present-day French; undergraduate level).

DOPPAGNE, A. 1966: *Trois aspects du français contemporain*. Larousse (Easy to read and quite interesting, although most of the material is well known by now).

DOPPAGNE, A. 1979: *Majuscules, abréviations, symboles et sigles*. Duculot (A practical guide).

DUBOIS, J. 1965: *Grammaire structurale du français: nom et pronom*. Larousse.

_____ 1967: *Grammaire structurale du français: verbe*. Larousse.

_____ 1969: *Grammaire structurale du français: la phrase et les transformations*. Larousse (The first volume is distributionalist in its approach, the two others are transformationalist, the passage from the one to the other being relatively gradual. Interesting from a purely theoretical point of view).

DUBOIS, J. and LAGANE, R. 1973: *Nouvelle grammaire du français*. Larousse (A school grammar used in French secondary schools; it attempts to be more 'modern' than previous ones, but ends up being very poor because of major omissions).

DUPRE, 1972: *Encylopédie du bon français dans l'usage contemporain*: *difficultés, subtilités, complexités, singularités* (3 vols.). Editions de Trevise (A useful synthesis of problems as analysed in 5 dictionaries).

ENGVER, K. 1972: *Place de l'adverbe déterminant un infinitif dans la prose française*. Acta Universitatis Uppsaliensis, Sweden. (Descriptive; useful).

FREI, H. 1929: *Grammaire des fautes*. Slatkine reprints, 1971, Geneva (Interesting as an example of what the French felt to be 'incorrect' forms of the language at that time).

FURUKAWA, N. 1977: *Nombre grammatical en français contemporain*. France-Tosho (A thesis written under the supervision of G. Moignet and based on G. Guillaume's principles).

GERTNER, M.H. 1973: *The morphology of the modern French verb*. Mouton (Interesting and easy to read).

GAATONE, D. 1971: *Etude descriptive du système de la négation en français contemporain*. Droz, Geneva (A descriptive work, easy to read and very informative).

GAIFFE, F., MAILLE, E., BREUIL, E., JAHAN, S., WAGNER, R., MARIJON, M. 1936: *Grammaire Larousse du XXe siècle*. Larousse (Detailed but old-fashioned).

GODIN, H.G.J. 1948: *Ressources stylistiques du français contemporain*. Blackwell (Some interesting points).

GOUGENHEIM, G. 1938: *Système grammatical de la langue française*. Ed. d'Artrey (Describes certain aspects of French in structuralist terms. Interesting).

GREVISSE, M. 1936: *Le bon usage*. Duculot, Belgium (A fund of information, particularly in respect of literary examples reedited many times since then; a 'must' in many French departments in France, although totally traditional in its approach and therefore lacking most of the facts brought to light by Modern Linguistics).

GROSS, M. 1968: *Grammaire transformationnelle du français: syntaxe du verbe*. Larousse.

_____ 1968: *Grammaire transformationnelle du français*. Larousse.

_____ 1977: *Grammaire transformationnelle du français: syntaxe du nom*. Larousse (All three works are highly praised by transformationalists).

GUILLAUME, G. 1919: *Le problème de l'article et sa solution dans la langue française*. Hachette (Interesting but some aspects of this work are not acceptable today).

_____ 1945: *Temps et verbe. Théorie des aspects, des modes et des temps* followed by *L'architectonique du temps dans les langues classiques*. H. Champion (A difficult work but of major importance).

HARMER, L.C. 1979: *Uncertainties in French grammar*. Cambridge University Press (Extremely interesting in its detail).

HARRIS, Z.S. 1976: *Notes du cours de syntaxe*. Editions du Seuil (Notes for a set of lectures given at the university of Vincennes in 1973 – 4; shows Harris's version of transformational grammar).

IMBS, P. 1968: *Emploi des temps verbaux en français moderne*. Klincksieck (A standard work, descriptive and very detailed).

LE BIDOIS, G., and LE BIDOIS, R. reprinted 1971: *Syntaxe du français moderne* (2 vols.). A. & J. Picard (A remarkable traditional grammar; suitable for advanced students).

MAROUZEAU, J. 1941: *Précis de stylistique française*. Masson (Readable and interesting; suitable for undergraduates).

MARTINET, A. 1979: *Grammaire fonctionnelle du français*. Didier (A rather disappointing grammar in that it does not say much that is new).

MAUGER, G. 1968: *Grammaire pratique du français d'aujourd'hui* 7th edn. Hachette (Popular with many anglophones).

MODDY, M.D. 1973: *Classification and analysis of Noun + de + Noun constructions in French*. Mouton, The Hague (Descriptive, academic and interesting).

PERSSON, B. 1974: *Etude sur la concurrence entre les groupes du type*: *les côtes de France, les côtes de la France, les côtes françaises*. Acta Universitatis Uppsaliensis, Sweden.

PICABIA, L. 1975: *Eléments de grammaire générative: applications au français*. A. Colin (Simple; contains a good analysis of tenses).

_____ 1978: *Constructions adjectivales en français*. Droz, Geneva (Study of the 'subject + *être* + adjective' construction, based on the work of Harris, Chomsky and Gross).

PINCHON, J. 1972: *Les pronoms adverbiaux en et y*. Droz, Geneva (comparison between their use in the 17th and 20th century; descriptive, based on distributionalism, but on the threshold of transformationalism).

POURADIER-DUTEIL, F. 1978: *Trois suffixes nominalisateurs*. Gunter Nar Verlag, Tübingen (A thesis, but very practical in its approach; useful).

REQUÉDAT, F. 1980: *Constructions verbales avec l'infinitif*. Hachette (deals with the problem of *à* or *de* + noun; useful and practical).

ROSENBERG, S.N. 1970: *Modern French ce: the neuter pronoun in adjectival predication*. Mouton, The Hague (Of academic interest).

RUWET, N. 1972: *Théorie syntaxique et syntaxe du français*. Editions du Seuil (Follows a generative approach).

SANDFELD, K. 1928, reprinted 1970: *Syntaxe du français contemporain: les pronoms*. Champion.

_____ 1936, reprinted 1965: *Syntaxe du français contemporain: les propositions subordonnées*. Champion.

_____ 1943, reprinted 1965: *Syntaxe du français contemporain: l'infinitif*. Droz, Geneva (Three volumes considered to be classics).

SAUVAGEOT, A. 1957: *Les procédés expressifs du français contemporain*. Klincksieck.

_____ 1962: *Français écrit, français parlé*. Larousse (Interesting and easy to read, but the material is no longer new).

SAYCE, R.A. 1953: *French prose*. The Clarendon Press (Old but still interesting; the approach is both systematic, i.e. one area of the language is studied at a time, and flexible since the analysis is based on texts).

SCHNEIDER (GIRY-SCHNEIDER), J. 1978: *Nominalisations en français: l'opérateur 'faire' dans le lexique*. Droz. Geneva (The approach is transformational).

SCHOGT, H.G. 1968: *Le système verbal du français contemporain*. Mouton (Practical and useful).

TESNIERE, L. 1965: *Eléments de syntaxe structurale* 2nd edn. Klincksieck. (A brilliant and revolutionary work, which stands on its own)

TOGEBY, K. 1965: *Structure immanente de la langue française*. Larousse (Interesting comparisons are made, in this highly academic work, between the different ways in which various schools of linguistics analyse the same problem).

TUTESCU, M. 1972: *Groupe nominal et la nominalisation en français moderne*. Klincksieck (The problem is analysed from a distributional point of view in Part I and from a generative point of view in Part II; very academic).

ULLMANN, S. 1964: Style in the French Novel. Blackwell (Interesting and pleasant to read).

WAGNER, R. and PINCHON, J. 1962: *Grammaire du français classique et moderne*. Hachette (An excellent grammar written for French university students; it does not contain the wealth of examples to be found in Grevisse's *Le bon usage*, but it is far more modern in its approach).

WAGNER, R. 1968: *La grammaire française: les niveaux et les domaines, les normes, les états de langue*. SEDES (Readable and interesting).

WARTBURG, W. VON, and ZUMTHOR, P. 1973: *Précis de syntaxe du français contemporain*. Editions Francke, Berne (A standard work).

Section 2: Basic works referring to the development of the Language:

ALLIÈRES, J. 1982: *Formation de la langue française*. Que sais-je, PUF (A very good introductory work).

ANGLADE, J. 1919: *Grammaire élémentaire de l'ancien français*. A. Colin (A very good introductory work).

BRUNOT, F. 1905 – 21 vols., the last by C. BRUNEAU, reprinted 1968: *Histoire de la langue française*. Colin (A monumental but somewhat dated work).

BRUNOT, F. and BRUNEAU, C. 1969: *Précis de grammaire historique de la langue française*. Masson (The most useful work of its type, particularly for those not having studied Old French).

FOULET, L. 1930: *Petite syntaxe de l'ancien français*. H. Champion (Still as useful as ever).

GOUGENHEIM, G. 1935, reprinted 1971: *Etudes sur les périphrases verbales de la langue française*. Nizet (A detailed and thorough doctoral thesis).

GOUGENHEIM, G. 1951, new edn 1973: *Grammaire de la langue française du seizième siècle*. A. & J. Picard (It examines the differences between 16th and 20th century French; it is meant for students 16th century literature; an invaluable work which is pleasant to read).

HAASE, A. edited by OBERT in 1914: *Syntaxe française du XVIIe siècle*. Delagrave (Old-fashioned in lay-out, but indispensable for the study of 17th century literature).

HARRIS, M. 1978: *The evolution of French syntax. A comparative approach* (Interesting).

MÉNARD, P. 1973: *Syntaxe de l'ancien français*. SOBODI (Easy to consult for non specialists).

MOIGNET, G. 1959: *Essai sur le mode subjonctif en latin post-classique et en ancien français*. PUF (A remarkable doctoral thesis).

_____ 1973: *Grammaire de l'ancien français*. Klincksieck (a synchronic description of 12th and 13th century French; easy to consult for non-specialists).

NYROP, K. 1899 – 1930, reprinted 1967: *Grammaire historique de la langue française*, 6 vols. Gyldendal, Denmark (A classic).

POPE, M.K. 1934: *From Latin to Modern French with especial consideration of anglonorman: phonology and morphology*. Manchester University Press (A classic still highly praised in France).

PRICE, G. 1971: *The French language: present and past*. Edward Arnold (A very readable introduction to the subject).

RAYNAUD DE LAGE, G. 1973: *Manuel pratique d'ancien français*. A & J. Picard (The study of Old French through the study of a text, *Le Charroi de Nimes*; excellent for those working on their own).

_____ 1975: *Introduction à l'ancien français*, 9th edn. CDU & SEDES (A convenient handbook for complete beginners).

RICKARD, P. 1974: *History of the French language*. Hutchinson (A very readable brief survey).

SEGUIN, J.P. 1972: *La langue française au XVIIIe siècle*. Bordas. (A modern approach to the topic; very useful for students of 18th century literature).

WARTBURG, W. VON 1946: *Evolution et structure de la langue française*. A. Francke, Berne (extremely interesting).

Section 3:   Contrastive studies in English and French:

This is a relatively new field of investigation; most work has been carried out in Quebec, and many of the results are published in periodicals rather than books, hence a rather short list.

ASTINGTON, E. 1980: *French structures: a manual for advanced students* Collins (Based on examples, very practical and useful).

DARBELNET, J. 1969: *Pensée et structure*. C. Scribner's Sons, New York (Easy book for first year students).

GUILLEMIN-FLESCHER, J. 1981: *Syntaxe comparée du français et de l'anglais*. Ophrys (An important academic work based on comparisons of translated texts).

TREMBLAY, J.P. 1972: *Grammaire comparative du français et de l'anglais à l'usage des anglophones*. Les Presses de l'Université de Laval, Québec (This comparison is done at a fairly low level).

VINAY, J.P. and DARBELNET, J. 1958: *Stylistique comparée du français et de l'anglais*. Didier (The first of its kind for French and English, although it is modelled on Malblanc's *Stylistique comparée du français et de l'allemand*. It is a pioneering work, of great use to teachers, although it is both too complex and too amorphous to be used with much success by students. It is rapidly becoming old-fashioned because of newer more modern work done in this field, although a number of workbooks have been written to go with it).

Index

General headings will be found in the Table of Contents; this index provides reference to French words and phrases which present particular problems, and to authors quoted. This index does not include irregular verbs, which are listed in alphabetical order on pp. 250–58.